This volume, a project of AEI's A Decade of Study of the Constitution, was funded in part by a bicentennial challenge grant from the National Endowment for the Humanities. A Decade of Study, directed by Robert A. Goldwin, was launched by AEI to help prepare the nation for a thoughtful observance of the bicentennial of the U.S. Constitution. Through its conferences, volumes, and television forums, AEI's program of constitutional studies is designed to assist scholars and the general public to recover and appreciate anew the principles of constitutional democracy.

* * *

ALEXANDER HAMILTON was born on the island of Nevis, in the British West Indies, probably on January 11, 1755 (or 1757). He was the illegitimate son of a Scottish trader, who abandoned his family in St. Croix in 1765. At the age of eleven, Hamilton went to work in a countinghouse, where he so impressed his employers that they sent him to New York to be educated. In 1773 he entered King's College (now Columbia) and soon began writing in favor of colonial causes against the crown. In the Revolutionary War, he served as aide-de-camp to George Washington, with the rank of lieutenant colonel. In 1780 he married Elizabeth Schuyler, who belonged to a prominent New York family. After studying law, Hamilton served as a delegate to the Continental Congress, to the Constitutional Convention in Philadelphia in 1787, and to the New York ratifying convention in 1788. He wrote about two-thirds of the eighty-five essays of *The Federalist,* in 1787–1788, supporting adoption of the newly drafted Constitution. When Washington became president in 1789, he appointed Hamilton the first secretary of the Treasury. He became a leader of the emerging Federalist party, won establishment of a national bank, and supported friendship with Britain, rather than France, through Jay's Treaty in 1794. His letter of July 30, 1796, contains a draft used by Washington for his Farewell Address. Hamilton kept Aaron Burr from becoming president in 1800 and governor of New York in 1804; after Burr wounded him in a duel, Hamilton died on July 12, 1804.

MORTON J. FRISCH is a professor of political science at Northern Illinois University and is the author of *Franklin D. Roosevelt: The Contribution of the New Deal to American Political Thought and Practice.* He is also a coeditor of *American Political Thought: The Philosophic Dimensions of American Statesmanship* and *The Political Thought of American Statesmen: Selected Writings and Speeches.*

ALEXANDER HAMILTON

Selected Writings and Speeches of ALEXANDER HAMILTON

Morton J. Frisch
editor

American Enterprise Institute for Public Policy Research
Washington and London

The entries in this volume were selected from *The Papers of Alexander Hamilton*, volumes 1–5, 8–16, 17–22, and 24–26, Harold C. Syrett, editor. © 1961–1979, Columbia University Press. Reprinted by permission.

Library of Congress Cataloging in Publication Data

Hamilton, Alexander, 1757–1804.
  Selected writings and speeches of Alexander Hamilton.

  (AEI studies ; 403)
  1. United States—Politics and government—1783–1809—
Addresses, essays, lectures.   2. United States—Politics
and government—Revolution, 1775–1783—Addresses, essays,
lectures.   I. Frisch, Morton J.   II. Title.   III. Series.
E302.Hss   1985   321.8   84-4620
ISBN 0-8447-3553-1
ISBN 0-8447-3551-5 (pbk.)

1 3 5 7 9 10 8 6 4 2

AEI Studies 403

Printed in the United States of America

COVER AND FRONTISPIECE: Engraving of Alexander Hamilton by W. Rollinson
from the portrait by Archibald Robertson, 1804. Courtesy of the Museum of
the City of New York.

Contents

Foreword

Alexander Hamilton was that rare combination—an active, influential politician and a powerful, original thinker. He played a critical role in the formation of the American republic as a delegate to the Constitutional Convention in 1787, as the coauthor, with James Madison and John Jay, of *The Federalist* papers, and as the first secretary of the Treasury. His speeches and writings are, therefore, essential reading if we are to understand the principles at the core of our regime.

Hamilton's "Report on Manufactures," for instance, was a blueprint for unleashing individual acquisitiveness and harnessing it to the goals of commercial prosperity and political freedom. It played an important role in the transformation of America from a handful of small, isolated, agrarian states into the powerful industrial nation of today, through the wise channeling of the energies of the free individual.

Hamilton's writings on the presidency explain a great deal about the character of that office today. Hamilton argued that an energetic executive was not only compatible with, it was essential for, the preservation of political liberty. A properly structured, complex arrangement of political institutions, Hamilton believed, could give to the presidential office the power and flexibility necessary to address the major problems of domestic and foreign policy, while ensuring that the presidency did not become a threat to individual liberty.

As we enter our third century of national existence, we would do well to recall the proper relationships between individual acquisitiveness and economic growth, between commercial prosperity and political liberty, and between an energetic executive office and individual rights. The interconnections of these principles are at the center of Hamilton's thought, as they have long been the focus of the work of the American Enterprise Institute and of its program of constitutional studies. We are pleased, therefore, to publish this volume, and we hope it will be useful to scholars and the general public, as our nation strives, on the occasion of the bicentennial of the Constitution, to recover and commit ourselves anew to the principles that undergird free and prosperous republics.

WILLIAM J. BAROODY, JR.
President
American Enterprise Institute

Preface

The time is propitious for the publication of a one-volume edition of the selected writings and speeches of Alexander Hamilton since the final volume of *The Papers of Alexander Hamilton* has recently been published by the Columbia University Press. The entire set, edited by Harold C. Syrett, contains twenty-six volumes. The intention of this one-volume edition is to reflect the penetrating and intense thought that Hamilton gave to the serious problems he faced by assembling a selected group of his writings and speeches. The volume attempts to provide coverage in the best sense, that is, one might hope to grasp, by reading Hamilton's writings and speeches, the whole of Hamilton's political thought and to be pointed toward a recovery of the most philosophic parts of it. As often as possible, the volume includes complete writings and speeches, which necessarily involves some repetition. This is not undesirable, however, for it is useful to see the continuing themes and the reaffirmation of certain principles over an extended period of time. The aim is to select writings and speeches that contain a maximum of principles, doctrines, and purposes. The volume also includes short introductions to many of the selections. These introductions tend to focus on his political thought and not on historical background and detail, matters that are fully treated in the twenty-six volume, definitive edition of *The Papers of Alexander Hamilton*.

Hamilton's Report on Public Credit of January 7, 1790, which proposes funding of the national debt and assumption of the state debts, and his Report on a National Bank of December 13, 1790, are not included in this volume because both are highly technical. The Vindication (of the Funding System) No. III, written between May and August 1792, and his letter to George Washington with an enclosure containing Objections and Answers respecting the Administration of Government, written on August 18, 1792, are theoretical treatments of the issues of the funding and assumption, so both are included in this volume. Morever, Hamilton's Opinion on the Constitutionality of the Bank of February 23, 1791, which covers in a more useful fashion the same topics he addressed in his Report on a National Bank, is also included in this volume. From Hamilton's early writing entitled "The Farmer Refuted," written on February 23, 1775, I have included only the passages that deal with natural right. The essay as a whole addresses the dispute between the American colonies and Great Britain and is, therefore, remote from Hamilton's later thought and practice.

Morton J. Frisch

NOTE:
Material in brackets provides dates and places of letters if these were missing or incomplete in the manuscript. ⟨-----⟩ indicates indecipherable words. Broken brackets around letters or words signify a guess about the letters or words in question.

Selected Writings and Speeches of ALEXANDER HAMILTON

Introduction: The Political Thought of Hamilton's Statesmanship

Alexander Hamilton, though never president himself, was one of the most important and influential statesmen of the American founding period. He is famous for having presented with great force and clarity the case for having a strong presidency. Moreover, as Washington's secretary of the Treasury, he did much to establish a presidency that accorded with the activist view of that office, which he so forcefully articulated in *The Federalist Papers*. Hamilton had no visionary expectations from politics but was essentially a man of affairs involved in the actual day-to-day working of the political system. He was principally concerned with the prosperity or financial well-being of the nation, for that was his job as secretary of the Treasury. He was not a theoretical politician who stressed principles to the detriment of experience, though he believed firmly in political principles. His view of the good society did not take the form of an imagined model. Instead, Hamilton took his bearings from American society as it existed and sought to make more reasonable the principles and possibilities imbedded in that society, with a view to what could be learned from English institutions and practices and from the English Constitution.

* * *

James Madison, Jefferson's antiadministration leader in the House until 1798, is reported to have said:

> I deserted Colonel Hamilton, or rather Colonel H. deserted me; in a word, the divergence between us took place—from his wishing to *administration*, or rather to administer the Government (these were Mr. M's very words), into what he thought it ought to be; while, on my part, I endeavored to make it conform to the Constitution as understood by the Convention that produced and recommended it, and particularly by the State conventions that *adopted* it.[1]

Hamilton became an administrator in the new American regime and, as secretary of the Treasury, was required to submit the principles of

1

the American Constitution to the test of day-to-day administrative practice.[2] He did not understand the problem, therefore, so much in terms of molding circumstance to principles (that is, making the government conform to the Constitution, as Madison had stated it), but rather in terms of adapting principles to circumstance. From that point of view, the Constitution had to be made to work, and that meant putting the principles of the Constitution into practice, or making accommodations to practical political necessities. As Hamilton wrote to Rufus King in 1798: "You know . . . how widely different the *business* of Government is from the *speculation* of it, and the energy of the imagination, dealing in general propositions, from that of *execution in detail.*"[3] He clearly wanted to distinguish the business of government from the speculation of it, that is, from political theorizing. Their functions are different. The suggestion is worth making that the problem of statesmanship for Hamilton was mainly a matter of determining what kinds of arrangements and policies under given circumstances would be the best means for securing the collective and permanent interests of the political community, and that would require a flexible constitution of powers. What appeared to Madison as unconstitutional was for Hamilton a different view of what constitutionalism requires.

The paramount problem of Washington's presidency was that of making the Constitution work, that is, constructing executive departments and putting into effect the economic measures that the Constitution's adoption implied. Hamilton recommended that "in construing a Constitution, it is wise, as far as possible, to pursue a course, which will reconcile essential principles with convenient modifications."[4] He understood the difference between constitutional principle and political practice: principles are fixed, but political practice is necessarily fluid. It is the fluidity of practice that requires the modification of principle.

> In my reasonings on the subject of government, I rely more on the interests and opinions of men, than on any speculative parchment provisions whatever. I have found, that Constitutions are more or less excellent, as they are more or less agreeable to the natural operation of things: I am therefore disposed not to dwell long on curious speculations, or pay much attention to modes and forms; but to adopt a system, whose principles have been sanctioned by experience; adapt it to the real state of our country; and depend on probable reasonings for its operation and result.[5]

Although Hamilton argued a broad rule of constitutional construction, he believed firmly in constitutional principles. He repeatedly emphasized, however, the difficulty of applying principles and the danger of applying them too rigidly to specific situations. Madison, by contrast, wanted "a system of administration corresponding with the purity of the theory." He wrote to J. K. Paulding in 1831 that "the criticism to which [Hamilton's] share in the administration of [the new system] was most liable was, that it had the aspect of an effort to give the instrument a constructive and practical bearing not warranted by its true and intended character."[6] As Hamilton saw it, however, Madison's strict emphasis on constitutional principles would have the effect of depriving the Constitution of its capacity to avail itself of experience and of accommodating its principles to circumstance. Hamilton perceived that, when the Constitution was submitted to the test of practice, many things would necessarily have to be worked out in the course of time that could not have been accounted for in the original document.

The most important aspect of the American Constitution, from the Hamiltonian perspective, was its strengthening of the executive. Even though the executive was subordinate to the legislature in principle, the constitutional design called for a relatively strong independent executive in competition with Congress and a presidential office that was to be in a significant sense a political office. The executive authority was to operate independently and with a wide range of discretion in its field, the Constitution and laws providing only broad guidelines and rules. Hence the traditional absolute supremacy of the legislature or assembly in democratic societies was qualified by an uneven balance between the legislative and executive powers. Beyond this uneven balance of divided power—divided between legislative and executive, giving an edge, but not complete preponderance, to the legislative—it could be said that the president was expected to exercise some positive political leadership.

Hamilton's contribution to the scheme of the Constitution was the preservation of the province of statesmanship, by an emphasis on executive energy and initiative. In the Hamiltonian scheme, statesmanship was called into existence out of the exigencies of fiscal reconstruction and foreign relations. The development of the presidency during the Washington administrations—the role of the presidency that Hamilton, under Washington's aegis, had forged for it at that time—can most immediately be understood as a strengthening of executive power, resulting from the need to *administer* the new government.

Hamilton's central concern during the Washington administrations was how statesmanship might be infused into a republican regime. The executive, he understood, must possess energy and

3

initiative. Those qualities were necessary to make republican government an effective instrument for providing security for the citizen and for ensuring the preservation of the government—that is, they were necessary for good government altogether. In response to Jefferson's opposition to the financial measures of the new government, Hamilton wrote in the *Gazette of the United States* in 1792 that "the success of every government—its capacity to combine the exertion of public strength with the preservation of personal right and private security, *qualities which define the perfection of a government,* must always naturally depend on the energy of the executive department."[7]

When the new government got under way in 1789, Hamilton naturally looked to the presidency for the formation of those policies that could not be expected from the legislative process alone. Statesmanship, he thought, would not arise from the legislature. It was necessary, therefore, for him to try to exert his influence on the Congress, and his financial reports became the principal means by which he sought to do so. The funding system, the assumption of state debts, the Bank of the United States, and other fiscal measures all originated in reports submitted by the secretary of the Treasury and were designed to fill the vacuum of leadership that the new regime exhibited. It was Hamilton's intention that legislative leadership would be exercised—as it has largely been exercised throughout American history—by the presidency.

Hamilton's principal political antagonist, Thomas Jefferson, believed that the policies of the new administration as they were defined in the system of legislation proposed by his adversary were the policies of a corrupt administration, which would destroy the essentials of the Constitution properly understood. He contended that the system proposed by the secretary of the Treasury was calculated to undermine the regime and move it toward the English monarchy and that "democratical" power, the power of the legislature, was the immediate target of the Hamiltonian scheme. As Jefferson wrote at a later time:

> the real ground of opposition which was made to the course of administration . . . was to preserve the legislature pure and independent of the executive, to restrain the administration to republican forms and principles, and not permit the constitution to be construed into a monarchy, and to be warped, in practice, into all the principles and pollutions of their favorite English model.[8]

Jefferson argued that Hamilton tried to use the Constitution as a basis for "administering the new government into a monarchy." He wrote to Elbridge Gerry in 1799 that he was "opposed to the monarchising [the Constitution's] features by the forms of its administration, with a view to conciliate a first transition to a President & Senate for life, & from that to an hereditary tenure of these offices, & thus to worm out the elective principle."[9] Jefferson believed that Hamilton, having failed to secure his plan of government at the Constitutional Convention, sought in a subtle and less visible (and therefore more dangerous) way to bring into being a monarchical system.

Jefferson was worried about the deterioration of our political institutions into less republican forms under Federalist leadership. Writing to Lafayette in 1792, he observed that

> a sect has shown itself among us, who declare they espoused our new constitution, not as a good & sufficient thing itself, but only as a step to an English constitution, the only thing good & sufficient in itself, in their eye. . . . Too many of these stock jobbers & king-jobbers have come into our legislature, or rather too many of our legislature have become stock jobbers and king-jobbers.[10]

Jefferson believed that Hamilton's financial policies, especially his method of funding the national debt, implied a design to introduce monarchy into the American regime, corrupting the legislative branch and making it subservient to the Treasury. He feared that such policies would create and sustain a wealthy privileged class. Jefferson not only believed that the existence of such a privileged class was antithetical to the requirements of democratic society, he also feared that an alliance of such a class with the executive part of the government would render it more than a match for the legislature, thereby breaking down the restraints of the Constitution. He was concerned, in other words, with executive aggrandizement.

The charge that Hamilton was a "monarchist" was prompted by his admiration for the English type of government. Hamilton was accused by Jefferson of acceding to the Constitution only to prepare the way for a change from the present republican form to a monarchy modeled after the English Constitution. As Jefferson later reflected on the monarchical tendencies of the Federalists:

> Among that section of our citizens called federalists, . . . the *leaders* consider the English Constitution as a model of perfection, some, with a correction of its vices, others, with all its corruptions and abuses. This last was Alexander Hamilton's opinion, which others, as well as myself, have often heard him declare, and that a correction of what are called its vices, would render the English an impracticable govern-

5

ment. This government they wished to have established here, and only accepted and held fast, *at first*, to the present constitution, as a steppingstone to the final establishment of their favorite model.[11]

Of all Hamilton's political opponents, none was more convinced of his attachment to monarchy or worked harder to convince others of that attachment than Jefferson, but Hamilton did not allow his attacks to go unanswered. He repeatedly reaffirmed his commitment to republican principles, though he surely contemplated a presidency stronger than that which the Constitution created.

The *basis* of the charge that Hamilton was a monarchist was that he had delivered a speech allegedly in praise of monarchy while outlining his proposed plan of government at the Constitutional Convention. In that speech, he asserted that "in his private opinion he had no scruple in declaring, supported as he was by the opinions of so many of the wise & good, that the British Govt. was the best in the world." But he prefaced that with the remark that "he was sensible at the same time that it would be unwise to propose one of any other form [than a Republican Govt.]."[12] Hamilton later affirmed that he had been fully committed to republican principles at the convention. He stated in a letter to the president that he had

> declared in strong terms that the republican theory ought to be adhered to in this Country as long as there was any chance of its success—that the idea of a perfect equality of political rights among the citizens, exclusive of all permanent hereditary distinctions, was of a nature to engage the good wishes of every good man, whatever might be his theoretic doubts—*that it merited his best efforts to give success to it in practice*—that hitherto from an incompetent structure of the Government it had not had a fair trial, and that the endeavor ought then to be to secure to it a better chance of success by a government more capable of energy and order.[13]

Hamilton further elaborated his position in a letter to Timothy Pickering written in 1803, saying that

> the highest toned propositions which I made in the Convention, were for a President, Senate, and Judges during good behaviour—a house of representatives for three years. . . . This plan was in my conception conformable with the strict theory of a Government purely republican; the essential criteria of which are that the principal organs of the Executive and Legislative departments be elected by the people, and hold their offices by a *responsible* and temporary or *defeasible* tenure.[14]

Throughout his entire political career, Hamilton remained subject to the charge that his real political sentiments and attachments lay with the English Constitution, to which he was undeniably attracted. But what becomes clear from Hamilton's remarks is that his sketch of a high-toned government was purely republican, for, unlike monarchies and aristocracies, all of the officers in that plan of government were chosen directly or indirectly by the people themselves and held their offices during good behavior. The English government was not his plan of government. He argued the desirability of a government devoted to public strength and individual security or rights, and he found the principles of this desired government in the Constitution of England. But despite his respect for that constitution, he never considered it a viable constitution for America. Hamilton could differ with Jefferson about what constituted "good government," but he made it perfectly clear that in restructuring the constitution of government "we ought to go as far in order to attain stability and permanency as republican government will admit"—and impliedly no further than that. The best practicable regime had been realized in England, but it was unfitted for America, and therefore Hamilton's view that it was the best that had thus far appeared cannot be understood as prescriptive. What we can say is that he saw immanent in the English Constitution those principles of executive strength and independence that were capable of rectifying republican government.

Hamilton, who as a matter of practice paid little attention to modes or forms of government, nevertheless dismissed the view that good government is simply reducible to good administration. In *Federalist* 68, he commented on a well-known verse written by Alexander Pope: "Though we cannot acquiesce in the political heresy of the poet who says—'For forms of government let fools contest—That which is best administered is best.'—yet we may safely pronounce, that the true test of a good government is its aptitude and tendency to produce a good administration." What Pope suggested was that it does not matter what the ends or purpose of government are, just so long as there is an efficient and orderly administration. By contrast, Hamilton would say that forms of government are important, and that the true test of good government, understood as free government, is its aptitude or tendency to foster a good administration. Therefore Pope was wrong, in Hamilton's thinking, in suggesting that the forms are absolutely unimportant. Hamilton was not neutral with regard to regimes, for he had a clear perception of what constitutes good government. For him, the Constitution contains within itself principles that are to be revered, principles that justify it, and its true test would be its ability to foster a good administration.

Hamilton believed that popular government was good but problematic—that is, he had a real sense of the problematic character of popular government. He expressed this concern in a letter to Edward Carrington written in 1792, at a time when the Washington administration was wracked by controversies:

> I am *affectionately* attached to Republican theory . . . & I add that I have strong hopes of the success of that theory; but in candor I ought also to add that I am far from being without doubts. I consider its success as yet a problem. It is yet to be determined by experience whether it be consistent with that *stability* and *order* in Government which are essential to public strength & private security and happiness.[15]

Both early and late in his political career, Hamilton was critical of the American Constitution, or at least skeptical about its survival,[16] but between those periods of doubt he did much to strengthen it, as was evidenced by his career as secretary of the Treasury. It is sometimes overlooked, moreover, that Jefferson also had reservations about the Constitution, but they were pointed in another direction.

Much has been made of Hamilton's remark in a letter to Gouverneur Morris in 1802 that the Constitution was a frail and worthless fabric, which, contrary to all his anticipations of its fate, he was still laboring to prop. Later in that same letter, however, he wrote that the time may come when the minds of men will be prepared to make an effort to *recover* the Constitution,[17] which would appear to suggest that the Jefferson administration had moved in the direction of changing the character of that instrument. Hamilton had in fact written in 1800 that "a new government, constructed on free principles, is always weak, *and must stand in need of the props of a firm and good administration;* till time shall have rendered its authority venerable, and fortified it by habits of obedience."[18] Hamilton would say that the Constitution contains sound principles and that the accommodation of these principles to circumstance by a good administration helps to protect it from the subsequent designs of those who would undermine it. But apparently, by the time of the Jeffersonian administration, the Constitution was not yet strong enough to resist what Hamilton regarded as that administration's undermining influence.[19]

The American Constitution was intended to secure, as far as republican principles would admit, the benefits of the traditional mixed regime by establishing a *complex* apparatus of government. But providing for the *benefits* of a mixed regime by means of complexity is not the same as providing for a mixed regime per se. From the point of view of simple democracy, the Constitution with its scheme of checks and balances appeared too complex—it appeared to guarantee what James MacGregor Burns was later to call "the deadlock of democracy." A similar charge moved through opposition opinion during the debate over the president's Neutrality Proclamation in 1793. Hamilton formulated that charge better than the opposition could themselves:

> The language in the confidential circles is that the constitution of the United States is too complex a system—that it savours too much of the pernicious doctrine of 'ballances and checks' that it requires to be simplified in its structure, to be purged of some monarchical and aristocratic ingredients which are said to have found their way into it and to be stripped of some dangerous prerogatives with which it is pretended to be invested.[20]

The Constitution acts in opposition to simple democracy, Hamilton would argue, through its skillfully contrived complexity, but that does not make it any less a popular government, as its critics would contend.

There is really no way, as it now appears, to understand Hamilton in his political thought without comparing him with Jefferson. Jefferson consistently opposed energetic government. He wrote to Madison concerning the proposed Constitution: "I own, I am not a friend to a very energetic government. It is *always* oppressive."[21] He thought that the proposed government was too centered in powers— that there were too many powers over too many things. The president has too much power, and Jefferson was especially disturbed about the indefinite reeligibility of the president. Jefferson understood the heart of the governmental process to be the legislative process, and this was a point of view he carried to the presidency, no matter what his later practice may have been. A clarification of the contrast between Hamilton and Jefferson would amount to the following: the lawmaking function was not the decisive political function for Hamilton, while for Jefferson it was. We could say, therefore, that much of the disagreement between Hamilton and Jefferson resulted from different interpretations of the proper balance between legislative and executive powers and different understandings of what those powers include. Hamilton wanted to provide the executive with the maximum freedom of action that the Constitution could be construed to allow. He therefore interpreted the enumeration of legislative powers in Article I as more *limiting* than the general grant of executive power in Article II. The executive power was to be subject only to the exceptions and qualifications expressed in that instrument.[22]

The following story was related by Jefferson to Dr. Benjamin Rush: President Washington asked Jefferson, in his capacity as secretary of state, to call together the heads of the other executive departments and the vice president to discuss an issue that required decision. Jefferson invited the group to dinner at his house, at which occasion Hamilton asked Jefferson the names of the men in the three portraits on his wall. Jefferson replied that they were his trinity of the greatest men the world had ever produced—Bacon, Newton, and Locke. Hamilton, after moments of studied silence, responded: "The greatest man that ever lived was Julius Caesar." Jefferson regarded this response as revealing of Hamilton's political principles, namely, his Caesarism.[23]

The very overstated character of Hamilton's remark about Caesar (for he often criticized him) was intended to make it clear to Jefferson that, from a purely political perspective, the practice of statesmanship is the highest human activity. The counterpoint of Jefferson's preference for scientists or philosopher-scientists over statesmen as his models[24] was his belief that rulers are incapable of ruling in the interests of the ruled, that is, of being guardians of the people's interests. Jefferson believed that enlightened statesmanship was problematic despite his famous dictum that the best form of government is that which provides most effectively for a natural *aristoi* of talent. He doubted the ability of the *aristoi* to rule in the best interests of the ruled.

Jefferson believed that power necessarily corrupts its possessor, while for Hamilton the consequences of a hiatus in power were just as dangerous as the evils that attend its unchecked accumulation. In a speech before the New York ratifying convention, he reflected:

> we are told it is dangerous to trust power any where; that *power* is liable to *abuse* with a variety of trite maxims of the same kind. General propositions of this nature are easily framed, the truth of which cannot be denied, but they rarely convey any precise idea. To these we might oppose other propositions equally true and equally indefinite. It might be said that too little power is as dangerous as too much, that it leads to anarchy, and from anarchy to despotism. But the question still recurs, what is this *too much or too little?* where is the measure or standard to ascertain the happy mean? Powers must be granted, or civil Society cannot exist; the possibility of abuse is no argument against the *thing*; this possibility is incident to every species of power however placed or modified.[25]

The Hamiltonian position tended to be more expansive than the Jeffersonian with regard to governmental functions and less apprehen-

10

sive about the exercise of political power. Jefferson looked to the reduction of government as such, for he believed that society would grow better by stripping governmental functions and hence power to the minimum. For Jefferson, there was ultimately little need for government, either as providing a broad political order within which economic activity is encouraged or as balancing the demands of constantly shifting factions and interests.

Hamilton emphasized that government is power to accomplish ends[26] and was convinced that the principal end of government was liberty. He is one of the great teachers of the necessity of energetic and efficient government for the preservation of a regime of liberty. Accordingly, Hamilton was no Machiavellian practitioner of unlimited government and political power. He believed that some fundamental limitations on the scope of government were indispensable to the American political system. As he wrote in answer to a letter from Washington stating objections to his financial policy: "There are some things which the General Government has clearly a right to do—there are others which it has clearly no right to meddle with, and there is a good deal of middle ground, about which honest and well disposed men might differ."[27] Hamilton defined "limited government" as the effort to limit the powers by means of which government performs the tasks assigned to it—the primary task being to secure individual rights (including the rights of property). But the need to limit government did not suggest to him the need to weaken government. He entertained a broader concept of limited government than that. Hamilton considered limited government rightly understood as limited energetic government, that is, a constitution with a strong, independent executive qualified by a system of separation of powers and checks and balances.

A substantial portion of Hamilton's political thought is devoted to showing that the way to limit government most effectively is not by niggardly grants of power or by a simple separation of powers that classifies all the powers of government in oversimple categories, but by a carefully designed complex structure of government. He laid down general rules for the operation of a system of checks and balances in 1802 that were consistent with his previous thought and practice:

> The means held out as proper to be employed for enabling the several departments to keep each other in their proper places are: 1. To give each an *organization* which will render them essentially independent of one another. 2. To secure to each a *support* which shall not be at the discretionary disposal of any other. 3. To establish between them *mutual relations of authority* as will make one a check upon another,

11

and enable them reciprocally to resist encroachments, and confine one another within their proper spheres.[28]

The complex or balanced government provided for in the Constitution depends, in other words, on an imprecision in the fundamental separation of powers that creates mutual relations of authority. This partial intermixture, says Hamilton, is necessary for the mutual defense of the several branches of government against one another.

The prevailing tendency among both Hamilton admirers and critics is to understand his political thought as well as his practice primarily in terms of energy or the strength of government. Much is attributed to his political thought on the basis of his remark that "energy in the executive is a leading character in the definition of good government."[29] But it has escaped attention that he said that energy is *a* leading character, and not *the* leading character, in the definition of good government. There is more to the definition of good government than energy in the executive, for Hamilton's political thought is one that gives double attention to energy in the administration and to liberty for the people. His formulation in the New York ratifying convention was as follows:

> There are two objects in forming systems of government—
> Safety for the people and energy in the administration.
> When these two objects are united, the certain tendency of
> the system will be to the public welfare. If the latter object be
> neglected, the people's security will be as certainly
> sacrificed, as by disregarding the former. Good constitutions
> are formed upon a comparison of the liberty of the indi-
> vidual with the strength of government: If the tone of either
> be too high, the other will be weakened too much.

The problem, therefore, consists in finding the best possible mode of conciliating these objects so that "the government will reach, in its regular operations, the perfect balance between liberty and power."[30] Hamilton was for liberty and not against power.

It becomes clear that Hamilton's aim was to render republicanism a defensible form of government by combining energy and liberty, and from this it follows that all the institutions of the American government are characterized by an attempt to balance their competing claims. Hamilton was clearly on the side of liberty, but the question is whether liberty can be achieved by absolute prohibitions on things that cause the loss of liberty or is secured by a kind of limited government that renders the abuse of power unlikely. He was against absolute prohibitions (that is, bills of rights) and in favor of giving power, but he was also in favor of making it unlikely that power would be abused. Hamilton's admonition that the maintenance of regimes and constitutions requires a perfect balance between liberty and power constitutes a new statement of the whole issue of balanced government. He asserted that energy was a leading character in the definition of good government but was not the sum and substance of good government. Hamilton understood that government is the power to accomplish ends. He was, therefore, able to make the connection between liberty and power, between ends and means.

In the political thought of Hamilton, the best guarantee of liberty rested in a government with competent powers to act and a complex structure arranged to make it act wisely and responsibly. The principle appealed to is: "Make the system complete in its structure; give a perfect proportion and balance to its parts; and the powers you give it will never affect your security."[31] Contrasted with Jefferson, it might appear that Hamilton was simply a loose constructionist, but great latitude of constitutional construction never meant for him that government has a right to do merely what it pleases. As he stated in his opinion on the constitutionality of the national bank in 1791:

> [The] criterion [of what is constitutional, and what is not so] is the *end*, to which the measure relates as a *mean*. If the end be clearly comprehended within any of the specified powers, & if the measure have an obvious relation to the end, and is not forbidden by any particular provision of the constitution—it may safely be deemed to come within the compass of the national authority.[32]

That the right to the end gives one a right to the means does not suggest that *any means* is appropriate—it must be a means in accordance with the end. Hamilton was a partisan of the strong executive, but he knew well its untoward tendencies; and to the extent that the government as a whole was limited by its ends, executive energy was limited too. Hamilton's presidency, as strong as it was, was intended to secure only limited ends.

The difference between Hamilton's and Jefferson's understandings of the right kind of republican government was reflected in their contrasting views of the proposed Constitution. The essence of Jefferson's objection to it was that it abandoned the necessity of rotation in office, which seemed to him to lead to the transformation of the republican executive into a monarch.[33] Hamilton, however, saw that the Jeffersonian alternative of rotation in office presupposed a political system significantly *different* from our present one, that of the unrestrained legislature and the subordinate executive, a system that tends to undermine separation of powers properly understood.[34]

Hamilton did not believe that we should have an executive who simply carries out the will of the legislature. He believed rather in the balance of a system of separation of powers and thought that the principle of rotation in office would serve to undermine that balance. Hamilton was for the balance of a well-ordered republican government, for the rightly understood kind of power and limits on power, with no one power capable of gaining the decisive advantage.

* * *

The problem of the "imperial presidency" as currently perceived is the problem of potential tyrannical rule within the context of American democratic society. It is no exaggeration to say that the first modern democracy at its outset attempted to liberate executive power, whereas today that democracy is far more concerned with circumscribing it. Perhaps this is because the liberal and conservative movements of political opinion in the United States have lost their sense of the connection between limited and energetic government, an understanding that animated the thought of Hamilton.

Commentators have too readily interpreted Hamilton's endorsement of strong, energetic government as signifying his agreement with unlimited government.[35] Hamilton believed that the perfection of republican government called for limited energetic government. He stated in the opening number of *The Federalist Papers* that "the vigour of government is *essential* to the security of liberty" and followed that with the remark that "in the contemplation of a sound and well informed judgment, their interest *can never be separated*,"[36] thereby indicating that the end of securing liberty should control governmental power. Hamilton argued in *Federalist* 70 that energetic executive power can be made compatible with republican government not by dispersing power to the greatest extent possible but by concentrating it in the hands of the executive. His reasoning was that concentrated power or unity in the executive can more easily be held accountable to popular opinion, whereas plurality in the executive tends to conceal faults and destroy responsibility, an idea inadmissible in free government. The sense of responsibility is always the greater the less it is divided.[37] The crucial point that Hamilton wanted to emphasize in *The Federalist Papers* was that executive energy was not outside the purview of republican or limited government. The fact is that energetic executive power, as that appears in Hamilton's political thought, was designed or intended to make republican theory successful in practice.

Hamilton was forced to rethink the basic premises of republicanism in the course of instituting a new constitution of government, and that was informed largely by an awareness of the defective character of our previous republican constitution, the Articles of Confederation. When he thought about what kind of political constitution ought to replace the articles, he measured republicanism by standards that transcended republicanism, in an effort to bring about a perfected republican constitution. He accordingly engaged in a more radical thinking through of republicanism than had been attempted by other founding statesmen, for he saw the need for a modification or strengthening of republicanism as it was traditionally understood.

From his experience with the articles, it became clear to Hamilton that the answer to the problem of inefficiency in republican government lay in energetic executive power accomplished through separation of power. Indeed, his defense of the presidency during the ratification debates, as well as his reflections and policies during his tenure as secretary of the Treasury, can be viewed as a sustained articulation of his attempt to structure or restructure republican government in such a way as to give it the necessary energy and stability. In the light of subsequent American history, it can be said that the executive office, often considered the most original contribution of the framers of modern republican government, was the institution designed to bring good administration to republican government.

Notes

1. "N. P. Trist Memoranda, September 27, 1834," in *The Records of the Federal Convention of 1787*, ed. Max Farrand, 4 vols. (New Haven, Conn.: Yale University Press, 1966), vol. 3, p. 534.

2. See Alexander Hamilton, "Explanation, November 11, 1795," in *The Papers of Alexander Hamilton*, ed. Harold C. Syrett, 26 vols. (New York: Columbia University Press, 1961–79), vol. 19, p. 423: "Preeminently hard in such circumstances, was the lot of the man who called to the head of the most arduous department in the public administration, in a new Government, without the guides of antecedent practice & precedent, had to trace out his own path and to adjust for himself the import and bearings of delicate and important provisions in the constitution & in the laws!" (Hereafter cited as *Papers.*)

3. Hamilton, "Hamilton to Rufus King, October 2, 1798," *Papers*, vol. 22, p. 192.

4. Hamilton, "The Examination, No. XVI, March 19, 1802," *Papers*, vol. 25, p. 567.

5. Hamilton, "Speech in the New York Ratifying Convention, June 21, 1788," *Papers*, vol. 5, pp. 36–37.

6. James Madison, "Spirit of Governments, from the National Gazette, February 20, 1792," *The Writings of James Madison*, ed. Gaillard Hunt, 9 vols.

(New York: G. P. Putnam's Sons, 1900–1910), vol. 6, p. 95; "Madison to J. K. Paulding, April 1831," *Letters and Other Writings of James Madison*, ed. Philip R. Fendall, 4 vols. (New York: R. Worthington, 1884), vol. 4, pp. 176–77.

7. Hamilton, "Metellus, October 24, 1792," *Papers*, vol. 12, p. 615. The italics are mine.

8. Thomas Jefferson, "The Anas," in *The Life and Selected Writings of Thomas Jefferson*, ed. Adrienne Koch and William Peden (New York: Modern Library, 1944), p. 125. (Hereafter cited as *Life and Selected Writings*.)

9. Jefferson, "Jefferson to Elbridge Gerry, January 26, 1799," in *Life and Selected Writings*, p. 545.

10. Jefferson, "Jefferson to Lafayette, June 16, 1792," in *The Works of Thomas Jefferson*, ed. Paul L. Ford, 12 vols. (New York: G. P. Putnam's Sons, 1904–1905), vol. 7, pp. 109–10. (Hereafter cited as *Works*.)

11. Jefferson. "Jefferson to John Melish, January 13, 1813," in *Life and Selected Writings*, p. 622.

12. Hamilton, "Speech on a Plan of Government, June 18, 1787," *Papers*, vol. 4, p. 192.

13. Hamilton, "Hamilton to George Washington, August 18, 1792," *Papers*, vol. 12, p. 253. The italics are mine.

14. Hamilton, "Hamilton to Timothy Pickering, September 16, 1802," *Papers*, vol. 26, pp. 147–48. See also Hamilton, "To the New York Evening Post, February 27, 1802," *Papers*, vol. 25, pp. 536–38.

15. Hamilton, "Hamilton to Edward Carrington, May 26, 1792," *Papers*, vol. 11, pp. 443–44.

16. See *Federalist* 71: "It is one thing to be subordinate to the laws, and another to be dependent on the legislative body. The first comports with, the last violates, the fundamental principles of good government."

17. Hamilton, "Hamilton to Gouverneur Morris, February 29, 1802," *Papers*, vol. 25, pp. 544–45.

18. Hamilton, "Letter concerning the Public Conduct and Character of John Adams, October 24, 1800," *Papers*, vol. 25, p. 233. The italics are mine.

19. See Hamilton's criticism of the policies of the Jefferson administration as they were defended in the president's annual message to Congress of December 8, 1801, and especially his criticism of the repeal of the Judiciary Act of 1801 as a violation of the Constitution, in Hamilton, "The Examination, Nos. IV–VI, December 26, 1801–January 2, 1802," *Papers*, vol. 25.

20. Hamilton, "Defense of the President's Neutrality Proclamation, May 1793," *Papers*, vol. 14, p. 503.

21. Jefferson, "Jefferson to James Madison, December 20, 1787," *The Papers of Thomas Jefferson*, ed. Julian P. Boyd, 20 vols. (Princeton, N.J.: Princeton University Press, 1950–1982), vol. 12, p. 442. The italics are mine. (Hereafter cited as *Papers*.)

22. Hamilton, "Pacificus No. 1, June 29, 1793," *Papers*, vol. 15, p. 39.

23. Jefferson, "Jefferson to Dr. Benjamin Rush, January 16, 1811," in *Life and Selected Writings*, p. 609.

24. Rousseau, Jefferson's mentor, recommended in his *First Discourse* that scientists or philosopher-scientists like Bacon, Descartes, and Newton should

be made advisers of princes and should help instruct peoples in their duties. Jefferson substitutes Locke for Descartes in the Rousseauean trilogy. See *First Discourse*, part 2 in *Jean Jacques Rousseau: The First and Second Discourses*, ed. Roger D. Masters (New York: Princeton University Press, 1964), pp. 63–64.

25. Hamilton, "Speech in the New York Assembly, January 19, 1787," *Papers*, vol. 4, p. 11.

26. Hamilton, "Tully, No. 3, August 28, 1794," *Papers*, vol. 17, p. 160: "Government supposes controul. It is the POWER by which individuals in society are kept from doing injury to each other and are bro't to cooperate to a common end."

27. Hamilton, "Hamilton to Washington, August 18, 1792," *Papers*, vol. 12, p. 251.

28. Hamilton, "The Examination No. XV, March 3, 1802," *Papers*, vol. 25, p. 525.

29. *Federalist* 70.

30. Hamilton, "Speech in the New York Ratifying Convention, June 25, 1788," *Papers*, vol. 5, p. 81.

31. Hamilton, "Remarks in the New York Ratifying Convention, June 27, 1788," *Papers*, vol. 5, p. 97.

32. Hamilton, "Opinion on Constitutionality of Bank, February 23, 1791," *Papers*, vol. 8, p. 107.

33. Jefferson, "Jefferson to Edward Carrington, May 27, 1788," *Papers*, vol. 13, pp. 208–9.

34. See Hamilton, "Catullus, No. IV, October 17, 1792," *Papers*, vol. 12, pp. 580–81.

35. See especially James MacGregor Burns's characterization of the Hamiltonian model of presidential leadership in his *Presidential Government: The Crucible of Leadership* (New York: Avon Books, 1965).

36. *Federalist* 1. The italics are mine.

37. See *Federalist* 70: "all multiplication of the executive is rather dangerous than friendly to liberty."

THE FARMER REFUTED
FEBRUARY 23, 1775

*The following passages from a tract Hamilton had written in 1775
contain his most explicit statements on natural rights. He was writing
in response to the Tory Samuel Seabury, who had held that the British
Parliament had a right to tax Britain's American colonies. Hamilton
based his argument for "no taxation without representation" on natural
rights. But the doctrine of natural rights for Hamilton was more than a
doctrine designed to serve the turn of a revolution. He understood that
every political society requires adherence to certain principles, that a
free society derives its character by looking up to freedom, and that civil
liberties or rights are ephemeral if they do not rest on a solid theoretical
foundation of natural rights.*

I shall . . . begin to make some allowance for that enmity, you have
discovered to the *natural rights* of mankind. For, though ignorance of
them in this enlightened age cannot be admitted, as a sufficient excuse for you; yet, it ought, in some measure, to extenuate your guilt.
If you will follow my advice, there still may be hopes of your reformation. Apply yourself, without delay, to the study of the law of nature.
I would recommend to your perusal, Grotius Puffendorf, Locke,
Montesquieu, and Burlemaqui. I might mention other excellent
writers on this subject; but if you attend, diligently, to these, you will
not require any others.

There is so strong a similitude between your political principles
and those maintained by Mr. Hobbs, that, in judging from them, a
person might very easily *mistake* you for a disciple of his. His opinion
was, exactly, coincident with yours, relative to man in a state of
nature. He held, as you do, that he was, then, perfectly free from all
restraint of *law* and *government*. Moral obligation, according to him, is
derived from the introduction of civil society; and there is no virtue,
but what is purely artificial, the mere contrivance of politicians, for
the maintenance of social intercourse. But the reason he run into this
absurd and impious doctrine, was, that he disbelieved the existence
of an intelligent superintending principle, who is the governor, and
will be the final judge of the universe.

As you, sometimes, swear *by him that made you,* I conclude, your sentiment does not correspond with his, in that which is the basis of the doctrine, you both agree in; and this makes it impossible to imagine whence this congruity between you arises. To grant, that there is a supreme intelligence, who rules the world, and has established laws to regulate the actions of his creatures; and, still, to assert, that man, in a state of nature, may be considered as perfectly free from all restraints of *law* and *government,* appear to a common understanding, altogether irreconcileable.

Good and wise men, in all ages, have embraced a very dissimilar theory. They have supposed, that the deity, from the relations, we stand in, to himself and to each other, has constituted an eternal and immutable law, which is, indispensibly, obligatory upon all mankind, prior to any human institution whatever.

This is what is called the law of nature, "which, being coeval with mankind, and dictated by God himself, is, of course, superior in obligation to any other. It is binding over all the globe, in all countries, and at all times. No human laws are of any validity, if contrary to this; and such of them as are valid, derive all their authority, mediately, or immediately, from this original." BLACKSTONE.

Upon this law, depend the natural rights of mankind, the supreme being gave existence to man, together with the means of preserving and beatifying that existence. He endowed him with rational faculties, by the help of which, to discern and pursue such things, as were consistent with his duty and interest, and invested him with an inviolable right to personal liberty, and personal safety.

Hence, in a state of nature, no man had any *moral* power to deprive another of his life, limbs, property or liberty; nor the least authority to command, or exact obedience from him; except that which arose from the ties of consanguinity.

Hence also, the origin of all civil government, justly established, must be a voluntary compact, between the rulers and the ruled; and must be liable to such limitations, as are necessary for the security of the *absolute rights* of the latter; for what original title can any man or set of man have, to govern others, except their own consent? To usurp dominion over a people, in their own despite, or to grasp at a more extensive power than they are willing to entrust, is to violate that law of nature, which gives every man a right to his personal liberty; and can, therefore, confer no obligation to obedience.

"The principal aim of society is to protect individuals, in the enjoyment of those absolute rights, which were vested in them by the immutable laws of nature; but which could not be preserved, in peace, without that mutual assistance, and intercourse, which is gained by the institution of friendly and social communities. Hence it follows, that the first and primary end of human laws, is to maintain and regulate these *absolute rights* of individuals." BLACKSTONE.

If we examine the pretensions of parliament, by this criterion, which is evidently, a good one, we shall, presently detect their injustice. First, they are subversive of our natural liberty, because an authority is assumed over us, which we by no means assent to. And secondly, they divest us of that moral security, for our lives and properties, which we are intitled to, and which it is the primary end of society to bestow. For such security can never exist, while we have no part in making the laws, that are to bind us; and while it may be the interest of our uncontroled legislators to oppress us as much as possible.

* * *

The fundamental source of all your errors, sophisms and false reasonings is a total ignorance of the natural rights of mankind. Were you once to become acquainted with these, you could never entertain a thought, that all men are not, by nature, entitled to a parity of privileges. You would be convinced, that natural liberty is a gift of the beneficent Creator to the whole human race, and that civil liberty is founded in that; and cannot be wrested from any people, without the most manifest violation of justice. *Civil liberty, is only natural liberty, modified and secured by the sanctions of civil society.* It is not a thing, in its own nature, precarious and dependent on human will and caprice; but is conformable to the constitution of man, as well as necessary to the *well-being* of society.

* * *

The sacred rights of mankind are not to be rummaged for, among old parchments, or musty records. They are written, as with a sun beam in the whole *volume* of human nature, by the hand of the divinity itself; and can never be erased or obscured by mortal power.

The nations of Turkey, Russia, France, Spain, and all other despotic kingdoms, in the world, have an inherent right, when ever they please, to shake off the yoke of servitude, (though sanctified by the immemorial usage of their ancestors;) and to model their government, upon the principles of civil liberty.

* * *

When the first principles of civil society are violated and the rights of a whole people are invaded, the common forms of municipal law are not to be regarded. Men may then betake themselves to the law of

21

nature; and, if they but conform their actions, to that standard, all cavils against them, betray either ignorance or dishonesty. There are some events in society, to which human laws cannot extend; but when applied to them lose all their force and efficacy. In short, when human laws contradict or discountenance the means, which are necessary to preserve the essential rights of any society, they defeat the proper end of all laws, and so become null and void.

LETTER TO JAMES DUANE
SEPTEMBER 3, 1780

Hamilton prepared a critical evaluation of the Confederation at the request of a New York delegate to the Continental Congress, which foreshadowed positions he was to take later on in The Federalist. *He was obviously concerned with strengthening the power of the confederal government over the states. But he was especially concerned with the strengthening of executive power within the confederal government itself, for legislative government under the Confederation was characterized by undifferentiated power or the dominance of the republican assembly. Hamilton was later to become a delegate to the Continental Congress in 1782.*

Liberty Pole, New Jersey, September 3, 1780

Dr. Sir

Agreeably to your request and my promise I sit down to give you my ideas of the defects of our present system, and the changes necessary to save us from ruin. They may perhaps be the reveries of a projector rather than the sober views of a politician. You will judge of them, and make what use you please of them.

The fundamental defect is a want of power in Congress. It is hardly worth while to show in what this consists, as it seems to be universally acknowledged, or to point out how it has happened, as the only question is how to remedy it. It may however be said that it has originated from three causes—an excess of the spirit of liberty which has made the particular states show a jealousy of all power not in their own hands; and this jealousy has led them to exercise a right of judging in the last resort of the measures recommended by Congress, and of acting according to their own opinions of their propriety or necessity, a diffidence in Congress of their own powers, by which they have been timid and indecisive in their resolutions, constantly making concession to the states, till they have scarcely left themselves the shadow of power; a want of sufficient means at their disposal to answer the public exigencies and of vigor to draw forth those means; which have occasioned them to depend on the states individually to fulfil their engagements with the army, and the consequence of which has been to ruin their influence and credit with the army, to establish its dependence on each state separately rather than *on them,* that is rather than on the whole collectively.

It may be pleaded, that Congress had never any definitive powers granted them and of course could exercise none—could do nothing more than recommend. The manner in which Congress was appointed would warrant, and the public good required, that they should have considered themselves as vested with full power *to preserve the republic from harm.* They have done many of the highest acts of sovereignty, which were always chearfully submitted to—the declaration of independence, the declaration of war, the levying an army, creating a navy, emitting money, making alliances with foreign powers, appointing a dictator &c. &c.—all these implications of a complete sovereignty were never disputed, and ought to have been a standard for the whole conduct of Administration. Undefined powers are discretionary powers, limited only by the object for which they were given—in the present case, the independence and freedom of America. The confederation made no difference; for as it has not been generally adopted, it had no operation. But from what I recollect of it, Congress have even descended from the authority which the spirit of that act gives them, while the particular states have no further attended to it than as it suited their pretensions and convenience. It would take too much time to enter into particular instances, each of which separately might appear inconsiderable; but united are of serious import. I only mean to remark, not to censure.

But the confederation itself is defective and requires to be altered; it is neither fit for war, nor peace. The idea of an uncontrolable sovereignty in each state, over its internal police, will defeat the other powers given to Congress, and make our union feeble and precarious. There are instances without number, where acts necessary for the general good, and which rise out of the powers given to Congress must interfere with the internal police of the states, and there are as many instances in which the particular states by arrangements of internal police can effectually though indirectly counteract the arrangements of Congress. You have already had examples of this for which I refer you to your own memory.

The confederation gives the states individually too much influence in the affairs of the army; they should have nothing to do with it. The entire formation and disposal of our military forces ought to belong to Congress. It is an essential cement of the union; and it ought to be the policy of Congress to des⟨troy⟩ all ideas of state attachments in the army and make it look up wholly to them. For this purpose all appointments promotions and provisions whatsoever ought to be made by them. It may be apprehended that this may be dangerous to liberty. But nothing appears more evident to me, than that we run much greater risk of having a weak and disunited federal government, than one which will be able to usurp upon the rights of the people. Already some of the lines of the army would obey their states in opposition to Congress notwithstanding the pains we have taken to preserve the unity of the army—if any thing would hinder this it would be the personal influence of the General, a melancholy and mortifying consideration.

The forms of our state constitutions must always give them great weight in our affairs and will make it too difficult to bend them to the persuit of a common interest, too easy to oppose whatever they do not like and to form partial combinations subversive of the general one. There is a wide difference between our situation and that of an empire under one simple form of government, distributed into counties provinces or districts, which have no legisla⟨tures⟩ but merely magistratical bodies to execute the laws of a common sovereign. Here the danger is that the sove[re]ign will have too much power to oppress the parts of which it is composed. In our case, that of an empire composed of confederated states each with a government completely organised within itself, having all the means to draw its subjects to a close dependence on itself—the danger is directly the reverse. It is that the common sovereign will not have power sufficient to unite the different members together, and direct the common forces to the interest and happiness of the whole.

The leagues among the old Grecian republics are a proof of this. They were continually at war with each other, and for want of union fell a prey to their neighbours. They frequently held general councils, but their resolutions were no further observed than as they suited the interests and inclinations of all the parties and at length, they sunk intirely into contempt.

The Swiss-cantons are another proof of the doctrine. They have had wars with each other which would have been fatal to them, had not the different powers in their neighbourhood been too jealous of one-another and too equally matched to suffer either to take advantage of their quarrels. That they have remained so long united at all is to be attributed to their weakness, to their poverty, and to the cause just mentioned. These ties will not exist in America; a little time hence, some of the states will be powerful empires, and we are so remote from other nations that we shall have all the leisure and opportunity we can wish to cut each others throats.

The Germanic corps might also be cited as an example in favour of the position.

The United provinces may be thought to be one against it. But the family of the stadtholders whose authority is interwoven with the whole government has been a strong link of union between them. Their physical necessities and the habits founded upon them have contributed to it. Each province is too inconsiderable by itself to undertake any thing. An analysis of their present constitutions would show that they have many ties which would not exist in ours; and that they are by no means a proper mode for us.

Our own experience should satisfy us. We have felt the difficulty of drawing out the resources of the country and inducing the states to combine in equal exertions for the common cause. The ill success of our last attempt is striking. Some have done a great deal, others little or scarcely any thing. The disputes about boundaries &c. testify how flattering a prospect we have of future tranquillity, if we do not frame in time a confederacy capable of deciding the differences and compelling the obedience of the respective members.

The confederation too gives the power of the purse too intirely to the state legislatures. It should provide perpetual funds in the disposal of Congress—by a land tax, poll tax, or the like. All imposts upon commerce ought to be laid by Congress and appropriated to their use, for without certain revenues, a government can have no power; that power, which holds the purse strings absolutely, must rule. This seems to be a medium, which without making Congress altogether independent will tend to give reality to its authority.

Another defect in our system is want of method and energy in the administration. This has partly resulted from the other defect, but in a great degree from prejudice and the want of a proper executive. Congress have kept the power too much into their own hands and have meddled too much with details of every sort. Congress is properly a deliberative corps and it forgets itself when it attempts to play the executive. It is impossible such a body, numerous as it is, constantly fluctuating, can ever act with sufficient decision, or with system. Two thirds of the members, one half the time, cannot know what has gone before them or what connection the subject in hand

25

has to what has been transacted on former occasions. The members, who have been more permanent, will only give information, that promotes the side they espouse, in the present case, and will as often mislead as enlighten. The variety of business must distract, and the proneness of every assembly to debate must at all times delay.

Lately Congress, convinced of these inconveniences, have gone into the measure of appointing boards. But this is in my opinion a bad plan. A single man, in each department of the administration, would be greatly preferable. It would give us a chance of more knowledge, more activity, more responsibility and of course more zeal and attention. Boards partake of a part of the inconveniencies of larger assemblies. Their decisions are slower their energy less their responsibility more diffused. They will not have the same abilities and knowledge as an administration by single men. Men of the first pretensions will not so readily engage in them, because they will be less cospicuous, of less importance, have less opportunity of distinguishing themselves. The members of boards will take less pains to inform themselves and arrive to eminence, because they have fewer motives to do it. All these reasons conspire to give a preference to the plan of vesting the great executive departments of the state in the hands of individuals. As these men will be of course at all times under the direction of Congress, we shall blend the advantages of a monarchy and republic in our constitution.

A question has been made, whether single men could be found to undertake these offices. I think they could, because there would be then every thing to excite the ambition of candidates. But in order to this Congress by their manner of appointing them and the line of duty marked out must show that they are in earnest in making these offices, offices of real trust and importance.

I fear a little vanity has stood in the way of these arrangements, as though they would lessen the importance of Congress and leave them nothing to do. But they would have precisely the same rights and powers as heretofore, happily disencumbered of the detail. They would have to inspect the conduct of their ministers, deliberate upon their plans, originate others for the public good—only observing this rule that they ought to consult their ministers, and get all the information and advice they could from them, before they entered into any new measures or made changes in the old.

A third defect is the fluctuating constitution of our army. This has been a pregnant source of evil; all our military misfortunes, three fourths of our civil embarrassments are to be ascribed to it. The General has so fully enumerated the mischief of it in a late letter of the to Congress that I could only repeat what he has said, and will therefore refer you to that letter.

The imperfect and unequal provision made for the army is a fourth defect which you will find delineated in the same letter. Without a speedy change the army must dissolve; it is now a mob, rather than an army, without cloathing, without pay, without provision, without morals, without discipline. We begin to hate the country for its neglect of us; the country begins to hate us for our oppressions of them. Congress have long been jealous of us; we have now lost all confidence in them, and give the worst construction to all they do. Held together by the slenderest ties we are ripening for a dissolution.

The present mode of supplying the army—by state purchases—is not one of the least considerable defects of our system. It is too precarious a dependence, because the states will never be sufficiently impressed with our necessities. Each will make its own ease a primary object, the supply of the army a secondary one. The variety of channels through which the business is transacted will multiply the number of persons employed and the opportunities of embezzling public money. From the popular spirit on which most of the governments turn, the state agents, will be men of less character and ability, nor will there be so rigid a responsibility among them as there might easily be among those in the employ of the continent, of course not so much diligence care or economy. Very little of the money raised in the several states will go into the Continental treasury, on pretence, that it is all exhausted in providing the quotas of supplies, and the public will be without funds for the other demands of governments. The expence will be ultimately much greater and the advantages much smaller. We actually feel the insufficiency of this plan and have reason to dread under it a ruinous extremity of want.

These are the principal defects in the present system that now occur to me. There are many inferior ones in the organization of particular departments and many errors of administration which might be pointed out; but the task would be troublesome and tedious, and if we had once remedied those I have mentioned the others would not be attended with much difficulty.

I shall now propose the remedies, which appear to me applicable to our circumstances, and necessary to extricate our affairs from their present deplorable situation.

The first step must be to give Congress powers competent to the public exigencies. This may happen in two ways, one by resuming and exercising the discretionary powers I suppose to have been originally vested in them for the safety of the states and resting their conduct on the candor of their country men and the necessity of the conjuncture: the other by calling immediately a convention of all the states with full authority to conclude finally upon a general confederation, stating to them beforehand explicity the evils arising from a want of power in Congress, and the impossibily of supporting the contest on its present footing, that the delegates may come possessed of proper sentiments as well as proper authority to give to the meeting. Their commission should include a right of vesting Congress with the whole or a proportion of the unoccupied lands, to be employed for the purpose of raising a revenue, reserving the jurisdiction to the states by whom they are granted.

The first plan, I expect will be thought too bold an expedient by the generality of Congress; and indeed their practice hitherto has so rivetted the opinion of their want of power, that the success of this experiment may very well be doubted.

I see no objection to the other mode, that has any weight in competition with the reasons for it. The Convention should assemble the 1st of November next, the sooner, the better; our disorders are too violent to admit of a common or lingering remedy. The reasons for which I require them to be vested with plenipotentiary authority are that the business may suffer no delay in the execution, and may in reality come to effect. A convention may agree upon a confederation; the states individually hardly ever will. We must have one at all events, and a vigorous one if we mean to succeed in the contest and be happy hereafter. As I said before, to engage the states to comply with this mode, Congress ought to confess to them plainly and unanimously the impracticability of supporting our affairs on the present footing and without a solid coercive union. I ask that the Convention should have a power of vesting the whole or a part of the unoccupied land in Congress, because it is necessary that body should have some property as a fund for the arrangements of finance, and I know of no other kind that can be given them.

The confederation in my opinion should give Congress complete sovereignty; except as to that part of internal police, which relates to the rights of property and life among individuals and to raising money by internal taxes. It is necessary, that every thing, belonging to this, should be regulated by the state legislatures. Congress should have complete sovereignty in all that relates to war, peace, trade, finance, and to the management of foreign affairs, the right of declaring war of raising armies, officering, paying them, directing their motions in every respect, of equipping fleets and doing the same with them, of building fortifications arsenals magazines &c. &c., of making peace on such conditions as they think proper, of regulating trade, determining with what countries it shall be carried on, granting indulgencies laying prohibitions on all the articles of export or import, imposing duties granting bounties & premiums for raising exporting importing and applying to their own use the product of these duties, only giving credit to the states on whom they are raised in the general account of revenues and expences, instituting Admiralty courts &c., of coining money, establishing banks on such terms, and with such privileges as they think proper, appropriating funds and doing whatever else relates to the operations of finance, transacting every thing with foreign nations, making alliances offensive and defensive, treaties of commerce, &c. &c.

The confederation should provide certain perpetual revenues, productive and easy of collection, a land tax, poll tax or the like, which together with the duties on trade and the unlocated lands would give Congress a substantial existence, and a stable foundation for their schemes of finance. What more supplies were necessary should be occasionally demanded of the states, in the present mode of quotas.

The second step I would recommend is that Congress should instantly appoint the following great officers of state—A secretary for foreign affairs—a President of war—A President of Marine—A Financier—A President of trade; instead of this last a board of Trade may be preferable as the regulations of trade are slow and gradual and require prudence and experience (more than other qualities), for which boards are very well adapted.

Congress should choose for these offices, men of the first abilities, property and character in the continent—and such as have had the best opportunities of being acquainted with the several branches. General Schuyler (whom you mentioned) would make an excellent President of War, General McDougall a very good President of Marine. Mr. Robert Morris would have many things in his favour for the department of finance. He could by his own personal influence give great weight to the measures he should adopt. I dare say men equally capable may be found for the other departments.

I know not, if it would not be a good plan to let the Financier be President of the Board of trade; but he should only have a casting voice in determining questions there. There is a connection between trade and finance, which ought to make the director of one acquainted with the other; but the Financier should not direct the affairs of trade, because for the sake of acquiring reputation by increasing the revenues, he might adopt measures that would depress trade. In what relates to finance he should be alone.

These offices should have nearly the same powers and functions as those in France analogous to them, and each should be chief in his department, with subordinate boards composed of assistant clerks &c. to execute his orders.

In my opinion a plan of this kind would be of inconceivable utility to our affairs; its benefits would be very speedily felt. It would give new life and energy to the operations of government. Business would be conducted with dispatch method and system. A million of abuses now existing would be corrected, and judicious plans would be formed and executed for the public good.

Another step of immediate necessity is to recruit the army for the war, or at least for three years. This must be done by a mode similar to that which is practiced in Sweeden. There the inhabitants are thrown into classes of sixteen, and when the sovereign wants men each of these classes must furnish one. They raise a fixed sum of money, and if one of the class is willing to become a soldier, he receives the money and offers himself a volunteer; if none is found to do this, a draft is made and he on whom the lot falls receives the money and is obliged to serve. The minds of the people are prepared for a thing of this kind; the heavy bounties they have been obliged to pay for men to serve a few months must have disgusted them with this mode, and made them desirous of another, that will once for all answer the public purposes, and obviate a repetition of the demand. It ought by all means to be attempted, and Congress should frame a general plan and press the execution upon the states. When the confederation comes to be framed, it ought to provide for this by a fundamental law, and hereafter there would be no doubt of the success. But we cannot now wait for this; we want to replace the men whose times of service will expire the 1st of January, for then, without this, we shall have no army remaining and the enemy may do what they please. The General in his letter already quoted has assigned the most substantial reasons for paying immediate attention to this point.

Congress should endeavour, both upon their credit in Europe, and by every possible exertion in this country, to provide cloathing for their officers, and should abolish the whole system of state supplies. The making good the depreciation of the currency and all other compensations to the army should be immediately taken up by Congress, and not left to the states; if they would have the accounts of depreciation liquidated, and governmental certificates given for what is due in specie or an equivalent to specie, it would give satisfaction; appointing periodical settlements for future depreciation.

The placing the officers upon half pay during life would be a great stroke of policy, and would give Congress a stronger tie upon them, than any thing else they can do. No man, that reflects a moment, but will prefer a permanent provision of this kind to any temporary compensation, nor is it opposed to economy; the difference between this and between what has been already done will be insignificant. The benefit of it to the widows should be confined to those whose husbands die during the war. As to the survivors, not more than one half on the usual calculation of mens lives will exceed the seven years for which the half pay is already established. Besides this whatever may be the visionary speculations of some men at this time, we shall find it indispensable after the war to keep on foot a considerable body of troops; and all the officers retained for this purpose must be deducted out of the half pay list. If any one will take the pains to calculate the expence on these principles, I am persuaded he will find the addition of expence from the establishment proposed, by no means a national object.

The advantages of securing the attachment of the army to Congress, and binding them to the service by substantial ties are immense. We should then have discipline, an army in reality, as well as in name. Congress would then have a solid basis of authority and consequence, for to me it is an axiom that in our constitution an army is essential to the American union.

The providing of supplies is the pivot of every thing else (though a well constituted army would not in a small degree conduce to this, by giving consistency and weight to government). There are four ways all which must be united—a foreign loan, heavy pecuniary taxes, a tax in kind, a bank founded on public and private credit.

As to a foreign loan I dare say, Congress are doing every thing in their power to obtain it. The most effectual way will be to tell France that without it, we must make terms with great Britain. This must be done with plainness and firmness, but with respect and without petulance, not as a menace, but as a candid declaration of our circumstances. We need not fear to be deserted by France. Her interest and honor are too deeply involved in our fate; and she can make no possible compromise. She can assist us, if she is convinced it is absolutely necessary, either by lending us herself or by becoming our surety or by influencing Spain. It has been to me astonishing how any man could have doubted at any period of our affairs of the necessity of a foreign loan. It was self evident, that we had not a fund of wealth in this country, capable of affording revenues equal to the expences. We must then create artificial revenues, or borrow; the first was done, but it ought to have been foreseen, that the expedient could not last; and we should have provided in time for its failure.

Here was an error of Congress. I have good reason to believe, that measures were not taken in earnest early enough, to procure a loan abroad. I give you my honor that from our first outset, I thought as I do now and wished for a foreign loan not only because I foresaw it would be essential but because I considered it as a tie upon the nation from which it was derived and as a mean to prop our cause in Europe.

Concerning the necessity of heavy pecuniary taxes I need say nothing, as it is a point in which everybody is agreed; nor is there any danger, that the product of any taxes raised in this way will over burthen the people, or exceed the wants of the public. Indeed if all the paper in circulation were drawn annually into the treasury, it would neither do one, nor the other.

As to a tax in kind, the necessity of it results from this principle— that the money in circulation is not a sufficient representative of the productions of the country, and consequently no revenues raised from it as a medium can be a competent representative of that part of the products of the country, which it is bound to contribute to the support of the public. The public therefore to obtain its due or satisfy its just demands and its wants must call for a part of those products themselves. This is done in all those countries which are not commercial, in Russia, Prussia, Denmark Sweden &c. and is peculiarly necessary in our case.

Congress in calling for specific supplies seem to have had this in view; but their intention has not been answered. The states in general have undertaken to furnish the supplies by purchase, a mode as I have observed, attended with every inconvenience and subverting the principle on which the supplies were demanded—the insufficiency of our circulating medium as a representative for the labour and commodities of the Country. It is therefore necessary that Congress should be more explicit, should form the outlines of a plan for a tax in kind, and recommend it to the states, as a measure of absolute necessity.

The general idea I have of a plan, is that a respectable man should be appointed by the state in each county to collect the taxes and form magazines, that Congress should have in each state an officer to superintend the whole and that the state collectors should be subordinate and responsible to them. This Continental superintendent might be subject to the general direction of the Quarter Master General, or not, as might be deemed best; but if not subject to him, he should be obliged to make monthly returns to the President at War, who should instruct him what proportion to deliver to the Quarter Master General. It may be necessary that the superintendents should sometimes have power to dispose of the articles in their possession on public account; for it would happen that the contributions in places remote from the army could not be transported to the theatre of operations without too great expence, in which case it would be eligible to dispose of them and purchase with the money so raised in the countries near the immediate scene of war.

I know the objections which may be raised to this plan—its tendency to discourage industry and the like; but necessity calls for it; we cannot proceed without [it], and less evils must give place to greater. It is besides practiced with success in other countries, and why not in this? It may be said, the examples cited are from nations under despotic governments and that the same would not be practicable with us; but I contend where the public good is evidently the object more may be effected in governments like ours than in any other. It has been a constant remark that free countries have ever paid the heaviest taxes. The obedience of a free people to general laws however hard they bear is ever more perfect than that of slaves to the arbitrary will of a prince. To this it may be added that Sweden was always a free government, and is so now in a great degree, notwithstanding the late revolution.

How far it may be practicable to erect a bank on the joint credit of the public and of individuals can only be certainly determined by the experiment; but it is of so much importance that the experiment ought to be fully tried. When I saw the subscriptions going on to the bank established for supplying the army, I was in hopes it was only the embryo of a more permanent and extensive establishment. But I have reason to believe I shall be disappointed. It does not seem to be at all conducted on the true principles of a bank. The directors of it are purchasing with their stock instead of bank notes as I expected; in consequence of which it must turn out to be a mere subscription of a particular sum of money for a particular purpose.

Paper credit never was long supported in any country, on a national scale, where it was not founded on the joint basis of public and private credit. An attempt to establish it on public credit alone in France under the auspices of Mr. Law had nearly ruined the kingdom; we have seen the effects of it in America, and every successive experiment proves the futility of the attempt. Our new money is depreciating almost as fast as the old, though it has in some states as real funds as paper money ever had. The reason is, that the monied men have not an immediate interest to uphold its credit. They may even in many ways find it their interest to undermine it. The only certain manner to obtain a permanent paper credit is to engage the monied interest immediately in it by making them contribute the whole or part of the stock and giving them the whole or part of the profits.

33

The invention of banks on the modern principle originated in Venice. There the public and a company of monied men are mutually concerned. The Bank of England unites public authority and faith with private credit; and hence we see what a vast fabric of paper credit is raised on a visionary basis. Had it not been for this, England would never have found sufficient funds to carry on her wars; but with the help of this she has done, and is doing wonders. The bank of Amsterdam is on a similar foundation.

And why can we not have an American bank? Are our monied men less enlightened to their own interest or less enterprising in the persuit? I believe the fault is in our government which does not exert itself to engage them in such a scheme. It is true, the individuals in America are not very rich, but this would not prevent their instituting a bank; it would only prevent its being done with such ample funds as in other countries. Have they not sufficient confidence in the government and in the issue of the cause? Let the Government endeavour to inspire that confidence, by adopting the measures I have recommended or others equivalent to them. Let it exert itself to procure a solid confederation, to establish a good plan of executive administration, to form a permanent military force, to obtain at all events a foreign loan. If these things were in a train of vigorous execution, it would give a new spring to our affairs; government would recover its respectability and individuals would renounce their diffidence.

The object I should propose to myself in the first instance from a bank would be an auxiliary mode of supplies; for which purpose contracts should be made between Government and the bank on terms liberal and advantageous to the latter. Every thing should be done in the first instance to encourage the bank; after it gets well established it will take care of itself and government may make the best terms it can for itself.

The first step to establishing the bank will be to engage a number of monied men of influence to relish the project and make it a business. The subscribers to that lately established are the fittest persons that can be found; and their plan may be interwoven.

The outlines of my plan would be to open subscriptions in all the states for the stock, which we will suppose to be one million of pounds. Real property of every kind, as well as specie should be deemed good stock, but at least a fourth part of the subscription should be in specie or plate. There should be one great company in three divisions in Virginia, Philadelphia, and at Boston or two at Philadelphia and Boston. The bank should have a right to issue bank notes bearing two per Cent interest for the whole of their stock; but not to exceed it. These notes may be payable every three months or oftener, and the faith of government must be pledged for the support of the bank. It must therefore have a right from time to time to inspect its operations, and must appoint inspectors for the purpose.

The advantages of the bank may consist in this, in the profits of the contracts made with government, which should bear interest to be annually paid in specie, in the loan of money at interest say six per Cent, in purchasing lives by annuities as practiced in England &c. The benefit resulting to the company is evident from the consideration, that they may employ in circulation a great deal more money than they have specie in stock, on the credit of the real property which they will have in other use; this money will be employed either in fulfilling their contracts with the public by which also they will gain a profit, or in loans at an advantageous interest or in annuities.

The bank may be allowed to purchase plate and bullion and coin money allowing government a part of the profit. I make the bank notes bear interest to obtain a readie currency and to induce the holders to prefer them to specie to prevent too great a run upon the bank at any time beyond its ability to pay.

If Government can obtain a foreign loan it should lend to the bank on easy terms to extend its influence and facilitate a compliance with its engagements. If government could engage the states to raise a sum of money in specie to be deposited in bank in the same manner, it would be of the greatest consequence. If government could prevail on the enthusiasm of the people to make a contribution in plate for the same purpose it would be a master stroke. Things of this kind sometimes succeed in popular contests; and if undertaken with address; I should not despair of its success; but I should not be sanguine.

The bank may be instituted for a term of years by way of trial and the particular privilege of coining money be for a term still shorter. A temporary transfer of it to a particular company can have no inconvenience as the government are in no condition to improve this resource nor could it in our circumstances be an object to them, though with the industry of a knot of individuals it might be.

A bank of this kind even in its commencement would answer the most valuable purposes to government and to the proprietors; in its progress the advantages will exceed calculation. It will promote commerce by furnishing a more extensive medium which we greatly want in our circumstances. I mean a more extensive valuable medium. We have an enormous nominal one at this time; but it is only a name.

In the present unsettled state of things in this country, we can hardly draw inferences from what has happened in others, otherwise I should be certain of the success of this scheme; but I think it has enough in its favour to be worthy of trial.

I have only skimmed the surface of the different subjects I have introduced. Should the plans recommended come into contemplation in earnest and you desire my further thoughts, I will endeavor to give them more form and particularity. I am persuaded a solid confederation a permanent army a reasonable prospect of subsisting it would give us treble consideration in Europe and produce a peace this winter.

If a Convention is called the minds of all the states and the people ought to be prepared to receive its determinations by sensible and popular writings, which should conform to the views of Congress. There are epochs in human affairs, when *novelty* even is useful. If a general opinion prevails that the old way is bad, whether true or false, and this obstructs or relaxes the operation of the public service, a change is necessary if it be but for the sake of change. This is exactly the case now. 'Tis an universal sentiment that our present system is a bad one, and that things do not go right on this account. The measure of a Convention would revive the hopes of the people and give a new direction to their passions, which may be improved in carrying points of substantial utility. The Eastern states have already pointed out this mode to Congress; they ought to take the hint and anticipate the others.

And, in future, My Dear Sir, two things let me recommend, as fundamental rules for the conduct of Congress—to attach the army to them by every motive, to maintain an air of authority (not domineering) in all their measures with the states. The manner in which a thing is done has more influence than is commonly imagined. Men are governed by opinion; this opinion is as much influenced by appearances as by realities; if a Government appears to be confident of its own powers, it is the surest way to inspire the same confidence in others; if it is diffident, it may be certain, there will be a still greater diffidence in others, and that its authority will not only be distrusted, controverted, but contemned.

I wish too Congress would always consider that a kindness consists as much in the manner as in the thing: the best things done hesitatingly and with an ill grace lose their effect, and produce disgust rather than satisfaction or gratitude. In what Congress have at any time done for the army, they have commonly been too late: They have seemed to yield to importunity rather than to sentiments of justice or to a regard to the accomodation of their troops. An attention to this idea is of more importance than it may be thought. I who have seen all the workings and progress of the present discontents, am convinced, that a want of this has not been among the most inconsiderable causes.

You will perceive My Dear Sir this letter is hastily written and with a confidential freedom, not as to a member of Congress, whose feelings may be sore at the prevailing clamours; but as to a friend who is in a situation to remedy public disorders, who wishes for nothing so much as truth, and who is desirous of information, even from those less capable of judging than himself. I have not even time to correct and copy and only enough to add that I am very truly and affectionately D Sir   Your most Obed ser   A. Hamilton

LETTER TO ROBERT MORRIS
APRIL 30, 1781

In the following passage from a letter to Robert Morris, the Confederation's recently appointed superintendent of finance, Hamilton recommends the institution of a national bank as a means of promoting national prosperity. Though aware of the worst tendencies of a society animated by the spirit of commerce and acquisitiveness, Hamilton believed that its virtues far outweighed its conceivable shortcomings. He was not insensitive to the meaner forms of self-interest and their evil effects, but he did not regard that as a serious threat to freedom. On the contrary, he regarded the commercial acquisitive spirit as in some measure a substitute for public spiritedness in a modern republican society.

De Peyster's Point, New York, April 30, 1781

Sir,
I was among the first who were convinced, that an administration by single men was essential to the proper management of the affairs of this country. I am persuaded now it is the only resource we have to extricate ourselves from the distresses, which threaten the subversion of our cause. It is palpable that the people have lost all confidence in our public councils, and it is a fact of which I dare say you are as well apprised as my self, that our friends in Europe are in the same disposition. I have been in a situation that has enabled me to obtain a better idea of this than most others; and I venture to assert,

that the Court of France will never give half the succours to this Country while Congress holds the reins of administration in their own hands, which they would grant, if these were intrusted to individuals of established reputation and con⟨spicuous⟩ for probity, abilities and fortune.

With respect to ourselves, there is so universal and rooted a diffidence of the government, that if we could be assured the future measures of Congress would be dictated by the most perfect wisdom and public spirit there would be still a necessity for a change in the forms of our administration to give a new spring and current to the passions and hopes of the people.

To me it appears evident that an executive ministry composed of men with the qualifications I have described would speedily restore the credit of government abroad and at home, would induce our allies to greater exertions in our behalf, would inspire confidence in monied men in Europe as well as in America to lend us ⟨those⟩ sums of which it may be demonstrated we ⟨stand⟩ in need from the disproportion of our national wealth to the expences of the War.

I hope Sir you will not consider it as a compliment when I assure you that I heard ⟨with⟩ the greatest satisfaction of your nomination ⟨to⟩ the department of finance. In a letter of mine last summer to Mr. Duane, urging among other things the plan of an executive ministry, I mentioned you as the person, who ought to fill that department. I know of no other in America who unites so many advantages, and of course, every impediment to your acceptance is to me a subject of chargine. I flatter my self Congress will not preclude the public from your services by an obstinate refusal of reasonable conditions; and as one deeply interrested in the event I am happy in believing you will not easily be discoureged from undertaking an office, by which you may render America and the world no less a service than the establishment of American independence! Tis by introducing order into our finances—by restoreing public credit—not by gaining battles, that we are finally to gain our object. Tis by putting ourselves in a condition to continue the war not by temporary, violent and unnatural efforts to bring it to a decisive issue, that we shall in reality bring it to a speedy and successful one. In the frankness of truth I believe, Sir, you are the Man best capable of performing this great work.

In expectation that all difficulties will be removed, and that you will ultimately act, on terms you approve, I take the liberty to submit to you some ideas, relative to the object of your department. . . .

. . . I regard [the institution of a National Bank] in some shape or other as an expedient essential to our safety and success, unless by a happy turn of European affairs the war should speedily terminate in a manner upon which it would be unwise to reckon. There is no other that can give to government that extensive and systematic credit, which the defect of our revenues makes indispensably necessary to its operations. The longer it is delayed, the more difficult it becomes; our affairs grow every day more relaxed and more involved; public credit hastens to a more irretrievable catastrophe; the means for executing the plan are exhausted in partial and temporary efforts. The loan now making in Massachusettes would have gone a great way in establishing the funds on which the bank must stand.

I am aware of all the objections that have been made to public banks and that they are not without enlightened and respectable opponents. But all that has been said against them only tends to prove that like all other good things they are subject to abuse and when abused become pernicious. The precious metals by similar arguments may be proved to be injurious; it is certain that the mines of South America have had great influence in banishing industry from Spain and sinking it in real wealth and importance. Great power, commerce and riches, or in other words great national prosperity, may in like manner be denominated evils; for they lead to insolence, an inordinate ambition, a vicious luxury, licentiousness of morals, and all those vices which corrupt government, enslave the people and precipitate the ruin of a nation. But no wise statesman will reject the good from an apprehension of the ill. The truth is in human affairs, there is no good, pure and unmixed; every advantage has two sides, and wisdom consists in availing ourselves of the good, and gua[r]ding as much as possible against the bad.

The tendency of a national bank is to increase public and private credit. The former gives power to the state for the protection of its rights and interests, and the latter facilitates and extends the operations of commerce among individuals. Industry is increased, commodities are multiplied, agriculture and manufactures flourish, and herein consist the true wealth and prosperity of a state.

Most commercial nations have found it necessary to institute banks and they have proved to be the happiest engines, that ever were invented for advancing trade. Venice Genoa Hamburgh Holland and England are examples of their utility. They owe their riches, commerce and the figure they have made at different periods in a great degree to this source. Great Britain is indebted for the immense efforts she has been able to make in so many illustrious and successful wars essentially to that vast fabric of credit raised on this foundation. Tis by this alone she now menaces our independence.

She has indeed abused the advantage and now stands on a precipice. Her example should both persuade and warn us. 'Tis in republics where banks are most easily established and supported and where they are least liable to abuse. Our situation will not expose us to frequent wars, and the public will have no temptation to overstrain its credit.

In my opinion we ought not to hesitate because we have no other resource. The long and expensive wars of King William had drained England of its specie, its commerce began to droop for want of a proper medium, its taxes were unproductive and its revenues declined. The Administration wisely had recourse to the institution of a bank and it relieved the national difficulties. We are in the same and still greater want of a sufficient medium; we have little specie; the paper we have is of small value and rapidly descending to less; we are immersed in a war for our exixtence as a nation, for our liberty and happiness as a people; we have no revenues nor no credit. A bank if practicable is the only thing that can give us either the one or the other.

THE CONTINENTALIST PAPERS, AN INTRODUCTION

In a series of six articles published in July and August 1781, Hamilton makes the case for strengthening the Articles of Confederation, which were drafted in 1777 and finally approved in February 1781. These articles should be read in conjunction with his letter to James Duane of September 3, 1780. Jack Rakove writes in The Beginnings of National Politics *(New York, 1979) that "no comparable commentary on the confederation was composed until Madison prepared his memorandum on the 'Vices of the Political System of the United States' in April 1787."*

THE CONTINENTALIST NO. I
JULY 12, 1781

Fishkill, New York, July 12, 1781

It would be the extreme of vanity in us not to be sensible, that we began this revolution with very vague and confined notions of the practical business of government. To the greater part of us it was a novelty: Of those, who under the former constitution had had opportunities of acquiring experience, a large proportion adhered to the opposite side, and the remainder can only be supposed to have possessed ideas adapted to the narrow coloneal sphere, in which they had been accustomed to move, not of that enlarged kind suited to the government of an INDEPENDENT NATION.

There were no doubt exceptions to these observations—men in all respects qualified for conducting the public affairs, with skill and advantage; but their number was small; they were not always brought forward in our councils; and when they were, their influence was too commonly borne down by the prevailing torrent of ignorance and prejudice.

On a retrospect however, of our transactions, under the disadvantages with which we commenced, it is perhaps more to be wondered at, that we have done so well, than that we have not done better. There are indeed some traits in our conduct, as conspicuous for sound policy, as others for magnanimity. But, on the other hand, it must also be confessed, there have been many false steps, many chimerical projects and utopian speculations, in the management of our civil as well as of our military affairs. A part of these were the natural effects of the spirit of the times dictated by our situation. An extreme jealousy of power is the attendant on all popular revolutions, and has seldom been without its evils. It is to this source we are to trace many of the fatal mistakes, which have so deeply endangered the common cause; particularly that defect, which will be the object of these remarks, A WANT OF POWER IN CONGRESS.

The present Congress, respectable for abilities and integrity, by experience convinced of the necessity of a change, are preparing several important articles to be submitted to the respective states, for augmenting the powers of the Confederation. But though there is hardly at this time a man of information in America, who will not acknowledge, as a general proposition, that in its present form, it is unequal, either to a vigorous prosecution of the war, or to the preser-

41

vation of the union in peace; yet when the principle comes to be applied to practice, there seems not to be the same agreement in the modes of remedying the defect; and it is to be feared, from a disposition which appeared in some of the states on a late occasion, that the salutary intentions of Congress may meet with more delay and opposition, than the critical posture of the states will justify.

It will be attempted to shew in a course of papers what ought to be done, and the mischiefs of a contrary policy.

In the first stages of the controversy it was excuseable to err. Good intentions, rather than great skill, were to have been expected from us. But we have now had sufficent time for reflection and experience, as ample as unfortunate, to rectify our errors. To persist in them, becomes disgraceful and even criminal, and belies that character of good sense and a quick discernment of our interests, which, in spite of our mistakes, we have been hitherto allowed. It will prove, that our sagacity is limited to interests of interior moment; and that we are incapable of those enlightened and liberal views, necessary to make us a great and a flourishing people.

History is full of examples, where in contests for liberty, a jealousy of power has either defeated the attempts to recover or preserve it in the first instance, or has afterwards subverted it by clogging government with too great precautions for its felicity, or by leaving too wide a door for sedition and popular licenciousness. In a government framed for durable liberty, not less regard must be paid to giving the magistrate a proper degree of authority, to make and execute the laws with rigour, than to guarding against encroachments upon the rights of the community. As too much power leads to despotism, too little leads to anarchy, and both eventually to the ruin of the people. These are maxims well known, but never sufficiently attended to, in adjusting the frames of governments. Some momentary interest or passion is sure to give a wrong biass, and pervert the most favourable opportunities.

No friend to order or to rational liberty, can read without pain and disgust the history of the commonwealth of Greece. Generally speaking, they were a constant scene of the alternate tyranny of one part of the people over the other, or of a few usurping demagogues over the whole. Most of them had been originally governed by kings, whose despotism (the natural disease of monarchy) had obliged their subjects to murder, expel, depose, or reduce them to a nominal existence, and institute popular governments. In these governments, that of Sparta excepted, the jealousy of power hindered the people from trusting out of their own hands a competent authority, to maintain the repose and stability of the commonwealth; whence originated the frequent revolutions and civil broils with which they were distracted. This, and the want of a solid fœderal union to restrain the ambition and rivalship of the different cities, after a rapid succession of bloody wars, ended in their total loss of liberty and subjugation to foreign powers.

In comparison of our governments with those of the ancient republics, we must, without hesitation, give the preference to our own; because, every power with us is exercised by representation, not in tumultuary assemblies of the collective body of the people, where the art or impudence of the ORATOR or TRIBUNE, rather than the utility or justice of the measure could seldom fail to govern. Yet whatever may be the advantage on our side, in such a comparison, men who estimate the value of institutions, not from prejudices of the moment, but from experience and reason, must be persuaded, that the same JEALOUSY of POWER has prevented our reaping all the advantages, from the examples of other nations, which we ought to have done, and has rendered our constitutions in many respects feeble and imperfect.

Perhaps the evil is not very great in respect to our constitutions; for notwithstanding their imperfections, they may, for some time, be made to operate in such a manner, as to answer the purposes of the common defence and the maintenance of order; and they seem to have, in themselves, and in the progress of society among us, the seeds of improvement.

But this is not the case with respect to the FOEDERAL GOVERNMENT; if it is too weak at first, it will continually grow weaker. The ambition and local interests of the respective members, will be constantly undermining and usurping upon its prerogatives, till it comes to a dissolution; if a partial combination of some of the more powerful ones does not bring it to a more SPEEDY and VIOLENT END.

THE CONTINENTALIST NO. II
JULY 19, 1781

Fishkill, New York, July 19, 1781

In a single state, where the sovereign power is exercised by delegation, whether it be a limited monarchy or a republic, the danger most commonly is, that the sovereign will become too powerful for his constituents; in fœderal governments, where different states are represented in a general council, the danger is on the other side—that the members will be an overmatch for the common head, or in other words, that it will not have sufficient influence and authority to secure the obedience of the several parts of the confederacy.

In a single state, the sovereign has the whole legislative power as well as the command of the national forces, of course, an immediate controul over the persons and property of the subjects. Every other power is subordinate and dependent. If he undertakes to subvert the constitution, it can only be preserved by a general insurrection of the people. The magistrates of the provinces, counties, or towns, into which the state is divided, having only an executive and police jurisdiction, can take no decisive measures for counteracting the first indications of tyranny; but must content themselves with the ineffectual weapon of petition and remonstrance. They cannot raise money, levy troops, nor form alliances. The leaders of the people must wait till their discontents have ripened into a general revolt, to put them in a situation to confer the powers necessary for their defence. It will always be difficult for this to take place; because the sovereign possessing the appearance and forms of legal authority, having the forces and revenues of the state at his command, and a large party among the people besides, which with those advantages he can hardly fail to acquire, he will too often be able to baffle the first motions of the discontented, and prevent that union and concert essential to the success of their opposition.

The security therefore of the public liberty, must consist in such a distribution of the sovereign power, as will make it morally impossible for one part to gain an ascendency over the others, or for the whole to unite in a scheme of usurpation.

In fœderal governments, each member has a distinct sovereignty, makes and executes laws, imposes taxes, distributes justice, and exercises every other function of government. It has always within itself the means of revenue, and on an emergency can levy forces. If the common sovereign should meditate, or attempt any thing unfavourable to the general liberty, each member, having all the proper organs of power, can prepare for defence with celerity and vigour. Each can immediately sound the alarm to the others, and enter into leagues for mutual protection. If the combination is general, as is to be expected, the usurpers will soon find themselves without the means of recruiting their treasury, or their armies; and for want of continued supplies of men and money, must, in the end fall a sacrifice to the attempt. If the combination is not general, it will imply, that some of the members are interested in that which is the cause of dissatisfaction to others, and this cannot be an attack upon the common liberty, but upon the interests of one part in favour of another part; and it will be a war between the members of the fœderal union with each other, not between them and the fœderal government.

From the plainest principles of human nature, two inferences are to be drawn, one, that each member of a political confederacy, will be more disposed to advance its own authority upon the ruins of that of the confederacy, than to make any improper concessions in its favour, or support it in unreasonable pretensions; the other, that the subjects of each member, will be more devoted in their attachments and obedience to their own particular governments, than to that of the union.

It is the temper of societies as well as of individuals to be impatient of constraint, and to prefer partial to general interest. Many cases may occur, where members of a confederacy have, or seem to have an advantage in things contrary to the good of the whole, or a disadvantage in others conducive to that end. The selfishness of every part will dispose each to believe, that the public burthens are unequally apportioned, and that itself is the victim. These, and other circumstances, will promote a disposition for abridging the authority of the fœderal government; and the ambition of men in office in each state, will make them glad to encourage it. They think their own consequence connected with the power of the government of which they are a part; and will endeavour to encrease the one as the mean of encreasing the other.

The particular governments will have more empire over the minds of their subjects, than the general one, because their agency will be more direct, more uniform, and more apparent. The people will be habituated to look up to them as the arbiters and guardians of their personal concerns, by which the passions of the vulgar, if not of all men are most strongly affected; and in every difference with the confederated body will side with them against the common sovereign.

Experience confirms the truth of these principles. The chief cities of Greece had once their council of Amphyctions, or States-General, with authority to decide and compose the differences of the several cities; and to transact many other important matters relative to the common interest and safety. At their first institution, they had great weight and credit; but never enough to preserve effectually the ballance and harmony of the confederacy; and in time their decrees only served as an additional pretext to that side, whose pretensions they favoured. When the cities were not engaged in foreign wars, they were at perpetual varience among themselves. Sparta and Athens contended twenty-seven years for the precedence, or rather dominion of Greece, till the former made herself mistress of the whole; and till in subsequent struggles, having had recourse to the pernicious expedient of calling in the aid of foreign enemies; the Macedonians first, and afterwards the Romans became their masters.

The German diet had formerly more authority than it now has, though like that of Greece never enough to hinder the great potentates from disturbing the repose of the empire, and mutually wasting their own territories and people.

The Helvetie league is another example. It is true it has subsisted near five hundred years; but in that period the cantons have had repeated and furious wars with each other, which would have made them an easy prey to their more powerful neighbours, had not the reciprocal jealousy of these prevented either from taking advantage of their dissentions. This and their poverty have hitherto saved them from total destruction, and kept them from feeling the miseries of foreign conquest, added to those of civil war. The fœderal government is too weak to hinder their renewal, whenever the ambition or fanaticism of the principal cantons shall be disposed to rekindle the flame. For some time past indeed, it has been in a great measure nominal; the Protestants and Catholics have had separate diets, to manage almost all matters of importance; so that in fact, the general diet is only kept up to regulate the affairs of the common bailliages, and preserve a semblance of union; and even this it is probable would cease, did not the extreme weakness of the cantons oblige them to a kind of coalition.

If the divisions of the United Provinces have not proceeded to equal extremities, there are peculiar causes to be assigned. The authority of the Stadtholder pervades the whole frame of the republic, and is a kind of common link by which the provinces are bound together. The jealousy of this progressive influence, in which more or less they all agree, operates as a check upon their ill-humours against one another. The inconsiderableness of each province separately, and the imminent danger to which the whole would be exposed of being overrun by their neighbours, in case of disunion, is a further preservative against the phrenzy of hostility; and their importance and even existence depending intirely upon frugality, industry and commerce; peace, both at home and abroad, is of necessity the predominant object of their policy.

THE CONTINENTALIST NO. III
AUGUST 9, 1781

Fishkill, New York, August 9, 1781

The situation of these states is very unlike that of the United Provinces. Remote as we are from Europe, in a little time, we should fancy ourselves out of the reach of attempts from abroad, and in full liberty, at our leisure and convenience, to try our strength at home. This might not happen at once; but if the FOEDERAL GOVERNMENT SHOULD LOSE ITS AUHORITY, it would CERTAINLY FOLLOW. Political societies, in close neighbourhood, must either be strongly united under one government, or there will infallibly exist emulations and quarrels. This is in human nature; and we have no reason to think ourselves wiser, or better, than other men. Some of the larger states, a small number of years hence, will be in themselves populous, rich and powerful, in all those circumstances calculated to inspire ambition and nourish ideas of separation and independence. Though it will ever be their true interest to preserve the union, their vanity and self importance, will be very likely to overpower that motive, and make them seek to place themselves at the head of particular confederacies independent of the general one. A schism once introduced, competitions of boundary and rivalships of commerce will easily afford pretexts for war. European powers may have inducements for fomenting these divisions and playing us off against each other. But without such a disposition in them, if separations once take place, we shall, of course, embrace different interests and connections. The particular confederacies, leaguing themselves with rival nations, will naturally be involved in their disputes; into which they will be the more readily tempted by the hope of making acquisitions upon each other, and upon the colonies of the powers with whom they are respectively at enmity.

WE ALREADY SEE SYMPTOMS OF THE EVILS TO BE APPREHENDED. In the midst of a war for our existence as a nation; in the midst of dangers too serious to be trifled with, some of the states have evaded, or refused, compliance with the demands of Congress in points of the greatest moment to the common safety. If they act such a part at this perilous juncture, what are we to expect in a time of peace and security? Is it not to be feared, that the resolutions of Congress would soon become like the decisions of the Greek amphyctions, or like the edicts of a German diet?

But as these evils are at a little distance, we may perhaps be insensible and short sighted enough to disregard them. There are others that threaten our immediate safety. Our whole system is in disorder; our currency depreciated, till in many places it will hardly obtain a circulation at all, public credit at its lowest ebb, our army deficient in numbers, and unprovided with every thing, the government, in its present condition, unable to command the means to pay, clothe, or feed their troops, the enemy making an alarming progress in the southern states, lately in complete possession of two of them, though now in part rescued by the genius and exertions of a General without an army, a force under Cornwallis still formidable to Virginia.

We ought to blush to acknowledge, that this is a true picture of our situation, when we reflect, that the enemy's whole force in the United States, including their American levies and the late reinforcement, is little more than fourteen thousand effective men; that our population, by recent examination, has been found to be greater, than at the commencement of the war; that the quantity of our specie has also increased, that the country abounds with all the necessaries of life, and has a sufficiency of foreign commodities, with a considerable and progressive commerce; that we have beyond comparison a better stock of warlike materials, than when we began the contest, and an ally as willing as able to supply our further wants: And that we have, on the spot, five thousand auxiliary troops, paid and subsisted by that ally, to assist in our defence.

Nothing but a GENERAL DISAFFECTION of the PEOPLE, or MISMANAGEMENT in their RULERS, can account for the figure we make, and for the distresses and perplexities we experience, contending against so small a force.

Our enemies themselves must now be persuaded, that the first is not the cause; and WE KNOW it is not. The most decided attachment of the people could alone have made them endure, without a convulsion, the successive shocks in our currency, added to the unavoidable inconveniences of war. There is perhaps not another nation in the world, that would have shown equal patience and perseverance in similar circumstances. The enemy have now tried the temper of almost every part of America; and they can hardly produce in their ranks a thousand men, who without their arts and seductions have voluntarily joined their standard. The miseries of a rigorous captivity, may perhaps have added half as many more to the number of the American levies, at this time in their armies. This small accession of force is the more extraordinary, as they have at some periods, been apparently in the full tide of success, while every thing wore an aspect tending to infuse despondency into the people of this country. This has been remarkably the case in the southern states. They for a time had almost undisturbed possession of two of them; and Cornwallis, after overruning a great part of a third; after two victorious battles, only brought with him into Virginia, about two hundred tories. In the state where he thought himself so well established, that he presumptuously ventured to assure the minister, there was not a rebel left, a small body of Continental troops, have been so effectually seconded by the militia of that vanquished country, as to have been able to capture a number of his troops more than equal to their own, and to repossess the principal part of the state.

As in the explanation of our embarrassments nothing can be alledged to the disaffection of the people, we must have recourse to the other cause of IMPOLICY and MISMANAGEMENT in their RULERS.

Where the blame of this may lie is not so much the question as what are the proper remedies; yet it may not be amiss to remark, that too large a share has fallen upon Congress. That body is no doubt chargeable with mistakes; but perhaps its greatest has been too much readiness to make concessions of the powers implied in its original trust. This is partly to be attributed to an excessive complaisance to the spirit, which has evidently actuated a majority of the states, a desire of monopolizing all power in themselves. Congress have been responsible for the administration of affairs, without the means of fulfilling that responsibility.

It would be too severe a reflection upon us to suppose, that a disposition to make the most of the friendship of others, and to exempt ourselves from a full share of the burthens of the war has had any part in the backwardness, which has appeared in many of the states, to confer powers and adopt measures adequate to the exigency. Such a sentiment would neither by wise, just, generous, nor honorable; nor do I believe the accusation would be well founded, yet our conduct makes us liable to a suspicion of this sort. It is certain, however, that too sanguine expectations from Europe have unintentionally relaxed our efforts, by diverting a sense of danger, and begetting an opinion, that the inequality of the contest would make every campaign the last.

We did not consider how difficult it must be to exhaust the resources of a nation circumstanced like that of Great Britain; whose government has always been distinguished for energy, and its people for enthusiasm. Nor did we, in estimating the superiority of our friends make sufficient allowance for that want of concert, which will ever characterise the operations of allies, or for the immense advantage to the enemy, of having their forces, though inferior, under a single direction. Finding the rest of Europe either friendly, or pacific, we never calculated the contingencies, which might alter that disposition; nor reflected that the death of a single prince, the change or caprice of a single minister, was capable of giving a new face to the whole system.

We are at this time more sanguine than ever. The war with the Dutch, we believe, will give such an addition of force to our side, as will make the superiority irresistible. No person can dispute this, if things remain in their present state; but the extreme disparity of the contest is the very reason, why this cannot be the case. The neutral powers will either effect a particular, or a general accommodation, or they will take their sides. There are three suppositions to be made: one, that there will be a compromise *between the united* provinces and England; for which we are certain the mediation of Austria and Russia have been offered; another, a pacification between all the belligerent powers, for which we have reason to believe the same mediation has been offered; the third, a rejection of the terms of mediation and a more general war.

Either of these suppositions is a motive for exertion. The first will place things in the same, probably in a worse situation, than before the declaration of the war against Holland. The composing of present differences may be accompanied with a revival of ancient connections; and at least would be productive of greater caution and restraint in a future intercourse with us.

The second, it is much to be dreaded, would hazard a dismemberment of a part of these states; and we are bound in honor, in duty and in interest, to employ every effort to dispossess the enemy of what they hold. A natural basis of the negociation, with respect to this continent, will be, that each party shall retain what it possesses at the conclusion of the treaty, qualified perhaps by a cession of particular points for an equivalent elsewhere. It is too delicate to dwell on the motives to this apprehension; but if such a compromise sometimes terminates the disputes of nations originally independent, it will be less extraordinary where one party was originally under the dominion of the other.

If we are determined, as we ought to be with the concurrence of our allies, not to accept such a condition, then we ought to prepare for the third event, a more general and more obstinate war.

Should this take place, a variety of new interests will be involved, and the affairs of America MAY CEASE TO BE OF PRIMARY IMPORTANCE. In proportion as the objects and operations of the war become complicated and extensive, the final success must become uncertain; and in proportion as the interests of others in our concerns may be weakened, or supplanted by more immediate interests of their own, ought our attention to ourselves, and exertions in our own behalf to be awakened and augmented.

We ought therefore, not only to strain every nerve for complying with the requisitions, to render the present campaign as decisive as possible; but we ought without delay, to ENLARGE THE POWERS OF CONGRESS. Every plan of which, this is not the foundation, will be illusory. The separate exertions of the states will never suffice. Nothing but a well-proportioned exertion of the resources of the whole, under the direction of a Common Council, with power sufficient to give efficacy to their resolutions, can preserve us from being a CONQUERED PEOPLE now, or can make us a HAPPY PEOPLE hereafter.

THE CONTINENTALIST NO. IV
AUGUST 30, 1781

Fishkill, New York, August 30, 1781

The preceding numbers are chiefly intended to confirm an opinion, already pretty generally received, that it is necessary to augment the powers of the confederation. The principal difficulty yet remains, to fix the public judgment, definitively, on the points, which ought to compose that augmentation.

It may be pronounced with confidence, that nothing short of the following articles can suffice.

1st, THE POWER OF REGULATING TRADE, comprehending a right of granting bounties and premiums by way of encouragement, of imposing duties of every kind, as well for revenue as regulation, of appointing all officers of the customs, and of laying embargoes, in extraordinary emergencies.

2d, A moderate land-tax throughout the United States, at a specific rate per pound, or per acre, granted to the FOEDERAL GOVERNMENT in perpetuity, and, if Congress think proper, to be levied by their own collectors.

3d, A moderate capitation tax on every male inhabitant above fifteen years of age; exclusive of common soldiers, common seamen, day-labourers, cottagers and paupers; to be also vested in perpetuity, and with the same condition of collection.

4th, The disposal of all unlocated land, for the benefit of the United States (so far as respects the profits of the first sale and the quit-rents) the jurisdiction remaining to the respective States in whose limits they are contained.

5th, A certain proportion of the product of all mines, discovered, or to be discovered, for the same duration and with the same right of collection, as in the second and third articles.

6th, The appointment of all land (as well as naval) officers of every rank.

The three first articles are of IMMEDIATE NECESSITY; the three last would be of great present but of much greater future utility; the whole combined would give solidity and permanency to the union.

The great defect of the confederation is, that it gives the United States no property, or in other words, no revenue, nor the means of acquiring it, inherent in themselves, and independent on the temporary pleasure of the different members; and power without revenue in political society is a name. While Congress continue altogether dependent on the occasional grants of the several States, for the means of defraying the expences of the FOEDERAL GOVERNMENT, it can neither have dignity vigour nor *credit*. CREDIT supposes specific and permanent funds for the punctual payment of interest, with a moral certainty of a final redemption of the principal. In our situation it will probably require more, on account of the general diffidence, which has been excited by the past disorder in our finances. It will perhaps be necessary, in the first instance, to appropriate funds for the redemption of the principal in a determinate period, as well as for the payment of interest.

It is essential, that the property in such funds should be in the contractor himself, and the appropriation dependent on his own will; if instead of this the possession, or disposal of them, is to float on the voluntary and occasional concurrence of a number of different wills, not under his absolute control, both the one and the other will be too precarious to be trusted.

The most wealthy and best established nations are obliged to pledge their funds to obtain credit; and it would be the height of absurdity in us, in the midst of a revolution, to expect to have it on better terms. This credit being to be procured through Congress, the funds ought to be provided, declared, and vested in them. It is a fact, that besides the want of specific funds, a circumstance which operates powerfully against our obtaining credit abroad, is, not a distrust of our becoming independent, but of our continuing united; and with our present confederation the distrust is natural. Both foreigners and the thinking men among ourselves, would have much more confidence in the duration of the union, if they were to see it supported on the foundation here proposed.

There are some among us ignorant enough to imagine, that the war may be carried on without credit; defraying the expences of the year with what may be raised within the year. But this is for want of a knowledge of our real resources and expenses. It may be demonstrated, that the whole amount of the revenue, which these States are capable of affording, will be deficient annually five or six millions of dollars, for the support of civil government and of the war. This is not a conjecture hazarded at random, but the result of experiment and calculation; nor can it appear surprising, when it is considered, that the revenues of the United Provinces equal to these States in population, beyond comparison superior in industry, commerce and riches, do not exceed twenty five millions of guilders, or about nine millions and an half of dollars. In times of war, they have raised a more considerable sum; but has been chiefly by gratuitous contributions of rich individuals; a resource we cannot employ, because there are few men of large fortunes in this country, and these for the most part in land. Taxes in the United Provinces are carried to an extreme, which would be impracticable here; not only the living are made to pay for every necessity of life; but even the dead are tributary to the public for the liberty of interment at particular hours. These considerations make it evident, that we could not raise an equal amount of revenue in these States; yet in seventy-six, when the currency was not depreciated, Congress emitted for the expences of the year fourteen millions of dollars. It cannot be denied, that there was a want of order and œconomy, in the expenditure of public money, nor that we had a greater military force to maintain at that time, than we now have; but, on the other hand, allowing for the necessary increase in our different civil lists, and for the advanced prices of many articles, it can hardly be supposed possible to reduce our annual expence very much below that sum. This simple idea of the subject, without entering into details, may satisfy us, that the deficiency which has been stated is not to be suspected of exaggeration.

Indeed nations the most powerful and opulent are obliged to have recourse to loans, in time of war; and hence it is, that most of the States of Europe are deeply immersed in debt. France is among the number, notwithstanding her immense population, wealth and resources. England owes the enormous sum of two hundred millions sterling. The United Provinces, with all their prudence and parsimony, owe a debt of the generality of fifty millions sterling, besides the particular debts of each province. Almost all the other powers are more or less in the same circumstances.

While this teaches us how contracted and uninformed are the views of those who expect to carry on the war, without running in debt; it ought to console us, with respect to the amount of that which we now owe, or may have occasion to incur, in the remainder of the war. The whole, without burthening the people, may be paid off in twenty years after the conclusion of peace.

The principal part of the deficient five or six millions must be procured by loans from private persons, at home and abroad.

Every thing may be hoped, from the generosity of France, which her means will permit; but she has full employment for her revenues and credit, in the prosecution of the war on her own part. If we judge of the future by the past, the pecuniary succours from her must continue to be far short of our wants: And the contingency of a war on the continent of Europe makes it possible, they may diminish rather than increase.

We have in a less degree experienced the friendship of Spain in this article.

The government of the United Provinces, if disposed to do it, can give us no assistance. The revenues of the Republic are chiefly mortgaged for former debts. Happily it has extensive credit, but it will have occasion for the whole to supply its own exigencies.

Private men, either foreigners, or natives, will not lend to a large amount, but on the usual security of funds properly established. This security Congress cannot give, till the several States vest them with revenue, or the means of revenue for that purpose.

Congress have wisely appointed a Superintendant of their Finances; a man of acknowledged abilities and integrity, as well as of great personal credit and pecuniary influence. It was impossible, that the business of finance could be ably conducted by a body of men, however well composed or well intentioned. Order in the future management of our monied concerns, a strict regard to the performance of public engagements, and of course, the restoration of public credit may be reasonably and confidently expected from Mr. Morris's administration, if he is furnished with materials upon which to operate—that is, if the fœderal government can acquire funds as the basis of his arrangements. He has very judiciously proposed a national bank, which, by uniting the influence and interest of the monied men with the resources of government, can alone give it that durable and extensive credit of which it stands in need. This is the best expedient he could have devised for relieving the public embarrassments, but to give success to the plan, it is essential, that Congress should have it in their power to support him with unexceptionable funds.

Had we begun the practice of funding four years ago, we should have avoided that depreciation of the currency, which has been as pernicious to the morals as to the credit of the nation: And there is no other method than this to prevent a continuance and multiplication of the evils flowing from that prolific source.

THE CONTINENTALIST NO. V
APRIL 18, 1782

Fishkill, New York, April 18, 1782

The vesting Congress with the power of regulating trade ought to have been a principal object of the confederation for a variety of reasons. It is as necessary for the purposes of commerce as of revenue. There are some, who maintain, that trade will regulate itself, and is not to be benefitted by the encouragements, or restraints of government. Such persons will imagine, that there is no need of a common directing power. This is one of those wild speculative paradoxes, which have grown into credit among us, contrary to the uniform practice and sense of the most enlightened nations. Contradicted by the numerous institutions and laws, that exist every where for the benefit of trade, by the pains taken to cultivate particular branches and to discourage others, by the known advantages derived from those measures, and by the palpable evils that would attend their discontinuance—it must be rejected by every man acquainted with commercial history. Commerce, like other things, has its fixed principles, according to which it must be regulated; if these are understood and observed, it will be promoted by the attention of government, if unknown, or violated, it will be injured—but it is the same with every other part of administration.

To preserve the ballance of trade in favour of a nation ought to be a leading aim of its policy. The avarice of individuals may frequently find its account in pursuing channels of traffic prejudicial to that ballance, to which the government may be able to oppose effectual impediments. There may, on the other hand, be a possibility of open-

55

ing new sources, which, though accompanied with great difficulties in the commencement, would in the event amply reward the trouble and expence of bringing them to perfection. The undertaking may often exceed the influence and capitals of individuals; and may require no small assistance, as well from the revenue, as from the authority of the state.

The contrary opinion, which has grown into a degree of vogue among us, has originated in the injudicious attempts made at different times to effect a REGULATION of PRICES. It became a cant phrase among the opposers of these attempts, that TRADE MUST REGULATE ITSELF; by which at first was only meant that it had its fundamental laws, agreeable to which its general operations must be directed; and that any violent attempts in opposition to these would commonly miscarry. In this sense the maxim was reasonable; but it has since been extended to militate against all interference by the sovereign; an extreme as little reconcileable with experience, or common sense, as the practice it was first framed to discredit.

The reasonings of a very ingenious and sensible writer,* by being misapprehended, have contributed to this mistake. The scope of his argument is not, as by some supposed, that trade will hold a certain invariable course independent on the aid, protection, care or concern of government; but that it will, in the main, depend upon the comparative industry moral and physical advantages of nations; and that though, for a while, from extraordinary causes, there may be a wrong ballance against one of them, this will work its own cure, and things will ultimately return to their proper level. His object was to combat that excessive jealousy on this head, which has been productive of so many unnecessary wars, and with which the British nation is particularly interested; but it was no part of his design to insinuate that the regulating hand of government was either useless, or hurtful. The nature of a government, its spirit, maxims and laws, with respect to trade, are among those constant moral causes, which influence its general results, and when it has by accident taken a wrong direction, assist in bringing it back to its natural course. This is every where admitted by all writers upon the subject; nor is there one who has asserted a contrary doctrine.

Trade may be said to have taken its rise in England under the auspices of Elizabeth; and its rapid progress there is in a great measure to be ascribed to the fostering care of government in that and succeeding reigns.

From a different spirit in the government, with superior advan-

*Hume. Essay Jealousy of Trade.

tages, France was much later in commercial improvements, nor would her trade have been at this time in so prosperous a condition had it not been for the abilities and indefatigable endeavours of the great COLBERT. He laid the foundation of the French commerce, and taught the way to his successors to enlarge and improve it. The establishment of the woolen manufacture, in a kingdom, where nature seemed to have denied the means, is one among many proofs, how much may be effected in favour of commerce by the attention and patronage of a wise administration. The number of useful edicts passed by Louis the 14th, and since his time, in spite of frequent interruptions from the jealous enmity of Great Britain, has advanced that of France to a degree which has excited the envy and astonishment of its neighbours.

The Dutch, who may justly be allowed a pre-eminence in the knowledge of trade, have ever made it an essential object of state. Their commercial regulations are more rigid and numerous, than those of any other country; and it is by a judicious and unremitted vigilance of government, that they have been able to extend their traffic to a degree so much beyond their natural and comparitive advantages.

Perhaps it may be thought, that the power of regulation will be left placed in the governments of the several states, and that a general superintendence is unnecessary. If the states had distinct interests, were unconnected with each other, their own governments would then be the proper and could be the only depositaries of such a power; but as they are parts of a whole with a common interest in trade, as in other things, there ought to be a common direction in that as in all other matters. It is easy to conceive, that many cases may occur, in which it would be beneficial to all the states to encourage, or suppress a particular branch of trade, while it would be detrimental to either to attempt it without the concurrence of the rest, and where the experiment would probably be left untried for fear of a want of that concurrence.

No mode can be so convenient as a source of revenue to the United States. It is agreed that imposts on trade, when not immoderate, or improperly laid, is one of the most eligible species of taxation. They fall in a great measure upon articles not of absolute necessity, and being partly transferred to the price of the commodity, are so far imperceptibly paid by the consumer. It is therefore that mode which may be exercised by the fœderal government with least exception or disgust. Congress can easily possess all the information necessary to impose the duties with judgment, and the collection can without difficulty be made by their own officers.

They can have no temptation to abuse this power, because the motive of revenue will check its own extremes. Experience has shown that moderate duties are more productive than high ones. When they are low, a nation can trade abroad on better terms—its imports and exports will be larger—the duties will be regularly paid, and arising on a greater quantity of commodities, will yield more in the aggregate, than when they are so high as to operate either as a prohibition, or as an inducement to evade them by illicit practices.

It is difficult to assign any good reason why Congress should be more liable to abuse the powers with which they are intrusted than the state-assemblies. The frequency of the election of the members is a full security against a dangerous ambition, and the rotation established by the confederation makes it impossible for any state, by continuing the same men, who may put themselves at the head of a prevailing faction, to maintain for any length of time an undue influence in the national councils. It is to be presumed, that Congress will be in general better composed for abilities, and as well for integrity as any assembly on the continent.

But to take away any temptation from a cabal to load particular articles, which are the principal objects of commerce to particular states, with a too great proportion of duties, to ease the others in the general distributions of expence; let all the duties whether for regulation or revenue, raised in each state, be creditted to that state, and let it in like manner be charged for all the bounties paid within itself for the encouragement of agriculture, manufactures, or trade. This expedient will remove the temptation; for as the quotas of the respective states are to be determined by a standard of land, agreeable to the [eighth] article of the confederation, each will have so much the less to contribute otherwise as it pays more on its commerce.

An objection has been made in a late instance to this principle. It has been urged, that as the consumer pays the duty, those states which are not equally well situated for foreign commerce, and which consume a great part of the imports of their neighbours, will become contributors to a part of their taxes. This objection is rather specious, than solid.

The maxim, that the consumer pays the duty has been admitted in theory with too little reserve; frequently contradicted in practice. It is true, the merchant will be unwilling to let the duty be a deduction from his profits, if the state of the market will permit him to incorporate it with the price of his commodity. But this is often not practicable. It turns upon the quantity of goods at market in proportion to the demand. When the latter exceeds the former, and the competition is among the buyers, the merchant can easily increase his price and make his customers pay the duty. When the reverse is the case, and the competition is among the sellers, he must then content himself with smaller profits, and lose the value of the duty or at least a part of it. Where a nation has a flourishing and well settled trade this more commonly happens than may be imagined, and it will, many times, be found that the duty is divided between the merchant and the consumer.

Besides this consideration, which greatly diminishes the force of the objection, there is another which intirely destroys it. There is strong reciprocal influence between the prices of all commodities in a state, by which they, sooner or later, attain a pretty exact ballance and proportion to each other. If the immediate productions of the soil rise, the manufacturer will have more for his manufacture, the merchant for his goods; and the same will happen with whatever class the increase of price begins. If duties are laid upon the imports in one state, by which the prices of foreign articles are raised, the products of land and labour within that state will take a proportionable rise; and if a part of those articles are consumed in a neighbouring state, it will have the same influence there as at home. The importing state must allow an advanced price upon the commodities, which it receives in exchange from its neighbor in a ratio to the increased price of the article it sells. To know then which is the gainer or loser, we must examine how the general ballance of trade stands between them. If the importing state takes more of the commodities of its neighbour, than it gives in exchange, that will be the loser by the reciprocal augmentation of prices—it will be the gainer, if it takes less—and neither will gain, or lose, if the barter is carried on upon equal terms. The ballance of trade, and consequently the gain, or loss, in this respect will be governed more by the relative industry and frugality of the parties, than by their relative advantages for foreign commerce.

Between separate nations, this reasoning will not apply with full force, because a multitude of local and extraneous circumstances may counteract the principal; but from the intimate connections of these states, the similitude of governments, situations, customs, manners—political and commercial causes will have nearly the same operation in the intercourse between the states, as in that between the different parts of the same state. If this should be controverted, the objection drawn from the hypothesis of the consumer paying the duty must fall at the same time: For as far as this is true it is as much confined in its application to a state within itself, as the doctrine of a reciprocal proportion of prices.

General principles in subjects of this nature ought always to be advanced with caution; in an experimental analysis there are found

59

such a number of exceptions as tend to render them very doubtful; and in questions which affect the existence and collective happiness of these states, all nice and abstract distinctions should give way to plainer interests and to more obvious and simple rules of conduct.

But the objection which has been urged ought to have no weight on another account. Which are the states, that have not sufficient advantages for foreign commerce, and that will not in time be their own carriers? Connecticut and Jersey are the least maritime of the whole; yet the sound which washes the coast of Connecticut has an easy outlet to the ocean, affords a number of harbours and bays, very commodious for trading vessels. New-London may be a receptacle for merchantmen of almost any burthen; and the fine rivers with which the state is intersected, by facilitating the transportation of commodities to and from every part, are extremely favorable both to its domestic and foreign trade. Jersey, by way of Amboy has a shorter communication with the ocean, than the city of New-York. Princes bay, which may serve as an out port to it, will admit and shelter in winter and summer vessels of any size. Egg-harbour on its southern coast is not to be despised. The Delaware may be made as subservient to its commerce as to that of Pennsylvania, Gloucester, Burlington, and Trenton, being all conveniently situated on that river. The United Provinces with inferior advantages of position to either of these states, have for centuries held the first rank among commercial nations.

The want of large trading cities has been sometimes objected as an obstacle to the commerce of these states; but this is a temporary deficiency that will repair itself with the encrease of population and riches. The reason that the states in question have hitherto carried on little foreign trade, is that they have found it equally beneficial to purchase the commodities imported by their neighbours. If the imposts on trade should work an inconvenience to them, it will soon cease by making it their interest to trade abroad.

It is too much characteristic of our national temper to be ingenious in finding out and magnifying the minutest disadvantages, and to reject measures of evident utility even of necessity to avoid trivial and sometimes imaginary evils. We seem not to reflect, that in human society, there is scarcely any plan, however salutary to the whole and to every part, by the share, each has in the common prosperity, but in one way, or another, and under particular circumstances, will operate more to the benefit of some parts, than of others. Unless we can overcome this narrow disposition and learn to estimate measures, by their general tendency, we shall never be a great or a happy people, if we remain a people at all.

THE CONTINENTALIST NO. VI
JULY 4, 1782

Fishkill, New York, July 4, 1782

Let us see what will be the consequences of not authorising the Fœderal Government to regulate the trade of these states.

Besides the want of revenue and of power, besides the immediate risk to our independence, the danger of all the future evils of a precarious union, besides the deficiency of a wholesome concert and provident superintendence to advance the general prosperity of trade, the direct consequence will be, that the landed interest and the labouring poor will in the first place fall a sacrifice to the trading interest, and the whole eventually to a bad system of policy, made necessary by the want of such regulating power.

Each state will be afraid to impose duties on its commerce, lest the other states, not doing the same, should enjoy greater advantages than itself; by being able to afford native commodities cheaper abroad, and foreign commodities cheaper at home.

A part of the evils resulting from this would be: A loss to the revenue of those moderate duties, which, without being injurious to commerce, are allowed to be the most agreeable species of taxes to the people.

Articles of foreign luxury while they would contribute nothing to the income of the state, being less dear by an exemption from duties, would have a more extensive consumption.

Many branches of trade hurtful to the common interest would be continued for want of proper checks and discouragements.

As revenues must be found to satisfy the public exigencies in peace and in war, too great a proportion of taxes will fall directly upon land and upon the necessaries of life, the produce of that land.

The influence of these evils will be, to render landed property fluctuating and less valuable, to oppress the poor by raising the prices of necessaries, to injure commerce by encouraging the consumption of foreign luxuries, by encreasing the value of labor, by lessening the quantity of home productions, enhancing their prices at foreign markets, of course, obstructing their sale and enabling other nations to supplant us.

Particular caution ought at present to be observed in this country, not to burthen the soil itself and its productions, with heavy impositions; because the quantity of unimproved land will invite the

husbandmen to abandon old settlements for new, and the disproportion of our population for some time to come, will necessarily make
labor dear, to reduce which, and not to increase it, ought to be a
capital object of our policy.

Easy duties therefore on commerce, especially on imports, ought
to lighten the burthens, which will unavoidably fall upon land.
Though it may be said, that on the principle of a reciprocal influence
of prices, whereon the taxes are laid in the first instance, they will in
the end be borne by all classes; yet it is of the greatest importance that
no one should sink under the immediate pressure. The great art is to
distribute the public burthens well and not suffer them, either first, or
last, to fall too heavily upon parts of the community; else distress and
disorder must ensue. A shock given to any part of the political machine vibrates through the whole.

As a sufficient revenue could not be raised from trade to answer
the public purposes, other articles have been proposed.

A moderate land and poll tax, being of easy and unexpensive
collection, and leaving nothing to discretion, are the simplest and
best, that could be devised.

It is to be feared, the avarice of many of the landholders will be
opposed to a perpetual tax upon land, however moderate. They will
ignorantly hope to shift the burthens of the national expence from
themselves to others; a disposition as iniquitous as it is fruitless. The
public necessities must be satisfied; this can only be done by the
contributions of the whole society. Particular classes are neither able
nor will be willing to pay for the protection and security of the others;
and where so selfish a spirit discovers itself in any member, the rest of
the community will unite to compel it to do its duty.

Indeed many theorists in political œconomy have held, that all
taxes, wherever they originate fall ultimately upon land; and have
therefore been of opinion, that it would be best to draw the whole
revenue of the state immediately from that source, to avoid the expence of a more diversified collection, and the accumulations which
will be heaped in their several stages upon the primitive sums advanced in those taxes, which are imposed on our trade. But though it
has been demonstrated, that this theory has been carried to an extreme, impracticable in fact, yet it is evident, in tracing the matter,
that a large part of all taxes, however remotely laid, will by an insensible circulation, come at last to settle upon land; the source of most of
the materials employed of commerce.

It appears from calculation made by the ablest masters of political
arithmetic, about sixty years ago, that the yearly product of all the
lands in England amounted to £42,000,000 sterling, and the whole

annual consumption, at that period, of foreign as well as domestic commodities, did not exceed £49,000,000, and the surplus of the exportation above the importation £2,000,000; on which sums, must arise all the revenues in whatever shape which go into the treasury. It is easy to infer from this, how large a part of them must directly, or indirectly be derived from land.

Nothing can be more mistaken, than the collision and rivalship, which almost always subsist between the landed and trading interests, for the truth is they are so inseparably interwoven, that one cannot be injured, without injury, nor benefitted, without benefit to the other. Oppress trade, lands sink in value, make it flourish, their value rises, incumber husbandry, trade declines, encourage agriculture, commerce revives. The progress of this mutual reaction might easily be delineated, but it is too obvious to every man, who turns his thoughts, however superficially, upon the subject, to require it. It is only to be regretted that it is too often lost sight of, when the seductions of some immediate advantage or exemption tempt us to sacrifice the future to the present.

But perhaps the class is more numerous than those, who not unwilling to bear their share of public burthens, are yet averse to the idea of perpetuity, as if there ever would arrive a period, when the state would cease to want revenues and taxes become unnecessary. It is of importance to unmask this delusion and open the eyes of the people to the truth. It is paying too great a tribute to the idol of popularity to flatter so injurious and so visionary an expectation. The error is too gross to be tolerated any where, but in the cottage of the peasant; should we meet with it in the senate house, we must lament the ignorance or despise the hypocrisy, on which it is ingrafted. Expence is in the present state of things entailed upon all governments. Though if we continue united, we shall be hereafter less exposed to wars by land, than most other countries; yet while we have powerful neighbours on either extremity, and our frontier is embraced by savages, whose alliance they may without difficulty command, we cannot, in prudence, dispense with the usual precautions for our interior security. As a commercial people, maritime power must be a primary object of our attention, and a navy cannot be created or maintained without ample revenues. The nature of our popular constitutions requires a numerous magistracy, for whom competent provision must be made; or we may be certain our affairs will always be committed to improper hands; and experience will teach us, that no government costs so much as a bad one.

We may preach till we are tired of the theme, the necessity of disinterestedness in republics, without making a single proselyte.

63

The virtuous declaimer will neither persuade himself nor any other person to be content with a double mess of porridge, instead of a reasonable stipend for his services. We might as soon reconcile ourselves to the Spartan community of goods and wives, to their iron coin, their long beards, or their black broth. There is a total dissimulation in the circumstances, as well as the manners, of society among us; and it is as ridiculous to seek for models in the simple ages of Greece and Rome, as it would be to go in quest of them among the Hottentots and Laplanders.

The public, for the different purposes, that have been mentioned, must always have large demands upon its constituents, and the only question is whether these shall be satisfied by annual grants perpetually renewed—by a perpetual grant once for all or by a compound of permanent and occasional supplies. The last is the wisest course. The Fœderal Government should neither be independent nor too much dependent. It should neither be raised above responsibility or controul, nor should it want the means of maintaining its own weight, authority, dignity and credit. To this end permanent funds are indispensable, but they ought to be of such a nature and so moderate in their amount, as never to be inconvenient. Extraordinary supplies can be the objects of extraordinary grants; and in this salutary medium will consist our true wisdom.

It would seem as if no mode of taxation could be relished but that worst of all modes which now prevails, by assessment. Every proposal for a specific tax is sure to meet with opposition. It has been objected to a poll tax, at a fixed rate, that it will be unequal, as the rich will pay no more than the poor. In the form under which it has been offered in these papers, the poor properly speaking are not comprehended, though it is true that beyond the exclusion of the indigent the tax has no reference to the proportion of property; but it should be remembered that it is impossible to devise any specific tax, that will operate equally on the whole community. It must be the province of the legislature to hold the scales with a judicious hand and ballance one by another. The rich must be made to pay for their luxuries; which is the only proper way of taxing their superior wealth.

Do we imagine that our assessments opperate equally? Nothing can be more contrary to the fact. Wherever a discretionary power is lodged in any set of men over the property of their neighbours, they will abuse it. Their passions, prejudices, partialities, dislikes, will have the principal lead in measuring the abilities of those over whom their power extends; and assessors will ever be a set of petty tyrants, too unskilful, if honest, to be possessed of so delicate a trust, and too seldom honest to give them the excuse of want of skill. The genius of liberty reprobates every thing arbitrary or discretionary in taxation. It exacts that every man by a definite and general rule should know what proportion of his property the state demands. Whatever liberty we may boast in theory, it cannot exist in fact, while assessments continue. The admission of them among us is a new proof, how often human conduct reconciles the most glaring opposites; in the present case the most vicious practice of despotic governments, with the freest constitutions and the greatest love of liberty.

The establishment of permanent funds would not only answer the public purposes infinitely better than temporary supplies; but it would be the most effectual way of easing the people. With this basis for procuring credit, the amount of present taxes might be greatly diminished. Large sums of money might be borrowed abroad at a low interest, and introduced into the country to defray the current expences and pay the public debts; which would not only lessen the demand for immediate supplies, but would throw more money into circulation, and furnish the people with greater means of paying the taxes. Though it be a just rule, that we ought not to run in debt to avoid present expence, so far as our faculties extend; yet the propriety of doing it cannot be disputed when it is apparent, that these are incompetent to the public necessities. Efforts beyond our abilities can only tend to individual distress and national disappointment.

The product of the three forgoing articles will be as little as can be required to enable Congress to pay their debts, and restore order into their finances. In addition to these—

The disposal of the unlocated lands will hereafter be a valuable source of revenue, and an immediate one of credit. As it may be liable to the same condition with the duties on trade, that is the product of the sales within each state, to be creditted to that state, and as the rights of jurisdiction are not infringed, it seems to be susceptible of no reasonable objection.

Mines in every country constitute a branch of the revenue. In this where nature has so richly impregnated the bowels of the earth, they may in time become a valuable one; and as they require the care and attention of government to bring them to perfection, this care and a share in the profits of it, will very properly devolve upon Congress. All the precious metals should absolutely be the property of the Fœderal Government, and with respect to the others, it should have a discretionary power of reserving in the nature of a tax, such part as it may judge not inconsistent with the encouragement due to so important an object. This is rather a future than a present resource.

The reason of allowing Congress to appoint its own officers of the customs, collectors of taxes, and military officers of every rank, is to create in the interior of each state a mass of influence in favour of the Fœderal Government. The great danger has been shown to be, that it will not have power enough to defend itself and preserve the union, not that it will ever become formidable to the general liberty. A mere regard to the interests of the confederacy will never be a principle sufficiently active to curb the ambition and intrigues of different members. Force cannot effect it: A contest of arms will seldom be between the common sovereign and a single refractory member; but between distinct combinations of the several parts against each other. A sympathy of situations will be apt to produce associates to the disobedient. The application of force is always disagreeable, the issue uncertain. It will be wise to obviate the necessity of it, by interesting such a number of individuals in each state in support of the Fœderal Government, as will be counterpoised to the ambition of others; and will make it difficult for them to unite the people in opposition to the just and necessary measures of the union.

There is something noble and magnificent in the perspective of a great Fœderal Republic, closely linked in the pursuit of a common interest, tranquil and prosperous at home, respectable abroad; but there is something proportionably diminutive and contemptible in the prospect of a number of petty states, with the appearance only of union, jarring, jealous and perverse, without any determined direction, fluctuating and unhappy at home, weak and insignificant by their dissentions, in the eyes of other nations. Happy America! if those, to whom thou hast intrusted the guardianship of thy infancy, know how to provide for thy future repose; but miserable and undone, if their negligence or ignorance permits the spirit of discord to erect her banners on the ruins of thy tranquillity!

SECOND LETTER FROM PHOCION
APRIL 1784

Hamilton believed that liberty is the perfection of civil society, that is, the deepest purpose or nature of government is securing the individual's rights and interests. In order to achieve the end of liberty, it is necessary to construct a regime that ensures the rule of law. The importance of the rule of law for liberty is that it ensures the goodness of the government's intention to protect every citizen from oppression. In the Phocion let-

ters, the second of which appears below, Hamilton shows that liberty depends especially on how governmental authority is applied to and affects individual rights and interests. He was criticizing the attempt of the New York legislature to refuse to restore confiscated Loyalist property in violation of the peace treaty with England.

New York, April 1784

The little hasty production, under the signature of PHOCION, has met with a more favourable reception from the public, than was expected. The force of plain truth has carried it along against the stream of prejudice; and the principles, it holds out, have gained ground, in spite of the opposition of those, who were either too angry, or too much interested to be convinced. Men of this description, have, till lately, contented themselves with virulent invectives against the Writer, without attempting to answer his arguments; but alarmed at the progress of the sentiments advocated by him, one of them has at last come forward with an answer; with what degree of success, let those, who are most partial to his opinion, determine.

To say, that the answer of Mentor is a feeble attempt, would be no derogation from his abilities; for, in fact, the cause he espouses, admits of nothing solid; and, as one of its partizans, he is only to be blamed for not knowing its weak sides better, than to have been tempted to expose it to the experiment of a defence.

But, before I enter farther into the subject, I shall take occasion to acknowledge, with regret, the injudicious appearance of warmth in my former letter; calculated, with many minds, to raise prejudices against the truths it contains, and liable to be misrepresented into a general censure on that part of the community, whose zeal, sacrifices and sufferings must ever render them respectable to the true friends of the revolution. I shall only observe in apology (as is truly the case) that whatever severity of animadversion may have been indulged, was wholly directed against a *very small* number of men, who are manifestly aiming at nothing, but the acquisition of power and profit to themselves; and who, to gratify their avidity for these objects, would trample upon every thing sacred in society, and overturn the foundations of public and private security. It is difficult for a man, conscious of a pure attachment to the public weal, who sees it invaded and endangered by such men, under specious but false pretenses, either to think, or to speak of their conduct, without indignation. It is equally difficult for one, who in questions that affect the community, regards *principles* only, and not *men*, to look with indifference on attempts to make the great principles of social right, justice and honour, the victims of personal animosity or party intrigue.

More tenderness is indeed due to the mistakes of those, who have suffered too much to reason with impartiality, whose honest prejudices, grown into habits by the impressions of an eight years war, cannot at once accommodate themselves to that system which the public good requires, and whose situations are less favourable to distinguishing between doctrines invented to serve the turn of a revolution, and those which must give permanent prosperity to the state.

These observations I have thought proper to premise, in justice to my own intentions, and I shall now proceed, as concisely as possible, to examine the suggestions of Mentor, interspersing as I go along, some remarks on objections which though omitted by him, have been urged in other shapes against the principles of Phocion.

Mentor proposes to treat the sentiments of Phocion as a political novelty, but if he is serious, it is a proof that he is not even "tolerably well informed." They are as old as any regular notions of free government among mankind, and are to be met with, not only in every speculative Writer, on these subjects, but are interwoven in the theory and practice of that code, which constitutes the law of the land. They speak the common language of this country at the beginning of the revolution, and are essential to its future happiness and respectability.

The principles of all the arguments I have used or shall use, lie within the compass of a few simple propositions, which, to be assented to, need only to be stated.

First, That no man can forfeit or be justly deprived, without his consent, of any right to which as a member of the community he is entitled, but for some crime incurring the forfeiture.

Secondly, That no man ought to be condemned unheard, or punished for supposed offences, without having an opportunity of making his defence.

Thirdly, That a crime is *an act* committed or omitted, in violation of a public law, either forbidding or commanding it.

Fourthly, That a prosecution is in its most precise signification, an *inquiry* or *mode of ascertaining*, whether a particular person has committed, or omitted such *act*.

Fifthly, That *duties* and *rights* as applied to subjects are reciprocal; or in other words, that a man cannot be a *citizen* for the purpose of punishment, and not a *citizen* for the purpose of privilege.

These propositions will hardly be controverted by any man professing to be a friend to civil liberty. The application of them will more fully appear hereafter.

By the declaration of Independence on the 4th of July, in the year 1776, acceded to by our Convention on the ninth, the late colony of New-York became an independent state. All the inhabitants, who were subjects under the former government, and who did not withdraw themselves upon the change which took place, were to be considered as citizens, owing allegiance to the new government. This, at least, is the legal presumption; and this was the principle, in fact, upon which all the measures of our public councils have been grounded. Duties have been exacted, and punishments inflicted according to this rule. If any exceptions to it were to be admitted, they could only flow from the *indulgence* of the state to such individuals, as from peculiar circumstances might desire to be permitted to stand upon a different footing.

The inhabitants of the southern district, before they fell under the power of the British army, were as much citizens of the state as the inhabitants of other parts of it. They must, therefore, continue to be such, unless they have been divested of that character by some posterior circumstance. This circumstance must, either be—

Their having, by the fortune of war, fallen under the power of the British army.

Their having forfeited their claim by their own misconduct.

Their having been left out of the compact by some subsequent association of the body of the state, or

Their having been dismembered by treaty.

The first of these circumstances according to the fundamental principles of government, and the constant practice of nations could have no effect in working a forfeiture of their citizenship. To allow it such an effect, would be to convert misfortune into guilt; it would be in many instances, to make the negligence of the society, in not providing adequate means of defence for the several parts, the crime of those parts which were the immediate sufferers by that negligence. It would tend to the dissolution of society, by loosening the ties which bind the different parts together, and justifying those who should for a moment fall under the power of a conqueror, not merely in yielding such a submission as was exacted from them, but in taking a willing, interested and decisive part with him.

It was the policy of the revolution, to inculcate upon every citizen the obligation of renouncing his habitation, property, and every private concern for the service of his country, and many of us have scarcely yet learned to consider it as less than treason to have acted in

69

a different manner. But it is time we should correct the exuberances of opinions propagated through policy, and embraced from enthusiasm; and while we admit, that those who did act so disinterested and noble a part, deserve the applause and, wherever they can be bestowed with propriety the rewards of their country, we should cease to impute indiscriminate guilt to those, who, submitting to the accidents of war, remained with their habitions and property. We should learn, that this conduct is tolerated by the general sense of mankind; and that according to that sense, whenever the state recovers the possession of such parts as were for a time subdued, the citizens return at once to all the rights, to which they were formerly entitled.

As to the second head of forfeiture by misconduct, there is no doubt, that all such as remaining within the British lines, did not merely yield an obedience, which they could not refuse, without ruin; but took a voluntary and interested part with the enemy, in carrying on the war, became subject to the penalties of treason. They could not however, by that conduct, make themselves aliens, because though they were bound to pay a temporary and qualified obedience to the conqueror, they could not transfer their eventual allegiance from the state to a foreign power. By becoming aliens too, they would have ceased to be traitors; and all the laws of the state passed during the revolution, by which they are considered and punished as subjects, would have been, by that construction, unintelligible and unjust. The idea indeed of citizens transforming themselves into aliens, by taking part against the state, to which they belong, is altogether of new-invention, unknown and inadmissible in law, and contrary to the nature of the social compact.

But were this not the case, an insurmountable difficulty would still remain, for how shall we ascertain who are aliens or traitors, let us call them which we will. It has been seen that the boundaries of the British lines cannot determine the question; for this would be to say, that the merely falling under the power of the British army, constituted every man a *traitor* or an *alien*. It would be to confound one third of the citizens of the state in promiscuous guilt and degradation, without evidence, or enquiry. It would be to make crimes, which are in their nature personal and individual, aggregate and territorial. Shall we go into an enquiry to ascertain the crime of each person? *This would be a prosecution;* and the treaty forbids all future prosecutions. Shall the Legislature take the map and make a geographical delineation of the rights and disqualifications of its citizens? This would be to measure innocence and guilt, by latitude and longitude. It would be to *condemn* and *punish,* not one man, but thousands for *supposed offences,* without giving them an opportunity of making their defence. God forbid that such an act of barefaced tyranny should ever disgrace our history! God forbid that the body of the people should be corrupt enough to wish it, or even to submit to it!

But here we are informed by Mentor, that the treaty, instead of offering any obstacles to the views of those, who wish to metamorphose their fellow citizens into aliens, is precisely the thing which removes the difficulty. Mentor is thus far right; that if they are aliens at all, it must be by some stipulations in the treaty, but it requires not a little dexterity to shew, that such a stipulation exists. If it exists at all, it must be collected from the 5th and 6th articles. Let us, by analyzing these articles, try if we can find it out.

The fifth article speaks in the first clause of *real British subjects* whose estates *had been confiscated*, and stipulates that Congress shall recommend a restitution.

In the second clause it speaks of *persons resident* in districts in the possession of the British forces, who had not borne arms against the United States of whose estates, *also confiscated*, Congress are in like manner to recommend a restitution.

In the third clause, persons of every other description are comprehended, who are to be permitted to remain twelve months unmolested, in any of the states, to solicit a restoration of their property, which *had been confiscated;* Congress recommending, even with respect to them, a restitution, on condition of their refunding to the present possessors, where there had been a sale, the bona fide price given by them for the estates in their possession.

It is apparent from the dissection of the article, that the inhabitants in the Southern district, possessed by the British army, are not confounded in one general mass of alienism, as has been asserted. We find the express words of description are *real British subjects*, and as contradistinguished from them, *persons resident* in districts within the possession of the British arms. These last, by the *letter* as well as the spirit of the article are deemed *not British subjects*.

There is no intelligible medium, between a real British subject, and one that is not a British subject at all. A man either *is* or *is not* the subject of a country. The word *real*, as applied to the affirmative, is a redundancy. Its natural contrasts are *fictitious* or *pretended*. If we should call the persons of other descriptions in the article *fictitious* or *pretended* British subjects, instead of justifying, it would exclude the construction given by Mentor. For if they were only *fictitious* or *pretended* British subjects, they must be real American subjects; or in other words, if they were not *real* British subjects, which by necessary implication they are declared not to be, they must of necessity be American subjects.

71

The phrase *real British subjects*, strictly considered, is innaccurate; but its practical import, with the help of a little candor, is easily fixed. It is well known that in this and other states, the property of persons, who had never been subjects of this country, before or after the revolution, but who had truly been subjects of Great-Britain, had in many instances been confiscated. Sir Henry Clinton, the late Governor Tryon, Lord Dunmore, are examples among us of the real British subjects in the contemplation of the treaty. All the rest are of course American subjects.

To understand the fifth and sixth articles relatively, it is necessary to remark that all the different classes described in the fifth article agree in one *common quality*; they are all persons whose *property had been already confiscated*. I have placed this fact in a pointed view; because it shews incontestibly, that the persons who are the objects of the fifth article, and those who are the objects of the sixth, are totally different. The one relates to persons whose property had been confiscated, and *aims* at restitution; the other relates to those whose property had not yet been confiscated, who were not actually suffering the sentence of the law, and has for object to prevent future prosecutions, confiscations, or injuries to individuals on account of their conduct in the war.

This distinction solves the seeming contradiction between the fifth and sixth articles; the former providing for the future residence of persons of a particular description within the state for a twelve month; the other prohibiting all future injury or damage to persons, liberty or property. At first sight, the great extent of the latter provision appears to supercede, and render absurd, the former; but the two articles are reconciled, by considering those, who had already suffered the sentence of the law, as not within the purview of the sixth article, to arrest or remit that sentence; while all others against whom sentence had not passed, are within the protection of the sixth article. It does not operate with a retrospective and restorative influence, but looks forward and stops the future current of prosecution and punishment.

To illustrate, in a more striking manner, the fallacy of Mentor's comment upon the treaty, I shall give a recital of it, with some explanatory additions, the fairness of which I think will not be disputed.

"In the sixth article (says he) it is provided that *no one shall suffer* in his person, liberty, or property, on account of the part he may have taken in the war;" and yet though no one, consistently with the treaty, can hereafter suffer in either of those respects, yet many, consistently with the treaty, may be declared aliens, may be stripped of the most valuable rights of citizenship, and may be banished from the state, without injury to person, liberty, or property, "The fifth article," though it speaks of none but those who have already had their estates confiscated, "describes the persons provided for by the sixth," which indeed says, that there *shall be* no future prosecutions, nor confiscations, nor injury to person, liberty, or property; but this only means, that there shall be no future prosecutions commenced against those, who have been already *attainted and banished*, nor confiscations made of the estates of those whose estates *have been already confiscated*, nor injuries done to the persons, liberty, and property, of those, who are already to be esteemed *dead in law* by attainder and exile; but with respect to all those who have not been already *attainted, banished*, and *subjected to confiscation*, (the only persons comprehended in the fifth article and provided for in the sixth) we may prosecute, banish, confiscate, disfranchise, and do whatever else we think proper. The fifth article stipulates the good offices of Congress for those, who have been already ruined, and the sixth benignly takes care that they shall not be ruined a second time; but leaves all others to their destiny and our mercy. "The fifth article, distinguishes, the persons who are the objects of it, into three classes—First, those who are real British subjects—The second, those" (meaning British subjects who were not real British subjects, described by the appellation of persons resident in districts in the possession of the British forces) "who had not taken arms against the country—The third class are described by the provision that is made for them, viz. They shall have liberty to go into any part of the United States for twelve months to solicit a restoration of their estates, that may have been confiscated. This class must be those who belonging to America, have taken arms against their country. The first and second class it is agreed, that Congress shall recommend to the states a restoration of their property. The third it seems were too infamous for the English minister to ask any consideration for, except the wretched privilege of asking it for themselves," though in fact, with respect even to them, it is expressly stipulated, that Congress shall recommend a restoration of their estates, rights and properties, on paying to the present possessors the bona fide price given for them, where there has been an actual sale. "But (continues he) I can find no where even a request, and that only implied, that any of the three classes may dwell among us, and enjoy the immunities and privileges of citizens; for the first class are considered as former subjects; the second and third as acquired subjects of England," *acquired* but not *real*.

Thus we see, by taking the out-lines of Mentor's construction, and filling up the canvass in a manner suited to the design, the whole

73

is a groupe of absurdities; or in other words by connecting the consequences with the principles of his comment, on the treaty, the result
is too ridiculous not to strike the meanest understanding.

It must appear by this time manifest, that there is nothing in the
terms of the treaty, which countenances the supposition, that those
who have been within the British lines are considered and stipulated
for as aliens. One ground, upon which this idea has been originally
adopted, was that it would have been improper to have stipulated for
them at all, if they were not aliens; but I have shown in my former
letter, that a stipulation for subjects, in similar circumstances, has
been far from unprecedented.

A good criterion by which to determine the meaning of the
treaty, in this respect, is to recur to the impressions that it made, on
its first appearance; before there had been time to contrive and substitute an artificial to the natural and obvious sense of the words. Every
man, by appealing to his own bosom, will recollect, that he was at
first struck with an opinion that the disaffected were secured from
every future deprivation and injury whatever; and however many
may have been chagrined at the idea, that they should be admitted to
a party of privileges with those who had supported the revolution,
none doubted that this was the sense of the treaty. Indeed the principal doubt seemed to be, in the first instance, whether the sixth article
was not so broad, as to protect even those, who had been attainted,
from personal injury, in case of their return within the state.

I shall not, in this place, revive the question of the power of
Congress to make this stipulation; not only because Mentor appears
to have conceded this point, and to acknowledge our obligation to a
faithful observance of the treaty; but because what has been offered in
my former letter on this head, must continue to appear to me to be
absolutely conclusive; until some satisfactory limits can be assigned to
the powers of war, peace and treaty, vested in Congress, other than
those I have mentioned,—the public safety and the fundamental constitutions of the society.

When any different and intelligible line shall be drawn—I will
give up the question, if I cannot shew it is inadmissible in practice.

The common interests of humanity, and the general tranquility
of the world, require that the power of making peace, wherever
lodged, should be construed and exercised liberally; and even in
cases where its extent may be doubtful, it is the policy of all wise
nations to give it latitude rather than confine it. The exigencies of a
community, in time of war, are so various and often so critical, that it
would be extremely dangerous to prescribe narrow bounds to that
power, by which it is to be restored. The consequence might fre-

quently be a diffidence of our engagements, and a prolongation of the calamities of war.

It may not be improper, in this place, to answer an objection which has been made to a position contained in my former letter. It is there laid down as a rule, that the breach of a single article of a treaty annuls the whole. The reason of this rule is, that every article is to be regarded as the consideration of some other article.

This has given occasion to observe, that a breach of the treaty on the part of the British, in sending away a great number of negroes, has upon my principles long since annihilated the treaty, and left us at perfect liberty to desert the stipulations, on our part.

This admits of an easy and solid answer. The breach of one article annuls the whole; if the side injured by it chooses to take advantage of it to dissolve the treaty; but if its interest dictates a different conduct it may wave the breach and let the obligation of the treaty continue. The power of determining whether the treaty has been broken properly belongs to that body who made it. Congress have wisely taken a different course, and instead of reviving the state of hostility by declaring the treaty void, have proceeded upon the presumption of its continuing in force; and by subsequent acts have given it additional validity and strength. The definitive treaty has been since concluded, and proclaimed with a remarkable solemnity and energy for the observance of the citizens of the United States.

The third mode mentioned, by which the inhabitants of the southern district may have lost their rights of citizenship, is their having been left out of the compact by some subsequent association of the body of the state. The fact however is directly the reverse; for not only the constitution makes provision for the representation of the people of the southern district in the Legislature, but during the whole war, by an ordinance of the Convention, who framed the constitution, an actual representation has been kept up in a manner, the regularity of which (whatever might have been the expedience of it) was more than questionable; as all elections were suspended in that part of the state. This circumstance of a constant representation of the inhabitants of the Southern district in the Legislature, during the war, is in a rational as well as a legal light a conclusive refutation of the pretended alienism of those inhabitants by any event of the war, or by any other matter that applies to them in a collective view antecedent to the treaty of peace. To this it may be added, that a variety of the laws of the state, in the course of the war, suppose and treat the inhabitants of the Southern district as subjects; owing allegiance to the state, and consequently having the rights which subjects in general enjoy under the government.

The argument is still stronger when we attend to what has been done by the government since the restoration of its jurisdiction in the Southern district. We did not wait till a bill of naturalization was passed, to remove the disabilities of the inhabitants, before we proceeded to elections. We did not confine those elections to such persons only, as had resided without the British lines, but left them open to all descriptions of persons, who would choose to take the oath prescribed for that purpose, by the Council. Few indeed in this city, besides those who had been absent, did in fact vote at the elections; but a considerable number did in the counties. And if we should admit the doctrine of the general alienism of the inhabitants of the Southern district, either before, or in consequence of the treaty of peace, a curious question not easy to be solved, would arise as to the validity of the election of many individuals now holding seats in Senate and Assembly. So far as an act of government can decide the point in controversy, it is already decided. The Council for the temporary government of the Southern district in appointing the mode of election—the conduct of the legislature since in admitting the members elected in that mode, are unconstitutional; or the inhabitants at large of the Southern district, either by the treaty, or any antecedent circumstance, are not aliens.

I have dwelt the more largely on this head, not only because the idea of a general alienism of the inhabitants of the Southern district is the ground Mentor has taken; but because some persons who have it in their power to make a mischievous use of it, are endeavouring to give it circulation, where, if it could prevail, it might lead to pernicious consequences. Pressed by the difficulty of discriminating those, who may have forfeited the rights of citizenship from those who have not, without a manifest violation as well of the constitution, as of the treaty of peace, they are willing if possible to devise some general expedient to evade both; and the one they have hit upon is, to declare all those aliens, who lived within the British lines during the war, on the miserable pretence that they are made such by the treaty.

Thus we have another example how easy it is for men to change their principles with their situations—to be zealous advocates for the rights of the citizens when they are invaded by others, and as soon as they have it in their power, to become the invaders themselves—to resist the encroachments of power, when it is the hands of others, and the moment they get it into their own to make bolder strides than those they have resisted. Are such men to be sanctified with the hallowed name of patriots? Are they not rather to be branded as men who make their passions, prejudices and interests the sole measure of their own and others rights?

This history of mankind is too full of these melancholy instances of human contradiction.

Having mentioned the oath directed to be prescribed to electors in the Southern district, by the Council for the temporary government; I shall take occasion, in this place, with freedom, but with respect, to examine the propriety of that measure.

This measure was founded upon an act of the legislature of this state passed in the year declaring, that persons who had been guilty of certain matters particularized in that act, should be forever after disqualified from voting at all public elections. I confine myself for the sake of brevity to the general idea of the act. The embarrassment with the Council, no doubt, was, how to ascertain the persons who had incurred the disability. As the matters, to which that disability related, were of a specific nature, it was necessary, they should be specifically ascertained before the law could have its effect.

The Council, therefore, could not satisfy that law, by declaring all those disqualified, who had resided within the British lines during the war. They would not leave the operation of it to a course of judicial investigation and decision, because this would be to fly in the face of the treaty, and appearances were to be preserved. This consideration was strengthened by another. The course of the law must have been dilatory. The elections were to be entered upon. It was deemed inexpedient, that the voice of the citizens at large (which must have been the case if the act of the legislature, in question, had been left to its natural course) should govern these elections. If the returning citizens were not at this juncture gratified, tumults were by some apprehended.

This was a plausible step, and on that account the more dangerous. If we examine it with an unprejudiced eye, we must acknowledge not only that it was an evasion of the treaty, but a subversion of one great principle of social security, to wit, that every man shall be presumed innocent until he is proved guilty: This was to invert the order of things; and instead of obliging the state to prove the guilt, in order to inflict the penalty, it was to oblige the citizen to establish his own innocence, to avoid the penalty. It was to excite scruples in the honest and conscientious, and to hold out a bribe to perjury.

That this was an evasion of the treaty, the fourth proposition already laid down will illustrate. It was a mode of inquiry who had committed any of those crimes to which the penalty of disqualification was annexed, with this aggravation, that it deprived the citizen of the benefit of that advantage which he would have enjoyed by leaving, as in all other cases, the burthen of the proof upon the prosecutor.

To place this matter in a still clearer light, let it be supposed, that instead of the mode of indictment and trial by jury, the legislature was to declare that every citizen who did not swear he had never adhered to the King of Great-Britain, should incur all the penalties which our treason laws prescribe. Would this not be a palpable evasion of the treaty, and a direct infringement of the constitution? The principle is the same in both cases, with only this difference in the consequences; that in the instance already acted upon, the citizen forfeits a part of his rights,—in the one supposed he would forfeit the whole. The degree of punishment is all that distinguishes the cases. In either justly considered, it is substituting a new and arbitrary mode of prosecution to that antient and highly esteemed one, recognized by the laws and the constitution of the state; I mean the trial by jury.

Let us not forget that the constitution declares that trial by jury in all cases in which it has been formerly used, should remain inviolate forever, and that the legislature should at no time, erect any new jurisdiction which should not proceed, according to the course of the common law. Nothing can be more repugnant to the true genius of the common law, than such an inquisition as has been mentioned into the consciences of men.

A share in the sovereignty of the state, which is exercised by the citizens at large, in voting at elections is one of the most important rights of the subject, and in a republic ought to stand foremost in the estimation of the law. It is that right, by which we exist a free people; and it certainly therefore will never be admitted, that less ceremony ought to be used in divesting any citizen of that right, than in depriving him of his property. Such a doctrine would ill suit the principles of the revolution, which taught the inhabitants of this country to risk their lives and fortunes in asserting their *liberty;* or in other words, their *right* to a *share* in the government. That portion of the soverignty, to which each individual is entitled, can never be too highly prized. It is that for which we have fought and bled; and we should cautiously guard against any precedents, however they may be immediately directed against those we hate, which may in their consequences render our title to this great privilege, precarious. Here we may find the criterion to distinguish the genuine from the pretended whig. The man that would attack that right, in whatever shape, is an enemy to whiggism.

If any oath, with retrospect to past conduct, were to be made the condition, on which individuals, who have resided within the British lines, should hold their estates; we should immediately see, that this proceeding would be tyrannical, and a violation of the treaty, and yet when the same mode is employed to divest that right, which ought to be deemed still more sacred, many of us are so infatuated as to over-look the mischief.

To say that the persons, who will be affected by it, have previously forfeited that right, and that therefore nothing is taken away from them, is a begging of the question. How do we know who are the persons in this situation? If it be answered, this is the mode taken to ascertain it, the objection returns, 'tis an improper mode, because it puts the most essential interests of the citizen upon a worse footing, than we should be willing to tolerate where inferior interests were concerned; and because to elude the treaty it substitutes to the established and legal mode of investigating crimes, and inflicting forfeitures, on that is unknown to the constitution, and repugnant to the genius of our law.

Much stress has been laid upon a couple of unmeaning words in the act, to enforce the penalties of which, the oath was invented. It is declared, that the persons, who have done the several things enumerated in the act, shall be *ipso facto* disqualified. These words of potent sound, but of little substance, have been supposed to include wonderful effects. Let us see if we can give them any definite meaning. If a man commits murder, by the very act *ipso facto*, he incurs the penalty of death; but before he can be hanged, we must enquire whether he has certainly committed the fact. If a man has done any of those things which are declared sufficient to disqualify him from voting, though by the very act, *ipso facto* he incurs the penalty of the law, yet before he can be actually disqualified, we must enquire whether he has really done the act. From this we perceive the words *ipso facto* are mere expletives, which add nothing to the force or efficacy of the law.

It has been said too, that an oath to determine the qualifications of electors, is an usual precaution in free governments; but we may challenge those who make the assertion, to show that retrospective oaths have ever been administered, requiring electors to swear that they have not been guilty of past offences. In all the violence of party which has at different periods agitated Great Britain, nothing of this kind has ever been adopted; but even where religious fanaticism has given an edge to political opposition, and in an undecided contest for the crown, they have never gone further than to prescribe oaths for testing present dispositions towards the government on general principles, without retrospection to particular instances of past malconduct. The practical notions of legal liberty established in that country by a series of time would make such an experiment too odious to be attempted by the government. Wise men have thought that even there, they have carried the business of oaths to an exceptionable length; but we who pretend a purer zeal for liberty, in a decided contest, after a formal renunciation of claims by the adverse party, are for carrying the matter to a still more blameable extreme.

Men, whose judgements and intentions I respect, were promoters of the measure, which has occasioned this digression; some from the contagion of popular opinion; others from the too strong impressions of momentary expedience, and a third class from the insensible bias of some *favourite pursuit*.

As to the fourth method in which the inhabitants of the Southern district may have lost their rights of citizenship, a dismemberment by treaty, I have naturally been drawn, under the third head, into a discussion of this, and I trust have shown to the full satisfaction of all candid men, that there is not a shadow of foundation to suppose that such a dismemberment, is in the contemplation of the treaty. A few short remarks shall conclude what I intend to say on this article.

It is a case, without precedent, that a nation in surrendering its acquisitions in war, to the state from which those acquisitions were made, should stipulate for the inhabitants of the country given up as for *its own* subjects. To do it would be both useless and absurd; unless, because the country being surrendered, no reasonable advantage could be derived from retaining the allegiance of its inhabitants; absurd, because the district of territory surrendered being given up as a part of the state, to which the surrender is made, it would be contradictory, by the same act, to acknowledge the right of that state to the *part* given up, and yet to hold up a claim to the allegiance of its inhabitants.

The surrender (for the question does not relate to *original cessions*) carries in itself a decisive implication, that the inhabitants of the country surrendered, are the subjects of the power to which the surrender is made; and the presumption in this case is so strong that nothing but the most positive and unequivocal exceptions in the treaty would be sufficient to defeat it. Laboured constructions to give the treaty that complexion are inadmissable; for if there were room to doubt, the doubt, in just reasoning, should be interpreted against the position, that the inhabitants of the country surrendered were the subjects of the power by which the surrender was made.

The only additional remark I shall make on this head is this: Though we are under great obligations to our ministers for the substance of the treaty, which comprehends all the essential interests of this country; we must acknowledge that the language of it is, in many respects, defective and obscure. The true rule in this case is, not to have recourse to artifical and far-fetched interpretation; but to admit such meanings as the simple and proper import of the words conveys. When therefore it is said in the sixth article, "that there shall be no future prosecutions commenced, nor confiscations made, nor damage done to person, liberty, or property, of any person or persons, on account of the part taken by them in the war," as the natural and obvious scope of the words presents a full amnesty and indemnity for the future; we should not torture our imaginations to pervert them to a different sense.

It has been urged, in support of the doctrines under consideration, that every government has a right to take precautions for its own security, and to prescribe the terms on which its rights shall be enjoyed.

All this is true when understood with proper limitations; but when rightly understood will not be found to justify the conclusions, which have been drawn from the premises.

In the first formation of a government the society may multiply its precautions as much, and annex as many conditions to the enjoyment of its rights, as it shall judge expedient; but when it has once adopted a constitution, that constitution must be the measure of its discretion, in providing for its own safety, and in prescribing the conditions upon which its privileges are to be enjoyed. If the constitution declares that persons possessing certain qualifications shall be entitled to certain rights, while that constitution remains in force, the government which is the mere creature of the constitution, can divest no citizen, who has the requisite qualifications, of his corresponding rights. It may indeed enact laws and annex to the breach of them the penalty of forfeiture; but before that penalty can operate, the existence of the fact, upon which it is to take place, must be ascertained in that mode which the constitution and the fundamental laws have provided. If trial by jury is the mode known and established by that constitution and those laws, the persons who administer the government in deviating from that course will be guilty of usurpation. If the constitution declares that the legislative power of the state shall be vested in one set of men and the judiciary power in another; and those who are appointed to act in a legislative capacity undertake the office of judges, if, instead of confining themselves to passing laws, with proper sanctions to enforce their observance, they go out of their province to decide who are the violators of those laws, they subvert the constitution and erect a tyranny. If the constitution were even silent on particular points those who are intrusted with its power, would be bound in exercising their discretion to consult and pursue its spirit, and to conform to the dictates of reason and equity; if, instead of this, they should undertake to declare whole classes of citizens disfranchised and excluded from the common rights of the

81

society, without hearing, trial, examination or proof; if, instead of waiting to take away the rights of citizenship from individuals, till the state has convicted them of crimes, by which they are to lose them, before the ordinary and regular tribunal, they institute an inquisition into mens consciences, and oblige them to give up their privileges, or undertake to interpret the law at the hazard of perjury; they expose themselves to the imputation of injustice and oppression.

The right of a government to prescribe the conditions on which its privileges shall be enjoyed, is bounded with respect to those who are already included in the compact, by its original conditions; in admitting strangers it may add new ones; but it cannot without a breach of the social compact deprive those, who have been once admitted of their rights, unless for some declared cause of forfeiture authenticated with the solemnities required by the subsisting compact.

The rights too of a republican government are to be modified and regulated by the principles of such a government. These principles dictate, that no man shall lose his rights without a hearing and conviction, before the proper tribunal; that previous to his disfranchisement, he shall have the full benefit of the laws to make his defence; and that his innocence shall be presumed till his guilt has been proved. These with many other maxims, never to be forgotten in any but tyrannical governments, oppose the aims of those who quarrel with the principles of Phocion.

Cases indeed of extreme necessity are exceptions to all general rules; but these only exist, when it is manifest the safety of the community is in imminent danger. Speculations of possible danger never can be justifying causes of departures from principles on which in the ordinary course of things all private security depends—from principles which constitute the essential distinction between free and arbitrary governments.

When the advocates for legislature discriminations are driven from one subterfuge to another, their last resting place is—that this is a new case, the case of a revolution. Your principles are all right say they, in the ordinary course of society, but they do not apply to a situation like ours. This is opening a wilderness, through all the labyrinths of which, it is impossible to pursue them: The answer to this must be, that there are principles eternally true and which apply to all situations; such as those that have been already enumerated—that we are not now in the midst of a revolution but have happily brought it to a successful issue—that we have a constitution formed as a rule of conduct—that the frame of our government is determined and the general principle of it is settled—that we have taken our station among nations have claimed the benefit of the laws which regulate them, and must in our turn be bound by the same laws—that those eternal principles of social justice forbid the inflicting punishment upon citizens, by an abridgement of rights, or in any other manner, without conviction of some specific offence by regular trial and condemnation—that the constitution we have formed makes the trial by jury the only proper mode of ascertaining the delinquences of individuals—that legislative discriminations, to supersede the necessity of inquiry and proof, would be an usurpation on the judiciary powers of the government, and a renunciation of all the maxims of civil liberty—that by the laws of nations and the rules of justice, we are bound to observe the engagements entered into on our behalf, by that power which is invested with the constitutional prerogative of treaty—and that the treaty we have made in its genuine sense, ties up the hands of government from any species of future prosecution or punishment, on account of the part taken by individuals in the war.

Among the extravagancies with which these prolific times abound, we hear it often said that the constitution being the creature of the people, their sense with respect to any measure, if it even stand in opposition to the constitution, will sanctify and make it right.

Happily, for us, in this country, the position is not to be controverted; that the constitution is the creature of the people; but it does not follow that they are not bound by it, while they suffer it to continue in force; nor does it follow, that the legislature, which is, on the other hand, a creature of the constitution, can depart from it, on any presumption of the contrary sense of the people.

The constitution is the compact made between the society at large and each individual. The society therefore, cannot without breach of faith and injustice, refuse to any individual, a single advantage which he derives under that compact, no more than one man can refuse to perform his agreement with another. If the community have good reasons for abrogating the old compact, and establishing a new one, it undoubtedly has a right to do it; but until the compact is dissolved with the same solemnity and certainty with which it was made, the society, as well as individuals, are bound by it.

All the authority of the legislature is delegated to them under the constitution; their rights and powers are there defined; if they exceed them, 'tis a treasonable usurpation upon the power and majesty of the people; and by the same rule that they may take away from a single individual the rights he claims under the constitution, they may erect themselves into perpetual dictators. The sense of the people, if urged in justification of the measure, must be considered as a mere pretext; for that sense cannot appear to them in a form so explicit and authoritative, as the constitution under which they act; and if it could appear with equal authenticity, it could only bind, when it had been preceded by a declared change in the form of government.

The contrary doctrine serves to undermine all those rules, by which individuals can know their duties and their rights, and to convert the government into a government of *will* not of *laws.*

There is only one light on Mentor's plan in which this subject remains to be considered—the danger to the government, from suffering persons to reside among us, who have an aversion to our constitution; either by their becoming auxiliaries to future attempts of the British nation to recover their lost authority; or by their contributing to corrupt the principles and change the form of our government.

My observations on this subject, in my former letter, I believe remain unshaken, by what Mentor has opposed to them. I shall however add a few others.

The restoration of British authority in this country, is too chimerical to be believed even by Mentor himself; though he makes some faint essays to induce the supposition.

Why did Great Britain make peace with America? Because the necessity of her affairs compelled her to it. In what did this necessity consist? In every species of embarrassment and disorder, that a nation could experience. Her public debt had almost arrived at that point, when the expences of a peace establishment were nearly equal to all the revenues they were able to extract from exhausting the sources of taxation. Had they carried on the war, 'till they had exceeded this point, a bankruptcy would have been the inevitable consequence. We perceive, as it is, the great difficulties that are acknowledged by every succession of ministers, in devising means to retrieve the affairs of the nation.

The distractions of the government, arising from those embarrassments, are scarcely paralleled in any period of British history. Almost every sitting of parliament is a signal of a change of ministry. The King at variance with his ministers—the ministers unsupported by parliament—the lords disagreeing with the commons; the nation execrating the King, ministers, lords and commons; all these are symptioms of a vital malady in the present state of the nation.

Externally the scene is not brighter: The affairs of the East India settlements are in the most perplexing confusion, and Ireland seems to be ready to dismember itself from the British empire.

It may be said that these are temporary mischiefs, which may be succeeded by greater tranquility, prosperity and power. The future situation of Great Britain is a problem which the wisest man cannot solve. In all appearance, it will be a considerable time, before she can recover from the pressure of the evils under which she now labours, to be in a condition to form enterprizes against others: When that period may arrive our strength and resources will have greatly increased—the habits of men attached to her will have worn out—and it is visionary to suppose that she will then entertain a disposition to renew her attempts upon a country, increased in strength and resources, exerting its forces under an established constitution, fortified by foreign alliances, which her acknowledged independence will at all times command; when she reflects that that country, in the tumult of a revolution, and in a state of comparative impotence, baffled all her efforts, in the zenith of her power.

To an enlightened mind it will be sufficient to say, upon this subject, that independent of our own means of repelling enterprises against us, Europe has been taught by this revolution to estimate the danger to itself of an union of the two countries, under the same government, in too striking a manner, ever to permit the re-union, or tolerate the attempts of Great Britain towards it.

The danger, from a corruption of the principles of our government, is more plausible, but not more solid. It is an axiom that governments form manners, as well as manners form governments. The body of the people of this state are too firmly attached to the democracy, to permit the principles of a small number to give a different tone to that spirit. The present law of inheritance making an equal division among the children, of the parents property, will soon melt down those great estates, which if they continued, might favour the power of the *few*. The number of the disaffected, who are so, from speculative notions of government, is small: The great majority of those, who took part against us, did it from accident, from the dread of the British power, and from the influence of others to whom they had been accustomed to look up. Most of the men, who had that kind of influence are already gone: The residue and their adherents must be carried along by the torrent; and with very few exception, if the government is mild and just, will soon come to view it with approbation and attachment.

Either the number of mal-contents in the state is small or it is considerable. If small, there can be no room for apprehensions; if great, then opposition to the government is only to be overcome by making it their interest to be its friends, or by extirpating them from the community. A middle line which will betray a spirit of persecution in the government, but will only extend its operation to a small number, will answer no other purpose than to disable a few, and inflame and rivet the prejudices of the rest; by exhibiting the temper of government in a harsh and unconciliating light. We shall then in truth have a considerable faction in the state ready for all innovations.

The impracticability of such a general extirpation suggests the opposite conduct as the only proper one.

There is a bigotry in politics, as well as in religions, equally pernicious in both. The zealots, of either description, are ignorant of the advantage of a spirit of toleration: It was a long time before the kingdoms of Europe were convinced of the folly of persecution, with respect to those, who were schismatics from the established church. The cry was, these men will be equally the disturbers of the hierarchy and of the state. While some kingdoms were impoverishing and depopulating themselves, by their severities to the non-conformists, their wiser neighbours were reaping the fruits of their folly, and augmenting their own numbers, industry and wealth, by receiving with open arms the persecuted fugitives. Time and experience have taught a different lesson; and there is not an enlightened nation, which does not now acknowledge the force of this truth, that whatever speculative notions of religion may be entertained, men will not on that account, be enemies to a government, that affords them protection and security. The same spirit of toleration in politics, and for the same reasons, has made great progress among mankind, of which the history of most modern revolutions is a proof. Unhappily for this state, there are some among us, who possess too much influence, that have motives of personal ambition and interest to shut their minds against the entrance of that moderation, which the real welfare of the community teaches.

Our neighbours seems to be in a disposition to benefit by our mistakes; and the time will not be very remote, if the schemes of some men can prevail, when we shall be ashamed of our own blindness, and heap infamy upon its promoters.

It is remarkable, though not extraordinary, that those characters, throughout the states, who have been principally instrumental in the revolution, are the most opposed to persecuting measures. Were it proper, I might trace the truth of this remark from that character, which has been the first in conspicuousness, through the several gradations of those, with very few exceptions, who either in the civil or military line have borne a distinguished part. On the other hand I might point out men who were reluctantly dragged into taking a part in the revolution; others who were furious zealots in the commencement of the dispute, that were not heard of to any public purpose, during the progress of it, and others who were fluctuating, according to the tide of good or ill-fortune, all of whom now join in the cry with a third class, more imprudent but much more respectable, and endeavour by the loudness of their clamours to atone for their past delinquencies.

As to Mentor's commercial reveries, I shall decline bestowing many remarks upon them, not only because they are not immediately connected with the general subject, but because there is little danger of their making any proselytes; while men are convinced that the prosperity of the national commerce depends as much upon the extent of its capital as that of an individual—that to confine trade to any particular description of men, in exclusion of others who have better means of carrying it on, would be, if practicable, to make the people at large tributary to the avarice of a small number, who were to have the benefit of the monopoly—that in the present situation of things, a very small proportion of those, intended to be benefited, who have the means to avail themselves of the advantage, would reap all its fruits even at the expence and to the prejudice of the greater part of those who were meant to be favoured—that the fewer hands trade is confined to the less will be its activity, and the less the degree of employment afforded to other classes of the community; and, in short, that all monopolies, exclusions and discriminations, in matters of traffick, are pernicious and absurd.

SINCE writing the foregoing, I have learned, that a bill is depending before the House of Assembly, for putting various descriptions of persons out of the protection of government. I have too much respect for the wisdom and virtue of that body to suppose a measure of this nature can obtain the sanction of the majority. What is the plain language of the proposal? There are certain persons, who are obnoxious to public resentment. The treaty forbids us to proceed against them in a legal way. Let us therefore by an unconstitutional exertion of power evade the treaty, however dangerous the precedent to the liberty of the subject, and however derogatory to the honour of the nation. By the treaty we stipulate, that *no person* or *persons* shall *suffer* on account of the part they may have taken in the war, any damage to person, liberty, or property; and yet by taking away the protection of government, which they would enjoy under the subsisting laws, we leave them to *suffer* whatever injury to either, the rashness of individuals who are the *subjects* of the state, may think proper to inflict. What would this be but to imitate the conduct of a certain General, who having promised that he would not spill the blood of some prisoners, who were about to surrender by capitulation, after he had them in his power, had them all strangled to death? Words in every contract are to be construed so as to give them a reasonable effect. When it is stipulated, that a man shall not suffer in person, liberty, or property, it does not merely mean, that the state will not

87

inflict any positive punishment upon him; but also that it will afford him protection and security from injury. The very *letter* as well as the *spirit* of the stipulation imports this. He *shall not suffer* any damage, are the words of the treaty.

The scheme of putting men out of the protection of the law, is calculated to transfer the scepter from the hands of government to those of individuals—it is to arm one part of the community against another; it is to *enact* a civil war. If unhappily for the state, this plan could succeed, no man can foresee the end of it. But the guardians of the rights of the community will certainly, on mature deliberation reject it.

Feeling for the honour of the state, if expulsions must take place, if the constitution and the faith of the United States, must be sacrificed to a supposed political expedience. I had much rather see an open avowal of the principles upon which we acted, than that we should cloth the design with a viel of artifice and disguise, too thin not to be penetrated by the most ordinary eye.

I shall now with a few general reflections conclude.

Those, who are at present entrusted with power, in all these infant republics, hold the most sacred deposit that ever was confided to human hands. 'Tis with governments as with individuals, first impressions and early habits give a lasting bias to the temper and character. Our governments hitherto have no habits. How important to the happiness not of America alone, but of mankind, that they should acquire good ones.

If we set out with justice, moderation, liberality, and a scrupulous regard to the constitution, the government will acquire a spirit and tone, productive of permanent blessings to the community. If on the contrary, the public councils are guided by humour, passion and prejudice; if from resentment to individuals, or a dread of partial inconveniences, the constitution is slighted or explained away, upon every frivolous pretext, the future spirit of government will be feeble, distracted and arbitrary. The rights of the subject will be the sport of every party vicissitude. There will be no settled rule of conduct, but every thing will fluctuate with the alternate prevalency of contending factions.

The world has its eye upon America. The noble struggle we have made in the cause of liberty, has occasioned a kind of revolution in human sentiment. The influence of our example has penetrated the gloomy regions of despotism, and has pointed the way to inquiries, which may shake it to its deepest foundations. Men begin to ask every where, who is this tyrant, that dares to build his greatness on our misery and degradation? What commission has he to sacrifice millions to the wanton appetites of himself and the few minions that surround his throne?

To ripen inquiry into action, it remains for us to justify the revolution by its fruits.

If the consequences prove, that we really have asserted the cause of human happiness, what may not be expected from so illustrious an example? In a greater or less degree, the world will bless and imitate!

But if experience, in this instance, verifies the lesson long taught by the enemies of liberty; that the bulk of mankind are not fit to govern themselves, that they must have a master, and were only made for the rein and the spur: We shall then see the final triumph of despotism over liberty. The advocates of the latter must acknowledge it to be an *ignis fatuus*, and abandon the pursuit. With the greatest advantages for promoting it, that ever a people had, we shall have betrayed the cause of human nature.

Let those in whose hands it is placed, pause for a moment, and contemplate with an eye of reverence, the vast trust committed to them. Let them retire into their own bosoms and examine the motives which there prevail. Let them ask themselves this solemn question— Is the sacrifice of a few mistaken, or criminal individuals, an object worthy of the shifts to which we are reduced to evade the constitution and the national engagements? Then let them review the arguments that have been offered with dispassionate candour; and if they even doubt the propriety of the measures, they may be about to adopt, let them remember, that in a doubtful case, the constitution ought never to be hazarded, without extreme necessity.

PHOCION

SPEECH IN THE NEW YORK ASSEMBLY
JANUARY 19, 1787

Hamilton was a delegate to the New York Assembly in 1787. In the following speech in that assembly, he is reacting to objections voiced against the states granting revenue powers to the Continental Congress. By 1786, twelve states had granted that congress the revenue powers it sought. New York, however, had imposed unacceptable conditions on its approval, and that provided the context of Hamilton's discussion.

. . ., we are told it is dangerous to trust power any where; that *power* is liable to *abuse* with a variety of trite maxims of the same kind. General propositions of this nature are easily framed, the truth of which cannot be denied, but they rarely convey any precise idea. To these we might oppose other propositions equally true and equally indefinite. It might be said that too little power is as dangerous as too much, that it leads to anarchy, and from anarchy to despotism. But the question still recurs, what is this *too much or too little?* where is the measure or standard to ascertain the happy mean?

Powers must be granted, or civil Society cannot exist; the possibility of abuse is no argument against the *thing;* this possibility is incident to every species of power however placed or modified.

SPEECH IN THE CONSTITUTIONAL CONVENTION ON A PLAN OF GOVERNMENT
JUNE 18, 1787

Hamilton, a delegate from New York to the Constitutional Convention in Philadelphia, offered his plan of government to the convention after the Virginia and New Jersey plans had been proposed. The speech outlining his plan (all four versions of which are included below) has a three-fold character: his praise of the English Constitution, though he recognizes that a simple transferral of the principles of that constitution to America would not work; his presentation of his plan of government, which was inserted into his speech; and his indication of the lines which a reform of the Virginia Plan should follow. The section of his speech that recommended an executive for life chosen by electors was actually part of a discussion of the necessity for independent and energetic executive power and must be understood as a corrective to the fundamental weakness of the Virginia Plan, namely, a weak executive chosen by the legislature. Hamilton concludes by saying that he did not mean to offer the plan he had sketched as a proposition to the Convention, but that it was meant only to give a more correct view of his ideas and to suggest the amendments which he should probably propose to the Virginia Plan in the proper stages of its future discussion. Hamilton was critical of the Virginia Plan, but he could remain satisfied with the reform of that plan.

Alexander Hamilton's Notes

Introduction

I   Importance of the occasion

II   Solid *plan* without regard to temporary *opinion*.

III   If an ineffectual plan be again proposed it will beget despair & no government will grow out of consent

IV   There seem to be but three lines of conduct

     I   A league offensive and defensive, treaty of commerce, & apportionment of the public debt.

     II   An amendment of the present confederation by adding such powers as the public mind seems nearest being matured to grant.

     III   The forming a new government to pervade the whole with decisive powers in short with complete sovereignty.

B   Last seems to be the prevailing sentiment—

I Its practicability to be examined—

Immense extent unfavourable to representation—

Vast expence—

double setts of officers—

Difficulty of judging of local circumstances—

☞ Distance has a physical effect upon mens minds—

Difficulty of drawing proper characters from home—

Execution of laws feeble at a distance from government—

particularly in the collection of revenue—

SENTIMENT of Obedience

Opinion

ı Objections to the present confederation

I Entrusts the great interests of the nation to hands incapable of managing them—

All matters in which foreigners are concerned—

The care of the public peace: DEBTS

Power of treaty without power of execution

Common defence without power to raise troops—have a fleet—raise money

Power to contract debts without the power to pay—

These great interests of the state must be well managed or the public prosperity must be the victim—

LEGISLATES upon communities—

Where the legislatures are to act,

they will deliberate—⎰ TO ASK MONEY

No sanction— ⎱ not to collect
& by an unjust
measur⟨e⟩

C   Amendment of CONFEDERATION according to present Ideas
    1—Difficult because not agreed upon any thing
       Ex—IMPOST
          COMMERCE different THEORIES
    To ascertain practicability of this let us examine the principles
of civil obedience—
SUPPORTS OF GOVERNMENT—
I   INTEREST to Support it
II   OPINION of Utility & necessity
III HABITUAL sense of obligation
IV   FORCE
V   INFLUENCE.

I   INTEREST
C   *Particular* & general *interests*
     Esprit de Corps—
     Vox populi *vox Dei*
II   Opinion of Utility & necessity
1—First will decrease with the growth of the *states.*
III *Necessity*
     This does not apply to Fœderal Government—
     This may dissolve & yet the order of the community con-
     tinue—
     Anarchy not a necessary consequence
IV   HABITUAL SENSE of obligation
     This results from administration of private justice—
     DEMAND of service or money odious.
V   FORCE of two kinds.
     COERTION of laws COERTION of arms.
     First does *not exist*—& the last *useless*—
     Attempt to *use it* a war between the states—
     FOREIGN aid—
     DELINQUENCY not confined to one.
VI   INFLUENCE
     1 from municipal Jurisdiction
     2 appointment of Officers
     4 Military Jurisdiction
     5 FISCAL Jurisdiction

D   All these now reside in particular states
Their governments are the chief sources of honor and emolument.

AMBITION   AVARICE

To effect any thing PASSIONS must be turned towa⟨rd⟩ general government?
PRESENT Confederation cannot be amended unless the most important powers be given to Congress constituted as they are—
This would be liable to all objections against any form of general government with the addition of the want of *Checks*—

E   PERPETUAL EFFORT in each member
Influence of Individuals in office employed to excite jealousy & clamour
STATE LEADERS
EXPERIENCE corresponds
Grecian Republics
Demosthenes says
    Athens 73 years
    Lacedaemon 27
    Thebans after battle of Leuctra

PHOCIANS consecrated ground
PHILIP

[F]   GERMANIC *Empire*
charlemagne & his successors
DIET Recesses—
ELECTORS now 7 excluding other

G   SWISS CANTONS
Two diets—
opposite *alliances*
BERNE LUCERNE
To strengthen the Foerderal government powers too great must be given to a single branch!

H   Leag[u]e Offensive & Defensive &c
particular Govs. might exert themselves in &c
But liable to usual VICISSI[tudes]—
        —INTERNAL PEACE affected—
PROXIMITY of situation—natural enemies—
Partial confederacies from unequal extent
Power inspires ambition—

Weakness begets jealousy

———————————————

Western territory

———————————————

Obj: Genius of republics pacific—

———————————————

Answer—Jealousy of commerce as well as jealousy of power
begets war—
Sparta Athens Thebes Rome
Carthage Venice Hanseatic League
ENGLAND as many
Popular as Royal Wars
Lewis the 14th—AUSTRIA BOURBON
William & Anne—

———————————————

Wars depend on triffling circumstances every where—
    Dutchess of Malboroughs Glov[es]

———————————————

FOREIGN CONQUEST
Dismemberment—POLAND—
FOREIGN INFLUENCE—
Distractions set afloat Vicious humours
STANDING armies by dissensions
DOMESTIC FACTIONS—
Montesquieu
Monarchy in Southern States—

———————————————

☞ Foederal Rights *Fisheries*—
Wars destructive

I   Loss of advantages
        —Foreign nations would not respect our rights nor grant us reci-
        procity—
        Would reduce us to a PASSIVE COMMERCE
        Fisheries Navigation of the lakes, of the MISSISSIPPI

———————————————

FLEET
    The general government must, in this case, not only have a
strong soul, but *strong organs* by which that soul is to operate.
    Here I shall give my sentiments of the best form of government—

not as a thing attainable by us, but as a model which we ought to approach as near as possible.

British constitution best form.

Aristotle—Cicero—Montesquieu—Neckar.

Society naturally divides itself into two political divisions—the *few* and the *many*, who have distinct interests.

If government in the hands of the *few*, they will tyrannize over the many.

If (in) the hands of the many, they will tyrannize over the few. It ought to be in the hands of both; and they should be separated.

This separation must be permanent.

Representation alone will not do.

Demagogues will generally prevail.

And if separated, they will need a mutual check.

This check is a monarch.

Each principle ought to exist in full force, or it will not answer its end.

The democracy must be derived immediately from the people.

The aristocracy ought to be entirely separated; their power should be permanent, and they should have the *caritas liberorum.*

They should be so circumstanced that they can have no interest in a change—as to have an effectual weight in the constitution.

Their duration should be the earnest of wisdom and stability.

'Tis essential there should be a permanent will in a community.

Vox populi, vox Dei.

Source of government—the unreasonableness of the people—separate interests—debtors and creditors, &c.

There ought to be a principle in government capable of resisting the popular current.

No periodical duration will come up to this.

This will always imply hopes and fears.

Creature and Creator.

Popular assemblies governed by a few individuals.

These individuals seeing their dissolution approach, will sacrifice.

The principle of representation will influence.

The most popular branch will acquire an influence over the other.

The other may check in ordinary cases, in which there is no strong public passion; but it will not in cases where there is—the cases in which such a principle is most necessary.

☞ Suppose duration seven years, and rotation.

One-seventh will have only one year to serve.

One-seventh————two years.

One-seventh————three years.

One-seventh————four years.

A majority will look to a dissolution in four years by instalments.

The monarch must have proportional strength. He ought to be hereditary, and to have so much power, that it will not be his interest to risk much to acquire more.

The advantage of a monarch is this—he is above corruption—he must always intend, in respect to foreign nations, the true interest and glory of the people.

Republics liable to foreign corruption and intrigue—Holland—Athens.

Effect of the British government.

A vigorous execution of the laws—and a vigorous defence of the people, will result.

Better chance for a good administration.

It is said a republican government does not admit a vigorous execution.

It is therefore bad; for the goodness of a government consists in a vigorous execution.

The principle chiefly intended to be established is this—that there must be a permanent *will*.

Gentlemen say we need to be rescued from the democracy. But what the means proposed?

A democratic assembly is to be checked by a democratic senate, and both these by a democratic chief magistrate.

The end will not be answered—the means will not be equal to the object.

It will, therefore, be feeble and inefficient.

Recapitulation

I. Impossible to secure the union by any modification of fœderal government.

II. League, offensive and defensive, full of certain evils and greater dangers.

III. General government, very difficult, if not impracticable, liable to various objections.

What is to be done?

Answer. Balance inconveniences and dangers, and choose that which seems to have the fewest objections.

Expence admits of this answer. The expense of the state governments will be proportionably diminished.

Interference of officers not so great, because the objects of the general government and the particular ones will not be the same— Finance—Administration of private justice. Energy will not be wanting in essential points, because the administration of private justice will be carried home to men's doors by the particular governments.

And the revenues may be collected from imposts, excises, &c. If necessary to go further, the general government may make use of the particular governments.

The attendance of members near the seat of government may be had in the lower branch.

And the upper branch may be so constructed as to induce the attendance of members from any part.

But this proves that the government must be so constituted as to offer strong motives.

In short, to interest all the *passions* of individuals.

And turn them into that channel.

James Madison's Version

Mr. HAMILTON, had been hitherto silent on the business before the Convention, partly from respect to others whose superior abilities age & experience rendered him unwilling to bring forward ideas dissimilar to theirs, and partly from his delicate situation with respect to his own State, to whose sentiments as expressed by his Colleagues, he could by no means accede. The crisis however which now marked our affairs, was too serious to permit any scruples whatever to prevail over the duty imposed on every man to contribute his efforts for the public safety & happiness. He was obliged therefore to declare himself unfriendly to both plans. He was particularly opposed to that from N. Jersey, being fully convinced, that no amendment of the Confederation, leaving the States in possession of their Sovereignty could possibly answer the purpose. On the other hand he confessed he was much discouraged by the amazing extent of Country in expecting the desired blessings from any general sovereignty that could be substituted. As to the powers of the Convention, he thought the doubts started on that subject had arisen from distinctions & reasonings too subtle. A *federal* Govt. he conceived to mean an association of independent Communities into one. Different Confederacies have different powers, and exercise them in different ways. In some instances the powers are exercised over collective bodies; in others over individuals, as in the German Diet—& among ourselves in cases of piracy. Great latitude therefore must be given to the signification of the term. The plan last proposed departs itself from the *federal* idea, as understood by some, since it is to operate eventually on individuals. He agreed moreover with the Honble gentleman from Va. (Mr. R.) that we owed it to our Country, to do on this emergency whatever we should deem essential to its happiness. The States sent us here to provide for the exigences of the Union. To rely on & propose any plan not adequate to these exigences, merely because it was not clearly within our powers, would be to sacrifice the means to the end. It may be said that the *States* can not *ratify* a plan not within the purview of the article of Confederation providing for alterations & amendments. But may not the States themselves in which no constitutional authority equal to this purpose exists in the Legislatures, have had in view a reference to the people at large. In the Senate of N. York, a proviso was moved, that no act of the Convention should be binding untill it should be referred to the people & ratified; and the motion was lost by a single voice only, the reason assigned agst. it being, that it might possibly be found an inconvenient shackle.

The great question is what provision shall we make for the happiness of our Country? He would first make a comparative examination of the two plans—prove that there were essential defects in both—and point out such changes as might render a *national one,* efficacious. The great & essential principles necessary for the support of Government are i. an active & constant interest in supporting it. This principle does not exist in the States in favor of the federal Govt. They have evidently in a high degree, the esprit de corps. They constantly pursue internal interests adverse to those of the whole. They have their particular debts—their particular plans of finance &c. All these when opposed to, invariably prevail over the requisitions & plans of Congress. 2. The love of power. Men love power. The same remarks are applicable to this principle. The States have constantly shewn a disposition rather to regain the powers delegated by them than to part with more, or to give effect to what they had parted with. The ambition of their demagogues is known to hate the controul of the Genl. Government. It may be remarked too that the Citizens have not that anxiety to prevent a dissolution of the Genl. Govt. as of the particular Govts. A dissolution of the latter would be fatal; of the former would still leave the purposes of Govt. attainable to a considerable degree. Consider what such a State as Virga. will be in a few years, a few compared with the life of nations. How strongly will it feel its importance & self-sufficiency? 3. An habitual attachment of the people. The whole force of this tie is on the side of the State Govt.

Its sovereignty is immediately before the eyes of the people: its protection is immediately enjoyed by them. From its hand distributive justice, and all those acts which familiarize & endear Govt. to a people, are dispensed to them. 4. *Force* by which may be understood a *coertion of laws* or *coertion of arms*. Congs. have not the former except in few cases. In particular States, this coercion is nearly sufficient; tho' he held it in most cases, not entirely so. A certain portion of military force is absolutely necessary in large communities. Masss. is now feeling this necessity & making provision for it. But how can this force be exerted on the States collectively. It is impossible. It amounts to a war between the parties. Foreign powers also will not be idle spectators. They will interpose, the confusion will increase, and a dissolution of the Union will ensue. 5. *influence*. he did not mean corruption, but a dispensation of those regular honors & emoluments, which produce an attachment to the Govt. Almost all the weight of these is on the side of the States; and must continue so as long as the States continue to exist. All the passions then we see, of avarice, ambition, interest, which govern most individuals, and all public bodies, fall into the current of the States, and do not flow in the stream of the Genl. Govt. The former therefore will generally be an overmatch for the Genl. Govt. and render any confederacy, in its very nature precarious. Theory is in this case fully confirmed by experience. The Amphyctionic Council had it would seem ample powers for general purposes. It had in particular the power of fining and using force agst. delinquent members. What was the consequence. Their decrees were mere signals of war. The Phocian war is a striking example of it. Philip at length taking advantage of their disunion, and insinuating himself into their Councils, made himself master of their fortunes. The German Confederacy affords another lesson. The authority of Charlemagne seemed to be as great as could be necessary. The great feudal chiefs however, exercising their local sovereignties, soon felt the spirit & found the means of, encroachments, which reduced the imperial authority to a nominal sovereignty. The Diet has succeeded, which tho' aided by a Prince at its head, of great authority independently of his imperial attributes, is a striking illustration of the weakness of Confederated Governments. Other examples instruct us in the same truth. The Swiss cantons have scarce any Union at all, and have been more than once at war with one another. How then are all these evils to be avoided? only by such a compleat sovereignty in the general Governmt. as will turn all the strong principles & passions above mentioned on its side. Does the scheme of N. Jersey produce this effect? does it afford any substantial remedy whatever? On the contrary it labors under great defects, and the defect of some of its provisions will destroy the efficacy of others. It gives a direct revenue to Congs. but this will not be sufficient. The balance can only be supplied by requisitions: which experience proves can not be relied on. If States are to deliberate on the mode, they will also deliberate on the object of the supplies, and will grant or not grant as they approve or disapprove of it. The delinquency of one will invite and countenance it in others. Quotas too must in the nature of things be so unequal as to produce the same evil. To what standard will you resort? Land is a fallacious one. Compare Holland with Russia: France or Engd. with other countries of Europe. Pena. with N. Carola. will the relative pecuniary abilities in those instances, correspond with the relative value of land. Take numbers of inhabitants for the rule and make like comparison of different countries, and you will find it to be equally unjust. The different degrees of industry and improvement in different Countries render the first object a precarious measure of wealth. Much depends too on *situation.* Cont. N. Jersey & N. Carolina, not being commercial States & contributing to the wealth of the commercial ones, can never bear quotas assessed by the ordinary rules of proportion. They will & must fail in their duty, their example will be followed, and the Union itself be dissolved. Whence then is the national revenue to be drawn? from Commerce? even from exports which notwithstanding the common opinion are fit objects of moderate taxation, from excise, &c &c. These tho' not equal, are less unequal than quotas. Another destructive ingredient in the plan, is that equality of suffrage which is so much desired by the small States. It is not in human nature that Va. & the large States should consent to it, or if they did that they shd. long abide by it. It shocks too much the ideas of Justice, and every human feeling. Bad principles in a Govt. tho slow are sure in their operation, and will gradually destroy it. A doubt has been raised whether Congs. at present have a right to keep Ships or troops in time of peace. He leans to the negative. Mr. Ps. plan provides no remedy. If the powers proposed were adequate, the organization of Congs. is such that they could never be properly & effectually exercised. The members of Congs. being chosen by the States & subject to recall, represent all the local prejudices. Should the powers be found effectual, they will from time to time be heaped on them, till a tyrannic sway shall be established. The general power whatever be its form if it preserves itself, must swallow up the State powers. Otherwise it will be swallowed up by them. It is agst. all the principles of a good Government to vest the requisite powers in such a body as Congs. Two Sovereignties can not co-exist within the same limits. Giving powers to Congs. must eventuate in a bad Govt. or in no Govt. The plan of N. Jersey therefore will not do. What then is to be done? Here he was embarrassed. The extent of the Country to be governed, discouraged him. The expence of a general Govt. was also formidable; unless there were such a diminution of expence on the side of the State Govts. as the case would admit. If they were extinguished, he was persuaded that great œconomy might be obtained by substituting a general Govt. He did not mean however to shock the public opinion by proposing such a measure. On the other hand he saw no *other* necessity for declining it. They are not necessary for any of the great purposes of commerce, revenue, or agriculture. Subordinate authorities he was aware would be necessary. There must be district tribunals: corporations for local purposes. But cui bono, the vast & expensive apparatus now appertaining to the States. The only difficulty of a serious nature which occurred to him, was that of drawing representatives from the extremes to the center of the Community. What inducements can be offered that will suffice? The moderate wages for the 1st. branch would only be a bait to little demagogues. Three dollars or thereabouts he supposed would be the utmost. The Senate he feared from a similar cause, would be filled by certain undertakers who wish for particular offices under the Govt. This view of the subject almost led him to despair that a Republican Govt. could be established over so great an extent. He was sensible at the same time that it would be unwise to propose one of any other form. In his private opinion he had no scruple in declaring, supported as he was by the opinions of so many of the wise & good, that the British Govt. was the best in the world: and that he doubted much whether any thing short of it would do in America. He hoped Gentlemen of different opinions would bear with him in this, and begged them to recollect the change of opinion on this subject which had taken place and was still going on. It was once thought that the power of Congs. was amply sufficient to secure the end of their institution. The error was now seen by every one. The members most tenacious of republicanism, he observed, were as loud as any in declaiming agst. the vices of democracy. This progress of the public mind led him to anticipate the time, when others as well as himself would join in the praise bestowed by Mr. Neckar on the British Constitution, namely, that it is the only Govt. in the world "which unites public strength with individual security." In every community where industry is encouraged, there will be a division of it into the few & the many. Hence separate interests will arise. There will be debtors & creditors &c. Give all power to the many, they will oppress the few. Give all power to the few, they will oppress the many. Both therefore ought to have power, that each may defend itself agst. the other. To the want of this check we owe our paper money, instalment laws &c.

To the proper adjustment of it the British owe the excellence of their Constitution. Their house of Lords is a most noble institution. Having nothing to hope for by a change, and a sufficient interest by means of their property, in being faithful to the national interest, they form a permanent barrier agst. every pernicious innovation, whether attempted on the part of the Crown or of the Commons. No temporary Senate will have the firmness eno' to answer the purpose. The Senate (of Maryland) which seems to be so much appealed to, has not yet been sufficiently tried. Had the people been unanimous & eager, in the late appeal to them on the subject of a paper emission they would have yielded to the torrent. Their acquiescing in such an appeal is a proof of it. Gentlemen differ in their opinions concerning the necessary checks, from the different estimates they form of the human passions. They suppose seven years a sufficient period to give the senate an adequate firmness, from not duly considering the amazing violence & turbulence of the democratic spirit. When a great object of Govt. is pursued, which seizes the popular passions, they spread like wild fire, and become irresistable. He appealed to the gentlemen from the N. England States whether experience had not there verified the remark. As to the Executive, it seemed to be admitted that no good one could be established on Republican principles. Was not this giving up the merits of the question: for can there be a good Govt. without a good Executive. The English model was the only good one on this subject. The Hereditary interest of the King was so interwoven with that of the Nation, and his personal emoluments so great, that he was placed above the danger of being corrupted from abroad—and at the same time was both sufficiently independent and sufficiently controuled, to answer the purpose of the institution at home. one of the weak sides of Republics was their being liable to foreign influence & corruption. Men of little character, acquiring great power become easily the tools of intermedling Neibours. Sweeden was a striking instance. The French & English had each their parties during the late Revolution which was effected by the predominant influence of the former. What is the inference from all these observations? That we ought to go as far in order to attain stability and permanency, as republican principles will admit. Let one branch of the Legislature hold their places for life or at least during good behaviour. Let the Executive also be for life. He appealed to the feelings of the members present whether a term of seven years, would induce the sacrifices of private affairs which an acceptance of public trust would require, so as to ensure the services of the best Citizens. On this plan we should have in the Senate a permanent will, a weighty interest, which would answer essential purposes. But is this a Republican Govt., it will be asked? Yes if all the Magistrates are appointed, and vacancies are filled, by the people, or a process of election originating with the people. He was sensible that an Executive constituted as he proposed would have in fact but little of the power and independence that might be necessary. On the other plan of appointing him for 7 years, he thought the Executive ought to have but little power. He would be ambitious, with the means of making creatures; and as the object of his ambition wd. be to *prolong* his power, it is probable that in case of a war, he would avail himself of the emergence, to evade or refuse a degradation from his place. An Executive for life has not this motive for forgetting his fidelity, and will therefore be a safer depository of power. It will be objected probably, that such an Executive will be an *elective Monarch*, and will give birth to the tumults which characterize that form of Govt. He wd. reply that *Monarch* is an indefinite term. It marks not either the degree or duration of power. If this Executive Magistrate wd. be a monarch for life— the other propd. by the Report from the Comtte of the whole, wd. be a monarch for seven years. The circumstance of being elective was also applicable to both. It had been observed by judicious writers that elective monarchies wd. be the best if they could be guarded agst. the *tumults* excited by the ambition and intrigues of competitors. He was not sure that tumults were an inseparable evil. He rather thought this character of Elective Monarchies had been taken rather from particular cases than from general principles. The election of Roman Emperors was made by the *Army*. In *Poland* the election is made by great rival *princes* with independent power, and ample means, of raising commotions. In the German Empire, the appointment is made by the Electors & Princes, who have equal motives & means, for exciting cabals & parties. Might not such a mode of election be devised among ourselves as will defend the community agst. these effects in any dangerous degree? Having made these observations he would read to the Committee a sketch of a plan which he shd. prefer to either of those under consideration. He was aware that it went beyond the ideas of most members. But will such a plan be adopted out of doors? In return he would ask will the people adopt the other plan? At present they will adopt neither. But he sees the Union dissolving or already dissolved—he sees evils operating in the States which must soon cure the people of their fondness for democracies—he sees that a great progress has been already made & is still going on in the public mind. He thinks therefore that the people will in time be unshackled from their prejudices; and whenever that happens, they will themselves not be satisfied at stopping where the plan of Mr. R. wd. place them, but be ready to go as far at least as he proposes. He did not mean to offer the paper he had sketched as a proposition to the Committee. It was meant only to give a more correct view of his ideas, and to suggest the amendments which he should probably propose to the plan of Mr. R. in the proper stages of its future discussion. He read his sketch in the words following: towit. . . ."

On these several articles he entered into explanatory observations corresponding with the principles of his introductory reasoning.

Robert Yates's Version

Mr. Hamilton. To deliver my sentiments on so important a subject, when the first characters in the union have gone before me, inspires me with the greatest diffidence, especially when my own ideas are so materially dissimilar to the plans now before the committee. My situation is disagreeable, but it would be criminal not to come forward on a question of such magnitude. I have well considered the subject, and am convinced that no amendment of the confederation can answer the purpose of a good government, so long as state sovereignties do, in any shape, exist; and I have great doubts whether a national government on the Virginia plan can be made effectual. What is federal? An association of several independent states into one. How or in what manner this association is formed, is not so clearly distinguishable. We find the diet of Germany has in some instances the power of legislation on individuals. We find the United States of America have it in an extensive degree in the cases of piracies.

Let us now review the powers with which we are invested. We are appointed for the *sole* and *express* purpose of revising the confederation, and to *alter* or *amend* it, so as to render it effectual for the purposes of a good government. Those who suppose it must be federal, lay great stress on the terms *sole* and *express,* as if these words intended a confinement to a federal government; when the manifest import is no more than that the institution of a good government must be the *sole* and *express* object of your deliberations. Nor can we suppose an annihilation of our powers by forming a national government, as many of the states have made in their constitutions no provision for any alteration; and thus much I can say for the state I have the honor to represent, that when our credentials were under consideration in the senate, some members were for inserting a restriction in the powers, to prevent an encroachment on the constitution: it was answered by others, and thereupon the resolve carried on the credentials, that it might abridge some of the constitutional powers of the state, and that possibly in the formation of a new union it would be found necessary. This appears reasonable, and therefore leaves us at liberty to form such a national government as we think best adapted for the good of the whole. I have therefore no difficulty as to the extent of our powers, nor do I feel myself restrained in the exercise of my judgment under them. We can only propose and recommend—the power of ratifying or rejecting is still in the states. But on this great question I am still greatly embarrassed. I have before observed my apprehension of the inefficacy of either plan, and I have great doubts whether a more energetic government can pervade this wide and extensive country. I shall now show, that both plans are materially defective.

1. A good government ought to be constant, and ought to contain an active principle.
2. Utility and necessity.
3. An habitual sense of obligation.
4. Force.
5. Influence.

I hold it, that different societies have all different views and interests to pursue, and always prefer local to general concerns. For example: New-York legislature made an external compliance lately to a requisition of congress; but do they not at the same time counteract their compliance by gratifying the local objects of the state so as to defeat their concession? And this will ever be the case. Men always love power, and states will prefer their particular concerns to the general welfare; and as the states become large and important, will they not be less attentive to the general government? What, in process of time will Virginia be? She contains now half a million inhabitants—in twenty-five years she will double the number. Feeling her own weight and importance, must she not become indifferent to the concerns of the union? And where, in such a situation, will be found national attachment to the general government?

By *force*, I mean the *coercion* of law and the coercion of arms. Will this remark apply to the power intended to be vested in the government to be instituted by theire plan? A delinquent must be compelled to obedience by force of arms. How is this to be done? If you are unsuccessful, a dissolution of your government must be the consequence; and in that case the individual legislatures will reassume their powers; nay, will not the interest of the states be thrown into the state governments?

By *influence*, I mean the regular weight and support it will receive from those who will find it their interest to support a government intended to preserve the peace and happiness of the community of the whole. The state governments, by either plan, will exert the means to counteract it. They have their state judges and militia all

105

combined to support their state interests; and these will be influenced to oppose a national government. Either plan is therefore precarious. The national government cannot long exist when opposed by such a weighty rival. The experience of ancient and modern confederacies evince this point, and throw considerable light on the subject. The amphyctionic council of Greece had a right to require of its members troops, money and the force of the country. Were they obeyed in the exercise of those powers? Could they preserve the peace of the greater states and republics? or where were they obeyed? History shows that their decrees were disregarded, and that the stronger states, regardless of their power, gave law to the lesser.

Let us examine the federal institution of Germany. It was instituted upon the laudable principle of securing the independency of the several states of which it was composed, and to protect them against foreign invasion. Has it answered these good intentions? Do we not see that their councils are weak and distracted, and that it cannot prevent the wars and confusions which the respective electors carry on against each other? The Swiss cantons, or the Helvetic union, are equally inefficient.

Such are the lessons which the experience of others affords us, and from whence results the evident conclusion that all federal governments are weak and distracted. To avoid the evils deducible from these observations, we must establish a general and national government, completely sovereign, and annihilate the state distinctions and state operations; and unless we do this, no good purpose can be answered. What does the Jersey plan propose? It surely has not this for its object. By this we grant the regulation of trade and a more effectual collection of the revenue, and some partial duties. These, at five or ten per cent, would only perhaps amount to a fund to discharge the debt of the corporation.

Let us take a review of the variety of important objects, which must necessarily engage the attention of a national government. You have to protect your rights against Canada on the north, Spain on the south, and your western frontier against the savages. You have to adopt necessary plans for the settlement of your frontiers, and to institute the mode in which settlements and good government are to be made.

How is the expense of supporting and regulating these important matters to be defrayed? By requisition on the states, according to the Jersey plan? Will this do it? We have already found it ineffectual. Let one state prove delinquent, and it will encourage others to follow the example; and thus the whole will fail. And what is the standard to quota among the states their respective proportions? Can lands be the standard? How would that apply between Russia and Holland? Compare Pennsylvania with North-Carolina, or Connecticut with New-York. Does not commerce or industry in the one or other make a great disparity between these different countries, and may not the comparative value of the states from these circumstances, make an unequal disproportion when the data is numbers? I therefore conclude that either system would ultimately destroy the confederation, or any other government which is established on such fallacious principles. Perhaps imposts, taxes on specific articles, would produce a more equal system of drawing a revenue.

Another objection against the Jersey plan is, the unequal representation. Can the great States consent to this? If they did it would eventually work its own destruction. How are forces to be raised by the Jersey plan? By quotas? Will the states comply with the requisition? As much as they will with the taxes.

Examine the present confederation, and it is evident they can raise no troops nor equip vessels before war is actually declared. They cannot therefore take any preparatory measure before an enemy is at your door. How unwise and inadequate their powers! and this must ever be the case when you attempt to define powers. Something will always be wanting. Congress, by being annually elected, and subject to recall, will ever come with the prejudices of their states rather than the good of the union. Add therefore additional powers to a body thus organized, and you establish a *sovereignty* of the worst kind, consisting of a single body. Where are the checks? None. They must either prevail over the state governments, or the prevalence of the state governments must end in their dissolution. This is a conclusive objection to the Jersey plan.

Such are the insuperable objections to both plans: and what is to be done on this occasion? I confess I am at a loss. I foresee the difficulty on a consolidated plan of drawing a representation from so extensive a continent to one place. What can be the inducements for gentlemen to come 600 miles to a national legislature? The expense would at least amount of £100,000. This however can be no conclusive objection if it eventuates in an extinction of state governments. The burthen of the latter would be saved, and the expense then would not be great. State distinctions would be found unnecessary, and yet I confess, to carry government to the extremities, the state governments reduced to corporations, and with very limited powers, might be necessary, and the expense of the national government become less burthensome.

Yet, I confess, I see great difficulty of drawing forth a good representation. What, for example, will be the inducements for gentlemen of fortune and abilities to leave their houses and business to attend annually and long? It cannot be the wages; for these, I presume, must be small. Will not the power, therefore, be thrown into the hands of the demagogue or middling politician, who, for the sake of a small stipend and the hopes of advancement, will offer himself as a candidate, and the real men of weight and influence, by remaining at home, add strength to the state governments? I am at a loss to know what must be done; I despair that a republican form of government can remove the difficulties. Whatever may be my opinion, I would hold it however unwise to change that form of government. I believe the British government forms the best model the world ever produced, and such has been its progress in the minds of the many, that this truth gradually gains ground. This government has for its object *public strength* and *individual security*. It is said with us to be unattainable. If it was once formed it would maintain itself. All communities divide themselves into the few and the many. The first are the rich and well born, the other the mass of the people. The voice of the people has been said to be the voice of God; and however generally this maxim has been quoted and believed, it is not true in fact. The people are turbulent and changing; they seldom judge or determine right. Give therefore to the first class a distinct, permanent share in the government. They will check the unsteadiness of the second, and as they cannot receive any advantage by a change, they therefore will ever maintain good government. Can a democratic assembly, who annually revolve in the mass of the people, be supposed steadily to pursue the public good? Nothing but a permanent body can check the imprudence of democracy. Their turbulent and uncontrouling disposition requires checks. The senate of New-York, although chosen for four years, we have found to be inefficient. Will, on the Virginia plan, a continuance of seven years do it? It is admitted, that you cannot have a good executive upon a democratic plan. See the excellency of the British executive. He is placed above temptation. He can have no distinct interests from the public welfare. Nothing short of such an executive can be efficient. The weak side of a republican government is the danger of foreign influence. This is unavoidable, unless it is so constructed as to bring forward its first characters in its support. I am therefore for a general government, yet would wish to go the full length of republican principles.

Let one body of the legislature be constituted during good behaviour or life.

Let one executive be appointed who dares execute his powers.

It may be asked is this a republican system? It is strictly so, as long as they remain elective.

And let me observe, that an executive is less dangerous to the liberties of the people when in office during life, than for seven years.

It may be said, this constitutes an elective monarchy? Pray, what is a monarchy? May not the governors of the respective states be considered in that light? But by making the executive subject to impeachment, the term monarchy cannot apply. These elective monarchs have produced tumults in Rome, and are equally dangerous to peace in Poland; but this cannot apply to the mode in which I would propose the election. Let electors be appointed in each of the states to elect the executive—*(Here Mr. H produced his plan, a copy whereof is hereunto annexed,)* to consist of two branches—and I would give them the unlimited power of passing *all laws* without exception. The assembly to be elected for three years by the people in districts— the senate to be elected by the electors to be chosen for that purpose by the people, and to remain in office during life. The executive to have the power of negativing all laws—to make war or peace, with the advice of the senate—to make treaties with their advice, but to have the sole direction of all military operations, and to send ambassadors and appoint all military officers, and to pardon all offenders, treason excepted, unless by advice of the senate. On his death or removal, the president of the senate to officiate, with the same powers, until another is elected. Supreme judicial officers to be appointed by the executive and the senate. The legislature to appoint courts in each state, so as to make the state governments unnecessary to it.

All state laws to be absolutely void which contravene the general laws. An officer to be appointed in each state to have a negative on all state laws. All the militia and the appointment of officers to be under the national government.

I confess that this plan and that from Virginia are very remote from the idea of the people. Perhaps the Jersey plan is nearest their expectation. But the people are gradually ripening in their opinions of government—they begin to be tired of an excess of democracy—and what even is the Virginia plan, but *pork still, with a little change of the sauce.*

John Lansing's Version

Hamilton—The Situation of the State he represents and the Diffidence he has of his own Judgment induced him to Silence tho his Ideas are dissimilar from both Plans.

No amendment of Confederation can answer the Exigencies of the States. State Sovereignties ought not to exist. Supposes we have Powers sufficient. Foederal an Association of States differently modified. Diet of Germany has Power to legislate for Individuals. In United States Confederacy legislate for States and in some Instances on Individuals—*Instances Piracies.* The Term *sole* he supposes was to impress an Idea only that we were not to govern ourselves, but to revise Government.

Another Difficulty that the Legislature cannot be supposed to have delegated a Power they did not possess themselves—So far as Respects the State of New York one of the Branches of the Legislature considered it—It was *said they might have Recourse to the People*—this had its Influence and it was carried by one Vote. We ought not to sacrafice the public Good to narrow Scruples. All America, all Europe, the World would condemn us. The only Enquiry ought to be what can we do to save our Country. Five Essentials indispensible in foederal Government.

1. A constant and active Interest.
2. Utility and Necessity.
3. A habitual Sense of Obligation.
4. Force.
5. Influence.

Every Set of men who associate acquire an *Esprit de Corps.* This will apply forcibly to States—they will have distinct Views—their own Obligations thwart general Good.

Do we not find a Jealousy subsisting? In the State of New York we had an Instance. The last Requisition was partially paid—the principal Part of their Funds applied to discharge State Obligations—the Individual States hostile to general Interest.

Virginia will in 25 Years contain a Million of Inhabitants—It may then be disposed to give up an Union only burthensome. The Distribution of Justice presents itself to every Eye—this has a powerful Influence and must particular attach Individuals to the State Governments.

Two modes of Coercion—of Laws—of Military.

Individuals are easily controuled—not so Society—You must carry the Force to Individuals—If only State delinquent it would cause a war—If more they would associate and make a common Cause of it.

We must resort to Influence—Dispensations of Honors and Emoluments of Office necessary—these are all in the Hands of the State Governments. If they exist in State Governments their Influence too great. our Situation is peculiar. *It leaves us Room to dream* as we think proper. Groecian Confederacy lost for Want of adequate Powers—German the same. Swiss Cantons—general Diet has lost its Powers. Cannot combine States but by absorbing the *Ambition and Avarice* of all.

Jersey Propositions—Regulating Trade—Revenue not adequate to meet our Debt—where are we to find it? Requisitions—the several States will deliberate on them. Requisitions founded on Quotas must always fail. There is no general Standard for Wealth in Communities—Pennsylvania and North Carolina—Connecticut and New York compared. New York derives great Wealth from Commerce—Connecticut none. Indirect Taxation must be multiplied.

Equality of Suffrage ruinous to the Union.

Doubts have been entertained whether the United States have a Right to build a Ship or raise a Reg(imen)t in Time of Peace—this Doubt might involve almost our Ruin.

The Organization of Congress exceptionable—They are annually appointed and subject to recal.—They will of Consequence represent the Prejudices of the States not general Interests. No Power will be executed if the States think proper to obstruct it. If general Government preserves itself it must extinguish State Governments.

If Congress remains Legislature the Sovereignty must ultimately vest in them.

The Expence of national Government is a Consideration with him—it will probably amount to £100,000 per ann.—this however surmountable. It will not do to propose formal Extinction of State Governments. It would shock public Opinion too much. Some subordinate Jurisdictions—something like limitted Corporations. If general Government properly modified it may extinguish State Governments gradually. Representation is another difficulty. British Government the best. Dispairs of ever uniting the great Objects of Government which have been so successfully attained by the British, public Strength and individual Safety, in any Republican System. He thinks here it would support itself—the Citizens of America may be distinguished into the wealthy well born and well educated—*and the many*. If Government in the hands of the latter they sacrafice the few—are as often in the wrong as right.

You can only protect the few by giving them exclusive Rights—they have Nothing to hope from Change. Monarchy is essential to them. One Branch of Legislature ought to be independent to check popular Frenzy—or Democracies will prevail. Seven Years is no Check—It is no Object for Men of first Importance. Little Daemagogues will fill Assembly. Undertakers your Senate.

In Republics trifling Characters obtrude—they are easily corrupted—the most Important Individuals ought to [be] drawn forth for Government—this can only be effected by establishing upper House for good Behaviour. Congress are Objects of foreign Corruption.

Executive ought to be during good Behaviour. He will part with his Power with Reluctance. You ought to interest him in the Government.

This may be objected to as establishing an elective Monarchy—but he will be liable to Impeachment for mal-conduct. The Election it supposed would cause Tumults. To avoid this the People in each District should chuse Electors—those should elect a few in that State who should meet with Electors from the other States and elect *the Governor*.

Roman Emperor—elective—by Army.

German Emperor—by great Electors.

Polish King—great Barons who have numerous Dependents.

These were tumultous from their Institutions. We may guard against it.

The principal Citizens of every State are tired of Democracy—he then read his Plan and expatiated on it—See

Rufus King's Version

Federal is an association of distinct Govt: into one—these fed. Govt. in some instances legislate on collective bodies, in others on individuals. The Confederation partakes of both—Piracies are cognizable by the Congress—&c.

Our powers have this object—the Freedom & Happiness of our Country—we must go all lengths to accomplish this Object—if the Legislatures have no powers to ratify because thereby they diminish their own Sovereignty, the people may come in on revolution principles—

We have power,

Upon the plan of the separation & indipendence of the States, you incourage those Habits, and opinions, that Esprit de Corps which is peculiar to the State and to every individual. These habits prefer their own State to those of the Genl. or fed. Govt. This has been the case, State Debts, State Crs. have always stood before the fedl. Debr or Cr.

Man loves power—State magistrates will desire to increase yr. own powers at the Expence of the Genl. or fed. Govt.

One great Objt. of Govt. is personal protection and the security of Property—if you establish a federal Govt. men will not be interested in the protection or preservation of the Genl. Govt. but they will in the existence of the State Govt. if the latter is dissolved and the former remains their persons & fortune will be safe—Besides the large States will be indisposed to remain connected.

Habits of Obedience

Men will see their fortunes secured, their persons protected, offenders punished by State laws and State magistrates—they will love the Govt. that is thus immediate—

Force

The Force of law or the strength of Arms—The former is inefficient unless the people have the habits of Obedience—in this case you must have Arms—if this doctrine is applied to States—the system is utopian—you could not coerce Virginia.—a fedl. Govt. is impracticable—you must call in foreign powers to aid the Genl. Govt. agt. the individual States—this will desolve the Union and destroy your Freedom.

Influence

No govt. will be good without Influence that is unless men of merit or the Pillars of Govt. are rewarded with Offices of Honor & profit—the State Govts. have this influence—the fed. Govt. will be without it—this being true the Genl. Govt. will fail—as long as the States are rivals of the Genl. Govt. so long the Genl. will be subordinate—

How does History illustrate this point

The *amphictions*—had power to levy money men &c on the States—it was peculiarly federal—when a State failed the Amphictions fined—this was the case of the Phocians when Philip interposed—

Germany

their Diets are as weak as the amphictions, although the Emperor is bound to carry their Decrees into Execution—they put an electorate under the Ban, & the Electorate puts the Diet & the Emperor at Defiance—

Switzerland

Their Diet is divided, their union is destroyed—part are in allaince wt. France and the other part wt. the U Netherlands.

The Result is that all the passions of avarice, pride, ambition &c. shd. depend on the Genl. & not the State Govts.—you must make the national Sovereignty transcendent & entire—

The plan of N. Jersey

It proposes Requisitions on the States for such monies as the Impost does not yield—States will not comply—they have not—you have no Standard to Quota

Numbers or Lands will not be a just Standard—an equal

Difficulty arises in the Quotas of men—the States find men only in proportion to their Zeal—this was the Case in the late war—they cannot now obtain an honest adjustment of ye. Expence—for this gave large pecuniary bounties—

The Hic labor the hoc Opus is the Genl. Government

The Extent of Territory, the variety of opinions, & numerous considerations, seem to prevent a General Govt: The expence of the Genl. Govt. is important—not less yn. 100,000 £ any.

How will you induce Genl. to come into the Genl Govt.—what will be ye. inducement: you can give them perhaps 3 Dols. pr. Diem. Men of first consequence will not come forward—it will be managed by undertakers & not by the most able hands. I fear Republicanism ⟨will⟩ not answr. and yet we cannot go beyond it—I think the British Govt. is the only proper one for such an extensive Country—This govt. unites the highest public strength with the most perfect individual security—we are not in a Situation to receive it—perhaps if it was established it wd. maintain itself—I am however sensible that it can't be established by consent, and we ought not to think of other means—We may attempt a general and not a federal Govt: let the senate hold ye. office for life or during good behaviour; so of the Executive—This is republican if the people elect and also fill vacancies.

HAMILTON'S PLAN OF GOVERNMENT
JUNE 18, 1787

Philadelphia, June 18, 1787

I The Supreme Legislative Power of the United States of America to be vested in two distinct bodies of men—the one to be called the *Assembly* the other the *senate;* who together shall form the Legislature of the United States, with power

A to pass all *laws whatsoever*, subject to the *negative* hereafter mentioned.

B II The Assembly to consist of persons elected *by the People* to serve for three years.

III The Senate to consist of persons elected to serve during

114

C   *good behaviour*. Their election to be made by *Electors* chosen for that purpose by the People. In order to this The States to be divided into election districts. On the death removal or resignation of any senator his place to be filled out of the district from which he came.

        IV   The Supreme Executive authority of the United States to

D   be vested in a *governor* to be elected to serve *during good*

E   *behaviour*. His election to be made by *Electors* chosen by *elec-*

F   *tors* chosen by the people in the election districts aforesaid or by electors chosen for that purpose by the respective legislatures—provided that [if] an election be not made within a limit⟨ed⟩ time the President of the Senate shall ⟨−⟩ be the Governor. The Governor to have *a negative* upon all laws about to be passed and to have the execution of all laws passed—to be the Commander in Chief of the land and naval forces and of the Militia of the United States—to have the direction of war, when authorised or began—to have with the *advice* and *approbation* of the Senate the power of making all treaties—to have the

G   appointment of the *heads or chief* officers of the departments of

H   finance war and foreign affairs—to have the *nomination* of all other officers (ambassadors to foreign nations included) subject to the approbation or rejection of the Senate—to have the power

I   of pardoning all offences but *treason,* which he shall not pardon without the approbation of the Senate.

        V   On the death resignation or removal of the Governor his authorities to be exercised by the President of the Senate.

K   VI   The Senate to have the sole power of *declaring war*—the power of advising and approving all treaties—the power of approving or rejecting all appointments of officers except the heads or chiefs of the departments of finance war and foreign affairs.

        VII   The Supreme Judicial authority of the United States to be vested in twelve Judges, to hold their offices during good behaviour with adequate and permanent salaries. This Court to have original jurisdiction in all causes of capture and an appellative jurisdiction (from the Courts of the several states) in all causes in which the revenues of the general government or the citizens of foreign nations are concerned.

L   VIII   The Legislature of the United States to have power to institute Courts in each state for the determination of all causes of capture and of all matters relating to their revenues, or in which the citizens of foreign nations are concerned.

        IX   The Governor Senators and all Officers of the United States

115

to be liable to impeachment for mal and corrupt conduct, and upon conviction to be removed from office and disqualified for holding any place of trust or profit. All impeachments to be tried by a Court to consist of the judges of the Supreme Court chief or Senior Judge of the superior Court of law of each state— provided that such judge hold his place during good behaviour and have a permanent salary.

X   All laws of the particular states contrary to the constitution or laws of the United States to be utterly void. And the better to prevent such laws being passed the Governor or President of each state shall *be appointed by the general government*

M   and shall have a *negative* upon the laws about to be passed in the state of which he is governor or President.

XI   No state to have any forces land or naval—and the *Militia*

N   of all the states to be under the sole and *exclusive direction* of the United States *the officers* of which to be appointed and commissioned by them.

REMARKS IN THE CONSTITUTIONAL CONVENTION ON THE TERM OF OFFICE FOR MEMBERS OF THE SECOND BRANCH OF THE LEGISLATURE
JUNE 26, 1787

The context of Hamilton's remarks is a debate over the term of office to be prescribed for members of the less popular branch of the legislature.

Philadelphia, June 26, 1787

Mr. HAMILTON. He did not mean to enter particularly into the subject. He concurred with Mr. Madison in thinking we were now to decide for ever the fate of Republican Government; and that if we did not give to that form due stability and wisdom, it would be disgraced & lost among ourselves, disgraced & lost to mankind for ever. He acknowledged himself not to think favorably of Republican Government; but addressed his remarks to those who did think favorably of it, in order to prevail on them to tone their Government as high as possible. He professed himself to be as zealous an advocate for liberty as any man whatever, and trusted he should be as willing a martyr to it though he differed as to the form in which it was most eligible. He concurred also in the general observations of (Mr. Madison) on the subject, which might be supported by others if it were necessary. It was certainly true: that nothing like an equality of property existed: that an inequality would exist as long as liberty existed, and that it would unavoidably result from that very liberty itself. This inequality of property constituted the great & fundamental distinction in Society. When the Tribunitial power had levelled the boundary between the *patricians* & *plebians*, what followed? The distinction between rich & poor was substituted. He meant not however to enlarge on the subject. He rose principally to remark that (Mr. Sherman) seemed not to recollect that one branch of the proposed Govt. was so formed, as to render it particularly the guardians of the poorer orders of Citizens; nor to have adverted to the true causes of the stability which had been exemplified in Cont. Under the British system as well as the federal, many of the great powers appertaining to Govt. particularly all those relating to foreign Nations were not in the hands of the Govt. there. Their internal affairs also were extremely simple, owing to sundry causes many of which were peculiar to that Country. Of late the Governt. had entirely given way to the people, and had in fact suspended many of its ordinary functions in order to prevent those turbulent scenes which had appeared elsewhere. He asks Mr. S. whether the State at this time, dare impose & collect a tax on ye. people? To these causes & not to the frequency of elections, the effect, as far as it existed ought to be chiefly ascribed.

REMARKS IN THE CONSTITUTIONAL CONVENTION ON THE EQUALITY OF REPRESENTATION IN THE CONGRESS

JUNE 29, 1787

The Virginia Plan proposed that representation in both houses of the Congress be in proportion to population. Hamilton addresses that issue in the following speech. The versions by James Madison and by Robert Yates and notes by John Lansing are included.

Philadelphia, June 29, 1787

Mr. HAMILTON observed that individuals forming political Societies modify their rights differently, with regard to suffrage. Examples of it are found in all the States. In all of them some individuals are deprived of the right altogether, not having the requisite qualifications of property. In some of the States the right of suffrage is allowed in some cases and refused in others. To vote for a member in one branch, a certain quantum of property, to vote for a member in another branch of the Legislature, a higher quantum of property is required. In like manner States may modify their right of suffrage differently, the larger exercising a larger, the smaller a smaller share of it. But as States are a collection of individual men which ought we to respect most, the rights of the people composing them, or of the artificial beings resulting from the composition. Nothing could be more preposterous or absurd than to sacrifice the former to the latter. It has been sd. that if the smaller States renounce their *equality*, they renounce at the same time their *liberty*. The truth is it is a contest for power, not for liberty. Will the men composing the small States be less free than those composing the larger. The State of Delaware having 40,000 souls will *lose power*, if she has ¹⁄₁₀th only of the votes allowed to Pa. having 400,000: but will the people of Del: *be less free*, if each citizen has an equal vote with each citizen of Pa. He admitted that common residence within the same State would produce a certain degree of attachment; and that this principle might have a certain influence in public affairs. He thought however that this might by some precautions be in a great measure excluded: and that no material inconvenience could result from it, as there could not be any ground for combination among the States whose influence was most dreaded. The only considerable distinction of interests, lay between the carrying & non-carrying States, which divide instead of uniting the largest States. No considerable inconvenience had been found from the division of the State of N. York into different districts of different sizes.

Some of the consequences of a dissolution of the Union, and the establishment of partial confederacies, had been pointed out. He would add another of a most serious nature. Alliances will immediately be formed with different rival & hostile nations of Europes, who will foment disturbances among ourselves, and make us parties to all their own quarrels. Foreign Nations having American dominions are & must be jealous of us. Their representatives betray the utmost anxiety for our fate, & for the result of this meeting, which must have an essential influence on it. It had been said that respectability in the eyes of foreign Nations was not the object at which we aimed; that the proper object of republican Government was domestic tranquility & happiness. This was an ideal distinction. No Governmt. could give us tranquility & happiness at home, which did not possess sufficient stability and strength to make us respectable abroad. This was the critical moment for forming such a Government. We should run every risk in trusting to future amendments. As yet we retain the habits of union. We are weak & sensible of our weakness. Henceforward the motives will become feebler, and the difficulties greater. It is a miracle that we were now here exercising our tranquil & free deliberations on the subject. It would be madness to trust to future miracles. A thousand causes must obstruct a reproduction of them.

Remarks Attributed to Hamilton by Robert Yates

"The course of my experience in human affairs might perhaps restrain me from saying much on this subject. I shall, however, give birth to some of the observations I have made during the course of this debate. The gentleman from Maryland [Luther Martin] has been at great pains to establish positions which are not denied. Many of them, as drawn from the best writers on government, are become almost self-evident principles. But I doubt the propriety of his application of those principles in the present discussion. He deduces from them the necessity that states entering into a confederacy must retain the equality of votes—this position cannot be correct—Facts plainly contradict it. The parliament of Great Britain asserted a supremacy over the whole empire, and the celebrated Judge Blackstone labors for the legality of it, although many parts were not represented. This parliamentary power we opposed as contrary to our colonial rights. With that exception, throughout that whole empire, it is submitted to. May not the smaller and greater states so modify their respective rights as to establish the general interest of the whole, without adhering to the right of equality? Strict representation is not observed in any of the state governments. The senate of New-York are chosen by persons of certain qualifications, to the exclusion of others. The question, after all is, is it our interest in modifying this general government to sacrifice individual rights to the preservation of the rights of an *artificial* being, called states? There can be no truer principle than this—that every individual of the community at large has an equal right to the protection of government. If therefore three states contain a majority of the inhabitants of America, ought they to be governed by a minority? Would the inhabitants of the great states ever submit

119

to this? If the smaller states maintain this principle, through a love of power, will not the larger, from the same motives, be equally tenacious to preserve their power? They are to surrender their rights—for what? for the preservation of an artificial being. We propose a free government—Can it be so if partial distinctions are maintained? I agree with the gentleman from Delaware [George Read], that if the state governments are to act in the general government, it affords the strongest reason for exclusion. In the state of New-York, five counties form a majority of representatives, and yet the government is in no danger, because the laws have a general operation. The small states exaggerate their danger, and on this ground contend for an undue proportion of power. But their danger is increased, if the larger states will not submit to it. Where will they form new alliances for their support? Will they do this with foreign powers? Foreigners are jealous of our encreasing greatness, and would rejoice in our distractions. Those who have had opportunities of conversing with foreigners respecting sovereigns in Europe, have discovered in them an anxiety for the preservation of our democratic governments, probably for no other reason, but to keep us weak. Unless your government is respectable, foreigners will invade your rights; and to maintain tranquillity, it must be respectable—even to observe neutrality, you must have a strong government. I confess our present situation is critical. We have just finished a war which has established our independency, and loaded us with a heavy debt. We have still every motive to unite for our common defence. Our people are disposed to have a good government, but this disposition may not always prevail. It is difficult to amend confederations—it has been attempted in vain, and it is perhaps a miracle that we are now met. We must therefore improve the opportunity, and render the present system as perfect as possible. Their good sense, and above all, the necessity of their affairs, will induce the people to adopt it."

Record of John Lansing, Jr., of Hamilton's Remarks

"Hamilton—In the Course of his Experience he has found it difficult to convince Persons who have been in certain Habits of thinking. Some desultory Remarks may not be improper. We can modify Representation as we think proper.

"The Question simply is, what is general Interest. Larger States may submit to an Inequality of Representation to their Prejudice for a short Time—but it cannot be durable. This is a Contest for Power— the People of all States have an Inequality of Representation.

"So long as State Governments prevail State Influence will be perpetuated.

"There may be a Distinction of Interests but it arises merely from the carrying and noncarrying States.

"Those Persons who have had frequent Opportunities of conversing with the Representatives of European Sovereignties know they are very anxious to perpetuate our Democracies. This is easily accounted for—Our weakness will make us more manageable. Unless your Government is respectable abroad your Tranquility cannot be preserved.

"This is a critical Moment of American Liberty—We are still too weak to exist without Union. It is a Miracle that we have met—they seldom occur.

"We must devise a System on the Spot—It ought to be strong and nervous, *hoping* that the good Sense and principally *the Necessity of our Affairs* will reconcile the People to it."

LETTER TO GEORGE WASHINGTON
JULY 3, 1787

Hamilton left the Constitutional Convention on June 30 to take care of some pressing legal business and did not return until August 6. The following letter to Washington was written during this period.

New York, July 3, 1787

Dr. Sir.

In my passage through the Jerseys and since my arrival here I have taken particular pains to discover the public sentiment and I am more and more convinced that this is the critical opportunity for establishing the prosperity of this country on a solid foundation. I have conversed with men of information not only of this City but from different parts of the state; and they agree that there has been an astonishing revolution for the better in the minds of the people. The prevailing apprehension among thinking men is that the Convention, from a fear of shocking the popular opinion, will not go far enough.

121

They seem to be convinced that a strong well mounted government will better suit the popular palate than one of a different complexion. Men in office are indeed taking all possible pains to give an unfavourable impression of the Convention; but the current seems to be running strongly the other way.

A plain but sensible man, in a conversation I had with him yesterday, expressed himself nearly in this manner. The people begin to be convinced that their "excellent form of government" as they have been used to call it, will not answer their purpose, and that they must substitute something not very remote from that which they have lately quitted.

These appearances though they will not warrant a conclusion that the people are yet ripe for such a plan as I advocate, yet serve to prove that there is no reason to despair of their adopting one equally energetic, if the Convention should think proper to propose it. They serve to prove that we ought not to allow too much weight to objections drawn from the supposed repugnancy of the people to an efficient constitution. I confess I am more and more inclined to believe that former habits of thinking are regaining their influence with more rapidity than is generally imagined.

Not having compared ideas with you, Sir, I cannot judge how far our sentiments agree; but as I persuade myself the genuineness of my representations will receive credit with you, my anxiety for the event of the deliberations of the Convention induces me to have this communication of what appears to be the tendency of the public mind. I own to you Sir that I am seriously and deeply distressed at the aspect of the Councils which prevailed when I left Philadelphia. I fear that we shall let slip the golden opportunity of rescuing the American empire from disunion anarchy and misery. No motley or feeble measure can answer the end or will finally receive the public support. Decision is true wisdom and will be not less reputable to the Convention than salutary to the community.

I shall of necessity remain here ten or twelve days; if I have reason to believe that my attendance at Philadelphia will not be mere waste of time, I shall after that period rejoin the Convention.

I remain with sincere esteem Dr Sir   Yr. Obed serv. A Hamilton

REMARKS IN THE CONSTITUTIONAL CONVENTION ON THE ELECTION OF THE PRESIDENT

SEPTEMBER 6, 1787

The seventh resolution of the Virginia Plan provided for a national executive to be chosen by the national legislature for an unspecified number of years. In the report of the Committee on Detail appointed to prepare a constitution, referred to by Hamilton as the "printed Report" of August 6, 1787, the president was to be elected by ballot by a national legislature and to hold office for seven years without reeligibility. Hamilton surely saw very clearly what the proposal for legislative selection with ineligibility for reelection would do. He wanted to avoid an undue dependence of the president on Congress resulting from legislative selection. Hamilton therefore supported what he calls the "new modification," that is, the proposal for the electoral college of the Committee of Eleven on September 4, 1787, which placed no limits on the president's eligibility for reelection.

Philadelphia, September 6, 1787

Mr. HAMILTON said that he had been restrained from entering into the discussions by his dislike of the Scheme of Govt. in General; but as he meant to support the plan to be recommended, as better than nothing, he wished in this place to offer a few remarks. He liked the new modification, on the whole, better than that in the printed Report. In this the President was a Monster elected for seven years, and ineligible afterwards; having great powers, in appointments to office, & continually tempted by this constitutional disqualification to abuse them in order to subvert the Government. Although he should be made re-eligible, still if appointed by the Legislature, he would be tempted to make use of corrupt influence to be continued in office. It seemed peculiarly desireable therefore that some other mode of election should be devised. Considering the different views of different States, & the different districts Northern Middle & Southern, he concurred with those who thought that the votes would not be concentered, and that the appointment would consequently in the present mode devolve on the Senate. The nomination to offices will give great weight to the President. Here then is a mutual connection & influence, that will perpetuate the President, and aggrandize both him

& the Senate. What is to be the remedy? He saw none better than to let the highest number of ballots, whether a majority or not, appoint the President. What was the objection to this? Merely that too small a number might appoint. But as the plan stands, the Senate may take the candidate having the smallest number of votes, and make him President.

REMARKS IN THE CONSTITUTIONAL CONVENTION ON THE SIGNING OF THE CONSTITUTION
SEPTEMBER 17, 1787

Hamilton was the only member of the New York delegation who signed the proposed Constitution because the other two delegates, John Lansing and Robert Yates, had left the convention. Although Hamilton had no power to sign for New York (the other two delegates being absent), he signed as an individual.

Philadelphia, September 17, 1787

Mr. HAMILTON expressed his anxiety that every member should sign. A few characters of consequence, by opposing or even refusing to sign the Constitution, might do infinite mischief by kindling the latent sparks which lurk under an enthusiasm in favor of the Convention which may soon subside. No man's ideas were more remote from the plan than his were known to be; but is it possible to deliberate between anarchy and Convulsion on one side, and the chance of good to be expected from the plan on the other.

CONJECTURES ABOUT THE NEW CONSTITUTION
SEPTEMBER 17–30, 1787

The following assessment of the Constitution's possibilities was written by Hamilton either at the time of or shortly after its signing, and before the publication of the first Federalist essay. It reveals a hesitancy about

124

the new Constitution that is not surprising, given his statement at the signing that no man's ideas were more remote from the plan than his own. He was the author of neither the Virginia Plan nor the Connecticut Compromise. On the other hand, his speech of June 18 on the plan of government, though critical of the Virginia Plan, could be understood as an effort to secure a strengthened Virginia Plan, and later in the convention he took a position on presidential selection and tenure, an issue that worked out to his liking.

September 17–30, 1787

The new constitution has in favour of its success these circumstances—a very great weight of influence of the persons who framed it, particularly in the universal popularity of General Washington—the good will of the commercial interest throughout the states which will give all its efforts to the establishment of a government capable of regulating protecting and extending the commerce of the Union—the good will of most men of property in the several states who wish a government of the union able to protect them against domestic violence and the depredations which the democratic spirit is apt to make on property; and who are besides anxious for the respectability of the nation—the hopes of the Creditors of the United States that a general government possessing the means of doing it will pay the debt of the Union—a strong belief in the people at large of the insufficiency of the present confederation to preserve the existence of the Union and of the necessity of the union to their safety and prosperity; of course a strong desire of a change and a predisposition to receive well the propositions of the Convention.

Against its success is to be put the dissent of two or three important men in the Convention; who will think their characters pleged to defeat the plan—the influence of many *inconsiderable* men in possession of considerable offices under the state governments who will fear a diminution of their consequence, power and emolument by the establishment of the general government and who can hope for nothing there—the influence of some *considerable* men in office possessed of talents and popularity who partly from the same motives and partly from a desire of *playing a part* in a convulsion for their own aggrandisement will oppose the quiet adoption of the new government—(some considerable men out of office, from motives of ⟨am⟩bition may be disposed to act the same part)—add ⟨to⟩ these causes the disinclination of the people to taxes, and of course to a strong government—the opposition of all men much in debt who will not wish to see a government established one object of which is to restrain the means of cheating Creditors—the democratical jealousy of the people which may be alarmed at the appearance of institutions that may seem calculated to place the power of the community in few hands and to raise a few individuals to stations of great preeminence—and the influence of some foreign powers who from different motives will not wish to see an energetic government established throughout the states.

In this view of the subject it is difficult to form any judgment whether the plan will be adopted or rejected. It must be essentially [a] matter of conjecture. The present appearances and all other circumstances considered the probability seems to be on the side of its adoption.

But the causes operating against its adoption are powerful and there will be nothing astonishing in the Contrary.

If it do not finally obtain, it is probable the discussion of the question will beget such struggles animosities and heats in the community that this circumstance conspiring with the *real necessity* of an essential change in our present situation will produce civil war. Should this happen, whatever parties prevail it is probable governments very different from the present in their principles will be established. A dismemberment of the Union and monarchies in different portions of it may be expected. It may however happen that no civil war will take place; but several republican confederacies be established between different combinations of the particular states.

A reunion with Great Britain, from universal disgust at a state of commotion, is not impossible, though not much to be feared. The most plausible shape of such a business would be the establishment of a son of the present monarch in the supreme government of this country with a family compact.

If the government be adopted, it is probable general Washington will be the President of the United States. This will insure a wise choice of men to administer the government and a good administration. A good administration will conciliate the confidence and affection of the people and perhaps enable the government to acquire more consistency than the proposed constitution seems to promise for so great a Country. It may then triumph altogether over the state governments and reduce them to an intire subordination, dividing the larger states into smaller districts. The *organs* of the general government may also acquire additional strength.

If this should not be the case, in the course of a few years, it is probable that the contests about the boundaries of power between the particular governments and the general government and the *momentum* of the larger states in such contests will produce a dissolution of the Union. This after all seems to be the most likely result.

But it is almost arrogance in so complicated a subject, depending so intirely on the incalculable fluctuations of the human passions, to attempt even a conjecture about the event.

It will be Eight or Nine months before any certain judgment can be formed respecting the adoption of the Plan.

THE FEDERALIST PAPERS, AN INTRODUCTION

Hamilton was not a political thinker comparable to Locke or Montesquieu, but he wrote with James Madison the most powerfully reasoned defense of the institution of free government in the modern world, a defense that was the culmination of reasoned reflection about the state of the American polity under the Articles of Confederation. The Federalist Papers were originally written as a series of essays appearing in the newspapers of New York between October 27, 1787, and April 4, 1788, for the purpose of influencing that state's ratification of the proposed Constitution. Shortly after their newspaper appearance, the essays were published as a book and circulated to the leading supporters of the proposed Constitution in other states. Although the authorship of the essays was essentially a collaborative effort, the project was conceived by Hamilton, and he is the author of the largest number of essays, some of which are included in this volume. It would not be misleading to say that The Federalist Papers represent a kind of first appearance of political philosophy on the American scene.

THE FEDERALIST NO. 1
OCTOBER 27, 1787

The opening paragraph of the first essay poses the important question whether societies of men are capable of establishing good government from reflection and choice. Then follows the suggestion that the American experiment, if it succeeds, would have a far-reaching effect on political practice, for it would set the tone for a new mode of political life throughout the world, presumably republican political life. Although there is no mention of republicanism in the opening paragraph but only

127

of good government, it soon becomes clear that the subject under consideration is the proposed republican Constitution. But while America is in a position to show mankind that good government can be established by reflection and choice, that will ultimately depend on the success of the experiment, not to mention its acceptance or ratification. The problem at hand is the acceptance of the proposed Constitution, for the founding of a regime surely touches on the deepest interests and passions of the parties concerned, and the way in which the regime is founded is bound to favor certain interests to the detriment of others. The first essay concentrates mainly on the motives of those interested parties opposed to the proposed Constitution with a view to disestablishing their credibility in the eyes of those who have not yet made up their minds. The essay ends up, however, with the suggestion that it would be wise to forget about motives and simply concentrate on an examination of the proposed Constitution's merits, for a discussion of motives could be counterproductive. Accordingly, a general plan for the entire series of essays is outlined in order to facilitate such an examination.

New York, October 27, 1787

To the People of the State of New-York.

AFTER an unequivocal experience of the inefficacy of the subsisting Fœderal Government, you are called upon to deliberate on a new Constitution for the United States of America. The subject speaks its own importance; comprehending in its consequences, nothing less than the existence of the UNION, the safety and welfare of the parts of which it is composed, the fate of an empire, in many respects, the most interesting in the world. It has been frequently remarked, that it seems to have been reserved to the people of this country, by their conduct and example, to decide the important question, whether societies of men are really capable or not, of establishing good government from ref[l]ection and choice, or whether they are forever destined to depend, for their political constitutions, on accident and force. If there be any truth in the remark, the crisis, at which we are arrived, may with propriety be regarded as the æra in which that decision is to be made; and a wrong election of the part we shall act, may, in this view, deserve to be considered as the general misfortune of mankind.

This idea will add the inducements of philanthropy to those of patriotism to heighten the sollicitude, which all considerate and good men must feel for the event. Happy will it be if our choice should be directed by a judicous estimate of our true interests, unperplexed and unbiassed by considerations not connected with the public good. But this is a thing more ardently to be wished, than seriously to be expected. The plan offered to our deliberations, affects too many particular interests, innovates upon too many local institutions, not to involve in its discussion a variety of objects foreign to its merits, and of views, passions and prejudices little favourable to the discovery of truth.

Among the most formidable of the obstacles which the new Constitution will have to encounter, may readily be distinguished the obvious interest of a certain class of men in every State to resist all changes which may hazard a diminution of the power, emolument and consequence of the offices they hold under the State-establishments—and the perverted ambition of another class of men, who will either hope to aggrandise themselves by the confusions of their country, or will flatter themselves with fairer prospects of elevation from the subdivision of the empire into several partial confederacies, than from its union under one government.

It is not, however, my design to dwell upon observations of this nature. I am well aware that it would be disingenuous to resolve indiscriminately the opposition of any set of men (merely because their situations might subject them to suspicion) into interested or ambitious views: Candour will oblige us to admit, that even such men may be actuated by upright intentions; and it cannot be doubted, that much of the opposition which has made its appearance, or may hereafter make its appearance, will spring from sources, blameless at least, if not respectable, the honest errors of minds led astray by preconceived jealousies and fears. So numerous indeed and so powerful are the causes, which serve to give a false bias to the judgment, that we upon many occasions, see wise and good men on the wrong as well as on the right side of questions, of the first magnitude to society. This circumstance, if duly attended to, would furnish a lesson of moderation of those, who are ever so much persuaded of their being in the right, in any controversy. And a further reason for caution, in this respect, might be drawn from the reflection, that we are not always sure, that those who advocate the truth are influenced by purer principles than their antagonists. Ambition, avarice, personal animosity, party opposition, and many other motives, not more laudable than these, are apt to operate as well upon those who support as upon those who oppose the right side of a question. Were there not even these inducements to moderation, nothing could be more ill-judged than that intolerant spirit, which has, at all times, characterised political parties. For, in politics as in religion, it is equally absurd to aim at making proselytes by fire and sword. Heresies in either can rarely be cured by persecution.

And yet however just these sentiments will be allowed to be, we

129

have already sufficient indications, that it will happen in this as in all former cases of great national discussion. A torrent of angry and malignant passions will be let loose. To judge from the conduct of the opposite parties, we shall be led to conclude, that they will mutually hope to evince the justness of their opinions, and to increase the number of their converts by the loudness of their declamations, and by the bitterness of their invectives. An enlightened zeal for the energy and efficiency of government will be stigmatised, as the offspring of a temper fond of despotic power and hostile to the principles of liberty. An overscrupulous jealousy of danger to the rights of the people, which is more commonly the fault of the head than of the heart, will be represented as mere pretence and artifice; the bait for popularity at the expence of public good. It will be forgotten, on the one hand, that jealousy is the usual concomitant of violent love, and that the noble enthusiasm of liberty is too apt to be infected with a spirit of narrow and illiberal distrust. On the other hand, it will be equally forgotten, that the vigour of government is essential to the security of liberty; that, in the contemplation of a sound and well informed judgment, their interest can never be separated; and that a dangerous ambition more often lurks behind the specious mask of zeal for the rights of the people, than under the forbidding appearance of zeal for the firmness and efficiency of government. History will teach us, that the former has been found a much more certain road to the introduction of despotism, than the latter, and that of those men who have overturned the liberties of republics the greatest number have begun their career, by paying an obsequious court to the people, commencing Demagogues and ending Tyrants.

In the course of the preceeding observations I have had an eye, my Fellow Citizens, to putting you upon your guard against all attempts, from whatever quarter, to influence your decision in a matter of the utmost moment to your welfare by any impressions other than those which may result from the evidence of truth. You will, no doubt, at the same time, have collected from the general scope of them that they proceed from a source not unfriendly to the new Constitution. Yes, my Countrymen, I own to you, that, after having given it an attentive consideration, I am clearly of opinion, it is your interest to adopt it. I am convinced, that this is the safest course for your liberty, your dignity, and your happiness. I effect not reserves, which I do not feel. I will not amuse you with an appearance of deliberation, when I have decided. I frankly acknowledge to you my convictions, and I will freely lay before you the reasons on which they are founded. The consciousness of good intentions disdains ambiguity. I shall not however multiply professions on this head. My motives must remain in the depository of my own breast: My arguments will be open to all, and may be judged of by all. They shall at least be offered in a spirit, which will not disgrace the cause of truth.

I propose in a series of papers to discuss the following interesting particulars—*The utility of the UNION to your political prosperity—The insufficiency of the present Confederation to preserve that Union—The necessity of a government at least equally energetic with the one proposed to the attainment of this object—The conformity of the proposed constitution to the true principles of republican government—Its analogy to your own state constitution*—and lastly, *The additional security, which its adoption will afford to the preservation of that species of government, to liberty and to property.*

In the progress of this discussion I shall endeavour to give a satisfactory answer to all the objections which shall have made their appearance that may seem to have any claim to your attention.

It may perhaps be thought superfluous to offer arguments to prove the utility of the UNION, a point, no doubt, deeply engraved on the hearts of the great body of the people in every state, and one, which it may be imagined has no adversaries. But the fact is, that we already hear it whispered in the private circles of those who oppose the new constitution, that the Thirteen States are of too great extent for any general system, and that we must of necessity resort to separate confederacies of distinct portions of the whole.* This doctrine will, in all probability, be gradually propagated, till it has votaries enough to countenance an open avowal of it. For nothing can be more evident, to those who are able to take an enlarged view of the subject than the alternative of an adoption of the new Constitution, or a dismemberment of the Union. It will therefore be of use to begin by examining the advantages of that Union, the certain evils and the probable dangers, to which every State will be exposed from its dissolution. This shall accordingly constitute the subject of my next address.

PUBLIUS.

The same idea, tracing the arguments to their consequences, is held out in several of the late publications against the New Constitution.

THE FEDERALIST NO. 9
NOVEMBER 21, 1787

It is possible to say that the rejection of classical politics culminates in the American Constitution, for that constitution, which provides the structure for modern democratic government, is surely the achievement of "the new science of politics." This new science was called into being to counteract the worst tendencies of ancient republicanism. As Hamilton states in the first part of Federalist 9, the various principles of the new science of politics are means "by which the excellencies of republican government may be retained and its imperfections lessened or avoided." In other words, the thrust of the new science of politics was to reconcile efficient government with republican principles and hence transform republicanism into a viable regime.

New York, November 21, 1787

To the People of the State of New-York.

A Firm Union will be of the utmost moment to the peace and liberty of the States as a barrier against domestic faction and insurrection. It is impossible to read the history of the petty Republics of Greece and Italy, without feeling sensations of horror and disgust at the distractions with which they were continually agitated, and at the rapid succession of revolutions, by which they were kept in a state of perpetual vibration, between the extremes of tyranny and anarchy. If they exhibit occasional calms, these only serve as short-lived contrasts to the furious storms that are to succeed. If now and then intervals of felicity open themselves to view, we behold them with a mixture of regret arising from the reflection that the pleasing scenes before us are soon to be overwhelmed by the tempestuous waves of sedition and party-rage. If momentary rays of glory break forth from the gloom, while they dazzle us with a transient and fleeting brilliancy, they at the same time admonish us to lament that the vices of government should pervert the direction and tarnish the lustre of those bright talents and exalted indowments, for which the favoured soils, that produced them, have been so justly celebrated.

From the disorders that disfigure the annals of those republics, the advocates of despotism have drawn arguments, not only against the forms of republican government, but against the very principles of civil liberty. They have decried all free government, as inconsistent with the order of society, and have indulged themselves in malicious exultation over its friends and partizans. Happily for mankind, stupendous fabrics reared on the basis of liberty, which have flourished for ages, have in a few glorious instances refuted their gloomy sophisms. And, I trust, America will be the broad and solid foundation of other edifices not less magnificent, which will be equally permanent monuments of their errors.

But it is not to be denied that the portraits, they have sketched of republican government, were too just copies of the originals from which they were taken. If it had been found impracticable, to have devised models of a more perfect structure, the enlightened friends to liberty would have been obliged to abandon the cause of that species of government as indefensible. The science of politics, however, like most other sciences has received great improvement. The efficacy of various principles is now well understood, which were either not known at all, or imperfectly known to the ancients. The regular distribution of power into distinct departments—the introduction of legislative ballances and checks—the institution of courts composed of judges, holding their offices during good behaviour—the representation of the people in the legislature by deputies of their own election—these are either wholly new discoveries or have made their principal progress toward perfection in modern times. They are means, and powerful means, by which the excellencies of republican government may be retained and its imperfections lessened or avoided. To this catalogue of circumstances, that tend to the amelioration of popular systems of civil government, I shall venture, however novel it may appear to some, to add one more on a principle, which has been made the foundation of an objection to the New Constitution, I mean the ENLARGEMENT of the ORBIT within which such systems are to revolve either in respect to the dimensions of a single State, or to the consolidation of several smaller States into one great confederacy. . . .

PUBLIUS

THE FEDERALIST NO. 23
DECEMBER 18, 1787

One of the principal difficulties in understanding that Hamilton's constitutionalism was directed toward limited ends is that he appears to be an exponent of unlimited power for the national government. But he never argues for national power without limitation. What he argues ought to exist without limitation are "the authorities essential to the care of the common defence"—those powers relating to raising armies, providing for a navy, governing the armed forces, directing their operations, and providing for their support. In other words, national powers with a view to certain ends ought to exist without limits.

New York, December 18, 1787

To the People of the State of New-York.

THE necessity of a Constitution, at least equally energetic with the one proposed, to the preservation of the Union, is the point, at the examination of which we are now arrived.

This enquiry will naturally divide itself into three branches—the objects to be provided for by a Fœderal Government—the quantity of power necessary to the accomplishment of those objects—the persons upon whom that power ought to operate. Its distribution and organization will more properly claim our attention under the succeeding head.

The principal purposes to be answered by Union are these—The common defence of the members—the preservation of the public peace as well against internal convulsions as external attacks—the regulation of commerce with other nations and between the States—the superintendence of our intercourse, political and commercial, with foreign countries.

The authorities essential to the care of the common defence are these—to raise armies—to build and equip fleets—to prescribe rules for the government of both—to direct their operations—to provide for their support. These powers ought to exist without limitation: *Because it is impossible to foresee or define the extent and variety of national exigencies, or the correspondent extent & variety of the means which may be necessary to satisfy them.* The circumstances that endanger the safety of nations are infinite; and for this reason no constitutional shackles can wisely be imposed on the power to which the care of it is committed. This power ought to be co-extensive with all the possible combinations of such circumstances; and ought to be under the direction of the same councils, which are appointed to preside over the common defence.

This is one of those truths, which to a correct and unprejudiced mind, carries its own evidence along with it; and may be obscured, but cannot be made plainer by argument or reasoning. It rests upon axioms as simple as they are universal. The *means* ought to be proportioned to the *end;* the persons, from whose agency the attainment of any *end* is expected, ought to possess the *means* by which it is to be attained.

Whether there ought to be a Fœderal Government intrusted with the care of the common defence, is a question in the first instance open to discussion; but the moment it is decided in the affirmative, it will follow, that that government ought to be cloathed with all the powers requisite to the complete execution of its trust. And unless it can be shewn, that the circumstances which may affect the public safety are reducible within certain determinate limits; unless the contrary of this position can be fairly and rationally disputed, it must be admitted, as a necessary consequence, that there can be no limitation of that authority, which is to provide for the defence and protection of the community, in any matter essential to its efficiency; that is, in any matter essential to the *formation, direction* or *support* of the NATIONAL FORCES.

Defective as the present Confederation has been proved to be, this principle appears to have been fully recognized by the framers of it; though they have not made proper or adequate provision for its exercise. Congress have an unlimited discretion to make requisitions of men and money—to govern the army and navy—to direct their operations. As their requisitions were made constitutionally binding upon the States, who are in fact under the most solemn obligations to furnish the supplies required of them, the intention evidently was, that the United States should command whatever resources were by them judged requisite to "the common defence and general welfare." It was presumed that a sense of their true interests, and a regard to the dictates of good faith, would be found sufficient pledges for the punctual performance of the duty of the members to the Fœderal Head.

The experiment has, however demonstrated, that this expectation was ill founded and illusory; and the observations made under the last head, will, I imagine, have sufficed to convince the impartial and discerning, that there is an absolute necessity for an entire change in the first principles of the system: That if we are in earnest about giving the Union energy and duration, we must abandon the vain project of legislating upon the States in their collective capacities: We must extend the laws of the Fœderal Government to the individual citizens of America: We must discard the fallacious scheme of quotas and requisitions, as equally impracticable and unjust. The result from all this is, that the Union ought to be invested with full power to levy troops; to build and equip fleets, and to raise the revenues, which will be required for the formation and support of an army and navy, in the customary and ordinary modes practiced in other governments.

If the circumstances of our country are such, as to demand a compound instead of a simple, a confederate instead of a sole government, the essential point which will remain to be adjusted, will be to discriminate the OBJECTS, as far as it can be done, which shall appertain to the different provinces or departments of power; allowing to each the most ample authority for fulfilling the objects committed to its charge. Shall the Union be constituted the guardian of the common safety? Are fleets and armies and revenues necessary to this purpose? The government of the Union must be empowered to pass all laws, and to make all regulations which have relation to them. The same must be the case, in respect to commerce, and to every other matter to which its jurisdiction is permitted to extend. Is the administration of justice between the citizens of the same State, the proper department of the local governments? These must possess all the authorities which are connected with this object, and with every other that may be allotted to their particular cognizance and direction. Not to confer in each case a degree of power, commensurate to the end, would be to violate the most obvious rules of prudence and propriety, and improvidently to trust the great interests of the nation to hands, which are disabled from managing them with vigour and success.

Who so likely to make suitable provisions for the public defence, as that body to which the guardianship of the public safety is confided—which, as the center of information, will best understand the extent and urgency of the dangers that threaten—as the representative of the WHOLE will feel itself most deeply interested in the preservation of every part—which, from the responsibility implied in the duty assigned to it, will be most sensibly impressed with the necessity of proper exertions—and which, by the extension of its authority throughout the States, can alone establish uniformity and concert in the plans and measures, by which the common safety is to be secured? Is there not a manifest inconsistency in devolving upon the Fœderal Government the care of the general defence, and leaving in the State governments the *effective* powers, by which it is to be provided for? Is not a want of co-operation the infallible consequence of such a system? And will not weakness, disorder, an undue distribution of the burthens and calamities of war, an unnecessary and intolerable increase of expence, be its natural and inevitable concomitants? Have we not had unequivocal experience of its effects in the course of the revolution, which we have just accomplished?

Every view we may take of the subject, as candid enquirers after truth, will serve to convince us, that it is both unwise and dangerous to deny the Fœderal Government an unconfined authority, as to all those objects which are intrusted to its management. It will indeed deserve the most vigilant and careful attention of the people, to see that it be modelled in such a manner, as to admit of its being safely vested with the requisite powers. If any plan which has been, or may be offered to our consideration, should not, upon a dispassionate inspection, be found to answer this description, it ought to be rejected. A government, the Constitution of which renders it unfit to be trusted with all the powers, which a free people *ought to delegate to any government*, would be an unsafe and improper depository of the NATIONAL INTERESTS, wherever THESE can with propriety be confided, the co-incident powers may safely accompany them. This is the true result of all just reasoning upon the subject. And the adversaries of the plan, promulgated by the Convention, ought to have confined themselves to showing that the internal structure of the proposed government, was such as to render it unworthy of the confidence of the people. They ought not to have wandered into inflammatory declamations, and unmeaning cavils about the extent of the powers. The POWERS are not too extensive for the OBJECTS of Fœderal administration, or in other words, for the management of our NATIONAL INTERESTS; nor can any satisfactory argument be framed to shew that they are chargeable with such an excess. If it be true, as has been insinuated by some of the writers on the other side, that the difficulty arises from the nature of the thing, and that the extent of the country will not permit us to form a government, in which such ample powers can safely be reposed, it would prove that we ought to contract our views, and resort to the expedient of separate Confederacies, which will move within more practicable spheres. For the absurdity must continually stare us in the face of confiding to a government, the direction of the most essential national interests, without daring to trust it with the authorities which are indispensable to their proper and efficient management. Let us not attempt to reconcile contradictions, but firmly embrace a rational alternative.

I trust, however, that the impracticability of one general system cannot be shewn. I am greatly mistaken, if any thing of weight, has yet been advanced of this tendency; and I flatter myself, that the observations which have been made in the course of these papers, have sufficed to place the reverse of that position in as clear a light as any matter still in the womb of time and experience can be susceptible of. This at all events must be evident, that the very difficulty itself drawn from the extent of the country, is the strongest argument in favor of an energetic government; for any other can certainly never preserve the Union of so large an empire. If we embrace the tenets of those, who oppose the adoption of the proposed Constitution, as the standard of our political creed, we cannot fail to verify the gloomy doctrines, which predict the impracticability of a national system, pervading the entire limits of the present Confederacy.

PUBLIUS.

THE FEDERALIST NO. 31
JANUARY 1, 1788

> *Hamilton states in the following essay that "a government ought to contain in itself every power requisite to the full accomplishment of the objects committed to its care, and to the complete execution of the trusts for which it is responsible, free from every other control, but a regard to the public good and to the sense of the people." It might appear from this statement, declaring the necessity of doing everything needful and possible for achieving the ends of government, that everything must be subordinated to authority in the interest of national self-preservation. But Hamilton believed that authority must condition itself or be conditioned by the ends or purposes of a free society and therefore be exercised under certain constraints or limitations.*

New York, January 1, 1788

To the People of the State of New-York.

IN disquisitions of every kind there are certain primary truths or first principles upon which all subsequent reasonings must depend. These contain an internal evidence, which antecedent to all reflection or combination commands the assent of the mind. Where it produces not this effect, it must proceed either from some defect or disorder in the organs of perception, or from the influence of some strong interest, or passion, or prejudice. Of this nature are the maxims in geometry, that "The whole is greater than its part; that things equal to the same are equal to one another; that two straight lines cannot inclose a space; and that all right angles are equal to each other." Of the same nature are these other maxims in ethics and politics, that there cannot be an effect without a cause; that the means ought to be proportioned to the end; that every power ought to be commensurate with its object; that there ought to be no limitation of a power destined to effect a purpose, which is itself incapable of limitation. And there are other truths in the two latter sciences, which if they cannot pretend to rank in the class of axioms, are yet such direct inferences from them, and so obvious in themselves, and so agreeable to the natural and unsophisticated dictates of common sense, that they challenge the assent of a sound and unbiassed mind, with a degree of force and conviction almost equally irresistable.

The objects of geometrical enquiry are so intirely abstracted from those pursuits which stir up and put in motion the unruly passions of the human heart, that mankind without difficulty adopt not only the more simple theorems of the science, but even those abstruse paradoxes, which however they may appear susceptible of demonstration, are at variance with the natural conceptions which the mind, without the aid of philosophy, would be led to entertain upon the subject. The INFINITE DIVISIBILITY of matter, or in other words, the INFINITE divisibility of a FINITE thing, extending even to the minutest atom, is a point agreed among geometricians; though not less incomprehensible to common sense, than any of those mysteries in religion, against which the batteries of infidelity have been so industriously levelled.

But in the sciences of morals and politics men are found far less tractable. To a certain degree it is right and useful, that this should be the case. Caution and investigation are a necessary armour against error and imposition. But this untractableness may be carried too far, and may degenerate into obstinacy, perverseness or disingenuity. Though it cannot be pretended that the principles of moral and political knowledge have in general the same degree of certainty with those of the mathematics; yet they have much better claims in this respect, than to judge from the conduct of men in particular situations, we should be disposed to allow them. The obscurity is much oftener in the passions and prejudices of the reasoner than in the subject. Men upon too many occasions do not give their own understandings fair play; but yielding to some untoward bias they entangle themselves in words and confound themselves in subtleties.

How else could it happen (if we admit the objectors to be sincere in their opposition) that positions so clear as those which manifest the necessity of a general power of taxation in the government of the union, should have to encounter any adversaries among men of discernment? Though these positions have been elsewhere fully stated, they will perhaps not be improperly recapitulated in this place, as introductory to an examination of what may have been offered by way of objection to them. They are in substance as follow:

A government ought to contain in itself every power requisite to the full accomplishment of the objects committed to its care, and to the complete execution of the trusts for which it is responsible; free from every other control, but a regard to the public good and to the sense of the people.

As the duties of superintending the national defence and of securing the public peace against foreign or domestic violence, involve a provision for casualties and dangers, to which no possible limits can be assigned, the power of making that provision ought to know no other bounds than the exigencies of the nation and the resources of the community.

As revenue is the essential engine by which the means of answering the national exigencies must be procured, the power of procuring that article in its full extent, must necessarily be comprehended in that of providing for those exigencies.

As theory and practice conspire to prove that the power of procuring revenue is unavailing, when exercised over the States in their collective capacities, the Federal government must of necessity be invested with an unqualified power of taxation in the ordinary modes.

Did not experience evince the contrary, it would be natural to conclude that the propriety of a general power of taxation in the national government might safely be permitted to rest on the evidence of these propositions, unassisted by any additional arguments or illustrations. But we find in fact, that the antagonists of the proposed constitution, so far from acquiescing in their justness or truth, seem to make their principal and most zealous effort against this part of the plan. It may therefore be satisfactory to analize the arguments with which they combat it.

Those of them, which have been most labored with that view, seem in substance to amount to this: "It is not true, because the exigencies of the Union may not be susceptible of limitation, that its power of laying taxes ought to be unconfined. Revenue is as requisite to the purposes of the local administrations as to those of the Union; and the former are at least of equal importance with the latter to the happiness of the people. It is therefore as necessary, that the State Governments should be able to command the means of supplying their wants, as, that the National Government should possess the like faculty, in respect to the wants of the Union. But an indefinite power of taxation in the *latter* might, and probably would in time deprive the former of the means of providing for their own necessities; and would subject them entirely to the mercy of the national Legislature. As the laws of the Union are to become the supreme law of the land; as it is to have power to pass all laws that may be NECESSARY for carrying into execution, the authorities with which it is proposed to vest it; the national government might at any time abolish the taxes imposed for State objects, upon the pretence of an interference with its own. It might alledge a necessity of doing this, in order to give efficacy to the national revenues: And thus all the resources of taxation might by degrees, become the subjects of fœderal monopoly, to the intire exclusion and destruction of the State Governments."

This mode of reasoning appears some times to turn upon the supposition of usurpation in the national government; at other times it seems to be designed only as a deduction from the constitutional operation of its intended powers. It is only in the latter light, that it can be admitted to have any pretensions to fairness. The moment we launch into conjectures about the usurpations of the fœderal Government, we get into an unfathomable abyss, and fairly put ourselves out of the reach of all reasoning. Imagination may range at pleasure till it gets bewildered amidst the labyrinths of an enchanted castle, and knows not on which side to turn to extricate itself from the perplexities into which it has so rashly adventured. Whatever may be the limits or modifications of the powers of the Union, it is easy to imagine an endless train of possible dangers; and by indulging an excess of jealousy and timidity, we may bring ourselves to a state of absolute scepticism and irresolution. I repeat here what I have observed in substance in another place that all observations founded upon the danger of usurpation, ought to be referred to the composition and structure of the government, not to the nature or extent of its powers. The State governments, by their original constitutions, are invested with complete sovereignty. In what does our security consist against usurpations from that quarter? Doubtless in the manner of their formation, and in a due dependence of those who are to administer them upon the people. If the proposed construction of the Fœderal Government, be found upon an impartial examination of it, to be such as to afford, to a proper extent, the same species of security, all apprehensions on the score of usurpation ought to be discarded.

It should not be forgotten, that a disposition in the State governments to encroach upon the rights of the Union, is quite as probable, as a disposition in the Union to encroach upon the rights of the State Governments. What side would be likely to prevail in such a conflict, must depend on the means which the contending parties could employ towards ensuring success. As in republics, strength is always on the side of the people; and as there are weighty reasons to induce a belief, that the State governments will commonly possess most influence over them, the natural conclusion is, that such contests will be most apt to end to the disadvantage of the Union; and that there is greater probability of encroachments by the members upon the Fœderal Head, than by the Fœderal Head upon the members. But it is evident, that all conjectures of this kind, must be extremely vague and fallible, and that it is by far the safest course to lay them altogether aside; and to confine our attention wholly to the nature and extent of the powers as they are delineated in the constitution. Every thing beyond this, must be left to the prudence and firmness of the people; who, as they will hold the scales in their own hands, it is to be hoped, will always take care to preserve the constitutional equilibrium between the General and the State Governments. Upon this ground, which is evidently the true one, it will not be difficult to obviate the objections, which have been made to an indefinite power of taxation in the United States.

PUBLIUS

THE FEDERALIST NOS. 70–77, AN INTRODUCTION

Federalist essays 70 through 77 constitute a treatise on energetic executive power. The problem of the American founding was the need to energize republican government, and Hamilton insisted that energetic executive power is not, despite first impressions, in tension with republicanism. What he wanted from executive power was to bring into government qualities of wisdom, common sense, and energy, which might otherwise be lacking in a republican regime. He did not, however, envision unlimited executive power, as exemplified by Schlesinger's Imperial Presidency.

THE FEDERALIST NO. 70
MARCH 15, 1788

New York, March 15, 1788

To the People of the State of New-York.

THERE is an idea, which is not without its advocates, that a vigorous executive is inconsistent with the genius of republican government. The enlightened well wishers to this species of government must at least hope that the supposition is destitute of foundation; since they can never admit its truth, without at the same time admitting the condemnation of their own principles. Energy in the executive is a leading character in the definition of good government. It is essential to the protection of the community against foreign attacks: It is not less essential to the steady administration of the laws, to the protection of property against those irregular and high handed combinations, which sometimes interrupt the ordinary course of justice to the security of liberty against the enterprises and assaults of ambition, of faction and of anarchy. Every man the least conversant in Roman story knows how often that republic was obliged to take refuge in the absolute power of a single man, under the formidable title of dictator, as well against the intrigues of ambitious individuals, who aspired to the tyranny, and the seditions of whole classes of the community, whose conduct threatened the existence of all government, as against the invasions of external enemies, who menaced the conquest and destruction of Rome.

There can be no need however to multiply arguments or examples on this head. A feeble executive implies a feeble execution of the government. A feeble execution is but another phrase for a bad execution: And a government ill executed, whatever it may be in theory, must be in practice a bad government.

Taking it for granted, therefore, that all men of sense will agree in the necessity of an energetic executive; it will only remain to inquire, what are the ingredients which constitute this energy—how far can they be combined with those other ingredients which constitute safety in the republican sense? And how far does this combination characterise the plan, which has been reported by the convention?

The ingredients, which constitute energy in the executive, are first unity, secondly duration, thirdly an adequate provision for its support, fourthly competent powers.

The circumstances which constitute safety in the republican

sense are, Ist. a due dependence on the people, secondly a due responsibility.

Those politicians and statesmen, who have been the most celebrated for the soundness of their principles, and for the justness of their views, have declared in favor of a single executive and a numerous legislature. They have with great propriety considered energy as the most necessary qualification of the former, and have regarded this as most applicable to power in a single hand; while they have with equal propriety considered the latter as best adapted to deliberation and wisdom, and best calculated to conciliate the confidence of the people and to secure their privileges and interests.

That unity is conducive to energy will not be disputed. Decision, activity, secrecy, and dispatch will generally characterise the proceedings of one man, in a much more eminent degree, than the proceedings of any greater number; and in proportion as the number is increased, these qualities will be diminished.

This unity may be destroyed in two ways; either by vesting the power in two or more magistrates of equal dignity and authority; or by vesting it ostensibly in one man, subject in whole or in part to the controul and co-operation of others, in the capacity of counsellors to him. Of the first the two consuls of Rome may serve as an example; of the last we shall find examples in the constitutions of several of the states. New-York and New-Jersey, if I recollect right, are the only states, which have entrusted the executive authority wholly to single men.* Both these methods of destroying the unity of the executive have their partisans; but the votaries of an executive council are the most numerous. They are both liable, if not to equal, to similar objections; and may in most lights be examined in conjunction.

The experience of other nations will afford little instruction on this head. As far however as it teaches any thing, it teaches us not to be inamoured of plurality in the executive. We have seen that the Achæans on an experiment of two Prætors, were induced to abolish one. The Roman history records many instances of mischiefs to the republic from the dissentions between the consuls, and between the military tribunes, who were at times substituted to the consuls. But it gives no specimens of any peculiar advantages derived to the state, from the circumstance of the plurality of those magistrates. That the dissentions between them were not more frequent, or more fatal, is matter of astonishment; until we advert to the singular position in

---

*New-York has no council except for the single purpose of appointing to offices; New-Jersey has a council, whom the governor may consult. But I think from the terms of the constitution their resolutions do not bind him.

which the republic was almost continually placed and to the prudent policy pointed out by the circumstances of the state, and pursued by the consuls, of making a division of the government between them. The Patricians engaged in a perpetual struggle with the Plebeians for the preservation of their antient authorities and dignities; the consuls, who were generally chosen out of the former body, were commonly united by the personal interest they had in the defence of the privileges of their order. In addition to this motive of union, after the arms of the republic had considerably expanded the bounds of its empire, it became an established custom with the consuls to divide the administration between themselves by lot; one of them remaining at Rome to govern the city and its environs; the other taking the command in the more distant provinces. This expedient must no doubt have had great influence in preventing those collisions and rivalships, which might otherwise have embroiled the peace of the republic.

But quitting the dim light of historical research, and attaching ourselves purely to the dictates of reason and good sense, we shall discover much greater cause to reject than to approve the idea of plurality in the executive, under any modification whatever.

Wherever two or more persons are engaged in any common enterprize or pursuit, there is always danger of difference of opinion. If it be a public trust or office in which they are cloathed with equal dignity and authority, there is peculiar danger of personal emulation and even animosity. From either and especially from all these causes, the most bitter dissentions are apt to spring. Whenever these happen, they lessen the respectability, weaken the authority, and distract the plans and operations of those whom they divide. If they should unfortunately assail the supreme executive magistracy of a country, consisting of a plurality of persons, they might impede or frustrate the most important measures of the government, in the most critical emergencies of the state. And what is still worse, they might split the community into the most violent and irreconcilable factions, adhering differently to the different individuals who composed the magistracy.

Men often oppose a thing merely because they have had no agency in planning it, or because it may have been planned by those whom they dislike. But if they have been consulted and have happened to disapprove, opposition then becomes in their estimation an indispensable duty of self love. They seem to think themselves bound in honor, and by all the motives of personal infallibility to defeat the success of what has been resolved upon, contrary to their sentiments. Men of upright, benevolent tempers have too many opportunities of remarking with horror, to what desperate lengths this disposition is sometimes carried, and how often the great interests of society are

145

sacrificed to the vanity, to the conceit and to the obstinacy of individuals, who have credit enough to make their passions and their caprices interesting to mankind. Perhaps the question now before the public may in its consequences afford melancholy proofs of the effects of this despicable frailty, or rather detestable vice in the human character.

Upon the principles of a free government, inconveniencies from the source just mentioned must necessarily be submitted to in the formation of the legislature; but it is unnecessary and therefore unwise to introduce them into the constitution of the executive. It is here too that they may be most pernicious. In the legislature, promptitude of decision is oftener an evil than a benefit. The differences of opinion, and the jarrings of parties in that department of the government, though they may sometimes obstruct salutary plans, yet often promote deliberations and circumspection; and serve to check excesses in the majority. When a resolution too is once taken, the opposition must be at an end. That resolution is a law, and resistance to it is punishable. But no favourable circumstances palliate or atone for the disadvantages of dissention in the executive department. Here they are pure and unmixed. There is no point at which they cease to operate. They serve to embarrass and weaken the execution of the plan or measure, to which they relate, from the first step to the final conclusion of it. They constantly counteract those qualities in the executive, which are the most necessary ingredients in its composition, vigour and expedition, and this without any counterballancing good. In the conduct of war, in which the energy of the executive is the bulwark of the national security, every thing would be to be apprehended from its plurality.

It must be confessed that these observations apply with principal weight to the first case supposed, that is to a plurality of magistrates of equal dignity and authority; a scheme the advocates for which are not likely to form a numerous sect: But they apply, though not with equal, yet with considerable weight, to the project of a council, whose concurrence is made constitutionally necessary to the operations of the ostensible executive. An artful cabal in that council would be able to distract and to enervate the whole system of administration. If no such cabal should exist, the mere diversity of views and opinions would alone be sufficient to tincture the exercise of the executive authority with a spirit of habitual feebleness and delatoriness.

But one of the weightiest objections to a plurality in the executive, and which lies as much against the last as the first plan, is that it tends to conceal faults, and destroy responsibility. Responsibility is of two kinds, to censure and to punishment. The first is the most important of the two; especially in an elective office. Man, in public trust, will much oftener act in such a manner as to render him unworthy of being any longer trusted, than in such a manner as to make him obnoxious to legal punishment. But the multiplication of the executive adds to the difficulty of detection in either case. It often becomes impossible, amidst mutual accusations, to determine on whom the blame or the punishment of a pernicious measure, or series of pernicious measures ought really to fall. It is shifted from one to another with so much dexterity, and under such plausible appearances, that the public opinion is left in suspense about the real author. The circumstances which may have led to any national miscarriage or misfortune are sometimes so complicated, that where there are a number of actors who may have had different degrees and kinds of agency, though we may clearly see upon the whole that there has been mismanagement, yet it may be impracticable to pronounce to whose account the evil which may have been incurred is truly chargeable.

"I was overruled by my council. The council were so divided in their opinions, that it was impossible to obtain any better resolution on the point." These and similar pretexts are constantly at hand, whether true or false. And who is there that will either take the trouble or incur the odium of a strict scrutiny into the secret springs of the transaction? Should there be found a citizen zealous enough to undertake the unpromising task, if there happen to be a collusion between the parties concerned, how easy is it to cloath the circumstances with so much ambiguity, as to render it uncertain what was the precise conduct of any of those parties?

In the single instance in which the governor of this state is coupled with a council, that is in the appointment to offices, we have seen the mischiefs of it in the view now under consideration. Scandalous appointments to important offices have been made. Some cases indeed have been so flagrant, that ALL PARTIES have agreed in the impropriety of the thing. When enquiry has been made, the blame has been laid by the governor on the members of the council; who on their part have charged it upon his nomination: While the people remain altogether at a loss to determine by whose influence their interests have been committed to hands so unqualified, and so manifestly improper. In tenderness to individuals, I forbear to descend to particulars.

It is evident from these considerations, that the plurality of the executive tends to deprive the people of the two greatest securities they can have for the faithful exercise of any delegated power; first, the restraints of public opinion, which lose their efficacy as well on account of the division of the censure attendant on bad measures among a number, as on account of the uncertainty on whom it ought to fall; and secondly, the opportunity of discovering with facility and clearness the misconduct of the persons they trust, in order either to their removal from office, or to their actual punishment, in cases which admit of it.

In England the king is a perpetual magistrate; and it is a maxim, which has obtained for the sake of the public peace, that he is unaccountable for his administration, and his person sacred. Nothing therefore can be wiser in that kingdom than to annex to the king a constitutional council, who may be responsible to the nation for the advice they give. Without this there would be no responsibility whatever in the executive department; an idea inadmissible in a free government. But even there the king is not bound by the resolutions of his council, though they are answerable for the advice they give. He is the absolute master of his own conduct, in the exercise of his office; and may observe or disregard the council given to him at his sole discretion.

But in a republic, where every magistrate ought to be personally responsible for his behaviour in office, the reason which in the British constitution dictates the propriety of a council not only ceases to apply, but turns against the institution. In the monarchy of Great-Britain, it furnishes a substitute for the prohibited responsibility of the chief magistrate; which serves in some degree as a hostage to the national justice for his good behaviour. In the American republic it would serve to destroy, or would greatly diminish the intended and necessary responsibility of the chief magistrate himself.

The idea of a council to the executive, which has so generally obtained in the state constitutions, has been derived from that maxim of republican jealousy, which considers power as safer in the hands of a number of men than of a single man. If the maxim should be admitted to be applicable to the case, I should contend that the advantage on that side would not counterballance the numerous disadvantages on the opposite side. But I do not think the rule at all applicable to the executive power. I clearly concur in opinion in this particular with a writer whom the celebrated Junius pronounces to be "deep, solid and ingenious," that, "the executive power is more easily confined when it is one:"* That it is far more safe there should be a single object for the jealousy and watchfulness of the people; and in a word that all multiplication of the executive is rather dangerous than friendly to liberty.

A little consideration will satisfy us, that the species of security

*De Lome.

sought for in the multiplication of the executive is unattainable. Numbers must be so great as to render combination difficult; or they are rather a source of danger than of security. The united credit and influence of several individuals must be more formidable to liberty than the credit and influence of either of them separately. When power therefore is placed in the hands of so small a number of men, as to admit of their interests and views being easily combined in a common enterprise, by an artful leader, it becomes more liable to abuse and more dangerous when abused, than if it be lodged in the hands of one man; who from the very circumstance of his being alone will be more narrowly watched and more readily suspected, and who cannot unite so great a mass of influence as when he is associated with others. The Decemvirs of Rome, whose name denotes their number,† were more to be dreaded in their usurpation than any ONE of them would have been. No person would think of proposing an executive much more numerous than that body, from six to a dozen have been suggested for the number of the council. The extreme of these numbers is not too great for an easy combination; and from such a combination America would have more to fear, than from the ambition of any single individual. A council to a magistrate, who is himself responsible for what he does, are generally nothing better than a clog upon his good intentions; are often the instruments and accomplices of his bad, and are almost always a cloak to his faults.

I forbear to dwell upon the subject of expence; though it be evident that if the council should be numerous enough to answer the principal end, aimed at by the institution, the salaries of the members, who must be drawn from their homes to reside at the seat of government, would form an item in the catalogue of public expenditures, too serious to be incurred for an object of equivocal utility.

I will only add, that prior to the appearance of the constitution, I rarely met with an intelligent man from any of the states, who did not admit as the result of experience, that the UNITY of the Executive of this state was one of the best of the distinguishing features of our constitution.

PUBLIUS.

†*Ten.*

THE FEDERALIST NO. 71
MARCH 18, 1788

New York, March 18, 1788

To the People of the State of New-York.

DURATION in office has been mentioned as the second requisite to the energy of the executive authority. This has relation to two objects: To the personal firmness of the Executive Magistrate in the employment of his constitutional powers; and to the stability of the system of administration which may have been adopted under his auspices. With regard to the first, it must be evident, that the longer the duration in office, the greater will be the probability of obtaining so important an advantage. It is a general principle of human nature, that a man will be interested in whatever he possesses, in proportion to the firmness or precariousness of the tenure, by which he holds it; will be less attached to what he holds by a momentary or uncertain title, than to what he enjoys by a durable or certain title; and of course will be willing to risk more for the sake of the one, than for the sake of the other. This remark is not less applicable to a political privilege, or honor, or trust, than to any article of ordinary property. The inference from it is, that a man acting in the capacity of Chief Magistrate, under a consciousness, that in a very short time he *must* lay down his office, will be apt to feel himself too little interested in it, to hazard any material censure or perplexity, from the independent exertion of his powers, or from encountering the ill-humors, however transient, which may happen to prevail either in a considerable part of the society itself, or even in a predominant faction in the legislative body. If the case should only be, that he *might* lay it down, unless continued by a new choice; and if he should be desirous of being continued, his wishes conspiring with his fears would tend still more powerfully to corrupt his integrity, or debase his fortitude. In either case feebleness and irresolution must be the characteristics of the station.

There are some, who would be inclined to regard the servile pliancy of the executive to a prevailing current, either in the community, or in the Legislature, as its best recommendation. But such men entertain very crude notions, as well of the purposes for which government was instituted, as of the true means by which the public happiness may be promoted. The republican principle demands, that the deliberate sense of the community should govern the conduct of those to whom they entrust the management of their affairs; but it does not require an unqualified complaisance to every sudden breese

150

of passion, or to every transient impulse which the people may receive from the arts of men, who flatter their prejudices to betray their interests. It is a just observation, that the people commonly *intend* the PUBLIC GOOD. This often applies to their very errors. But their good sense would despise the adulator, who should pretend that they always *reason right* about the *means* of promoting it. They know from experience, that they sometimes err; and the wonder is, that they so seldom err as they do; beset as they continually are by the wiles of parasites and sycophants, by the snares of the ambitious, the avaricious, the desperate; by the artifices of men, who possess their confidence more than they deserve it, and of those who seek to possess, rather than to deserve it. When occasions present themselves in which the interests of the people are at variance with their inclinations, it is the duty of the persons whom they have appointed to be the guardians of those interests, to withstand the temporary delusion, in order to give them time and opportunity for more cool and sedate reflection. Instances might be cited, in which a conduct of this kind has saved the people from very fatal consequences of their own mistakes, and has procured lasting monuments of their gratitude to the men, who had courage and magnanimity enough to serve them at the peril of their displeasure.

But however inclined we might be to insist upon an unbounded complaisance in the executive to the inclinations of the people, we can with no propriety contend for a like complaisance to the humors of the Legislature. The latter may sometimes stand in opposition to the former; and at other times the people may be entirely neutral. In either supposition, it is certainly desirable that the executive should be in a situation to dare to act his own opinion with vigor and decision.

The same rule, which teaches the propriety of a partition between the various branches of power, teaches us likewise that this partition ought to be so contrived as to render the one independent of the other. To what purpose separate the executive, or the judiciary, from the legislative, if both the executive and the judiciary are so constituted as to be at the absolute devotion of the legislative? Such a separation must be merely nominal and incapable of producing the ends for which it was established. It is one thing to be subordinate to the laws, and another to be dependent on the legislative body. The first comports with, the last violates, the fundamental principles of good government; and whatever may be the forms of the Constitution, unites all power in the same hands. The tendency of the legislative authority to absorb every other, has been fully displayed and illustrated by examples, in some preceding numbers. In governments purely republican, this tendency is almost irresistable. The repre-

151

sentatives of the people, in a popular assembly, seem sometimes to fancy that they are the people themselves; and betray strong symptoms of impatience and disgust at the least sign of opposition from any other quarter; as if the exercise of its rights by either the executive or judiciary, were a breach of their privilege and an outrage to their dignity. They often appear disposed to exert an imperious controul over the other departments; and as they commonly have the people on their side, they always act with such momentum as to make it very difficult for the other members of the government to maintain the balance of the Constitution.

It may perhaps be asked how the shortness of the duration in office can affect the independence of the executive on the legislature, unless the one were possessed of the power of appointing or displacing the other? One answer to this enquiry may be drawn from the principle already remarked, that is from the slender interest a man is apt to take in a short lived advantage, and the little inducement it affords him to expose himself on account of it to any considerable inconvenience or hazard. Another answer, perhaps more obvious, though not more conclusive, will result from the consideration of the influence of the legislative body over the people, which might be employed to prevent the re-election of a man, who by an upright resistance to any sinister project of that body, should have made himself obnoxious to its resentment.

It may be asked also whether a duration of four years would answer the end proposed, and if it would not, whether a less period which would at least be recommended by greater security against ambitious designs, would not for that reason be preferable to a longer period, which was at the same time too short for the purpose of inspiring the desired firmness and independence of the magistrate?

It cannot be affirmed, that a duration of four years or any other limited duration would completely answer the end proposed; but it would contribute towards it in a degree which would have a material influence upon the spirit and character of the government. Between the commencement and termination of such a period there would always be a considerable interval, in which the prospect of annihilation would be sufficiently remote not to have an improper effect upon the conduct of a man endued with a tolerable portion of fortitude; and in which he might reasonably promise himself, that there would be time enough, before it arrived, to make the community sensible of the propriety of the measures he might incline to pursue. Though it be probable, that as he approached the moment when the public were by a new election to signify their sense of his conduct, his confidence and with it, his firmness would decline; yet both the one and the other would derive support from the opportunities, which his previ-

ous continuance in the station had afforded him of establishing himself in the esteem and good will of his constituents. He might then
hazard with safety, in proportion to the proofs he had given of his
wisdom and integrity, and to the title he had acquired to the respect
and attachment of his fellow citizens. As on the one hand, a duration
of four years will contribute to the firmness of the executive in a
sufficient degree to render it a very valuable ingredient in the composition; so on the other, it is not long enough to justify any alarm for
the public liberty. If a British House of Commons, from the most
feeble beginnings, *from the mere power of assenting or disagreeing to the
imposition of a new tax*, have by rapid strides, reduced the prerogatives
of the crown and the privileges of the nobility within the limits they
conceived to be compatible with the principles of a free government;
while they raised themselves to the rank and consequence of a coequal branch of the Legislature; if they have been able in one instance
to abolish both the royalty and the aristocracy, and to overturn all the
ancient establishments as well in the church as State; if they have
been able on a recent occasion to make the monarch tremble at the
prospect of an innovation* attempted by them; what would be to be
feared from an elective magistrate of four years duration, with the
confined authorities of a President of the United States? What but that
he might be unequal to the task which the Constitution assigns him? I
shall only add that if his duration be such as to leave a doubt of his
firmness, that doubt is inconsistent with a jealousy of his encroachments.

PUBLIUS.

THE FEDERALIST NO. 72
MARCH 19, 1788

New York, March 19, 1788

To the People of the State of New-York.

THE ADMINISTRATION of government, in its largest sense, comprehends all the operations of the body politic, whether legislative,
executive or judiciary, but in its most usual and perhaps in its most
precise signification, it is limited to executive details, and falls pecu-

---

*This was the case with respect to Mr. Fox's India bill which was carried in the House of
Commons, and rejected in the House of Lords, to the entire satisfaction, as it is said, of the people.*

liarly within the province of the executive department. The actual conduct of foreign negotiations, the preparatory plans of finance, the application and disbursement of the public monies, in conformity to the general appropriations of the legislature, the arrangement of the army and navy, the direction of the operations of war; these and other matters of a like nature constitute what seems to be most properly understood by the administration of government. The persons therefore, to whose immediate management these different matters are committed, ought to be considered as the assistants or deputies of the chief magistrate; and, on this account, they ought to derive their offices from his appointment, at least from his nomination, and ought to be subject to his superintendence. This view of the subject will at once suggest to us the intimate connection between the duration of the executive magistrate in office, and the stability of the system of administration. To reverse and undo what has been done by a predecessor is very often considered by a successor, as the best proof he can give of his own capacity and desert; and, in addition to this propensity, where the alteration has been the result of public choice, the person substituted is warranted in supposing, that the dismission of his predecessor has proceeded from a dislike to his measures, and that the less he resembles him the more he will recommend himself to the favor of his constituents. These considerations, and the influence of personal confidences and attachments, would be likely to induce every new president to promote a change of men to fill the subordinate stations; and these causes together could not fail to occasion a disgraceful and ruinous mutability in the administration of the government.

With a positive duration of considerable extent, I connect the circumstance of re-eligibility. The first is necessary to give to the officer himself the inclination and the resolution to act his part well, and to the community time and leisure to observe the tendency of his measures, and thence to form an experimental estimate of their merits. The last is necessary to enable the people, when they see reason to approve of his conduct, to continue him in the station, in order to prolong the utility of his talents and virtues, and to secure to the government, the advantage of permanency in a wise system of administration.

Nothing appears more plausible at first sight, nor more ill founded upon close inspection, than a scheme, which in relation to the present point has had some respectable advocates—I mean that of continuing the chief magistrate in office for a certain time, and then excluding him from it, either for a limited period, or for ever after. This exclusion whether temporary or perpetual would have nearly the same effects; and these effects would be for the most part rather pernicious than salutary.

One ill effect of the exclusion would be a diminution of the inducements to good behaviour. There are few men who would not feel much less zeal in the discharge of a duty, when they were conscious that the advantages of the station, with which it was connected, must be relinquished at a determinate period, than when they were permitted to entertain a hope of *obtaining* by *meriting* a continuance of them. This position will not be disputed, so long as it is admitted that the desire of reward is one of the strongest incentives of human conduct, or that the best security for the fidelity of mankind is to make their interest coincide with their duty. Even the love of fame, the ruling passion of the noblest minds, which would prompt a man to plan and undertake extensive and arduous enterprises for the public benefit, requiring considerable time to mature and perfect them, if he could flatter himself with the prospect of being allowed to finish what he had begun, would on the contrary deter him from the undertaking, when he foresaw that he must quit the scene, before he could accomplish the work, and must commit that, together with his own reputation, to hands which might be unequal or unfriendly to the task. The most to be expected from the generality of men, in such a situation, is the negative merit of not doing harm instead of the positive merit of doing good.

Another ill effect of the exclusion would be the temptation to sordid views, to peculation, and in some instances, the usurpation. An avaricious man, who might happen to fill the offices, looking forward to a time when he must at all events yield up the emoluments he enjoyed, would feel a propensity, not easy to be resisted by such a man, to make the best use of the opportunity he enjoyed, while it lasted; and might not scruple to have recourse to the most corrupt expedients to make the harvest as abundant as it was transitory; though the same man probably, with a different prospect before him, might content himself with the regular perquisites of his station, and might even be unwilling to risk the consequences of an abuse of his opportunities. His avarice might be a guard upon his avarice. Add to this, that the same man might be vain or ambitious as well as avaricious. And if he could expect to prolong his honors, by his good conduct, he might hesitate to sacrifice his appetite for them to his appetite for gain. But with the prospect before him of approaching and inevitable annihilation, his avarice would be likely to get the victory over his caution, his vanity or his ambition.

An ambitious man too, when he found himself seated on the summit of his country's honors, when he looked forward to the time

155

at which he must descend from the exalted eminence forever; and reflected that no exertion of merit on his part could save him from the unwelcome reverse: Such a man, in such a situation, would be much more violently tempted to embrace a favorable conjuncture for attempting the prolongation of his power, at every personal hazard, than if he had the probability of answering the same end by doing his duty.

Would it promote the peace of the community, or the stability of the government, to have half a dozen men who had had credit enough to be raised to the seat of the supreme magistracy, wandering among the people like discontented ghosts, and sighing for a place which they were destined never more to possess?

A third ill effect of the exclusion would be the depriving the community of the advantage of the experience gained by the chief magistrate in the exercise of his office. That experience is the parent of wisdom is an adage, the truth of which is recognized by the wisest as well as the simplest of mankind. What more desirable or more essential than this quality in the governors of nations? Where more desirable or more essential than in the first magistrate of a nation? Can it be wise to put this desirable and essential quality under the ban of the constitution; and to declare that the moment it is acquired, its possessor shall be compelled to abandon the station in which it was acquired, and to which it is adopted? This nevertheless is the precise import of all those regulations, which exclude men from serving their country, by the choice of their fellow citizens, after they have, by a course of service fitted themselves for doing it with a greater degree of utility.

A fourth ill effect of the exclusion would be the banishing men from stations, in which in certain emergencies of the state their presence might be of the greatest moment to the public interest or safety. There is no nation which has not at one period or another experienced an absolute necessity of the services of particular men, in particular situations, perhaps it would not be too strong to say, to the preservation of its political existence. How unwise therefore must be every such self-denying ordinance, as serves to prohibit a nation from making use of its own citizens, in the manner best suited to its exigences and circumstances! Without supposing the personal essentiality of the man, it is evident that a change of the chief magistrate, at the breaking out of a war, or at any similar crisis, for another even of equal merit, would at all times be detrimental to the community; inasmuch as it would substitute inexperience to experience, and would tend to unhinge and set afloat the already settled train of the administration.

A fifth ill effect of the exclusion would be, that it would operate as a constitutional interdiction of stability in the administration. *By necessitating* a change of men, in the first office in the nation, it would necessitate a mutability of measures. It is not generally to be expected, that men will vary; and measures remain uniform. The contrary is the usual course of things. And we need not be apprehensive there will be too much stability, while there is even the option of changing; nor need we desire to prohibit the people from continuing their confidence, where they think it may be safely placed, and where by constancy on their part, they may obviate the fatal inconveniences of fluctuating councils and a variable policy.

These are some of the disadvantages, which would flow from the principle of exclusion. They apply most forcibly to the scheme of a perpetual exclusion; but when we consider that even a partial exclusion would always render the re-admission of the person a remote and precarious object, the observations which have been made will apply nearly as fully to one case as to the other.

What are the advantages promised to counterballance these disadvantages? They are represented to be 1st. Greater independence in the magistrate: 2dly. Greater security to the people. Unless the exclusion be perpetual there will be no pretence to infer the first advantage. But even in that case, may he have no object beyond his present station to which he may sacrifice his independence? May he have no connections, no friends, for whom he may sacrifice it? May he not be less willing, by a firm conduct, to make personal enemies, when he acts under the impression, that a time is fast approaching, on the arrival of which he not only MAY, but MUST be exposed to their resentments, upon an equal, perhaps upon an inferior footing? It is not an easy point to determine whether his independence would be most promoted or impaired by such an arrangement.

As to the second supposed advantage, there is still greater reason to entertain doubts concerning it. If the exclusion were to be perpetual, a man of irregular ambition, of whom alone there could be reason in any case to entertain apprehensions, would with infinite reluctance yield to the necessity of taking his leave forever of a post, in which his passion for power and pre-eminence had acquired the force of habit. And if he had been fortunate or adroit enough to conciliate the good will of people he might induce them to consider as a very odious and unjustifiable restraint upon themselves, a provision which was calculated to debar them of the right of giving a fresh proof of their attachment to a favorite. There may be conceived circumstances, in which this disgust of the people, seconding the thwarted ambition of such a favourite, might occasion greater danger

157

to liberty, than could ever reasonably be dreaded from the possibility of a perpetuation in office, by the voluntary suffrages of the community, exercising a constitutional privilege.

There is an excess of refinement in the idea of disabling the people to continue in office men, who had entitled themselves, in their opinion, to approbation and confidence; the advantages of which are at best speculative and equivocal; and are over-balanced by disadvantages far more certain and decisive.

PUBLIUS.

THE FEDERALIST NO. 73
MARCH 21, 1788

New York, March 21, 1788

To the People of the State of New-York.

THE third ingredient towards constituting the vigor of the executive authority is an adequate provision for its support. It is evident that without proper attention to this article, the separation of the executive from the legislative department would be merely nominal and nugatory. The Legislature, with a discretionary power over the salary and emoluments of the Chief Magistrate, could render him as obsequious to their will, as they might think proper to make him. They might in most cases either reduce him by famine, or tempt him by largesses, to surrender at discretion his judgment to their inclinations. These expressions taken in all the latitude of the terms would no doubt convey more than is intended. There are men who could neither be distressed nor won into a sacrifice of their duty; but this stern virtue is the growth of few soils: And in the main it will be found, that a power over a man's support is a power over his will. If it were necessary to confirm so plain a truth by facts, examples would not be wanting, even in this country, of the intimidation or seduction of the executive by the terrors, or allurements, of the pecuniary arrangements of the legislative body.

It is not easy therefore to commend too highly the judicious attention which has been paid to this subject in the proposed Constitution. It is there provided that "The President of the United States shall, at stated times, receive for his services a compensation, *which shall neither be increased nor diminished, during the period for which he shall have been elected,* and he shall *not receive within that period any other emolument* from the United States or any of them." It is impossible to imagine any provision which would have been more eligible than this. The Legislature on the appointment of a President is once for all to declare what shall be the compensation for his services during the time for which he shall have been elected. This done, they will have no power to alter it either by increase or diminution, till a new period of service by a new election commences. They can neither weaken his fortitude by operating upon his necessities; nor corrupt his integrity, by appealing to his avarice. Neither the Union nor any of its members will be at liberty to give, nor will he be at liberty to receive any other emolument, than that which may have been determined by the first act. He can of course have no pecuniary inducement to renounce or desert the independence intended for him by the Constitution.

The last of the requisites to energy which have been enumerated are competent powers. Let us proceed to consider those which are proposed to be vested in the President of the United States.

The first thing that offers itself to our observation, is the qualified negative of the President upon the acts or resolutions of the two Houses of the Legislature; or in other words his power of returning all bills with objections; to have the effect of preventing their becoming laws, unless they should afterwards be ratified by two thirds of each of the component members of the legislative body.

The propensity of the legislative department to intrude upon the rights and to absorb the powers of the other departments, has been already suggested and repeated; the insufficiency of a mere parchment delineation of the boundaries of each, has also been remarked upon; and the necessity of furnishing each with constitutional arms for its own defence, has been inferred and proved. From these clear and indubitable principles results the propriety of a negative, either absolute or qualified, in the executive, upon the acts of the legislative branches. Without the one or the other the former would be absolutely unable to defend himself against the depredations of the latter. He might gradually be stripped of his authorities by successive resolutions, or annihilated by a single vote. And in the one mode or the other, the legislative and executive powers might speedily come to be blended in the same hands. If even no propensity had ever discovered itself in the legislative body, to invade the rights of the executive, the rules of just reasoning and theoretic propriety would of themselves teach us, that the one ought not to be left at the mercy of the other, but ought to possess a constitutional and effectual power of self defence.

159

But the power in question has a further use. It not only serves as a shield to the executive, but it furnishes an additional security against the enaction of proper laws. It establishes a salutary check upon the legislative body calculated to guard the community against the effects of faction, precipitancy, or of any impulse unfriendly to the public good, which may happen to influence a majority of that body.

The propriety of a negative, has upon some occasions been combated by an observation, that it was not to be presumed a single man would possess more virtue or wisdom, than a number of men; and that unless this presumption should be entertained, it would be improper to give the executive magistrate any species of controul over the legislative body.

But this observation when examined will appear rather specious than solid. The propriety of the thing does not turn upon the supposition of superior wisdom or virtue in the executive: But upon the supposition that the legislative will not be infallible: That the love of power may sometimes betray it into a disposition to encroach upon the rights of the other members of the government; that a spirit of faction may sometimes pervert its deliberations; that impressions of the moment may sometimes hurry it into measures which itself on maturer reflection would condemn. The primary inducement to conferring the power in question upon the executive, is to enable him to defend himself; the secondary one is to encrease the chances in favor of the community, against the passing of bad laws, through haste, inadvertence, or design. The oftener a measure is brought under examination, the greater the diversity in the situations of those who are to examine it, the less must be the danger of those errors which flow from want of due deliberation, or of those missteps which proceed from the contagion of some common passion or interest. It is far less probable, that culpable views of any kind should infect all the parts of the government, at the same moment and in relation to the same object, than that they should by turns govern and mislead every one of them.

It may perhaps be said, that the power of preventing bad laws includes that of preventing good ones; and may be used to the one purpose as well as to the other. But this objection will have little weight with those who can properly estimate the mischiefs of that inconstancy and mutability in the laws, which form the greatest blemish in the character and genius of our governments. They will consider every institution calculated to restrain the excess of lawmaking, and to keep things in the same state, in which they may happen to be at any given period, as much more likely to do good than harm; because it is favorable to greater stability in the system of legislation.

The injury which may possibly be done by defeating a few good laws will be amply compensated by the advantage of preventing a number of bad ones.

Nor is this all. The superior weight and influence of the legislative body in a free government, and the hazard to the executive in a trial of strength with that body, afford a satisfactory security, that the negative would generally be employed with great caution, and that there would oftener be room for a charge of timidity than of rashness, in the exercise of it. A King of Great-Britain, with all his train of sovereign attributes, and with all the influence he draws from a thousand sources, would at this day hesitate to put a negative upon the joint resolutions of the two houses of Parliament. He would not fail to exert the utmost resources of that influence to strangle a measure disagreeable to him, in its progress to the throne, to avoid being reduced to the dilemma of permitting it to take effect, or of risking the displeasure of the nation, by an opposition to the sense of the legislative body. Nor is it probable that he would ultimately venture to exert his prerogative, but in a case of manifest propriety, or extreme necessity. All well informed men in that kingdom will accede to the justness of this remark. A very considerable period has elapsed since the negative of the crown has been exercised.

If a magistrate, so powerful and so well fortified as a British monarch, would have scruples about the exercise of the power under consideration, how much greater caution may be reasonably expected in a President of the United States, cloathed for the short period of four years with the executive authority of a government wholly and purely republican?

It is evident that there would be greater danger of his not using his power when necessary, than of his using it too often, or too much. An argument indeed against its expediency has been drawn from this very source. It has been represented on this account as a power odious in appearance; useless in practice. But it will not follow, that because it might be rarely exercised, it would never be exercised. In the case for which it is chiefly designed, that of an immediate attack upon the constitutional rights of the executive, or in a case in which the public good was evidently and palpably sacrificed, a man of tolerable firmness would avail himself of his constitutional means of defence, and would listen to the admonitions of duty and responsibility. In the former supposition, his fortitude would be stimulated by his immediate interest in the power of his office; in the latter by the probability of the sanction of his constituents; who though they would naturally incline to the legislative body in a doubtful case, would hardly suffer their partiality to delude them in a very plain case. I speak now with an eye to a magistrate possessing only a common share of firmness. There are men, who under any circumstances will have the courage to do their duty at every hazard.

But the Convention have pursued a mean in this business; which will both facilitate the exercise of the power vested in this respect in the executive magistrate, and make its efficacy to depend on the sense of a considerable part of the legislative body. Instead of an absolute negative, it is proposed to give the executive the qualified negative already described. This is a power, which would be much more readily exercised than the other. A man who might be afraid to defeat a law by his single VETO, might not scruple to return it for reconsideration; subject to being finally rejected only in the event of more than one third of each house concurring in the sufficiency of his objections. He would be encouraged by the reflection, that if his opposition should prevail, it would embark in it a very respectable proportion of the legislative body, whose influence would be united with his in supporting the propriety of his conduct, in the public opinion. A direct and categorical negative has something in the appearance of it more harsh, and more apt to irritate, than the mere suggestion of argumentative objections to be approved or disapproved, by those to whom they are addressed. In proportion as it would be less apt to offend, it would be more apt to be exercised; and for this very reason it may in practice be found more effectual. It is to be hoped that it will not often happen, that improper views will govern so large a proportion as two-thirds of both branches of the Legislature at the same time; and this too in defiance of the counterpoising weight of the executive. It is at any rate far less probable, that this should be the case, than that such views should taint the resolutions and conduct of a bare majority. A power of this nature, in the executive, will often have a silent and unperceived though forcible operation. When men engaged in unjustifiable pursuits are aware, that obstructions may come from a quarter which they cannot controul, they will often be restrained, by the bare apprehension of opposition, from doing what they would with eagerness rush into, if no such external impediments were to be feared.

This qualified negative, as has been elsewhere remarked, is in this State vested in a council, consisting of the Governor, with the Chancellor and Judges of the Supreme Court, or any two of them. It has been freely employed upon a variety of occasions, and frequently with success. And its utility has become so apparent, that persons who in compiling the Constitution were violent opposers of it, have from experience become its declared admirers.*

*Mr. Abraham Yates, a warm opponent of the plan of the Convention, is of this number.

I have in another place remarked, that the Convention in the formation of this part of their plan, had departed from the model of the Constitution of this State, in favor of that of Massachusetts—two strong reasons may be imagined for this preference. One is that the Judges, who are to be the interpreters of the law, might receive an improper bias from having given a previous opinion in their revisionary capacities. The other is that by being often associated with the executive they might be induced to embark too far in the political views of that magistrate, and thus a dangerous combination might by degrees be cemented between the executive and judiciary departments. It is impossible to keep the Judges too distinct from every other avocation than that of expounding the laws. It is peculiarly dangerous to place them in a situation to be either corrupted or influenced by the executive.

PUBLIUS.

THE FEDERALIST NO. 74
MARCH 25, 1788

New York, March 25, 1788

To the People of the State of New-York.

THE President of the United States is to be "Commander in Chief of the army and navy of the United States, and of the militia of the several States *when called into the actual service* of the United States." The propriety of this provision is so evident in itself; and it is at the same time so consonant to the precedents of the State constitutions in general, that little need be said to explain or enforce it. Even those of them, which have in other respects coupled the Chief Magistrate with a Council, have for the most part concentrated the military authority in him alone. Of all the cares or concerns of government, the direction of war most peculiarly demands those qualities which distinguish the exercise of power by a single hand. The direction of war implies the direction of the common strength; and the power of directing and employing the common strength, forms an usual and essential part in the definition of the executive authority.

"The President may require the opinion in writing of the principal officer in each of the executive departments upon any subject relating to the duties of their respective offices." This I consider as a mere redundancy in the plan; as the right for which it provides would result of itself from the office.

He is also to be authorised "to grant reprieves and pardons for offences against the United States *except in cases of impeachment.*" Humanity and good policy conspire to dictate, that the benign prerogative for pardoning should be as little as possible fettered or embarrassed. The criminal code of every country partakes so much of necessary severity, that without an easy access to exceptions in favor of unfortunate guilt, justice would wear a countenance too sanguinary and cruel. As the sense of responsibility is always strongest in proportion as it is undivided, it may be inferred that a single man would be most ready to attend to the force of those motives, which might plead for a mitigation of the rigor of the law, and least apt to yield to considerations, which were calculated to shelter a fit object of its vengeance. The reflection, that the fate of a fellow creature depended on his *sole fiat,* would naturally inspire scrupulousness and caution: The dread of being accused of weakness or connivance would beget equal circumspection, though of a different kind. On the other hand, as men generally derive confidence from their numbers, they might often encourage each other in an act of obduracy, and might be less sensible to the apprehension of suspicion or censure for an injudicious or affected clemency. On these accounts, one man appears to be a more eligible dispenser of the mercy of the government than a body of men.

The expediency of vesting the power of pardoning in the President has, if I mistake not, been only contested in relation to the crime of treason. This, it has been urged, ought to have depended upon the assent of one or both of the branches of the legislative body. I shall not deny that there are strong reasons to be assigned for requiring in this particular the concurrence of that body or of a part of it. As treason is a crime levelled at the immediate being of the society, when the laws have once ascertained the guilt of the offender, there seems a fitness in refering the expediency of an act of mercy towards him to the judgment of the Legislature. And this ought the rather to be the case, as the supposition of the connivance of the Chief Magistrate ought not to be entirely excluded. But there are also strong objections to such a plan. It is not to be doubted that a single man of prudence and good sense, is better fitted, in delicate conjunctures, to balance the motives, which may plead for and against the remission of the punishment, than any numerous body whatever. It deserves particular attention, that treason will often be connected with seditions, which embrace a large proportion of the community; as lately happened in Massachusetts. In every such case, we might expect to see the representation of the people tainted with the same spirit, which had given birth to the offense. And when parties were pretty equally matched, the secret sympathy of the friends and favorers of the condemned person, availing itself of the good nature and weakness of others, might frequently bestow impunity where the terror of an example was necessary. On the other hand, when the sedition had proceeded from causes which had inflamed the resentments of the major party, they might often be found obstinate and inexorable, when policy demanded a conduct of forbearance and clemency. But the principal argument for reposing the power of pardoning in this case in the Chief Magistrate is this—In seasons of insurrection or rebellion, there are often critical moments, when a well timed offer of pardon to the insurgents or rebels may restore the tranquility of the commonwealth; and which, if suffered to pass unimproved, it may never be possible afterwards to recall. The dilatory process of convening the Legislature, or one of its branches, for the purpose of obtaining its sanction to the measure, would frequently be the occasion of letting slip the golden opportunity. The loss of a week, a day, an hour, may sometimes be fatal. If it should be observed that a discretionary power with a view to such contingencies might be occasionally conferred upon the President; it may be answered in the first place, that it is questionable whether, in a limited constitution, that power could be delegated by law; and in the second place, that it would generally be impolitic before-hand to take any step which might hold out the prospect of impunity. A proceeding of this kind, out of the usual course, would be likely to be construed into an argument of timidity or of weakness, and would have a tendency to embolden guilt.

PUBLIUS.

THE FEDERALIST NO. 75
MARCH 26, 1788

Hamilton reveals the difficulty of classifying the treaty-making power as either an executive or a legislative power. He suggests that the treaty-making power is neither executive nor legislative in character, but federative, and that, moreover, does not preclude the primacy of executive responsibility in exercising that function. Though the treaty-

making function is not peculiarly an executive function, the Constitution wisely places it in the class of executive authorities, for the executive is the most fit agent in the management of foreign relations. Surely executive energy would not be impaired by legislative participation in the executive power of making treaties, since the Senate restrains only by virtue of concurring or not.

Hamilton makes it perfectly clear that the only reason the Senate participates in treaty making is to provide a greater prospect for security, but it has nothing to do with the actual exercise of negotiations. The Senate's role in the formation of treaties is limited to advice and consent, and the executive may determine how much and what kind of advice it wishes to accept. The treaty-making power is clearly presidential despite the Senate's power to ratify treaties.

Where Hamilton discusses the participation of the Senate in treaty making, he appears as much more a spokesman of limited government than he does later on in "Pacificus I" where he defends the president's exclusive authority to issue a neutrality proclamation. Hamilton defends the president's power to issue such a proclamation by pointing out that the Senate's participation in treaty making is simply a qualification of the general grant of executive power to the president, that the Senate cannot claim an equal share in the exercise of that power, and that, therefore, the president has the exclusive right to determine the nature of the obligations treaties impose upon the government, the Senate's power of advice and consent notwithstanding. The president exercises the treaty-making power even though the Senate is given a check on that power, for the Constitution intended to vest general executive power in the president alone.

New York, March 26, 1788

To the People of the State of New-York.

THE president is to have power "by and with the advice and consent of the senate, to make treaties, provided two-thirds of the senators present concur." Though this provision has been assailed on different grounds, with no small degree of vehemence, I scruple not to declare my firm persuasion, that it is one of the best digested and most unexceptionable parts of the plan. One ground of objection is, the trite topic of the intermixture of powers; some contending that the president ought alone to possess the power of making treaties; and others, that it ought to have been exclusively deposited in the senate. Another source of objection is derived from the small number of persons by whom a treaty may be made: Of those who espouse this objection, a part are of opinion that the house of representatives ought to have been associated in the business, while another part seem to think that nothing more was necessary than to have substituted two-thirds of *all* the members of the senate to two-thirds of the members *present*. As I flatter myself the observations made in a preceding number, upon this part of the plan, must have sufficed to place it to a discerning eye in a very favourable light, I shall here content myself with offering only some supplementary remarks, principally with a view to the objections which have been just stated.

With regard to the intermixture of powers, I shall rely upon the explanations already given, in other places of the true sense of the rule, upon which that objection is founded; and shall take it for granted, as an inference from them, that the union of the executive with the senate, in the article of treaties, is no infringement of that rule. I venture to add that the particular nature of the power of making treaties indicates a peculiar propriety in that union. Though several writers on the subject of government place that power in the class of executive authorities, yet this is evidently an arbitrary disposition: For if we attend carefully to its operation, it will be found to partake more of the legislative than of the executive character, though it does not seem strictly to fall within the definition of either of them. The essence of the legislative authority is to enact laws, or in other words to prescribe rules for the regulation of the society, while the execution of the laws and the employment of the common strength, either for this purpose or for the common defence, seem to comprise all the functions of the executive magistrate. The power of making treaties is plainly neither the one nor the other. It relates neither to the execution of the subsisting laws, nor to the enaction of new ones, and still less to an exertion of the common strength. Its objects are CONTRACTS with foreign nations, which have the force of law, but derive it from the obligations of good faith. They are not rules prescribed by the sovereign to the subject, but agreements between sovereign and sovereign. The power in question seems therefore to form a distinct department, and to belong properly neither to the legislative nor to the executive. The qualities elsewhere detailed, as indispensable in the management of foreign negotiations, point out the executive as the most fit agent in those transactions; while the vast importance of the trust, and the operation of treaties as laws, plead strongly for the participation of the whole or a part of the legislative body in the office of making them.

However proper or safe it may in governments where the executive magistrate is an hereditary monarch, to commit to him the entire power of making treaties, it would be utterly unsafe and improper to

167

entrust that power to an elective magistrate for four years duration. It has been remarked upon another occasion, and the remark is unquestionably just, that an hereditary monarch, though often the oppressor of his people, has personally too much at stake in the government to be in any material danger of being corrupted by foreign powers. But a man raised from the station of a private citizen to the rank of chief magistrate, possessed of but a moderate or slender fortune, and looking forward to a period not very remote, when he may probably be obliged to return to the station from which he was taken, might sometimes be under temptations to sacrifice his duty to his interest, which it would require superlative virtue to withstand. An avaricious man might be tempted to betray the interests of the state to the acquisition of wealth. An ambitious man might make his own aggrandizement, by the aid of a foreign power, the price of his treachery to his constituents. The history of human conduct does not warrant that exalted opinion of human virtue which would make it wise in a nation to commit interests of so delicate and momentous a kind as those which concern its intercourse with the rest of the world to the sole disposal of a magistrate, created and circumstanced, as would be a president of the United States.

To have entrusted the power of making treaties to the senate alone, would have been to relinquish the benefits of the constitutional agency of the president, in the conduct of foreign negotiations. It is true, that the senate would in that case have the option of employing him in this capacity; but they would also have the option of letting it alone; and pique or cabal might induce the latter rather than the former. Besides this, the ministerial servant of the senate could not be expected to enjoy the confidence and respect of foreign powers in the same degree with the constitutional representative of the nation; and of course would not be able to act with an equal degree of weight or efficacy. While the union would from this cause lose a considerable advantage in the management of its external concerns, the people would lose the additional security, which would result from the co-operation of the executive. Though it would be imprudent to confide in him solely so important a trust; yet it cannot be doubted, that his participation in it would materially add to the safety of the society. It must indeed be clear to a demonstration, that the joint possession of the power in question by the president and senate would afford a greater prospect of security, than the separate possession of it by either of them. And whoever has maturely weighed the circumstances, which must concur in the appointment of a president will be satisfied, that the office will always bid fair to be filled by men of such characters as to render their concurrence in the formation of treaties peculiarly desirable, as well on the score of wisdom as on that of integrity.

The remarks made in a former number, which has been alluded to in an other part of this paper, will apply with conclusive force against the admission of the house of representatives to a share in the formation of treaties. The fluctuating and taking its future increase into the account, the multitudinous composition of that body, forbid us to expect in it those qualities which are essential to the proper execution of such a trust. Accurate and comprehensive knowledge of foreign politics; a steady and systematic adherence to the same views; a nice and uniform sensibility to national character, decision, *secrecy* and dispatch; are incompatible with the genius of a body so variable and so numerous. The very complication of the business by introducing a necessity of the concurrence of so many different bodies, would of itself afford a solid objection. The greater frequency of the calls upon the house of representatives, and the greater length of time which it would often be necessary to keep them together when convened, to obtain their sanction in the progressive stages of a treaty, would be source of so great inconvenience and expence, as alone ought to condemn the project.

The only objection which remains to be canvassed is that which would substitute the proportion of two thirds of all the members composing the senatorial body to that of two thirds of the members *present*. It has been shewn under the second head of our inquiries that all provisions which require more than the majority of any body to its resolutions have a direct tendency to embarrass the operations of the government and an indirect one to subject the sense of the majority to that of the minority. This consideration seems sufficient to determine our opinion, that the convention have gone as far in the endeavour to secure the advantage of numbers in the formation of treaties as could have been reconciled either with the activity of the public councils or with a reasonable regard to the major sense of the community. If two thirds of the whole number of members had been required, it would in many cases from the non attendance of a part amount in practice to a necessity of unanimity. And the history of every political establishment in which this principle has prevailed is a history of impotence, perplexity and disorder. Proofs of this position might be adduced from the examples of the Roman tribuneship, the Polish diet and the states general of the Netherlands; did not an example at home render foreign precedents unnecessary.

To require a fixed proportion of the whole body would not in all probability contribute to the advantages of a numerous agency, better than merely to require a proportion of the attending members. The

169

former by making a determinate number at all times requisite to a resolution diminishes the motives to punctual attendance. The latter by making the capacity of the body to depend on a *proportion* which may be varied by the absence or presence of a single member, has the contrary effect. And as, by promoting punctuality, it tends to keep the body complete, there is great likelihood that its resolutions would generally be dictated by as great a number in this case as in the other; while there would be much fewer occasions of delay. It ought not to be forgotten that under the existing confederation two members *may* and usually *do* represent a state; whence it happens that Congress, who now are solely invested with *all the powers* of the union, rarely consists of a greater number of persons than would compose the intended senate. If we add to this, that as the members vote by states, and that where there is only a single member present from a state, his vote is lost, it will justify a supposition that the active voices in the senate, where the members are to vote individually, would rarely fall short in number of the active voices in the existing Congress. When in addition to these considerations we take into view the co-operation of the president, we shall not hesitate to infer that the people of America would have greater security against an improper use of the power of making treaties, under the new constitution, than they now enjoy under the confederation. And when we proceed still one step further, and look forward to the probable augmentation of the senate, by the erection of new states, we shall not only perceive ample ground of confidence in the sufficiency of the numbers, to whose agency that power will be entrusted; but we shall probably be led to conclude that a body more numerous than the senate would be likely to become, would be very little fit for the proper discharge of the trust.

PUBLIUS.

THE FEDERALIST NO. 76
APRIL 1, 1788

New York, April 1, 1788

To the People of the State of New-York.

THE President is "to *nominate* and by and with the advice and consent of the Senate to appoint Ambassadors, other public Ministers and Consuls, Judges of the Supreme Court, and all other officers of the United States, whose appointments are not otherwise provided for in the Constitution. But the Congress may by law vest the appointment of such inferior officers as they think proper in the President alone, or in the Courts of law, or in the heads of departments. The President shall have power to fill up *all vacancies* which may happen *during the recess of the Senate,* by granting commissions which shall *expire* at the end of their next session."

It has been observed in a former paper, "that the true test of a good government is its aptitude and tendency to produce a good administration." If the justness of this observation be admitted, the mode of appointing the officers of the United States contained in the foregoing clauses, must when examined be allowed to be entitled to particular commendation. It is not easy to conceive a plan better calculated than this, to produce a judicious choice of men for filling the offices of the Union; and it will not need proof, that on this point must essentially depend the character of its administration.

It will be agreed on all hands, that the power of appointment in ordinary cases ought to be modified in one of three ways. It ought either to be vested in a single man—or in a *select* assembly of a moderate number—or in a single man with the concurrence of such an assembly. The exercise of it by the people at large, will be readily admitted to be impracticable; as, waving every other consideration it would leave them little time to do any thing else. When therefore mention is made in the subsequent reasonings of an assembly or body of men, what is said must be understood to relate to a select body or assembly of the description already given. The people collectively from their number and from their dispersed situation cannot be regulated in their movements by that systematic spirit of cabal and intrigue, which will be urged as the chief objections to reposing the power in question in a body of men.

Those who have themselves reflected upon the subject, or who have attended to the observations made in other parts of these papers, in relation to the appointment of the President, will I presume agree to the position that there would always be great probability of having the place supplied by a man of abilities, at least respectable. Premising this, I proceed to lay it down as a rule, that one man of discernment is better fitted to analise and estimate the peculiar qualities adapted to particular offices, than a body of men of equal, or perhaps even of superior discernment.

The sole and undivided responsibility of one man will naturally beget a livelier sense of duty and a more exact regard to reputation. He will on this account feel himself under stronger obligations, and more interested to investigate with care the qualities requisite to the stations to be filled, and to prefer with impartiality the persons who

171

may have the fairest pretentions to them. He will have *fewer* personal attachments to gratify than a body of men, who may each be supposed to have an equal number, and will be so much the less liable to be misled by the sentiments of friendship and of affection. A single well directed man by a single understanding, cannot be distracted and warped by that diversity of views, feelings and interests, which frequently distract and warp the resolutions of a collective body. There is nothing so apt to agitate the passions of mankind as personal considerations, whether they relate to ourselves or to others, who are to be the objects of our choice or preference. Hence, in every exercise of the power of appointing to offices by an assembly of men, we must expect to see a full display of all the private and party likings and dislikes, partialities and antipathies, attachments and animosities, which are felt by those who compose the assembly. The choice which may at any time happen to be made under such circumstances will of course be the result either of a victory gained by one party over the other, or of a compromise between the parties. In either case, the intrinsic merit of the candidate will be too often out of sight. In the first, the qualifications best adapted to uniting the suffrages of the party will be more considered than those which fit the person for the station. In the last the coalition will commonly turn upon some interested equivalent—"Give us the man we wish for this office, and you shall have the one you wish for that." This will be the usual condition of the bargain. And it will rarely happen that the advancement of the public service will be the primary object either of party victories or of party negociations.

The truth of the principles here advanced seems to have been felt by the most intelligent of those who have found fault with the provision made in this respect by the Convention. They contend that the President ought solely to have been authorized to make the appointments under the Fœderal Government. But it is easy to shew that every advantage to be expected from such an arrangement would in substance be derived from the power of *nomination*, which is proposed to be conferred upon him; while several disadvantages which might attend the absolute power of appointment in the hands of that officer, would be avoided. In the act of nomination his judgment alone would be exercised; and as it would be his sole duty to point out the man, who with the approbation of the Senate should fill an office, his responsibility would be as complete as if he were to make the final appointment. There can in this view be no difference between nominating and appointing. The same motives which would influence a proper discharge of his duty in one case would exist in the other. And as no man could be appointed, but upon his previous nomination, every man who might be appointed would be in fact his choice.

But might not his nomination be overruled? I grant it might, yet this could only be to make place for another nomination by himself. The person ultimately appointed must be the object of his preference, though perhaps not in the first degree. It is also not very probable that his nomination would often be overruled. The Senate could not be tempted by the preference they might feel to another to reject the one proposed; because they could not assure themselves that the person they might wish would be brought forward by a second or by any subsequent nomination. They could not even be certain that a future nomination would present a candidate in any degree more acceptable to them: And as their dissent might cast a kind of stigma upon the individual rejected; and might have the appearance of a reflection upon the judgment of the chief magistrate; it is not likely that their sanction would often be refused, where there were not special and strong reasons for the refusal.

To what purpose then require the co-operation of the Senate? I answer that the necessity of their concurrence would have a powerful, though in general a silent operation. It would be an excellent check upon a spirit of favoritism in the President, and would tend greatly to preventing the appointment of unfit characters from State prejudice, from family connection, from personal attachment, or from a view to popularity. And, in addition to this, it would be an efficacious source of stability in the administration.

It will readily be comprehended, that a man, who had himself the sole disposition of offices, would be governed much more by his private inclinations and interests, than when he was bound to submit the propriety of his choice to the discussion and determination of a different and independent body; and that body an entire branch of the Legislature. The possibility of rejection would be a strong motive to care in proposing. The danger to his own reputation, and, in the case of an elective magistrate, to his political existence, from betraying a spirit of favoritism, or an unbecoming pursuit of popularity, to the observation of a body, whose opinion would have great weight in forming that of the public, could not fail to operate as a barrier to the one and to the other. He would be both ashamed and afraid to bring forward for the most distinguished or lucrative stations, candidates who had no other merit, than that of coming from the same State to which he particularly belonged, or of being in some way or other personally allied to him, or of possessing the necessary insignificance and pliancy to render them the obsequious instruments of his pleasure.

173

To this reasoning, it has been objected, that the President by the influence of the power of nomination may secure the compliance of the Senate to his views. The supposition of universal venality in human nature is little less an error in political reasoning than the supposition of universal rectitude. The institution of delegated power implies that there is a portion of virtue and honor among mankind, which may be a reasonable foundation of confidence. And experience justifies the theory: It has been found to exist in the most corrupt periods of the most corrupt governments. The venality of the British House of Commons has been long a topic of accusation against that body, in the country to which they belong, as well as in this; and it cannot be doubted that the charge is to a considerable extent well founded. But it is as little to be doubted that there is always a large proportion of the body, which consists of independent and public spirited men, who have an influential weight in the councils of the nation. Hence it is (the present reign not excepted) that the sense of that body is often seen to controul the inclinations of the monarch, both with regard to men and to measures. Though it might therefore be allowable to suppose, that the executive might occasionally influence some individuals in the Senate; yet the supposition that he could in general purchase the integrity of the whole body would be forced and improbable. A man disposed to view human nature as it is, without either flattering its virtues or exaggerating its vices, will see sufficient ground of confidence in the probity of the Senate, to rest satisfied not only that it will be impracticable to the Executive to corrupt or seduce a majority of its members; but that the necessity of its co-operation in the business of appointments will be a considerable and salutary restraint upon the conduct of that magistrate. Nor is the integrity of the Senate the only reliance. The constitution has provided some important guards against the danger of executive influence upon the legislative body: It declares that "No Senator, or representative shall, during the time *for which he was elected*, be appointed to any civil office under the United States, which shall have been created, or the emoluments whereof shall have been encreased during such time; and no person holding any office under the United States shall be a member of either house during his continuance in office."

PUBLIUS.

THE FEDERALIST NO. 77
APRIL 2, 1788

New York, April 2, 1788

To the People of the State of New-York.

IT has been mentioned as one of the advantages to be expected from the co-operation of the senate, in the business of appointments, that it would contribute to the stability of the administration. The consent of that body would be necessary to displace as well as to appoint. A change of the chief magistrate therefore would not occasion so violent or so general a revolution in the officers of the government, as might be expected if he were the sole disposer of offices. Where a man in any station had given satisfactory evidence of his fitness for it, a new president would be restrained from attempting a change, in favour of a person more agreeable to him, by the apprehension that the discountenance of the senate might frustrate the attempt, and bring some degree of discredit upon himself. Those who can best estimate the value of a steady administration will be most disposed to prize a provision, which connects the official existence of public men with the approbation or disapprobation of that body, which from the greater permanency of its own composition, will in all probability be less subject to inconstancy, than any other member of the government.

To this union of the senate with the president, in the article of appointments, it has in some cases been objected, that it would serve to give the president an undue influence over the senate; and in others, that it would have an opposite tendency; a strong proof that neither suggestion is true.

To state the first in its proper form is to refute it. It amounts to this—The president would have an improper *influence over* the senate; because the senate would have the power of *restraining* him. This is an absurdity in terms. It cannot admit of a doubt that the intire power of appointment would enable him much more effectually to establish a dangerous empire over that body, than a mere power of nomination subject to their controul.

Let us take a view of the converse of the proposition—"The senate would influence the executive." As I have had occasion to remark in several other instances, the indistinctness of the objection forbids a precise answer. In what manner is this influence to be exerted? In relation to what objects? The power of influencing a person, in the sense in which it is here used, must imply a power of conferring a benefit upon him. How could the senate confer a benefit upon the president by the manner of employing their right of negative upon his nominations? If it be said they might sometimes gratify him by an acquiesence in a favorite choice, when public motives might dictate a different conduct; I answer that the instances in which the president could be personally interested in the result, would be too few to admit of his being materially affected by the compliances of the senate. The POWER which can *originate* the disposition of honors and emoluments, is more likely to attract than to be attracted by the POWER which can merely obstruct their course. If by influencing the president be meant *restraining* him, this is precisely what must have been intended. And it has been shewn that the restraint would be salutary, at the same time that it would not be such as to destroy a single advantage to be looked for from the uncontrouled agency of that magistrate. The right of nomination would produce all the good of that of appointment, and would in a great measure avoid its ills.

Upon a comparison of the plan for the appointment of the officers of the proposed government with that which is established by the constitution of this state a decided preference must be given to the former. In that plan the power of nomination is unequivocally vested in the executive. And as there would be a necessity for submitting each nomination to the judgment of an entire branch of the legislature, the circumstances attending an appointment, from the mode of conducting it, would naturally become matters of notoriety; and the public would be at no loss to determine what part had been performed by the different actors. The blame of a bad nomination would fall upon the president singly and absolutely. The censure of rejecting a good one would lie entirely at the door of the senate; aggravated by the consideration of their having counteracted the good intentions of the executive. If an ill appointment should be made the executive for nominating and the senate for approving would participate though in different degrees in the opprobrium and disgrace.

The reverse of all this characterises the manner of appointment in this state. The council of appointment consists of from three to five persons, of whom the governor is always one. This small body, shut up in a private apartment, impenetrable to the public eye, proceed to the execution of the trust committed to them. It is known that the governor claims the right of nomination, upon the strength of some ambiguous expressions in the constitution; but it is not known to what extent, or in what manner he exercises it; nor upon what occasions he is contradicted or opposed. The censure of a bad appointment, on account of the uncertainty of its author, and for want of a determinate object, has neither poignancy nor duration. And while an unbounded field for cabal and intrigue lies open, all idea of responsibility is lost. The most that the public can know is, that the governor claims the right of nomination: That *two* out of the considerable number of *four* men can too often be managed without much difficulty: That if some of the members of a particular council should happen to be of an uncomplying character, it is frequently not impossible to get rid of their opposition, by regulating the times of meeting in such a manner as to render their attendance inconvenient: And that, from whatever cause it may proceed, a great number of very improper appointments are from time to time made. Whether a governor of this state avails himself of the ascendant he must necessarily have, in this delicate and important part of the administration, to prefer to offices men who are best qualified for them: Or whether he prostitutes that advantage to the advancement of persons, whose chief merit is their implicit devotion to his will, and to the support of a despicable and dangerous system of personal influence, are questions which unfortunately for the community can only be the subjects of speculation and conjecture.

Every mere council of appointment, however constituted, will be a conclave, in which cabal and intrigue will have their full scope. Their number, without an unwarrantable increase of expence, cannot be large enough to preclude a facility of combination. And as each member will have his friends and connections to provide for, the desire of mutual gratification will beget a scandalous bartering of votes and bargaining for places. The private attachments of one man might easily be satisfied; but to satisfy the private attachments of a dozen, or of twenty men, would occasion a monopoly of all the principal employments of the government, in a few families, and would lead more directly to an aristocracy or an oligarchy, than any measure that could be contrived. If to avoid an accumulation of offices, there was to be a frequent change in the persons, who were to compose the council, this would involve the mischiefs of a mutable administration in their full extent. Such a council would also be more liable to executive influence than the senate, because they would be fewer in number, and would act less immediately under the public inspection. Such a council in fine as a substitute for the plan of the convention, would be productive of an increase of expence, a multiplication of the evils which spring from favouritism and intrigue in the distribution of the public honors, a decrease of stability in the administration of the government, and a diminution of the security against an undue influence of the executive. And yet such a council has been warmly contended for as an essential amendment in the proposed constitution.

I could not with propriety conclude my observations on the subject of appointments, without taking notice of a scheme, for which there has appeared some, though but a few advocates; I mean that of uniting the house of representatives in the power of making them. I shall however do little more than mention it, as I cannot imagine that it is likely to gain the countenance of any considerable part of the community. A body so fluctuating, and at the same time so numerous, can never be deemed proper for the exercise of that power. Its unfitness will appear manifest to all, when it is recollected that in half a century it may consist of three or four hundred persons. All the advantages of the stability, both of the executive and of the senate, would be defeated by this union; and infinite delays and embarrassments would be occasioned. The example of most of the states in their local constitutions, encourages us to reprobate the idea.

The only remaining powers of the executive, are comprehended in giving information to congress of the state of the union; in recommending to their consideration such measures as he shall judge expedient; in convening them, or either branch, upon extraordinary occasions; in adjourning them when they cannot themselves agree upon the time of adjournment; in receiving ambassadors and other public ministers; in faithfully executing the laws; and in commissioning all the officers of the United States.

Except some cavils about the power of convening *either* house of the legislature and that of receiving ambassadors, no objection has been made to this class of authorities; nor could they possibly admit of any. It required indeed an insatiable avidity for censure to invent exceptions to the parts which have been excepted to. In regard to the power of convening either house of the legislature, I shall barely remark, that in respect to the senate at least, we can readily discover a good reason for it. As this body has a concurrent power with the executive in the article of treaties, it might often be necessary to call it together with a view to this object, when it would be unnecessary and improper to convene the house of representatives. As to the reception of ambassadors, what I have said in a former paper will furnish a sufficient answer.

We have now compleated a survey of the structure and powers of the executive department, which, I have endeavoured to show, combines, as far as republican principles would admit, all the requisites to energy. The remaining enquiry is; does it also combine the requisites to safety in the republican sense—a due dependence on the people—a due responsibility? The answer to this question has been anticipated in the investigation of its other characteristics, and is satisfactorily deducible from these circumstances, from the election of the president once in four years by persons immediately chosen by the people for that purpose; and from his being at all times liable to impeachment, trial, dismission from office, incapacity to serve in any other; and to the forfeiture of life and estate by subsequent prosecution in the common course of law. But these precautions, great as they are, are not the only ones, which the plan of the convention has provided in favor of the public security. In the only instances in which the abuse of the executive authority was materially to be feared, the chief magistrate of the United States would by that plan be subjected to the controul of a branch of the legislative body. What more could be desired by an enlightened and reasonable people?

PUBLIUS.

THE FEDERALIST NO. 78
MAY 28, 1788

Hamilton presented the classic argument for judicial review in Federalist 78, an argument that was restated by Chief Justice John Marshall in Marbury v. Madison in 1803. His reasoning, simply stated, was that the Constitution is the fundamental law of the land and, hence, is superior to legislative law, that the courts are charged with the interpretation of the law, and that, therefore, they have the authority to invalidate legislative law when in conflict with constitutional law. The members of the Constitutional Convention never directly raised the question of the grant of such a power to the judiciary, but that did not prevent Hamilton from making the argument in the context of his defense of the proposed Constitution. He was concerned with the lack of adequate constitutional limits on legislative authority.

Hamilton thought that the Constitution could be made more stable by achieving a shift in the respective strengths of the three branches of government. The qualified negative of the executive was the major bulwark against legislative encroachment in the proposed Constitution, but it was not fully adequate to its task. To offset this inherent weakness of the executive, a more rational distribution of power between these three branches required the judiciary's function of declaring unconstitutional laws void. By the introduction of judicial review, the two-way balance between the legislative and executive was transformed into a three-way balance.

New York, May 28, 1788

To the People of the State of New-York.

WE proceed now to an examination of the judiciary department of the proposed government.

In unfolding the defects of the existing confederation, the utility and necessity of a federal judicature have been clearly pointed out. It is the less necessary to recapitulate the considerations there urged; as the propriety of the institution in the abstract is not disputed: The only questions which have been raised being relative to the manner of constituting it, and to its extent. To these points therefore our observations shall be confined.

The manner of constituting it seems to embrace these several objects— 1st. The mode of appointing the judges— 2d. The tenure by which they are to hold their places— 3d. The partition of the judiciary authority between different courts, and their relations to each other.

First. As to the mode of appointing the judges: This is the same with that of appointing the officers of the union in general, and has been so fully discussed in the two last numbers, that nothing can be said here which would not be useless repetition.

Second. As to the tenure by which the judges are to hold their places: This chiefly concerns their duration in office; the provisions for their support; and the precautions for their responsibility.

According to the plan of the convention, all the judges who may be appointed by the United States are to hold their offices *during good behaviour,* which is conformable to the most approved of the state constitutions; and among the rest, to that of this state. Its propriety having been drawn into question by the adversaries of that plan, is no light symptom of the rage for objection which disorders their imaginations and judgments. The standard of good behaviour for the continuance in office of the judicial magistracy is certainly one of the most valuable of the modern improvements in the practice of government. In a monarchy it is an excellent barrier to the despotism of the prince: In a republic it is a no less excellent barrier to the encroachments and oppressions of the representative body. And it is the best expedient which can be devised in any government, to secure a steady, upright and impartial administration of the laws.

Whoever attentively considers the different departments of

power must perceive, that in a government in which they are separated from each other, the judiciary, from the nature of its functions, will always be the least dangerous to the political rights of the constitution; because it will be least in a capacity to annoy or injure them. The executive not only dispenses the honors, but holds the sword of the community. The legislature not only commands the purse, but prescribes the rules by which the duties and rights of every citizen are to be regulated. The judiciary on the contrary has no influence over either the sword or the purse, no direction either of the strength or of the wealth of the society, and can take no active resolution whatever. It may truly be said to have neither FORCE nor WILL, but merely judgment; and must ultimately depend upon the aid of the executive arm even for the efficacy of its judgments.

This simple view of the matter suggests several important consequences. It proves incontestibly that the judiciary is beyond comparison the weakest of the three departments of power;* that it can never attack with success either of the other two; and that all possible care is requisite to enable it to defend itself against their attacks. It equally proves, that though individual oppression may now and then proceed from the courts of justice, the general liberty of the people can never be endangered from that quarter; I mean, so long as the judiciary remains truly distinct from both the legislative and executive. For I agree that "there is no liberty, if the power of judging be not separated from the legislative and executive powers." And it proves, in the last place, that as liberty can have nothing to fear from the judiciary alone, but would have every thing to fear from its union with either of the other departments; that as all the effects of such an union must ensue from a dependence of the former on the latter, notwithstanding a nominal and apparent separation; that as from the natural feebleness of the judiciary, it is in continual jeopardy of being overpowered, awed or influenced by its coordinate branches; and that as nothing can contribute so much to its firmness and independence, as permanency in office, this quality may therefore be justly regarded as an indispensable ingredient in its constitution; and in a great measure as the citadel of the public justice and the public security.

The complete independence of the courts of justice is peculiarly essential in a limited constitution. By a limited constitution I understand one which contains certain specified exceptions to the legislative authority; such for instance as that it shall pass no bills of

---

*The celebrated Montesquieu speaking of them says, "of the three powers above mentioned, the JUDICIARY is next to nothing." Spirit of Laws, vol. I, page 186.

181

attainder, no *ex post facto* laws, and the like. Limitations of this kind can be preserved in practice no other way than through the medium of the courts of justice; whose duty it must be to declare all acts contrary to the manifest tenor of the constitution void. Without this, all the reservations of particular rights or privileges would amount to nothing.

Some perplexity respecting the right of the courts to pronounce legislative acts void, because contrary to the constitution, has arisen from an imagination that the doctrine would imply a superiority of the judiciary to the legislative power. It is urged that the authority which can declare the acts of another void, must necessarily be superior to the one whose acts may be declared void. As this doctrine is of great importance in all the American constitutions, a brief discussion of the grounds on which it rests cannot be unacceptable.

There is no position which depends on clearer principles, than that every act of a delegated authority, contrary to the tenor of the commission under which it is exercised, is void. No legislative act therefore contrary to the constitution can be valid. To deny this would be to affirm that the deputy is greater than his principal; that the servant is above his master; that the representatives of the people are superior to the people themselves; that men acting by virtue of powers may do not only what their powers do not authorise, but what they forbid.

If it be said that the legislative body are themselves the constitutional judges of their own powers, and that the construction they put upon them is conclusive upon the other departments, it may be answered, that this cannot be the natural presumption, where it is not to be collected from any particular provision in the constitution. It is not otherwise to be supposed that the constitution could intend to enable the representatives of the people to substitute their *will* to that of their constituents. It is far more rational to suppose that the courts were designed to be an intermediate body between the people and the legislature, in order, among other things, to keep the latter within the limits assigned to their authority. The interpretation of the laws is the proper and peculiar province of the courts. A constitution is in fact, and must be, regarded by the judges as a fundamental law. It therefore belongs to them to ascertain its meaning as well as the meaning of any particular act proceeding from the legislative body. If there should happen to be an irreconcileable variance between the two, that which has the superior obligation and validity ought of course to be preferred; or in other words, the constitution ought to be preferred to the statute, the intention of the people to the intention of their agents.

Nor does this conclusion by any means suppose a superiority of the judicial to the legislative power. It only supposes that the power of the people is superior to both; and that where the will of the legislature declared in its statutes, stands in opposition to that of the people declared in the constitution, the judges ought to be governed by the latter, rather than the former. They ought to regulate their decisions by the fundamental laws, rather than by those which are not fundamental.

This exercise of judicial discretion in determining between two contradictory laws, is exemplified in a familiar instance. It not uncommonly happens, that there are two statutes existing at one time, clashing in whole or in part with each other, and neither of them containing any repealing clause or expression. In such a case, it is the province of the courts to liquidate and fix their meaning and operation: So far as they can by any fair construction be reconciled to each other; reason and law conspire to dictate that this should be done: Where this is impracticable, it becomes a matter of necessity to give effect to one, in exclusion of the other. The rule which has obtained in the courts for determining their relative validity is that the last in order of time shall be preferred to the first. But this is mere rule of construction, not derived from any positive law, but from the nature and reason of the thing. It is a rule not enjoined upon the courts by legislative provision, but adopted by themselves, as consonant to truth and propriety, for the direction of their conduct as interpreters of the law. They thought it reasonable, that between the interfering acts of an *equal* authority, that which was the last indication of its will, should have the preference.

But in regard to the interfering acts of a superior and subordinate authority, of an original and derivative power, the nature and reason of the thing indicate the converse of that rule as proper to be followed. They teach us that the prior act of a superior ought to be prefered to the subsequent act of an inferior and subordinate authority; and that, accordingly, whenever a particular statute contravenes the constitution, it will be the duty of the judicial tribunals to adhere to the latter, and disregard the former.

It can be of no weight to say, that the courts on the pretence of a repugnancy, may substitute their own pleasure to the constitutional intentions of the legislature. This might as well happen in the case of two contradictory statutes; or it might as well happen in every adjudication upon any single statute. The courts must declare the sense of the law; and if they should be disposed to exercise *will* instead of *judgment*, the consequence would equally be the substitution of their pleasure to that of the legislative body. The observation, if it proved

183

any thing, would prove that there ought to be no judges distinct from that body.

If then the courts of justice are to be considered as the bulwarks of a limited constitution against legislative encroachments, this consideration will afford a strong argument for the permanent tenure of judicial offices, since nothing will contribute so much as this to that independent spirit in the judges, which must be essential to the faithful performance of so arduous a duty.

This independence of the judges is equally requisite to guard the constitution and the rights of individuals from the effects of those ill humours which the arts of designing men, or the influence of particular conjunctures, sometimes disseminate among the people themselves, and which, though they speedily give place to better information and more deliberate reflection, have a tendency in the mean time to occasion dangerous innovations in the government, and serious oppressions of the minor party in the community. Though I trust the friends of the proposed constitution will never concur with its enemies* in questioning that fundamental principle of republican government, which admits the right of the people to alter or abolish the established constitution whenever they find it inconsistent with their happiness; yet it is not to be inferred from this principle, that the representatives of the people, whenever a momentary inclination happens to lay hold of a majority of their constituents incompatible with the provisions in the existing constitution, would on that account be justifiable in a violation of those provisions; or that the courts would be under a greater obligation to connive at infractions in this shape, than when they had proceeded wholly from the cabals of the representative body. Until the people have by some solemn and authoritative act annulled or changed the established form, it is binding upon themselves collectively, as well as individually; and no presumption, or even knowledge of their sentiments, can warrant their representatives in a departure from it, prior to such an act. But it is easy to see that it would require an uncommon portion of fortitude in the judges to do their duty as faithful guardians of the constitution, where legislative invasions of it had been instigated by the major voice of the community.

But it is not with a view to infractions of the constitution only that the independence of the judges may be an essential safeguard against the effects of occasional ill humours in the society. These sometimes extend no farther than to the injury of the private rights of particular classes of citizens, by unjust and partial laws. Here also the firmness

*Vide Protest of the minority of the convention of Pennsylvania, Martin's speech, &c.

of the judicial magistracy is of vast importance in mitigating the severity, and confining the operation of such laws. It not only serves to moderate the immediate mischiefs of those which may have been passed, but it operates as a check upon the legislative body in passing them; who, perceiving that obstacles to the success of an iniquitous intention are to be expected from the scruples of the courts, are in a manner compelled by the very motives of the injustice they meditate, to qualify their attempts. This is a circumstance calculated to have more influence upon the character of our governments, than but few may be aware of. The benefits of the integrity and moderation of the judiciary have already been felt in more states than one; and though they may have displeased those whose sinister expectations they may have disappointed, they must have commanded the esteem and applause of all the virtuous and disinterested. Considerate men of every description ought to prize whatever will tend to beget or fortify that temper in the courts; as no man can be sure that he may not be to-morrow the victim of a spirit of injustice, by which he may be a gainer to-day. And every man must now feel that the inevitable tendency of such a spirit is to sap the foundations of public and private confidence, and to introduce in its stead, universal distrust and distress.

That inflexible and uniform adherence to the rights of the constitution and of individuals, which we perceive to be indispensable in the courts of justice, can certainly not be expected from judges who hold their offices by a temporary commission. Periodical appointments, however regulated, or by whomsoever made, would in some way or other be fatal to their necessary independence. If the power of making them was committed either to the executive or legislature, there would be danger of an improper complaisance to the branch which possessed it; if to both, there would be an unwillingness to hazard the displeasure of either; if to the people, or to persons chosen by them for the special purpose, there would be too great a disposition to consult popularity, to justify a reliance that nothing would be consulted but the constitution and the laws.

There is yet a further and a weighty reason for the permanency of the judicial offices; which is deducible from the nature of the qualifications they require. It has been frequently remarked with great propriety, that a voluminous code of laws is one of the inconveniences necessarily connected with the advantages of a free government. To avoid an arbitrary discretion in the courts, it is indispensable that they should be bound down by strict rules and precedents, which serve to define and point out their duty in every particular case that comes before them; and it will readily be con-

185

ceived from the variety of controversies which grow out of the folly and wickedness of mankind, that the records of those precedents must unavoidably swell to a very considerable bulk, and must demand long and laborious study to acquire a competent knowledge of them. Hence it is that there can be but few men in the society, who will have sufficient skill in the laws to qualify them for the stations of judges. And making the proper deductions for the ordinary depravity of human nature, the number must be still smaller of those who unite the requisite integrity with the requisite knowledge. These considerations apprise us, that the government can have no great option between fit characters; and that a temporary duration in office, which would naturally discourage such characters from quitting a lucrative line of practice to accept a seat on the bench, would have a tendency to throw the administration of justice into hands less able, and less well qualified to conduct it with utility and dignity. In the present circumstances of this country, and in those in which it is likely to be for a long time to come, the disadvantages on this score would be greater than they may at first sight appear; but it must be confessed that they are far inferior to those which present themselves under the other aspects of the subject.

Upon the whole there can be no room to doubt that the convention acted wisely in copying from the models of those constitutions which have established *good behaviour* as the tenure of their judicial offices in point of duration; and that so far from being blameable on this account, their plan would have been inexcuseably defective if it had wanted this important feature of good government. The experience of Great Britain affords an illustrious comment on the excellence of the institution.

PUBLIUS.

THE FEDERALIST NO. 84
MAY 28, 1788

Jefferson wrote to Francis Hopkinson in March 1789 that what he "disapproved from the first moment [in the new Constitution] was the want of a bill of rights to guard liberty against the legislative as well as the executive branches of the government, that is to say to secure freedom in religion, freedom of the press, freedom from monopolies, freedom from unlawful imprisonment, freedom from a permanent military, and a trial by jury in all cases determinable by the laws of the land." Hamilton was concerned with securing the greatest amount of individual liberty that the constitution of a society could establish. He believed that the best way to establish liberty for the people was through the right kind of formal constitutional arrangements—separation of powers and checks and balances, and a government equipped with the power to govern—and not through absolute prohibitions, that is, through bills of rights.

New York, May 28, 1788

To the People of the State of New-York.

IN the course of the foregoing review of the constitution I have taken notice of, and endeavoured to answer, most of the objections which have appeared against it. There however remain a few which either did not fall naturally under any particular head, or were forgotten in their proper places. These shall now be discussed; but as the subject has been drawn into great length, I shall so far consult brevity as to comprise all my observations on these miscellaneous points in a single paper.

The most considerable of these remaining objections is, that the plan of the convention contains no bill of rights. Among other answers given to this, it has been upon different occasions remarked, that the constitutions of several of the states are in a similar predicament. I add, that New-York is of this number. And yet the opposers of the new system in this state, who profess an unlimited admiration for its constitution, are among the most intemperate partizans of a bill of rights. To justify their zeal in this matter, they alledge two things; one is, that though the constitution of New-York has no bill of rights prefixed to it, yet it contains in the body of it various provisions in favour of particular privileges and rights, which in substance amount to the same thing; the other is, that the constitution adopts in their full extent the common and statute law of Great-Britain, by which many other rights not expressed in it are equally secured.

To the first I answer, that the constitution proposed by the convention contains, as well as the constitution of this state, a number of such provisions.

Independent of those, which relate to the structure of the government, we find the following: Article I. section 3. clause 7. "Judgment in cases of impeachment shall not extend further than to removal from office, and disqualification to hold and enjoy any office

187

of honour, trust or profit under the United States; but the party convicted shall nevertheless be liable and subject to indictment, trial, judgment and punishment, according to law." Section 9. of the same article, clause 2. "The privilege of the writ of *habeas corpus* shall not be suspended, unless when in cases of rebellion or invasion the public safety may require it." Clause 3. "No bill of attainder or *ex post facto* law shall be passed." Clause 7. "No title of nobility shall be granted by the United States: And no person holding any office of profit or trust under them, shall, without the consent of congress, accept of any present, emolument, office or title, of any kind whatever, from any king, prince or foreign state." Article III. section 2. clause 3. "The trial of all crimes, except in cases of impeachment, shall be by jury; and such trial shall be held in the state where the said crimes shall have been committed; but when not committed within any state, the trial shall be at such place or places as the congress may by law have directed." Section 3, of the same article, "Treason against the United States shall consist only in levying war against them, or in adhering to their enemies, giving them aid and comfort. No person shall be convicted of treason unless on the testimony of two witness to the same overt act, or on confession in open court." And clause 3, of the same section. "The congress shall have power to declare the punishment of treason, but no attainder of treason shall work corruption of blood, or forfeiture, except during the life of the person attainted."

It may well be a question whether these are not upon the whole, of equal importance with any which are to be found in the constitution of this state. The establishment of the writ of *habeas corpus,* the prohibition of *ex post facto* laws, and of TITLES OF NOBILITY, *to which we have no corresponding provisions in our constitution,* are perhaps greater securities to liberty and republicanism than any it contains. The creation of crimes after the commission of the fact, or in other words, the subjecting of men to punishment for things which, when they were done, were breaches of no law, and the practice of arbitrary imprisonments have been in all ages the favourite and most formidable instruments of tyranny. The observations of the judicious Blackstone* in reference to the latter, are well worthy of recital. "To bereave a man of life (says he) or by violence to confiscate his estate, without accusation or trial, would be so gross and notorious an act of despotism, as must at once convey the alarm of tyranny throughout the whole nation; but confinement of the person by secretly hurrying to goal, where his sufferings are unknown or forgotten, is a less public, a less striking, and therefore *a more dangerous engine* of arbi-

*Vide Blackstone's Commentaries, vol. I, page 136.

trary government." And as a remedy for this fatal evil, he is every where peculiarly emphatical in his encomiums on the *habeas corpus* act, which in one place he calls "the BULWARK of the British constitution."

Nothing need be said to illustrate the importance of the prohibition of titles of nobility. This may truly be denominated the corner stone of republican government; for so long as they are excluded, there can never be serious danger that the government will be any other than that of the people.

To the second, that is, to the pretended establishment of the common and statute law by the constitution, I answer, that they are expressly made subject "to such alterations and provisions as the legislature shall from time to time make concerning the same." They are therefore at any moment liable to repeal by the ordinary legislative power, and of course have no constitutional sanction. The only use of the declaration was to recognize the ancient law, and to remove doubts which might have been occasioned by the revolution. This consequently can be considered as no part of a declaration of rights, which under our constitutions must be intended as limitations of the power of the government itself.

It has been several times truly remarked, that bills of rights are in their origin, stipulations between kings and their subjects, abridgments of prerogative in favor of privilege, reservations of rights not surrendered to the prince. Such was MAGNA CHARTA, obtained by the Barons, sword in hand, from king John. Such were the subsequent confirmations of that charter by subsequent princes. Such was the *petition of right* assented to by Charles the First, in the beginning of his reign. Such also was the declaration of right presented by the lords and commons to the prince of Orange in 1688, and afterwards thrown into the form of an act of parliament, called the bill of rights. It is evident, therefore, that according to their primitive signification, they have no application to constitutions professedly founded upon the power of the people, and executed by their immediate representatives and servants. Here, in strictness, the people surrender nothing, and as they retain every thing, they have no need of particular reservations. "WE THE PEOPLE of the United States, to secure the blessings of liberty to ourselves and our posterity, do *ordain* and *establish* this constitution for the United States of America." Here is a better recognition of popular rights than volumes of those aphorisms which make the principal figure in several of our state bills of rights, and which would sound much better in a treatise of ethics than in a constitution of government.

But a minute detail of particular rights is certainly far less applicable to a constitution like that under consideration, which is merely intended to regulate the general political interests of the nation, than to a constitution which has the regulation of every species of personal and private concerns. If therefore the loud clamours against the plan of the convention on this score, are well founded, no epithets of reprobation will be too strong for the constitution of this state. But the truth is, that both of them contain all, which in relation to their objects, is reasonably to be desired.

I go further, and affirm that bills of rights, in the sense and in the extent in which they are contended for, are not only unnecessary in the proposed constitution, but would even be dangerous. They would contain various exceptions to powers which are not granted; and on this very account, would afford a colourable pretext to claim more than were granted. For why declare that things shall not be done which there is no power to do? Why for instance, should it be said, that the liberty of the press shall not be restrained, when no power is given by which restrictions may be imposed? I will not contend that such a provision would confer a regulating power; but it is evident that it would furnish, to men disposed to usurp, a plausible pretence for claiming that power. They might urge with a semblance of reason, that the constitution ought not to be charged with the absurdity of providing against the abuse of an authority, which was not given, and that the provision against restraining the liberty of the press afforded a clear implication, that a power to prescribe proper regulations concerning it, was intended to be vested in the national government. This may serve as a specimen of the numerous handles which would be given to the doctrine of constructive powers, by the indulgence of an injudicious zeal for bills of rights.

On the subject of the liberty of the press, as much has been said, I cannot forbear adding a remark or two: In the first place, I observe that there is not a syllable concerning it in the constitution of this state, and in the next, I contend that whatever has been said about it in that of any other state, amounts to nothing. What signifies a declaration that "the liberty of the press shall be inviolably preserved?" What is the liberty of the press? Who can give it any definition which would not leave the utmost latitude for evasion? I hold it to be impracticable; and from this, I infer, that its security, whatever fine declarations may be inserted in any constitution respecting it, must altogether depend on public opinion, and on the general spirit of the people and of the government.* And here, after all, as intimated

---

*To show that there is a power in the constitution by which the liberty of the press may be affected, recourse has been had to the power of taxation. It is said that duties

upon another occasion, must we seek for the only solid basis of all our rights.

There remains but one other view of this matter to conclude the point. The truth is, after all the declamation we have heard, that the constitution is itself in every rational sense, and to every useful purpose, A BILL OF RIGHTS. The several bills of rights, in Great-Britain, form its constitution, and conversely the constitution of each state is its bill of rights. And the proposed constitution, if adopted, will be the bill of rights of the union. Is it one object of a bill of rights to declare and specify the political privileges of the citizens in the structure and administration of the government? This is done in the most ample and precise manner in the plan of the convention, comprehending various precautions for the public security, which are not to be found in any of the state constitutions. Is another object of a bill of rights to define certain immunities and modes of proceeding, which are relative to personal and private concerns? This we have seen has also been attended to, in a variety of cases, in the same plan. Adverting therefore to the substantial meaning of a bill of rights, it as absurd to allege that it is not to be found in the work of the convention. It may be said that it does not go far enough, though it will not be easy to make this appear; but it can with no propriety be contended that there is no such thing. It certainly must be immaterial what mode is observed as to the order of declaring the rights of the citizens, if they are to be found in any part of the instrument which establishes the government. And hence it must be apparent that much of what has been said on this subject rests merely on verbal and nominal distinctions, which are entirely foreign from the substance of the thing.

Another objection, which has been made, and which from the frequency of its repetition it is to be presumed is relied on, is of this

---

may be laid upon publications so high as to amount to a prohibition. I know not by what logic it could be maintained that the declarations in the state constitutions, in favour of the freedom of the press, would be a constitutional impediment to the imposition of duties upon publications by the state legislatures. It cannot certainly be pretended that any degree of duties, however low, would be an abrigement of the liberty of the press. We know that newspapers are taxed in Great-Britain, and yet it is notorious that the press no where enjoys greater liberty than in that country. And if duties of any kind may be laid without a violation of that liberty, it is evident that the extent must depend on legislative discretion, regulated by public opinion; so that after all, general declarations respecting the liberty of the press will give it no greater security than it will have without them. The same invasions of it may be effected under the state constitutions which contain those declarations through the means of taxation, as under the proposed constitution which has nothing of the kind. It would be quite as significant to declare that government ought to be free, that taxes ought not to be excessive, &c., as that the liberty of the press ought not to be restrained.

nature: It is improper (say the objectors) to confer such large powers, as are proposed, upon the national government; because the seat of that government must of necessity be too remote from many of the states to admit of a proper knowledge on the part of the constituent, of the conduct of the representative body. This argument, if it proves any thing, proves that there ought to be no general government whatever. For the powers which it seems to be agreed on all hands, ought to be vested in the union, cannot be safely intrusted to a body which is not under every requisite controul. But there are satisfactory reasons to shew that the objection is in reality not well founded. There is in most of the arguments which relate to distance a palpable illusion of the imagination. What are the sources of information by which the people in Montgomery county must regulate their judgment of the conduct of their representatives in the state legislature? Of personal observation they can have no benefit. This is confined to the citizens on the spot. They must therefore depend on the information of intelligent men, in whom they confide—and how must these men obtain their information? Evidently from the complection of public measures, from the public prints, from correspondences with their representatives, and with other persons who reside at the place of their deliberation. This does not apply to Montgomery county only, but to all the counties, at any considerable distance from the seat of government.

It is equally evident that the same sources of information would be open to the people, in relation to the conduct of their representatives in the general government; and the impediments to a prompt communication which distance may be supposed to create, will be overballanced by the effects of the vigilance of the state governments. The executive and legislative bodies of each state will be so many centinels over the persons employed in every department of the national administration; and as it will be in their power to adopt and pursue a regular and effectual system of intelligence, they can never be at a loss to know the behaviour of those who represent their constituents in the national councils, and can readily communicate the same knowledge to the people. Their disposition to apprise the community of whatever may prejudice its interests from another quarter, may be relied upon, if it were only from the rivalship of power. And we may conclude with the fullest assurance, that the people, through that channel, will be better informed of the conduct of their national representatives, than they can be by any means they now possess of that of their state representatives.

It ought also to be remembered, that the citizens who inhabit the country at and near the seat of government, will in all questions that affect the general liberty and prosperity, have the same interest with those who are at a distance; and that they will stand ready to sound the alarm when necessary, and to point out the actors in any pernicious project. The public papers will be expeditious messengers of intelligence to the most remote inhabitants of the union.

Among the many extraordinary objections which have appeared against the proposed constitution, the most extraordinary and the least colourable one, is derived from the want of some provision respecting the debts due *to* the United States. This has been represented as a tacit relinquishment of those debts, and as a wicked contrivance to screen public defaulters. The newspapers have teemed with the most inflammatory railings on this head; and yet there is nothing clearer than that the suggestion is entirely void of foundation, and is the offspring of extreme ignorance or extreme dishonesty. In addition to the remarks I have made upon the subject in another place, I shall only observe, that as it is a plain dictate of common sense, so it is also an established doctrine of political law, that *"States neither lose any of their rights, nor are discharged from any of their obligations by a change in the form of their civil government."**

The last objection of any consequence which I at present recollect, turns upon the article of expence. If it were even true that the adoption of the proposed government would occasion a considerable increase of expence, it would be an objection that ought to have no weight against the plan. The great bulk of the citizens of America, are with reason convinced that union is the basis of their political happiness. Men of sense of all parties now, with few exceptions, agree that it cannot be preserved under the present system, nor without radical alterations; that new and extensive powers ought to be granted to the national head, and that these require a different organization of the federal government, a single body being an unsafe depository of such ample authorities. In conceding all this, the question of expence must be given up, for it is impossible, with any degree of safety, to narrow the foundation upon which the system is to stand. The two branches of the legislature are in the first instance, to consist of only sixty-five persons, which is the same number of which congress, under the existing confederation, may be composed. It is true that this number is intended to be increased; but this is to keep pace with the increase of the population and resources of the country. It is evident, that a less number would, even in the first instance, have been unsafe; and that a continuance of the present number

*Vide Rutherford's Institutes, vol. 2, book II. chap. x. sec. xiv, and xv. Vide also Grotius, book II, chap. ix, sect. viii, and ix.

would, in a more advanced stage of population, be a very inadequate representation of the people.

Whence is the dreaded augmentation of expence to spring? One source pointed out, is the multiplication of offices under the new government. Let us examine this a little.

It is evident that the principal departments of the administration under the present government, are the same which will be required under the new. There are now a secretary at war, a secretary for foreign affairs, a secretary for domestic affairs, a board of treasury consisting of three persons, a treasurer, assistants, clerks, &c. These offices are indispensable under any system, and will suffice under the new as well as under the old. As to ambassadors and other ministers and agents in foreign countries, the proposed constitution can make no other difference, than to render their characters, where they reside, more respectable, and their services more useful. As to persons to be employed in the collection of the revenues, it is unquestionably true that these will form a very considerable addition to the number of federal officers; but it will not follow, that this will occasion an increase of public expence. It will be in most cases nothing more than an exchange of state officers for national officers. In the collection of all duties, for instance, the persons employed will be wholly of the latter description. The states individually will stand in no need of any for this purpose. What difference can it make in point of expence, to pay officers of the customs appointed by the state, or those appointed by the United States? There is no good reason to suppose, that either the number or the salaries of the latter, will be greater than those of the former.

Where then are we to seek for those additional articles of expence which are to swell the account to the enormous size that has been represented to us? The chief item which occurs to me, respects the support of the judges of the United States. I do not add the president, because there is now a president of congress, whose expences may not be far, if any thing, short of those which will be incurred on account of the president of the United States. The support of the judges will clearly be an extra expence, but to what extent will depend on the particular plan which may be adopted in practice in regard to this matter. But it can upon no reasonable plan amount to a sum which will be an object of material consequence.

Let us now see what there is to counterballance any extra expences that may attend the establishment of the proposed government. The first thing that presents itself is, that a great part of the business, which now keeps congress sitting through the year, will be transacted by the president. Even the management of foreign negociations will naturally devolve upon him according to general principles concerted with the senate, and subject to their final concurrence. Hence it is evident, that a portion of the year will suffice for the session of both the senate and the house of representatives: We may suppose about a fourth for the latter, and a third or perhaps a half for the former. The extra business of treaties and appointments may give this extra occupation to the senate. From this circumstance we may infer, that until the house of representatives shall be increased greatly beyond its present number, there will be a considerable saving of expence from the difference between the constant session of the present, and the temporary session of the future congress.

But there is another circumstance, of great importance in the view of the economy. The business of the United States has hitherto occupied the state legislatures as well as congress. The latter has made requisitions which the former have had to provide for. Hence it has happened that the sessions of the state legislatures have been protracted greatly beyond what was necessary for the execution of the mere local business of the states. More than half their time has been frequently employed in matters which related to the United States. Now the members who compose the legislatures of the several states amount to two thousand and upwards; which number has hitherto performed what under the new system will be done in the first instance by sixty-five persons, and probably at no future period by above a fourth or a fifth of that number. The congress under the proposed government will do all the business of the United States themselves, without the intervention of the state legislatures, who thenceforth will have only to attend to the affairs of their particular states, and will not have to sit in any proportion as long as they have heretofore done. This difference, in the time of the sessions of the state legislatures, will be all clear gain, and will alone form an article of saving, which may be regarded as an equivalent for any additional objects of expence that may be occasioned by the adoption of the new system.

The result from these observations is, that the sources of additional expence from the establishment of the proposed constitution are much fewer than may have been imagined, that they are counterbalanced by considerable objects of saving, and that while it is questionable on which side the scale will preponderate, it is certain that a government less expensive would be incompetent to the purposes of the union.

PUBLIUS.

HAMILTON'S REMARKS AND SPEECHES
AT THE NEW YORK RATIFYING CONVENTION, AN INTRODUCTION

When the New York Ratifying Convention convened on June 17, 1788, eight states had already approved the Constitution (including Virginia). The acceptance of nine states was required for the Constitution to go into effect. Hamilton's speeches and remarks in the New York Ratifying Convention may be regarded as an appendix to the Hamiltonian Federalist, for they extend and amplify positions he took in the previous document. They contain some of Hamilton's most theoretical statements on the American Constitution.

REMARKS IN THE NEW YORK RATIFYING CONVENTION
JUNE 20, 1788

Poughkeepsie, New York, June 20, 1788

The hon. Mr. *Hamilton* then rose. Mr. Chairman the honorable Member, who spoke yesterday, went into an explanation of a variety of circumstances to prove the expediency of a change in our national government, and the necessity of a firm union: At the same time he described the great advantages which this State, in particular, receives from the confederacy, and its peculiar weaknesses when abstracted from the Union. In doing this, he advanced a variety of arguments, which deserve serious consideration. Gentlemen have this day come forward, to answer him. He has been treated as having wandered in the flowery fields of fancy; and attempts have been made, to take off from the minds of the committee, that sober impression, which might be expected from his arguments. I trust, sir, that observations of this kind are not thrown out to cast a light air on this important subject; or to give any personal bias, on the great question before us. I will not agree with gentlemen, who trifle with the weaknesses of our country; and suppose, that they are enumerated to answer a party purpose, and to terrify with ideal dangers. No; I believe these weaknesses to be real, and pregnant with destruction.

Yet, however weak our country may be, I hope we shall never sacrifice our liberties. If, therefore, on a full and candid discussion, the proposed system shall appear to have that tendency, for God's sake, let us reject it! But, let us not mistake words for things, nor accept doubtful surmises as the evidence of truth. Let us consider the Constitution calmly and dispassionately, and attend to those things only which merit consideration.

No arguments drawn from embarrassment or inconvenience, ought to prevail upon us to adopt a system of government radically bad; yet it is proper that these arguments, among others, should be brought into view. In doing this, yesterday, it was necessary to reflect upon our situation; to dwell upon the imbecility of our Union; and to consider whether we, as a State, could stand alone. Although I am persuaded this Convention will be resolved to adopt nothing that is bad; yet I think every prudent man will consider the merits of the plan in connection with the circumstances of our country; and that a rejection of the Constitution may involve most fatal consequences. I make these remarks to shew, that tho' we ought not to be actuated by unreasonable fear, yet we ought to be prudent.

This day, sir, one gentleman has attempted to answer the arguments advanced by my honorable friend; another has treated him as having wandered from the subject: This being the case, I trust I shall be equally indulged in reviewing the remarks which have been made.

Sir, it appears to me extraordinary, that while gentlemen in one breath acknowledge, that the old confederation requires many material amendments, they should in the next deny, that its defects have been the cause of our political weakness, and the consequent calamities of our country. I cannot but infer from this, that there is still some lurking favorite imagination, that this system, with corrections, might become a safe and permanent one. It is proper that we should examine this matter. We contend that the radical vice in the old confederation is, that the laws of the Union apply only to States in their corporate capacity. Has not every man, who has been in our legislature, experienced the truth of this position? It is inseparable from the disposition of bodies, who have a constitutional power of resistance, to examine the merits of a law. This has ever been the case with the federal requisitions. In this examination, not being furnished with those lights, which directed the deliberations of the general government; and incapable of embracing the general interests of the Union, the States have almost uniformly weighed the requisitions by their own local interests; and have only executed them so far as answered their particular conveniency or advantage. Hence there have ever been thirteen different bodies to judge of the measures of Congress—and the operations of government have been distracted by their taking different courses: Those, which were to be benefited have complied with the requisitions; others have totally disregarded them. Have not all of us been witnesses to the unhappy embarrassments which resulted from these proceedings? Even during the late war, while the pressure of common danger connected strongly the bond of our union, and incited to vigorous exertions, we have felt many distressing effects of the impotent system. How have we seen this State, though most exposed to the calamities of the war, complying, in an unexampled manner, with the federal requisitions, and compelled by the delinquency of others, to bear most unusual burthens! Of this truth we have the most solemn proof on our records. In 1779 and 1780, when the State, from the ravages of war, and from her great exertions to resist them, became weak, distressed and forlorn, every man avowed the principle which we now contend for; that our misfortunes, in a great degree, proceeded from the want of vigor in the continental government. These were our sentiments when we did not speculate, but feel. We saw our weakness, and found ourselves its victims. Let us reflect that this may again in all probability be our situation. This is a weak State; and its relative station is dangerous. Your capital is accessible by land, and by sea is exposed to every daring invader; and on the North West, you are open to the inroads of a powerful foreign nation. Indeed this State, from its situation, will, in time of war, probably be the theatre of its operations.

Gentlemen have said that the non-compliance of the States has been occasioned by their sufferings. This may in part be true. But has this State been delinquent? Amidst all our distresses, *we* have fully complied. If New-York could comply wholly with the requisitions, is it not to be supposed, that the other States, could in part comply? Certainly every State in the Union might have executed them in some degree. But New Hampshire, who has not suffered at all, is totally delinquent: North-Carolina is totally delinquent: Many others have contributed in a very small proportion; and Pennsylvania and New-York are the only states, which have perfectly discharged their Federal duty.

From the delinquency of those States who have suffered little by the war, we naturally conclude, that they have made no efforts; and a knowledge of human nature will teach us, that their ease and security have been a principal cause of their want of exertion. While danger is distant, its impression is weak, and while it affects only our neighbours we have few motives to provide against it. Sir, if we have national objects to pursue, we must have national revenues. If you make requisitions and they are not complied with, what is to be done? It has been well observed, that to coerce the States is one of the maddest projects that was ever devised. A failure of compliance will never be confined to a single State: This being the case, can we suppose it wise to hazard a civil war? Suppose Massachusetts or any large State should refuse; and Congress should attempt to compel them; would they not have influence to procure assistance, especially from those states who are in the same situation as themselves? What picture does this idea present to our view? A complying state at war with a non-complying state: Congress marching the troops of one state into the bosom of another: This state collecting auxiliaries and forming perhaps a majority against its Federal head. Here is a nation at war with itself. Can any reasonable man be well disposed towards a government which makes war and carnage the only means of supporting itself? a government that can exist only by the sword? Every such war must involve the innocent with the guilty. This single consideration should be sufficient to dispose every peaceable citizen against such a government.

But can we believe that one state will ever suffer itself to be used as an instrument of coercion? The thing is a dream. It is impossible. Then we are brought to this dilemma: Either a federal standing army is to enforce the requisitions, or the Federal Treasury is left without supplies, and the government without support. What, Sir, is the cure for this great evil? Nothing, but to enable the national laws to operate on individuals, in the same manner as those of the states do. This is the true reasoning upon the subject, Sir. The gentlemen appear to acknowledge its force; and yet while they yield to the principle, they seem to fear its application to the government.

What then shall we do? Shall we take the Old Confederation, as the basis of a new system? Can this be the object of the gentlemen? certainly not. Will any man who entertains a wish for the safety of his country, trust the sword and the purse with a single Assembly organized on principles so defective—so rotten? Though we might give to such a government certain powers with safety, yet to give them the full and unlimited powers of taxation and the national forces would be to establish a despotism; the definition of which is, a government, in which all power is concentred in a single body. To take the Old Confederation, and fashion it upon these principles, would be establishing a power which would destroy the liberties of the people. These considerations show clearly, that a government totally different must be instituted. They had weight in the convention who formed the new system. It was seen, that the necessary powers were too great to be trusted to a single body: They therefore formed two branches; and divided the powers, that each might be a check upon the other. This was the result of their wisdom; and I presume that every reasonable man will agree to it. The more this subject is explained, the more clear and convincing it will appear to every member of this body. The fundamental principle of the Old Confederation is defective. We must totally eradicate and discard this principle before we can expect an efficient government. The gentlemen who have spoken to day have taken up the subject of the antient Confederacies: But their view of them has been extremely partial and erroneous: The fact is, the same false and impracticable principle ran through most of the antient governments. The first of these governments that we read of, was the Amphyctionic confederacy. The council which managed the affairs of this league possessed powers of a similar complexion to those of our present Congress. The same feeble mode of legislation in the head, and the same power of resistance in the members, prevailed. When a requisition was made, it rarely met a compliance; and a civil war was the consequence. Those which were attacked called in foreign aid to protect them; and the ambitious Philip under the mask of an ally to one, invaded the liberties of each, and finally subverted the whole.

The operation of this principle appears in the same light in the Dutch Republics. They have been obliged to levy taxes by an armed force. In this confederacy, one large province, by its superior wealth and influence, is commonly a match for all the rest; and when they do not comply, the province of Holland is obliged to compel them. It is observed, that the United Provinces have existed a long time; but they have been constantly the sport of their neighbors; and have been supported only by the external pressure of the surrounding powers. The policy of Europe, not the policy of their government, has saved them from dissolution. Besides, the powers of the Stadholder have served to give an energy to the operations of this government, which is not to be found in ours. This prince has a vast personal influence: He has independent revenues: He commands an army of forty thousand men.

The German confederacy has also been a perpetual source of wars: They have a diet, like our Congress, who have authority to call for supplies: These calls are never obeyed; and in time of war, the Imperial army never takes the field, till the enemy are returning from it. The Emperor's Austrian dominions, in which he is an absolute prince, alone enable him to make head against the common foe. The members of this confederacy are ever divided and opposed to each other. The king of Prussia is a member; yet he has been constantly in opposition to the Emperor. Is this a desirable government?

I might go more particularly into the discussion of examples, and shew, that wherever this fatal principle has prevailed, even as far back as the Lycian and Achæan leagues, as well as the Amphyctionic confederacy; it has proved the destruction of the government. But I think observations of this kind might have been spared. Had they not been entered into by others, I should not have taken up so much of the time of the committee. No inference can be drawn from these examples, that republics cannot exist: We only contend that they have hitherto been founded on false principles. We have shewn how they have been conducted, and how they have been destroyed. Weakness in the head has produced resistence in the members: This has been the immediate parent of civil war: Auxiliary force has been invited, and a foreign power has annihilated their liberties and their name. Thus Philip subverted the Amphyctionic, and Rome the Achæan Republic.

We shall do well, sir, not to deceive ourselves with the favorable events of the late war. Common danger prevented the operation of the ruinous principle, in its full extent: But since the peace, we have experienced the evils; we have felt the poison of the system in its unmingled purity.

Without dwelling any longer on this subject, I shall proceed to the question immediately before the committee.

In order that the committee may understand clearly the principles on which the general convention acted, I think it necessary to explain some preliminary circumstances.

Sir, the natural situation of this country seems to divide its interests into different classes. There are navigating and non-navigating States. The Northern are properly the navigating States: The Southern appear to possess neither the means nor the spirit of navigation. This difference of situation naturally produces a dissimilarity of interests and views respecting foreign commerce. It was the interest of the Northern States, that there should be no restraints on their navigation, and that they should have full power, by a majority in Congress, to make commercial regulations in favour of their own, and in restraint of the navigation of foreigners. The Southern States wished to impose a restraint on the Northern, by requiring that two thirds in Congress, should be requisite to pass an act in regulation of commerce: They were apprehensive that the restraints of a navigation law, would discourage foreigners, and by obliging them to employ the shipping of the Northern States would probably enhance their freight. This being the case, they insisted strenuously on having this provision engrafted in the constitution; and the Northern States were as anxious in opposing it. On the other hand, the small states seeing themselves embraced by the confederation upon equal terms, wished to retain the advantages which they already possessed: The large states, on the contrary, thought it improper that Rhode Island and Delaware should enjoy an equal suffrage with themselves: From these sources a delicate and difficult contest arose. It became necessary, therefore, to compromise; or the Convention must have dissolved without affecting any thing. Would it have been wise and prudent in that body, in this critical situation, to have deserted their country? No. Every man who hears me—every wise man in the United States, would have condemned them. The Convention were obliged to appoint a Committee for accommodation: In this Committee, the arrangement was formed, as it now stands; and their report was accepted. It was a delicate point; and it was necessary that all parties should be indulged. Gentlemen will see, that if there had not been a unanimity, nothing could have been done: For the Convention had no power to establish, but only to recommend a government. Any other system would have been impracticable. Let a Convention be called to-morrow. Let them meet twenty times; nay, twenty thousand times; they will have the same difficulties to encounter; the same clashing interests to reconcile.

But dismissing these reflections, let us consider how far the arrangement is in itself entitled to the approbation of this body. We will examine it upon its own merits.

The first thing objected to, is that clause which allows a representation for three fifths of the negroes. Much has been said of the impropriety of representing men, who have no will of their own. Whether this be reasoning or declamation, I will not presume to say. It is the unfortunate situation of the Southern States, to have a great part of their population, as well as property in blacks. The regulation complained of was one result of the spirit of accommodation, which governed the Convention; and without this indulgence, no union could possibly have been formed. But, Sir, considering some peculiar advantages which we derive from them, it is entirely just that they should be gratified. The Southern States possess certain staples, tobacco, rice, indigo, &c. which must be capital objects in treaties of commerce with foreign nations; and the advantage which they necessarily procure in these treaties, will be felt throughout all the States. But the justice of this plan will appear in another view. The best writers on government have held that representation should be compounded of persons and property. This rule has been adopted, as far as it could be, in the Constitution of New-York. It will however by no means be admitted, that the slaves are considered altogether as property. They are men, though degraded to the condition of slavery.

They are persons known to the municipal laws of the states which they inhabit, as well as to the laws of nature. But representation and taxation go together—and one uniform rule ought to apply to both. Would it be just to compute these slaves in the assessment of taxes; and discard them from the estimate in the apportionment of representatives? Would it be just to impose a singular burthen, without conferring some adequate advantage?

Another circumstance ought to be considered. The rule we have been speaking of is a general rule, and applies to all the States. Now, you have a great number of people in your State, which are not represented at all; and have no voice in your government: These will be included in the enumeration—not two fifths—nor three fifths, but the whole. This proves that the advantages of the plan are not confined to the southern States, but extend to other parts of the Union.

I now proceed to consider the objection with regard to the number of representatives, as it now stands: I am persuaded the system, in this respect, stands on a better footing than the gentlemen imagine.

It has been asserted that it will be in the power of Congress to reduce the number. I acknowledge, that there are no direct words of prohibition. But, I contend, that the true and genuine construction of the clause gives Congress no power whatever to reduce the representation below the number, as it now stands. Although they may limit, they can never diminish the number. One representative for every thirty thousand inhabitants is fixed as the standard of increase; till, by the natural course of population, it shall become necessary to limit the ratio. Probably at present, were this standard to be immediately applied, the representation would considerably exceed sixty-five: In three years it would exceed a hundred. If I understand the gentlemen, they contend that the number may be enlarged or may not. I admit that this is in the discretion of Congress; and I submit to the committee whether it be not necessary and proper. Still, I insist, that an immediate limitation is not probable; nor was it in the contemplation of the Convention. But, Sir, who will presume to say to what precise point the representation ought to be increased? This is a matter of opinion; and opinions are vastly different upon the subject. A proof of this is drawn from the representations in the state legislatures. In Massachusetts, the Assembly consists of about three hundred, In South-Carolina, of nearly one hundred, In New-York there are sixty five. It is observed generally that the number ought to be large. Let the gentlemen produce their criterion. I confess it is difficult for me to say what number may be said to be sufficiently large. On one hand, it ought to be considered, that a small number will act with more facility, system, and decision: On the other, that a large one may enhance the difficulty of corruption. The Congress is to consist at first of ninety-one members. This, to a reasonable man, may appear to be as near the proper medium as any number whatever; at least for the present. There is one source of increase, also, which does not depend upon any constructions of the Constitution; it is the creation of new states. Vermont, Kentuckey, and Franklin, will probably soon become independent: New members of the Union will also be formed from the unsettled tracts of Western Territory. These must be represented; and will all contribute to swell the federal legislature. If the whole number in the United States be, at present, three millions, as is commonly supposed, according to the ratio of one for thirty thousand, we shall have, on the first census, a hundred representatives: In ten years, thirty more will be added; and in twenty-five years, the number will double: Then, Sir, we shall have two hundred; if the increase goes on in the same proportion. The Convention of Massachusetts who made the same objection, have fixed upon this number as the point at which they chose to limit the representation. But can we pronounce with certainty, that it will not be expedient to go beyond this number? We cannot. Experience alone must determine. This matter may, with more safety, be left to the discretion of the legislature, as it will be the interest of the larger and increasing states, of Massachusetts, New-York, Pennsylvania, &c. to augment the representation. Only Connecticut, Rhode-Island, Delaware, and Maryland, can be interested in limiting it. We may therefore safely calculate upon a growing representation, according to the advance of population, and the circumstances of the country.

The State governments possess inherent advantages, which will ever give them an influence and ascendency over the national government; and will forever preclude the possibility of federal encroachments. That their liberties indeed can be subverted by the federal head, is repugnant to every rule of political calculation. Is not this arrangement then, Sir, a most wise and prudent one? Is not the present representation fully adequate to our present exigencies; and sufficient to answer all the purposes of the Union? I am persuaded that an examination of the objects of the federal government will afford a conclusive answer.

Many other observations might be made on this subject, but I cannot now pursue them; for I feel myself not a little exhausted: I beg leave therefore to wave for the present the further discussion of this question.

FIRST SPEECH OF JUNE 21 IN THE NEW YORK RATIFYING CONVENTION

JUNE 21, 1788

Poughkeepsie, New York, June 21, 1788

Mr. *Hamilton* then reassumed his argument. When, said he, I had the honor to address the committee yesterday, I gave a history of the circumstances which attended the Convention, when forming the Plan before you. I endeavored to point out to you the principles of accommodation, on which this arrangement was made; and to shew that the contending interests of the States led them to establish the representation as it now stands. In the second place I attempted to prove, that, in point of number, the representation would be perfectly secure.

Sir, no man agrees more perfectly than myself to the main principle for which the gentlemen contend. I agree that there should be a broad democratic branch in the national legislature. But this matter, Sir, depends on circumstances; It is impossible, in the first instance to be precise and exact with regard to the number; and it is equally impossible to determine to what point it may be proper in future to increase it. On this ground I am disposed to acquiesce. In my reasonings on the subject of government, I rely more on the interests and the opinions of men, than on any speculative parchment provisions whatever. I have found, that Constitutions are more or less excellent, as they are more or less agreeable to the natural operation of things: I am therefore disposed not to dwell long on curious speculations, or pay much attention to modes and forms; but to adopt a system, whose principles have been sanctioned by experience; adapt it to the real state of our country; and depend on probable reasonings for its operation and result. I contend that sixty-five and twenty-six in two bodies afford perfect security, in the present state of things; and that the regular progressive enlargement, which was in the contemplation of the General Convention, will leave not an apprehension of danger in the most timid and suspicious mind. It will be the interest of the large states to increase the representation: This will be the standing instruction to their delegates. But, say the gentlemen, the Members of Congress will be interested not to increase the number, as it will diminish their relative influence. In all their reasoning upon the subject, there seems to be this fallacy: They suppose that the representative will have no motive of action, on the one side, but a sense of duty; or on the other, but corruption: They do not reflect, that he is to return to the community; that he is dependent on the will of the people, and that it cannot be his interest to oppose their wishes. Sir, the general sense of the people will regulate the conduct of their representatives. I admit that there are exceptions to this rule: There are certain conjunctures, when it may be necessary and proper to disregard the opinions which the majority of the people have formed: But in the general course of things, the popular views and even prejudices will direct the actions of the rulers.

All governments, even the most despotic, depend, in a great degree, on opinion. In free republics, it is most peculiarly the case: In these, the will of the people makes the essential principle of the government; and the laws which control the community, receive their tone and spirit from the public wishes. It is the fortunate situation of our country, that the minds of the people are exceedingly enlightened and refined: Here then we may expect the laws to be proportionably agreeable to the standard of perfect policy; and the wisdom of public measures to consist with the most intimate conformity between the views of the representative and his constituent. If the general voice of the people be for an increase, it undoubtedly must take place: They have it in their power to instruct their representatives; and the State Legislatures, which appoint the Senators, may enjoin it also upon them. Sir, if I believed that the number would remain at sixty-five, I confess I should give my vote for an amendment; though in a different form from the one proposed.

The amendment proposes a ratio of one for twenty thousand: I would ask, by what rule or reasoning it is determined, that one man is a better representative for twenty than thirty thousand? At present we have three millions of people; in twenty-five years, we shall have six millions; and in forty years, nine millions: And this is a short period, as it relates to the existence of States. Here then, according to the ratio of one for thirty thousand, we shall have, in forty years, three hundred representatives. If this be true, and if this be a safe representation, why be dissatisfied? why embarrass the Constitution with amendments, that are merely speculative and useless. I agree with the gentleman, that a very small number might give some colour for suspicion: I acknowledge, that ten would be unsafe; on the other hand, a thousand would be too numerous. But I ask him, why will not ninety-one be an adequate and safe representation? This at present appears to be the proper medium. Besides, the President of the United States will be himself the representative of the people. From the competition that ever subsists between the branches of government, the President will be induced to protect their rights, whenever they are invaded by either branch. On whatever side we view this subject, we discover various and powerful checks to the encroachments of Congress. The true and permanent interests of the members are opposed to corruption: Their number is vastly too large for easy combination: The rivalship between the houses will forever prove an insuperable obstacle: The people have an obvious and powerful protection in their own State governments: Should any thing dangerous be attempted, these bodies of perpetual observation, will be capable of forming and conducting plans of regular opposition. Can we suppose the people's love of liberty will not, under the incitement of their legislative leaders, be roused into resistance, and the madness of tyranny be extinguished at a blow? Sir, the danger is too distant; it is beyond all rational calculations.

It has been observed by an honorable gentleman, that a pure democracy, if it were practicable, would be the most perfect government. Experience has proved, that no position in politics is more false than this. The ancient democracies, in which the people themselves deliberated, never possessed one feature of good government. Their very character was tyranny; their figure deformity: When they assembled, the field of debate presented an ungovernable mob, not only incapable of deliberation, but prepared for every enormity. In these assemblies, the enemies of the people brought forward their plans of ambition systematically. They were opposed by their enemies of another party; and it became a matter of contingency, whether the people subjected themselves to be led blindly by one tyrant or by another.

It was remarked yesterday, that a numerous representation was necessary to obtain the confidence of the people. This is not generally true. The confidence of the people will easily be gained by a good administration. This is the true touchstone. I could illustrate the position, by a variety of historical examples, both ancient and modern. In Sparta, the Ephori were a body of magistrates, instituted as a check upon the senate, and representing the people. They consisted of only five men: But they were able to protect their rights, and therefore enjoyed their confidence and attachment. In Rome, the people were represented by three Tribunes, who were afterwards increased to ten. Every one acquainted with the history of that republic, will recollect how powerful a check to the senatorial encroachments, this small body proved; how unlimited a confidence was placed in them by the people whose guardians they were; and to what a conspicuous station in the government, their influence at length elevated the Plebians. Massachusetts has three hundred representatives; New York has sixty-five. Have the people in this state less confidence in their representation, than the people of that? Delaware has twenty-one: Do the inhabitants of New-York feel a higher confidence than those of Delaware? I have stated these examples, to prove that the gentleman's principle is not just. The popular confidence depends on circumstances very distinct from considerations of number. Probably the public attachment is more strongly secured by a train of prosperous events, which are the result of wise deliberation and vigorous execution, and to which large bodies are much less competent than small ones. If the representative conducts with propriety, he will necessarily enjoy the good will of the constituent. It appears then, if my reasoning be just, that the clause is perfectly proper, upon the principles of the gentleman who contends for the amendment: as there is in it the greatest degree of present security, and a moral certainty of an increase equal to our utmost wishes.

It has been farther, by the gentlemen in opposition, observed, that a large representation is necessary to understand the interests of the people. This principle is by no means true in the extent to which the gentleman seems to carry it. I would ask, why may not a man understand the interests of thirty as well as of twenty? The position appears to be made upon the unfounded presumption, that all the interests of all parts of the community must be represented. No idea is more erroneous than this. Only such interests are proper to be represented, as are involved in the powers of the General Government. These interests come compleatly under the observation of one, or a few men; and the requisite information is by no means augmented in proportion to the increase of number. What are the objects of the Government? Commerce, taxation, &c. In order to comprehend the interests of commerce, is it necessary to know how wheat is raised, and in what proportion it is produced in one district and in another? By no means. Neither is this species of knowledge necessary in general calculations upon the subject of taxation. The information necessary for these purposes, is that which is open to every intelligent enquirer; and of which, five men may be as perfectly possessed as fifty. In royal governments, there are usually particular men to whom the business of taxation is committed. These men have the forming of systems of finance; and the regulation of the revenue. I do not mean to commend this practice. It proves however, this point; that a few individuals may be competent to these objects; and that large numbers are not necessary to perfection in the science of taxation. But granting, for a moment, that this minute and local knowledge the gentlemen contend for, is necessary, let us see, if under the New Constitution, it will not probably be found in the representation.

The natural and proper mode of holding elections, will be to divide the state into districts, in proportion to the number to be elected. This state will consequently be divided at first into six. One man from each district will probably possess all the knowledge the gentlemen can desire. Are the senators of this state more ignorant of the interests of the people, than the assembly? Have they not ever enjoyed their confidence as much? Yet, instead of six districts, they are elected in four; and the chance of their being collected from the smaller divisions of the state consequently diminished. Their number is but twenty-four; and their powers are co-extensive with those of the assembly, and reach objects, which are most dear to the people—life, liberty and property.

Sir, we hear constantly a great deal, which is rather calculated to awake our passions, and create prejudices, than to conduct us to truth, and teach us our real interests. I do not suppose this to be the design of the gentlemen. Why then are we told so often of an aristocracy? For my part, I hardly know the meaning of this word as it is applied. If all we hear be true, this government is really a very bad one. But who are the aristocracy among us? Where do we find men elevated to a perpetual rank above their fellow citizens; and possessing powers entirely independent of them? The arguments of the gentlemen only go to prove that there are men who are rich, men who are poor, some who are wise, and others who are not—That indeed every distinguished man is an aristocrat. This reminds me of a description of the aristocrats, I have seen in a late publication, styled the Federal Farmer. The author reckons in the aristocracy, all governors of states, members of Congress, chief magistrates, and all officers of the militia. This description, I presume to say, is ridiculous. The image is a phantom. Does the new government render a rich man more eligible than a poor one? No. It requires no such qualification. It is bottomed on the broad and equal principle of your state constitution.

Sir, if the people have it in their option, to elect their most meritorious men; is this to be considered as an objection? Shall the constitution oppose their wishes, and abridge their most invaluable privilege? While property contines to be pretty equally divided, and a considerable share of information pervades the community; the tendency of the people's suffrages, will be to elevate merit even from obscurity. As riches increase and accumulate in few hands; as luxury prevails in society; virtue will be in a greater degree considered as only a graceful appendage of wealth, and the tendency of things will be to depart from the republican standard. This is the real disposition of human nature: It is what, neither the honorable member nor myself can correct. It is a common misfortune, that awaits our state constitution, as well as all others.

There is an advantage incident to large districts of election, which perhaps the gentlemen, amidst all their apprehensions of influence and bribery, have not adverted to. In large districts, the corruption of the electors is much more difficult: Combinations for the purposes of intrigue are less easily formed: Factions and cabals are little known. In a small district, wealth will have a more complete influence; because the people in the vicinity of a great man, are more immediately his dependants, and because this influence has fewer objects to act upon. It has been remarked, that it would be disagreeable to the middle class of men to go to the seat of the new government. If this be so, the difficulty will be enhanced by the gentleman's proposal. If his argument be true, it proves, that the larger the representation is, the less will be your choice of having it filled. But, it appears to me frivolous to bring forward such arguments as these. It has answered no other purpose, than to induce me, by way of reply, to enter into discussions, which I consider as useless, and not applicable to our subject.

It is a harsh doctrine, that men grow wicked in proportion as they improve and enlighten their minds. Experience has by no means justified us in the supposition, that there is more virtue in one class of men than in another. Look through the rich and the poor of the community; the learned and the ignorant. Where does virtue predominate? The difference indeed consists, not in the quantity but kind of vices, which are incident to the various classes; and here the advantage of character belongs to the wealthy. Their vices are probably more favorable to the prosperity of the state, than those of the indigent; and partake less of moral depravity.

After all, Sir, we must submit to this idea, that the true principle of a republic is, that the people should choose whom they please to govern them. Representation is imperfect, in proportion as the current of popular favour is checked. This great source of free government, popular election, should be perfectly pure, and the most unbounded liberty allowed. Where this principle is adhered to; where, in the organization of the government, the legislative, executive and judicial branches are rendered distinct; where again the legislative is divided into separate houses, and the operations of each are controuled by various checks and balances, and above all, by the vigilance and weight of the state governments; to talk of tyranny, and the subversion of our liberties, is to speak the language of enthusiasm. This balance between the national and state governments ought to be dwelt on with peculiar attention, as it is of the utmost importance. It forms a double security to the people. If one encroaches on their rights, they will find a powerful protection in the other. Indeed they will both be prevented from overpassing their constitutional limits, by a certain rivalship, which will ever subsist between them. I am persuaded, that a firm union is as necessary to perpetuate our liberties, as it is to make us respectable; and experience will probably prove, that the national government will be as natural a guardian of our freedom, as the state legislatures themselves.

Suggestions, Sir, of an extraordinary nature, have been frequently thrown out in the course of the present political controversy. It gives me pain to dwell on topics of this kind; and I wish they might be dismissed. We have been told, that the old Confederation has proved inefficacious, only because intriguing and powerful men, aiming at a revolution, have been forever instigating the people, and rendering them disaffected with it. This, Sir, is a false insinuation. The thing is impossible. I will venture to assert, that no combination of designing men under Heaven, will be capable of making a government unpopular, which is in its principles a wise and good one; and vigorous in its operations.

The Confederation was framed amidst the agitation and tumult of society. It was composed of unfound materials put together in haste. Men of intelligence discovered the feebleness of the structure, in the first stages of its existence; but the great body of the people, too much engrossed with their distresses, to contemplate any but the immediate causes of them, were ignorant of the defects of their Constitution. But, when the dangers of war were removed, they saw clearly what they had suffered, and what they had yet to suffer from a feeble form of government. There was no need of discerning men to convince the people of their unhappy situation—the complaint was co-extensive with the evil, and both were common to all classes of the community. We have been told, that the spirit of patriotism and love of liberty are almost extinguished among the people; and that it has become a prevailing doctrine, that republican principles ought to be hooted out of the world. Sir, I am confident that such remarks as these are rather occasioned by the heat of argument, than by a cool conviction of their truth and justice. As far as my experience has extended, I have heard no such doctrine, nor have I discovered any diminution of regard for those rights and liberties, in defence of which, the people have fought and suffered. There have been, undoubtedly, some men who have had speculative doubts on the subject of government; but the principles of republicanism are founded on too firm a basis to be shaken by a few speculative and sceptical

211

reasoners. Our error has been of a very different kind. We have erred through excess of caution, and a zeal false and impracticable. Our counsels have been destitute of consistency and stability. I am flattered with a hope, Sir, that we have now found a cure for the evils under which we have so long labored. I trust, that the proposed Constitution affords a genuine specimen of representative and republican government—and that it will answer, in an eminent degree, all the beneficial purposes of society.

THIRD SPEECH OF JUNE 21 IN THE NEW YORK RATIFYING CONVENTION
JUNE 21, 1788

Poughkeepsie, New York, June 21, 1788

The Hon. Mr. *Hamilton.* Mr. Chairman I rise to take notice of the observations of the hon. member from Ulster. I imagine the objections he has stated, are susceptible of a complete and satisfactory refutation. But before I proceed to this, I shall attend to the arguments advanced by the gentlemen from Albany and Dutchess. These arguments have been frequently urged, and much confidence has been placed in their strength: The danger of corruption has been dwelt upon with peculiar emphasis, and presented to our view in the most heightened and unnatural colouring: Events, merely possible have been magnified by distempered imagination into inevitable realities; and the most distant and doubtful conjectures have been formed into a serious and infallible prediction. In the same spirit, the most fallacious calculations have been made: The lowest possible quorum has been contemplated as the number to transact important business; and a majority of these to decide in all cases on questions of infinite moment. Allowing, for the present, the propriety and truth of these apprehensions, it would be easy, in comparing the two constitutions, to prove that the chances of corruption under the new, are much fewer that those to which the old one is exposed. Under the old confederation, the important powers of declaring war, making peace, &c. can be exercised by nine states. On the presumption that the smallest constitutional number will deliberate and decide, those interesting powers will be committed to fewer men, under the ancient than under the new government. In the former, eighteen members, in the latter, not less than twenty-four may determine all great questions. Thus on the principles of the gentlemen, the fairer prospect of safety is clearly visible in the new government. That we may have the fullest conviction of the truth of this position, it ought to be suggested, as a decisive argument, that it will ever be the interest of the several states to maintain, under the new government, an ample representation: For, as every member has a vote, the relative influence and authority of each state will be in proportion to the number of representatives she has in Congress. There is not therefore a shadow of probability, that the number of acting members in the general legislature, will be ever reduced to a bare quorum; especially as the expence of their support is to be defrayed from a federal treasury: But under the existing confederation, as each state has but one vote, it will be a matter of indifference, on the score of influence, whether she delegates two or six representatives: And the maintenance of them forming a striking article in the state expenditures, will forever prove a capital inducement to retain or withdraw from the federal legislature, those delegates which her selfishness may too often consider as superfluous.

There is another source of corruption, in the old government, which the proposed plan is happily calculated to remedy. The concurrence of nine states, as has been observed, is necessary to pass resolves the most important, and on which, the safety of the republic may depend. If these nine states are at any time assembled, a foreign enemy, by dividing a state and gaining over and silencing a single member, may frustrate the most indispensible plan of national policy, and totally prevent a measure, essential to the welfare or existence of the empire. Here, then, we find a radical, dangerous defect, which will forever embarrass and obstruct the machine of government; and suspend our fate on the uncertain virtue of an individual. What a difference between the old and new constitution strikes our view! In the one, corruption must embrace a majority; in the other, her poison administered to a single man, may render the efforts of a majority totally vain. This mode of corruption is still more dangerous, as its operations are more secret and imperceptible: The exertions of active villainy are commonly accompanied with circumstances, which tend to its own exposure: But this negative kind of guilt has so many plausible apologies as almost to elude suspicion.

In all reasonings on the subject of corruption, much use has been made of the examples furnished by the British house of commons. Many mistakes have arisen from fallacious comparisons between our government and theirs. It is time, that the real state of this matter should be explained. By far the greatest part of the house of commons is composed of representatives of towns or boroughs: These towns had antiently no voice in parliament; but on the extension of commercial wealth and influence, they were admitted to a seat. Many of them are in the possession and gift of the king; and from their dependence on him, and the destruction of the right of free election, they are stigmatized with the appellation of rotten boroughs. This is the true source of the corruption, which has so long excited the severe animadversion of zealous politicians and patriots. But the knights of the shire, who form another branch of the house of commons, and who are chosen from the body of the counties they represent, have been generally esteemed a virtuous and incorruptible set of men. I appeal, Sir, to the history of that house: This will shew us, that the rights of the people have been ever very safely trusted to their protection; that they have been the ablest bulwarks of the British commons; and that in the conflict of parties, by throwing their weight into one scale or the other, they have uniformly supported and strengthened the constitutional claims of the people. Notwithstanding the cry of corruption that has been perpetually raised against the house of commons, it has been found, that that house, sitting at first without any constitutional authority, became, at length, an essential member of the legislature, and have since, by regular gradations, acquired new and important accessions of privilege: That they have, on numerous occasions, impaired the overgrown prerogative, and limited the incroachments of monarchy.

An honorable member from Dutchess, (*Mr. Smith*) has observed, that the delegates from New-York, (for example) can have very little information of the local circumstances of Georgia or South-Carolina, except from the representatives of those states; and on this ground, insists upon the expediency of an enlargment of the representation; since, otherwise, the majority must rely too much on the information of a few. In order to determine whether there is any weight in this reasoning, let us consider the powers of the national government, and compare them with the objects of state legislation. The powers of the new government are general, and calculated to embrace the aggregate interest of the Union, and the general interest of each state, so far as it stands in relation to the whole. The object of the state governments is to provide for their internal interests, as unconnected with the United States, and as composed of minute parts or districts. A particular knowledge, therefore, of the local circumstances of any state, as they may vary in different districts, is unnecessary for the federal representative. As he is not to represent the interests or local wants of the county of Dutchess or Montgomery; neither is it necessary that he should be acquainted with their particular resources: But in the state governments, as the laws regard the interests of the people, in all their various minute divisions; it is necessary, that the smallest interests should be represented. Taking these distinctions into view, I think it must appear evident, that one discerning and intelligent man will be as capable of understanding and representing the general interests of a state, as twenty; because, one man can be as fully acquainted with the general state of the commerce, manufactures, population, production and common resources of a state, which are the proper objects of federal legislation. It is to be presumed, that few men originally possess a complete knowledge of the circumstances of other states; They must rely, therefore, on the information, to be collected from the representatives of those states: And if the above reasoning be just, it appears evident, I imagine, that this reliance will be as secure as can be desired.

Sir, in my experience of public affairs, I have constantly remarked, in the conduct of members of Congress, a strong and uniform attachment to the interests of their own state: These interests have, on many occasions, been adhered to, with an undue and illiberal pertinacity; and have too often been preferred to the welfare of the Union. This attachment has given birth to an unaccommodating spirit of party, which has frequently embarrassed the best measures: It is by no means, however, an object of surprize. The early connections we have formed; the habits and prejudices in which we have been bred, fix our affection so strongly, that no future objects of association can easily eradicate them: This, together with the entire and immediate dependence the representative feels on his constituent, will generally incline him to prefer the particular before the public good.

The subject, on which this argument of a small representation has been most plausibly used, is taxation. As to internal taxation, in which the difficulty principally rests, it is not probable, that any general regulation will originate in the national legislature. If Congress in times of great danger and distress, should be driven to this resource, they will undoubtedly adopt such measures, as are most conformable to the laws and customs of each state: They will take up your own codes and consult your own systems: This is a source of information which cannot mislead, and which will be equally accessible to every member. It will teach them the most certain, safe and expeditious mode of laying and collecting taxes in each state. They will appoint the officers of revenue agreeably to the spirit of your particular establishments; or they will make use of your own.

Sir, the most powerful obstacle to the members of Congress betraying the interests of their constituents, is the state legislatures themselves; who will be standing bodies of observation, possessing the confidence of the people, jealous of federal encroachments, and armed with every power to check the first essays of treachery. They will institute regular modes of enquiry: The complicated domestic attachments, which subsist between the state legislators and their electors, will ever make them vigilant guardians of the people's rights: Possessed of the means, and the disposition of resistance, the spirit of opposition will be easily communicated to the people; and under the conduct of an organized body of leaders, will act with weight and system. Thus it appears, that the very structure of the confederacy affords the surest preventives from error, and the most powerful checks to misconduct.

Sir, there is something in an argument, that has been urged, which, if it proves any thing, concludes against all union and all government; it goes to prove, that no powers should be entrusted to any body of men, because they may be abused. This is an argument of possibility and chance; one that would render useless all reasonings upon the probable operation of things, and defeat the established principles of natural and moral causes. It is a species of reasoning, sometimes used to excite popular jealousies, but is generally discarded by wise and discerning men. I do not suppose that the honorable member who advanced the idea, had any such design: He, undoubtedly, would not wish to extend his argument to the destruction of union or government; but this, Sir, is its real tendency. It has been asserted, that the interests, habits and manners of the Thirteen States are different; and hence it is inferred, that no general free government can suit them. This diversity of habits, &c. has been a favorite theme with those who are disposed for a division of our empire; and like many other popular objections, seems to be founded on fallacy. I acknowledge, that the local interests of the states are in some degree various; and that there is some difference in their habits and manners: But this I will presume to affirm; that, from New-Hampshire to Georgia, the people of America are as uniform in their interests and manners, as those of any established in Europe. This diversity, to the eye of a speculatist, may afford some marks of characteristic discrimination, but cannot form an impediment to the regular operation of those general powers, which the Constitution gives to the united government. Were the laws of the union to new-model the internal police of any state; were they to alter, or abrogate at a blow, the whole of its civil and criminal institutions; were they to penetrate the recesses of domestic life, and controul, in all respects, the private conduct of individuals, there might be more force in the objection:

And the same constitution, which was happily calculated for one state, might sacrifice the wellfare of another. Though the difference of interests may create some difficulty and apparent partiality, in the first operations of government, yet the same spirit of accommodation, which produced the plan under discussion, would be exercised in lessening the weight of unequal burthens. Add to this that, under the regular and gentle influence of general laws, these varying interests will be constantly assimilating, till they embrace each other, and assume the same complexion.

REMARKS IN THE NEW YORK RATIFYING CONVENTION
JUNE 24, 1788

Poughkeepsie, New York, June 24, 1788

Honorable Mr. *Hamilton*. I am persuaded, Mr. Chairman, that I in my turn, shall be indulged, in addressing the committee. We all, with equal sincerity, profess to be anxious for the establishment of a republican government, on a safe and solid basis. It is the object of the wishes of every honest man in the United States, and I presume I shall not be disbelieved, when I declare, that it is an object of all others the nearest and most dear to my own heart. The means of accomplishing this great purpose become the most important study, which can interest mankind. It is our duty to examine all those means with peculiar attention, and to chuse the best and most effectual. It is our duty to draw from nature, from reason, from examples, the justest principles of policy, and to pursue and apply them in the formation of our government. We should contemplate and compare the systems, which, in this examination, come under our view, distinguish, with a careful eye, the defects and excellencies of each, and discarding the former, incorporate the latter, as far as circumstances will admit, into our constitution. If we pursue a different course and neglect this duty, we shall probably disappoint the expectations of our country and of the world.

In the commencement of a revolution, which received its birth from the usurpations of tyrannny, nothing was more natural, than that the public mind should be influenced by an extreme spirit of jealousy. To resist these encroachments, and to nourish this spirit, was the great object of all our public and private institutions. The zeal for liberty became predominant and excessive. In forming our confederation, this passion alone seemed to actuate us, and we appear to have had no other view than to secure ourselves from despotism. The object certainly was a valuable one, and deserved our utmost attention: But, Sir, there is another object, equally important, and which our enthusiasm rendered us little capable of regarding. I mean a principle of strength and stability in the organization of our government, and vigor in its operations. This purpose could never be accomplished but by the establishment of some select body, formed peculiarly upon this principle. There are few positions more demonstrable than that there should be in every republic, some permanent body to correct the prejudices, check the intemperate passions, and regulate the fluctuations of a popular assembly. It is evident that a body instituted for these purposes must be formed as to exclude as much as possible from its own character, those infirmities, and that mutability which it is designed to remedy. It is therefore necessary that it should be small, that it should hold its authority during a considerable period, and that it should have such an independence in the exercise of its powers, as will divest it as much as possible of local prejudices. It should be so formed as to be the center of political knowledge, to pursue always a steady line of conduct, and to reduce every irregular propensity to system. Without this establishment, we may make experiments without end, but shall never have an efficient government.

It is an unquestionable truth, that the body of the people in every country desire sincerely its prosperity: But it is equally unquestionable, that they do not possess the discernment and stability necessary for systematic government. To deny that they are frequently led into the grossest errors by misinformation and passion, would be a flattery which their own good sense must despise. That branch of administration especially, which involves our political relation with foreign states, a community will ever be incompetent to. These truths are not often held up in public assemblies—but they cannot be unknown to any who hear me. From these principles it follows that there ought to be two distinct bodies in our government—one which shall be immediately constituted by and peculiarly represent the people, and possess all the popular features; another formed upon the principles, and for the purposes before explained. Such considerations as these induced the convention who formed your state constitution, to institute a senate upon the present plan. The history of ancient and modern republics had taught them, that many of the evils which these republics suffered arose from the want of a certain balance and mutual controul indispensible to a wise administration. They were convinced that popular assemblies are frequently, misguided by ignorance, by sudden impulses and the intrigues of ambitious men; and that some firm barrier against these operations was necessary: They, therefore, instituted your senate, and the benefits we have experienced, have fully justified their conceptions.

Now, Sir, what is the tendency of the proposed amendment? To take away the stability of government by depriving the senate of its permanency: To make this body subject to the same weakness and prejudices, which are incident to popular assemblies, and which it was instituted to correct; and by thus assimilating the complexion of the two branches, destroy the balance between them. The amendment will render the senator a slave to all the capricious humors among the people. It will probably be here suggested, that the legislatures—not the people—are to have the power of recall. Without attempting to prove that the legislatures must be in a great degree the image of the multitude, in respect to federal affairs, and that the same prejudices and factions will prevail; I insist, that in whatever body the power of recall is vested, the senator will perpetually feel himself in such a state of vassalage and dependence, that he never can possess that firmness which is necessary to the discharge of his great duty to the union.

Gentlemen, in their reasoning, have placed the interests of the several states, and those of the United States in contrast. This is not a fair view of the subject. They must necessarily be involved in each other. What we apprehend is, that some sinister prejudice, or some prevailing passion, may assume the form of a genuine interest. The influence of these is as powerful as the most permanent conviction of the public good; and against this influence we ought to provide. The local interests of a state ought in every case to give way to the interests of the Union: For when a sacrifice of one or the other is necessary, the former becomes only an apparent, partial interest, and should yield, on the principle that the small good ought never to oppose the great one. When you assemble from your several counties in the legislature, were every member to be guided only by the apparent interest of his county, government would be impracticable. There must be a perpetual accommodation and sacrifice of local advantage to general expediency. But the spirit of a mere popular assembly would rarely be actuated by this important principle. It is therefore absolutely necessary that the senate should be so formed, as to be unbiassed by false conceptions of the real interests, or undue attachment to the apparent good of their several states.

219

Gentlemen indulge too many unreasonable apprehensions of danger to the state governments. They seem to suppose, that the moment you put men into the national council, they become corrupt and tyrannical, and lose all their affection for their fellow-citizens. But can we imagine that the senators will ever be so insensible of their own advantage, as to sacrifice the genuine interest of their constituents? The state governments are essentially necessary to the form and spirit of the general system. As long, therefore, as Congress have a full conviction of this necessity, they must, even upon principles purely national, have as firm an attachment to the one as to the other. This conviction can never leave them, unless they become madmen. While the constitution continues to be read, and its principles known, the states must, by every rational man, be considered as essential component parts of the union; and therefore the idea of sacrificing the former to the latter is totally inadmissible.

The objectors do not advert to the natural strength and resources of the state governments, which will ever give them an important superiority over the general government. If we compare the nature of their different powers, or the means of popular influence which each possesses, we shall find the advantage entirely on the side of the states. This consideration, important as it is, seems to have been little attended to. The aggregate number of representatives throughout the states may be two thousand. Their personal influence will therefore be proportionably more extensive than that of one or two hundred men in Congress. The state establishments of civil and military officers of every description, infinitely surpassing in number any possible correspondent establishments in the general government, will create such an extent and complication of attachments, as will ever secure the predilection and support of the people. Whenever, therefore, Congress shall meditate any infringement of the state constitutions, the great body of the people will naturally take part with their domestic representatives. Can the general government withstand such a united opposition? Will the people suffer themselves to be stripped of their privileges? Will they suffer their legislatures to be reduced to a shadow and a name? The idea is shocking to common sense.

From the circumstances already explained, and many others which might be mentioned, results a complicated, irresistable check, which must ever support the existence and importance of the state governments. The danger, if any exists, flows from an opposite source. The probable evil is, that the general government will be too dependent on the state legislatures, too much governed by their prejudices, and too obsequious to their humours; that the states, with every power in their hands, will make encroachments on the national authority, till the union is weakened and dissolved.

Every member must have been struck with an observation of a gentleman from Albany. Do what you will, says he, local prejudices and opinions will go into the government. What! shall we then form a constitution to cherish and strengthen these prejudices? Shall we confirm the distemper instead of remedying it? It is undeniable that there must be a controul somewhere. Either the general interest is to controul the particular interests, or the contrary. If the former, then certainly the government ought to be so framed, as to render the power of controul efficient to all intents and purposes; if the latter, a striking absurdity follows: The controuling powers must be as numerous as the varying interests, and the operations of government must therefore cease: For the moment you accommodate these differing interests, which is the only way to set the government in motion, you establish a general controuling power. Thus, whatever constitutional provisions are made to the contrary, every government will be at last driven to the necessity of subjecting the partial to the universal interest. The gentlemen ought always, in their reasoning, to distinguish between the real, genuine good of a state, and the opinions and prejudices which may prevail respecting it: The latter may be opposed to the general good, and consequently ought to be sacrificed; the former is so involved in it, that it never can be sacrificed. Sir, the main design of the convention, in forming the senate, was to prevent fluctuations and cabals: With this view, they made that body small, and to exist for a considerable period. Have they executed this design too far? The senators are to serve six years. This is only two years longer than the senators of this state hold their place. One third of the members are to go out every two years; and in six, the whole body may be changed. Prior to the revolution, the representatives in the several colonies were elected for different periods; for three years, for seven years, &c. Were those bodies ever considered as incapable of representing the people, or as too independent of them? There is one circumstance which will have a tendency to increase the dependence of the senators on the states, in proportion to the duration of their appointments. As the state legislatures are in continual fluctuation, the senator will have more attachments to form, and consequently a greater difficulty of maintaining his place, than one of shorter duration. He will therefore be more cautious and industrious to suit his conduct to the wishes of his constituents.

Sir, when you take a view of all the circumstances which have been recited, you will certainly see, that the senators will constantly look up to the state governments, with an eye of dependence and

221

affection. If they are ambitious to continue in office, they will make every prudent arrangement for this purpose, and, whatever may be their private sentiments of politics, they will be convinced, that the surest means of obtaining a re-election will be a uniform attachment to the interests of their several states.

The gentlemen to support their amendment have observed that the power of recall, under the old government, has never been exercised. There is no reasoning from his. The experience of a few years, under peculiar circumstances, can afford no probable security that it never will be carried into execution, with unhappy effects. A seat in congress has been less an object of ambition; and the arts of intrigue, consequently, have been less practised. Indeed, it has been difficult to find them, who were willing to suffer the mortifications, to which so feeble a government and so dependent a station exposed them.

Sir, if you consider but a moment the purposes, for which the senate was instituted, and the nature of the business which they are to transact, you will see the necessity of giving them duration. They, together with the President, are to manage all our concerns with foreign nations: They must understand all their interests, and their political systems. This knowledge is not soon acquired. But a very small part is gained in the closet. Is it desirable then that new and unqualified members should be continually thrown into that body? When public bodies are engaged in the exercise of general powers, you cannot judge of the propriety of their conduct, but from the result of their systems. They may be forming plans, which require time and diligence to bring to maturity. It is necessary, therefore, that they should have a considerable and fixed duration, that they may make their calculations accordingly. If they are to be perpetually fluctuating, they can never have that responsibility which is so important in republican governments. In bodies subject to frequent changes, great political plans must be conducted by members in succession: A single assembly can have but a partial agency in them, and consequently cannot properly be answerable for the final event. Considering the senate therefore with a view to responsibility, duration is a very interesting and essential quality. There is another view, in which duration in the senate appears necessary. A government, changeable in its policy, must soon lose its sense of national character, and forfeit the respect of foreigners. Senators will not be solicitous for the reputation of public measures, in which they have had but a temporary concern, and will feel lightly the burthen of public disapprobation, in proportion to the number of those who partake of the censure. Our political rivals will ever consider our mutable counsels as evidence of deficient wisdom, and will be little apprehensive of our arriving at any exalted station in the scale of power. Such are the internal and external disadvantages which would result from the principle contended for. Were it admitted, I am firmly persuaded, Sir, that prejudices would govern the public deliberations, and passions rage in the counsels of the union. If it were necessary, I could illustrate my subject by historical facts: I could travel through an extensive field of detail, and demonstrate that wherever the fatal principle of the head suffering the controul of the members, has operated, it has proved a fruitful source of commotions and disorders.

This, Sir, is the first fair opportunity that has been offered, of deliberately correcting the errors in government. Instability has been a prominent and very defective feature in most republican systems. It is the first to be seen, and the last to be lamented by a philosophical enquirer. It has operated most banefully in our infant republics. It is necessary that we apply an immediate remedy, and eradicate the poisonous principle from our government. If this be not done, Sir, we shall feel, and posterity will be convulsed by a painful malady.

SPEECH IN THE NEW YORK RATIFYING CONVENTION
JUNE 25, 1788

Poughkeepsie, New York, June 25, 1788

The Hon. Mr. *Hamilton.* Mr. Chairman, in debates of this kind it is extremely easy, on either side, to say a great number of plausible things. It is to be acknowledged, that there is even a certain degree of truth in the reasonings on both sides. In this situation, it is the province of judgment and good sense to determine their force and application, and how far the arguments advanced on one side, are balanced by those on the other. The ingenious dress, in which both may appear, renders it a difficult task to make this decision, and the mind is frequently unable to come to a safe and solid conclusion. On the present question, some of the principles on each side are admitted, and the conclusions drawn from them denied, while other principles, with their inferences, are rejected altogether. It is the business of the committee to seek the truth in this labyrinth of argument.

There are two objects in forming systems of government—Safety

223

for the people, and energy in the administration. When these objects are united, the certain tendency of the system will be to the public welfare. If the latter object be neglected, the people's security will be as certainly sacrificed, as by disregarding the former. Good constitutions are formed upon a comparison of the liberty of the individual with the strength of government: If the tone of either be too high, the other will be weakened too much. It is the happiest possible mode of conciliating these objects, to institute one branch peculiarly endowed with sensibility, another with knowledge and firmness. Through the opposition and mutual controul of these bodies, the government will reach, in its regular operations, the perfect balance between liberty and power. The arguments of the gentlemen chiefly apply to the former branch—the house of representatives. If they will calmly consider the different nature of the two branches, they will see that the reasoning which justly applies to the representative house, will go to destroy the essential qualities of the senate. If the former is calculated perfectly upon the principles of caution, why should you impose the same principle upon the latter, which is designed for a different operation? Gentlemen, while they discover a laudable anxiety for the safety of the people, do not attend to the important distinction I have drawn. We have it constantly held up to us, that as it is our chief duty to guard against tyranny, it is our policy to form all the branches of government for this purpose. Sir, it is a truth sufficiently illustrated by experience, that when the people act by their representatives, they are commonly irresistable. The gentleman admits the position, that stability is essential to the government, and yet enforces principles, which if true, ought to banish stability from the system. The gentleman observes that there is a fallacy in my reasoning, and informs us that the legislatures of the states—not the people, are to appoint the senators. Does he reflect, that they are the immediate agents of the people; that they are so constituted, as to feel all their prejudices and passions, and to be governed, in a great degree, by their misapprehensions? Experience must have taught him the truth of this. Look through their history. What factions have arisen from the most trifling causes? What intrigues have been practiced for the most illiberal purposes? Is not the state of Rhode-Island, at this moment, struggling under difficulties and distresses, for having been led blindly by the spirit of the multitude? What is her legislature but the picture of a mob? In this state we have a senate, possessed of the proper qualities of a permanent body: Virginia, Maryland, and a few other states, are in the same situation: The rest are either governed by a single democratic assembly, or have a senate constituted entirely upon democratic principles. These have been more or less embroiled in factions, and have generally been the image and echo of the multitude. It is difficult to reason on this point, without touching on certain delicate cords. I could refer you to periods and conjunctures, when the people have been governed by improper passions, and led by factious and designing men. I could shew that the same passions have infected their representatives. Let us beware that we do not make the state legislatures a vehicle, in which the evil humors may be conveyed into the national system. To prevent this, it is necessary that the senate should be so formed, as in some measure to check the state governments, and preclude the communication of the false impressions which they receive from the people. It has been often repeated, that the legislatures of the states can have only a partial and confined view of national affairs; that they can form no proper estimate of great objects which are not in the sphere of their interests. The observation of the gentleman therefore cannot take off the force of my argument.

Sir, the senators will constantly be attended with a reflection, that their future existence is absolutely in the power of the states. Will not this form a powerful check? It is a reflection which applies closely to their feelings and interests; and no candid man, who thinks deliberately, will deny that it would be alone a sufficient check. The legislatures are to provide the mode of electing the President, and must have a great influence over the electors. Indeed they convey their influence, through a thousand channels, into the general government. Gentlemen have endeavoured to shew that there will be no clashing of local and general interests. They do not seem to have sufficiently considered the subject. We have in this state a duty of six pence per pound on salt, and it operates lightly and with advantage: But such a duty would be very burthensome to some of the states. If Congress should, at any time, find it convenient to impose a salt tax, would it not be opposed by the eastern states? Being themselves incapable of feeling the necessity of the measure, they could only feel its apparent injustice. Would it be wise to give the New-England states a power to defeat this measure by recalling their senators who may be engaged for it? I beg the gentlemen once more to attend to the distinction between the real and apparent interests of the states. I admit that the aggregate of individuals constitutes the government— yet every state is not the government: Every petty district is not the government. Sir, in our state legislatures, a compromise is frequently necessary between the interests of counties: The same must happen in the general government between states. In this, the few must yield to the many; or, in other words, the particular must be sacrificed to the general interest. If the members of Congress are too dependent on the state legislatures, they will be eternally forming secret combinations from local views. This is reasoning from the plainest principles. Their interest is interwoven with their dependence, and they will necessarily yield to the impression of their situation. Those who have been in Congress have seen these operations. The first question has been—How will such a measure affect my constituents, and consequently, how will the part I take affect my re-election? This consideration may be in some degree proper; but to be dependent from day to day, and to have the idea perpetually present would be the source of innumerable evils. Six years, sir, is a period short enough for a proper degree of dependence. Let us consider the peculiar state of this body, and see under what impressions they will act. One third of them are to go out at the end of two years; two thirds at four years, and the whole at six years. When one year is elapsed, there is a number who are to hold their places for one year, others for three, and others for five years. Thus, there will not only be a constant and frequent change of members; but there will be some whose office is near the point of expiration, and who from this circumstance, will have a lively sense of their dependence. The biennial change of members is an excellent invention for increasing the difficulty of combination. Any scheme of usurpation will lose, every two years, a number of its oldest advocates, and their places will be supplied by an equal number of new, unaccommodating and virtuous men. When two principles are equally important, we ought if possible to reconcile them, and sacrifice neither. We think that safety and permanency in this government are completely reconcileable. The state governments will have, from the causes I have described, a sufficient influence over the senate, without the check for which the gentlemen contend.

It has been remarked that there is an inconsistency in our admitting that the equal vote in the senate was given to secure the rights of the states, and at the same time holding up the idea, that their interests should be sacrificed to those of the union. But the committee certainly perceive the distinction between the rights of a state and its interests. The rights of a state are defined by the constitution, and cannot be invaded without a violation of it; but the interests of a state have no connection with the constitution, and may be in a thousand instances constitutionally sacrificed. A uniform tax is perfectly constitutional; and yet it may operate oppressively upon certain members of the union. The gentlemen are afraid that the state governments will be abolished. But, Sir, their existence does not depend upon the laws of the United States. Congress can no more abolish the state governments, than they can dissolve the union. The whole constitution is repugnant to it, and yet the gentlemen would introduce an additional useless provision against it. It is proper that the influence of the states should prevail to a certain extent. But shall the individual states be the judges how far? Shall an unlimited power be left them to determine in their own favor? The gentlemen go into the extreme: Instead of a wise government, they would form a fantastical Utopia: But, Sir, while they give it a plausible, popular shape, they would render it impracticable. Much has been said about factions. As far as my observation has extended, factions in Congress have arisen from attachment to state prejudices. We are attempting by this constitution to abolish factions, and to unite all parties for the general welfare. That a man should have the power, in private life, of recalling his agent, is proper; because in the business in which he is engaged, he has no other object but to gain the approbation of his principal. Is this the case with the senator? Is he simply the agent of the state? No: He is an agent for the union, and he is bound to perform services necessary to the good of the whole, though his state should condemn them.

Sir, in contending for a rotation, the gentlemen carry their zeal beyond all reasonable bounds. I am convinced that no government, founded on this feeble principle, can operate well. I believe also that we shall be singular in this proposal. We have not felt the embarrassments resulting from rotation, that other states have; and we hardly know the strength of their objections to it. There is no probability that we shall ever persuade a majority of the states to agree to this admendment. The gentlemen deceive themselves. The amendment would defeat their own design. When a man knows he must quit his station, let his merit be what it may; he will turn his attention chiefly to his own emolument: Nay, he will feel temptations, which few other situations furnish; to perpetuate his power by unconstitutional usurpations. Men will pursue their interests. It is as easy to change human nature, as to oppose the strong current of the selfish passions. A wise legislator will gently divert the channel, and direct it, if possible, to the public good.

It has been observed, that it is not possible there should be in a state only two men qualified for senators. But, sir, the question is not, whether there may be no more than two men; but whether, in certain emergencies, you could find two equal to those whom the amendment would discard. Important negociations, or other business to which they shall be most competent, may employ them, at the moment of their removal. These things often happen. The difficulty of obtaining men, capable of conducting the affairs of a nation in dangerous times, is much more serious than the gentlemen imagine.

As to corruption, sir, admitting in the president a disposition to corrupt; what are the instruments of bribery? It is said, he will have in his disposal a great number of offices: But how many offices are there, for which a man would relinquish the senatorial dignity? There may be some in the judicial, and some in the other principal departments: But there are very few, whose respectability can in any measure balance that of the office of senator. Men who have been in the senate once, and who have a reasonable hope of a reelection, will not be easily bought by offices. This reasoning shews that a rotation would be productive of many disadvantages. Under particular circumstances, it might be extremely inconvenient, if not fatal to the prosperity of our country.

REMARKS IN THE NEW YORK RATIFYING CONVENTION
JUNE 27, 1788

Poughkeepsie, New York, June 27, 1788

The hon. Mr. *Hamilton.* This is one of those subjects, Mr. Chairman, on which objections very naturally arise, and assume the most plausible shape. Its address is to the passions, and its first impressions create a prejudice, before cool examination has an opportunity for exertion. It is more easy for the human mind to calculate the evils, than the advantages of a measure; and vastly more natural to apprehend the danger, than to see the necessity, of giving powers to our rulers. Hence I may justly expect, that those who hear me, will place less confidence in those arguments which oppose, than in those which favour, their prepossessions.

After all our doubts, our suspicions and speculations, on the subject of government, we must return at last to this important truth—that when we have formed a constitution upon free principles, when we have given a proper balance to the different branches of administration, and fixed representation upon pure and equal principles, we may with safety furnish it with all the powers, necessary to answer, in the most ample manner, the purposes of government. The great desiderata are a free representation, and mutual checks: When these are obtained, all our apprehension of the extent of powers are unjust and imaginary. What then is the structure of this constitution? One branch of the legislature is to be elected by the people—by the

same people, who choose your state representatives: Its members are
to hold their office two years, and then return to their constituents.
Here, sir, the people govern: Here they act by their immediate representatives. You have also a senate, constituted by your state legislatures—by men, in whom you place the highest confidence; and
forming another representative branch. Then again you have an executive magistrate, created by a form of election, which merits universal admiration. In the form of this government, and in the mode of
legislation, you find all the checks which the greatest politicians and
the best writers have ever conceived. What more can reasonable men
desire? Is there any one branch, in which the whole legislative and
executive powers are lodged? No. The legislative authority is lodged
in three distinct branches properly balanced: The executive authority
is divided between two branches; and the judicial is still reserved for
an independent body, who hold their office during good behaviour.
This organization is so complex, so skillfully contrived, that it is next
to impossible that an impolitic or wicked measure should pass the
great scrutiny with success. Now what do gentlemen mean by coming forward and declaiming against this government? Why do they
say we ought to limit its powers, to disable it, and to destroy its
capacity of blessing the people? Has philosophy suggested—has experience taught, that such a government ought not to be trusted with
every thing necessary for the good of society? Sir, when you have
divided and nicely balanced the departments of government; When
you have strongly connected the virtue of your rulers with their interest; when, in short, you have rendered your system as perfect as
human forms can be; you must place confidence; you must give
power.

   We have heard a great deal of the sword and the purse: It is said,
our liberties are in danger, if both are possessed by Congress. Let us
see what is the true meaning of this maxim, which has been so much
used, and so little understood. It is, that you shall not place these
powers in either the legislative or executive singly: Neither one nor
the other shall have both; Because this would destroy that division of
powers, on which political liberty is founded; and would furnish one
body with all the means of tyranny. But where the purse is lodged in
one branch, and the sword in another, there can be no danger. All
governments have possessed these powers. They would be monsters
without them, and incapable of exertion. What is your state government? Does not your legislature command what money it pleases?
Does not your executive execute the laws without restraint? These
distinctions between the purse and the sword have no application to
the system, but only to its separate branches. Sir, when we reason

229

about the great interests of a great people, it is high time that we dismiss our prejudices and banish declamation.

In order to induce us to consider the powers given by this constitution as dangerous; In order to render plausible an attempt to take away the life and spirit of the most important power in government; the gentleman complains that we shall not have a true and safe representation. I have asked him, what a safe representation is; and he has given no satisfactory answer. The assembly of New-York has been mentioned as a proper standard: But if we apply this standard to the general government, our Congress will become a mere mob, exposed to every irregular impulse, and subject to every breeze of faction. Can such a system afford security? Can you have confidence in such a body? The idea of taking the ratio of representation, in a small society, for the ratio of a great one, is a fallacy which ought to be exposed. It is impossible to ascertain to what point our representation will increase: It may vary from one, to two, three or four hundred. It depends upon the progress of population. Suppose it to rest at two hundred. Is not this number sufficient to secure it against corruption? Human nature must be a much more weak and despicable thing, than I apprehend it to be, if two hundred of our fellow citizens can be corrupted in two years. But suppose they are corrupted; can they in two years accomplish their designs? Can they form a combination, and even lay a foundation for a system of tyranny, in so short a period? It is far from my intention to wound the feelings of any gentleman; but I must, in this most interesting discussion, speak of things as they are; and hold up opinions in the light in which they ought to appear: and I maintain, that all that has been said of corruption, of the purse and the sword, and of the danger of giving powers, is not supported by principle or fact—That it is mere verbage, and idle declamation. The true principle of government is this—Make the system compleat in its structure; give a perfect proportion and balance to its parts; and the powers you give it will never affect your security. The question then, of the division of powers between the general and state governments, is a question of convenience: It becomes a prudential enquiry, what powers are proper to be reversed to the latter; and this immediately involves another enquiry into the proper objects of the two governments. This is the criterion, by which we shall determine the just distribution of powers.

The great leading objects of the federal government, in which revenue is concerned, are to maintain domestic peace, and provide for the common defence. In these are comprehended the regulation of commerce; that is, the whole system of foreign intercourse; the support of armies and navies, and of the civil administration. It is useless to go into detail. Every one knows that the objects of the general government are numerous, extensive and important. Every one must acknowledge the necessity of giving powers, in all respects and in every degree, equal to these objects. This principle assented to, let us enquire what are the objects of the state governments. Have they to provide against foreign invasion? Have they to maintain fleets and armies? Have they any concern in the regulation of commerce, the procuring alliances, or forming treaties of peace? No: Their objects are merely civil and domestic; to support the legislative establishment, and to provide for the administration of the laws. Let any one compare the expence of supporting the civil list in a state, with the expence of providing for the defence of the union. The difference is almost beyond calculation. The experience of Great-Britain will throw some light on this subject. In that kingdom, the ordinary expences of peace to those of war, are as one to fourteen: But there they have a monarch, with his splendid court, and an enormous civil establishment, with which we have nothing in this country to compare. If, in Great-Britain, the expences of war and peace are so disproportioned; how wide will be their disparity in the United States; How infinitely wider between the general government and each individual state! Now, Sir, where ought the great resources to be lodged? Every rational man will give an immediate answer. To what extent shall these resources be possessed? Reason says as far as possible exigencies can require; that is, without limitation. A constitution cannot set bounds to a nation's wants; it ought not therefore to set bounds to its resources. Unexpected invasions—long and ruinous wars, may demand all the possible abilities of the country: Shall not your government have power to call these abilities into action? The contingencies of society are not reducible to calculations: They cannot be fixed or bounded, even in imagination. Will you limit the means of your defence, when you cannot ascertain the force or extent of the invasion? Even in ordinary wars, a government is frequently obliged to call for supplies, to the temporary oppression of the people.

Sir, if we adopt the idea of exclusive revenues, we shall be obliged to fix some distinguishing line, which neither government shall overpass. The inconveniencies of this measure must appear evident, on the slightest examination. The resources appropriated to one, may diminish or fail; while those of the other may increase, beyond the wants of government: One may be destitute of revenues, while the other shall possess an unnecessary abundance: and the constitution will be an eternal barrier to a mutual intercourse and relief. In this case, will the individual states stand on so good a ground, as if the objects of taxation were left free and open to the embrace of both the governments? Possibly, in the advancement of commerce, the imposts may increase to such a degree, as to render direct taxes unnecessary; These resources then, as the constitution stands, may be occasionally relinquished to the states: But on the gentleman's idea of prescribing exclusive limits, and precluding all reciprocal communication, this would be entirely improper. The laws of the states must not touch the appropriated resources of the United States, whatever may be their wants. Would it not be of more advantage to the states, to have a concurrent jurisdiction extending to all the sources of revenue, than to be confined to such a small resource, as, on calculation of the objects of the two governments, should appear to be their due proportion? Certainly you cannot hesitate on this question. The gentleman's plan would have a further ill effect; It would tend to dissolve the connexion and correspondence of the two governments, to estrange them from each other, and to destroy that mutual dependence, which forms the essence of union.

Sir, a number of arguments have been advanced by an honorable member from New-York, which to every unclouded mind must carry conviction. He has stated, that in sudden emergencies, it may be necessary to borrow; and that it is impossible to borrow, unless you have funds to pledge for the payment of your debts. Limiting the powers of government to certain resources, is rendering the fund precarious; and obliging the government to ask, instead of empowering them to command, is to destroy all confidence and credit. If the power of taxing is restricted, the consequence is, that on the breaking out of a war, you must divert the funds, appropriated to the payment of debts, to answer immediate exigencies. Thus you violate your engagements, at the very time you increase the burthen of them. Besides, sound policy condemns the practice of accumulating debts. A government, to act with energy, should have the possession of all its revenues to answer present purposes. The principle, for which I contend, is recognized in all its extent by our old constitution. Congress is authorized to raise troops, to call for supplies without limitation, and to borrow money to any amount. It is true, they must use the form of recommendations and requisitions: but the states are bound by the solemn ties of honor, of justice, of religion, to comply without reserve.

Mr. Chairman, it has been advanced as a principle, that no government but a despotism can exist in a very extensive country. This is a melancholy consideration indeed. If it were founded on truth, we ought to dismiss the idea of a republican government, even for the state of New-York. This idea has been taken from a celebrated writer, who, by being misunderstood, has been the occasion of frequent fallacies in our reasoning on political subjects. But the position has been misapprehended; and its application is entirely false and unwarrantable: It relates only to democracies, where the whole body of the people meet to transact business; and where representation is unknown. Such were a number of antient, and some modern independent cities. Men who read without attention, have taken these maxims respecting the extent of country; and, contrary to their proper meaning, have applied them to republics in general. This application is wrong, in respect to all representative governments; but especially in relation to a confederacy of states, in which the supreme legislature has only general powers, and the civil and domestic concerns of the people are regulated by the laws of the several states. This distinction being kept in view, all the difficulty will vanish, and we may easily conceive, that the people of a large country may be represented as truly, as those of a small one. An assembly constituted for general purposes, may be fully competent to every federal regulation, without being too numerous for deliberate conduct. If the state governments were to be abolished, the question would wear a different face: but this idea is inadmissible. They are absolutely necessary to the system. Their existence must form a leading principle in the most perfect constitution we could form. I insist, that it never can be the interest or desire of the national legislature, to destroy the state governments. It can derive no advantage from such an event; But, on the contrary, would lose an indispensable support, a necessary aid in executing the laws, and conveying the influence of government to the doors of the people. The union is dependent on the will of the state governments for its chief magistrate, and for its senate. The blow aimed at the members, must give a fatal wound to the head; and the destruction of the states must be at once a political suicide. Can the national government be guilty of this madness? what inducements, what temptations can they have? Will they attach new honors to their station; will they increase the national strength; will they multiply the national resources; will they make themselves more respectable, in the view of foreign nations, or of their fellow citizens, by robbing the states of their constitutional privileges? But imagine, for a moment, that a political frenzy should seize the government. Suppose they should make the attempt. Certainly, Sir, it would be forever impracticable. This has been sufficiently demonstrated by reason and experience. It has been proved, that the members of republics have been, and ever will be, stronger than the head. Let us attend to one general historical example. In the antient feudal governments of Europe, there were, in the first place a monarch; subordinate to him, a body of nobles; and subject to these, the vassals or the whole body of the

233

people. The authority of the kings was limited, and that of the barons considerably independent. A great part of the early wars in Europe were contests between the king and his nobility. In these contests, the latter possessed many advantages derived from their influence, and the immediate command they had over the people; and they generally prevailed. The history of the feudal wars exhibits little more than a series of successful encroachments on the prerogatives of monarchy. Here, Sir, is one great proof of the superiority, which the members in limited governments possess over their head. As long as the barons enjoyed the confidence and attachment of the people, they had the strength of the country on their side, and were irresistable. I may be told, that in some instances the barons were overcome: But how did this happen? Sir, they took advantage of the depression of the royal authority, and the establishment of their own power, to oppress and tyrannise over their vassals. As commerce enlarged, and as wealth and civilization encreased, the people began to feel their own weight and consequence: They grew tired of their oppressions; united their strength with that of the prince; and threw off the yoke of aristocracy. These very instances prove what I contend for: They prove, that in whatever direction the popular weight leans, the current of power will flow: Wherever the popular attachments lie, there will rest the political superiority. Sir, can it be supposed that the state governments will become the oppressors of the people? Will they forfeit their affections? Will they combine to destroy the liberties and happiness of their fellow citizens, for the sole purpose of involving themselves in ruin? God forbid! The idea, Sir, is shocking! It outrages every feeling of humanity, and every dictate of common sense!

There are certain social principles in human nature, from which we may draw the most solid conclusions with respect to the conduct of individuals, and of communities. We love our families, more than our neighbours: We love our neighbours, more than our countrymen in general. The human affections, like the solar heat, lose their intensity, as they depart from the center; and become languid, in proportion to the expansion of the circle, on which they act. On these principles, the attachment of the individual will be first and forever secured by the states governments: They will be a mutual protection and support. Another source of influence, which has already been pointed out, is the various official connections in the states. Gentlemen endeavour to evade the force of this, by saying that these offices will be insignificant. This is by no means true. The state officers will ever be important, because they are necessary and useful. Their powers are such, as are extremely interesting to the people; such as affect their property, their liberty and life. What is more important, than the administration of justice, and the execution of the civil and criminal laws? Can the state governments become insignificant, while they have the power of raising money independently and without controul? If they are really useful; If they are calculated to promote the essential interests of the people; they must have their confidence and support. The states can never lose their powers, till the whole people of America are robbed of their liberties. These must go together, they must support each other, or meet one common fate. On the gentleman's principle, we may safely trust the state governments, tho' we have no means of resisting them: but we cannot confide in the national government, tho' we have an effectual, constitutional guard against every encroachment. This is the essence of their argument, and it is false and fallacious beyond conception.

With regard to the jurisdiction of the two governments, I shall certainly admit that the constitution ought to be so formed, as not to prevent the states from providing for their own existence; and I maintain that it is so formed; and that their power of providing for themselves is sufficiently established. This is conceded by one gentleman, and in the next breath, the concession is retracted. He says, Congress have but one exclusive right in taxation; that of duties on imports: Certainly then, their other powers are only concurrent. But to take off the force of this obvious conclusion, he immediately says that the laws of the United States are supreme; and that where there is one supreme, there cannot be a concurrent authority: and further, that where the laws of the union are supreme, those of the states must be subordinate; because, there cannot be two supremes. This is curious sophistry. That two supreme powers cannot act together, is false. They are inconsistent only when they are aimed at each other, or at one indivisible object. The laws of the United States are supreme, as to all their proper, constitutional objects: The laws of the states are supreme in the same way. These supreme laws may act on different objects, without clashing; or they may operate on different parts of the same common object, with perfect harmony. Suppose both governments should lay a tax of a penny on a certain article: Has not each an independent and uncontrolable power to collect its own tax? The meaning of the maxim—that there can not be two supremes—is simply this:—Two powers cannot be supreme over each other. This meaning is entirely perverted by the gentlemen. But, it is said, disputes between collectors are to be referred to the federal courts. This is again wandering in the field of conjecture. But suppose the fact certain: Is it not to be presumed, that they will express the true meaning of the constitution and the laws? Will they not be bound to consider the concurrent jurisdiction; to declare that both the taxes shall

235

have equal operation; that both the powers, in that respect, are sovereign and co-extensive? If they transgress their duty, we are to hope that they will be punished. Sir, we can reason from probabilities alone. When we leave common sense, and give ourselves up to conjecture, there can be no certainty, no security in our reasonings.

I imagine I have stated to the committee abundant reasons to prove the entire safety of the state governments and of the people. I would go into a more minute consideration of the nature of the concurrent jurisdiction, and the operation of the laws, in relation to revenue; but at present I feel too much indisposed to proceed. I shall, with the leave of the committee, improve another opportunity of expressing to them more fully my ideas on this point. I wish the committee to remember, that the constitution under examination is framed upon truly republican principles; and that, as it is expressly designed to provide for the common protection and the general welfare of the United States, it must be utterly repugnant to this constitution, to subvert the state governments, or oppress the people.

SPEECH IN THE NEW YORK RATIFYING CONVENTION
JUNE 28, 1788

Poughkeepsie, New York, June 28, 1788

Mr. *Hamilton.* The honorable gentleman from Ulster has given a turn to the introduction of those papers, which was never in our contemplation. He seems to insinuate that they were brought forward, with a view of shewing an inconsistency in the conduct of some gentlemen—perhaps of himself. Sir, the exhibition of them had a very different object. It was to prove that this state once experienced hardships and distresses to an astonishing degree, for want of the assistance of the other states. It was to shew the evils we suffered since, as well as before the establishment of the confederation, from being compelled to support the burthen of the war; That requisitions have been unable to call forth the resources of the country; That requisitions have been the cause of a principal part of our calamities; that the system is defective and rotten, and ought forever to be banished from our government. It was necessary, with deference to the honorable gentleman, to bring forward these important proofs of our argument, without consulting the feelings of any man.

That the human passions should flow from one extreme to another, I allow is natural. Hence the mad project of creating a dictator. But it is equally true, that this project was never ripened into a deliberate and extensive design. When I heard of it, it met my instant disapprobation. The honorable gentleman's opposition too is known and applauded. But why bring these things into remembrance? Why affect to compare this temporary effusion with the serious sentiments our fellow citizens entertained of the national weaknesses? The gentleman has made a declaration of his wishes for a strong federal government. I hope this is the wish of all. But why has he not given us his ideas of the nature of this government, which is the object of his wishes? Why does he not describe it? We have proposed a system, which we supposed would answer the purposes of strength and safety. The gentleman objects to it, without pointing out the grounds, on which his objections are founded, or shewing us a better form. These general surmises, never lead to the discovery of truth. It is to be desired, that the gentleman would explain particularly the errors in this system, and furnish us with their proper remedies. The committee remember that a grant of an impost to the United States, for twenty-five years, was requested by Congress. Though this was a very small addition of power to the federal government, it was opposed in this state, without any reasons being offered. The dissent of New-York and Rhode-Island frustrated a most important measure. The gentleman says, he was for granting the impost; yet he acknowleges, he could not agree to the mode recommended. But it was well known, that Congress had declared, that they could not receive the accession of the states, upon any other plan than that proposed. In such case, propositions for altering the plan amounted to a positive rejection. At this time, Sir, we were told it was dangerous to grant powers to Congress. Did this general argument indicate a disposition to grant the impost in any shape? I should myself have been averse to the granting of very extensive powers: But the impost was justly considered as the only means of supporting the union. We did not then contemplate a fundamental change in government. From my sense of the gentlemen's integrity, I am bound to believe, that they are attached to a strong united government; and yet I find it difficult to draw this conclusion from their conduct or their reasonings.

Sir, with respect to the subject of revenue, which was debated yesterday, it was asserted that in all matters of taxation, except in the article of imposts, the united and individual states had a concurrent jurisdiction; that the state governments had an independent authority, to draw revenues from every source but one. The truth of these positions will appear on a slight investigation. I maintain, that the word *supreme* imports no more than this; that the constitution, and laws made in pursuance thereof, cannot be controuled or defeated by any other law. The acts of the United States therefore will be absolutely obligatory, as to all the proper objects and powers of the general government. The states as well as individuals are bound by these laws. But the laws of Congress are restricted to a certain sphere, and when they depart from this sphere, they are no longer supreme or binding. In the same manner the states have certain independent powers, in which their laws are supreme: For example, in making and executing laws concerning the punishment of certain crimes, such as murder, theft, &c. the states cannot be controuled. With respect to certain other objects, the powers of the two governments are concurrent, and yet supreme. I instanced, yesterday, a tax on any specific article. Both might lay the tax; both might collect it without clashing or interference. If the individual should be unable to pay both, the first seizure would hold the property. Here the laws are not in the way of each other; they are independent and supreme. The case is like that of two creditors: Each has a distinct demand; the debtor is held equally for the payment of both. Their suits are independent; and if the debtor cannot pay both, he who takes the first step, secures his debt. The individual is precisely in the same situation, whether he pays such a sum to one, or to two. No more will be required of him to supply the public wants, than he has ability to afford. That the states have an undoubted right to lay taxes in all cases in which they are not prohibited, is a position founded on the obvious and important principle in confederated governments, that whatever is not expressly given to the federal head, is reserved to the members. The truth of this principle must strike every intelligent mind. In the first formation of government by the association of individuals, every power of the community is delegated, because the government is to extend to every possible object; Nothing is reserved, but the unalienable rights of mankind: But when a number of these societies unite for certain purposes, the rule is different, and from the plainest reason: They have already delegated their sovereignty, and their powers to their several governments; and these cannot be recalled, and given to another, without an express act. I submit to the committee whether this reasoning is not conclusive. Unless therefore we find that the powers of taxation are exclusively granted, we must conclude, that there remains a concurrent authority. Let us then enquire if the constitution gives such exclusive powers to the general government. Sir, there is not a syllable in it, that favours this idea: Not a word importing an exclusive grant, except in the article of imposts. I am supported in my general position, by this very exception. If the states are prohibited from laying duties on imports, the implication is clear. Now, what proportion will the duties on imports bear to the other ordinary resources of the country? We may now say, one third; but this will not be the case long. As our manufactures increase, foreign importations must lessen. Here are two thirds at least of the resources of our country open to the state governments. Can it be imagined then, that the states will lose their existence or their importance for want of revenues? The propriety of Congress possessing an exclusive power over the impost appears from the necessity of their having a considerable portion of our resources, to pledge as a fund for the reduction of the debts of the United States. When you have given a power of taxation to the general government, none of the states individually will be holden for the discharge of the federal obligations: The burthen will be on the union.

The gentleman says, that the operation of the taxes will exclude the states, on this ground, that the demands of the community are always equal to its resources; that Congress will find a use for all the money the people can pay. This observation, if designed as a general rule, is in every view unjust. Does he suppose the general government will want all the money the people can furnish; and also that the state governments will want all the money the people can furnish? What contradiction is this? But if this maxim be true, how does the wealth of a country ever increase? How are the people enabled to accumulate fortunes? Do the burthens regularly augment, as its inhabitants grow prosperous and happy. But if indeed all the resources are required for the protection of the people, it follows that the protecting power should have access to them. The only difficulty lies in the want of resources: If they are adequate, the operation will be easy: If they are not, taxation must be restrained: Will this be the fate of the state taxes alone? Certainly not. The people will say no. What will be the conduct of the national rulers? The consideration will not be, that our imposing the tax will destroy the states, for this cannot be effected; but that it will distress the people, whom we represent, and whose protectors we are. It is unjust to suppose that they will be altogether destitute of virtue and prudence: it is unfair to presume that the representatives of the people will be disposed to tyrannize, in one government more than in another. If we are convinced that the national legislature will pursue a system of measures unfavorable to the interests of the people, we ought to have no general government at all. But if we unite, it will be for the accomplishment of great purposes: These demand great resources, and great powers. There are certain extensive and uniform objects of revenue, which the United States will improve, and to which, if possible they will confine themselves. Those objects which are more limited, and in respect to which, the circumstances of the states differ, will be reserved for their use: A great variety of articles will be in this last class of objects, to which only the state laws will properly apply. To ascertain this division of objects is the proper business of legislation: It would be absurd to fix it in the constitution, both because it would be too extensive and intricate, and because alteration of circumstances must render a change of the division indispensible. Constitutions should consist only of general provisions: The reason is, that they must necessarily be permanent, and that they cannot calculate for the possible changes of things. I know that the states must have their resources; but I contend that it would be improper to point them out particularly in the constitution.

Sir, it has been said that a poll-tax is a tyrannical tax: But the legislature of this state can lay it, whenever they please. Does then our constitution authorize tyranny? I am as much opposed to a capitation as any man: Yet who can deny, that there may exist certain circumstances, which will render this tax necessary. In the course of a war, it may be necessary to lay hold of every resource: and, for a certain period, the people may submit to it. But on removal of the danger, or the return of peace, the general sense of the community would abolish it. The United Netherlands were obliged, on a emergency, to give up one half of their property to the government. It has been said, that it will be impossible to exercise this power of taxation: If it cannot be exercised, why be alarmed at it? But the gentlemen say that the difficulty of executing it with moderation will necessarily drive the government into despotic measures. Here again they are in the old track of jealousy and conjecture. Whenever the people feel the hand of despotism, they will not regard forms and parchments. But the gentlemen's premises are as false as their conclusion. No one reason can be offered, why the exercise of the power should be impracticable: No one difficulty can be pointed out, which will not apply to our state governments. Congress will have every means of knowledge, that any legislature can have. From general observation, and from the revenue systems of the several states, they will derive information as to the most eligible modes of taxation. If a land tax is the object, cannot Congress procure as perfect a valuation as any other assembly? Can they not have all the necessary officers for assessment and collection? Where is the difficulty? Where is the evil? They never can oppress a particular state, by an unequal imposition; because the constitution has provided a fixed ratio, a uniform rule, by which this must be regulated. The system will be founded upon the most easy and equal principles—to draw as much as possible from direct taxation; to lay the principal burthens on the wealthy, &c. Even ambitious and unprincipled men will form their system so, as to draw forth the resources of the country in the most favorable and gentle methods; because such will be ever the most productive. They never can hope for success, by adopting those arbitrary modes, which have been used in some of the states.

A gentleman yesterday passed many enconiums on the character and operations of the state governments. The question has not been, whether their laws have produced happy or unhappy effects: The character of our confederation is the subject of our controversy. But the gentleman concludes too hastily. In many of the states, government has not had a salutary operation. Not only Rhode-Island, but several others have been guilty of indiscretions and misconduct—of acts, which have produced misfortune and dishonor. I grant that the government of New-York has operated well; and I ascribe it to the influence of those excellent principles, in which the proposed constitution and our own are so congenial. We are sensible that private credit is much lower in some states, than it is in ours. What is the cause of this? Why is it at the present period, so low even in this state? Why is the value of our land depreciated? It is said there is a scarcity of money in the community: I do not believe this scarcity to be so great, as is represented. It may not appear; It may be retained by its holders; but nothing more than stability and confidence in the government is requisite to draw it into circulation. It is acknowledged that the general government has not answered its purposes. Why? We attribute it to the defects of the revenue system. But the gentlemen say, the requisitions have not been obeyed, because the states were impoverished. This is a kind of reasoning that astonishes me. The records of this state—the records of Congress prove that, during the war, New-York had the best reason to complain of the non-compliance of the other states. I appeal to the gentlemen. Have the states, who have suffered least, contributed most? No sir—the fact is directly the reverse. This consideration is sufficient entirely to refute the gentlemen's reasoning. Requisitions will ever be attended with the same effects. This depends on principles of human nature, that are as infallible as any mathematical calculations. States will contribute or not, according to their circumstances and interests: They will all be inclined to throw off the burthens of government upon their neighbours. These positions have been so fully illustrated and proved in former stages of this debate, that nothing need be added. Unanswerable experience—stubborn facts have supported and fixed them.

241

Sir, to what situation is our Congress now reduced! It is notorious, that with the utmost difficulty they maintain their ordinary officers, and support the mere form of a federal government. How do we stand with respect to foreign nations? It is a fact, that should strike us with surprize and with shame, that we are obliged to borrow money, in order to pay the interests of our debts. It is a fact, that these debts are every day accumulating by compound interest. This, sir, will one day endanger the peace of our country, and expose us to vicisitudes the most alarming. Such is the character of requisitions; Such the melancholy, dangerous condition, to which they have reduced us. Now, sir, after this full and fair experiment, with what countenance do gentlemen come forward, to recommend the ruinous principle, and make it the basis of a new government? Why do they affect to cherish this political demon, and present it once more to our embraces? The gentleman observes, that we cannot, even in a single state, collect the whole of a tax; Some counties will necessarily be deficient: In the same way, says he, some states will be delinquent. If this reasoning were just, I should expect to see the states pay, like the counties, in proportion to their ability; which is not the fact.

I shall proceed now more particularly to the proposition before the committee. This clearly admits, that the unlimited power of taxation, which I have been contending for, is proper. It declares that after the states have refused to comply with the requisitions, the general government may enforce its demands. While the gentlemen's proposal admits my principle, in its fullest latitude, the whole course of their argument is against it. The mode they point out would involve all the inconveniences, against which they would wish to guard. Suppose the gentlemen's scheme should be adopted; Would not all the resources of the country be equally in the power of Congress? The states cannot have but one opportunity of refusal. After having passed through the empty ceremony of a requisition, the general government can enforce all its demands, without limitation or resistance. The states will either comply, or they will not. If they comply, they are bound to collect the whole of the tax from the citizens. The people must pay it. What then will be the disadvantage of its being levied and collected by Congress, in the first instance? It has been proved, as far as probabilities can go, that the federal government will, in general, take the laws of the several states as its rule, and pursue those measures, to which the people are most accustomed. But if the states do not comply, what is the consequence? If the power of compulsion be a misfortune to the states, they must now suffer it, without opposition or complaint. I shall shew too, that they feel it in an aggravated degree. It may frequently happen, that, though the states formally comply with the requisitions, the avails will not be fully realized by Congress: The states may be dilatory in the collection and payment, and may form excuses for not paying the whole: There may be also partial compliances, which will subject the Union to inconveniences. Congress therefore in laying the tax will calculate for these losses and inconveniences: They will make allowances for the delays and delinquencies of the states, and apportion their burthens accordingly: They will be induced to demand more than their actual wants. In these circumstances the requisitions will be made upon calculations in some measure arbitrary. Upon the constitutional plan, the only enquiry will be—how much is actually wanted; and how much can the object bear, or the people pay? On the gentlemen's scheme, it will be—what will be the probable deficiencies of the states? for we must increase our demands in proportion, whatever the public wants may be, or whatever may be the abilities of the people. Now suppose the requisition is totally rejected, it must be levied upon the citizens, without reserve. This will be like inflicting a penalty upon the states: It will place them in the light of criminals. Will they suffer this? Will Congress presume so far? If the states solemnly declare they will not comply, does not this imply a determination not to permit the exercise of the coercive power? The gentlemen cannot escape the dilemma, into which their own reasoning leads them. If the states comply, the people must be taxed; If they do not comply, the people must equally be taxed: The burthen, in either case, will be the same; the difficulty of collecting the same. Sir, if these operations are merely harmless and indifferent, why play the ridiculous farce? If they are inconvenient, why subject us to their evils? It is infinitely more eligible, to lay a tax originally, which will have uniform effects throughout the Union; which will operate equally and silently. The United States will then be able to ascertain their resources, and to act with vigor and decision: All hostility between the governments will be prevented: The people will contribute regularly and gradually, for the support of government; and all odious, retrospective enquiries will be precluded.

But, the ill effects of the gentlemen's plan do not terminate here. Our own state will suffer peculiar disadvantages from the measure. One provision in the amendment is, that no direct taxes shall be laid till after the impost and excise shall be found insufficient for the public exigencies; and that no excise shall be laid on articles of the growth or manufacture of the United States. Sir, the favorable maritime situation of this state, and our large and valuable tracts of unsettled land, will ever lead us to commerce and agriculture as our proper objects. Unconfined, and tempted by the prospect of easy subsistance and independence, our citizens, as the country populates, will retreat back, and cultivate the western parts of our state. Our population, though extensive, will never be crowded, and consequently we shall remain an importing and agricultural state. Now, what will be the operation of the proposed plan? The general government, restrained by the constitution from a free application to other resources, will push imposts to an extreme. Will excessive impositions on our commerce be favorable to the policy of this state? Will they not directly oppose our interests. Similar will be the operation of the other clause of the amendment, relative to excise. Our neighbours not possessed of our advantages for commerce and agriculture, will become manufacturers: Their property will, in a great measure, be vested in the commodities of their own production: But a small proportion will be in trade, or in lands. Thus, on the gentlemen's scheme, they will be almost free from burthens, while we shall be loaded with them. Does not the partiality of this strike every one? Can gentlemen, who are laboring for the interest of their state, seriously bring forward such propositions? It is the interest of New-York, that those articles should be taxed, in the production of which, the other states exceed us. If we are not a manufacturing people, excises on manufactures will ever be for our advantage. This position is indisputable. Sir, I agree, that it is not good policy to lay excises to any considerable amount, while our manufactures are in their infancy— but are they always to be so? In some of the states, they already begin to make considerable progress. In Connecticut such encouragement is given, as will soon distinguish that state. Even at the present period, there is one article, from which, a revenue may very properly be drawn: I speak of ardent spirits. New-England manufactures more than a hundred gallons to our one. Consequently, an excise on spirits at the still-head would make those states contribute in a vastly greater proportion than ourselves. In every view, excises on domestic manufactures would benefit New-York. But the gentlemen would defeat the advantages of our situation, by drawing upon us all the burthens of government. The nature of our union requires, that we should give up our state impost: The amendment would forfeit every other advantage. This part of the constitution should not be touched. The excises were designed as a recompence to the importing states, for relinquishing their imposts. Why then should we reject the benefits conferred upon us? Why should we run blindly against our own interest?

Sir, I shall no further enlarge on this argument. My exertions have already exhausted me. I have persevered, from an anxious desire to give the committee the most complete conception of this subject. I fear however, that I have not been so successful, as to bestow upon it that full and clear light, of which it is susceptible. I shall conclude with a few remarks, by way of apology. I am apprehensive, Sir, that in the warmth of my feelings, I may have uttered expressions, which were too vehement. If such has been my language, it was from the habit of using strong phrases to express my ideas; and, above all, from the interesting nature of the subject. I have ever condemned those cold, unfeeling hearts, which no object can animate. I condemn those indifferent mortals, who either never form opinions, or never make then known. I confess, Sir, that on no subject, has my breast been filled with stronger emotions, or more anxious concern. If any thing has escaped me, which may be construed into a personal reflection, I beg the gentlemen, once for all, to be assured, that I have no design to wound the feelings of any one who is opposed to me. While I am making these observations, I cannot but take notice of some expressions, which have fallen, in the course of the debate. It has been said, that ingenious men may say ingenious things, and that those, who are interested in raising the few upon the ruins of the many, may give to every cause an appearance of justice. I know not whether these insinuations allude to the characters of any, who are present, or to any of the reasonings in this house. I presume that the gentlemen would not ungenerously impute such motives to those, who differ from themselves. I declare I know not any set of men who are to derive peculiar advantages from this constitution. Were any permanent honors or emoluments to be secured to the families of those who have been active in this cause, there might be some ground for suspicion. But what reasonable man, for the precarious enjoyment of rank and power, would establish a system, which would reduce his nearest friends and his posterity to slavery and ruin? If the gentlemen reckon me among the obnoxious few; If they imagine, that I contemplate, with an ambitious eye, the immediate honors of the government; yet, let them consider, that I have my friends—my family—my children, to whom the ties of nature and of habit have attached me. If, to day, I am among the favoured few; my children, tomorrow, may be among the oppressed many: These dearest pledges of my patriotism may, at a future day, be suffering the severe distresses, to which my ambition has reduced them. The changes in the human conditions are uncertain and frequent. Many, on whom fortune has bestowed her favours, may trace their family to a more unprosperous station; and many who are now in obscurity, may look back upon the affluence and exalted rank of their ancestors. But I will no longer trespass on your indulgence. I have troubled the committee with these observations, to shew that it cannot be the wish of any reasonable man, to establish a government unfriendly to the liberties of the people. Gentlemen ought not then to presume, that the advocates of this constitution are influenced by ambitious views. The suspicion, Sir, is unjust; the charge is uncharitable.

LETTER TO GEORGE WASHINGTON
SEPTEMBER 1788

The following letter discusses the possibility of Washington's being offered and accepting the presidency and emphasizes how much Hamilton thought that the initial success of the new government would depend upon his willingness to serve in that capacity.

New York, September 1788

Dear Sir

Your Excellency's friendly and obliging letter of the 28th Ulto. came safely to hand. I thank you for your assurance of seconding my application to General Morgan. The truth of that affair is, that he purchased the watch for a trifle of a British soldier, who plundered Major Cochran at the moment of his fall at York Town.

I should be deeply pained my Dear Sir if your scruples in regard to a certain station should be matured into a resolution to decline it; though I am neither surprised at their existence nor can I but agree in opinion that the caution you observe in deferring an ultimate determination is prudent. I have however reflected maturely on the subject and have come to a conclusion, (in which I feel no hesitation) that every public and personal consideration will demand from you an acquiescence in what will *certainly* be the unanimous wish of your country. The absolute retreat which you meditated at the close of the late war was natural and proper. Had the government produced by the revolution gone on in a *tolerable* train, it would have been most adviseable to have persisted in that retreat. But I am clearly of opinion that the crisis which brought you again into public view left you no alterative but to comply—and I am equally clear in the opinion that you are by that act *pledged* to take a part in the execution of the government. I am not less convinced that the impression of this necessity of your filling the station in question is so universal that you run no risk of any uncandid imputation, by submitting to it. But even if this were not the case, a regard to your own reputation as well as to the public good, calls upon you in the strongest manner to run that risk.

It cannot be considered as a compliment to say that on your acceptance of the office of President the success of the new government in its commencement may materially depend. Your agency and influence will be not less important in preserving it from the future attacks of its enemies than they have been in recommending it in the first instance to the adoption of the people. Independent of all considerations drawn from this source the point of light in which you stand at home and abroad will make an infinite difference in the respectability with which the government will begin its operations in the alternative of your being or not being at the head of it. I forbear to urge considerations which might have a more personal application. What I have said will suffice for the inferences I mean to draw.

First—In a matter so essential to the well being of society as the prosperity of a newly instituted government a citizen of so much consequence as yourself to its success has no option but to lend his services if called for. Permit me to say it would be inglorious in such a situation not to hazard the glory however great, which he might have previously acquired.

Secondly. Your signature to the proposed system pledges your judgment for its being such an one as upon the whole was worthy of the public approbation. If it should miscarry (as men commonly decide from success or the want of it) the blame will in all probability be laid on the system itself. And the framers of it will have to encounter the disrepute of having brought about a revolution in government, without substituting any thing that was worthy of the effort. They pulled down one Utopia, it will be said, to build up another. This view of the subject, if I mistake not my dear Sir will suggest to your mind greater hazard to that fame, which must be and ought to be dear to you, in refusing your future aid to the system than in affording it. I will only add that in my estimate of the matter that aid is indispensable.

I have taken the liberty to express these sentiments to lay before you my view of the subject. I doubt not the considerations mentioned have fully occurred to you, and I trust they will finally produce in your mind the same result, which exists in mine. I flatter myself the frankness with which I have delivered myself will not be displeasing to you. It has been prompted by motives which you would not disapprove.

I remain My Dear Sir With the sincerest respect and regard   Your
Obd & hum serv   A Hamilton

OPINION ON THE CONSTITUTIONALITY OF AN ACT TO ESTABLISH A NATIONAL BANK
FEBRUARY 23, 1791

Hamilton was secretary of the Treasury during the first and part of the second Washington administration, from September 11, 1789, through January 31, 1795. As secretary of the Treasury, Hamilton submitted to Congress on December 13, 1790, a report recommending the establishment of a national bank. The bill passed both houses of Congress and was submitted to President Washington for his approval on February 14,1791. Because there had been considerable controversy over the bill, and because the issue of its constitutionality had been raised, the president asked for the opinions of his attorney general and secretary of state, both of which were negative. Washington sent their opinions to Hamilton with a request for his response. Hamilton's response follows.

The Secretary of the Treasury having perused with attention the papers containing the opinions of the Secretary of State and Attorney General concerning the constitutionality of the bill for establishing a National Bank proceeds according to the order of the President to submit the reasons which have induced him to entertain a different opinion.

It will naturally have been anticipated that, in performing this task he would feel uncommon solicitude. Personal considerations alone arising from the reflection that the measure originated with him would be sufficient to produce it: The sense which he has manifested of the great importance of such an institution to the successful administration of the department under his particular care; and an expectation of serious ill consequences to result from a failure of the measure, do not permit him to be without anxiety on public accounts. But the chief solicitude arises from a firm persuasion, that principles of construction like those espoused by the Secretary of State and the Attorney General would be fatal to the just & indispensible authority of the United States.

In entering upon the argument it ought to be premised, that the objections of the Secretary of State and Attorney General are founded on a general denial of the authority of the United States to erect corporations. The latter indeed expressly admits, that if there be any thing in the bill which is not warranted by the constitution, it is the clause of incorporation.

Now it appears to the Secretary of the Treasury, that this *general principle* is *inherent* in the very *definition* of *Government* and *essential* to every step of the progress to be made by that of the United States; namely—that every power vested in a Government is in its nature *sovereign*, and includes by *force* of the *term*, a right to employ all the *means* requisite, and fairly *applicable* to the attainment of the *ends* of such power; and which are not precluded by restrictions & exceptions specified in the constitution; or not immoral, or not contrary to the essential ends of political society.

This principle in its application to Government in general would be admitted as an axiom. And it will be incumbent upon those, who may incline to deny it, to *prove* a distinction; and to shew that a rule which in the general system of things is essential to the preservation of the social order is inapplicable to the United States.

The circumstances that the powers of sovereignty are in this country divided between the National and State Governments, does not afford the distinction required. It does not follow from this, that each of the *portions* of powers delegated to the one or to the other is not sovereign *with regard to its proper objects*. It will only *follow* from it, that each has sovereign power as to *certain things*, and not as to *other things*. To deny that the Government of the United States has sovereign power as to its declared purposes & trusts, because its power does not extend to all cases, would be equally to deny, that the State Governments have sovereign power in any case; because their power does not extend to every case. The tenth section of the first article of the constitution exhibits a long list of very important things which they may not do. And thus the United States would furnish the singular spectacle of a *political society* without *sovereignty*, or of a people *governed* without *government*.

If it would be necessary to bring proof to a proposition so clear as that which affirms that the powers of the fœderal government, *as to its objects*, are sovereign, there is a clause of its constitution which would be decisive. It is that which declares, that the constitution and the laws of the United States made in pursuance of it, and all treaties made or which shall be made under their authority shall be the supreme law of the land. The power which can create the *Supreme law* of the land, in any case, is doubtless sovereign *as to such case*.

This general & indisputable principle puts at once an end to the *abstract* question—Whether the United States have power to *erect a corporation?* that is to say, to give a *legal* or *artificial capacity* to one or more persons, distinct from the natural. For it is unquestionably incident to *sovereign power* to erect corporations, and consequently to *that* of the United States, in *relation to the objects* intrusted to the management of the government. The difference is this—where the authority of the government is general, it can create corporations in *all cases;* where it is confined to certain branches of legislation, it can create corporations only in those cases.

Here then as far as concerns the reasonings of the Secretary of State & the Attorney General, the affirmative of the constitutionality of the bill might be permitted to rest. It will occur to the President that the principle here advanced has been untouched by either of them.

For a more complete elucidation of the point nevertheless, the arguments which they have used against the power of the government to erect corporations, however foreign they are to the great & fundamental rule which has been stated, shall be particularly examined. And after shewing that they do not tend to impair its force, it shall also be shewn, that the power of incorporation incident to the government in certain cases, does fairly extend to the particular case which is the object of the bill.

The first of these arguments is, that the foundation of the constitution is laid on this ground "that all powers not delegated to the United States by the Constitution nor prohibited to it by the States are reserved to the States or to the people", whence it is meant to be inferred, that congress can in no case exercise any power not included in those enumerated in the constitution. And it is affirmed that the power of erecting a corporation is not included in any of the enumerated powers.

The main proposition here laid down, in its true signification is not to be questioned. It is nothing more than a consequence of this republican maxim, that all government is a delegation of power. But how much is delegated in each case, is a question of fact to be made out by fair reasoning & construction upon the particular provisions of the constitution—taking as guides the general principles & general ends of government.

It is not denied, that there are *implied*, as well as *express* powers, and that the former are as effectually delegated as the latter. And for the sake of accuracy it shall be mentioned, that there is another class of powers, which may be properly denominated *resulting* powers. It will not be doubted that if the United States should make a conquest of any of the territories of its neighbours, they would possess sovereign jurisdiction over the conquered territory. This would rather be a result from the whole mass of the powers of the government & from the nature of political society, than a consequence of either of the powers specially enumerated.

But be this as it may, it furnishes a striking illustration of the general doctrine contended for. It shews an extensive case, in which a power of erecting corporations is either implied in, or would result from some or all of the powers, vested in the National Government. The jurisdiction acquired over such conquered territory would certainly be competent to every species of legislation.

To return—It is conceded, that implied powers are to be considered as delegated equally with express ones.

Then it follows, that as a power of erecting a corporation may as well be *implied* as any other thing; it may as well be employed as an *instrument* or *mean* of carrying into execution any of the specified powers, as any other instrument or mean whatever. The only question must be, in this as in every other case, whether the mean to be employed, or in this instance the corporation to be erected, has a natural relation to any of the acknowledged objects or lawful ends of the government. Thus a corporation may not be erected by congress, for superintending the police of the city of Philadelphia because they are not authorised to *regulate* the *police* of that city; but one may be erected in relation to the collection of the taxes, or to the trade with foreign countries, or to the trade between the States, or with the Indian Tribes, because it is the province of the fœderal government to regulate those objects & because it is incident to a general *sovereign* or *legislative power* to *regulate* a thing, to employ all the means which relate to its regulation to the *best & greatest advantage*.

A strange fallacy seems to have crept into the manner of thinking & reasoning upon the subject. Imagination appears to have been unusually busy concerning it. An incorporation seems to have been regarded as some great, independent, substantive thing—as a political end of peculiar magnitude & moment; whereas it is truly to be considered as a *quality, capacity,* or *mean* to an end. Thus a mercantile company is formed with a certain capital for the purpose of carrying on a particular branch of business. Here the business to be prosecuted is the *end;* the association in order to form the requisite capital is the primary mean. Suppose that an incorporation were added to this; it would only be to add a new *quality* to that association; to give it an artificial capacity by which it would be enabled to prosecute the business with more safety & convenience.

That the importance of the power of incorporation has been exaggerated, leading to erroneous conclusions, will further appear from tracing it to its origin. The roman law is the source of it, according to which a *voluntary* association of individuals at *any time* or *for any purpose* was capable of producing it. In England, whence our notions of it are immediately borrowed, it forms a part of the executive authority, & the exercise of it has been often *delegated* by that authority. Whence therefore the ground of the supposition, that it lies beyond the reach of all those very important portions of sovereign power, legislative as well as executive, which belong to the government of the United States?

To this mode of reasoning respecting the right of employing all the means requisite to the execution of the specified powers of the Government, it is objected that none but *necessary* & proper means are to be employed, & the Secretary of State maintains, that no means are to be considered as *necessary*, but those without which the grant of the power would be *nugatory*. Nay so far does he go in his restrictive interpretation of the word, as even to make the case of *necessity* which shall warrant the constitutional exercise of the power to depend on *casual* & *temporary* circumstances, an idea which alone refutes the construction. The *expediency* of exercising a particular power, at a particular time, must indeed depend on *circumstances;* but the constitutional right of exercising it must be uniform & invariable—the same to day, as to morrow.

All the arguments therefore against the constitutionality of the bill derived from the accidental existence of certain State-banks: institutions which *happen* to exist to day, & for ought that concerns the government of the United States, may disappear to morrow, must not only be rejected as fallacious, but must be viewed as demonstrative, that there is a *radical* source of error in the reasoning.

It is essential to the being of the National government, that so erroneous a conception of the meaning of the word *necessary*, should be exploded.

It is certain, that neither the grammatical, nor popular sense of the term requires that construction. According to both, *necessary* often means no more than *needful, requisite, incidental, useful,* or *conducive to.* It is a common mode of expression to say, that it is *necessary* for a government or a person to do this or that thing, when nothing more is intended or understood, than that the interests of the government or person require, or will be promoted, by the doing of this or that thing. The imagination can be at no loss for exemplifications of the use of the word in this sense.

And it is the true one in which it is to be understood as used in the constitution. The whole turn of the clause containing it, indicates, that it was the intent of the convention, by that clause to give a liberal latitude to the exercise of the specified powers. The expressions have peculiar comprehensiveness. They are—"to make *all laws*, necessary & proper for *carrying into execution* the foregoing powers & all *other powers* vested by the constitution in the *government* of the United States, or in any *department* or *officer* thereof." To understand the word as the Secretary of State does, would be to depart from its obvious & popular sense, and to give it a *restrictive* operation; an idea never before entertained. It would be to give it the same force as if the word *absolutely* or *indispensibly* had been prefixed to it.

Such a construction would beget endless uncertainty & embarassment. The cases must be palpable & extreme in which it could be pronounced with certainty, that a measure was absolutely necessary, or one without which the exercise of a given power would be nugatory. There are few measures of any goverment, which would stand so severe a test. To insist upon it, would be to make the criterion of the exercise of any implied power a *case of extreme necessity;* which is rather a rule to justify the overleaping of the bounds of constitutional authority, than to govern the ordinary exercise of it.

It may be truly said of every government, as well as of that of the United States, that it has only a right, to pass such laws as are necessary & proper to accomplish the objects intrusted to it. For no government has a right to do *merely what it pleases.* Hence by a process of reasoning similar to that of the Secretary of State, it might be proved, that neither of the State governments has a right to incorporate a bank. It might be shewn, that all the public business of the State, could be performed without a bank, and inferring thence that it was unnecessary it might be argued that it could not be done, because it is against the rule which has been just mentioned. A like mode of reasoning would prove, that there was no power to incorporate the Inhabitants of a town, with a view to a more perfect police: For it is certain, that an incorporation may be dispensed with, though it is better to have one. It is to be remembered, that there is no *express* power in any State constitution to erect corporations.

The *degree* in which a measure is necessary, can never be a test of the *legal* right to adopt it. That must ever be a matter of opinion; and can only be a test of expediency. The *relation* between the *measure* and the *end*, between the *nature* of *the mean* employed towards the execution of a power and the object of that power, must be the criterion of constitutionality not the more or less of *necessity* or *utility.*

The practice of the government is against the rule of construction advocated by the Secretary of State. Of this the act concerning light houses, beacons, buoys & public piers, is a decisive example. This doubtless must be referred to the power of regulating trade, and is fairly relative to it. But it cannot be affirmed, that the exercise of that power, in this instance, was strictly necessary; or that the power itself would be *nugatory* without that of regulating establishments of this nature.

This restrictive interpretation of the word *necessary* is also contrary to this sound maxim of construction namely, that the powers contained in a constitution of government, especially those which concern the general administration of the affairs of a country, its finances, trade, defence &c ought to be construed liberally, in advancement of the public good. This rule does not depend on the particular form of a government or on the particular demarkation of the boundaries of its powers, but on the nature and objects of government itself. The means by which national exigencies are to be provided for, national inconveniencies obviated, national prosperity promoted, are of such infinite variety, extent and complexity, that there must, of necessity, be great latitude of discretion in the selection & application of those means. Hence consequently, the necessity & propriety of exercising the authorities intrusted to a government on principles of liberal construction.

The Attorney General admits the *rule,* but takes a distinction between a State, and the fœderal constitution. The latter, he thinks, ought to be construed with greater strictness, because there is more danger of error in defining partial than general powers.

But the reason of the *rule* forbids such a distinction. This reason is—the variety & extent of public exigencies, a far greater proportion of which and of a far more critical kind, are objects of National than of State administration. The greater danger of error, as far as it is supposeable, may be a prudential reason for caution in practice, but it cannot be a rule of restrictive interpretation.

In regard to the clause of the constitution immediately under consideration, it is admitted by the Attorney General, that no *restrictive* effect can be ascribed to it. He defines the word necessary thus. "To be necessary is to be *incidental,* and may be denominated the natural means of executing a power."

But while, on the one hand, the construction of the Secretary of State is deemed inadmissible, it will not be contended on the other, that the clause in question gives any *new* or *independent* power. But it gives an explicit sanction to the doctrine of *implied* powers, and is equivalent to an admission of the proposition, that the government, *as to its specified powers* and *objects,* has plenary & sovereign authority, in some cases paramount to that of the States, in others coordinate with it. For such is the plain import of the declaration, that it may pass *all laws* necessary & proper to carry into execution those powers.

It is no valid objection to the doctrine to say, that it is calculated to extend the powers of the general government throughout the entire sphere of State legislation. The same thing has been said, and may be said with regard to every exercise of power by *implication* or *construction*. The moment the literal meaning is departed from, there is a chance of error and abuse. And yet an adherence to the letter of its powers would at once arrest the motions of the government. It is not only agreed, on all hands, that the exercise of constructive powers is indispensible, but every act which has been passed is more or less an exemplification of it. One has been already mentioned, that relating to light houses &c. That which declares the power of the President to remove officers at pleasure, acknowlidges the same truth in another, and a signal instance.

The truth is that difficulties on this point are inherent in the nature of the fœderal constitution. They result inevitably from a division of the legislative power. The consequence of this division is, that there will be cases clearly within the power of the National Government; others clearly without its power; and a third class, which will leave room for controversy & difference of opinion, & concerning which a reasonable latitude of judgment must be allowed.

But the doctrine which is contended for is not chargeable with the consequence imputed to it. It does not affirm that the National government is sovereign in all respects, but that it is sovereign to a certain extent: that is, to the extent of the objects of its specified powers.

It leaves therefore a criterion of what is constitutional, and of what is not so. This criterion is the *end* to which the measure relates as a *mean*. If the end be clearly comprehended within any of the specified powers, & if the measure have an obvious relation to that end, and is not forbidden by any particular provision of the constitution—it may safely be deemed to come within the compass of the national authority. There is also this further criterion which may materially assist the decision. Does the proposed measure abridge a preexisting right of any State, or of any individual? If it does not, there is a strong presumption in favour of its constitutionality; & slighter relations to any declared object of the constitution may be permitted to turn the scale.

The general objections which are to be inferred from the reasonings of the Secretary of State and of the Attorney General to the doctrine which has been advanced, have been stated and it is hoped satisfactorily answered. Those of a more particular nature shall now be examined.

The Secretary of State introduces his opinion with an observa-

255

tion, that the proposed incorporation undertakes to create certain capacities properties or attributes which are *against* the laws of *alienage, descents, escheat* and *forfeiture, distribution* and *monopoly*, and to confer a power to make laws paramount to those of the States. And nothing says he, in another place, but a *necessity invincible by other means* can justify such a *prostration* of *laws* which constitute the pillars of our whole system of jurisprudence, and are the foundation laws of the State Governments.

If these are truly the foundation laws of the several states, then have most of them subverted their own foundations. For there is scarcely one of them which has not, since the establishment of its particular constitution, made material alterations in some of those branches of its jurisprudence especially the law of descents. But it is not conceived how any thing can be called the fundamental law of a State Government which is not established in its constitution unalterable by the ordinary legislature. And with regard to the question of necessity it has been shewn, that this can only constitute a question of expediency, not of right.

To erect a corporation is to substitute a *legal* or *artificial* to a *natural* person, and where a number are concerned to give them *individuality*. To that legal or artificial person once created, the common law of every state of itself *annexes* all those incidents and attributes, which are represented as a prostration of the main pillars of their jurisprudence. It is certainly not accurate to say, that the erection of a corporation is *against* those different *heads* of the State laws; because it is rather to create a kind of person or entity, to which *they* are inapplicable, and to which the general rule of those laws assign a different regimen. The laws of alienage cannot apply to an artificial person, because it can have no country. Those of descent cannot apply to it, because it can have no heirs. Those of escheat are foreign from it for the same reason. Those of forfeiture, because it cannot commit a crime. Those of distribution, because, though it may be dissolved, it cannot die. As truly might it be said, that the exercise of the power of prescribing the rule by which foreigners shall be naturalised, is *against* the law of alienage; while it is in fact only to put them in a situation to cease to be the subject of that law. To do a thing which is *against* a law, is to do something which it forbids or which is a violation of it.

But if it were even to be admitted that the erection of a corporation is a direct alteration of the State laws in the enumerated particulars; it would do nothing towards proving, that the measure was unconstitutional. If the government of the United States can do no act, which amounts to an alteration of a State law, all its powers are nugatory. For almost every new law is an alteration, in some way or other of an old *law*, either *common*, or *statute*.

256

There are laws concerning bankruptcy in some states—some states have laws regulating the values of foreign coins. Congress are empowered to establish uniform laws concerning bankruptcy throughout the United States, and to regulate the values of foreign coins. The exercise of either of these powers by Congress necessarily involves an alteration of the laws of those states.

Again: Every person by the common law of each state may export his property to foreign countries, at pleasure. But Congress, in pursuance of the power of regulating trade, may prohibit the exportation of commodities: in doing which, they would alter the common law of each state in abridgement of individual rights.

It can therefore never be good reasoning to say—this or that act is unconstitutional, because it alters this or that law of a State. It must be shewn, that the act which makes the alteration is unconstitutional on other accounts, not *because* it makes the alteration.

There are two points in the suggestions of the Secretary of State which have been noted that are peculiarly incorrect. One is, that the proposed incorporation is against the laws of monopoly, because it stipulates an exclusive right of banking under the national authority. The other that it gives power to the institution to make laws paramount to those of the states.

But with regard to the first point, the bill neither prohibits any State from erecting as many banks as they please, nor any number of Individuals from associating to carry on the business: & consequently is free from the charge of establishing a monopoly: for monopoly implies a *legal impediment* to the carrying on of the trade by others than those to whom it is granted.

And with regard to the second point, there is still less foundation. The bye-laws of such an institution as a bank can operate only upon its own members; can only concern the disposition of its own property and must essentially resemble the rules of a private mercantile partnership. They are expressly not to be contrary to law; and law must here mean the law of a State as well as of the United States. There never can be a doubt, that a law of the corporation, if contrary to a law of a state, must be overruled as void; unless the law of the State is contrary to that of the United States; and then the question will not be between the law of the State and that of the corporation, but between the law of the State and that of the United States.

Another argument made use of by the Secretary of State, is, the rejection of a proposition by the convention to empower Congress to make corporations, either generally, or for some special purpose.

What was the precise nature or extent of this proposition, or what the reasons for refusing it, is not ascertained by any authentic document, or even by accurate recollection. As far as any such docu-

257

ment exists, it specifies only canals. If this was the amount of it, it would at most only prove, that it was thought inexpedient to give a power to incorporate for the purpose of opening canals, for which purpose a special power would have been necessary; except with regard to the Western Territory, there being nothing in any part of the constitution respecting the regulation of canals. It must be confessed however, that very different accounts are given of the import of the proposition and of the motives for rejecting it. Some affirm that it was confined to the opening of canals and obstructions in rivers; others, that it embraced banks; and others, that it extended to the power of incorporating generally. Some again alledge, that it was disagreed to, because it was thought improper to vest in Congress a power of erecting corporations—others, because it was thought unnecessary to *specify* the power, and inexpedient to furnish an additional topic of objection to the constitution. In this state of the matter, no inference whatever can be drawn from it.

But whatever may have been the nature of the proposition or the reasons for rejecting it concludes nothing in respect to the real merits of the question. The Secretary of State will not deny, that whatever may have been the intention of the framers of a constitution, or of a law, that intention is to be sought for in the instrument itself, according to the usual & established rules of construction. Nothing is more common than for laws to *express* and *effect*, more or less than was intended. If then a power to erect a corporation, in any case, be deducible by fair inference from the whole or any part of the numerous provisions of the constitution of the United States, arguments drawn from extrinsic circumstances, regarding the intention of the convention, must be rejected.

Most of the arguments of the Secretary of State which have not been considered in the foregoing remarks, are of a nature rather to apply to the expediency than to the constitutionality of the bill. They will however be noticed in the discussions which will be necessary in reference to the particular heads of the powers of the government which are involved in the question.

Those of the Attorney General will now properly come under review.

His first observation is, that the power of incorporation is not *expressly* given to congress. This shall be conceded, but in *this sense* only, that it is not declared in *express terms* that congress may erect a *corporation*. But this cannot mean, that there are not certain *express* powers, which *necessarily* include it.

For instance, Congress have express power "to exercise exclusive legislation in all cases whatsoever, over such *district* (not exceeding ten miles square) as may by cession of particular states, & the acceptance of Congress become the seat of the government of the United states; and to exercise *like authority* over all places purchased by consent of the legislature of the State in which the same shall be for the erection of forts, arsenals, dock yards & other needful buildings."

Here then is express power to exercise *exclusive legislation in all cases whatsoever over certain places;* that is to do in respect to those places, all that any government whatever may do: For language does not afford a more complete designation of sovereign power, than in those comprehensive terms. It is in other words a power to pass all laws whatsoever, & consequently to pass laws for erecting corporations, as well as for any other purpose which is the proper object of law in a free government. Surely it can never be believed, that Congress with *exclusive power of legislation in all cases whatsoever,* cannot erect a corporation within the district which shall become the seat of government, for the better regulation of its police. And yet there is an unqualified denial of the power to erect corporations in every case on the part both of the Secretary of State and of the Attorney General. The former indeed speaks of that power in these emphatical terms, that it is *a right remaining exclusively with the states.*

As far then as there is an express power to do any *particular act of legislation,* there is an express one to erect corporations in the cases above described. But accurately speaking, no *particular power* is more than *implied* in a *general one.* Thus the power to lay a duty on a *gallon of rum,* is only a particular *implied* in the general power to lay and collect taxes, duties, imposts and excises. This serves to explain in what sense it may be said, that congress have not an express power to make corporations.

This may not be an improper place to take notice of an argument which was used in debate in the House of Representatives. It was there urged, that if the constitution intended to confer so important a power as that of erecting corporations, it would have been expressly mentioned. But the case which has been noticed is clearly one in which such a power exists, and yet without any specification or express grant of it, further than as every *particular implied* in a general power, can be said to be so granted.

But the argument itself is founded upon an exaggerated and erroneous conception of the nature of the power. It has been shewn, that it is not of so transcendent a kind as the reasoning supposes; and that viewed in a just light it is a mean which ought to have been left to *implication,* rather than an *end* which ought to have been *expressly* granted.

Having observed, that the power of erecting corporations is not

259

expressly granted to Congress, the Attorney General proceeds thus. . . .

"If it can be exercised by them, it must be
1. because the nature of the fœderal government implies it.
2. because it is involved in some of the specified powers of legislation or
3. because it is necessary & proper to carry into execution some of the specified powers."

To be implied in the *nature of the fœderal government,* says he, would beget a doctrine so indefinite, as to grasp every power.

This proposition it ought to be remarked is not precisely, or even substantially, that, which has been relied upon. The proposition relied upon is, that the *specified powers* of Congress are in their nature sovereign—that it is incident to sovereign power to erect corporations; & that therefore Congress have a right within the *sphere & in relation to the objects of their power, to erect corporations.*

It shall however be supposed, that the Attorney General would consider the two propositions in the same light, & that the objection made to the one, would be made to the other.

To this objection an answer has been already given. It is this; that the doctrine is stated with this express *qualification,* that the right to erect corporations does *only* extend to *cases & objects* within the *sphere* of the *specified powers* of the government. A general legislative authority implies a power to erect corporations *in all cases*—a particular legislative power implies authority to erect corporations, in relation to cases arising under that power only. Hence the affirming, that as an *incident* to sovereign power, congress may erect a corporation in relation to the *collection* of their taxes, is no more than to affirm that they may do whatever else they please; than the saying that they have a power to regulate trade would be to affirm that they have a power to regulate religion: or than the maintaining that they have sovereign power as to taxation, would be to maintain that they have sovereign power as to every thing else.

The Attorney General undertakes, in the next place, to shew, that the power of erecting corporations is not involved in any of the specified powers of legislation confided to the National government.

In order to this he has attempted an enumeration of the particulars which he supposes to be comprehended under the several heads of the *powers* to lay & collect taxes &c—to borrow money on the credit of the United States—to regulate commerce with foreign nations—between the states, and with the Indian Tribes—to dispose of and make all needful rules & regulations respecting the territory or other property belonging to the United States; the design of which enumeration is to shew *what is* included under those different heads of power, & *negatively*, that the power of erecting corporations is not included.

The truth of this inference or conclusion must depend on the accuracy of the enumeration. If it can be shewn that the enumeration is *defective*, the inference is destroyed. To do this will be attended with no difficulty.

The heads of the power to lay & collect taxes, he states to be

1. To ascertain the subject of taxation &c
2. to declare the quantum of taxation &c
3. to prescribe the *mode* of *collection*.
4. to ordain the manner of accounting for the taxes &c

The defectiveness of this enumeration consists in the generality of the third division *"to prescribe the mode* of collection"; which is in itself an immense chapter. It will be shewn hereafter, that, among a vast variety of particulars, it comprises the very power in question; namely to *erect corporations*.

The heads of the power to borrow money are stated to be

1. to stipulate the sum to be lent.
2. an interest or no interest to be paid.
3. the time & manner of repaying, unless the loan be placed on an irredeemable fund.

This enumeration is liable to a variety of objections. It omits, in the first place, the *pledging* or *mortgaging* of a fund for the security of the money lent, an usual and in most cases an essential ingredient.

The idea of a stipulation of *an interest or no interest* is too confined. It should rather have been said, to stipulate *the consideration* of the loan. Individuals often borrow upon considerations other than the payment of interest. So may government; and so they often find it necessary to do. Every one reCollects the lottery tickets & other douceurs often given in Great Britain, as collateral inducements to the lending of money to the Government.

There are also frequently collateral conditions, which the enumeration does not contemplate. Every contract which has been made for monies borrowed in Holland includes stipulations that the sum due shall be *free from taxes*, and from sequestration in time of war, and mortgages all the land & property of the United States for the reimbursement.

It is also known, that a lottery is a common expedient for borrowing money, which certainly does not fall under either of the enumerated heads.

The heads of the power to regulate commerce with foreign nations are stated to be

1. to prohibit them or their commodities from our ports.
2. to impose duties on *them* where none existed before, or to increase existing duties on them.
3. to subject *them* to any species of custom house regulation
4. to grant *them* any exemptions or privileges which policy may suggest

This enumeration is far more exceptionable than either of the former. It omits *every thing* that relates to the *citizens vessels* or *commodities* of the United States. The following palpable omissions occur at once.

1. Of the power to prohibit the exportation of commodities which not only exists at all times, but which in time of war it would be necessary to exercise, particularly with relation to naval and warlike stores.
2. Of the power to prescribe rules concerning the *characteristics* & *priviledges* of an american bottom—how she shall be navigated, as whether by citizens or foreigners, or by a proportion of each.
3. Of the power of regulating the manner of contracting with seamen, the police of ships on their voyages &c of which the act for the government & regulation of seamen in the merchants service is a specimen.

That the three preceding articles are omissions, will not be doubted. There is a long list of items in addition, which admit of little, if any question; of which a few samples shall be given.

1. The granting of bounties to certain kinds of vessels, & certain species of merchandise. Of this nature is the allowance on dried & pickled fish & salted provisions.
2. The prescribing of rules concerning the *inspection* of commodities to be exported. Though the states individually are competent to this regulation, yet there is no reason, in point of authority at least, why a general system might not be adopted by the United States.
3. The regulation of policies of insurance; of salvage upon goods found at sea, and the disposition of such goods.
4. The regulation of pilots.
5. The regulation of bills of exchange drawn by a merchant of *one state* upon a merchant of *another state.* This last rather belongs to the regulation of trade between the states, but is equally omitted in the specification under that head.

The last enumeration relates to the power "to dispose of & make *all needful rules and regulations* respecting the territory *or other property* belonging to the United States."

The heads of this power are said to be

1. to exert an ownership over the territory of the United States, which may be properly called the property of the United States, as in the Western Territory, and to *institute a government therein:* or

2. to exert an ownership over the other property of the United States.

This idea of exerting an ownership over the Territory or other property of the United States, is particularly indefinite and vague. It does not at all satisfy the conception of what must have been intended by a power, to make all needful *rules* and *regulations;* nor would there have been any use for a special clause which authorised nothing more. For the right of exerting an ownership is implied in the very definition of property.

It is admitted that in regard to the western territory some thing more is intended—even the institution of a government; that is the creation of a body politic, or corporation of the highest nature; one, which in its maturity, will be able itself to create other corporations. Why then does not the same clause authorise the erection of a corporation in respect to the regulation or disposal of any other of the property of the United States? This idea will be enlarged upon in another place.

Hence it appears, that the enumerations which have been attempted by the Attorney General are so imperfect, as to authorise no conclusion whatever. They therefore have no tendency to disprove, that each and every of the powers to which they relate, includes that of erecting corporations; which they certainly do, as the subsequent illustrations will more & more evince.

It is presumed to have been satisfactorily shewn in the course of the preceding observations

1. That the power of the government, *as to* the objects intrusted to its management, is in its nature sovereign.

2. That the right of erecting corporations is one, inherent in & inseparable from the idea of sovereign power.

3. That the position, that the government of the United States can exercise no power but such as is delegated to it by its constitution, does not militate against this principle.

4. That the word *necessary* in the general clause can have no *restrictive* operation, derogating from the force of this principle, indeed, that the degree in which a measure is, or is not necessary, cannot be a *test* of *constitutional* right, but of expediency only.

5. That the power to erect corporations is not to be considered,

as an *independent* & *substantive* power but as an *incidental* & *auxiliary* one; and was therefore more properly left to implication, than expressly granted.

6. that the principle in question does not extend the power of the government beyond the prescribed limits, because it only affirms a power to *incorporate* for *purposes within the sphere of the specified powers.*

And lastly that the right to exercise such a power, in certain cases, is unequivocally granted in the most *positive* & *comprehensive* terms.

To all which it only remains to be added that such a power has actually been exercised in two very eminent instances: namely in the erection of two governments, One, northwest of the river Ohio, and the other south west—*the last, independent of any antecedent compact.*

And there results a full & complete demonstration, that the Secretary of State & Attorney General are mistaken, when they deny generally the power of the National government to erect corporations.

It shall now be endeavoured to be shewn that there is a power to erect one of the kind proposed by the bill. This will be done, by tracing a natural & obvious relation between the institution of a bank, and the objects of several of the enumerated powers of the government; and by shewing that, *politically* speaking, it is necessary to the effectual execution of one or more of those powers. In the course of this investigation, various instances will be stated, by way of illustration, of a right to erect corporations under those powers.

Some preliminary observations maybe proper.

The proposed bank is to consist of an association of persons for the purpose of creating a joint capital to be employed, chiefly and essentially, in loans. So far the object is not only lawful, but it is the mere exercise of a right, which the law allows to every individual. The bank of New York which is not incorporated, is an example of such an association. The bill proposes in addition, that the government shall become a joint proprietor in this undertaking, and that it shall permit the bills of the company payable on demand to be receivable in its revenues & stipulates that it shall not grant privileges similar to those which are to be allowed to this company, to any others. All this is incontrovertibly within the compass of the discretion of the government. The only question is, whether it has a right to incorporate this company, in order to enable it the more effectually to accomplish *ends,* which are in themselves lawful.

To establish such a right, it remains to shew the relation of such an institution to one or more of the specified powers of the government.

Accordingly it is affirmed, that it has a relation more or less direct to the power of collecting taxes; to that of borrowing money; to that of regulating trade between the states; and to those of raising, supporting & maintaining fleets & armies. To the two former, the relation may be said to be *immediate*.

And, in the last place, it will be argued, that it is, *clearly*, within the provision which authorises the making of all *needful* rules & *regulations* concerning the *property* of the United States, as the same has been practiced upon by the Government.

A Bank relates to the collection of taxes in two ways; *indirectly*, by increasing the quantity of circulating medium & quickening circulation, which facilitates the means of paying—*directly*, by creating a *convenient species of medium* in which they are to be paid.

To designate or appoint the money or *thing* in which taxes are to be paid, is not only a proper, but a necessary *exercise* of the power of collecting them. Accordingly congress in the law concerning the collection of the duties on imports & tonnage, have provided that they shall be payable in gold & silver. But while it was an indispensible part of the work to say in what they should be paid, the choice of the specific thing was mere matter of discretion. The payment might have been required in the commodities themselves. Taxes in kind, however ill judged, are not without precedents, even in the United States. Or it might have been in the paper money of the several states; or in the bills of the bank of North America, New York and Massachusetts, all or either of them: or it might have been in bills issued under the authority of the United States.

No part of this can, it is presumed, be disputed. The appointment, then, of the *money* or *thing*, in which the taxes are to be paid, is an incident to the power of collection. And among the expedients which may be adopted, is that of bills issued under the authority of the United States.

Now the manner of issuing these bills is again matter of discretion. The government might, doubtless, proceed in the following manner. It might provide, that they should be issued under the direction of certain officers, payable on demand; and in order to support their credit & give them a ready circulation, it might, besides giving them a currency in its taxes, set apart out of any monies in its Treasury, a given sum and appropriate it under the direction of those officers as a fund for answering the bills as presented for payment.

The constitutionality of all this would not admit of a question.

And yet it would amount to the institution of a bank, with a view to the more convenient collection of taxes. For the simplest and most precise idea of a bank, is, a deposit of coin or other property, as a fund for *circulating* a *credit* upon it, which is to answer the purpose of money. That such an arrangement would be equivalent to the establishment of a bank would become obvious, if the place where the fund to be set apart was kept should be made a receptacle of the monies of all other persons who should incline to deposit them there for safe keeping; and would become still more so, if the Officers charged with the direction of the fund were authorised to make discounts at the usual rate of interest, upon good security. To deny the power of the government to add these ingredients to the plan, would be to refine away all government.

This process serves to exemplify the natural & direct relation which may subsist between the institution of a bank and the collection of taxes. It is true that the species of bank which has been designated, does not include the idea of incorporation. But the argument intended to be founded upon it, is this: that the institution comprehended in the idea of a bank being one immediately relative to the collection of taxes, *in regard to the appointment* of *the money or thing* in which they are to be paid; the sovereign power of providing for the collection of taxes necessarily includes the right of granting a corporate capacity to such an institution, as a requisite to its greater security, utility and more convenient management.

A further process will still more clearly illustrate the point. Suppose, when the species of bank which has been described was about to be instituted, it were to be urged, that in order to secure to it a due degree of confidence the fund ought not only to be set apart & appropriated generally, but ought to be specifically vested in the officers who were to have the direction of it, and in their *successors* in office, to the end that it might acquire the character of *private property* incapable of being resumed without a violation of the sanctions by which the rights of property are protected & occasioning more serious & general alarm, the apprehension of which might operate as a check upon the government—such a proposition might be opposed by arguments against the expediency of it or the solidity of the reason assigned for it, but it is not conceivable what could be urged against its constitutionality.

And yet such a disposition of the thing would amount to the erection of a corporation. For the true definition of a corporation seems to be this. It is a *legal* person, or a person created by act of law, consisting of one or more natural persons authorised to hold property or a franchise in succession in a legal as contradistinguished from a natural capacity.

Let the illustration proceed a step further. Suppose a bank of the nature which has been described with or without incorporation, had been instituted, & that experience had evinced as it probably would, that being wholly under public direction it possessed not the confidence requisite to the credit of its bills—Suppose also that by some of those adverse conjunctures which occasionally attend nations, there had been a very great drain of the specie of the country, so as not only to cause general distress for want of an adequate medium of circulation, but to produce, in consequence of that circumstance, considerable defalcations in the public revenues—suppose also, that there was no bank instituted in any State—in such a posture of things, would it not be most manifest that the incorporation of a bank, like that proposed by the bill, would be a measure immediately relative to the *effectual collection* of the taxes and completely within the province of the sovereign power of providing by all laws necessary & proper for that collection?

If it be said, that such a state of things would render that necessary & therefore constitutional, which is not so now—the answer to this, and a solid one it doubtless is, must still be, that which has been already stated—Circumstances may affect the expediency of the measure, but they can neither add to, nor diminish its constitutionality.

A Bank has a direct relation to the power of borrowing money, because it is an usual and in sudden emergencies an essential instrument in the obtaining of loans to Government.

A nation is threatened with a war. Large sums are wanted, on a sudden, to make the requisite preparations. Taxes are laid for the purpose, but it requires time to obtain the benefit of them. Anticipation is indispensible. If there be a bank, the supply can, at once be had; if there be none loans from Individuals must be sought. The progress of these is often too slow for the exigency: in some situations they are not practicable at all. Frequently when they are, it is of great consequence to be able to anticipate the product of them by advances from a bank.

The essentiality of such an institution as an instrument of loans is exemplified at this very moment. An Indian expedition is to be prosecuted. The only fund out of which the money can arise consistently with the public engagements, is a tax which will only begin to be collected in July next. The preparations, however, are instantly to be made. The money must therefore be borrowed. And of whom could it be borrowed; if there were no public banks?

It happens, that there are institutions of this kind, but if there were none, it would be indispensible to create one.

Let it then be supposed, that the necessity existed, (as but for a casualty would be the case) that proposals were made for obtaining a loan; that a number of individuals came forward and said, we are willing to accommodate the government with this money; with what we have in hand and the credit we can raise upon it we doubt not of being able to furnish the sum required: but in order to this, it is indispensible, that we should be incorporated as a bank. This is essential towards putting it in our power to do what is desired and we are obliged on that account to make it the *consideration* or condition of the loan.

Can it be believed, that a compliance with this proposition would be unconstitutional? Does not this alone evince the contrary? It is a necessary part of a power to borrow to be able to stipulate the consideration or conditions of a loan. It is evident, as has been remarked elsewhere, that this is not confined to the mere stipulation of a sum of money by way of interest—why may it not be deemed to extend, where a government is the contracting party, to the stipulation of a *franchise?* If it may, & it is not perceived why it may not, then the grant of a corporate capacity may be stipulated as a consideration of the loan? There seems to be nothing unfit, or foreign from the nature of the thing in giving individuality or a corporate capacity to a number of persons who are willing to lend a sum of money to the government, the better to enable them to do it, and make them an ordinary instrument of loans in future emergencies of the state.

But the more general view of the subject is still more satisfactory. The legislative power of borrowing money, & of making all laws necessary & proper for carrying into execution that power, seems obviously competent to the appointment of the *organ* through which the abilities and wills of individuals may be most efficaciously exerted, for the accommodation of the government by loans.

The Attorney General opposes to this reasoning, the following observation. "To borrow money presupposes the accumulation of a fund to be lent, and is secondary to the creation of an ability to lend." This is plausible in theory, but it is not true in fact. In a great number of cases, a previous accumulation of a fund equal to the whole sum required, does not exist. And nothing more can be actually presupposed, than that there exist resources, which put into activity to the greatest advantage by the nature of the operation with the government, will be equal to the effect desired to be produced. All the provisions and operations of government must be presumed to contemplate things as they *really* are.

The institution of a bank has also a natural relation to the regulation of trade between the States: in so far as it is conducive to the creation of a convenient medium of *exchange* between them, and to the keeping up a full circulation by preventing the frequent displacement of the metals in reciprocal remittances. Money is the very hinge on which commerce turns. And this does not mean merely gold & silver, many other things have served the purpose with different degrees of utility. Paper has been extensively employed.

It cannot therefore be admitted with the Attorney General, that the regulation of trade between the States, as it concerns the medium of circulation & exchange ought to be considered as confined to coin. It is even supposeable in argument, that the whole, or the greatest part of the coin of the country, might be carried out of it.

The Secretary of State objects to the relation here insisted upon, by the following mode of reasoning—"To erect a bank, says he, & to regulate commerce, are very different acts. He who erects a bank, creates a subject of commerce, so does he, who makes a bushel of wheat, or digs a dollar out of the mines. Yet neither of these persons regulates commerce thereby. To make a thing which may be bought & sold is not to *prescribe* regulations for *buying* & *selling:* thus making the regulation of commerce to consist in prescribing rules for *buying* & *selling.*

This indeed is a species of regulation of trade; but is one which falls more aptly within the province of the local jurisdictions than within that of the general government, whose care must be presumed to have been intended to be directed to those general political arrangements concerning trade on which its aggregate interests depend, rather than to the details of buying and selling.

Accordingly such only are the regulations to be found in the laws of the United States; whose objects are to give encouragement to the entreprise of our own merchants, and to advance our navigation and manufactures.

And it is in reference to these general relations of commerce, that an establishment which furnishes facilities to circulation and a convenient medium of exchange & alienation, is to be regarded as a regulation of trade.

The Secretary of State futher argues, that if this was a regulation of commerce, it would be void, *as extending as much to the internal commerce of every state as to its external.* But what regulation of commerce does not extend to the internal commerce of every state? What are all the duties upon imported articles amounting to prohibitions, but so many bounties upon domestic manufactures affecting the interests of different classes of citizens in different ways? What are all

269

the provisions in the coasting act, which relate to the trade between district and district of the same State? In short what regulation of trade between the States, but must affect the internal trade of each State? What can operate upon the whole but must extend to every part!

The relation of a bank to the execution of the powers, that concern the common defence, has been anticipated. It has been noted, that at this very moment the aid of such an institution is essential to the measures to be pursued for the protection of our frontier.

It now remains to shew, that the incorporation of a bank is within the operation of the provision which authorises Congress to make all needful rules & regulations concerning the property of the United States. But it is previously necessary to advert to a distinction which has been taken by the Attorney General.

He admits, that the word *property* may signify personal property however acquired. And yet asserts, that it cannot signify money arising from the sources of revenue pointed out in the constitution; because, says he, "the disposal & regulation of money is the final cause for raising it by taxes."

But it would be more accurate to say, that the *object* to which money is intended to be applied is the *final cause* for raising it, than that the disposal and regulation of it is *such*. The support of Government; the support of troops for the common defence; the payment of the public debt, are the true *final causes* for raising money. The disposition & regulation of it when raised, are the steps by which it is applied to the *ends* for which it was raised, not the ends themselves. Hence therefore the money to be raised by taxes as well as any other personal property, must be supposed to come within the meaning as they certainly do within the letter of the authority, to make all needful rules & regulations concerning the property of the United States.

A case will make this plainer: suppose the public debt discharged, and the funds now pledged for it liberated. In some instances it would be found expedient to repeal the taxes, in others, the repeal might injure our own industry, our agriculture and manufactures. In these cases they would of course be retained. Here then would be monies arising from the authorised sources of revenue which would not fall within the rule by which the Attorney General endeavours to except them from other personal property, & from the operation of the clause in question.

The monies being in the coffers of the government, what is to hinder such a disposition to be made of them as is contemplated in the bill or what an incorporation of the parties concerned under the clause which has been cited.

It is admitted that with regard to the Western territory they give a power to erect a corporation—that is to institute a government. And by what rule of construction can it be maintained, that the same words in a constitution of government will not have the same effect when applied to one species of property, as to another, as far as the subject is capable of it? or that a legislative power to make all needful rules & regulations, or to pass all laws necessary & proper concerning the public property which is admitted to authorise an incorporation in one case will not authorise it in another? will justify the institution of a government over the western territory & will not justify the incorporation of a bank, for the more useful management of the money of the nation? If it will do the last, as well as the first, then under this provision alone the bill is constitutional, because it contemplates that the United States shall be joint proprietors of the stock of the bank.

There is an observation of the secretary of state to this effect, which may require notice in this place. Congress, says he, are not to lay taxes *ad libitum for any purpose they please*, but only to pay the debts, or provide for the *welfare* of the Union. Certainly no inference can be drawn from this against the power of applying their money for the institution of a bank. It is true, that they cannot without breach of trust, lay taxes for any other purpose than the general welfare but so neither can any other government. The welfare of the community is the only legitimate end for which money can be raised on the community. Congress can be considered as under only one restriction, which does not apply to other governments—They cannot rightfully apply the money they raise to any purpose *merely* or purely local. But with this exception they have as large a discretion in relation to the *application* of money as any legislature whatever. The constitutional *test* of a right application must always be whether it be for a purpose of *general* or *local* nature. If the former, there can be no want of constitutional power. The quality of the object, as how far it will really promote or not the welfare of the union, must be matter of conscientious discretion. And the arguments for or against a measure in this light, must be arguments concerning expediency or inexpediency, not constitutional right. Whatever relates to the general order of the finances, to the general interests of trade &c being general objects are constitutional ones for *the application* of *money*.

A Bank then whose bills are to circulate in all the revenues of the country, is *evidently* a general object, and for that very reason a constitutional one as far as regards the appropriation of money to it. Whether it will really be a beneficial one, or not, is worthy of careful examination, but is no more a constitutional point, in the particular referred to; than the question whether the western lands shall be sold for twenty or thirty cents ℔ acre.

A hope is entertained, that it has by this time been made to

271

appear, to the satisfaction of the President, that a bank has a natural relation to the power of collecting taxes; to that of borrowing money; to that of regulating trade; to that of providing for the common defence: and that as the bill under consideration contemplates the government in the light of a joint proprietor of the stock of the bank, it brings the case within the provision of the clause of the constitution which immediately respects the property of the United States.

Under a conviction that such a relation subsists, the Secretary of the Treasury, with all deference conceives, that it will result as a necessary consequence from the position, that all the specified powers of the government are sovereign as to the proper objects; that the incorporation of a bank is a constitutional measure, and that the objections taken to the bill, in this respect, are ill founded.

But from an earnest desire to give the utmost possible satisfaction to the mind of the President, on so delicate and important a subject, the Secretary of the Treasury will ask his indulgence while he gives some additional illustrations of cases in which a power of erecting corporations may be exercised, under some of those heads of the specified powers of the Government, which are alledged to include the right of incorporating a bank.

1. It does not appear susceptible of a doubt, that if Congress had thought proper to provide in the collection law, that the bonds to be given for the duties should be given to the collector of each district in the name of the collector of the district A. or B. as the case might require, to enure to him & his successors in office, in trust for the United States, that it would have been consistent with the constitution to make such an arrangement. And yet this it is conceived would amount to an incorporation.

2. It is not an unusual expedient of taxation to farm particular branches of revenue, that is to mortgage or sell the product of them for certain definite sums, leaving the collection to the parties to whom they are mortgaged or sold. There are even examples of this in the United States. Suppose that there was any particular branch of revenue which it was manifestly expedient to place on this footing, & there were a number of persons willing to engage with the Government, upon condition, that they should be incorporated & the funds vested in them, as well for their greater safety as for the more convenient recovery & management of the taxes. Is it supposeable, that there could be any constitutional obstacle to the measure? It is presumed that there could be none. It is certainly a mode of collection which it would be in the discretion of the Government to adopt; though the circumstances must be very extra-

ordinary, that would induce the Secretary to think it expedient.

3. suppose a new & unexplored branch of trade should present itself with some foreign country. Suppose it was manifest, that, to undertake it with advantage, required an union of the capitals of a number of individuals; & that those individuals would not be disposed to embark without an incorporation, as well to obviate that consequence of a private partnership, which makes every individual liable in his whole estate for the debts of the company to their utmost extent, as for the more convenient management of the business—what reason can there be to doubt, that the national government would have a constitutional right to institute and incorporate such a company? None.

They possess a general authority to regulate trade with foreign countries. This is a mean which has been practiced to that end by all the principal commercial nations; who have trading companies to this day which have subsisted for centuries. Why may not the United States *constitutionally* employ the means *usual* in the other countries for attaining the ends entrusted to them?

A power to make all needful rules & regulations concerning territory has been construed to mean a power to erect a government. A power to *regulate* trade is a power to make all needful rules & regulations concerning trade. Why may it not then include that of erecting a trading company as well as in the other case to erect a Government?

It is remarkable, that the State Conventions who have proposed amendments in relation to this point, have most, if not all of them, expressed themselves nearly thus—"Congress shall not grant monopolies, nor *erect any company* with exclusive advantages of commerce;" thus at the same time expressing their sense, that the power to erect trading companies or corporations, was inherent in Congress, & objecting to it no further, than as to the grant of *exclusive* priviledges.

The Secretary entertains all the doubts which prevail concerning the utility of such companies; but he cannot fashion to his own mind a reason to induce a doubt, that there is a constitutional authority in the United States to establish them. If such a reason were demanded, none could be given unless it were this—that congress cannot erect a corporation; which would be no better than to say they cannot do it, because they cannot do it: first presuming an inability, without reason, & then assigning that *inability* as the cause of itself.

Illustrations of this kind might be multiplied without end. They shall however be pursued no further.

There is a sort of evidence on this point, arising from an aggregate view of the constitution, which is of no inconsiderable weight. The very general power of laying & collecting taxes & appropriating their proceeds—that of borrowing money indefinitely—that of coining money & regulating foreign coins—that of making all needful rules and regulations respecting the property of the United States— these powers combined, as well as the reason & nature of the thing speak strongly this language: That it is the manifest design and scope of the constitution to vest in congress all the powers requisite to the effectual administration of the finances of the United States. As far as concerns this object, there appears to be no parsimony of power.

To suppose then, that the government is precluded from the employment of so usual as well as so important an instrument for the administration of its finances as that of a bank, is to suppose, what does not coincide with the general tenor & complexion of the constitution, and what is not agreeable to impressions that any mere spectator would entertain concerning it. Little less than a prohibitory clause can destroy the strong presumptions which result from the general aspect of the government. Nothing but demonstration should exclude the idea, that the power exists.

In all questions of this nature the practice of mankind ought to have great weight against the theories of Individuals.

The fact, for instance, that all the principal commercial nations have made use of trading corporations or companies for the purposes of *external commerce,* is a satisfactory proof, that the Establishment of them is an incident to the regulation of that commerce.

This other fact, that banks are an usual engine in the administration of national finances, & an ordinary & the most effectual instrument of loans & one which in this country has been found essential, pleads strongly against the supposition, that a government clothed with most of the most important prerogatives of sovereignty in relation to the revenues, its debts, its credit, its defence, its trade, its intercourse with foreign nations—is forbidden to make use of that instrument as an appendage to its own authority.

It has been stated as an auxiliary test of constitutional authority, to try, whether it abridges any preexisting right of any state, or any Individual. The proposed incorporation will stand the most severe examination on this point. Each state may still erect as many banks as it pleases; every individual may still carry on the banking business to any extent he pleases.

Another criterion may be this, whether the institution or thing has a more direct relation as to its uses, to the objects of the reserved powers of the State Governments, than to those of the powers delegated by the United States. This rule indeed is less precise than the former, but it may still serve as some guide. Surely a bank has more reference to the objects entrusted to the national government, than to those, left to the care of the State Governments. The common defence is decisive in this comparison.

It is presumed, that nothing of consequence in the observations of the Secretary of State and Attorney General has been left unnoticed.

There are indeed a variety of observations of the Secretary of State designed to shew that the utilities ascribed to a bank in relation to the collection of taxes and to trade, could be obtained without it, to analyse which would prolong the discussion beyond all bounds. It shall be forborne for two reasons—first because the report concerning the Bank may speak for itself in this respect; and secondly, because all those observations are grounded on the erroneous idea, that the *quantum* of necessity or utility is the test of a constitutional exercise of power.

One or two remarks only shall be made: one is that he has taken no notice of a very essential advantage to trade in general which is mentioned in the report, as peculiar to the existence of a bank circulation equal, in the public estimation to Gold & silver. It is this, that it renders it unnecessary to *lock* up the money of the country to accumulate for months successively in order to the periodical payment of interest. The other is this; that his arguments to shew that treasury orders & bills of exchange from the course of trade will prevent any considerable displacement of the metals, are founded on a partial view of the subject. A case will prove this: The sums collected in a state may be small in comparison with the debt due to it. The balance of its trade, direct & circuitous, with the seat of government may be even or nearly so. Here then without bank bills, which in that state answer the purpose of coin, there must be a displacement of the coin, in proportion to the difference between the sum collected in the State and that to be paid in it. With bank bills no such displacement would take place, or, as far as it did, it would be gradual & insensible. In many other ways also, would there be at least a temporary & inconvenient displacement of the coin, even where the course of trade would eventually return it to its proper channels.

The difference of the two situations in point of convenience to the Treasury can only be appreciated by one, who experiences the embarassments of making provision for the payment of the interest on a stock continually changing place in thirteen different places.

One thing which has been omitted just occurs, although it is not very material to the main argument. The Secretary of State affirms, that the bill only contemplates a re-payment, not a loan to the government. But here he is, certainly mistaken. It is true, the government invests in the stock of the bank a sum equal to that which it receives on loan. But let it be remembered, that it does not, therefore, cease to be a proprietor of the stock; which would be the case, if the money received back were in the nature of a repayment. It remains a proprietor still, & will share in the profit, or loss, of the institution, according as the dividend is more or less than the interest it is to pay on the sum borrowed. Hence that sum is manifestly, and, in the strictest sense, a loan.

Philadelphia February 23d. 1791.

CONVERSATION WITH THOMAS JEFFERSON
AUGUST 13, 1791

In the following notes made by Jefferson of his conversation with Hamilton, the "J.A." referred to is John Adams. A series of letters signed "Publicola" had appeared in a Boston newspaper attacking Thomas Paine's Rights of Man *and supporting John Adams's* Discourses on Davila. *Jefferson thought that John Adams had written these letters, but it turned out that John Quincy Adams had written them.*

Philadelphia, August 13, 1791

Aug. 13. 1791. Notes of a conversn between A. Hamilton & Th: J.

Th. J. mentioned to him a lre recd. from J. A. disavowing Publicola, & denying that he ever entertd. a wish to bring this country under a hereditary executive, or introduce an hereditary branch of legislature &c. See his lre. A. H. condemning mr A's writings & most particularly Davila, as having a tendency to weaken the present govmt declared in substance as follows. "I own it is my own opn, tho' I do not publish it in Dan & Bersheba, that the present govmt is not that which will answer the ends of society by giving stability & protection to it's rights, and that it will probably be found expedient to go into the British form. However, since we have undertaken the experiment, I am for giving it a fair course, whatever my expectns may be. The success indeed so far is greater than I had expected, & therefore at present success seems more possible than it had done heretofore,

& there are still other & other stages of improvemt which, if the present does not succeed, may be tried & ought to be tried before we give up the republican form altogether for that mind must be really depraved which would not prefer the equality of political rights which is the foundn of pure republicanism, if it can be obtained consistently with order. Therefore whoever by his writings disturbs the present order of things, is really blameable, however pure his intentns may be, & he was sure mr Adams's were pure." This is the substance of a declaration made in much more lengthy terms, & which seemed to be more formal than usual for a private conversn. between two, & as if intended to qualify some less guarded expressions which had been dropped on former occasions. Th: J. has committed it to writing in the moment of A.H.'s leaving the room.

REPORT ON MANUFACTURES
DECEMBER 5, 1791

Hamilton's "Report on Manufactures," submitted to the House of Representatives on January 15, 1790, reveals more than any other of his writings the kind of society he envisioned for America. Hamilton's argument in the report is that the general welfare requires the encouragement of manufactures in the United States. But he goes further than that. His defense of manufacturing is a defense of the acquisitive principle. Hamilton felt compelled to emphasize the applicability of the spirit of acquisitiveness to the American experience. The acquisitive faculties that found protection under the combined influence of commerce and the Constitution would be further enhanced by manufacturing, the new economic force in American politics. Hamilton's report, moreover, is based on the principles of modern political philosophy. His understanding of government is reminiscent of Locke's, that is, he concurred in Locke's vision of a wide community of industrious men with much opportunity to pursue their private interests. He believed that the welfare or well-being of a political society cannot be separated from its wealth, and that a society's wealth can be increased by the diversification of industrious pursuits, the exercise of a great variety of arts and occupations. Through the diversification of occupations, individuals would be led to seek ever greater tests of their capacities and ever greater opportunities to exercise their faculties. Men are improved by their diversified labor through the enlargement of their capacities. There is, according to Hamilton, more productive exertion of the human mind in a manufacturing commercial society than in a society dominated by agrarianism. Hamilton sought to mingle excellence with acquisitiveness.

Philadelphia, December 5, 1791
Communicated on December 5, 1791

[To the Speaker of the House of Representatives]

The Secretary of the Treasury in obedience to the order of ye House of Representatives, of the 15th day of January 1790, has applied his attention, at as early a period as his other duties would permit, to the subject of Manufactures; and particularly to the means of promoting such as will tend to render the United States, independent on foreign nations, for military and other essential supplies. And he there[upon] respectfully submits the following Report.

The expediency of encouraging manufactures in the United States, which was not long since deemed very questionable, appears at this time to be pretty generally admitted. The embarrassments, which have obstructed the progress of our external trade, have led to serious reflections on the necessity of enlarging the sphere of our domestic commerce: the restrictive regulations, which in foreign markets abrige the vent of the increasing surplus of our Agricultural produce, serve to beget an earnest desire, that a more extensive demand for that surplus may be created at home: And the complete success, which has rewarded manufacturing enterprise, in some valuable branches, conspiring with the promising symptoms, which attend some less mature essays, in others, justify a hope, that the obstacles to the growth of this species of industry are less formidable than they were apprehended to be; and that it is not difficult to find, in its further extension; a full indemnification for any external disadvantages, which are or may be experienced, as well as an accession of resources, favourable to national independence and safety.

There still are, nevertheless, respectable patrons of opinions, unfriendly to the encouragement of manufactures. The following are, substantially, the arguments, by which these opinions are defended.

"In every country (say those who entertain them) Agriculture is the most beneficial and *productive* object of human industry. This position, generally, if not universally true, applies with peculiar emphasis to the United States, on account of their immense tracts of fertile territory, uninhabited and unimproved. Nothing can afford so advantageous an employment for capital and labour, as the conversion of this extensive wilderness into cultivated farms. Nothing equally with this, can contribute to the population, strength and real riches of the country."

"To endeavor by the extraordinary patronage of Government, to accelerate the growth of manufactures, is in fact, to endeavor, by force and art, to transfer the natural current of industry, from a more, to a less beneficial channel. Whatever has such a tendency must necessarily be unwise. Indeed it can hardly ever be wise in a government, to attempt to give a direction to the industry of its citizens. This under the quicksighted guidance of private interest, will, if left to itself, infallibly find its own way to the most profitable employment: and 'tis by such employment, that the public prosperity will be most effectually promoted. To leave industry to itself, therefore, is, in almost every case, the soundest as well as the simplest policy."

"This policy is not only recommended to the United States, by considerations which affect all nations, it is, in a manner, dictated to them by the imperious force of a very peculiar situation. The smallness of their population compared with their territory—the constant allurements to emigration from the settled to the unsettled parts of the country—the facility, with which the less independent condition of an artisan can be exchanged for the more independent condition of a farmer, these and similar causes conspire to produce, and for a length of time must continue to occasion, a scarcity of hands for manufacturing occupation, and dearness of labor generally. To these disadvantages for the prosecution of manufactures, a deficiency of pecuniary capital being added, the prospect of a successful competition with the manufactures of Europe must be regarded as little less than desperate. Extensive manufactures can only be the offspring of a redundant, at least of a full population. Till the latter shall characterise the situation of this country, 'tis vain to hope for the former."

"If contrary to the natural course of things, an unseasonable and premature spring can be given to certain fabrics, by heavy duties, prohibitions, bounties, or by other forced expedients; this will only be to sacrifice the interests of the community to those of particular classes. Besides the misdirection of labour, a virtual monopoly will be given to the persons employed on such fabrics; and an enhancement of price, the inevitable consequence of every monopoly, must be defrayed at the expence of the other parts of the society. It is far preferable, that those persons should be engaged in the cultivation of the earth, and that we should procure, in exchange for its productions, the commodities, with which foreigners are able to supply us in greater perfection, and upon better terms."

279

This mode of reasoning is founded upon facts and principles, which have certainly respectable pretensions. If it had governed the conduct of nations, more generally than it has done, there is room to suppose, that it might have carried them faster to prosperity and greatness, than they have attained, by the pursuit of maxims too widely opposite. Most general theories, however, admit of numerous exceptions, and there are few, if any, of the political kind, which do not blend a considerable portion of error, with the truths they inculcate.

In order to an accurate judgement how far that which has been just stated ought to be deemed liable to a similar imputation, it is necessary to advert carefully to the considerations, which plead in favour of manufactures, and which appear to recommend the special and positive encouragement of them; in certain cases, and under certain reasonable limitations.

It ought readily to be conceded, that the cultivation of the earth—as the primary and most certain source of national supply—as the immediate and chief source of subsistence to man—as the principal source of those materials which constitute the nutriment of other kinds of labor—as including a state most favourable to the freedom and independence of the human mind—one, perhaps, most conducive to the multiplication of the human species—has *intrinsically a strong claim to pre-eminence over every other kind of industry.*

But, that it has a title to any thing like an exclusive predilection, in any country, ought to be admitted with great caution. That it is even more productive than every other branch of Industry requires more evidence, than has yet been given in support of the position. That its real interests, precious and important as without the help of exaggeration, they truly are, will be advanced, rather than injured by the due encouragement of manufactures, may, it is believed, be satisfactorily demonstrated. And it is also believed that the expediency of such encouragement in a general view may be shewn to be recommended by the most cogent and persuasive motives of national policy.

It has been maintained, that Agriculture is, not only, the most productive, but the only productive species of industry. The reality of this suggestion in either aspect, has, however, not been verified by any accurate detail of facts and calculations; and the general arguments, which are adduced to prove it, are rather subtil and paradoxical, than solid or convincing.

Those which maintain its exclusive productiveness are to this effect.

Labour, bestowed upon the cultivation of land produces enough, not only to replace all the necessary expences incurred in the business, and to maintain the persons who are employed in it, but to afford together with the *ordinary profit* on the stock or capital of the Farmer, a nett surplus, or *rent* for the landlord or proprietor of the soil. But the labor of Artificers does nothing more, than replace the Stock which employs them (or which furnishes materials tools and wages) and yield the *ordinary profit* upon that Stock. It yields nothing equivalent to the *rent* of land. Neither does it add any thing to the *total value* of the *whole annual produce* of the land and labour of the country. The additional value given to those parts of the produce of land, which are wrought into manufactures, is counter-balanced by the value of those other parts of that produce, which are consumed by the manufacturers. It can therefore only be by saving, or *parsimony* not by the positive *productiveness* of their labour, that the classes of Artificers can in any degree augment the revenue of the Society.

To this it has been answered—

I "That inasmuch as it is acknowledged, that manufacturing labour reproduces a value equal to that which is expended or consumed in carrying it on, and continues in existence the original Stock or capital employed—it ought on that account alone, to escape being considered as wholly unproductive: That though it should be admitted, as alleged, that the consumption of the produce of the soil, by the classes of Artificers or Manufacturers, is exactly equal to the value added by their labour to the materials upon which it is exerted; yet it would not thence follow, that it added nothing to the Revenue of the Society, or to the aggregate value of the annual produce of its land and labour. If the consumption for any given period amounted to a *given sum* and the *increased* value of the produce manufactured, in the same period, to a *like sum*, the total amount of the consumption and production during that period, would be equal to the *two sums*, and consequently double the value of the agricultural produce consumed. And though the increment of value produced by the classes of Artificers should at no time exceed the value of the produce of the land consumed by them, yet there would be at every moment, in consequence of their labour, a greater value of goods in the market than would exist independent of it."

II—"That the position, that Artificers can augment the revenue of a Society, only by parsimony, is true, in no other sense, than in one, which is equally applicable to Husbandmen or Cultivators. It may be alike affirmed of all these classes, that the fund acquired by their labor and destined for their support is not, in an ordinary way, more than equal to it. And hence it will follow, that augmentations of the wealth or capital of the community (except in the instances of some extraor-

281

dinary dexterity or skill) can only proceed, with respect to any of them, from the savings of the more thrifty and parsimonious."

III—"That the annual produce of the land and labour of a country can only be encreased, in two ways—by some improvement in the *productive powers* of the useful labour, which actually exists within it, or by some increase in the quantity of such labour: That with regard to the first, the labour of Artificers being capable of greater subdivision and simplicity of operation, than that of Cultivators, it is susceptible, in a proportionably greater degree, of improvement in its *productive powers,* whether to be derived from an accession of Skill, or from the application of ingenious machinery; in which particular, therefore, the labour employed in the culture of land can pretend to no advantage over that engaged in manufactures: That with regard to an augmentation of the quantity of useful labour, this, excluding adventitious circumstances, must depend essentially upon an increase of *capital,* which again must depend upon the savings made out of the revenues of those, who furnish or manage *that,* which is at any time employed, whether in Agriculture, or in Manufactures, or in any other way."

But while the *exclusive* productiveness of Agricultural labour has been thus denied and refuted, the superiority of its productiveness has been conceded without hesitation. As this concession involves a point of considerable magnitude, in relation to maxims of public administration, the grounds on which it rests are worthy of a distinct and particular examination.

One of the arguments made use of, in support of the idea may be pronounced both quaint and superficial. It amounts to this—That in the productions of the soil, nature co-operates with man; and that the effect of their joint labour must be greater than that of the labour of man alone.

This however, is far from being a necessary inference. It is very conceivable, that the labor of man alone laid out upon a work, requiring great skill and art to bring it to perfection, may be more productive, *in value,* than the labour of nature and man combined, when directed towards more simple operations and objects: And when it is recollected to what an extent the Agency of nature, in the application of the mechanical powers, is made auxiliary to the prosecution of manufactures, the suggestion, which has been noticed, loses even the appearance of plausibility.

It might also be observed, with a contrary view, that the labour employed in Agriculture is in a great measure periodical and occasional, depending on seasons, liable to various and long intermissions; while that occupied in many manufactures is constant and regular, extending through the year, embracing in some instances night as well as day. It is also probable, that there are among the cultivators of land more examples of remissness, than among artificers. The farmer, from the peculiar fertility of his land, or some other favorable circumstance, may frequently obtain a livelihood, even with a considerable degree of carelessness in the mode of cultivation; but the artisan can with difficulty effect the same object, without exerting himself pretty equally with all those, who are engaged in the same pursuit. And if it may likewise be assumed as a fact, that manufactures open a wider field to exertions of ingenuity than agriculture, it would not be a strained conjecture, that the labour employed in the former, being at once more *constant,* more uniform and more ingenious, than that which is employed in the latter, will be found at the same time more productive.

But it is not meant to lay stress on observations of this nature— they ought only to serve as a counterbalance to those of a similar complexion. Circumstances so vague and general, as well as so abstract, can afford little instruction in a matter of this kind.

Another, and that which seems to be the principal argument offered for the superior productiveness of Agricultural labour, turns upon the allegation, that labour employed in manufactures yields nothing equivalent to the rent of land; or to that nett surplus, as it is called, which accrues to the proprietor of the soil.

But this distinction, important as it has been deemed, appears rather *verbal* than *substantial.*

It is easily discernible, that what in the first instance is divided into two parts under the denominations of the *ordinary profit* of the Stock of the farmer and *rent* to the landlord, is in the second instance united under the general appellation of the *ordinary profit* on the Stock of the Undertaker; and that this formal or verbal distribution constitutes the whole difference in the two cases. It seems to have been overlooked, that the land is itself a Stock or capital, advanced or lent by its owner to the occupier or tenant, and that the rent he receives is only the ordinary profit of a certain Stock in land, not managed by the proprietor himself, but by another to whom he lends or lets it, and who on his part advances a second capital to stock & improve the land, upon which he also receives the usual profit. The rent of the landlord and the profit of the farmer are therefore nothing more than the *ordinary profits* of *two* capitals belonging to *two* different persons, and united in the cultivation of a farm: As in the other case, the surplus which arises upon any manufactory, after replacing the expences of carrying it on, answers to the ordinary profits of *one* or *more* capitals engaged in the prosecution of such manufactory. It is said *one*

283

or *more* capitals; because in fact, the same thing which is contemplated, in the case of the farm, sometimes happens in that of a manufactory. There is one, who furnishes a part of the capital, or lends a part of the money, by which it is carried on, and another, who carries it on, with the addition of his own capital. Out of the surplus, which remains, after defraying expences, an interest is paid to the money lender for the portion of the capital furnished by him, which exactly agrees with the rent paid to the landlord; and the residue of that surplus constitutes the profit of the undertaker or manufacturer, and agrees with what is denominated the ordinary profits on the Stock of the farmer. Both together make the ordinary profits of two capitals [employed in a manufactory; as in the other case the rent of the landlord and the revenue of the farmer compose the ordinary profits of two Capitals] employed in the cultivation of a farm.

The rent therefore accruing to the proprietor of the land, far from being a criterion of *exclusive* productiveness, as has been argued, is no criterion even of superior productiveness. The question must still be, whether the surplus, after defraying expences, of a *given capital*, employed in the *purchase* and *improvement* of a piece of land, is greater or less, than that of a like capital employed in the prosecution of a manufactory: or whether the *whole value produced* from a *given capital* and a *given quantity of labour*, employed in one way, be greater or less, than the *whole value produced* from an *equal capital* and an *equal quantity of labour* employed in the other way: or rather, perhaps whether the business of Agriculture or that of Manufactures will yield the greatest product, according to a *compound ratio* of the quantity of the Capital and the quantity of labour, which are employed in the one or in the other.

The solution of either of these questions is not easy; it involves numerous and complicated details, depending on an accurate knowledge of the objects to be compared. It is not known that the comparison has ever yet been made upon sufficient data properly ascertained and analised. To be able to make it on the present occasion with satisfactory precision would demand more previous enquiry and investigation, than there has been hitherto either leisure or opportunity to accomplish.

Some essays however have been made towards acquiring the requisite information; which have rather served to throw doubt upon, than to confirm the Hypothesis, under examination: But it ought to be acknowledged, that they have been too little diversified, and are too imperfect, to authorise a definitive conclusion either way; leading rather to probable conjecture than to certain deduction. They render it probable, that there are various branches of manufactures, in which a given Capital will yield a greater *total* product, and a considerably greater *nett* product, than an equal capital invested in the purchase and improvement of lands; and that there are also *some* branches, in which both the *gross* and the *nett* produce will exceed that of Agricultural industry; according to a compound ratio of capital and labour: But it is on this last point, that there appears to be the greatest room for doubt. It is far less difficult to infer generally, that the *nett produce* of Capital engaged in manufacturing enterprises is greater than that of Capital engaged in Agriculture.

In stating these results, the purchase and improvement of lands, under previous cultivation are alone contemplated. The comparison is more in favour of Agriculture, when it is made with reference to the settlement of new and waste lands; but an argument drawn from so temporary a circumstance could have no weight in determining the general question concerning the permanent relative productiveness of the two species of industry. How far it ought to influence the policy of the United States, on the score of particular situation, will be adverted to in another place.

The foregoing suggestions are *not designed to inculcate an opinion that manufacturing industry is more productive than that of Agriculture.* They are intended rather to shew that the reverse of this proposition is not ascertained; that the general arguments which are brought to establish it are not satisfactory; and consequently that a supposition of the superior productiveness of Tillage ought to be no obstacle to listening to any substantial inducements to the encouragement of manufactures, which may be otherwise perceived to exist, through an apprehension, that they may have a tendency to divert labour from a more to a less profitable employment.

It is extremely probable, that on a full and accurate devellopment of the matter, on the ground of fact and calculation, it would be discovered that there is no material difference between the aggregate productiveness of the one, and of the other kind of industry; and that the propriety of the encouragements, which may in any case be proposed to be given to either ought to be determined upon considerations irrelative to any comparison of that nature.

II   But without contending for the superior productiveness of Manufacturing Industry, it may conduce to a better judgment of the policy, which ought to be pursued respecting its encouragement, to contemplate the subject, under some additional aspects, tending not only to confirm the idea, that this kind of industry has been improperly represented as unproductive in itself; but [to] evince in addition that the establishment and diffusion of manufactures have the effect of rendering the total mass of useful and productive labor in a com-

285

munity, *greater than it would otherwise be.* In prosecuting this discussion, it may be necessary briefly to resume and review some of the topics, which have been already touched.

To affirm, that the labour of the Manufacturer is unproductive, because he consumes as much of the produce of land, as he adds value to the raw materials which he manufactures, is not better founded, than it would be to affirm, that the labour of the farmer, which furnishes materials to the manufacturer, is unproductive, *because he consumes an equal value of manufactured articles.* Each furnishes a certain portion of the produce of his labor to the other, and each destroys a correspondent portion of the produce of the labour of the other. In the mean time, the maintenance of two Citizens, instead of one, is going on; the State has two members instead of one; and they together consume twice the value of what is produced from the land.

If instead of a farmer and artificer, there were a farmer only, he would be under the necessity of devoting a part of his labour to the fabrication of cloathing and other articles, which he would procure of the artificer, in the case of there being such a person; and of course he would be able to devote less labor to the cultivation of his farm; and would draw from it a proportionably less product. The whole quantity of production, in this state of things, in provisions, raw materials and manufactures, would certainly not exceed in value the amount of what would be produced in provisions and raw materials only, if there were an artificer as well as a farmer.

Again—if there were both an artificer and a farmer, the latter would be left at liberty to pursue exclusively the cultivation of his farm. A greater quantity of provisions and raw materials would of course be produced—equal at least—as has been already observed, to the whole amount of the provisions, raw materials and manufactures, which would exist on a contrary supposition. The artificer, at the same time would be going on in the production of manufactured commodities; to an amount sufficient not only to repay the farmer, in those commodities, for the provisions and materials which were procured from him, but to furnish the Artificer himself with a supply of similar commodities for his own use. Thus then, there would be two quantities or values in existence, instead of one; and the revenue and consumption would be double in one case, what it would be in the other.

If in place of both these suppositions, there were supposed to be two farmers, and no artificer, each of whom applied a part of his labour to the culture of land, and another part to the fabrication of Manufactures—in this case, the portion of the labour of both bestowed upon land would produce the same quantity of provisions and raw materials only, as would be produced by the intire sum of the labour of one applied in the same manner, and the portion of the labour of both bestowed upon manufactures, would produce the same quantity of manufactures only, as would be produced by the intire sum of the labour of one applied in the same manner. Hence the produce of the labour of the two farmers would not be greater than the produce of the labour of the farmer and artificer; and hence, it results, that the labour of the artificer is as possitively productive as that of the farmer, and, as positively, augments the revenue of the Society.

The labour of the Artificer replaces to the farmer that portion of his labour, with which he provides the materials of exchange with the Artificer, and which he would otherwise have been compelled to apply to manufactures: and while the Artificer thus enables the farmer to enlarge his stock of Agricultural industry, a portion of which he purchases for his own use, *he also supplies himself with the manufactured articles of which he stands in need.*

He does still more—Besides this equivalent which he gives for the portion of Agricultural labour consumed by him, and this supply of manufactured commodities for his own consumption—he furnishes still a surplus, which compensates for the use of the Capital advanced either by himself or some other person, for carrying on the business. This is the ordinary profit of the Stock employed in the manufactory, and is, in every sense, as effective an addition to the income of the Society, as the rent of land.

The produce of the labour of the Artificer consequently, may be regarded as composed of three parts; one by which the provisions for his subsistence and the materials for his work are purchased of the farmer, one by which he supplies himself with manufactured necessaries, and a third which constitutes the profit on the Stock employed. The two last portions seem to have been overlooked in the system, which represents manufacturing industry as barren and unproductive.

In the course of the preceding illustrations, the products of equal quantities of the labour of the farmer and artificer have been treated as if equal to each other. But this is not to be understood as intending to assert any such precise equality. It is merely a manner of expression adopted for the sake of simplicity and perspicuity. Whether the value of the produce of the labour of the farmer be somewhat more or less, than that of the artificer, is not material to the main scope of the argument, which hitherto has only aimed at shewing, that the one, as well as the other, occasions a possitive augmentation of the total produce and revenue of the Society.

It is now proper to proceed a step further, and to enumerate the principal circumstances, from which it may be inferred—That manufacturing establishments not only occasion a possitive augmentation of the Produce and Revenue of the Society, but that they contribute essentially to rendering them greater than they could possibly be, without such establishments. These circumstances are—

1. The division of Labour.
2. An extension of the use of Machinery.
3. Additional employment to classes of the community not ordinarily engaged in the business.
4. The promoting of emigration from foreign Countries.
5. The furnishing greater scope for the diversity of talents and dispositions which discriminate men from each other.
6. The affording a more ample and various field for enterprize.
7. The creating in some instances a new, and securing in all, a more certain and steady demand for the surplus produce of the soil.

Each of these circumstances has a considerable influence upon the total mass of industrious effort in a community. Together, they add to it a degree of energy and effect, which are not easily conceived. Some comments upon each of them, in the order in which they have been stated, may serve to explain their importance.

I. As to the Division of Labour.

It has justly been observed, that there is scarcely any thing of greater moment in the œconomy of a nation, than the proper division of labour. The seperation of occupations causes each to be carried to a much greater perfection, than it could possible acquire, if they were blended. This arises principally from three circumstances.

1st—The greater skill and dexterity naturally resulting from a constant and undivided application to a single object. It is evident, that these properties must increase, in proportion to the separation and simplification of objects and the steadiness of the attention devoted to each; and must be less, in proportion to the complication of objects, and the number among which the attention is distracted.

2nd. The œconomy of time—by avoiding the loss of it, incident to a frequent transition from one operation to another of a different nature. This depends on various circumstances—the transition itself—the orderly disposition of the impliments, machines and materials employed in the operation to be relinquished—the preparatory steps to the commencement of a new one—the interruption of the impulse, which the mind of the workman acquires, from being engaged in a particular operation—the distractions hesitations and reluctances, which attend the passage from one kind of business to another.

3rd. An extension of the use of Machinery. A man occupied on a single object will have it more in his power, and will be more naturally led to exert his imagination in devising methods to facilitate and abrige labour, than if he were perplexed by a variety of independent and dissimilar operations. Besides this, the fabrication of Machines, in numerous instances, becoming itself a distinct trade, the Artist who follows it, has all the advantages which have been enumerated, for improvement in his particular art; and in both ways the invention and application of machinery are extended.

And from these causes united, the mere separation of the occupation of the cultivator, from that of the Artificer, has the effect of augmenting the *productive powers* of labour, and with them, the total mass of the produce or revenue of a Country. In this single view of the subject, therefore, the utility of Artificers or Manufacturers, towards promoting an increase of productive industry, is apparent.

II. As to an extension of the use of Machinery a point which though partly anticipated requires to be placed in one or two additional lights.

The employment of Machinery forms an item of great importance in the general mass of national industry. 'Tis an artificial force brought in aid of the natural force of man; and, to all the purposes of labour, is an increase of hands; an accession of strength, *unincumbered too by the expence of maintaining the laborer*. May it not therefore be fairly inferred, that those occupations, which give greatest scope to the use of this auxiliary, contribute most to the general Stock of industrious effort, and, in consequence, to the general product of industry?

It shall be taken for granted, and the truth of the position referred to observation, that manufacturing pursuits are susceptible in a greater degree of the application of machinery, than those of Agriculture. If so all the difference is lost to a community, which, instead of manufacturing for itself, procures the fabrics requisite to its supply from other Countries. The substitution of foreign for domestic manufactures is a transfer to foreign nations of the advantages accruing from the employment of Machinery, in the modes in which it is capable of being employed, with most utility and to the greatest extent.

The Cotton Mill invented in England, within the last twenty years, is a signal illustration of the general proposition, which has been just advanced. In consequence of it, all the different processes for spining Cotton are performed by means of Machines, which are put in motion by water, and attended chiefly by women and Children; [and by a smaller] number of [persons, in the whole, than are] requisite in the ordinary mode of spinning. And it is an advantage of great moment that the operations of this mill continue with convenience, during the night, as well as through the day. The prodigious affect of such a Machine is easily conceived. To this invention is to be attributed essentially the immense progress, which has been so suddenly made in Great Britain in the various fabrics of Cotton.

III. As to the additional employment of classes of the community, not ordinarily engaged in the particular business.

This is not among the least valuable of the means, by which manufacturing institutions contribute to augment the general stock of industry and production. In places where those institutions prevail, besides the persons regularly engaged in them, they afford occasional and extra employment to industrious individuals and families, who are willing to devote the leisure resulting from the intermissions of their ordinary pursuits to collateral labours, as a resource of multiplying their acquisitions or [their] enjoyments. The husbandman himself experiences a new source of profit and support from the encreased industry of his wife and daughters; invited and stimulated by the demands of the neighboring manufactories.

Besides this advantage of occasional employment to classes having different occupations, there is another of a nature allied to it [and] of a similar tendency. This is—the employment of persons who would otherwise be idle (and in many cases a burthen on the community), either from the byass of temper, habit, infirmity of body, or some other cause, indisposing, or disqualifying them for the toils of the Country. It is worthy of particular remark, that, in general, women and Children are rendered more useful and the latter more early useful by manufacturing establishments, than they would otherwise be. Of the number of persons employed in the Cotton Manufactories of Great Britain, it is computed that $\frac{4}{7}$ nearly are women and children; of whom the greatest proportion are children and many of them of a very tender age.

And thus it appears to be one of the attributes of manufactures, and one of no small consequence, to give occasion to the exertion of a greater quantity of Industry, even by the *same number* of persons, where they happen to prevail, than would exist, if there were no such establishments.

IV. As to the promoting of emigration from foreign Countries.

Men reluctantly quit one course of occupation and livelihood for another, unless invited to it by very apparent and proximate advantages. Many, who would go from one country to another, if they had a prospect of continuing with more benefit the callings, to which they have been educated, will often not be tempted to change their situation, by the hope of doing better, in some other way. Manufacturers, who listening to the powerful invitations of a better price for their fabrics, or their labour, of greater cheapness of provisions and raw materials, of an exemption from the chief part of the taxes burthens and restraints, which they endure in the old world, of greater personal independence and consequence, under the operation of a more equal government, and of what is far more precious than mere religious toleration—a perfect equality of religious privileges; would probably flock from Europe to the United States to pursue their own trades or professions, if they were once made sensible of the advantages they would enjoy, and were inspired with an assurance of encouragement and employment, will, with difficulty, be induced to transplant themselves, with a view to becoming Cultivators of Land.

If it be true then, that it is the interest of the United States to open every possible [avenue to] emigration from abroad, it affords a weighty argument for the encouragement of manufactures; which for the reasons just assigned, will have the strongest tendency to multiply the inducements to it.

Here is perceived an important resource, not only for extending the population, and with it the useful and productive labour of the country, but likewise for the prosecution of manufactures, without deducting from the number of hands, which might otherwise be drawn to tillage; and even for the indemnification of Agriculture for such as might happen to be diverted from it. Many, whom Manufacturing views would induce to emigrate, would afterwards yield to the temptations, which the particular situation of this Country holds out to Agricultural pursuits. And while Agriculture would in other respects derive many signal and unmingled advantages, from the growth of manufactures, it is a problem whether it would gain or lose, as to the article of the number of persons employed in carrying it on.

V. As to the furnishing greater scope for the diversity of talents and dispositions, which discriminate men from each other.

This is a much more powerful mean of augmenting the fund of national Industry than may at first sight appear. It is a just observation, that minds of the strongest and most active powers for their proper objects fall below mediocrity and labour without effect, if confined to uncongenial pursuits. And it is thence to be inferred, that the results of human exertion may be immensely increased by diversifying its objects. When all the different kinds of industry obtain in a community, each individual can find his proper element, and can call

291

into activity the whole vigour of his nature. And the community is benefitted by the services of its respective members, in the manner, in which each can serve it with most effect.

If there be anything in a remark often to be met with—namely that there is, in the genius of the people of this country, a peculiar aptitude for mechanic improvements, it would operate as a forcible reason for giving opportunities to the exercise of that species of talent, by the propagation of manufactures.

VI. As to the affording a more ample and various field for enterprise.

This also is of greater consequence in the general scale of national exertion, than might perhaps on a superficial view be supposed, and has effects not altogether dissimilar from those of the circumstance last noticed. To cherish and stimulate the activity of the human mind, by multiplying the objects of enterprise, is not among the least considerable of the expedients, by which the wealth of a nation may be promoted. Even things in themselves not positively advantageous, sometimes become so, by their tendency to provoke exertion. Every new scene, which is opened to the busy nature of man to rouse and exert itself, is the addition of a new energy to the general stock of effort.

The spirit of enterprise, useful and prolific as it is, must necessarily be contracted or expanded in proportion to the simplicity or variety of the occupations and productions, which are to be found in a Society. It must be less in a nation of mere cultivators, than in a nation of cultivators and merchants; less in a nation of cultivators and merchants, than in a nation of cultivators, artificers and merchants.

VII. As to the creating, in some instances, a new, and securing in all a more certain and steady demand, for the surplus produce of the soil.

This is among the most important of the circumstances which have been indicated. It is a principal mean, by which the establishment of manufactures contributes to an augmentation of the produce or revenue of a country, and has an immediate and direct relation to the prosperity of Agriculture.

It is evident, that the exertions of the husbandman will be steady or fluctuating, vigorous or feeble, in proportion to the steadiness or fluctuation, adequateness, or inadequateness of the markets on which he must depend, for the vent of the surplus, which may be produced by his labour; and that such surplus in the ordinary course of things will be greater or less in the same proportion.

For the purpose of this vent, a domestic market is greatly to be preferred to a foreign one; because it is in the nature of things, far more to be relied upon.

It is a primary object of the policy of nations, to be able to supply themselves with subsistence from their own soils; and manufacturing nations, as far as circumstances permit, endeavor to procure, from the same source, the raw materials necessary for their own fabrics. This disposition, urged by the spirit of monopoly, is sometimes even carried to an injudicious extreme. It seems not always to be recollected, that nations, who have neither mines nor manufactures, can only obtain the manufactured articles, of which they stand in need, by an exchange of the products of their soils; and that, if those who can best furnish them with such articles are unwilling to give a due course to this exchange, they must of necessity make every possible effort to manufacture for themselves, the effect of which is that the manufacturing nations abrige the natural advantages of their situation, through an unwillingness to permit the Agricultural countries to enjoy the advantages of theirs, and sacrifice the interests of a mutually beneficial intercourse to the vain project of *selling every thing* and *buying nothing*.

But it is also a consequence of the policy, which has been noted, that the foreign demand for the products of Agricultural Countries, is, in a great degree, rather casual and occasional, than certain or constant. To what extent injurious interruptions of the demand for some of the staple commodities of the United States, may have been experienced, from that cause, must be referred to the judgment of those who are engaged in carrying on the commerce of the country; but it may be safely assumed, that such interruptions are at times very inconveniently felt, and that cases not unfrequently occur, in which markets are so confined and restricted, as to render the demand very unequal to the supply.

Independently likewise of the artificial impediments, which are created by the policy in question, there are natural causes tending to render the external demand for the surplus of Agricultural nations a precarious reliance. The differences of seasons, in the countries, which are the consumers make immense differences in the produce of their own soils, in different years; and consequently in the degrees of their necessity for foreign supply. Plentiful harvests with them, especially if similar ones occur at the same time in the countries, which are the furnishers, occasion of course a glut in the markets of the latter.

Considering how fast and how much the progress of new settlements in the United States must increase the surplus produce of the soil, and weighing seriously the tendency of the system, which prevails among most of the commercial nations of Europe; whatever dependence may be placed on the force of natural circumstances to counteract the effects of an artificial policy; there appear strong reasons to regard the foreign demand for that surplus as too uncertain a reliance, and to desire a substitute for it, in an extensive domestic market.

To secure such a market, there is no other expedient, than to promote manufacturing establishments. Manufacturers who constitute the most numerous class, after the Cultivators of land, are for that reason the principal consumers of the surplus of their labour.

This idea of an extensive domestic market for the surplus produce of the soil is of the first consequence. It is of all things, that which most effectually conduces to a flourishing state of Agriculture. If the effect of manufactories should be to detach a portion of the hands, which would otherwise be engaged in Tillage, it might possibly cause a smaller quantity of lands to be under cultivation but by their tendency to procure a more certain demand for the surplus produce of the soil, they would, at the same time, cause the lands which were in cultivation to be better improved and more productive. And while, by their influence, the condition of each individual farmer would be meliorated, the total mass of Agricultural production would probably be increased. For this must evidently depend as much, if not more, upon the degree of improvement; than upon the number of acres under culture.

It merits particular observation, that the multiplication of manufactories not only furnishes a Market for those articles, which have been accustomed to be produced in abundance, in a country; but it likewise creates a demand for such as were either unknown or produced in inconsiderable quantities. The bowels as well as the surface of the earth are ransacked for articles which were before neglected. Animals, Plants and Minerals acquire an utility and value, which were before unexplored.

The foregoing considerations seem sufficient to establish, as general propositions, That it is the interest of nations to diversify the industrious pursuits of the individuals, who compose them—That the establishment of manufactures is calculated not only to increase the general stock of useful and productive labour; but even to improve the state of Agriculture in particular; certainly to advance the interests of those who are engaged in it. There are other views, that will be hereafter taken of the subject, which, it is conceived, will serve to confirm these inferences.

III   Previously to a further discussion of the objections to the encouragement of manufactures which have been stated, it will be of use to see what can be said, in reference to the particular situation of the United States, against the conclusions appearing to result from what has been already offered.

It may be observed, and the idea is of no inconsiderable weight, that however true it might be, that a State, which possessing large tracts of vacant and fertile territory, was at the same time secluded from foreign commerce, would find its interest and the interest of Agriculture, in diverting a part of its population from Tillage to Manufactures; yet it will not follow, that the same is true of a State, which having such vacant and fertile territory, has at the same time ample opportunity of procuring from abroad, on good terms, all the fabrics of which it stands in need, for the supply of its inhabitants. The power of doing this at least secures the great advantage of a division of labour; leaving the farmer free to pursue exclusively the culture of his land, and enabling him to procure with its products the manufactured supplies requisite either to his wants or to his enjoyments. And though it should be true, that in settled countries, the diversification of Industry is conducive to an increase in the productive powers of labour, and to an augmentation of revenue and capital; yet it is scarcely conceivable that there can be any [thing] of so solid and permanent advantage to an uncultivated and unpeopled country as to convert its wastes into cultivated and inhabited districts. If the Revenue, in the mean time, should be less, the Capital, in the event, must be greater.

To these observations, the following appears to be a satisfactory answer—

1. If the system of perfect liberty to industry and commerce were the prevailing system of nations—the arguments which dissuade a country in the predicament of the United States, from the zealous pursuits of manufactures would doubtless have great force. It will not be affirmed, that they might not be permitted, with few exceptions, to serve as a rule of national conduct. In such a state of things, each country would have the full benefit of its peculiar advantages to compensate for its deficiencies or disadvantages. If one nation were in condition to supply manufactured articles on better terms than another, that other might find an abundant indemnification in a superior capacity to furnish the produce of the soil. And a free exchange, mutually beneficial, of the commodities which each was able to supply, on the best terms, might be carried on between them, supporting in full vigour the industry of each. And though the circumstances which have been mentioned and others, which will be unfolded hereafter render it probable, that nations merely Agricultural would not enjoy the same degree of opulence, in proportion to

295

their numbers, as those which united manufactures with agriculture; yet the progressive improvement of the lands of the former might, in the end, atone for an inferior degree of opulence in the mean time: and in a case in which opposite considerations are pretty equally balanced, the option ought perhaps always to be, in favour of leaving Industry to its own direction.

But the system which has been mentioned, is far from characterising the general policy of Nations. [The prevalent one has been regulated by an opposite spirit.]

The consequence of it is, that the United States are to a certain extent in the situation of a country precluded from foreign Commerce. They can indeed, without difficulty obtain from abroad the manufactured supplies, of which they are in want; but they experience numerous and very injurious impediments to the emission and vent of their own commodities. Nor is this the case in reference to a single foreign nation only. The regulations of several countries, with which we have the most extensive intercourse, throw serious obstructions in the way of the principal staples of the United States.

In such a position of things, the United States cannot exchange with Europe on equal terms; and the want of reciprocity would render them the victim of a system, which should induce them to confine their views to Agriculture and refrain from Manufactures. A constant and encreasing necessity, on their part, for the commodities of Europe, and only a partial and occasional demand for their own, in return, could not but expose them to a state of impoverishment, compared with the opulence to which their political and natural advantages authorise them to aspire.

Remarks of this kind are not made in the spirit of complaint. 'Tis for the nations, whose regulations are alluded to, to judge for themselves, whether, by aiming at too much they do not lose more than they gain. 'Tis for the United States to consider by what means they can render themselves least dependent, on the combinations, right or wrong of foreign policy.

It is no small consolation, that already the measures which have embarrassed our Trade, have accelerated internal improvements, which upon the whole have bettered our affairs. To diversify and extend these improvements is the surest and safest method of indemnifying ourselves for any inconveniences, which those or similar measures have a tendency to beget. If Europe will not take from us the products of our soil, upon terms consistent with our interest, the natural remedy is to contract as fast as possible our wants of her.

2. The conversion of their waste into cultivated lands is certainly a point of great moment in the political calculations of the United

States. But the degree in which this may possibly be retarded by the encouragement of manufactories does not appear to countervail the powerful inducements to affording that encouragement.

An observation made in another place is of a nature to have great influence upon this question. If it cannot be denied, that the interests even of Agriculture may be advanced more by having such of the lands of a state as are occupied under good cultivation, than by having a greater quantity occupied under a much inferior cultivation, and if Manufactories, for the reasons assigned, must be admitted to have a tendency to promote a more steady and vigorous cultivation of the lands occupied than would happen without them—it will follow, that they are capable of indemnifying a country for a diminution of the progress of new settlements; and may serve to increase both the capital [value] and the income of its lands, even though they should abrige the number of acres under Tillage.

But it does, by no means, follow, that the progress of new settlements would be retarded by the extension of Manufactures. The desire of being an independent proprietor of land is founded on such strong principles in the human breast, that where the opportunity of becoming so is as great as it is in the United States, the proportion will be small of those, whose situations would otherwise lead to it, who would be diverted from it towards Manufactures. And it is highly probable, as already intimated, that the accessions of foreigners, who originally drawn over by manufacturing views would afterwards abandon them for Agricultural, would be more than equivalent for those of our own Citizens, who might happen to be detached from them.

The remaining objections to a particular encouragement of manufactures in the United States now require to be examined.

One of these turns on the proposition, that Industry, if left to itself, will naturally find its way to the most useful and profitable employment: whence it is inferred, that manufactures without the aid of government will grow up as soon and as fast, as the natural state of things and the interest of the community may require.

Against the solidity of this hypothesis, in the full latitude of the terms, very cogent reasons may be offered. These have relation to—the strong influence of habit and the spirit of imitation—the fear of want of success in untried enterprises—the intrinsic difficulties incident to first essays towards a competition with those who have previously attained to perfection in the business to be attempted—the bounties premiums and other artificial encouragements, with which foreign nations second the exertions of their own Citizens in the branches, in which they are to be rivalled.

Experience teaches, that men are often so much governed by what they are accustomed to see and practice, that the simplest and most obvious improvements, in the [most] ordinary occupations, are adopted with hesitation, reluctance and by slow gradations. The spontaneous transition to new pursuits, in a community long habituated to different ones, may be expected to be attended with proportionably greater difficulty. When former occupations ceased to yield a profit adequate to the subsistence of their followers, or when there was an absolute deficiency of employment in them, owing to the superabundance of hands, changes would ensue; but these changes would be likely to be more tardy than might consist with the interest either of individuals or of the Society. In many cases they would not happen, while a bare support could be ensured by an adherence to ancient courses; though a resort to a more profitable employment might be practicable. To produce the desireable changes, as early as may be expedient, may therefore require the incitement and patronage of government.

The apprehension of failing in new attempts is perhaps a more serious impediment. There are dispositions apt to be attracted by the mere novelty of an undertaking—but these are not always those best calculated to give it success. To this, it is of importance that the confidence of cautious sagacious capitalists both citizens and foreigners, should be excited. And to inspire this description of persons with confidence, it is essential, that they should be made to see in any project, which is new, and for that reason alone, if, for no other, precarious, the prospect of such a degree of countenance and support from government, as may be capable of overcoming the obstacles, inseperable from first experiments.

The superiority antecedently enjoyed by nations, who have preoccupied and perfected a branch of industry, constitutes a more formidable obstacle, than either of those, which have been mentioned, to the introduction of the same branch into a country, in which it did not before exist. To maintain between the recent establishments of one country and the long matured establishments of another country, a competition upon equal terms, both as to quality and price, is in most cases impracticable. The disparity in the one, or in the other, or in both, must necessarily be so considerable as to forbid a successful rivalship, without the extraordinary aid and protection of government.

But the greatest obstacle of all to the successful prosecution of a new branch of industry in a country, in which it was before unknown, consists, as far as the instances apply, in the bounties premiums and other aids which are granted, in a variety of cases, by the nations, in which the establishments to be imitated are previously introduced. It is well known (and particular examples in the course of this report will be cited) that certain nations grant bounties on the exportation of particular commodities, to enable their own workmen to undersell and supplant all competitors, in the countries to which those commodities are sent. Hence the undertakers of a new manufacture have to contend not only with the natural disadvantages of a new undertaking, but with the gratuities and remunerations which other governments bestow. To be enabled to contend with success, it is evident, that the interference and aid of their own government are indispensible.

Combinations by those engaged in a particular branch of business in one country, to frustrate the first efforts to introduce it into another, by temporary sacrifices, recompensed perhaps by extraordinary indemnifications of the government of such country, are believed to have existed, and are not to be regarded as destitute of probability. The existence or assurance of aid from the government of the country, in which the business is to be introduced, may be essential to fortify adventurers against the dread of such combinations, to defeat their effects, if formed and to prevent their being formed, by demonstrating that they must in the end prove fruitless.

Whatever room there may be for an expectation that the industry of a people, under the direction of private interest, will upon equal terms find out the most beneficial employment for itself, there is none for a reliance, that it will struggle against the force of unequal terms, or will of itself surmount all the adventitious barriers to a successful competition, which may have been erected either by the advantages naturally acquired from practice and previous possession of the ground, or by those which may have sprung from positive regulations and an artificial policy. This general reflection might alone suffice as an answer to the objection under examination; exclusively of the weighty considerations which have been particularly urged.

The objections to the pursuit of manufactures in the United States, which next present themselves to discussion, represent an impracticability of success, arising from three causes—scarcity of hands—dearness of labour—want of capital.

The two first circumstances are to a certain extent real, and, within due limits, ought to be admitted as obstacles to the success of manufacturing enterprize in the United States. But there are various considerations, which lessen their force, and tend to afford an assurance that they are not sufficient to prevent the advantageous prosecution of many very useful and extensive manufactories.

With regard to scarcity of hands, the fact itself must be applied with no small qualification to certain parts of the United States. There are large districts, which may be considered as pretty fully peopled; and which notwithstanding a continual drain for distant settlement, are thickly interspersed with flourishing and increasing towns. If these districts have not already reached the point, at which the complaint of scarcity of hands ceases, they are not remote from it, and are approaching fast towards it: And having perhaps fewer attractions to agriculture, than some other parts of the Union, they exhibit a proportionably stronger tendency towards other kinds of industry. In these districts, may be discerned, no inconsiderable maturity for manufacturing establishments.

But there are circumstances, which have been already noticed with another view, that materially diminish every where the effect of a scarcity of hands. These circumstances are—the great use which can be made of women and children; on which point a very pregnant and instructive fact has been mentioned—the vast extension given by late improvements to the employment of Machines, which substituting the Agency of fire and water, has prodigiously lessened the necessity for manual labor—the employment of persons ordinarily engaged in other occupations, during the seasons, or hours of leisure; which, besides giving occasion to the exertion of a greater quantity of labour by the same number of persons, and thereby encreasing the general stock of labour, as has been elsewhere remarked, may also be taken into the calculation, as a resource for obviating the scarcity of hands— lastly the attraction of foreign emigrants. Whoever inspects, with a careful eye, the composition of our towns will be made sensible to what an extent this resource may be relied upon. This exhibits a large proportion of ingenious and valuable workmen, in different arts and trades, who, by expatriating from Europe, have improved their own condition, and added to the industry and wealth of the United States. It is a natural inference from the experience, we have already had, that as soon as the United States shall present the countenance of a serious prosecution of Manufactures—as soon as foreign artists shall be made sensible that the state of things here affords a moral certainty of employment and encouragement—competent numbers of European workmen will transplant themselves, effectually to ensure the success of the design. How indeed can it otherwise happen considering the various and powerful inducements, which the situation of this country offers; addressing themselves to so many strong passions and feelings, to so many general and particular interests?

It may be affirmed therefore, in respect to hands for carrying on manufactures, that we shall in a great measure trade upon a foreign Stock; reserving our own, for the cultivation of our lands and the manning of our Ships; as far as character and circumstances [shall] incline. It is not unworthy of remark, that the objection to the success of manufactures, deduced from the scarcity of hands, is alike applicable to Trade and Navigation; and yet these are perceived to flourish, without any sensible impediment from that cause.

As to the dearness of labour (another of the obstacles alledged) this has relation principally to two circumstances, one that which has been just discussed, or the scarcity of hands, the other, the greatness of profits.

As far as it is a consequence of the scarcity of hands, it is mitigated by all the considerations which have been adduced as lessening that deficiency.

It is certain too, that the disparity in this respect, between some of the most manufacturing parts of Europe and a large proportion of the United States, is not nearly so great as is commonly imagined. It is also much less in regard to Artificers and manufacturers than in regard to country labourers; and while a careful comparison shews, that there is, in this particular, much exaggeration; it is also evident that the effect of the degree of disparity, which does truly exist, is diminished in proportion to the use which can be made of machinery.

To illustrate this last idea—Let it be supposed, that the difference of price, in two Countries, of a given quantity of manual labour requisite to the fabrication of a given article is as 10; and that some *mechanic power* is introduced into both countries, which performing half the necessary labour, leaves only half to be done by hand, it is evident, that the difference in the cost of the fabrication of the article in question, in the two countries, as far as it is connected with the price of labour, will be reduced from 10. to 5, in consequence of the introduction of that *power*.

This circumstance is worthy of the most particular attention. It diminishes immensely one of the objections most strenuously urged, against the success of manufactures in the United States.

To procure all such machines as are known in any part of Europe, can only require a proper provision and due pains. The knowledge of several of the most important of them is already possessed. The preparation of them here, is in most cases, practicable on nearly equal terms. As far as they depend on Water, some superiority of advantages may be claimed, from the uncommon variety and greater cheapness of situations adapted to Mill seats, with which different parts of the United States abound.

So far as the dearness of labour may be a consequence of the greatness of profits in any branch of business, it is no obstacle to its success. The Undertaker can afford to pay the price.

301

There are grounds to conclude that undertakers of Manufactures in this Country can at this time afford to pay higher wages to the workmen they may employ than are paid to similar workmen in Europe. The prices of foreign fabrics, in the markets of the United States, which will for a long time regulate the prices of the domestic ones, may be considered as compounded of the following ingredients—The first cost of materials, including the Taxes, if any, which are paid upon them where they are made: the expence of grounds, buildings machinery and tools: the wages of the persons employed in the manufactory: the profits on the capital or Stock employed: the commissions of Agents to purchase them where they are made; the expence of transportation to the United States [including insurance and other incidental charges;] the taxes or duties, if any [and fees of office] which are paid on their exportation: the taxes or duties [and fees of office] which are paid on their importation.

As to the first of these items, the cost of materials, the advantage upon the whole, is at present on the side of the United States, and the difference, in their favor, must increase, in proportion as a certain and extensive domestic demand shall induce the proprietors of land to devote more of their attention to the production of those materials. It ought not to escape observation, in a comparison on this point, that some of the principal manufacturing Countries of Europe are much more dependent on foreign supply for the materials of their manufactures, than would be the United States, who are capable of supplying themselves, with a greater abundance, as well as a greater variety of the requisite materials.

As to the second item, the expence of grounds buildings machinery and tools, an equality at least may be assumed; since advantages in some particulars will counterbalance temporary disadvantages in others.

As to the third item, or the article of wages, the comparison certainly turns against the United States, though as before observed not in so great a degree as is commonly supposed.

The fourth item is alike applicable to the foreign and to the domestic manufacture. It is indeed more properly a *result* than a particular, to be compared.

But with respect to all the remaining items, they are alone applicable to the foreign manufacture, and in the strictest sense extraordinaries; constituting a sum of extra charge on the foreign fabric, which cannot be estimated, at less than [from 15 to 30] ℔ Cent. on the cost of it at the manufactory.

This sum of extra charge may confidently be regarded as more than a Counterpoise for the real difference in the price of labour; and is a satisfactory proof that manufactures may prosper in defiance of it in the United States. To the general allegation, connected with the circumstances of scarcity of hands and dearness of labour, that extensive manufactures can only grow out of a redundant or full population, it will be sufficient, to answer generally, that the fact has been otherwise—That the situation alleged to be an essential condition of success, has not been that of several nations, at periods when they had already attained to maturity in a variety of manufactures.

The supposed want of Capital for the prosecution of manufactures in the United States is the most indefinite of the objections which are usually opposed to it.

It is very difficult to pronounce any thing precise concerning the real extent of the monied capital of a Country, and still more concerning the proportion which it bears to the objects that invite the employment of Capital. It is not less difficult to pronounce how far the *effect* of any given quantity of money, as capital, or in other words, as a medium for circulating the industry and property of a nation, may be encreased by the very circumstance of the additional motion, which is given to it by new objects of employment. That effect, like the momentum of descending bodies, may not improperly be represented, as in a compound ratio to *mass* and *velocity*. It seems pretty certain, that a given sum of money, in a situation, in which the quick impulses of commercial activity were little felt, would appear inadequate to the circulation of as great a quantity of industry and property, as in one, in which their full influence was experienced.

It is not obvious, why the same objection might not as well be made to external commerce as to manufactures; since it is manifest that our immense tracts of land occupied and unoccupied are capable of giving employment to more capital than is actually bestowed upon them. It is certain, that the United States offer a vast field for the advantageous employment of Capital; but it does not follow, that there will not be found, in one way or another, a sufficient fund for the successful prosecution of any species of industry which is likely to prove truly beneficial.

The following considerations are of a nature to remove all inquietude on the score of want of Capital.

The introduction of Banks, as has been shewn on another occasion has a powerful tendency to extend the active Capital of a Country. Experience of the Utility of these Institutions is multiplying them in the United States. It is probable that they will be established wherever they can exist with advantage; and wherever, they can be supported, if administered with prudence, they will add new energies to all pecuniary operations.

The aid of foreign Capital may safely, and, with considerable latitude be taken into calculation. Its instrumentality has been long experienced in our external commerce; and it has begun to be felt in various other modes. Not only our funds, but our Agriculture and other internal improvements have been animated by it. It has already in a few instances extended even to our manufactures.

It is a well known fact, that there are parts of Europe, which have more Capital, than profitable domestic objects of employment. Hence, among other proofs, the large loans continually furnished to foreign states. And it is equally certain that the capital of other parts may find more profitable employment in the United States, than at home. And notwithstanding there are weighty inducements to prefer the employment of capital at home even at less profit, to an investment of it abroad, though with greater gain, yet these inducements are overruled either by a deficiency of employment or by a very material difference in profit. Both these Causes operate to produce a transfer of foreign capital to the United States. 'Tis certain, that various objects in this country hold out advantages, which are with difficulty to be equalled elsewhere; and under the increasingly favorable impressions, which are entertained of our government, the attractions will become more and More strong. These impressions will prove a rich mine of prosperity to the Country, if they are confirmed and strengthened by the progress of our affairs. And to secure this advantage, little more is now necessary, than to foster industry, and cultivate order and tranquility, at home and abroad.

It is not impossible, that there may be persons disposed to look with a jealous eye on the introduction of foreign Capital, as if it were an instrument to deprive our own citizens of the profits of our own industry: But perhaps there never could be a more unreasonable jealousy. Instead of being viewed as a rival, it ought to be Considered as a most valuable auxiliary; conducing to put in Motion a greater Quantity of productive labour, and a greater portion of useful enterprise than could exist without it. It is at least evident, that in a Country situated like the United States, with an infinite fund of resources yet to be unfolded, every farthing of foreign capital, which is laid out in internal ameliorations, and in industrious establishments of a permanent nature, is a precious acquisition.

And whatever be the objects which originally attract foreign Capital, when once introduced, it may be directed towards any purpose of beneficial exertion, which is desired. And to detain it among us, there can be no expedient so effectual as to enlarge the sphere, within which it may be usefully employed: Though induced merely with views to speculations in the funds, it may afterwards be rendered subservient to the Interests of Agriculture, Commerce & Manufactures.

But the attraction of foreign Capital for the direct purpose of Manufactures ought not to be deemed a chimerial expectation. There are already examples of it, as remarked in another place. And the examples, if the disposition be cultivated can hardly fail to multiply. There are also instances of another kind, which serve to strengthen the expectation. Enterprises for improving the Public Communications, by cutting canals, opening the obstructions in Rivers and erecting bridges, have received very material aid from the same source.

When the Manufacturing Capitalist of Europe shall advert to the many important advantages, which have been intimated, in the Course of this report, he cannot but perceive very powerful inducements to a transfer of himself and his Capital to the United States. Among the reflections, which a most interesting peculiarity of situation is calculated to suggest, it cannot escape his observation, as a circumstance of Moment in the calculation, that the progressive population and improvement of the United States, insure a continually increasing domestic demand for the fabrics which he shall produce, not to be affected by any external casualties or vicissitudes.

But while there are Circumstances sufficiently strong to authorise a considerable degree of reliance on the aid of foreign Capital towards the attainment of the object in view, it is satisfactory to have good grounds of assurance, that there are domestic resources of themselves adequate to it. It happens, that there is a species of Capital actually existing within the United States, which relieves from all inquietude on the score of want of Capital—This is the funded Debt.

The effect of a funded debt, as a species of Capital, has been Noticed upon a former Occasion; but a more particular elucidation of the point seems to be required by the stress which is here laid upon it. This shall accordingly be attempted.

Public Funds answer the purpose of Capital, from the estimation in which they are usually held by Monied men; and consequently from the Ease and dispatch with which they can be turned into money. This capacity of prompt convertibility into money causes a transfer of stock to be in a great number of Cases equivalent to a payment in coin. And where it does not happen to suit the party who is to receive, to accept a transfer of Stock, the party who is to pay, is never at a loss to find elsewhere a purchaser of his Stock, who will furnish him in lieu of it, with the Coin of which he stands in need. Hence in a sound and settled state of the public funds, a man possessed of a sum in them can embrace any scheme of business, which offers, with as much confidence as if he were possessed of an equal sum in Coin.

This operation of public funds as capital is too obvious to be denied; but it is objected to the Idea of their operating as an *augmentation* of the Capital of the community, that they serve to occasion the *destruction* of some other capital to an equal amount.

The Capital which alone they can be supposed to destroy must consist of—The annual revenue, which is applied to the payment of Interest on the debt, and to the gradual redemption of the principal—The amount of the Coin, which is employed in circulating the funds, or, in other words, in effecting the different alienations which they undergo.

But the following appears to be the true and accurate view of this matter.

1st. As to the point of the Annual Revenue requisite for Payment of interest and redemption of principal.

As a determinate proportion will tend to perspicuity in the reasoning, let it be supposed that the annual revenue to be applied, corresponding with the modification of the 6 per Cent stock of the United States, is in the ratio of eight upon the hundred, that is in the first instance six on Account of interest, and two on account of Principal.

Thus far it is evident, that the Capital destroyed to the capital created, would bear no greater proportion, than 8 to 100. There would be withdrawn from the total mass of other capitals a sum of eight dollars to be paid to the public creditor; while he would be possessed of a sum of One Hundred dollars, ready to be applied to any purpose, to be embarked in any enterprize, which might appear to him eligible. Here then the *Augmentation* of Capital, or the excess of that which is produced, beyond that which is destroyed is equal to Ninety two dollars. To this conclusion, it may be objected, that the sum of Eight dollars is to be withdrawn annually, until the whole hundred is extinguished, and it may be inferred, that in process of time a capital will be destroyed equal to that which is at first created.

But it is nevertheless true, that during the whole of the interval, between the creation of the Capital of 100 dollars, and its reduction to a sum not greater than that of the annual revenue appropriated to its redemption—there will be a greater active capital in existence than if no debt had been Contracted. The sum drawn from other Capitals *in any one year* will not exceed eight dollars; but there will be *at every instant of time* during the whole period, in question a sum corresponding *with so much of the principal*, as remains *unredeemed*, in the hands of some person, or other, employed, or ready to be employed in some profitable undertaking. There will therefore constantly be more capital, in capacity to be employed, than capital taken from employment. The excess for the first year has been stated to be Ninety two dollars; it will diminish yearly, but there always will be an excess, until the principal of the debt is brought to a level with the *redeeming annuity*, that is, in the case which has been assumed by way of example, to *eight dollars*. The reality of this excess becomes palpable, if it be supposed, as often happens, that the citizen of a foreign Country imports into the United States 100 dollars for the purchase of an equal sum of public debt. Here is an absolute augmentation of the mass of Circulating Coin to the extent of 100 dollars. At the end of a year the foreigner is presumed to draw back eight dollars on account of his Principal and Interest, but he still leaves, Ninety two of his original Deposit in circulation, as he in like manner leaves Eighty four at the end of the second year, drawing back then also the annuity of Eight Dollars: And thus the Matter proceeds; The capital left in circulation diminishing each year, and coming nearer to the level of the annuity drawnback. There are however some differences in the ultimate operation of the part of the debt, which is purchased by foreigners, and that which remains in the hands of citizens. But the general effect in each case, though in different degrees, is to add to the active capital of the Country.

Hitherto the reasoning has proceeded on a concession of the position, that there is a destruction of some other capital, to the extent of the annuity appropriated to the payment of the Interest and the redemption of the principal of the deb⟨t⟩ but in this, too much has been conceded. There is at most a temp⟨orary⟩ transfer of some other capital, to the amount of the Annuity, from those who pay to the Creditor who receives; which he again restor⟨es⟩ to the circulation to resume the offices of a capital. This he does ei⟨ther⟩ immediately by employing the money in some branch of Industry, or mediately by lending it to some other person, who does so employ ⟨it⟩ or by spending it on his own maintenance. In either sup⟨position⟩ there is no destruction of capital, there is nothing more ⟨than a⟩ suspension of its motion for a time; that is, while it is ⟨passing⟩ from the hands of those who pay into the Public coffers, & thence ⟨through⟩ the public Creditor into some other Channel of circulation. ⟨When⟩ the payments of interest are periodical and quick and made by instrumentality of Banks the diversion or suspension of capita⟨l⟩ may almost be denominated momentary. Hence the deduction on this Account is far less, than it at first sight appears to be.

There is evidently, as far as regards the annuity no destruction nor transfer of any other Capital, than that por⟨tion⟩ of the income of each individual, which goes to make up the Annuity. The land which furnishes the Farmer with the s⟨um⟩ which he is to contribute remains the same; and the like m⟨ay⟩ be observed of other Capitals. Indeed as far as the Tax, w⟨hich⟩ is the object of contribution (as frequently happens, when it doe⟨s⟩ not oppress, by its weight) may have been a Motive to *greate⟨r⟩ exertion* in any occupation; it may even serve to encrease the contributory Capital: This idea is not without importanc(e) in the general view of the subject.

It remains to see, what further deduction ought to be mad⟨e⟩ from the capital which is created, by the existence of the Debt; on account of the coin, which is employed in its circulation. This is susceptible of much less precise calculation, than the Article which has been just discussed. It is impossible to say what proportion of coin is necessary to carry on the alienations which any species of property usually undergoes. The quantity indeed varies according to circumstances. But it may still without hesitation be pronounced, from the quickness of the rotation, or rather of the transitions, that the *medium* of circulation always bears but a small proportion to the amount of the *property* circulated. And it is thence satisfactorily deducible, that the coin employed in the Negociations of the funds and which serves to give them activity, as capital, is incomparably less than the sum of the debt negotiated for the purposes of business.

It ought not, however, to be omitted, that the negotiation of the funds becomes itself a distinct business; which employs, and by employing diverts a portion of the circulating coin from other pursuits. But making due allowance for this circumstance there is no reason to conclude, that the effect of the diversion of coin in the whole operation bears any considerable proportion to the amount of the Capital to which it gives activity. The sum of the debt in circulation is continually at the Command, of any useful enterprise—the coin itself which circulates it, is never more than momentarily suspended from its ordinary functions. It experiences an incessant and rapid flux and reflux to and from the Channels of industry to those of speculations in the funds.

There are strong circumstances in confirmation of this Theory. The force of Monied Capital which has been displayed in Great Britain, and the height to which every species of industry has grown up under it, defy a solution from the quantity of coin which that kingdom has ever possessed. Accordingly it has been Coeval with its funding system, the prevailing opinion of the men of business, and of the generality of the most sagacious theorists of that country, that the operation of the public funds as capital has contributed to the effect in question. Among ourselves appearances thus far favour the same Conclusion. Industry in general seems to have been reanimated. There are symptoms indicating an extention of our Commerce. Our navigation has certainly of late had a Considerable spring, and there appears to be in many parts of the Union a command of capital, which till lately, since the revolution at least, was unknown. But it is at the same time to be acknowledged, that other circumstances have concurred, (and in a great degree) in producing the present state of things, and that the appearances are not yet sufficiently decisive, to be intirely relied upon.

In the question under discussion, it is important to distinguish between an *absolute increase of Capital, or an accession of real wealth*, and *an artificial increase of Capital*, as an engine of business, or as an instrument of industry and Commerce. In the first sense, a funded debt has no pretensions to being deemed an increase of Capital; in the last, it has pretensions which are not easy to be controverted. Of a similar nature is bank credit and in an inferior degree, every species of private credit.

But though a funded debt is not in the first instance, an absolute increase of Capital, or an augmentation of real wealth; yet by serving as a New power in the operation of industry, it has within certain bounds a tendency to increase the real wealth of a Community, in like manner as money borrowed by a thrifty farmer, to be laid out in the improvement of his farm may, in the end, add to his Stock of real riches.

There are respectable individuals, who from a just aversion to an accumulation of Public debt, are unwilling to concede to it any kind of utility, who can discern no good to alleviate the ill with which they suppose it pregnant; who cannot be persuaded that it ought in any sense to be viewed as an increase of capital lest it should be inferred, that the more debt the more capital, the greater the burthens the greater the blessings of the community.

But it interests the public Councils to estimate every object as it truly is; to appreciate how far the good in any measure is compensated by the ill; or the ill by the good, Either of them is seldom unmixed.

Neither will it follow, that an accumulation of debt is desireable, because a certain degree of it operates as capital. There may be a plethora in the political, as in the Natural body; There may be a state of things in which any such artificial capital is unnecessary. The debt too may be swelled to such a size, as that the greatest part of it may cease to be useful as a Capital, serving only to pamper the dissipation of idle and dissolute individuals: as that the sums required to pay the

Interest upon it may become oppressive, and beyond the means, which a government can employ, consistently with its tranquility, to raise them; as that the resources of taxation, to face the debt, may have been strained too far to admit of extensions adequate to exigencies, which regard the public safety.

Where this critical point is, cannot be pronounced, but it is impossible to believe, that there is not such a point.

And as the vicissitudes of Nations beget a perpetual tendency to the accumulation of debt, there ought to be in every government a perpetual, anxious and unceasing effort to reduce that, which at any time exists, as fast as shall be practicable consistently with integrity and good faith.

Reasonings on a subject comprehending ideas so abstract and complex, so little reducible to precise calculation as those which enter into the question just discussed, are always attended with a danger of runing into fallacies. Due allowance ought therefore to be made for this possibility. But as far as the Nature of the subject admits of it, there appears to be satisfactory ground for a belief, that the public funds operate as a resource of capital to the Citizens of the United States, and, if they are a resource at all, it is an extensive one. . . .

There remains to be noticed an objection to the encouragement of manufactures, of a nature different from those which question the probability of success. This is derived from its supposed tendency to give a monopoly of advantages to particula⟨r⟩ classes at the expence of the rest of the community, who, it is affirmed, would be able to procure the requisite supplies of manufactured articles on better terms from foreigners, than from our own Citizens, and who it is alledged, are reduced to a necessity of paying an enhanced price for whatever they want, by every measure, which obstructs the free competition of foreign commoditi⟨es⟩.

It is not an unreasonable supposition, that measures, which serve to abridge the free competition of foreign Articles, have a tendency to occasion an enhancement of prices and it is not to be denied that such is the effect in a number of Cases; but the fact does not uniformly correspond with the theory. A reduction of prices has in several instances immediately succeeded the establishment of a domestic manufacture. Whether it be that foreign Manufacturers endeavour to suppla⟨nt⟩ by underselling our own, or whatever else be the cause, the effect has been such as is stated, and the reverse of what mig⟨ht⟩ have been expected.

But though it were true, that the immedi⟨ate⟩ and certain effect of regulations controuling the competition of foreign with domestic fabrics was an increase of price, it is universally true, that the contrary is the ultimate effect with every successful manufacture. When a domestic manufacture has attained to perfection, and has engaged in the prosecution of it a competent number of Persons, it invariably becomes cheaper. Being free from the heavy charges, which attend the importation of foreign commodities, it can be afforded, and accordingly seldom or never fails to be sold Cheaper, in process of time, than was the foreign Article for which it is a substitute. The internal competition, which takes place, soon does away every thing like Monopoly, and by degrees reduces the price of the Article to the *minimum* of a reasonable profit on the Capital employed. This accords with the reason of the thing and with experience.

Whence it follows, that it is the interest of a community with a view to eventual and permanent œconomy, to encourage the growth of manufactures. In a national view, a temporary enhancement of price must always be well compensated by a permanent reduction of it.

It is a reflection, which may with propriety be indulged here, that this eventual diminution of the prices of manufactured Articles; which is the result of internal manufacturing establishments, has a direct and very important tendency to benefit agriculture. It enables the farmer, to procure with a smaller quantity of his labour, the manufactured produce of which he stan⟨ds⟩ in need, and consequently increases the value of his income and property.

The objections which are commonly made to the expediency of encouraging, and to the probability of succeeding in manufacturing pursuits, in the United states, having now been discussed; the Considerations which have appeared in the Course of the discussion, recommending that species of industry to the patronage of the Government, will be materially strengthened by a few general and some particular topics, which have been naturally reserved for subsequent Notice.

I There seems to be a moral certainty, that the trade of a country which is both manufacturing and Agricultural will be more lucrative and prosperous, than that of a Country, which is, merely Agricultural.

One reason for this is found in that general effort of nations (which has been already mentioned) to procure from their own soils, the articles of prime necessity requisite to their own consumption and use; and which serves to render their demand for a foreign supply of such articles in a great degree occasional and contingent. Hence, while the necessities of nations exclusively devoted to Agriculture, for the fabrics of manufacturing st⟨ates⟩ are constant and regular, the wants of the latter for the products of the former, are liable to very considerable fluctuations and interruptions. The great inequalities resulting from difference of seasons, have been elsewhere remarked: This uniformity of deman⟨d⟩ on one side, and unsteadiness of it, on the other, must necessarily ha⟨ve⟩ a tendency to cause the general course of the exchange of commodit⟨ies⟩ between the parties to turn to the disadvantage of the merely agricultural States. Peculiarity of situation, a climate and soil ada⟨pted⟩ to the production of peculiar commodities, may, sometimes, contradi⟨ct⟩ the rule; but there is every reason to believe that it will be fou⟨nd⟩ in the Main, a just one.

Another circumstance which gives a superiority of commercial advantages to states, that manufact⟨ure⟩ as well as cultivate, consists in the more numerous attractions, which a more diversified market offers to foreign Customers, and greater scope, which it affords to mercantile enterprise. It is ⟨a⟩ position of indisputable truth in Commerce, depending too on very obvious reasons, that the greatest resort will ever be to those mar⟨ts⟩ where commodities, while equally abundant, are most various. Each difference of kind holds out an additional inducement. And it is a position not less clear, that the field of enterprise must be enlarged to the Merchants of a Country, in proportion ⟨to⟩ the variety as well as the abundance of commodities which they find at home for exportation to foreign Markets.

A third circumstance, perhaps not inferior to either of the other two, conferring the superiority which has been stated has relation to the stagnations of demand for certain commodities which at some time or other interfere more or less with the sale of all. The Nation which can bring to Market, but few articles is likely to be more quickly and sensibly affected by such stagnations, than one, which is always possessed of a great variety of commodities. The former frequently finds too great a proportion of its stock of materials, for sale or exchange, lying on hand—or is obliged to make injurious sacrifices to supply its wants of foreign articles, which are *Numerous* and *urgent,* in proportion to the smallness of the number of its own. The latter commonly finds itself indemnified, by the high prices of some articles, for the low prices of others—and the Prompt and advantageous sale of those articles which are in demand enables its merchant the better to wait for a favorable change, in respect to those which are not. There is ground to believe, that a difference of situation, in this particular, has immensely different effec⟨ts⟩ upon the wealth and prosperity of Nations.

From these circumstances collectively, two important inferences are to be drawn, one, that there is always a higher probability of a favorable balance of Trade, in regard to countries in which manufactures founded on the basis of a thriving Agriculture flourish, than in regard to those, which are confined wholly or almost wholly to Agriculture; the other (which is also a consequence of the first) that countries of the former description are likely to possess more pecuniary wealth, or money, than those of the latter.

Facts appear to correspond with this conclusion. The importations of manufactured supplies seem invariably to drain the merely Agricultural people of their wealth. Let the situation of the manufauring countries of Europe be compared in this particular, with that of Countries which only cultivate, and the disparity will be striking. Other causes, it is true, help to Account for this disparity between some of them; and among these causes, the relative state of Agriculture; but between others of them, the most prominent circumstance of dissimilitude arises from the Comparative state of Manufactures. In corroboration of the same idea, it ought not to escape remark, that the West India Islands, the soils of which are the most fertile, and the Nation, which in the greatest degree supplies the rest of the world, with the precious metals, exchange to a loss with almost every other Country.

As far as experience at home may guide, it will lead to the same conclusion. Previous to the revolution, the quantity of coin, possessed by the colonies, which now compose the United states, appeared, to be inadequate to their circulation; and their debt to Great-Britain was progressive. Since the Revolution, the States, in which manufactures have most increased, have recovered fastest from the injuries of the late War, and abound most in pecuniary resources.

It ought to be admitted, however in this as in the preceding case, that causes irrelative to the state of manufactures account, in a degree, for the Phœnomena remarked. The continual progress of new settlements has a natural tendency to occasion an unfavorable balance of Trade; though it indemnifies for the inconvenience, by that increase of the national capital which flows from the conversion of waste into improved lands: And the different degrees of external commerce, which are carried on by the different States, may make material differences in the comparative state of their wealth. The first circumstance has reference to the deficien⟨cy⟩ of coin and the increase of debt previous to the revolution; the last to the advantages which the most manufacturing states appear to have enjoyed, over the others, since the termination of the late War.

But the uniform appearance of an abundance of specie, as the concomitant of a flourishing state of manufacture⟨s⟩ and of the reverse, where they do not prevail, afford a strong presumption of their favourable operation upon the wealth of a Country.

Not only the wealth; but the independence and security of a

Country, appear to be materially connected with the prosperity of manufactures. Every nation, with a view to those great objects, ought to endeavour to possess within itself all the essentials of national supply. These comprise the means of *Subsistence habitation clothing* and *defence.*

The possession of these is necessary to the perfection of the body politic, to the safety as well as to the welfare of the society; the want of either, is the want of an important organ of political life and Motion; and in the various crises which await a state, it must severely feel the effects of any such deficiency. The extreme embarrassments of the United States during the late War, from an incapacity of supplying themselves, are still matter of keen recollection: A future war might be expected again to exemplify the mischiefs and dangers of a situation, to which that incapacity is still in too great a degree applicable, unless changed by timely and vigorous exertion. To effect this change as fast as shall be prudent, merits all the attention and all the Zeal of our Public Councils; 'tis the next great work to be accomplished.

The want of a Navy to protect our external commerce, as long as it shall Continue, must render it a peculiarly precarious reliance, for the supply of essential articles, and must serve to strengthen prodigiously the arguments in favour of manufactures.

To these general Considerations are added some of a more particular nature.

Our distance from Europe, the great fountain of manufactured supply, subjects us in the existing state of things, to inconvenience and loss in two Ways.

The bulkiness of those commodities which are the chief productions of the soil, necessarily imposes very heavy charges on their transportation, to distant markets. These charges, in the Cases, in which the nations, to whom our products are sent, maintain a Competition in the supply of their own markets, principally fall upon us, and form material deductions from the primitive value of the articles furnished. The charges on manufactured supplies, brought from Europe are greatly enhanced by the same circumstance of distance. These charges, again, in the cases in which our own industry maintains no competition, in our own markets, also principally fall upon us; and are an additional cause of extraordinary deduction from the primitive value of our own products; these bei⟨ng⟩ the materials of exchange for the foreign fabrics, which we consume.

The equality and moderation of individual prope⟨rty⟩ and the growing settlements of new districts, occasion in this country an unusual demand for coarse manufactures; The charges of which being greater in proportion to their greater bulk augment the disadvantage, which has been just described.

As in most countries domestic supplie⟨s⟩ maintain a very considerable competition with such foreign productions of the soil, as are imported for sale; if the extensive establishment of Manufactories in the United states does not create a similar competition in respect to manufactured articles, it appears to be clearly deducible, from the Considerations which have been mentioned, that they must sustain a double loss in their exchanges with foreign Nations; strongly conducive to an unfavorable balance of Trade, and very prejudicial to their Interests.

These disadvantages press with no small weight, on the landed interest of the Country. In seasons of peace, they cause a serious deduction from the intrinsic value of the products of the soil. In the time of a War, which shou'd either involve ourselves, or another nation, possessing a Considerable share of our carrying trade, the charges on the transportation of our commodities, bulky as most of them are, could hardly fail to prove a grievous burthen to the farmer; while obliged to depend in so great degree as he now does, upon foreign markets for the vent of the surplus of his labour.

As far as the prosperity of the Fisheries of the United states is impeded by the want of an adequate market, there arises another special reason for desiring the extension of manufactures. Besides the fish, which in many places, would be likely to make a part of the subsistence of the persons employed; it is known that the oils, bones and skins of marine animals, are of extensive use in various manufactures. Hence the prospect of an additional demand for the produce of the Fisheries.

One more point of view only remains in which to Consider the expediency of encouraging manufactures in the United states.

It is not uncommon to meet with an opin⟨ion⟩ that though the promoting of manufactures may be the interest of a part of the Union, it is contrary to that of another part. The Northern & southern regions are sometimes represented as having adverse interests in this respect. Those are called Manufacturing, these Agricultural states; and a species of opposition is imagined to subsist between the Manufacturing a⟨nd⟩ Agricultural interests.

This idea of an opposition between those two interests is the common error of the early periods of every country, but experience gradually dissipates it. Indeed they are perceived so often to succour and to befriend each other, that they come at length to be considered as one: a supposition which has been frequently abused and is not universally true. Particular encouragements of particular manufac-

315

tures may be of a Nature to sacrifice the interests of landholders to those of manufacturers; But it is nevertheless a maxim well established by experience, and generally acknowledged, where there has been sufficient experience, that the *aggregate* prosperity of manufactures, and the *aggregate* prosperity of Agriculture are intimately connected. In the Course of the discussion which has had place, various weighty considerations have been adduced operating in support of that maxim. Perhaps the superior steadiness of the demand of a domestic market for the surplus produce of the soil, is alone a convincing argument of its truth.

Ideas of a contrariety of interests between the Northern and southern regions of the Union, are in the Main as unfounded as they are mischievous. The diversity of Circumstances on which such contrariety is usually predicated, authorises a directly contrary conclusion. Mutual wants constitute one of the strongest links of political connection, and the extent of the⟨se⟩ bears a natural proportion to the diversity in the means of mutual supply.

Suggestions of an opposite complexion are ever to be deplored, as unfriendly to the steady pursuit of one great common cause, and to the perfect harmony of all the parts.

In proportion as the mind is accustomed to trace the intimate connexion of interest, which subsists between all the parts of a Society united under the *same* government—the infinite variety of channels which serve to Circulate the prosper⟨ity⟩ of each to and through the rest—in that proportion will it be little apt to be disturbed by solicitudes and Apprehensions which originate in local discriminations. It is a truth as important as it is agreeable, and one to which it is not easy to imagine exceptions, that every thing tending to establish *substantial* and *permanent order*, in the affairs of a Country, to increase the total mass of industry and opulence, is ultimately beneficial to every part of it. On the Credit of this great truth, an acquiescence may safely be accorded, from every quarter, to all institutions & arrangements, which promise a confirmation of public order, and an augmentation of National Resource.

But there are more particular considerations which serve to fortify the idea, that the encouragement of manufactures is the interest of all parts of the Union. If the Northern and middle states should be the principal scenes of such establishments, they would immediately benefit the more southern, by creating a demand for productions; some of which they have in common with the other states, and others of which are either peculiar to them, or more abundant, or of better quality, than elsewhere. These productions, principally are Timber, flax, Hemp, Cotton, Wool, raw silk, Indigo, iron, lead, furs, hides, skins and coals. Of these articles Cotton & Indigo are peculiar to the southern states; as are hitherto *Lead & Coal*. Flax and Hemp are or may be raised in greater abundance there, than in the More Northern states; and the Wool of Virginia is said to be of better quality than that of any other state: a Circumstance rendered the more probable by the reflection that Virginia embraces the same latitudes with the finest Wool Countries of Europe. The Climate of the south is also better adapted to the production of silk.

The extensive cultivation of Cotton can perhaps hardly be expected, but from the previous establishment of domestic Manufactories of the Article; and the surest encouragement and vent, for the others, would result from similar establishments in respect to them.

If then, it satifactorily appears, that it is the Interest of the United states, generally, to encourage manufactures, it merits particular attention, that there are circumstances, which Render the present a critical moment for entering with Zeal upon the important business. The effort cannot fail to be materially seconded by a considerable and encreasing influx of money, in consequence of foreign speculations in the funds—and by the disorders, which exist in different parts of Europe.

The first circumstance not only facilita⟨tes⟩ the execution of manufacturing enterprises; but it indicates them as a necessary mean to turn the thing itself to advantage, and to prevent its being eventually an evil. If useful employment be not found for the Money of foreigners brought to the country to be invested in purchase⟨s⟩ of the public debt, it will quickly be reexported to defray the expence of an extraordinary consumption of foreign luxuries; and distressing drains of our specie may hereafter be experienced to pay the interest and redeem the principal of the purchased debt.

This useful employment too ought to be of a Nature to produce solid and permanent improvements. If the money merely serves to give a temporary spring to foreign commerce; as it cannot procure new and lasting outlets for the products of the Country; there will be no real or durable advantage gained. As far as it shall find its way in Agricultural ameliorations, in opening canals, and in similar improvements, it will be productive of substantial utility. But there is reason to doubt, whether in such channels it is likely to find sufficient employment, and still more whether many of those who possess it, would be as readily attracted to objects of this nature, as to manufacturing pursuits; which bear greater analogy to those to which they are accustomed, and to the spirit generated by them.

317

To open the one field, as well as the other, will at least secure a better prospect of useful employment, for whatever accession of money, there has been or may be.

There is at the present juncture a certain fermentation of mind, a certain activity of speculation and enterprise which if properly directed may be made subservient to useful purposes; but which if left entirely to itself, may be attended with pernicious effects.

The disturbed state of Europe, inclining its citizens to emigration, the requisite workmen, will be more easily acquired, than at another time; and the effect of multiplying the opportunities of employment to those who emigrate, may be an increase of the number and extent of valuable acquisitions to the population arts and industry of the Country. To find pleasure in the calamities of other nations, would be criminal; but to benefit ourselves, by opening an asylum to those who suffer, in consequence of them, is as justifiable as it is pol⟨itic⟩. . . .

LETTER TO EDWARD CARRINGTON
MAY 26, 1792

The best exposition of the circumstances that, from Hamilton's point of view, led to his conflict with Jefferson and Madison appears in the following letter to Edward Carrington. Hamilton concludes this letter by confronting the often repeated charge that he was an enemy of republicanism, for more than any other leading American statesman he felt compelled to emphasize the problematic character of republicanism. Hamilton surely endorsed the principles and practices of free government, but the establishment of a republican government, a government based on wholly popular principles, on a safe and solid basis, was still an experiment. Hamilton considered its success yet a problem.

Philadelphia, May 26, 1792

My Dear Sir

Believing that I possess a share of your personal friendship and confidence and yielding to that which I feel towards you—persuaded also that our political creed is the same on *two essential points,* 1st the necessity of *Union* to the respectability and happiness of this Country and 2 the necessity of an *efficient* general government to maintain that Union—I have concluded to unbosom myself to you on the present state of political parties and views. I ask no reply to what I shall say. I only ask that you will be persuaded, the representations I shall make are agreable to the real and sincere impressions of my mind. You will make the due allowances for the influence of circumstances upon it— you will consult your own observations and you will draw such a conclusion as shall appear to you proper.

When I accepted the Office, I now hold, it was under a full persuasion, that from similarity of thinking, conspiring with personal goodwill, I should have the firm support of Mr. Madison, in the *general course* of my administration. Aware of the intrinsic difficulties of the situation and of the powers of Mr. Madison, I do not believe I should have accepted under a different supposition.

I have mentioned the similarity of thinking between that Gentleman and myself. This was relative not merely to the general principles of National Policy and Government but to the leading points which were likely to constitute questions in the administration of the finances. I mean 1 the expediency of *funding* the debt 2 the inexpediency of *discrimination* between original and present holders 3 The expediency of *assuming* the state Debts.

As to the first point, the evidence of Mr. Madisons sentiments at one period is to be found in the address of Congress of April 26th 1783, which was planned by him in conformity to his own ideas and without any previous suggestions from the Committee and with his hearty cooperation in every part of the business. His conversations upon various occasions since have been expressive of a continuance in the same sentiment, nor indeed, has he yet contradicted it by any part of his official conduct. How far there is reason to apprehend a change in this particular will be stated hereafter.

As to the second part, the same address is an evidence of Mr. Madison's sentiments at the same period. And I had been informed that at a later period he had been in the Legislature of Virginia a strenuous and successful opponent of the principle of discrimination. Add to this that a variety of conversations had taken place between him and myself respecting the public debt down to the commencement of the New Government in none of which had he glanced at the idea of a change of opinion. I wrote him a letter after my appointment in the recess of Congress to obtain his sentiments on the subject of the Finances. In his answer there is not a lisp of his new system.

As to the third point, the question of an assumption of the state Debts by the U States was in discussion when the Convention that framed the present Government was sitting at Philadelphia; and in a long conversation, which I had with Mr. Madison in an afternoon's walk I well remember that we were perfectly agreed in the expediency and propriety of such a measure, though we were both of opinion that it would be more adviseable to make it a measure of administration than an article of constitution; from the impolicy of multiplying obstacles to its reception on collateral details.

Under these circumstances, you will naturally imagine that it must have been matter of surprize to me, when I was apprised, that it was Mr. Madison's intention to oppose my plan on both the last mentioned points.

Before the debate commenced, I had a conversation with him on my report, in the course of which I alluded to the calculation I had made of his sentiments and the grounds of that calculation. He did not deny them, but alledged in his justification that the very considerable alienation of the debt, subsequent to the periods at which he had opposed a discrimination, had essentially changed the state of the question—and that as to the assumption, he had contemplated it to take place *as matters stood at the peace.*

While the change of opinion avowed on the point of discrimination diminished my respect for the force of Mr. Madison's mind and the soundness of his judgment—and while the idea of reserving and setting afloat a vast mass of already extinguished debt as the condition of a measure the leading objects of which were an accession of strength to the National Government and an assurance of order and vigour in the national finances by doing away the necessity of thirteen complicated and conflicting systems of finance—appeared to me somewhat extraordinary: Yet my previous impressions of the fairness of Mr. Madison's character and my reliance on his good will towards me disposed me to believe that his suggestions were sincere; and even, on the point of an assumption of the debts of the States as they stood at the peace, to lean towards a cooperation in his view; 'till on feeling the ground I found the thing impracticable, and on further reflection I thought it liable to immense difficulties. It was tried and failed with little countenance.

At this time and afterwards repeated intimations were given to me that Mr. Madison, from a spirit of rivalship or some other cause had become personally unfriendly to me; and one Gentleman in particular, whose honor I have no reason to doubt, assured me, that Mr. Madison in a conversation with him had made a pretty direct attempt to insinuate unfavourable impressions of me.

Still I suspended my opinion on the subject. I knew the malevolent officiousness of mankind too well to yield a very ready acquiescience to the suggestions which were made, and resolved to wait 'till time and more experience should afford a solution.

It was not 'till the last session that I became unequivocally convinced of the following truth—"*That Mr. Madison cooperating with Mr. Jefferson is at the head of a faction decidedly hostile to me and my administration, and actuated by views in my judgment subversive of the principles of good government and dangerous to the union, peace and happiness of the Country.*"

These are strong expressions; they may pain your friendship for one or both of the Gentlemen whom I have named. I have not lightly resolved to hazard them. They are the result of a *Serious alarm* in my mind for the public welfare, and of a full conviction that what I have alledged is a truth, and a truth, which ought to be told and well attended to, by all the friends of Union and efficient National Government. The suggestion will, I hope, at least awaken attention, free from the byass of former prepossessions.

This conviction in my mind is the result of a long train of circumstances; many of them minute. To attempt to detail them all would fill a volume. I shall therefore confine myself to the mention of a few.

First—As to the point of opposition to me and my administration.

Mr. Jefferson with very little reserve manifests his dislike of the funding system generally; calling in question the expediency of funding a debt at all. Some expressions which he has dropped in my own presence (sometimes without sufficient attention to delicacy) will not permit me to doubt on this point, representations, which I have had from various respectable quarters. I do not mean, that he advocates directly the undoing of what has been done, but he censures the whole on principles, which if they should become general, could not but end in the subversion of the system.

In various conversations with *foreigners* as well as citizens, he has thrown censure on my *principles* of government and on my measures of administration. He has predicted that the people would not long tolerate my proceedings & that I should not long maintain my ground. Some of those, whom he *immediately* and *notoriously* moves, have *even* whispered suspicions of the rectitude of my motives and conduct. In the question concerning the Bank he not only delivered an opinion in writing against its constitutionality & expediency; but he did it *in a stile and manner* which I felt as partaking of asperity and ill humour towards me. As one of the trustees of the sinking fund, I have experienced in almost every leading question opposition from him. When any turn of things in the community has threatened either odium or embarrassment to me, he has not been able to suppress the satisfaction which it gave him.

A part of this is of course information, and might be misrepresentation. But it comes through so many channels and so well accords with what falls under my own observation that I can entertain no doubt.

I find a strong confirmation in the following circumstances. *Freneau* the present Printer of the National Gazette, who was a journeyman with Childs & Swain at New York, was a known antifederalist. It is reduced to a certainty that he was brought to Philadelphia by Mr. Jefferson to be the conductor of a News Paper. It is notorious that cotemporarily with the commencement of his paper he was a Clerk in the department of state for foreign languages. Hence a clear inference that his paper has been set on foot and is conducted under the patronage & not against the views of Mr. Jefferson. What then is the complexion of this paper? Let any impartial man peruse all the numbers down to the present day; and I never was more mistaken, if he does not pronounce that it is a paper devoted to the subversion of me & the measures in which I have had an Agency; and I am little less mistaken if he do not pronounce that it is a paper of a tendency *generally unfriendly* to the Government of the U States.

It may be said, that a News Paper being open to all the publications, which are offered to it, its complexion may be influenced by other views than those of the Editor. But the fact here is that wherever the Editor appears it is in a correspondent dress. The paragraphs which appear as his own, the publications, not original which are selected for his press, are of the same malignant and unfriendly aspect, so as not to leave a doubt of the temper which directs the publication.

Again *Brown*, who publishes an Evening paper called *The Federal Gazette* was originally a zealous federalist and personally friendly to me. He has been employed by Mr. Jefferson as a Printer to the Government for the publication of the laws; and for some time past 'till lately the complexion of his press was equally bitter and unfriendly to me & to the Government.

Lately, Col Pickering in consequence of certain attacks upon him, got hold of some instances of malconduct of his which have served to hold him in Check and seemed to have varied his tone a little. I dont lay so much stress on this last case as on the former. There, I find an internal evidence which is as conclusive as can be expected in any similar case. Thus far, as to Mr. Jefferson.

With regard to Mr. Madison—the matter stands thus. I have not heard, but in the one instance to which I have alluded, of his having held language unfriendly to me in private conversation. But in his public conduct there has been a more uniform & persevering opposition than I have been able to resolve into a sincere difference of opinion. I cannot persuade myself that Mr. Madison and I, whose politics had formerly so much the *same point of departure*, should now diverge so widely in our opinions of the measures which are proper to be pursued. The opinion I once entertained of the candour and simplicity and fairness of Mr. Madisons character has, I acknowledge, given way to a decided opinion that *it is one of a peculiarly artificial and complicated kind.*

For a considerable part of the last session, Mr. Madison lay in a great measure *perdu*. But it was evident from his votes & a variety of little movements and appearances, that he was the prompter of Mr. Giles & others, who were the open instruments of opposition. Two facts occurred, in the course of the session, which I view as unequivocal demonstrations of his disposition towards me. In one, a direct and decisive blow was aimed. When the department of the Treasury was established Mr. Madison was an unequivocal advocate of the principles which prevailed in it and of the powers and duties which were assigned by it to the head of the department. This appeared both from his private and public discourses; and I will add, that I have personal evidence that Mr. Madison is as well convinced as any man in the U States of the necessity of the arrangement which characterizes that establishment to the orderly conducting of the business of the Finances.

Mr. Madison nevertheless opposed directly a reference to me to report *ways* & *means* for the Western expedition, & combatted *on principle* the propriety of such references.

He well knew, that, if he had prevailed, a certain consequence was, my *resignation*—that I would not be fool enough to make pecuniary sacrifices and endure a life of extreme drudgery without opportunity either to do material good or to acquire reputation; and frequently with a responsibility in reputation for measures in which I had no hand, and in respect to which, the part I had acted, if any, could not be known.

To accomplish this point, an effectual train, as was supposed, was laid. Besides those who ordinarily acted under Mr. Madison's banners, several, who had generally acted with me from various motives, vanity, self importance, &c. &c. were enlisted.

My overthrow was anticipated as certain and Mr. Madison, *laying aside his wonted caution*, boldly led his troops as he imagined to a certain victory. He was disappointed. Though, *late* I became apprized of the danger. Measures of counteraction were adopted, & when the

Question was called, Mr. Madison was confounded to find characters voting against him, whom he had counted upon as certain.

Towards the close of the Session, another, though a more covert, attack was made. It was in the shape of a proposition to insert in the supplementary Act respecting the public Debt something by way of instruction to the Trustees "to make their purchases of the debt at the *lowest* market price." In the course of the discussion of this point, Mr. Madison dealt much in *insidious insinuations* calculated to give an impression that the public money under my particular direction had been unfaithfully applied to put undue advantages in the pockets of speculators, & to support the debt at an *artificial* price for their benefit. The whole manner of this transaction left no doubt in any ones mind that Mr. Madison was actuated by *personal* & political animosity.

As to this last instance, it is but candid to acknowledge, that Mr. Madison had a better right to act the enemy than on any former occasion. I had some short time before, subsequent to his conduct respecting the reference, declared openly my opinion of the views, by which he was actuated towards me, & my determination to consider & treat him as a political enemy.

An intervening proof of Mr. Madisons unfriendly intrigues to my disadvantage is to be found in the following incident which I relate to you upon my honor but from the nature of it, you will perceive in the *strictest confidence*. The president having prepared his speech at the commencement of the ensuing session communicated it to Mr. Madison for his remarks. It contained among other things a *clause* concerning weights & measures, hinting the advantage of an invariable standard, which *preceded*, in the original state of the speech, a clause concerning the Mint. Mr. Madison suggested a transposition of these clauses & the addition of certain words, which I now forget importing an *immediate connection* between the two subjects. You may recollect that Mr. Jefferson proposes that the *unit of weight* & the *unit in the coins* shall be the same, & that my propositions are to preserve the Dollar as the Unit, adhering to its present quantity of Silver, & establishing the same proportion of alloy in the silver as in the gold Coins. The evident design of this manoeuvre was to connect the Presidents opinion in favour of Mr. Jefferson's idea, in contradiction to mine, &, the worst of it is, *without his being aware of the tendency of the thing*. It happened, that the President shewed me the Speech, altered in conformity to Mr. Madisons suggestion, just before it was copied for the purpose of being delivered. I remarked to him the tendency of the alteration. *He declared that he had not been aware of it & had no such intention; & without hesitation agreed to expunge the words which were designed to connect the two subjects.*

This transaction, in my opinion, not only furnishes a proof of Mr. Madisons *intrigues*, in opposition to my measures, but charges him with an *abuse* of the Presidents confidence in him, by endeavouring to make him, without his knowledge, take part with one officer against another, in a case in which they had given different opinions to the Legislature of the Country. *I forebore to awaken the President's mind to this last inference;* but it is among the circumstances which have convinced me that Mr. Madisons true character is the reverse of that *simple, fair, candid one,* which he has assumed.

I have informed you, that Mr. Freneau was brought to Philadelphia, by Mr. Jefferson, to be the Conductor of a News Paper. My information announced Mr. Madison as the mean of negotiation while he was at New York last summer. This and the general coincidence & close intimacy between the two Gentlemen leave no doubt that their views are substantially the same.

Secondly As to the tendency of the views of the two Gentlemen who have been named.

Mr. Jefferson is an avowed enemy to a funded debt. Mr. Madison disavows in public any intention to *undo* what has been done; but in a private conversation with Mr. Charles Carroll (Senator), this Gentlemans name I mention confidentially though he mentioned the matter to Mr. King & several other Gentlemen as well as myself; & if any chance should bring you together you would easily bring him to repeat it to you, he favoured the sentiment in Mr. Mercers speech that a Legislature had no right to *fund* the debt by mortgaging permanently the public revenues because they had no right to bind posterity. The inference is that what has been unlawfully done may be undone.

The discourse of partizans in the Legislature & the publications in the party news-papers direct their main battery against the *principle* of a funded debt, & represent it in the most odious light as a perfect *Pandoras box.*

If Mr. Barnewell of St. Carolina, who appears to be a man of nice honor, may be credited, Mr. Giles declared in a conversation with him that if there was a question for reversing the funding system on the abstract point of the right of pledging & the futility of preserving public faith, he should be for reversal; merely to demonstrate his sense of the defect of right & the inutility of the thing. If positions equally extravagant were not publicly advanced by some of the party & secretly countenanced by the most guarded & *discreet* of them, one would be led, from the absurdity of the declaration, to suspect misapprehension. But from what is *known* any thing may be *believed.*

Whatever were the original merits of the funding system, after having been so solemnly adopted, & after so great a transfer of property under it, what would become of the Government should it be reversed? What of the National Reputation? Upon what system of morality can so atrocious a doctrine be maintained? In me, I confess it excites *indignation* & *horror!*

What are we to think of those maxims of Government by which the power of a Legislature is denied to bind the Nation by a *Contract* in an affair of *property* for twenty four years? For this is precisely the case of the debt. What are to become of all the legal rights of property, of all charters to corporations, nay, of all grants to a man his heirs & assigns for ever, if this doctrine be true? What is the term for which a government is in capacity to *contract?* Questions might be multiplied without end to demonstrate the perniciousness & absurdity of such a doctrine.

In almost all the questions great & small which have arisen, since the first session of Congress, Mr. Jefferson & Mr. Madison have been found among those who were disposed to narrow the Federal authority. The question of a National Bank is one example. The question of bounties to the Fisheries is another. Mr. Madison resisted it on the ground of constitutionality, 'till it was evident, by the intermediate questions taken, that the bill would pass & he then under the wretched subterfuge of a change of a single word "bounty" for "allowance" went over to the Majority & voted for the bill. In the Militia bill & in a variety of minor cases he has leaned to abridging the exercise of foederal authority, & leaving as much as possible to the States & he has lost no opportunity of *sounding the alarm* with great affected solemnity at encroachments meditated on the rights of the States, & of holding up the bugbear of a faction in the Government having designs unfriendly to Liberty.

This kind of conduct has appeared to me the more extraordinary on the part of Mr. Madison as I know for a certainty it was a primary article in his Creed that the real danger in our system was the subversion of the National authority by the preponderancy of the State Governments. All his measures have proceeded on an opposite supposition.

I recur again to the instance of Freneaus paper. In matters of this kind one cannot have direct proof of men's latent views; they must be inferred from circumstances. As the coadjutor of Mr. Jefferson in the establishment of this paper, I include Mr. Madison in the consequences imputable to it.

In respect to our foreign politics the views of these Gentlemen are in my judgment equally unsound & dangerous. *They have a womanish attachment to France and a womanish resentment against Great*

Britain. They would draw us into the closest embrace of the former & involve us in all the consequences of her politics, & they would risk the peace of the country in their endeavours to keep us at the greatest possible distance from the latter. This disposition goes to a length particularly in Mr. Jefferson of which, till lately, I had no adequate Idea. Various circumstances prove to me that if these Gentlemen were left to pursue their own course there would be in less than six months *an open War between the U States & Great Britain.*

I trust I have a due sense of the conduct of France towards this Country in the late Revolution, & that I shall always be among the foremost in making her every suitable return; but there is a wide difference between this & implicating ourselves in all her politics; between bearing good will to her, & hating and wrangling with all those whom she hates. The Neutral & the Pacific Policy appear to me to mark the true path to the U States.

Having now delineated to you what I conceive to be the true complexion of the politics of these Gentlemen, I will now attempt a solution of these strange appearances.

Mr. Jefferson, it is known, did not in the first instance cordially acquiesce in the new constitution for the U States; he had many doubts & reserves. He left this Country before we had experienced the imbicillities of the former.

In France he saw government only on the side of its abuses. He drank deeply of the French Philosophy, in Religion, in Science, in politics. He came from France in the moment of a fermentation which he had had a share in exciting, & in the passions and feelings of which he shared both from temperament and situation.

He came here probably with a too partial idea of his own powers, and with the expectation of a greater share in the direction of our councils than he has in reality enjoyed. I am not sure that he had not peculiarly marked out for himself the department of the Finances.

He came electrified *plus* with attachment to France and with the project of knitting together the two Countries in the closest political bands.

Mr. Madison had always entertained an exalted opinion of the talents, knowledge and virtues of Mr. Jefferson. The sentiment was probably reciprocal. A close correspondence subsisted between them during the time of Mr. Jefferson's absence from this country. A close intimacy arose upon his return.

Whether any peculiar opinions of Mr. Jefferson concerning the public debt wrought a change in the sentiments of Mr. Madison (for it is certain that the former is more radically wrong than the latter) or whether Mr. Madison seduced by the expectation of popularity and possibly by the calculation of advantage to the state of Virginia was led to change his own opinion—certain it is, that a very material *change* took place, & that the two Gentlemen were united in the new ideas. Mr. Jefferson was indiscreetly open in his approbation of Mr. Madison's principles, upon his first coming to the seat of Government. I say indiscreetly, because a Gentleman in the administration in one department ought not to have taken sides against another, in another department.

The course of this business & a variety of circumstances which took place left Mr. Madison a very discontented & chagrined man and begot some degree of ill humour in Mr. Jefferson.

Attempts were made by these Gentlemen in different ways to produce a Commercial Warfare with Great Britain. In this too they were disappointed. And as they had the liveliest wishes on the subject their dissatisfaction has been proportionally great; and as I had not favoured the project, I was comprehended in their displeasure.

These causes and perhaps some others created, much sooner than I was aware of it, a systematic opposition to me on the part of those Gentlemen. My subversion, I am now satisfied, has been long an object with them.

Subsequent events have encreased the Spirit of opposition and the feelings of personal mortification on the part of these Gentlemen.

A mighty stand was made on the affair of the Bank. There was much *commitment* in that case. I prevailed.

On the Mint business I was opposed from the same Quarter, & with still less success. In the affair of ways & means for the Western expedition—on the supplementary arrangements concerning the debt except as to the additional assumption, my views have been equally prevalent in opposition to theirs. This current of success on one side & defeat on the other have rendered the Opposition furious, & have produced a disposition to subvert their Competitors even at the expence of the Government.

Another circumstance has contributed to widening the breach. 'Tis evident beyond a question, from every movement, that Mr. Jefferson aims with ardent desire at the Presidential Chair. This too is an important object of the party-politics. It is supposed, from the nature of my former personal & political connexions, that I may favour some other candidate more than Mr. Jefferson when the Question shall occur by the retreat of the present Gentleman. My influence therefore with the Community becomes a thing, on ambitious & personal grounds, to be resisted & destroyed.

You know how much it was a point to establish the Secretary of State as the Officer who was to administer the Government in defect of the President & Vice President. Here I acknowledge, though I took far less part than was supposed, I run counter to Mr. Jefferson's wishes; but if I had had no other reason for it, I had already *experienced opposition* from him which rendered it a measure of *self defence.*

It is possible too (for men easily heat their imaginations when their passions are heated) that they have by degrees persuaded themselves of what they may have at first only sported to influence others—namely that there is some dreadful combination against State Government & republicanism; which according to them, are convertible terms. But there is so much absurdity in this supposition, that the admission of it tends to apologize for their hearts, at the expence of their heads.

Under the influence of all these circumstances, the attachment to the Government of the U States originally weak in Mr. Jeffersons mind has given way to something very like dislike; in Mr. Madisons, it is so counteracted by personal feelings, as to be more an affair of the head than of the heart—more the result of a conviction of the necessity of Union than of cordiality to the thing itself. I hope it does not stand worse than this with him.

In such a state of mind, both these Gentlemen are prepared to hazard a great deal to effect a change. Most of the important measures of every Government are connected with the Treasury. To subvert the present head of it they deem it expedient to risk rendering the Government itself odious; perhaps foolishly thinking that they can easily recover the lost affections & confidence of the people, and not appreciating as they ought to do the natural resistance to Government which in every community results from the human passions, the degree to which this is strengthened by the *organised rivality* of State Governments, & the infinite danger that the National Government once rendered odious will be kept so by these powerful & indefatigable enemies.

They forget an old but a very just, though a coarse saying—That it is much easier to raise the Devil than to lay him.

Poor *Knox* has come in for a share of their persecution as a man who generally thinks with me & who has a portion of the Presidents good Will & confidence.

In giving you this picture of political parties, my design is I confess, to awaken your attention, if it has not yet been awakened to the conduct of the Gentlemen in question. If my opinion of them is founded, it is certainly of great moment to the public weal that they should be understood. I rely on the strength of your mind to appreciate men as they merit—when you have a clue to their real views.

A word on another point. I am told that serious apprehensions are disseminated in your state as to the existence of a Monarchical party meditating the destruction of State & Republican Government.

329

If it is possible that so absurd an idea can gain ground it is necessary that it should be combatted. I assure you on my *private faith* and *honor* as a Man that there is not in my judgment a shadow of foundation of it. A very small number of men indeed may entertain theories less republican than Mr Jefferson & Mr. Madison; but I am persuaded there is not a Man among them who would not regard as both *criminal* & *visionary* any attempt to subvert the republican system of the Country. Most of these men rather *fear* that it may not justify itself by its fruits, than feel a predilection for a different form; and their fears are not diminished by the factions & fanatical politics which they find prevailing among a certain set of Gentlemen and threatening to disturb the tranquillity and order of the Government.

As to the destruction of State Governments, the *great* and *real* anxiety is to be able to preserve the National from the too potent and counteracting influence of those Governments. As to my own political Creed, I give it to you with the utmost sincerity. I am *affectionately* attached to the Republican theory. I desire *above all things* to see the *equality* of political rights exclusive of all *hereditary* distinction firmly established by a practical demonstration of its being consistent with the order and happiness of society.

As to State Governments, the prevailing byass of my judgment is that if they can be circumscribed within bounds consistent with the preservation of the National Government they will prove useful and salutary. If the States were all of the size of Connecticut, Maryland or New Jersey, I should decidedly regard the local Governments as both safe & useful. As the thing now is, however, I acknowledge the most serious apprehensions that the Government of the U States will not be able to maintain itself against their influence. I see that influence already penetrating into the National Councils & preverting their direction.

Hence a disposition on my part towards a liberal construction of the powers of the National Government and to erect every fence to guard it from depredations, which is, in my opinion, consistent with constitutional propriety.

As to any combination to prostrate the State Governments I disavow and deny it. From an apprehension lest the Judiciary should not work efficiently or harmoniously I have been desirous of seeing some rational scheme of connection adopted as an amendment to the constitution, otherwise I am for maintaining things as they are, though I doubt much the possibility of it, from a tendency in the nature of things towards the preponderancy of the State Governments.

I said, that I was *affectionately* attached to the Republican theory. This is the real language of my heart which I open to you in the sincerity of friendship; & I add that I have strong hopes of the success of that theory; but in candor I ought also to add that I am far from being without doubts. I consider its success as yet a problem.

It is yet to be determined by experience whether it be consistent with that *stability* and *order* in Government which are essential to public strength & private security and happiness. On the whole, the only enemy which Republicanism has to fear in this Country is in the Spirit of faction and anarchy. If this will not permit the ends of Government to be attained under it—if it engenders disorders in the community, all regular & orderly minds will wish for a change—and the demagogues who have produced the disorder will make it for their own aggrandizement. This is the old Story.

If I were disposed to promote Monarchy & overthrow State Governments, I would mount the hobby horse of popularity—I would cry out usurpation—danger to liberty &c. &c—I would endeavour to prostrate the National Government—raise a ferment—and then "ride in the Whirlwind and direct the Storm." That there are men acting with Jefferson & Madison who have this in view I verily believe. I could lay my finger on some of them. That Madison does *not* mean it I also verily believe, and I rather believe the same of Jefferson; but I read him upon the whole thus—"A man of profound ambition & violent passions."

You must be by this time tired of my epistle. Perhaps I have treated certain characters with too much severity. I have however not meant to do them injustice—and from the bottom of my soul believe I have drawn them truly and that it is of the utmost consequence to the public weal they should be viewed in their true colors. I yield to this impression. I will only add that I make no clandestine attacks on the gentlemen concerned. They are both apprized indirectly from myself of the opinion I entertain of their views. With the truest regard and esteem.

THE VINDICATION [OF THE FUNDING SYSTEM] NO. III

MAY–AUGUST, 1792

In January 1790, Hamilton presented to Congress his Report on Public Credit recommending that the existing domestic and foreign debt incurred by the previous government be funded and that the revolutionary debts of the states be assumed by the new central government. The

331

objections to Hamilton's funding plan were as much moral as economic, and in the following paper Hamilton deals with the moral issues involved.

Philadelphia, May–August, 1792

My last number contained a concise and simple statement of facts tending to shew that the public Debt was neither created nor increased by the Funding system, and consequently that it is not responsible either for the existence or the magnitude of the Debt.

It will be proper next to examine the allegations which have been made of a contrary tendency.

In the first place it is asserted that the debt is greater than it ought to be, because from the state of depreciation in which the government found it a much less provision for it than that which was made might have sufficed. A saving of nearly one half it is said might have been made by providing for it in the hands of Alienees at least, at 8 or 10/ in the pound; who having come by it at a much less rate would have been well compensated by such a provision.

To a man who entertains correct notions of public faith, and who feels as he ought to feel for the reputation & dignity of the country, it is mortifying to reflect that there are partisans enough of such a doctrine to render it worth the while to combat it. It is still more mortifying to know that in that class are comprehended some men who are in other respects soberminded and upright, friends to order, and strenuous advocates for the rights of property.

In reasoning upon all subjects it is necessary to take as a point of departure some principle in which reasonable and sound minds will agree. Without this, there can be no argument, no conclusion, in moral or political any more than in physical or mathematical disquisitions.

The principle which shall be assumed here is this—that the established *rules of morality and justice are applicable to nations as well as to Individuals; that the former as well as the latter are bound to keep their promises, to fulfil their engagements, to respect the rights of property* which others have acquired under contracts with them.

Without this, there is an end of all distinct ideas of right or wrong justice or injustice in relation to Society or Government. There can be no such thing as rights—no such thing as property or liberty. All the boasted advantages of a constitution of Government vanish in air. Every thing must float on the variable and vague opinions of the Governing party of whomsoever composed.

To this it may be answered, that the doctrine as a general one is true; but that there are certain great cases which operate as exceptions to the rule and in which the public good may demand and justify a departure from it.

It shall not be denied that there are such cases; but as the admission of them is one of the most common as well as the most fruitful sources of error and abuse it is of the greatest importance that just ideas should be formed of their true nature foundation and extent. To Minds which are either depraved or feeble, or under the influence of any particular passion or prejudice it is enough that cases are only attended with some *extraordinary circumstances* to induce their being considered as among the exceptions. *Convenience* is with them a substitute for *necessity*, and some temporary partial advantage is an equivalent for a fundamental and permanent interest of Society. We have too often seen in the United States examples of this species of levity. The treaties of the UStates the sacred rights of private property have been too frequently sported with from a too great facility in admitting exceptions to the maxims of public faith, and the general rules of property. A desire to escape from this evil was a principal cause of the Union which took place among good men to establish the National Government, and it behoved to friends to have been particularly cautious how they set an example of equal relaxation in the practice of that very Government.

The characteristics of the only admissible exception to the principle that has been assumed are I—*Necessity.* IId there being some intrinsic and inherent quality in the thing which is to constitute the exception, contrary to the Social Order and to the permanent good of society.

Necessity is admitted in all moral reasonings as an exception to general rules. It is of two kinds, as applied to Nations—where there is want of ability to perform a duty and then it is involuntary, and where the general rule cannot be observed without some manifest and *great* national calamity.

If from extraordinary circumstances a nation is disabled from performing its stipulations, or its duty in any other respect, it is then excuseable on the score of inability. But the inability must be a real not a pretended one—one that has been experimentally ascertained, or that can [be] demonstrated to the satisfaction of all honest and discerning men. And the deviation ought to be as small as possible. All that is practicable ought to be done.

A nation is alike excuseable in certain extraordinary cases for not observing a right or performing a duty if the one or the other would involve a *manifest* and *great* national calamity. But here also an extreme case is intended; the calamity to be avoided must not only be evident and considerable, it must be such an one as is like to prove fatal to the nation, as threatens its existence or at least its permanent welfare.

War for instance is almost always a national calamity of a serious kind; but it ought often to be encountered in protection *even* of a *part* of the community injured or annoyed; or in performance of the condition of a defensive alliance with some other nation. But if such special circumstances exist in either case that the going to war would eminently endanger the existence or permanent welfare of the Nation, it may excuseably be foreborne.

Of the second class of exceptions the case of certain fœdal rights which once oppressed all Europe and still oppresses too great a part of it may serve as an example; rights which made absolute slaves of a part of the community and rendered the condition of the greatest proportion of the remainder not much more eligible.

These rights, though involving that of property, being contrary to the Social order and to the permanent welfare of Society were justifiably abolished, in the instances, in which abolitions have taken place, and may be abolished in all the remaining vestiges.

Wherever indeed a right of property is infringed for the general good, if the nature of the case admits of compensation, it ought to be made; but if compensation be impracticable, that impracticability ought to be an obstacle to a clearly essential reform.

In what has been said the cases of exception have been laid down as broad as they ought to be. They are cases of extremity—where these is a palpable necessity where some great and permanent national evil is to be avoided—where some great & permanent national good is to be obtained.

It must not be to avoid a temporary burthen or inconvenience, to get rid of a particular though a considerable one or to secure a partial advantage. A relaxation of this kind would tend to dissolve all social obligations, to render all rights precarious and to introduce a general dissoluteness and corruption of morals.

A single glance will suffice to convince that the case of the Debt of the UStates was not one of those cases which could justify a clear infraction of the fundamental rules of good faith and a clear invasion of rights of property acquired under the most unequivocal national stipulation. If there was any doubt before the real facility with which a provision for the debt has been made removes it; a provision which touches no internal source of revenue but the single article of distilled spirits, and lays upon that a *very moderate* duty.

But a history of the real state of the Debt when it was taken up by the Government will put the matter out of all doubt. This shall constitute the subject of my next number.

GEORGE WASHINGTON TO ALEXANDER HAMILTON
JULY 29, 1792

Thomas Jefferson wrote to President Washington in May 1792 listing criticisms that had been made of the administration with a view to making the president aware of current expressions of discontent. Washington's letter to Hamilton, which follows, repeats that list of criticisms almost verbatim and requests explanations that one could use to counter such criticisms.

Mount Vernon July 29th. 1792.

My dear Sir,   (Private & confidential)
I have not yet received the new regulation of allowances to the Surveyors, or Collectors of the duties on Spirituous liquors; but this by the bye. My present purpose is to write you a letter on a more interesting and important subject. I shall do it in strict confidence, & with frankness & freedom.

On my way home, and since my arrival here, I have endeavoured to learn from sensible & moderate men—known friends to the Government—the sentiments which are entertained of public measures. These all agree that the Country is prosperous & happy; but they seem to be alarmed at that system of policy, and those interpretations of the Constitution which have taken place in Congress.

Others, less friendly perhaps to the Government, and more disposed to arraign the conduct of its Officers (among whom may be classed my neighbour, & quandom friend Colo M) go further, & enumerate a variety of matters, wch. as well as I can recollect, may be adduced under the following heads. Viz.

First   That the public debt is greater than we can possibly pay before other causes of adding new debt to it will occur; and that this has been artificially created by adding together the whole amount of the debtor & creditor sides of the accounts, instead of taking only their balances; which could have been paid off in a short time.

2d.   That this accumulation of debt has taken for ever out of our power those easy sources of revenue, which, applied to the ordinary necessities and exigencies of Government, would have answered them habitually, and covered us from habitual murmerings against taxes and tax gatherers; reserving extraordinary calls, for extraordinary occasions, would animate the People to meet them.

3d.   That the calls for money have been no greater than we must generally expect, for the same or equivalent exigencies; yet we are already obliged to strain the *impost* till it produces clamour, and will produce evasion, and war on our citizens to collect it, and even to resort to an *Excise* law, of odious character with the people; partial in its operation; unproductive unless enforced by arbitrary & vexatious means; and committing the authority of the Government in parts where resistance is most probable, & coercion least practicable.

4th   They cite propositions in Congress, and suspect other projects on foot, still to encrease the mass of the debt.

5th.   They say that by borrowing at ⅔ of the interest, we might have paid of[f] the principal in ⅔ of the time; but that from this we are precluded by its being made irredeemable but in small portions, & long terms.

6th.   That this irredeemable quality was given it for the avowed purpose of inviting its transfer to foreign Countries.

7th.   They predict that this transfer of the principal, when compleated, will occasion an exportation of 3 Millions of dollars annually for the interest; a drain of Coin, of which as there has been no example, no calculation can be made of its consequences.

8th.   That the banishment of our Coin will be compleated by the creation of 10 millions of paper money, in the form of Bank-bills now issuing into circulation.

9th.   They think the 10 or 12 pr Ct. annual profit, paid to the lenders of this paper medium, are taken out of the pockets of the people, who would have had without interest the coin it is banishing.

10th.   That all the Capitol employed in paper speculation is barren & useless, producing, like that on a gaming table, no accession to itself, and is withdrawn from Commerce and Agriculture where it would have produced addition to the common mass.

11th   That it nourishes in our citizens vice & idleness instead of industry & morality.

12th.   That it has furnished effectual means of corrupting such a portion of the legislature, as turns the balance between the honest Voters which ever way it is directed.

13th.   That this corrupt squadron, deciding the voice of the legislature, have manifested their dispositions to get rid of the limitations imposed by the Constitution on the general legislature; limitations, on the faith of which, the States acceded to that instrument.

14th   That the ultimate object of all this is to prepare the way for a change, from the present republican form of Government, to that of a monarchy; of which the British Constitution is to be the model.

15th.   That this was contemplated in the Convention, they say is no secret, because its partisans have made none of it—to effect it then was impracticable; but they are still eager after their object, and are predisposing every thing for its ultimate attainment.

16th.   So many of them have got into the legislature, that, aided by the corrupt squadron of paper dealers, who are at their devotion, they make a majority in both houses.

17th   The republican party who wish to preserve the Government in its present form, are fewer even when joined by the two, three, or half a dozen antifederalists, who, tho' they dare not avow it, are still opposed to any general Government: but being less so to a republican than a Monarchical one, they naturally join those whom they think pursuing the lesser evil.

18th.   Of all the mischiefs objected to the system of measures beforementioned, none they add is so afflicting, & fatal to every honest hope, as the corruption of the legislature. As it was the earliest of these measures it became the instrument for producing the rest, and will be the instrument for producing in future a King, Lords & Commons; or whatever else those who direct it may chuse. Withdrawn such a distance from the eye of their Constituents, and these so dispersed as to be inaccessible to public information, and particularly to that of the conduct of their own Representatives, they will form the worst Government upon earth, if the means of their corruption be not prevented.

19th.   The only hope of safety they say, hangs now on the numerous representation which is to come forward the ensuing year; but should the majority of the new members be still in the same principles with the present—shew so much deriliction to republican government, and such a disposition to encroach upon, or explain away the limited powers of the constitution in order to change it, it is not easy to conjecture what would be the result, nor what means would be resorted to for correction of the evil. True wisdom they acknowledge should direct temperate & peaceable measures; but add, the division of sentiment & interest happens unfortunately, to be so geographical, that no mortal can say that what is most wise & temperate, would prevail against what is more easy & obvious; they declare, they can contemplate no evil more incalculable than the breaking of the Union into two, or more parts; yet, when they view the mass which opposed the original coalescence, when they consider that it lay chiefly in the Southern quarter—that the legislature have availed themselves of no occasion of allaying it, but on the contrary whenever Northern & Southern prejudices have come into conflict, the latter have been sacraficed and the former soothed.

20th.   That the owers of the debt are in the Southern and the holders of it in the Northern division.

21st.   That the antifederal champions are now strengthened in argument by the fulfilment of their predictions, which has been brought about by the Monarchical federalists themselves; who, having been for the new government merely as a stepping stone to Monarchy, have themselves adopted the very construction, of which, when advocating its acceptance before the tribunal of the people, they declared it insuceptable; whilst the republican federalists, who espoused the same government for its intrinsic merits, are disarmed of their weapons, that which they denied as prophecy being now become true history. Who, therefore, can be sure they ask, that these things may not proselyte the small number which was wanting to place the majority on the other side—and this they add is the event at which they tremble.

These, as well as my memory serves me, are the sentiments which, directly and indirectly, have been disclosed to me.

To obtain light, and to pursue truth, being my sole aim; and wishing to have before me *explanations* of as well as the *complaints* on measures in which the public interest, harmony and peace is so deeply concerned, and my public conduct so much involved; it is my request, and you would oblige me in furnishing me, with your ideas upon the discontents here enumerated—and for this purpose I have thrown them into heads or sections, and numbered them that those ideas may apply to the corrispondent numbers. Although I do not mean to hurry you in giving your thoughts on the occasion of this letter, yet, as soon as you can make it convenient to yourself it would—for more reasons than one—be agreeable, & very satisfactory to me.

The enclosure in your letter of the 16th. was sent back the Post after I received it, with my approving signature; and in a few days I will write to the purpose mentioned in your letter of the 22d. both to the Secretary of War & yourself. At present all my business—public & private—is on my own shoulders, the two young Gentlemen who came home with me, being on visits to their friends—and my Nephew, the Major, too much indisposed to afford me any aid, in copying or in other matters.

With affectionate regard I am always—Yours Go: Washington

Alexr. Hamilton Esqr.

LETTER TO GEORGE WASHINGTON CONTAINING OBJECTIONS AND ANSWERS RESPECTING THE ADMINISTRATION OF GOVERNMENT
AUGUST 18, 1792

The following letter is Hamilton's reply to President Washington's request for explanations that could be used to counter criticisms of his administration. Washington's letter to Hamilton of July 29, 1792 (the preceding selection in this volume) contains a list of the objections Hamilton attempts to answer.

Philadelphia Aug 18. 1792

Sir

I am happy to be able, at length, to send you, answers to the objections, which were communicated in your letter of the 29th of July.

They have unavoidably been drawn in haste, too much so, to do perfect justice to the subject, and have been copied just as they flowed from my heart and pen, without revision or correction. You will observe, that here and there some severity appears. I have not fortitude enough always to hear with calmness, calumnies, which necessarily include me, as a principal Agent in the measures censured, of the falsehood of which, I have the most unqualified consciousness. I trust that I shall always be able to bear, as I ought, imputations of error of Judgment; but I acknowledge that I cannot be intirely patient under charges, which impeach the integrity of my

339

public motives or conduct. I feel, that I merit them *in no degree;* and expressions of indignation sometimes escape me, in spite of every effort to suppress them. I rely on your goodness for the proper allowances.

With high respect and the most affectionate attachment, I have the honor to be, Sir Your most Obedient & humble servant

Alexander Hamilton

The President of The United States

Objections and Answers respecting the Administration of the Government

1   Object. The public Debt is greater than we can possibly pay before other causes of adding to it will occur; and this has been artificially created by adding together the *whole amount* of the Debtor and Creditor sides of the Account.

Answer. The public Debt was produced by the late war. It is not the fault of the present government that it exists; unless it can be proved, that public morality and policy do not require of a Government an honest provision for its debts. Whether it is greater than can be paid before new causes of adding to it will occur is a problem incapable of being solved, but by experience; and this would be the case if it were not one fourth as much as it is. If the policy of the Country be prudent, cautious and *neutral* towards foreign nations, there is a rational probability, that war may be avoided long enough to wipe off the debt. The Dutch in a situation, not near so favourable for it as that of the UStates have enjoyed intervals of peace, longer than with proper exertions would suffice for the purpose. The Debt of the UStates compared with its present and growing abilities is really a very light one. It is little more than 15.000000 of pounds Sterling, about the annual expenditure of Great Britain.

But whether the public Debt shall be extinguished or not within a moderate period depends on the temper of the people. If they are rendered dissatisfied by misrepretations of the measures of the government, the Government will be deprived of an efficient command of the resources of the community towards extinguishing the Debt. And thus, those who clamour are likely to be the principal causes of protracting the existence of the debt.

As to having been artificially increased, this is denied; perhaps indeed the true reproach of the system, which has been adopted, is that it has artificially diminished the debt as will be explained by and by.

The assertion, that the Debt has been increased, by adding together the whole amount of the Debtor and Creditor sides of the account, not being very easy to be understood is not easy to be answered.

But an answer shall be attempted.

The thirteen States in their *joint* capacity owed a *certain* sum. The same states, in their separate capacities, owed *another sum.* These two sums constituted the *aggregate* of the *public Debt*. The PUBLIC, in a political sense, compounded of the Governments of the Union and of the several states, was the DEBTOR. The individuals who held the various evidences of debt were the CREDITORS. It would be non-sense to say, that the combining of *the two parts* of the public Debt is adding together the Debtor and Creditor sides of the account. So great an absurdity cannot be supposed to be intended by the objection. Another meaning must therefore be sought for.

It may possibly exist in the following misconception. The states individually, when they liquidated the accounts of Individuals for services and supplies towards the common defence during the late war, and gave certificates for the sums due would naturally charge them to the UStates as contributions to the common cause. The UStates in assuming to pay those certificates charge themselves with them. And it may be supposed that here is a double charge for the same thing.

But as the amount of the sum assumed for each state is by the system adopted to be charged to such state, it of course goes in extinguishment of so much of the first charge as is equal to the sum assumed, and leaves the UStates chargeable only once, as ought to be the case.

Or perhaps the meaning of the objection may be found in the following mode of reasoning. Some states, from having disproportionately contributed during the war, would probably on a settlement of accounts be found debtors, independently of the Assumption. The assuming of the debts of such states increases the ballances against them, and as these ballances will ultimately be remitted from the impracticability of enforcing their payment, the sums assumed will be an extra charge upon the U States increasing the mass of the debt.

This objection takes it for granted that the ballances of the Debtor States will not be exacted; which by the way is no part of the system and if it should eventually not prove true, the foundation of the reasoning would fail. For it is evident if the ballances are to be collected (unless there be some undiscovered error in the principle by which the accounts are to be adjusted) that one side of the accounts will counterpoise the other. And every thing as to the quantum of debt will remain *in statu quo.*

But it shall be taken for granted that the ballances will be remitted; and still the consequence alleged does not result. The reverse of it may even take place. In reasoning upon this point, it must be remembered that impracticability would be alike an obstacle to the collection of ballances without as with the Assumption.

This being the case, whether the ballances to be remitted will be increased or diminished must depend on the relative proportions of outstanding debts. If a former *debtor* State owes to individuals a smaller sum in proportion to its contributive faculty, than a former *Creditor* state, the assumption of the debts of both to be provided for out of a *common fund* raised upon them proportionally must necessarily, on the idea of a remission of ballances, tend to restore equality between them, and lessen the ballance of the debtor state to be remitted.

How the thing may work upon the whole, cannot be pronounced without a knowledge of the situation of the account of each State, but all circumstances that are known render it probable that the ultimate effect will be favourable to justice between the states and that there will be inconsiderable ballances either on one side or on the other.

It was observed that perhaps the true reproach of the system which has been adopted is that it has artificially decreased the Debt. This is explained thus—

In the case of the debt of the UStates interest upon two thirds of the principal only at 6 ₱ Cent is immediately paid—interest upon the remaining third was deferred for ten years—and only three ₱ Cent has been allowed upon the arrears of interest, making one third of the whole debt.

In the case of the separate debts of the States interest upon 4/9 only of the intire sum is immediately paid; interest upon 2/9 was deferred for 10 years and only three per Cent allowed on 3/9.

The Market rate of interest at the time of adopting the funding system was 6 ₱ Cent. Computing according to this rate of interest—the then present value of 100 Dollars of debt upon an average, principal and interest, was about 73 Dollars.

And The present *actual* value, in the Market, of 100 Dollars, as the several kinds of Stock are sold, is no more than 83 Dollars & 61 Cents. This computation is not made on equal sums of the several kinds of Stock according to which the average value of 100 Dollars would be only 78.75 but it is made on the proportions which constitute the Mass of the debt.

At 73 to 100 The diminution of 60 000 000 is 16.200 000 Dollars; at 83.61 to 100 it is 9.834 000 Dollars.

But as the UStates having a right to redeem in certain proportions need never give more than par for the 6 ⅌ Cent, the diminution to them as purchasers at the present market prices is 12.168 000 Dollars.

If it be said that the UStates are engaged to pay the whole sum at the Nominal value, the answer is that they are always at liberty if they have the means to purchase at the market prices and in all those purchases they gain the difference between the nominal sums and the lesser market rates.

If the whole debt had been provided for at 6 ⅌ Cent the market rate of Interest when the funding system passed the market value throughout would undoubtedly have been 100 for 100. The Debt may then rather be said to have been artificially decreased by the Nature of the provision.

The conclusion from the whole, is that assuming it as a principle that the public debts of the different descriptions were honestly to be provided for and paid—it is the reverse of true that there has been an artificial increase of them. To argue on a different principle is to presuppose dishonesty, and make it an objection to doing right.

Objection II This accumulation of debt has taken for ever out of our power those easy sources of revenue which applied &c.

Answer. There having been no accumulation of debt, if what is here pretended to have been the consequence were true, it would only be to be regretted as the unavoidable consequence of an unfortunate state of things. But the supposed consequence does by *no means* exist. The only sources of taxation which have been touched are imported articles and the single internal object of distilled spirits. Lands, houses, the great mass of personal as well as the whole of real property remain essentially free. In short, the chief sources of taxation are free for extraordinary conjunctures; and it is one of the distinguishing merits of the system which has been adopted, that it has rendered this far more the case than it was before. It is only to look into the different states to be convinced of it. In most of them real estate is wholly exempted. In some very small burthens rest upon it for the purpose of the internal Governments. In all the burthens of the people have been lightened. It is a mockery of truth to represent the U States as a community burthened and exhausted by taxes.

Objection 3

Answer. This is a mere painting and exaggeration. With the Exception of a very few articles, the duties on imports are still moderate, lower than in any Country of whose regulations we have knowledge, except perhaps Holland, where having few productions or commodities of their own, their export trade depends on the reexportation of foreign articles.

It is true the Merchants have complained, but so they did of the first impost law for a time and so men always will do at an augmentation of taxes which touch the business they carry on, especially in a country where no or scarcely any *such* taxes before existed. The Collection, it is not doubted will be essentially secure. Evasions have existed in a degree and will continue to exist. Perhaps they may be somewhat increased; to what extent can only be determined by experience, but there are no symptoms to induce an opinion that they will materially increase. As to the idea of a war upon the citizens to collect the impost duties, it can only be regarded as a figure of rhetoric.

The Excise law no doubt is a good topic of declamation. But can it be doubted that it is an excellent and a very fit mean of revenue?

As to the partiality of its operation, it is no more so than any other tax on a consumeable commodity; adjusting itself upon exactly the same principles. The consumer in the main pays the tax—and if some parts of the U States consume more domestic spirits, others consume more foreign—and both are taxed. There is perhaps, upon the whole, no article of more *general* and *equal consumption* than distilled spirits.

As to its *unproductiveness*, unless inforced by *arbitrary* and *vexatious* means, facts testify the contrary. Already, under all the obstacles arising from its novelty and the prejudices against it in some states, it has been considerably productive. And it is not inforced by any arbitrary or vexatious means; at least the precautions in the existing laws for the collection of the tax will not appear in that light but to men who regard all taxes and all the means of enforcing them as arbitrary and vexatious. Here however there is abundant room for fancy to operate. The standard is in the mind, and different minds will have different standards.

The observation relating to the commitment of the authority of the Government, in parts where resistance is most probable and coertion least practicable has more weight than any other part of this objection. It must be confessed that a hazard of this nature has been run but if there were motives sufficiently cogent for it, it was wisely run. It does not follow that a measure is bad because it is attended with a degree of danger.

The general inducements to a provision for the public Debt are—
I   To preserve the public faith and integrity by fulfilling as far as was

practicable the public engagements. II To manifest a due respect for property by satisfying the public obligations in the hands of the public Creditors and which were as much their property as their houses or their lands their hats or their coats. III To revive and establish public Credit; the palladium of public safety. IV To preserve the Government itself by shewing it worthy of the confidence which was placed in it, to procure to the community the blessings which in innumerable ways attend confidence in the Government and to avoid the evils which in as many ways attend the want of confidence in it.

The particular inducements to an assumption of the state Debts were I To consolidate the finances of the country and give an assurance of permanent order in them; avoiding the collisions of thirteen different and independent systems of finance under concurrent and coequal authorities and the scramblings for revenue which would have been incident to so many different systems. II To secure to the Government of the Union, by avoiding those entanglements, an effectual command of the resources of the Union for present and future exigencies. III To *equalize the condition* of the *citizens* of the several states in the important article of taxation; rescuing a part of them from being oppressed with burthens, beyond their strength, on account of extraordinary exertions in the war and through the want of certain adventitious resources, which it was the good fortune of others to possess.

A mind naturally attached to order and system and capable of appreciating their immense value, unless misled by particular feelings, is struck at once with the prodigious advantages which in the course of time must attend such a simplification of the financial affairs of the Country as results from placing all the parts of the public debt upon one footing—under one direction—regulated by one provision. The want of this sound policy has been a continual source of disorder and embarrassment in the affairs of the United Netherlands.

The true justice of the case of the public Debt consists in that equalization of the condition of the Citizens of all the states which must arise from a consolidation of the debt and common contributions towards its extinguishment. Little inequalities, as to the past, can bear no comparison with the more lasting inequalities, which, without the assumption, would have characterised the future condition of the people of the UStates; leaving upon those who had done most or suffered most a great additional weight of burthen.

If the foregoing inducements to a provision for the public Debt (including an assumption of the state debts) were sufficiently cogent—then the justification of the Excise law lies within a narrow compass. Some further source of revenue, besides the duties on imports, was indispensable, and none equally productive, would have been so little exceptionable to the Mass of the People.

Other reasons cooperated in the minds of some able men to render an excise at an early period desireable. They thought it well to lay hold of so valuable a resource of revenue before it was generally preoccupied by the State Governments. They supposed it not amiss that the authority of the National Government should be visible in some branch of internal Revenue; lest a total non-exercise of it should beget an impression that it was never to be exercised & next that it ought not to be exercised. It was supposed too that a thing of the kind could not be introduced with a greater prospect of easy success than at a period when the Government enjoyed the advantage of first impressions—when state-factions to resist its authority were not yet matured—when so much aid was to be derived from the popularity and firmness of the actual chief Magistrate.

Facts hitherto do not indicate the measure to have been rash or ill advised. The law is in operation with perfect acquiescence in all the states North of New York, though they contribute most largely. In New York and New Jersey it is in full operation with some very partial complainings fast wearing away. In the greatest part of Pensylvania it is in operation and with increasing good humour towards it. The four Western Counties continue exceptions. In Delaware it has had some struggle, which by the last accounts was surmounted. In Maryland and Virginia, it is in operation and without material conflict. In South Carolina it is now in pretty full operation, though in the interior parts it has had some serious opposition to overcome. In Georgia no material difficulty has been experienced. North Carolina Kentucke & the four Western Counties of Pensylvania present the only remaining impediments of any consequence to the full execution of the law. The latest advices from NC & Kentuke were more favourable than the former.

It may be added as a well established fact that the effect of the law has been to encourage new enterprises in most of the states in the business of domestic distillation. A proof that it is perceived to operate favourably to the manufacture, and that the measure cannot long remain unpopular any where.

Objection IV Propositions have been made in Congress & projects are on foot still to increase the Mass of the Debt.

Ans. Propositions have been made, and no doubt will be renewed by the States interested to complete the assumption of the State Debts. This would add in the first instance to the mass of the *Debt of the UStates* between three and four Millions of Dollars but it would not increase the mass of the *public Debt* at all. It would only

346

transfer from particular States to the Union debts which already exist and which if the states indebted are honest must be provided for. It happens that Massachusettes and South Carolina would be chiefly benefitted. And there is a moral certainty that Massachusettes will have a ballance in her favour more than equal to her remaining debt and a probability that South Carolina will have a ballance sufficient to cover hers—so that there is not likely to be an eventual increase even of the *debt of the United States* by the further assumption. The immense exertions of Massachusettes during the late war and particularly in the latter periods of it when too many of the States failed in their fœderal Duty are known to every well informed man. It would not be too strong to say, that they were in a great degree the pivot of the revolution. The exertions sufferings sacrifices and losses of South Carolina need not be insisted upon. The other States have compari-tively none or inconsiderable Debts. Can that policy be condemned which aims at putting the burthened states upon an equal footing with the rest? Can that policy be very liberal which resists so equitable an arrangement? It has been said that if they had exerted themselves since the peace their situation would have been different. But Mas-sachusettes threw her Citizens into Rebellion by heavier taxes than were paid in any other State and South Carolina has done as much since the peace as could have been expected considering the ex-hausted state in which the War left her.

The only proposition during the last session or at any antecedent one which would truly have swelled the debt artificially was one which Mr Maddison made in the first session & which was renewed in the last and generally voted for by those who oppose the system that has prevailed. The object of this proposition was *that all the parts* of the State debts which have been *paid* or other*wise absorbed by them* should be assumed for the benefit of the States, and funded by the UStates. This measure if it had succeeded would truly have produced an immense artificial increase of the debt; but it has twice failed & there is no probability that it will ever succeed.

Objection 5. By borrowing at ⅔ &c.

Answer. First—All the foreign loans which were made by the UStates prior to the present Government taking into the calculation charges & premiums cost them more than 6 ⅌ Cent. Since the estab-lishment of the present Government they borrowed first at about 5¼ including charges & since at about 4¼ including charges. And it is questionable in the present state of Europe whether they can obtain any further loans at so low a rate.

The System which is reprobated is the very cause that we have been able to borrow monies on so good terms. If one, that would have

347

inspired less confidence, certainly if the substitutes which have been proposed, from a certain quarter, had obtained, we could not have procured loans even at six per Cent. The Dutch were largely adventurers in our domestic debt before the present Government. They did not embark far till they had made inquiries of influential public characters, as to the light in which the Debt was & would be considered in the hands of alienees—and had received assurances that Assignees would be regarded in the same light as original holders. What would have been the state of our Credit with them, if they had been disappointed, or indeed if our conduct had been in any respect inconsistent with the notions entertained in Europe concerning the maxims of public Credit?

The inference is that our being able to borrow on low terms is a consequence of the system which is the object of censure and that the thing itself, which is made the basis of another system, would not have existed under it.

Secondly. It will not be pretended that we could have borrowed at the proposed low rate of interest in the UStates; and all our exertions to borrow in Europe which have been unremitted, as occasions presented, have not hitherto produced above   of Dollars in space of   ; not even a sufficient sum to change the form of our foreign debt.

Thirdly If it were possible to borrow the whole sum abroad within a short period, to pay off our debt, it is not easy to imagine a more pernicious operation than this would have been. It would first have transferred to foreigners by a violent expedient the whole amount of our debt; and creating a money plethora in the Country a momentary scene of extravagance would have followed & the excess would quickly have flowed back: The evils of which situation need not be enlarged upon. If it be said that the operation might have been gradual, then the end proposed would not have been attained.

Lastly The plan which has been adopted secures in the first instance the *identical advantage,* which in the other plan would have been *eventual* and *contingent.* It puts one third of the whole Debt at an interest of 3 ℔Ct. only—and by deferring the payment of interest on a third of the remainder effectually reduces the interest on that part. It is evident that a *suspension* of interest is in fact a *reduction* of interest. The money which would go towards paying interest in the interval of suspension is an accumulating fund to be applied towards payment of it when it becomes due, proportionably reducing the provision then to be made.

In reality, on the principles of the funding system, the United States reduced the interest on their whole Debt upon *an average* to about 4½ ⅌ Cent, nearly the lowest rate they have any chance to borrow at, and lower than they could possibly have borrowed at, in an attempt to reduce the interest on the whole Capital by borrowing and paying; probably by one ⅌ Cent. A demand for large loans by forcing the market would unavoidably have raised their price upon the borrower. The above average of 4½ ⅌ Ct. is found by calculation, computing the then present value of the deferred Stock at the time of passing the funding Act and of course 3 ⅌ Cent on the three per Cent Stock.

The funding system, then, secured in the very outset the *precise advantage* which it is alleged would have accrued from leaving the whole debt redeemable at pleasure. But this is not all. It did more. It left the Government still in a condition to enjoy upon ⅚ of the intire debt the advantage of extinguishing it, by loans at a low rate of interest, if they are obtainable. The 3 ⅌ Cents which are one third of the whole may always be purchased in the market below par, till the market rate of interest falls to 3 ⅌ Ct. The deferred will be purchaseable below par till near the period of the actual payment of interest. And this further advantage will result; in all these purchases the public will enjoy not only the advantage of a reduction of interest on the sums borrowed but the additional advantage of purchasing the debt under par, that is for less than 20/ in the pound.

If it be said that the like advantage might have been enjoyed under another system, the assertion would be without foundation. Unless some equivalent had been given for the reduction of interest in the irredeemable quality annexed to the Debt, nothing was left consistently with the principles of public Credit but to provide for the whole debt at 6 ⅌ Cent. This evidently would have kept the whole at par, and no advantage could have been derived by purchases under the nominal value. The reduction of interest by borrowing at a lower rate is all that would have been practicable and this advantage has been secured by the funding system in the very outset and without any second process.

If no provision for the interest had been made, not only public Credit would have been sacrificed; but by means of it the borrowing at a low rate of interest or at any rate would have been impracticable.

There is no reproach which has been thrown upon the funding system so unmerited as that which charges it with being a bad bargain for the public or with a tendency to prolong the extinguishment of the Debt. The bargain has if any thing been too good on the side of the public; and it is impossible for the debt to be in a more convenient form than it is for a rapid extinguishment.

Some Gentlemen seem to forget that the faculties of every Country are limited. They talk as if the Government could extend its revenue *ad libitum* to pay off the debt. Whereas every rational calculation of the abilities of the Country will prove that the power of redemption which has been reserved over the debt is quite equal to those abilities, and that a greater power would be useless. If happily the abilities of the Country should exceed this estimate, there is nothing to hinder the surplus being employed in purchases. As long as the three ⅌ Cents & deferred exist those purchases will be under par. If for the Stock bearing an immediate interest of six ⅌ Cent more than par is given—the Government can afford it from the saving made in the first instance.

Upon the whole then it is the merit of the funding System to have conciliated these three important points—the restoration of public Credit—a reduction of the rate of interest—and an organisation of the Debt convenient for speedy extinguishment.

Object 6   The irredeemeable quality was given to the debt for the *avowed* purpose of inviting its transfer to foreign countries.

This assertion is a palpable misrepresentation. The *avowed purpose* of that quality of the Debt, as explained in the report of the Secretary of the Treasury, and in the arguments in Congress was to give an *equivalent* for the reduction of Interest, that is for deferring the payment of interest on ⅓ of the principal for three years and for allowing only 3 ⅌ Cent on the arrears of Interest.

It was indeed argued, in confirmation of the reality of the equivalent, that foreigners would be willing to give more, where a high rate of Interest was *fixed*, than where it was liable to fluctuate with the market. And this has been verified by the fact—for the 6 ⅌ Cents could not have risen for a moment above par, if the rate could have been lowered by redeeming the Debt at pleasure. But the inviting of the transfer to foreigners was never assigned as a motive to the arrangement.

And what is more, that transfer will be probably slower with the portion of irredeemability which is attached to the Debt than without it because a larger capital would be requisite to purchase 100 Dollars in the former than in the latter case. And the Capital of foreigners is limited as well as our own.

It appears to be taken for granted that if the Debt had not been funded in its present shape foreigners would not have purchased it as they now do; than which nothing can be more ill founded or more contrary to experience. Under the old Confederation when there was no provision at all foreigners had purchased five or six millions of the Debt. If any provision had been made, capable of producing confidence, their purchases would have gone on just as they now do; and the only material difference would have been that what they got from us then would have cost them less than what they now get from us does cost them. Whether it is to the disadvantage of the Country that they pay more is submitted.

Even a provision which should not have inspired full confidence would not have prevented foreign purchases. The commodity would have been cheap in proportion to the risks to be run. And fullhanded Dutchmen would not have scrupled to amass large sums, for trifling considerations, in the hope, that time & experience would introduce juster notions into the public councils.

Our Debt would still have gone from us & with it our reputation & Credit.

Objection 7

Answer. The same glooming forebodings were heard in England in the early periods of its funding system. But they have never been realized. The money invested by foreigners in the purchase of its Debt being employed in its commerce agriculture and manufactures increased the wealth and Capital of the Nation, more than in proportion to the annual drain for the payment of interest and created the ability to bear it.

The objection seems to forget that the Debt is not transferred for Nothing—that the Capital paid for the Debt is always an equivalent for the interest to be paid to the purchasers. If that Capital is well employed in a young country, like this, it must be considerably increased so as to yield a greater revenue than the interest of the money. The Country therefore will be a gainer by it and will be able to pay the interest without inconvenience.

But the objectors suppose that all the money which come in goes out again in an increased consumption of foreign luxuries. This however is taking for granted what never happened in any industrious country & what appearances among us do not warrant. The expense of living generally speaking is not sensibly increased. Large investments are every day making in ship building, house building, manufactures & other improvements public & private.

The transfer too of the whole debt is a very improbable supposition. A large part of it will continue to be holden by our own citizens. And the interest of that part which is owned by foreigners will not be annually exported as is supposed. A considerable part will be invested in new speculations, in lands canals roads manufactures commerce. Facts warrant this supposition. The Agents of the Dutch have actually made large investments in a variety of such speculations. A young Country like this is peculiarly attractive. New objects will be continually opening and the money of foreigners will be made instrumental to their advancement.

8.th Object

Ans This is a mere hypothesis in which theorists differ. There are no decisive facts on which to rest the question.

The supposed tendency of bank paper to banish specie is from its capacity of serving as a substitute for it in circulation. But as the quantity circulated is proportioned to the demand for it, in circulation, the presumption is that a greater quantity of industry is put in motion by it, so as to call for a proportionably greater quantity of *circulating medium* and prevent the banishment of the specie.

But however this may be it is agreed among sound theroists that Banks more than compensate for the loss of the specie in other ways. SMITH who was witness to their effects in Scotland; where too a very adverse fortune attended some of them bears his testimony to their beneficial effects in these strong Terms (Wealth of Nations Vol. I Book II. Ch. II. Page 441. to 444).

9 Objection

The 10 or 12 ℔ Ct &c.

Answer   1   The profits of the Bank have not hitherto exceeded the rate of 8 ℔ Ct. per annum & perhaps never may. It is questionable whether they can legally make more than *10 ℔ Ct.*

2   These profits can in no just sense be said to be taken out of the pockets of the people. They are compounded of two things—1   the interest paid by the Government on that part of the public Debt which is incorporated in the stock of the Bank—2   the interest paid by those *Individuals who borrow* money of the Bank on the *sums they borrow.*

As to the first, it is no *new grant* to the bank. It is the old interest on a part of the old Debt of the Country, subscribed by the proprietors of that Debt towards constituting the Stock of the Bank. It would have been equally payable if the Bank had never existed. It is therefore nothing new taken out of the pockets of the people.

As to the second, it may with equal propriety be said, when one individual borrows money of another, that the interest, which the borrower pays to the lender, is taken out of the *pockets of the people.* The case here is not only parallel but the same. It is a case of one or more individuals borrowing money of a company of individuals associated to lend. None but the actual borrowers pay in either case. The rest of the community have nothing to do with it.

If a man receives a bank bill for the ox or the bushel of wheat which he sells he pays no more interest upon it than upon the same sum in gold or silver; that is he pays none at all.

So that whether the paper banishes specie or not it is the same thing to every individual through whose hands it circulates, as to the point of Interest. Specie no more than Bank paper can be borrowed without paying interest for it, and when either is not borrowed no interest is paid. As far as the Government is a sharer in the profits of the Bank which is in the proportion of ⅕ the contrary of what is supposed happens. *Money is put into the pockets of the People.*

All this is so plain and so palpable that the assertion which is made betrays extreme ignorance or extreme disingenuousness. It is destitute even of colour.

10 Objection

This is a copious subject which has been fully discussed in the report of the Secretary of the Treasury on the subject of Manufactures from Page   to   . It is true that the Capital, that is the *specie*, which is employed in paper speculation, while so employed, is barren and useless, but the paper itself constitutes a *new Capital*, which being saleable and transferrable at any moment, enables the proprietor to undertake any piece of business as well as an equal sum in Coin. And as the amount of the Debt circulated is much greater than the amount of the *specie* which circulates it, the new Capital put in motion by it considerably exceeds the old one which is *suspended*. And there is more capital to carry on the productive labour of the Society. Every thing that has value is Capital—an acre of ground a horse or a cow or a public or a private obligation; which may with different degrees of convenience be applied to industrious enterprise. That which, like public Stock, can at any instant be turned into money is of equal utility with money as Capital.

Let it be examined whether at those places where there is most debt afloat and most money employed in its circulation, there is not at the same time a greater plenty of money for every other purpose. It will be found that there is.

But it is in fact quite immaterial to the Government, as far as regards the propriety of its measures.

The Debt existed. It was to be provided for. In whatever shape the provision was made the object of speculation and the speculation would have existed. Nothing but abolishing the Debt could have obviated it. It is therefore the fault of the Revolution not of the Government that paper speculation exists.

An unsound or precarious provision would have increased this species of speculation in its most odious forms. The defects & casualties of the system would have been as much subjects of speculation as the Debt itself.

The difference is that under a bad system the public Stock would have been too uncertain an article to be a substitute for money & all the money employed in it would have been diverted from useful employment without any thing to compensate for it. Under a good system the Stock becomes more than a substitute for the money employed in negotiating it.

Objection 11 Paper Speculation nourishes in our Citizens &c.

Answer This proposition within certain limits is true. Jobbing in the funds has some bad effects among those engaged in it. It fosters a spirit of gambling, and diverts a certain number of individuals from other pursuits. But if the proposition be true, that Stock operates as Capital, the effect upon the Citizens at large is different. It promotes among them industry by furnishing a larger field of employment. Though this effect of a funded debt has been called in question in England by some theorists yet most theorists & all practical men allow its existence. And there is no doubt, as already intimated, that if we look into those scenes among ourselves where the largest portions of the Debt are accumulated we shall perceive that a new spring has been given to Industry in various branches.

But be all this as it may, the observation made under the last head applies here. The Debt was the creature of the Revolution. It was to be provided for. Being so, in whatever form, it must have become an object of speculation and jobbing.

Objection 12

The funding of the Debt has furnished effectual means of corrupting &c.

Answer This is one of those assertions which can only be denied and pronounced to be malignant and false. No facts exist to support it, and being a mere matter of fact, no *argument* can be brought to repel it.

The Assertors beg the question. They assume to themselves and to those who think with them infallibility. Take their words for it, they are the only honest men in the community. But compare the tenor of mens lives and *at least* as large a proportion of virtuous and independent characters will be found among those whom they malign as among themselves.

A member of a majority of the Legislature would say to these Defamers—

"In your vocabulary, Gentlemen, *creditor* and *enemy* appear to be synonimous terms—the *support of public credit* and *corruption* of similar import—an *enlarged* and *liberal* construction of the constitution for the public good and for the maintenance of the due energy of the national authority of the same meaning with usurpation and a conspiracy to overturn the republican government of the Country—every man of a different opinion from your own an ambitious despot or a corrupt knave. You bring every thing to the standard of your narrow and depraved ideas, and you condemn without mercy or even decency whatever does not accord with it. Every man who is either too long or two short for your political couch must be stretched or lopped to suit it. But your pretensions must be rejected. Your insinuations despised. Your Politics originate in immorality, in a disregard of the maxims of good faith and the rights of property, and if they could prevail must end in national disgrace and confusion. Your rules of construction for the authorities vested in the Government of the Union would arrest all its essential movements and bring it back in practice to the same state of imbecility which rendered the old confederation contemptible. Your principles of liberty are principles of licentiousness incompatible with all government. You sacrifice every thing that is venerable and substantial in society to the vain reveries of a false and new fangled philosophy. As to the motives by which I have been influenced, I leave my general conduct in private and public life to speak for them. Go and learn among my *fellow citizens* whether I have not uniformly maintained the character of an honest man. As to the love of liberty and Country you have given no stronger proofs of being actuated by it than I have done. Cease then to arrogate to yourself and to your party all the patriotism and virtue of the Country. Renounce if you can the intolerant spirit by which you are governed—and begin to reform yourself instead of reprobating others, by beginning to doubt of your own infallibility."

Such is the answer which would naturally be given by a member of the Majority in the Legislature to such an Objector. And it is the only one that could be given; until some evidence of the supposed corruption should be produced.

As far as I know, there is not a member of the Legislature who can properly be called a Stock-jobber or a paper Dealer. There are several of them who were proprietors of public debt in various ways. Some for money lent & property furnished for the use of the public during the War others for sums received in payment of Debts—and it is supposeable enough that some of them had been purchaser[s] of the public Debt, with intention to hold it, as a valuable & convenient property; considering an honorable provision for it as matter of course.

It is a strange perversion of ideas, and as novel as it is extraordinary, that men should be deemed corrupt & criminal for becoming proprietors in the funds of their Country. Yet I believe the number of members of Congress is very small who have ever been considerably proprietors in the funds.

355

And as to improper speculations on measures depending before Congress, I believe never was any *body* of men freer from them.

There are indeed several members of Congress, who have become proprietors in the Bank of the United States, and a *few* of them to a pretty large amount say 50 or 60 shares; but all operations of this kind were necessarily subsequent to the determination upon the measure. The subscriptions were of course subsequent & purchases still more so. Can there be any thing really blameable in this? Can it be culpable to invest property in an institution which has been established for the most important national purposes? Can that property be supposed to corrupt the holder? It would indeed tend to render him friendly to the preservation of the Bank; but in this there would be no collision between duty & interest and it could give him no improper byass in other questions.

To uphold public credit and to be friendly to the Bank must be presupposed to be *corrupt things* before the being a proprietor in the funds or of bank Stock can be supposed to have a *corrupting influence*. The being a proprietor in either case is a very different thing from being, in a proper sense of the term, a Stock jobber. On this point of the corruption of the Legislature one more observation of great weight remains. Those who oppose a *funded* debt and mean any provision for it contemplate an *annual* one. Now, it is impossible to conceive a more fruitful source of legislative corruption than this. All the members of it who should incline to speculate would have an annual opportunity of speculating upon their influence in the legislature to promote or retard or put off a provision. Every session the question whether the annual provision should be continued would be an occasion of pernicious caballing and corrupt bargaining. In this very view when the subject was in deliberation, it was impossible not to wish it declared upon once for all & out of the way.

Objection the 13   The Corrupt Squadron &c

Here again the objectors beg the question. They take it for granted that their constructions of the constitution are right and that the opposite ones are wrong, and with great good nature and candor ascribe the effect of a difference of opinion to a disposition to get rid of the limitations on the Government.

Those who have advocated the constructions which have obtained have met their opponents on the ground of fair argument and they think have refuted them. How shall it be determined which side is right?

There are some things which the General Government has clearly a right to do—there are others which it has clearly no right to meddle with, and there is a good deal of middle ground, about which honest & well disposed men may differ. The most that can be said is that some of this middle ground may have been occupied by the National Legislature; and this surely is no evidence of a disposition to get rid of the limitations in the constitution; nor can it be viewed in that light by men of candor.

The truth is one description of men is disposed to do the essential business of the Nation by a liberal construction of the powers of the Government; another from disaffection would fritter away those powers—a third from an overweening jealousy would do the same thing—a fourth from party & personal opposition are torturing the constitution into objections to every thing they do not like.

The Bank is one of the measures which is deemed by some the greatest stretch of power; and yet its constitutionality has been established in the most satisfactory manner.

And the most incorrigible theorist among its opponents would in one months experience as head of the Department of the Treasury be compelled to acknowlege that it is an absolutely indispensable engine in the management of the Finances and would quickly become a convert to its perfect constitutionality.

Objection XIV   The ultimate object of all

To this there is no other answer than a flat denial—except this that the project from its absurdity refutes itself.

The idea of introducing a monarchy or aristocracy into this Country, by employing the influence and force of a Government continually changing hands, towards it, is one of those visionary things, that none but madmen could meditate and that no wise men will believe.

If it could be done at all, which is utterly incredible, it would require a long series of time, certainly beyond the life of any individual to effect it. Who then would enter into such a plot? For what purpose of interest or ambition?

To hope that the people may be cajoled into giving their sanctions to such institutions is still more chimerical. A people so enlightened and so diversified as the people of this Country can surely never be brought to it, but from convulsions and disorders, in consequence of the acts of popular demagogues.

The truth unquestionably is, that the only path to a subversion of the republican system of the Country is, by flattering the prejudices of the people, and exciting their jealousies and apprehensions, to throw affairs into confusion, and bring on civil commotion. Tired at length of anarchy, or want of government, they may take shelter in the arms of monarchy for repose and security.

Those then, who resist a confirmation of public order, are the true Artificers of monarchy—not that this is the intention of the generality of them. Yet it would not be difficult to lay the finger upon some of their party who may justly be suspected. When a man unprincipled in private life desperate in his fortune, bold in his temper, possessed of considerable talents, having the advantage of military habits—despotic in his ordinary demeanour—known to have scoffed in private at the principles of liberty—when such a man is seen to mount the hobby horse of popularity—to join in the cry of danger to liberty—to take every opportunity of embarrassing the General Government & bringing it under suspicion—to flatter and fall in with all the non sense of the zealots of the day—It may justly be suspected that his object is to throw things into confusion that he may "ride the storm and direct the whirlwind."

It has aptly been observed that *Cato* was the Tory—*Cæsar* the whig of his day. The former frequently resisted—the latter always flattered the follies of the people. Yet the former perished with the Republic the latter destroyed it.

No popular Government was ever without its Catalines & its Cæsars. These are its true enemies.

As far as I am informed the anxiety of those who are calumniated is to keep the Government in the state in which it is, which they fear will be no easy task, from a natural tendency in the state of things to exalt the local on the ruins of the National Government. Some of them appear to wish, in a constitutional way, a change in the judiciary department of the Government, from an apprehension that an orderly and effectual administration of Justice cannot be obtained without a more intimate connection between the state and national Tribunals. But even this is not an object of any set of men as a party. There is a difference of opinion about it on various grounds among those who have generally acted together. As to any other change of consequence, I believe nobody dreams of it.

Tis curious to observe the anticipations of the different parties. One side appears to believe that there is a serious plot to overturn the state Governments and substitute monarchy to the present republican system. The other side firmly believes that there is a serious plot to overturn the General Government & elevate the separate power of the states upon its ruins. Both sides may be equally wrong & their mutual jealousies may be materially causes of the appearances which mutually disturb them, and sharpen them against each other.

Objection the 15   This change was contemplated &c

This is a palpable misrepresentation. No man, that I know of, contemplated the introducing into this country of a monarchy. A very small number (not more than three or four) manifested theoretical opinions favourable in the abstract to a constitution like that of Great

Britain, but every one agreed that such a constitution except as to the general distribution of departments and powers was out of the Question in reference to this Country. The Member who was most explicit on this point (a Member from New York) declared in strong terms that the republican theory ought to be adhered to in this Country as long as there was any chance of its success—that the idea of a perfect equality of political rights among the citizens, exclusive of all permanent or hereditary distinctions, was of a nature to engage the good wishes of every good man, whatever might be his theoretic doubts— that it merited his best efforts to give success to it in practice—that hitherto from an incompetent structure of the Government it had not had a fair trial, and that the endeavour ought then to be to secure to it a better chance of success by a government more capable of energy and order.

There is not a man at present in either branch of the Legislature who, that I recollect, had held language in the Convention favourable to Monarchy.

The basis therefore of this suggestion fails.

16   So many of them &c.

This has been answered above. Neither description of character is to be found in the Legislature. In the Senate there are 9 or ten who were members of the Convention; in the house of Representatives not more than six or seven. Of those who are in the lastmentioned house—none can be considered as influential but Mr. Madison and Mr. Gerry. Are they monarchy men?

As to the 17. 18th and 19th heads—They are rather inferences from and comments upon what is before suggested than specific objections. The answer to them must therefore be derived from what is said under other heads.

It is certainly much to be regretted that party discriminations are so far Geographical as they have been; and that ideas of a severance of the Union are creeping in both North and South. In the South it is supposed that more government than is expedient is desired by the North. In the North, it is believed, that the prejudices of the South are incompatible with the necessary degree of Government and with the attainment of the essential ends of National Union. In both quarters there are respectable men who talk of separation, as a thing dictated by the different geniusses and different prejudices of the parts. But happily their number is not considerable—& the prevailing sentiment of the people is in favour of their true interest, UNION. And it is to be hoped that the Efforts of wise men will be able to prevent a scism, which would be injurious in different degrees to different portions of the Union; but would seriously wound the prosperity of all.

As to the sacrifice of Southern to Northern prejudices—if the conflict has been between *prejudices* and *prejudices*, it is certainly to be wished for mutual gratification that there had been mutual concession; but if the conflict has been between *great* and *substantial* national objects on the one hand, and theoretical prejudices on the other, it is difficult to desire that the former should in any instance have yielded.

Objection 20   The Owers of the Debt are in the Southern and the holders of it in the Northern Division.

Answer. If this were literally true, it would be no argument for or against any thing. It would be still politically and morally right for the Debtors to pay their Creditors.

But it is in *no sense* true. The OWERS of the Debt are the people of *every* State, South Middle North. The holders are the Individual Creditors—citizens of the United Netherlands, Great Britain, France & of these States, North, Middle, South. Though some men, who constantly substitute hypothesis to fact, imagination to evidence, assert and reassert that the inhabitants of the South contribute *more* than those of the North; yet there is no pretence that they contribute *all;* and even the assertion of greater contribution is unsupported by documents facts, or, it may be added, probab[il]ities. Though the inhabitants of the South manufacture less than those of the North, which is the great argument, yet it does not follow that they consume more of taxable articles. It is a solid answer to this, that *whites* live better, wear more and better cloaths, and consume more luxuries, than blacks who constitute so considerable a part of the population of the South—that the Inhabitants of Cities and Towns, which abound so much more in the North than in the South, consume more of foreign articles, than the inhabitants of the Country—that it is a general rule that communities consume & contribute in proportion to their active or circulating wealth and that the Northern Regions have more active or circulating wealth than the Southern.

If official documents are consulted, though for obvious reasons they are not decisive, they contradict rather than confirm the hypothesis of greater proportional contribution in the Southern Division.

But to make the allegation in the objection true, it is necessary not merely that the Inhabitants of the South should contribute more, but that they should contribute *all.*

It must be confessed that a much larger proportion of the Debt is *owned* by inhabitants of the States from Pensylvania to New Hampshire inclusively than in the States South of Pensylvania.

But as to the primitive Debt of the United States, that was the case in its original concoction. This arose from two causes. I, from the war having more constantly been carried on in the Northern Quarter, which led to obtaining more men and greater supplies in that quarter, and credit having been, for a considerable time, the main instrument of the Government, a consequent accumulation of debt in that quarter took place. II from the greater ability of the Northern and middle States to furnish men money and other supplies; and from the greater quantity of men money and other supplies which they did furnish. The loan office Debt; the army debt, the debt of the five great departments was *contracted* in a much larger proportion in the Northern and middle, than in the Southern States.

It must be confessed too that by the attractions of a superior monied Capital the disparity has increased, but it was great in the beginning.

As to the assumed debt the proportion in the South was at the first somewhat larger than in the North; and it must be acknowledged that this has since, from the same superiority of monied Capital in the North, ceased to be the case.

But if the Northern people who were originally greater Creditors than the Southern have become still more so, as purchasers, is it any reason that an honorable provision should not be made for their Debt? Or is the Government to blame for having made it? Did the Northern people take their property by violence from the Southern, or did they purchase and pay for it?

It may be answered that they obtained a considerable part of it by speculation, taking advantage of superior opportunities of information.

But admitting this to be true in all the latitude in which it is commonly stated—Is a government to bend the general maxims of policy and to mould its measures according to the accidental course of private speculations? Is it to do this or omit that in cases of great national importance, because one set of Individuals may gain, another lose, from unequal opportunities of information, from unequal degrees of resource, craft confidence or enterprise?

More over—There is much exaggeration in stating the manner of the alienation of the Debt. The principal speculations in state debt, whatever may be pretended certainly began, after the promulgation of the plan for assuming by the Report of the Secy of the Treasury to the House of Representatives. The resources of Individuals in this Country are too limited to have admitted of much progress in purchases before the knowledge of that plan was diffused throughout the Country. After that, purchasers and sellers were upon equal ground. If the purchasers speculated upon the sellers, in many instances, the sellers speculated upon the purchasers. Each made his calculation of chances, and founded upon it an exchange of money for certificates. It has turned out generally that the buyer had the best of the bargain; but the seller got the value of his commodity according to his estimate of it, and probably in a great number of instances more. This shall be explained:

It happened that Mr. Maddison and some other distinguished characters of the South started in opposition to the Assumption. The high opinion entertained of them made it be taken for granted in that quarter, that the opposition would be successful. The securities quickly rose by means of purchases beyond their former prices. It was imagined that they would soon return to their old station by a rejection of the proposition for assuming. And the certificate holders were eager to part with them at their current prices; calculating on a loss to the Purchasers from their future fall. The representation is not conjectural; it is founded in information from respectable and intelligent Southern characters—And may be ascertained by Inquiry.

Hence it happened, that the inhabitants of the Southern states sustained a considerable loss, by the opposition to the assumption from Southern Gentlemen, and their too great confidence in the efficacy of that opposition.

Further—A great part of the Debt which has been purchased by Northern of Southern Citizens has been at high prices; in numerous instances beyond the true value. In the late delirium of speculation large sums were purchased at 25 ⅌Cent above par and upwards.

The Southern people upon the whole have not parted with their property for nothing. They parted with it voluntarily—in most cases, upon fair terms, without surprize or deception, in many cases for more than its value. Tis their own fault, if the purchase money has not been beneficial to them—and the presumption is that it has been so in a material degree.

Let then any candid and upright mind, weighing all the circumstances, pronounce whether there be any real hardship in the inhabitants of the South being required to contribute their proportion to a provision for the Debt as it now exists—whether, if at liberty, they could honestly dispute the doing of it, or whether they can even in candor and good faith complain of being obliged to do it.

If they can, it is time to unlearn all the ancient notions of justice and morality, and to adopt a new system of Ethics.

Observation 21   The Antifœderal Champions &c

Answer   All that can be said in answer to this has been already said.

It is much to be wished, that the true state of the case may not have been, that the Antifœderal Champions have been encouraged in their activity, by the countenance which has been given to their principles, by certain fœderalists, who in an envious and ambitious struggle for power influence and preeminence have imbraced as auxiliaries the numerous party originally disaffected to the Government in the hope that these united with the factious and feeble minded fœderalists whom they can detach will give them the prœdominancy. This would be nothing more than the old story of personal and party emulation.

The Antifœderal Champions alluded to may be taught to abate their exultation by being told that the great body of the fœderalists, or rather the great body of the people are of opinion that none of their predictions have been fulfilled—That the beneficial effects of the Goverment have exceeded expectation and are witnessed by the general prosperity of the Nation.

LETTER TO GEORGE WASHINGTON
SEPTEMBER 9, 1792

President Washington wrote a letter to Hamilton on August 26, 1792, about the differences of opinion among members of his cabinet and the pernicious effect they were having on the overall administration of government. He was referring to the feud between Jefferson and Hamilton and hoped that Hamilton would attempt to moderate his attacks on Jefferson. He wrote a similar letter to Jefferson urging him to do the same. The following is Hamilton's reply.

Philadelphia September 9
1792

Sir

I have the pleasure of your private letter of the 26th of August.

The feelings and views which are manifested in that letter are such as I expected would exist. And I most sincerely regret the causes of the uneasy sensations you experience. It is my most anxious wish, as far as may depend upon me, to smooth the path of your administration, and to render it prosperous and happy. And if any prospect shall open of healing or terminating the differences which exist, I shall most chearfully embrace it; though I consider myself as the deeply injured party. The recommendation of such a spirit is worthy of the moderation and wisdom which dictated it; and if your endeavours should prove unsucessful, I do not hesitate to say that in my opinion the period is not remote when the public good will require *substitutes* for the *differing members* of your administration. The continuance of a division there must destroy the energy of Government, which will be little enough with the strictest Union. On my part there will be a most chearful acquiescence in such a result.

I trust, Sir, that the greatest frankness has always marked and will always mark every step of my conduct towards you. In this disposition, I cannot conceal from you that I have had some instrumentality of late in the retaliations which have fallen upon certain public characters and that I find myself placed in a situation not to be able to recede *for the present*.

I considered myself as compelled to this conduct by reasons public as well as personal of the most cogent nature. I *know* that I have been a object of uniform opposition from Mr. Jefferson, from the first moment of his coming to the City of New York to enter upon his present office. I *know,* from the most authentic sources, that I have been the frequent subject of the most unkind whispers and insinuating from the same quarter. I have long seen a formed party in the Legislature, under his auspices, bent upon my subversion. I cannot doubt, from the evidence I possess, that the National Gazette was instituted by him for political purposes and that one leading object of it has been to render me and all the measures connected with my department as odious as possible.

Nevertheless I can truly say, that, except explanations to confidential friends, I never directly or indirectly retaliated or countenanced retaliation till very lately. I can even assure you, that I was instrumental in preventing a very severe and systematic attack upon Mr. Jefferson, by an association of two or three individuals, in consequence of the persecution, which he brought upon the Vice President, by his indiscreet and light letter to the Printer, transmitting *Paine's* pamphlet.

As long as I saw no danger to the Government, from the machinations which were going on, I resolved to be a silent sufferer of the injuries which were done me. I determined to avoid giving occasion to any thing which could manifest to the world dissentions among the principal characters of the government; a thing which can never happen without weakening its hands, and in some degree throwing a stigma upon it.

But when I no longer doubted, that there was a formed party deliberately bent upon the subversion of measures, which in its consequences would subvert the Government—when I saw, that the undoing of the funding system in particular (which, whatever may be the original merits of that system, would prostrate the credit and the honor of the Nation, and bring the Government into contempt with that description of Men, who are in every society the only firm supporters of government) was an avowed object of the party; and that all possible pains were taking to produce that effect by rendering it odious to the body of the people—I considered it as a duty, to endeavour to resist the torrent, and as an essential mean to this end, to draw aside the veil from the principal Actors. To this strong impulse, to this decided conviction, I have yielded. And I think events will prove that I have judged rightly.

Nevertheless I pledge my honor to you Sir, that if you shall hereafter form a plan to reunite the members of your administration, upon some steady principle of cooperation, I will faithfully concur in executing it during my continuance in office. And I will not directly or indirectly say or do a thing, that shall endanger a feud.

I have had it very much at heart to make an excursion to Mount Vernon, by way of the Fœderal City in the course of this Month—and have been more than once on the point of asking your permission for it. But I now despair of being able to effect it. I am nevertheless equally obliged by your kind invitation.

The subject mentioned in the Postscript of your letter shall with great pleasure be carefully attended to. With the most faithful and affectionate attachment I have the honor to remain

Sir   Your most Obed & humble servant   A Hamilton

AMICUS
SEPTEMBER 11, 1792

During the period of intense feuding between Hamilton and Jefferson, Hamilton was forced on a number of occasions to answer charges that he was secretly promoting monarchy in America when he put forward his plan of government in the Constitutional Convention. Hamilton defends his position in the following article.

Philadelphia, September 11, 1792

For the National Gazette

A writer in the Gazette of Saturday last, after several observations, with regard to certain charges, which have lately been brought forward against the Secretary of State, proceeds to make or insinuate several charges against another public character.

As to the observations which are designed to exculpate the Secretary of State, I shall do nothing more than refer to the discussions which have taken place and appear to be in a train to be pursued, in the Gazette of the United States.

As to the charges which have been bro't against the other public character alluded to, I shall assert generally, from a long, intimate, and confidential acquaintance with him, added to some other means of information, that the matters charged, as far as they are intelligible, are either grossly misrepresented or palpably untrue.

A part of them, is of a nature to speak itself, without comment, the malignity and turpitude of the accuser, denoting clearly the personal enemy in the garb of the political opponent.

The subject and the situation of the parties naturally impose silence—but this is not the first attempt of the kind that has been made; fruitlessly hitherto, and I doubt not equally fruitlessly in time to come. An opinion on the experience of fifteen years, the greatest part of the time, under circumstances affording the best opportunity for an accurate estimate of character, cannot be shaken by slanderous surmises. The charge of which I shall take more particular notice, is contained in the following passage—"Let him explain the public character, who, if uncontradicted fame is to be regarded, *opposed* the Constitution in the Grand Convention, because it was *too republican,* and advocated the *British monarchy as the perfect standard* to be approached as nearly as the people could be *made to bear."*

This I affirm, to be a gross misrepresentation. To prove it so, it were sufficient to appeal to a single fact, that the gentleman alluded to, was the only member from the state to which he belonged who signed the Constitution, and, it is notorious, against the prevailing weight of the official influence of the state, and against what would probably be the opinion of a large majority of his fellow-citizens, till better information should correct their first impressions—how then can he be believed to have opposed a thing, which he actually agreed to, and that, in so unsupported a situation, and under circumstances of such peculiar responsibility? To this I shall add two more facts; one, that the member in question, never made a single proposition to the Convention, which was not conformable to the republican theory; the other, that the highest-toned of any of the propositions made by him was actually voted for by the representations of several states, including some of the principal ones; and including individuals, who, in the estimation of those who deem themselves the only republicans, are pre-eminent for republican character—more than this I am not at liberty to say. It is a matter generally understood, that the deliberations of the Convention which were carried on in private, were to remain undisturbed. And every prudent man must be convinced of the propriety both of the one and the other. Had the deliberations been open while going on, the clamours of faction would have prevented any satisfactory result. Had they been afterwards disclosed, much food would have been afforded to inflammatory declamation. Propositions made without due reflection, and perhaps abandoned by the proposers themselves, on more mature reflection, would have been handles for a profusion of il-natured accusation.

Every infallible declaimer taking his own ideas as the perfect standard, would have railed without measure or mercy at every member of the Convention who had gone a single line beyond his standard.

The present is a period fruitful in accusation. Much anonymous slander has and will be vented. No man's reputation can be safe, if charges in this form are to be lightly listened to. There are but two kinds of anonymous charges that can merit attention—where the evidence goes along with the charge—and where reference is made to *specific facts*, the evidence of the truth or falsehood of which, is in the power or possession of the party accused, and he at liberty to make a free use of it. None of the charges brought forward in the present instance, fall within either of these rules.

AMICUS.

Sept. 11.

THE CATULLUS ESSAYS, AN INTRODUCTION

The following essays contain what may be regarded as Hamilton's strongest attack on Jefferson's character and motives, written when the tension between them was at its peak. Jefferson had accused Hamilton of contemplating monarchy through a "corps of interested persons who should be steadily at the orders of the Treasury." Hamilton had accused

Jefferson of originally being opposed to the Constitution and subsequently undermining the programs and policies of the Washington administration. Catullus No. III contains Hamilton's defense of his own character; the piece is virtually a comparison of the two statesmen (made, of course, by Hamilton).

CATULLUS NO. II
SEPTEMBER 19, 1792

Philadelphia, September 19, 1792

For the Gazette of the United States

To *Aristides*

The *"American"* to confirm the inference resulting from the official connection between the Secretary of State and the Editor of the National Gazette, appeals to a conformity of the political principles and views of that officer, with those which are sedulously inculcated in that Gazette. If this conformity exists, it certainly affords a strong presumption, in aid of direct facts, of the operation of his influence on the complexion of that paper.

The circumstances of conformity alleged fall under two heads; one—That the Secretary of State was in the origin opposed to that constitution, which it is the evident object of the National Gazette to discredit—the other That he has been and is opposed to those measures which it is the unremitted and it may be said the avowed endeavour of that paper to censure and subvert.

In contradiction to the first suggestion, Aristides cites an authority, which the *American* appears to have relied upon in support of his assertion,—the Speech of Mr. Pendleton in the Convention of Virginia. Let an analasis of this speech shew whether it supports or contradics the assertion.

Mr. Pendleton represents a certain letter of Mr. Jefferson as containing these particulars 1 a strong wish that the *first nine conventions* may accept the new constitution, because it would secure the *good* it contains, which is *great* and *important* 2 a wish that the four latest, whichever they should be, might refuse to accede to it, 'til *amendments were secured* 3 caution to take care that no objection to the form of the Government should produce a scism in the Union; which Mr. Jefferson admits to be an *incurable evil*.

From this it appears, that, though Mr. Jefferson was of opinion, that the Constitution contained "great and important good"—and was desirous, that the first nine deliberating states should consent to it, for the sake of preserving the existence of the Union; yet he had *strong objections* to the constitution—*so strong* that he was willing to risk *an ultimate dismemberment* in an *experiment* to obtain the alterations, which he deemed necessary.

If the four last deliberating States (particularly if they had happened to be states in Geographical contiguity, which was very possible) had refused to ratify the constitution, what might not have been the consequence? Who knows whether the assenting states would have been willing to have been *coerced* into the amendments which the non-assenting states might have been disposed to dictate? Calculating the intrigues and machinations, which were to have been expected to stand in the way, who can say, if even *two thirds* of *both* houses of Congress should have been found willing to propose—that *three fourths* of the Legislature—or Conventions in *three fourths*—of the States—would have been brought to adopt—the required amendments?

Could any thing but objections to the constitution of the most *serious* kind, have justified the hazarding an eventual scism in the Union, in so great a degree, as would have attended an adherence to the advice given by Mr. Jefferson? Can there be any perversion of truth, in affirming, that the person, who entertained those objections, was *opposed* to the Constitution?

The opposition, which was experienced in every part of the UStates, acknowledged the necessity and utility of *Union;* and generally speaking, that the Constitution contained many valuable features; contending only that it wanted some essential alterations to render it upon the whole a safe and a good government.

It may be satisfactory to review what was said, in the same Convention of Virginia, by some other members, on the subject of the letter in question—

Mr. Henry (Page 109 of the Debates) replies thus to Mr. Pendleton—"The Honorable Gentleman has endeavoured to *explain* the opinion of *Mr. Jefferson,* our common friend, *into* an advice to adopt this new Government. *He* wishes Nine States to adopt, and that four states may be found somewhere to reject it. Now Sir, I say, if we pursue his advice, what are we to do? To prefer form to substance? For, give me leave to ask, what is the substantial part of his counsel?

369

It is, Sir, that four States should *reject*. They tell us, that from the most authentic accounts, New Hampshire will adopt it. Where then will four states be found to reject, if we adopt it? If we do, the counsel of this worthy and enlightened countryman of ours will be thrown away &c." Whether this Gentleman argued sincerely from his impression of the true import of the letter; or made an attempt "to *pervert* Mr. Jefferson's sentiments" as Aristides affirms, must be referred to his own consciousness, and to the candid construction of an impartial public.

Mr. Madison, in reply to Mr. Henry (Page 122 of the same debates) expresses himself thus—"The Honorable Member, in order to influence our decision, has mentioned the opinion of a Citizen, who is an ornament to this state. When the name of this distinguished character was introduced, I was much surprised. *Is it come to this then, that we are not to follow our own reason?* Is it proper to adduce the opinions of respectable men, not within these walls? If the opinion of an important character were to weigh on this occasion, could we not adduce a character equally great on our side? Are we who (in the Honorable Gentleman's opinion are not to be guided by an *erring world*) *now to submit to the opinion of a Citizen, beyond the Atlantic?* I believe, that were that Gentleman now on this floor, he would be *for* the adoption of this constitution. I wish his name had never been mentioned. I wish every thing spoken here, relative to his opinion, may be suppressed, if our debates should be published. I know that the delicacy of his feelings will be wounded, when he will see in Print what has, and may be said concerning him on this occasion. I am in some measure acquainted with his sentiments on this subject. *It is not right for me to unfold what he has informed me.* But I will venture to assert that the clause now discussed is not objected to by Mr. Jefferson. He approves of it, because it enables the Government to carry on its operations &c."

It is observable, that Mr. Madison neither advocates the accuracy of Mr. Pendletons comment, nor denies the justness of that of Mr. Henry. His solicitude appears to be to destroy the influence of what he impliedly admits to be the opinion of Mr. Jefferson, to press out of sight the authority of that opinion, and to get rid of the subject as fast as possible. He confesses a knowledge of Mr. Jeffersons sentiments, but prudently avoids disclosure; wrapping the matter in mysterious reserve; and leaving the Public to this day to conjecture what was the precise import of the sentiments communicated.

Enough however is seen to justify the conclusion that if the spirit of Mr. Jefferson's advice had prevailed with the Convention, and full credence had been given to the expected adoption by New Hampshire—Virginia, North Carolina, New York and Rhode Island would temporarily have thrown themselves out of the Union. And whether in that event, they would have been at this day reunited to it, or whether there would be now any Union at all is happily a speculation which need only be pursued to derive the pleasing reflection, that the danger was wisely avoided.

To understand more accurately what the *American* meant, in asserting that Mr. Jefferson had been opposed to the constitution, let him be compared with himself. In his first paper he expresses himself thus—"While the Constitution of the United States was depending before the People of this Country, for their consideration and decision, Mr. Jefferson being in France was *opposed* to it, *in some of its most important features,* and wrote his objections to some of his friends in Virginia. He *at first* went so far as to *discountenance its adoption;* though he *afterwards recommended* it on the ground of expediency, in certain contingencies."

From this, it is evident, that so far from denying, he has even admitted, that Mr. Jefferson, at *one stage* of the business, *recommended* the adoption of the Constitution to his *fellow Citizens,* but upon a contingency. And this is literally the fact as established by the letter quoted in the debates of the Convention. The advice is to adopt, if nine states had not previously adopted; to reject if that number of states had previously adopted. This clearly is to adopt, or not, upon a contingency. Thus the authority appealed to by Aristides confirms the latter part of the *American's* assertion, without contradicting the former part of it.

Aristides has not denied, nor do I believe he will deny—that Mr. Jefferson in his early communications discountenanced the adoption of the constitution in its primitive form. I know the source of the *American's* information. It is equally authentie and friendly to Mr. Jefferson. Allowing for the bare possibility of misapprehension, it exactly accords with the statement, which has been made of it. If the fact shall be denied, the source of information will be indicated under due guards for the delicacy of the proceeding. This will serve, either to confirm, or, in case of misconception to correct.

I add, that some of Mr. Jefferson's objections to the constitution have not been removed, by the amendments, which have been proposed. Part of his objections went to the structure of particular parts of the government.

As to the second fact, with which the American corroborates the charge of Mr. Jefferson's participation in the views of the National Gazette, it is in a degree conceded by Aristides. He confesses, nay he even *boasts,* Mr. Jeffersons *abhorrence* of some of the leading principles

371

of Mr. Hamiltons fiscal administration, that is the leading principles of those measures, which have provided for the public debt, & restored public Credit.

It would have been well, if Aristides had told us what those leading principles are, which are the objects of so much *abhorrence* to Mr. Jefferson.

The leading principles of Mr. Hamilton's fiscal administration have been—that the Public debt ought to be provided for in favour of those, who, according to the express terms of the contract, were the *true legal proprietors* of it; that it ought to be provided for in other respects, according to the terms of the contract, except so far as deviations from it should be assented to by the Creditors, upon the condition of a fair equivalent—that it ought to be *funded* on *ascertained* revenues *pledged* for the payment of interest, and the gradual redemption of principal—that the debts of the several states ought to be comprised in the provision, on the same terms with that of the United States—that to render this great operation practicable avoid the oppression of Trade and industry, and facilitate loans to the government, in cases of emergency, it was necessary to institute a National Bank—that indirect taxes were, in the actual circumstances of the country, the most eligible means of revenue, and that direct taxes ought to be avoided as much and as long as possible.

I aver, from competent opportunities of knowing Mr. Jeffersons ideas, that he has been hostile to all these positions, except, perhaps, the last; and that even in regard to that, his maxims would oblige the government, in practice, speedily to resort to direct taxes.

I aver, moreover, that Mr. Jefferson's opposition to the administration of the Government has not been confined to the measures connected with the Treasury Department; but has extended, to use the words of the American "to almost all the important measures of the Government."

The *exceptions* to the generality of both the preceding assertions, I am content to rest on a designation by Mr. Jefferson, or by any person, who shall speak from a knowlege of his sentiments, of those principles of the Fiscal department, or of those measures of the Government of any importance which he *does approve*. I insist only, that the designation be precise and explicit, and come with such marks of authenticity, as are adapted to the nature of an anonymous discussion.

To give an idea of the accuracy with which Aristides discloses Mr. Jefferson's opinions, I shall cite one of his phrases, with a short observation. He asserts, that a suggestion against Mr. Jefferson, which he states, is "made on no better foundation than his being opposed to *some* of the principles of the funding system, of the National Bank, and of certain other measures of the Secretary of the Treasury." It is matter of general notoriety and unquestionable certainty, that Mr. Jefferson has been opposed to the National Bank in *toto*, to its *constitutionality* and to its *expediency*. With what propriety, is it then said, that he has been opposed only to "*some of* the principles of that Institution"?

I proceed now, to state the exact tenor of the advice, which Mr. Jefferson gave to Congress, respecting the transfer of the debt due to France to a company of Hollanders. After mentioning an offer, which had been made by such a company for the purchase of the debt, he concludes with these extraordinary expressions—"If there *is a danger* of the public payments *not being punctual*, I submit whether it may not be better, that *the discontents, which would then arise,* should be *transferred* from a *Court,* of whose *good will we have so much need,* to the *breasts* of a *private company.*"

The above is an extract which was made from the letter, in February 1787. The date of it was not noted, but the original, being on the files of the department of state, will ascertain that and all other particulars relating to its contents. The genuineness of the foregoing extract may be depended upon.

This letter was the subject of a Report from the Board of Treasury in February 1787. That Board treated the idea of the Transfer proposed as both unjust and impolitic: *unjust,* because the Nation would contract an engagement which there was no well grounded prospect of fulfilling; *impolitic,* because a failure in the payment of interest, on the debt transferred (which was *inevitable*) would *justly blast* all hopes of credit with the citizens of the United Netherlands, in future pressing exigencies of the Union: and gave it as their opinion that it would be adviseable for Congress, *without delay,* to instruct their Minister, at the Court of France, to forbear giving his sanction to any such transfer

Congress agreeing in the ideas of the Board caused an instruction to that effect to be sent to Mr. Jefferson*. Here then was a solemn act of Government condeming the principle, as unjust and impolitic.

---

*Note at *foot*

What is here said *with regard to Congress* is from a recollection of more than 5 years standing & so far liable to error though none is apprehended to exist. The Secret Journals in the possession of the Department of State, if there is one, may correct it.

If the sentiment contained in the extract, which has been recited, can be vindicated from the imputation of political *profligacy—then is it necessary to unlearn* all the ancient notions of justice, and to substitute some new fashioned scheme of morality in their stead.

Here is no complicated problem, which sophistry may entangle or obscrure—here is a plain question of *moral feeling*. A Government is encouraged, on the express condition of *not having a prospect* of making a due provision for a debt, which it owes, to concur in a transfer of that debt from a Nation well able to bear the inconveniences of failure or delay, to Individuals, whose total ruin might have been the consequence of it; and that upon the *interested* consideration of having need of the good will of the Creditor-Nation, and, with the dishonorable motive as is clearly implied, of having more to apprehend from the discontents of that Nation, than from those of disappointed and betrayed individuals. Let every honest and impartial mind, consulting its own spontaneous emotions, pronounce for itself upon the rectitude of such a suggestion. Let every sober and independent member of the community decide, whether it is likely to be a misfortune to the country, that the maxims of the Officer at the head of its Treasury Department are materially variant from those of the Author of that suggestion.

And let Aristides prove if he can, that Mr. Jefferson gave advice *"expressly contrary* to that which has been ascribed to him." Amidst the excentric ramblings of this political comet, its station, in another revolution, will not prove, that its appearance was not, at one time, at the place, which has been assigned for it.

The *American* it ought to be confessed, has, in this instance, drawn larger than the life. This he has done, by blending with the fact the sudden, though natural, comments of an honest indignation. But the original itself, in its true size and shape, without the help of the least exaggeration, is to the moral eye a deformed and hideous monster.

Say *Aristides!* did the Character, to whom you are so partial, imitate, in this case, the sublime virtue of that venerable Athenian, whose name you have assumed? Did he dissuade his countrymen from adopting a proposition, because though "nothing could be more advantageous nothing was more unjust"? Did he not rather advise them to do what was both *disadvantageous* and *unjust?* May he not, as a public man, discard all apprehension of *ostracism*, for being the *superlatively just?*

Catulus

CATULLUS NO. III
SEPTEMBER 29, 1792

Philadelphia, September 29, 1792

FOR THE GAZETTE OF THE UNITED STATES.

ARISTIDES complains that the AMERICAN has charged Mr. Jefferson with being the patron and promoter of *national disunion, national insignificance, public disorder and discredit.* The American however, has only affirmed, that "the real or pretended political tenets of that gentleman *tend*" to those points.

The facts which have been established clearly demonstrate, that in the form in which it is made, the charge is well founded.

If Mr. Jefferson's opposition to the funding system, to the bank, and to the other measures which are connected with the administration of the national finances had ceased, when those measures had received the sanction of law; nothing more could have been said, than, that he had transgressed the rules of official decorum, in entering the lists against the head of another department (between whom and himself, there was a reciprocal duty to cultivate harmony) that he had been culpable in pursuing a line of conduct, which was calculated to sow the seeds of discord in the executive branch of the government, in the infancy of its existence.

But when his opposition extended beyond that point; when it was apparent, that he wished to *render odious,* and of course to *subvert* (for in a popular government these are convertible terms) all those deliberate and solemn acts of the legislature, which had become the pillars of the public credit, his conduct deserved to be regarded with a still severer eye.

Whatever differences of opinion may have preceded those acts—however exceptionable particular features in them may have appeared to certain characters, there is no enlightened nor discreet citizen but must agree, that they ought *now* to remain *undisturbed.* To set afloat the funding system, after the faith of the nation had been so deliberately and solemnly pledged to it—after such numerous and extensive alienations of property for full value have been made under its sanction—with adequate revenues, little burthensome to the people—in a time of profound peace—with not even the shadow of any public necessity—on no better ground than that of theoretical and paradoxical dogmas—would be one of the most wanton and flagitious acts, that ever stained the annals of a civilized nation.

Yet positions tending to that disgraceful result have been maintained in public discourses, by individuals known to be devoted to the Secretary of State; and have been privately smiled upon as profound discoveries in political science.

Yet the less discreet, though not least important partizans of that officer, talk familiarly of undoing the funding system as a meritorious work: Yet his Gazette (which may fairly be regarded as the mirror of his views) after having labored for months to make it an object of popular detestation, has at length told us in plain and triumphant terms, that "the funding system has had its day;" and very clearly, if not expressly, that it is the object of the party to overthrow it.

The American, then, has justly, and from sufficient data, inferred, that Mr. Jefferson's politics, whatever may be the motives of them *tend* to national disunion, insignificance, disorder and discredit. That the subversion of the funding system would produce national discredit, proves itself. Loss of credit, the reason being the same, must attend nations, as well as individuals who voluntarily and without necessity, violate their formal and positive engagements.

Insignificance and disorder, as applied to communities, equally with individuals, are the natural offspring of a loss of credit, premeditatedly and voluntarily incurred.

Disunion would not long lag behind. Sober-minded and virtuous men in every State would lose all confidence in, and all respect for a government, which had betrayed so much levity and inconsistency, so profligate a disregard to the *rights of property*, and to the obligations of good faith. Their support would of course be so far withdrawn or relaxed, as to leave it an easy prey to its enemies. These comprise the advocates for separate confederacies; the jealous partizans of unlimited sovereignty, in the State governments—the never to be satiated lovers of innovation and change—the tribe of pretended philosophers, but real fabricators of chimeras and paradoxes—the Catalines and the Cæsars of the community (a description of men to be found in every republic) who leading the dance to the tune of liberty without law, endeavor to intoxicate the people with delicious but poisonous draughts to render them the easier victims of their rapacious ambition; the vicious and the fanatical of every class who are ever found the willing or the deluded followers of those seducing and treacherous leaders.

But this is not all—the invasion of sixty millions of property could not be perpetrated without violent concussions. The States, whose citizens, both as *original* creditors and *purchasers* own the largest portions of the debt (and several such there are) would not remain long bound in the trammels of a party which had so grossly violated their rights. The consequences in experiment would quickly awaken to a sense of injured right, and interest such of them whose representatives may have wickedly embarked, or been ignorantly betrayed into the atrocious and destructive project.

Where would all this end but in disunion and anarchy? in national disgrace and humiliation?

ARISTIDES insinuates that the AMERICAN has distinguished Mr. Jefferson as "the CATALINE of the day—the ambitious incendiary." Those epithets are not to be found in either of the papers, under that signature. But the American has said, that Mr. Jefferson "has been the prompter, open or secret, of unwarrantable aspersions on men, who as long as actions, not merely professions, shall be the true test of patriotism and integrity need never decline a comparison with him of their titles to the public esteem," and he is supported in the assertion by facts.

Not to cite or trace those foul and pestilent whispers, which clandestinely circulating through the country, have, as far as was practicable, contaminated some of its fairest and worthiest characters, an appeal to known circumstances will justify the charge.

Some time since, there appeared in print certain speculations, which have been construed into an advocation of hereditary distinctions in government. These (whether with, or without foundation, is to this moment matter of conjecture) were ascribed to a particular character—pre-eminent for his early, intrepid, faithful, presevering and comprehensively useful services to his country—a man pure and unspotted in private life, a citizen having a high and solid title to the esteem, the gratitude and the confidence of his fellow-citizens.

The first volume of the "Rights of man" makes its appearance— The opportunity is eagerly seized, to answer the double purpose of wounding a competitor and of laying in an additional stock of popularity; by associating and circulating the name of Thomas Jefferson, with a popular production of a favorite writer, on a favorite subject.

For this purpose the Secretary of State sits down and pens an epistle to a printer in the city of Philadelphia, transmitting the work for republication, and expressing his approbation of it in a way, which we learn, from the preface of that printer to his edition of the work, was calculated not only to do justice to the writings of Mr. Paine, but to do honor to Mr. Jefferson; *by directing the mind* to a contemplation of that *republican firmness* and *democratic simplicity*, which ought to *endear him* to every friend to the "Rights of Man."

The letter, as we learn from the same preface, contained the following passages: "I am extremely pleased to find it will be re-printed here, and that something is at length to be publicly said against the *political heresies*, which have sprung up among us. I have no doubt our citizens will *rally* a second time round the *standard* of common sense."

There was not a man in the United States, acquainted with the insinuations, which had been propagated, who did not instantly ap-ply the remark—and the signal was so well understood by the parti-zans of the writer, that a general attack immediately commenced. The newspapers in different States resounded with invective and scurril-ity against the patriot, who was marked out as the object of persecu-tion, and if possible of degradation.

Under certain circumstances general expressions designate a per-son or an object as clearly as an indication of it by name. So it hap-pened in the present case. The Javelin went directly to its destination.

But it was quickly perceived, that discerning and respectable men disapproved the step. It was of consequence to endeavor to maintain their good opinion. Protestations, and excuses as frivolous as awkward were multiplied to veil the real design.

"The gentleman alluded to, never once entered into the mind! It was never imagined, that the printer would be so incautious as to publish the letter or any part of it—nothing more was in view than to turn a handsome period, and to avoid the *baldness* of a note that did nothing but present the compliments of the writer!"

Thus a solemn invocation to the people of America, on the most serious and important subject, dwindled at once into a brilliant con-ceit, that tickled the imagination too much to be resisted. The imputa-tion of levity was preferred to that of malice.

But when the people of America presented themselves to the disturbed patriotic fancy, as a routed host, scattered and dispersed by political sorcerers; how was it possible to resist the heroic, the chival-rous desire, of erecting for them some magic standard of orthodoxy, and endeavoring to *rally* them round it, for mutual protection and safety.

In so glorious a cause, the considerations—that a citizen of the United States had written in a foreign country a book containing strictures on the government of that country, which would be re-garded by it, as libellous and seditious—that he had *dedicated* this book to the chief magistrate of the union—that a republication of it under the auspices of the Secretary of State, would wear the appear-ance of its having been promoted, at least of its being patronized by the government of this country—were considerations too light and un-important to occasion a moment's hesitation or pause.

Those who, after an attentive review of circumstances, can be deceived by the artifices, which have been employed to varnish over this very exceptionable proceeding must understand little of human nature—must be little read in the history of those arts, which in all countries, and at all times have served to disguise the machinations of factious and intriguing men.

The remaining circumstance of public notoriety, which fixes upon Mr. Jefferson the imputation of being the prompter, or instigator of detraction, exists in his patronage of the National Gazette.

Can any attentive reader of that Gazette doubt, for a moment, that it has been systematically devoted to the calumniating and blackening of public characters? Can it be a question, that a main object of the paper is to destroy the public confidence in a particular public character, who it seems is to be *hunted down* at all events, for the unpardonable sin of having been the steady, invariable and decided friend of broad national principles of government? Can it be a question, that the persecution of the officer alluded to, is agreeable to the views of the institutor of the paper?

Does all this proceed from motives purely disinterested and patriotic? Can none of a different complexion be imagined, that may at least have operated to give a *stimulous* to *patriotic* zeal?

No. Mr. Jefferson has hitherto been distinguished as the quiet modest, retiring philosopher—as the plain simple unambitious republican. He shall not now for the first time be regarded as the intriguing incendiary—the aspiring turbulent competitor.

How long it is since that gentleman's real character may have *divined*, or whether this is only the *first time* that the *secret* has been disclosed, I am not sufficiently acquainted with the history of his political life to determine; But there is always "a *first time*," when characters studious of artful disguises are unveiled; When the vizor of stoicism is plucked from the brow of the Epicurean; when the plain garb of Quaker simplicity is stripped from the concealed voluptuary; when Cæsar *coyley refusing* the proffered diadem, is seen to be Cæsar *rejecting* the trappings, but tenaciously grasping the substance of imperial domination.

It is not unusual to defend one post, by attacking another. Aristides has shewn a disposition to imitate this policy. He by clear implication tells us, and doubtless means it as a justification of the person whom he defends—that attachment to *aristocracy, monarchy, hereditary succession,* a *titled order of nobility* and all the *mock pageantry* of Kingly government form the *appropriate* and *prominent* features in the character to which he boasts Mr Jefferson's opposition, and which it seems to be a principal part of the business of his Gazette to depreciate. This

379

is no more than what has been long matter for malevolent insinuation; I mistake however the man, to whom it is applied, if he fears the strictest scrutiny into his political principles and conduct; if he does not wish there "were windows in the breast," and that assembled America might witness the inmost springs of his public actions. I mistake him, however a turn of mind less addicted to *dogmatising* than *reasoning*, less fond of *hypotheses* than *experience*, may have led to speculative doubts concerning the probable success of the republican theory—if he has not uniformly and ardently, since the experiment of it began in the United States, *wished* it success—if he is not sincerely desirous that the sublime idea of a perfect equality of rights among citizens, exclusive of hereditary distinctions, may be practically justified and realized—and if, among the sources of the regret, which his language and conduct have testified, at the overdriven maxims and doctrines that too long withstood the establishment of firm government in the United States, and now embarrass the execution of the government which has been established, a *principal one* has not been their tendency to counteract a *fair trial* of the theory, to which he is represented to be adverse. I mistake him if his measures, proceeding upon the ground of a liberal and efficient exercise of the powers of the national government have had any other object than to give to it stability and duration; *the only solid and rational expedient for preserving republican government in the United States.*

It has been pertinently remarked by a judicious writer, that *Cæsar,* who *overturned* the republic, was the WHIG, *Cato,* who *died* for it, the TORY of Rome; such at least was the common cant of political harangues; the insidious tale of hypocritical demagogues.

CATULLUS.

CATULLUS NO. IV
OCTOBER 17, 1792

Philadelphia, October 17, 1792

Attempts in different shapes have been made to repel the charges which have been brought against the Secretary of State. The defence of him however in the quarter in which he has been principally assailed, has hitherto gone no further than a mere shew of defending him. I speak as to his improper connection with the Editor of the National Gazette. But a more serious and more plausible effort has been made to obviate the impression, which arises from his having been originally an objector to the present Constitution of the United States.

For this purpose several letters said to have been written, by Mr. Jefferson, while in Europe, have been communicated. How far they are genuine letters or mere fabrications—how far they may have been altered or multilated is liable from the manner of their appearance to question and doubt. It is observable, also, that the extract of a letter of the 6 of July contained in the American Dayly Advertiser of the 10th instant though it seems to be intended as part of the one, which is mentioned in the debates of the Virginia Convention, does not answer to the description given of it by Mr. Pendleton, who professes to have seen it. For Mr. Pendleton expressly states with regard to that letter that Mr. Jefferson, after having declared his wish, respecting the issue of the deliberations upon the constitution, proceeds to *enumerate the amendments which he wishes to be secured*. The extract, which is published, speaks only of *a bill of rights*, as the essential amendment to be obtained by the rejection of four states; which by no means satisfies the latitude of Mr. Pendleton's expressions.

Such nevertheless, as it is, it affords an additional confirmation of that part of the American's statement, which represents Mr. Jefferson as having advised the people of Virginia to adopt or not *upon a contingency*.

It happens likewise that the letters, which have been communicated ⟨tend⟩ to confirm the only parts of the American's statement of the sentiments and conduct of Mr. Jefferson in relation to the Constitution, which remained to be supported; namely "that he was opposed to it *in some of its most important features*, and at first went so far as to discountenance its adoption." By this I understand, without previous amendments.

From the first of those letters dated "Paris the 20th of December 1787" it appears, that Mr. Jefferson among other topics of objection "disliked and *greatly* disliked the abandonment of the principle of *rotation* in office and *most particularly* in the case of the President": From which, the inference is clear, that he would have wished the principle of rotation to have extended not only to the executive, but to other branches of the Government—to the Senate at least, as is explained by a subsequent letter. This objection goes to the structure of the government in a very important article, and while it justifies the assertion, that Mr. Jefferson was opposed to the Constitution, *in some of its most important features*, it is a specimen of the visionary system of

381

politics of its Author. Had it been confined to the office of Chief Magistrate, it might have pretended not only to plausibility but to a degree of weight and respecta[bility. By being extended to other branches of the government, it assumes a different character, and evinces a mind prone to projects, which are incompatible with the principles of stable and systematic government; disposed to multiply the outworks, and leave the citadel weak and tottering.

But the *fact* not the *merit* of the objection is the material point. In this particular, it comes fully up to the suggestion which has been made.

It now only remains to see how far it is proved; that Mr. Jefferson at first *discountenanced* the adoption of the constitution in its primitive form.

Of this a person acquainted with the manner of that gentleman, and with the force of terms, will find sufficient evidence in the following passage: "*I do not pretend to decide,* what would be the best method of procuring the establishment of the manifold good things in the constitution, and of *getting rid of the bad:* whether by adopting it *in hopes* of future amendment; or after it has been duly weighed and canvassed by the people; after seeing the parts they generally dislike, and those they generally approve to say to them; 'we see now what you wish—send together your deputies again—let them frame a constitution for you; omitting what you have condemned, and establishing the powers you approve.' "

Mr. Jefferson did not explicitly decide which of these two modes was best; and while *it is clear,* that he had not *determined in favor* of an adoption without previous amendments, it is not difficult to infer from the terms of expression employed, that he preferred the last of the two modes; a recurrence to a second convention. The faintness of the phrase "*in hopes* of future amendment," and the emphatical method of displaying the alternative are sufficient indications of the preference he entertained.

The pains which he takes in the same letter to remove the alarm naturally inspired by the insurrection which had happened in Massachusetts, are an additional illustration of the same bias. It is not easy to understand what other object his comments on that circumstance] could have, but to obviate the anxiety, which it was calculated to inspire, for an adoption of the constitution, without a previous experiment to amend it.

It is not possible to avoid remarking by the way, that these comments afford a curious and characteristic sample of logic and calculation. "One Rebellion in *thirteen* states, in the course of *eleven* years is but one for each state in a Century and a half": While *France,* it seems, had had three insurrections in three years. In the latter instance the subdivisions of the intire nation are confounded in one mass. In the former, they are the ground of calculation. And thus a miserable sophism is gravely made a basis of political consolation and conduct. For according to the data stated, it was as true that the *U States* had had one rebellion in eleven years, endangering their common safety and welfare, as that *France* had had three insurrections in three years.

Thus it appears from the very documents produced in exculpation of Mr. Jefferson—that he in fact discountenanced in the first instance the adoption of the Constitution; favouring the idea of an attempt at previous amendments by a second Convention; which is the only part of the allegations of the American that remained to be established.

As to those letters of Mr. Jefferson which are subsequent to his knowledge of the ratification of the Constitution by the requisite number of states, they prove nothing, but that Mr Jefferson was willing to play the politician. They can at best only be viewed as acts of submission to the opinion of a Majority, which he professes to believe infallible—resigning to it, with all possible humility, not only his *conduct* but his *judgment*.

It will be remarked, that there appears to have been no want of versatility in his opinions. They kept pace tolerably well with the progress of the business; and were quite as accommodating as circumstances seemed to require. On the 31st of July 1788, when the adoption of the Constitution was known, the various and weighty objections of March 1787 had resolved themselves into the single want of a bill of rights. In November following, on the strength of the authority of three states (overruling in this instance the maxim of implicit deference for the opinion of a majority) that lately solitary defect acquires a companion, in a revival of the objection to the perpetual reeligibility of the President. And another Convention, which appeared no very alarming expedient while the intire constitution was in jeopardy, became an object *to be deprecated*, when partial amendments to an already established constitution were alone in question.

From the fluctuations ⟨of sentiment⟩ which appear in the letters that have ⟨been published,⟩ it is natural to infer, that had the whole of Mr Jefferson'[s] correspondence on the subject been given to the public much greater diversities would have been discovered.

In the preface to the publication of the letters under consideration, this question is put—"Wherein was the merit or offence of a favourable or unfavourable opinion of the constitution and to whom rendered?"

It is a sufficient answer to this question—as it relates to the present discussion, to say, that the intimation which was given of Mr. Jeffersons dislike of the Constitution, in the first instance, was evidently not intended as the imputation of a positive crime, but as one link in a chain of evidence tending to prove that the National Gazette was conducted under his auspices, and in conformity to his views. After shewing that the Editor of that paper was in his pay, and had been taken into it some short time previous to the commencement of the publication, the inference resulting, from this circumstance, of that paper being a political engine, in his hands, is endeavoured to be corroborated, first by the suggestion, that Mr Jefferson had originally serious objections to the Constitution, secondly by the further suggestion, that he has disapproved of most of the important measures adopted in the course of the administration of the Government.

In this light and with this special reference were these suggestions made. And certainly as far as they are founded in fact the argument they afford is fair and forcible. A correspondency of the principles and opinions of Mr. Jefferson with the complexion of a paper, the conductor of which is in the regular pay of his department—is surely a strong confirmation of the conclusion—that the paper is conducted under his influence and agreeably to his views.

Nothing but a known opposition of sentiment on the part of Mr. Jefferson to the doctrines inculcated in the National Gazette could obviate the inference deducible from his ascertained and very extraordinary connection with it. A coincidence of sentiments is a direct and irresistible confirmation of that inference.

An effort scarcely plausible has been made by *another* Aristides, to explain away the turpitude of the advice, which was given respecting the French Debt. It is represented that a Company of adventuring Speculators had offered to purchase the debt at a discount, foreseeing the delay of payment, calculating the probable loss, and willing to encounter the hazard. The terms employed by Mr. Jefferson refute this species of apology. His words are "If there is a *danger* of the public payments *not being punctual,* I submit whether it may not be better, that *the discontents which would then arise,* should be *transferred* from a *Court,* of whose *good will we have so much need,* to the *breasts* of a *private Company."*

He plainly takes it for granted that *discontents would arise* from the want of an adequate provision and proposes that they should be *transferred* to the breasts of Individuals. This he could not have taken for granted, if in his conception, the purchasers had calculated on delay and loss.

The true construction then is that the Company expected to purchase, at an under value, from the probability, that the Court of

France might be willing to raise a sum of money on this fund at a sacrifice—supposing that the U. States counting on her friendly indulgence might be less inclined to press the reimbursement; not that they calculated on material delay or neglect, when the transfer should be made to them. They probably made a very different calculation (to wit) that as it would be ruinous to the credit of the U. States abroad to neglect any part of its debt, which was contracted there with *Individuals*, from the impossibility of one part being distinguishable from another in the public apprehension; this consideration would stimulate to exertions to provide for it. And so it is evident from his own words that Mr. Jefferson understood it.

But the persons, who offered to purchase, were *speculators*. The cry of Speculation as usual is raised; and this with some people is the *panacea*, the *universal cure* for fraud and breach of faith.

It is true, as alleged, that Mr. Jefferson mentioned an alternative, the obtaining of the money by new loans to reimburse the Court of France; but this is not mentioned in any way that derogates from or waves the advice given in the first instance. He merely presents an alternative, in case the first idea should be disapproved.

It may be added, that the advice respecting the transfer of the Debt was little more honorable to the U.States, as it regarded the Court of France, than as it respected the Dutch Company. What a blemish on our National character that a debt of so sacred a nature should have been transferred at so considerable a loss to so meritorious a Creditor!

A still less plausible effort has been made to vindicate the National Gazette, from the charge of being a paper devoted to the calumniating and depreciating the Government of the UStates. No original performance, in defence of the Government, or its measures, has, it is said, been refused by the Editor of that paper. A few publications of this tendency have appeared in it—principally if not wholly since the public detection of the situation of its conductor.

What a wretched apology! Because the partiality has not been so daring and unprecedented, as to extend to a refusal of original publications in defence of the Government, a paper which industriously copies every inflammatory publication against it, that appears in any part of the United States, and carefully avoids every answer which is given to them, even when specially handed to the Editor for the purpose is not to be accounted a malicious and pernicious engine of detraction and calumny towards the Government!!!

But happily here no proof nor argument is necessary. The true character and tendency of the paper may be left to the evidence of every Reader's senses and feelings. And Aristides as often as he looks over that paper must blush, if he can blush, at the assertion "that it has *abounded,* since its commencemt. with publications in ⟨favor⟩ of the measures of the Government."

Deception, however artfully vieled, seldom fails to betray some unsound part. Aristides assures us—that Mr. Jefferson *"has actually refused* in any instance to mark a single paragraph, which appeared in the foreign prints for republication in the National Gazette." On what ground was such an application to Mr. Jefferson made, if he was not considered as the Patron of the Paper? What Printer would make a similar application to the head of any other department? I verily believe none. And I consider the circumstance stated as a confirmation of the Relation of *Patron* and *Client,* between the Secretary of State and the Editor of the National Gazette.

The refusal, if it happened, is one of those little under plots, with which the most intriguing man in the United States is at no loss, to keep out of sight the main design of the Drama.

Catullus

METELLUS
OCTOBER 24, 1792

Hamilton's thoughts on the responsibilities of the heads of the executive departments were largely a reaction to Jefferson's differences with Washington's administration. He contended that Jefferson, by opposing Treasury measures that Washington approved, violated his responsibility to the chief executive. Hamilton held that heads of executive departments were auxiliaries to the president, and, as subordinates to him, it was their responsibility to promote the program of the administration as far as their duty and conscience indicated and to abstain from interference in matters outside their jurisdiction.

Philadelphia, October 24, 1792

FOR THE GAZETTE OF THE UNITED STATES.

The votaries of Mr. Jefferson, whose devotion for their idol kindles at every form, in which he deigns to present himself, have deduced matter of panegyric from his opposition to the measures of the government. 'Tis according to them the sublimest pitch of virtue in him, not only to have extra-officially embarrassed plans, originating with his colleagues, in the course of their progress, but to have continued his opposition to them, after they had been considered and enacted by the legislature, with such modifications as appeared to them proper, and had been approved by the chief magistrate. Such conduct it seems, marks "a firm and virtuous independence of character." If any proof were wanting of that strange inversion of the ideas of decorum, propriety and order, which characterizes a certain party, this making a theme of encomium of what is truly a demonstration of a caballing, self-sufficient and refractory temper, would afford it.

In order to shew that the epithets have been misapplied, I shall endeavor to state what course a firm and virtuous independence of character, guided by a just and necessary sense of decorum, would dictate to a man in the station of Mr. Jefferson.

This has been rendered more particularly requisite, by the formal discussion of the point, which appears to be the object of a continuation of a defence of that gentleman, in the American Daily Advertiser of the 10th inst.

The position must be reprobated that a man who had accepted an office in the executive department, should be held to throw the weight of his character into the scale, to support a measure, which in his *conscience he disapproved,* and *in his station had opposed*—Or that the members of the administration should form together *a close and secret combination, into whose measures the profane eye of the public should in no instance pry.* But there is a very obvious medium between *aiding* or *countenancing,* and *intriguing* and *machinating* against a measure; between opposing it in the discharge of an official duty, or volunteering an opposition to it in the discharge of no duty; between entering into a close and secret combination with the other members of an administration, and being the active leader of an opposition to its measures.

The true line of propriety appears to me to be the following: A member of the administration, in one department, ought only to *aid* those measures of another, which he approves—where he disapproves, if called upon to *act officially,* he ought to manifest his disapprobation, and avow his opposition; but out of an official line he ought not to interfere, *as long as he thinks fit to continue a part of the administration.* When the measure in question has become a law of the land, especially with a direct sanction of the chief magistrate, it is peculiarly his duty to acquiesce. A contrary conduct is inconsistent with his relations as an officer of the government, and with a due respect as such, for the decisions of the legislature, and of the head of the executive department. The line here delineated, is drawn from obvious and very important considerations. The success of every gov-

387

ernment—its capacity to combine the exertion of public strength with the preservation of personal right and private security, qualities which define the perfection of a government, must always naturally depend on the energy of the executive department. This energy, again, must materially depend on the union and mutual deference, which subsist between the members of that department, and the conformity of their conduct with the views of the executive chief.

Difference of opinion between men engaged in any common pursuit, is a natural appendage of human nature. When only exerted *in the discharge of a duty,* with delicacy and temper, among liberal and sensible men, it can create no animosity; but when it produces officious interferences, dictated by no call of duty—when it volunteers a display of itself in a quarter, where there is no responsibility, to the obstruction and embarrassment of one who is charged with an immediate and direct responsibility—it must necessarily beget ill humour and discord between the parties.

Applied to the members of the executive administration of any government, it must necessarily tend to occasion, more or less, distracted councils, to foster factions in the community, and practically to weaken the government.

Moreover the heads of the several executive departments are justly to be viewed as auxiliaries to the executive chief. Opposition to any measure of his, by either of those heads of departments, except in the shape of frank, firm, and independent advice to himself, is evidently contrary to the relations which subsist between the parties. And it cannot well be controverted that a measure becomes his, so as to involve the duty of acquiescence on the part of the members of his administration, as well by its having received his sanction in the form of a law, as by its having previously received his approbation.

In the theory of our government, the chief magistrate is himself responsible for the exercise of every power vested in him by the constitution. One of the powers entrusted to him, is that of objecting to bills which have passed the two houses of Congress. This supposes the duty of objecting, when he is of opinion, that the object of any bill is either *unconstitutional* or *pernicious.* The approbation of a bill implies, that he does not think it either the one or the other. And it makes him responsible to the community for this opinion. The measure becomes his by adoption. Nor could he escape a portion of the blame, which should finally attach itself to a bad measure, to which he had given his consent.

I am prepared for some declamation against the principles which have been laid down. Some plausible flourishes have already been indulged. And it is to be expected, that the public ear will be still further assailed with the commonplace topics, that so readily present themselves, and are so dexterously retailed by the traffickers in popular prejudice. But it need never be feared to submit a solid truth to the deliberate and final opinion of an enlightened and sober people.

What! (it will probably be asked) is a man to sacrifice his conscience and his judgement to an office? Is he to be a dumb spectator of measures which he deems subversive of the rights or interests of his fellow-citizens? Is he to postpone to the frivolous rules of a false complaisance, or the arbitrary dictates of a tyrannical decorum, the higher duty, which he owes to the community?

I answer, No! he is to do none of these things. If he cannot coalesce with those, with whom he is associated, as far as the rules of official decorum, propriety & obligation may require, without abandoning what he conceives to be the true interest of the community, let him place himself in a situation in which he will experience no collision of opposite duties. Let him not cling to the honor of emolument of an office whichever it may be that attracts him, and content himself with defending the injured rights of the people by obscure or indirect means. Let him renounce a situation which is a clog upon his patriotism; tell the people that he could no longer continue in it without forfeiting his duty to them, and that he had quitted it to be more at liberty to afford them his best services.

Such is the course which would be indicated by a firm and virtuous independence of character. Such the course that would be pursued by a man attentive to unite the sense of delicacy with the sense of duty—in earnest about the pernicious tendency of public measures, and more solicitous to act the disinterested friend of the people, than the interested ambitious and intriguing head of a party.

METULLUS.

THE DEFENCE NO. I
1792–1795

Although no precise date can be assigned to the following draft, it is clear that Hamilton's criticism of the spirit of faction was written with a view to the attacks of the Jeffersonian faction on the Hamiltonian programs and policies of Washington's administration.

Party-Spirit is an inseparable appendage of human nature. It grows naturally out of the rival passions of Men, and is therefore to be found in all Governments. But there is no political truth better established by experience nor more to be deprecated in itself, than that this most dangerous spirit is apt to rage with greatest violence, in governments of the popular kind, and is at once their most common and their most fatal disease. Hence the disorders, convulsions, and tumults, which have so often disturbed the repose, marred the happiness, and overturned the liberties of republics; enabling the leaders of the parties to become the Masters & oppressors of the People.

It is the lot of all human institutions, even those of the most perfect kind, to have defects as well as excellencies—ill as well as good propensities. This results from the imperfection of the Institutor, Man.

Thus it happens, that admidst the numerous and transcendant advantages of republican systems of government, there are some byasses which tend to counteract their advantages, and which to render these permanent, require to be carefully guarded against. That which has been noticed, a too strong tendency toward party divisions, does not require least a vigilant circumspection.

What then ought to be & will be the conduct of wise and good men? Will it be their constant effort to nourish this propensity—to stimulate the restless and uneasy passions of the community—to sow groundless jealousies of public men—to destroy the confidence of the people in their tried and faithful friends—to agitate their minds with constant apprehensions of visionary danger—to disseminate their own ignorant and rash suspicions as authentic proofs of criminality in those with whom they differ in opinion—to blast with the foulest stains on the slightest pretences reputations which were unsullied till they began to invent their calumnies.

There can be no difficulty in answering these questions in the Negative.

Wise and virtuous men could not fail to pursue an opposite course. They will endeavour to repress the spirit of faction, as one of the most dangerous enemies to republican liberty—to calm and sooth those angry sensations, which in the best administered governments will spring up from the dissimilar manner in which different laws will affect different Interests of the Community. Instead of imputing crime and misconduct to public men where none exists they will rather endeavour to palliate their errors, when connected with good intention and an honest zeal, and will be ready to excuse those lesser deviations from strict rules, which in the complicated affairs of gov-

390

ernment will more or less occur at all times but which in the infant establishments of a new governmt. were to be calculated upon as inevitable. Instead of labouring to destroy they will endeavour to strengthen the confidence of the people in those to whom they have entrusted their affairs—if there is reasonable evidence that their conduct is the main guided by upright intelligent & disinterested zeal for the public interest. They will be cautious of censure and the censure which they may be at any time compelled to bestow will be preceded by due examination and tempered with moderation and candour. They would shudder at the idea of exhibiting as a Culprit & Plunderer of the Nation a man who is sacrificing the interests of himself & his family to an honest zeal for

with no motive more selfish than that of acquiring the esteem & applause of his fellow Citizens.

But how it may be asked shall we distinguish the virtuous Patriot, who is endeavouring to inflict punishment upon delinquency and disgrace upon demerit from the factious Partisan who is labouring to undermine the faithful friend of his Country and to destroy the Rival he envies & the Competitor he fears?

There are different ways of making the distinction. From the matter and from the manner of the attack which is at any time made—

DEFENSE OF THE PRESIDENT'S NEUTRALITY PROCLAMATION
MAY 1793

In the following paper, Hamilton attacks the motives of those who opposed President Washington's Neutrality Proclamation of 1793 relative to the war between England and revolutionary France. It should be read in conjunction with Hamilton's Pacificus Papers, which attempt to counter the criticisms of the president's issuance of that proclamation.

Philadelphia, May, 1793

1. It is a melancholy truth, which every new political occurrence more and more unfolds, that there is a discription of men in this country, irreconcileably adverse to the government of the United

States; whose exertions, whatever be the springs of them, whether infatuation or depravity or both, tend to disturb the tranquillity order and prosperity of this now peaceable flourishing and truly happy land. A real and enlightened friend to public felicity cannot observe new confirmations of this fact, without feeling a deep and poignant regret, that human nature should be so refractory and perverse; that amidst a profusion of the bounties and blessings of Providence, political as well as natural, inviting to contentment and gratitude, there should still be found men disposed to cherish and propagate disquietude and alarm; to render suspected and detested the instruments of the felicity, in which they partake; to sacrifice the most substantial advantages, that ever fell to the lot of a people at the shrine of personal envy rivalship and animosity, to the instigations of a turbulent and criminal ambition, or to the treacherous phantoms of an ever craving and never to be satisfied spirit of innovation; a spirit, which seems to suggest to its votaries that the most natural and happy state of Society is a state of continual revolution and change—that the welfare of a nation is in exact ratio to the rapidity of the political vicissitudes, which it undergoes—to the frequency and violence of the tempests with which it is agitated.

2 Yet so the fact unfortunately is—such men there certainly are—and it is essential to our dearest interests to the preservation of peace and good order to the dignity and independence of our public councils—to the real and permanent security of liberty and property—that the Citizens of the UStates should open their eyes to the true characters and designs of the men alluded to—should be upon their guard against their insidious and ruinous machinations.

3 At this moment a most dangerous combination exists. Those who for some time past have been busy in undermining the constitution and government of the UStates, by indirect attacks, by labouring to render its measures odious, by striving to destroy the confidence of the people in its administration—are now meditating a more direct and destructive war against it—a⟨nd⟩ embodying and arranging their forces and systematising their efforts. Secret clubs are formed and private consultations held. Emissaries are dispatched to distant parts of the United States to effect a concert of views and measures, among the members and partisans of the disorganising corps, in the several states. The language in the confidential circles is that the constitution of the United States is too complex a system—that it savours too much of the pernicious doctrine of "ballances and checks" that it requires to be simplified in its structure, to be purged of some monarchical and aristocratic ingredients which are said to have found their way into it and to be stripped of some dangerous prerogatives, with which it is pretended to be invested.

392

4 The noblest passion of the human soul, which no where burns with so pure and bright a flame, as in the breasts of the people of the UStates, is if possible to be made subservient to this fatal project. That zeal for the liberty of mankind, which produced so universal a sympathy in the cause of France in the first stages of its revolution, and which, it is supposed, has not yet yielded to the just reprobation, which a sober temperate and humane people, friends of religion, social order, and justice, enemies to tumult and massacre, to the wanton and lawless shedding of human blood cannot but bestow upon those extravagancies excesses and outrages, which have sullied and which endanger that cause—that laudable, it is not too much to say that holy zeal is intended by every art of misrepresentation and deception to be made the instrument first of controuling finally of overturning the Government of the Union.

5 The ground which has been so wisely taken by the Executive of the UStates, in regard to the present war of Europe against France, is to be the pretext of this mischievous attempt. The people are if possible to be made to believe, that the Proclamation of neutrality issued by the President of the US was unauthorised illegal and officious— inconsistent with the treaties and plighted faith of the Nation— inconsistent with a due sense of gratitude to France for the services rendered us in our late contest for independence and liberty— inconsistent with a due regard for the progress and success of republican principles. Already the presses begin to groan with invective against the Chief Magistrate of the Union, for that prudent and necessary measure; a measure calculated to manifest to the World the pacific position of the Government and to caution the citizens of the UStates against practices, which would tend to involve us in a War the most unequal and calamitous, in which it is possible for a Country to be engaged—a war which would not be unlikely to prove pregnant with still greater dangers and disasters, than that by which we established our existence as an Independent Nation.

6 What is the true solution of this extraordinary appearance? Are the professed the real motives of its authors? They are not. The true object is to disparage in the opinion and affections of his fellow citizens that man who at the head of our armies fought so successfully for the Liberty and Independence, which are now our pride and our boast—who during the war supported the hopes, united the hearts and nerved the arm of his countrymen—who at the close of it, unseduced by ambition & the love of power, soothed and appeased the discontents of his suffering companions in arms, and with them left the proud scenes of a victorious field for the modest retreats of private life—who could only have been drawn out of these favourite retreats, to aid in the glorious work of ingrafting that liberty, which his sword

393

had contributed to win, upon a stock of which it stood in need and without which it could not flourish—endure—a firm adequate national Government—who at this moment sacrifices his tranquillity and every favourite pursuit to the peremptory call of his country to aid in giving solidity to a fabric, which he has assisted in rearing—whose whole conduct has been one continued proof of his rectitude moderation disinterestedness and patriotism, who whether the evidence of a uniform course of virtuous public actions be considered, or the motives likely to actuate a man placed precisely in his situation be estimated, it may safely be pronounced, can have no other ambition than that of doing good to his Country & transmitting his fame unimpaired to posterity. For what or for whom is he to hazard that rich harvest of glory, which he has acquired that unexampled veneration and love of his fellow Citizens, which he so eminently possesses?

7 Yet the men alluded to, while they contend with affected zeal for gratitude towards a foreign Nation, which in assisting us was and ought to have been influenced by considerations relative to its own interest—forgetting what is due to a fellow Citizen, who at every hazard rendered essential services to his Country from the most patriotic motives—insidiously endeavour to despoil him of that precious reward of his services, the confidence and approbation of his fellow Citizens.

8 The present attempt is but the renewal in another form of an attack some time since commenced, and which was only dropped because it was perceived to have excited a general indignation. Domestic arrangements of mere convenience, calculated to reconcile the œconomy of time with the attentions of decorum and civility were then the topics of malevolent declamation. A more serious article of charge is now opened and seems intended to be urged with greater earnestness and vigour. The merits of it shall be examined in one or two succeeding papers, I trust in a manner, that will evince to every candid mind to futility.

9 To be an able and firm supporter of the Government of the Union is in the eyes of the men referred to a crime sufficient to justify the most malignant persecution. Hence the attacks which have been made and repeated with such persevering industry upon more than one public Character in that Government. Hence the effort which is now going on to depreciate in the eyes and estimation of the People the man whom their unanimous suffrages have placed at the head of it.

10 Hence the pains which are taking to inculcate a discrimination between *principles* and *men* and to represent an attachment to the one as a species of war against the other; an endeavour, which has a tendency to stifle or weaken one of the best and most useful feelings

of the human heart—a reverence for merit—and to take away one of the strongest incentives to public virtue—the expectation of public esteem.

11 A solicitude for the character who is attacked forms no part of the motives to this comment. He has deserved too much, and his countrymen are too sensible of it to render any advocation of him necessary. If his virtues and services do not secure his fame and ensure to him the unchangeable attachment of his fellow Citizens, twere in vain to attempt to prop them by anonymous panygeric.

12 The design of the observations which have been made is merely to awaken the public attention to the views of a party engaged in a dangerous conspiracy against the tranquillity and happiness of their country. Aware that their hostile aims against the Government can never succeed til they have subverted the confidence of the people in its present Chief Magistrate, they have at length permitted the suggestions of their enmity to betray them into this hopeless and culpable attempt. If we can destroy his popularity (say they) our work is more than half completed.

13 In proportion as the Citizens of the UStates value the constitution on which their union and happiness depend, in proportion as they tender the blessings of peace and deprecate the calamities of War—ought to be their watchfulness against this success of the artifices which will be employed to endanger that constitution and those blessings. A mortal blow is aimed at both.

14 It imports them infinitely not to be deceived by the protestations which are made—that no harm is meditated against the Constitution—that no design is entertained to involve the peace of the Country. These appearances are necessary to the accomplishment of the plan which has been formed. It is known that the great body of the People are attached to the constitution. It would therefore defeat the intention of destroying it to avow that it exists. It is also known that the People of the UStates are firmly attached to peace. It would consequently frustrate the design of engaging them in the War to tell them that such an object is in contemplation.

15 A more artful course has therefore been adopted. Professions of good will to the Constitution are made without reserve: But every possible art is employed to render the administration and the most zealous and useful friends of the Government odious. The reasoning is obvious. If the people can be persuaded to dislike all the measures of the Government and to dislike all or the greater part of those who have [been] most conspicuous in establishing or conducting it—the passage from this to the dislike and change of the constitution will not be long nor difficult. The abstract idea of regard for a constitution on paper will not long resist a thorough detestation of its practice.

395

16 In like manner, professions of a disposition to preserve the peace of the Country are liberally made. But the means of effecting the end are condemned; and exertions are used to prejudice the community against them. A proclamation of neutrality in the most cautious form is represented as illegal—contrary to our engagements with and our duty towards one of the belligerent powers. The plain inference is that in the opinion of these characters the UStates are under obligations which do not permit them to be neutral. Of course they are in a situation to become a party in the War from duty.

17 Pains are likewise taken to inflame the zeal of the people for the cause of France and to excite their resentments against the powers at War with her. To what end all this—but to beget if possible a temper in the community which may overrule the moderate or pacific views of the Government.

PACIFICUS NO. I
JUNE 29, 1793

One of the most controversial opinions of Hamilton's political career was his justification of executive independence in foreign policy questions in the debate over Washington's Neutrality Proclamation. That proclamation was criticized as an encroachment on the powers of the Senate, because the Senate has a right to be consulted in matters of foreign policy, and as an encroachment on the powers of Congress, because the proclamation could in effect commit the nation to war without the consent of Congress. Hamilton argues in the following essay that the president's power to make such a proclamation issues from the general grant of executive power, which includes conducting foreign relations, from the president's primary responsibility in the formation of treaties, and from the power of the execution of the laws, of which treaties form a part.

Philadelphia, June 29, 1793

As attempts are making very dangerous to the peace, and it is to be feared not very friendly to the constitution of the UStates—it becomes the duty of those who wish well to both to endeavour to prevent their success.

The objections which have been raised against the Proclamation of Neutrality lately issued by the President have been urged in a spirit of acrimony and invective, which demonstrates, that more was in view than merely a free discussion of an important public measure; that the discussion covers a design of weakening the confidence of the People in the author of the measure; in order to remove or lessen a powerful obstacle to the success of an opposition to the Government, which however it may change its form, according to circumstances, seems still to be adhered to and pursued with persevering Industry.

This Reflection adds to the motives connected with the measure itself to recommend endeavours by proper explanations to place it in a just light. Such explanations at least cannot but be satisfactory to those who may not have leisure or opportunity for pursuing themselves an investigation of the subject, and who may wish to perceive that the policy of the Government is not inconsistent with its obligations or its honor.

The objections in question fall under three heads—

1   That the Proclamation was without authority

2   That it was contrary to our treaties with France

3   That it was contrary to the gratitude, which is due from this to that country; for the succours rendered us in our own Revolution.

4   That it was out of time & unnecessary.

In order to judge of the solidity of the first of these objection[s], it is necessary to examine what is the nature and design of a proclamation of neutrality.

The true nature & design of such an act is—to *make known* to the powers at War and to the Citizens of the Country, whose Government does the Act that such country is in the condition of a Nation at Peace with the belligerent parties, and under no obligations of Treaty, to become an *associate in the war* with either of them; that this being its situation its intention is to observe a conduct conformable with it and to perform towards each the duties of neutrality; and as a consequence of this state of things, to give warning to all within its jurisdiction to abstain from acts that shall contravene those duties, under the penalties which the laws of the land (of which the law of Nations is a part) annexes to acts of contravention.

This, and no more, is conceived to be the true import of a Proclamation of Neutrality.

It does not imply, that the Nation which makes the declaration will forbear to perform to any of the warring Powers any stipulations in Treaties which can be performed without rendering it an *associate* or *party* in the War. It therefore does not imply in our case, that the

397

UStates will not make those distinctions, between the present belligerent powers, which are stipulated in the 17th and 22d articles of our
Treaty with France; because these distinctions are not incompatible
with a state of neutrality; they will in no shape render the UStates an
associate or *party* in the War. This must be evident, when it is considered, that even to furnish *determinate* succours, of a certain number
of Ships or troops, to a Power at War, in consequence of *antecedent
treaties having no particular reference to the existing war*, is not inconsistent with neutrality; a position well established by the doctrines of
Writers and the practice of Nations.*

But no special aids, succours or favors having relation to war, not
positively and precisely stipulated by some Treaty of the above description, can be afforded to either party, without a breach of neutrality.

In stating that the Proclamation of Neutrality does not imply the
non performance of any stipulations of Treaties which are not of a
nature to make the Nation an associate or party in the war, it is
conceded that an execution of the clause of Guarantee contained in
the 11th article of our Treaty of Alliance with France would be contrary to the sense and spirit of the Proclamation; because it would
engage us with our whole force as an *associate* or *auxiliary* in the War;
it would be much more than the case of a definite limited succour,
previously ascertained.

It follows that the Proclamation is virtually a manifestation of the
sense of the Government that the UStates are, *under the circumstances
of the case, not bound* to execute the clause of Guarantee.

If this be a just view of the true force and import of the Proclamation, it will remain to see whether the President in issuing it acted
within his proper sphere, or stepped beyond the bounds of his constitutional authority and duty.

It will not be disputed that the management of the affairs of this
country with foreign nations is confided to the Government of the
UStates.

It can as little be disputed, that a Proclamation of Neutrality,
where a Nation is at liberty to keep out of a War in which other
Nations are engaged and means so to do, is a *usual* and a *proper*
measure. *Its main object and effect are to prevent the Nation being immediately responsible for acts done by its citizens, without the privity or
connivance of the Government, in contravention of the principles of neutrality.**

*See Vatel Book III Chap. VI §101.
*See Vatel Book III Chap VII § 113.

An object this of the greatest importance to a Country whose true interest lies in the preservation of peace.

The inquiry then is—what department of the Government of the UStates is the prop⟨er⟩ one to make a declaration of Neutrality in the cases in which the engagements ⟨of⟩ the Nation permit and its interests require such a declaration.

A correct and well informed mind will discern at once that it can belong neit⟨her⟩ to the Legislative nor Judicial Department and of course must belong to the Executive.

The Legislative Department is not the *organ* of intercourse between the UStates and foreign Nations. It is charged neither with *making* nor *interpreting* Treaties. It is therefore not naturally that Organ of the Government which is to pronounce the existing condition of the Nation, with regard to foreign Powers, or to admonish the Citizens of their obligations and duties as founded upon that condition of things. Still less is it charged with enforcing the execution and observance of these obligations and those duties.

It is equally obvious that the act in question is foreign to the Judiciary Department of the Government. The province of that Department is to decide litigations in particular cases. It is indeed charged with the interpretation of treaties; but it exercises this function only in the litigated cases; that is where contending parties bring before it a specific controversy. It has no concern with pronouncing upon the external political relations of Treaties between Government and Government. This position is too plain to need being insisted upon.

It must then of necessity belong to the Executive Department to exercise the function in Question—when a proper case for the exercise of it occurs.

It appears to be connected with that department in various capacities, as the *organ* of intercourse between the Nation and foreign Nations—as the interpreter of the National Treaties in those cases in which the Judiciary is not competent, that is in the cases between Government and Government—as that Power, which is charged with the Execution of the Laws, of which Treaties form a part—as that Power which is charged with the command and application of the Public Force.

This view of the subject is so natural and obvious—so analogous to general theory and practice—that no doubt can be entertained of its justness, unless such doubt can be deduced from particular provisions of the Constitution of the UStates.

Let us see then if cause for such doubt is to be found in that constituion.

399

The second Article of the Constitution of the UStates, section 1st, establishes this general Proposition, That "The EXECUTIVE POWER shall be vested in a President of the United States of America."

The same article in a succeeding Section proceeds to designate particular cases of Executive Power. It declares among other things that the President shall be Commander in Cheif of the army and navy of the UStates and of the Militia of the several states when called into the actual service of the UStates, that he shall have power by and with the advice of the senate to make treaties; that it shall be his duty to receive ambassadors and other public Ministers and to take care that the laws be faithfully executed.

It would not consist with the rules of sound construction to consider this enumeration of particular authorities as derogating from the more comprehensive grant contained in the general clause, further than as it may be coupled with express restrictions or qualifications; as in regard to the cooperation of the Senate in the appointment of Officers and the making of treaties; which are qualifica⟨tions⟩ of the general executive powers of appointing officers and making treaties: Because the difficulty of a complete and perfect specification of all the cases of Executive authority would naturally dictate the use of general terms—and would render it improbable that a specification of certain particulars was designd as a substitute for those terms, when antecedently used. The different mode of expression employed in the constitution in regard to the two powers the Legislative and the Executive serves to confirm this inference. In the article which grants the legislative powers of the Governt. the expressions are—"*All Legislative powers herein granted shall be vested in a Congress of the UStates;*" in that which grants the Executive Power the expressions are, as already quoted "The EXECUTIVE PO⟨WER⟩ shall be vested in a President of the UStates of America."

The enumeration ought rather therefore to be considered as intended by way of greater caution, to specify and regulate the principal articles implied in the definition of Executive Power; leaving the rest to flow from the general grant of that power, interpreted in conformity to other parts ⟨of⟩ the constitution and to the principles of free government.

The general doctrine then of our constitution is, that the EXECUTIVE POWER of the Nation is vested in the President; subject only to the *exceptions* and *qu[a]lifications* which are expressed in the instrument.

Two of these have been already noticed—the participation of the Senate in the appointment of Officers and the making of Treaties. A third remains to be mentioned the right of the Legislature "to declare war and grant letters of marque and reprisal."

With these exceptions the EXECUTIVE POWER of the Union is completely lodged in the President. This mode of construing the Constitution has indeed been recognized by Congress in formal acts, upon full consideration and debate. The power of removal from office is an inportant instance.

And since upon general principles for reasons already given, the issuing of a proclamation of neutrality is merely an Executive Act; since also the general Executive Power of the Union is vested in the President, the conclusion is, that the step, which has been taken by him, is liable to no just exception on the score of authority.

It may be observed that this Inference w⟨ould⟩ be just if the power of declaring war had ⟨not⟩ been vested in the Legislature, but that ⟨this⟩ power naturally includes the right of judg⟨ing⟩ whether the Nation is under obligations to m⟨ake⟩ war or not.

The answer to this is, that however true it may be, that th⟨e⟩ right of the Legislature to declare wa⟨r⟩ includes the right of judging whether the N⟨ation⟩ be under obligations to make War or not—it will not follow that the Executive is in any case excluded from a similar right of Judgment, in the execution of its own functions.

If the Legislature have a right to make war on the one hand—it is on the other the duty of the Executive to preserve Peace till war is declared; and in fulfilling that duty, it must necessarily possess a right of judging what is the nature of the obligations which the treaties of the Country impose on the Government; and when in pursuance of this right it has concluded that there is nothing in them inconsistent with a *state* of neutrality, it becomes both its province and its duty to enforce the laws incident to that state of the Nation. The Executive is charged with the execution of all laws, the laws of Nations as well as the Municipal law, which recognises and adopts those laws. It is consequently bound, by faithfully executing the laws of neutrality, when that is the state of the Nation, to avoid giving a cause of war to foreign Powers.

This is the direct and proper end of the proclamation of neutrality. It declares to the UStates their situation with regard to the Powers at war and makes known to the Community that the laws incident to that situation will be enforced. In doing this, it conforms to an established usage of Nations, the operation of which as before remarked is to obviate a responsibility on the part of the whole Society, for secret and unknown violations of the rights of any of the warring parties by its citizens.

Those who object to the proclamation will readily admit that it is the right and duty of the Executive to judge of, or to interpret, those articles of our treaties which give to France particular privileges, in order to the enforcement of those privileges: But the necessary consequence of this is, that the Executive must judge what are the proper bounds of those privileges—what rights are given to other nations by our treaties with them—what rights the law of Nature and Nations gives and our treaties permit, in respect to those Nations with whom we have no treaties; in fine what are the reciprocal rights and obligations of the United States & of all & each of the powers at War.

The right of the Executive to receive ambassadors and other public Ministers may serve to illustrate the relative duties of the Executive and Legislative Departments. This right includes that of judging, in the case of a Revolution of Government in a foreign Country, whether the new rulers are competent organs of the National Will and ought to ⟨be⟩ recognised or not: And where a treaty antecedently exists between the UStates and such nation that right involves the power of giving operation or not to such treaty. For until the new Government is *acknowledged*, the treaties between the nations, as far at least as regards *public* rights, are of course suspended.

This power of determ[in]ing virtually in the case supposed upon the operation of national Treaties as a consequence, of the power to receive ambassadors and other public Ministers, is an important instance of the right of the Executive to decide the obligations of the Nation with regard to foreign Nations. To apply it to the case of France, if the⟨re⟩ had been a Treaty of alliance *offensive* ⟨and⟩ defensive between the UStates and that Coun⟨try,⟩ the unqualified acknowlegement of the new Government would have put the UStates in a condition to become an associate in the War in which France was engaged—and would have laid the Legislature under an obligation, if required, and there was otherwise no valid excuse, of exercising its power of declaring war.

This serves as an example of the right of the Executive, in certain cases, to determine the condition of the Nation, though it may consequentially affect the proper or improper exercise of the Power of the Legislature to declare war. The Executive indeed cannot control the exercise of that power—further than by the exer[c]ise of its general right of objecting to all acts of the Legislature; liable to being overruled by two thirds of both houses of Congress. The Legislature is free to perform its own duties according to its own sense of them— though the Executive in the exercise of its constitutional powers, may establish an antecedent state of things which ought to weigh in the legislative decisions. From the division of the Executive Power there results, in referrence to it, a *concurrent* authority, in the distributed cases.

Hence in the case stated, though treaties can only be made by the President and Senate, their activity may be continued or suspended by the President alone.

No objection has been made to the Presidents having acknowleged the Republic of France, by the Reception of its Minister, without having consulted the Senate; though that body is connected with him in the making of Treaties, and though the consequence of his act of reception is to give operation to the Treaties heretofore made with that Country: But he is censured for having declared the UStates to be in a state of peace & neutrality, with regard to the Powers at War; because the right of *changing* that state & *declaring war* belongs to the Legislature.

It deserves to be remarked, that as the participation of the senate in the making of Treaties and the power of the Legislature to declare war are exceptions out of the general "Executive Power" vested in the President, they are to be construed strictly—and ought to be extended no further than is essential to their execution.

While therefore the Legislature can alone declare war, can alone actually transfer the nation from a state of Peace to a state of War—it belongs to the "Executive Power," to do whatever else the laws of Nations cooperating with the Treaties of the Country enjoin, in the intercourse of the UStates with foreign Powers.

In this distribution of powers the wisdom of our constitution is manifested. It is the province and duty of the Executive to preserve to the Nation the blessings of peace. The Legislature alone can interrupt those blessings, by placing the Nation in a state of War.

But though it has been thought adviseable to vindicate the authority of the Executive on this broad and comprehensive ground—it was not absolutely necessary to do so. That clause of the constitution which makes it his duty to "take care that the laws be faithfully executed" might alone have been relied upon, and this simple process of argument pursued.

The President is the constitutional EXECUTOR of the laws. Our Treaties and the laws of Nations form a part of the law of the land. He who is to execute the laws must first judge for himself of their meaning. In order to the observance of that conduct, which the laws of nations combined with our treaties prescribed to this country, in reference to the present War in Europe, it was necessary for the President to judge for himself whether there was any thing in our treaties incompatible with an adherence to neutrality. Having judged that there was not, he had a right, and if in his opinion the interests of the

Nation required it, it was his duty, as Executor of the laws, to proclaim the neutrality of the Nation, to exhort all persons to observe it, and to warn them of the penalties which would attend its non observance.

The Proclamation has been represented as enacting some new law. This is a view of it entirely erroneous. It only proclaims a *fact* with regard to the *existing state* of the Nation, informs the citizens of what the laws previously established require of them in that state, & warns them that these laws will be put in execution against the Infractors of them.

PACIFICUS NO. IV
JULY 10, 1793

Washington's Neutrality Proclamation had the effect of annulling the eleventh article of America's 1778 Treaty of Alliance with France. One of the arguments made in opposition to the proclamation was that it was inconsistent with the gratitude due France for assistance to America during its war with England. Hamilton maintains in the following essay that mutual interest and reciprocal advantage are much sounder bases for relations among nations than gratitude. This is an important statement because it appears to call for a concentration less on moralism than on the realities of power. Hamilton confronts moralism or the doctrine that individual morality should be the standard for international conduct with the demand for the preservation of the state. He does not, however, divorce politics from morality. He says simply that the rule of morality is not the same between nations as between individuals. He never asserts that political life is less moral than private life. What Hamilton clearly states is that political life, generally speaking, is more moral than private life in the sense that it offers a greater opportunity for moral action. That moral action is directed toward collective rather than individual conduct.

Philadelphia, July 10, 1793

A third objection to the Proclamation is, that it is inconsistent with the gratitude due to France, for the services rendered us in our own Revolution.

Those who make this objection disavow at the same time all intention to advocate the position that the United States *ought to take part in the War*. They profess to be friends to our remaining at Peace. What then do they mean by the objection?

If it be no breach of gratitude to refrain from joining France in the War—how can it be a breach of gratitude to declare that such is our disposition and intention?

The two positions are at variance with each other; and the true inference is either that those who make the objection really wish to engage this country in the war, or that they seek a pretext for censuring the conduct of the chief Magistrate, for some purpose, very different from the public good.

They endeavour in vain to elude this inference by saying, that the Proclamation places France upon an *equal* footing with her enemies; while our Treaties require distinctions in her favour, and our relative situation would dictate kind offices to her, which ought not to be granted to her adversaries.

They are not ignorant, that the Proclamation is reconcileable with both those objects, as far as they have any foundation in truth or propriety.

It has been shewn, that the promise of "a *friendly* and *impartial* conduct" towards all the belligerent powers is not inconsistent with the performance of any stipulations in our treaties, which would not include our becoming an associate in the Wars, and it has been observed, that the conduct of the Executive, in regard to the 17th and 22 articles of the Treaty of Commerce, is an unequivocal comment upon those terms. The expressions indeed were naturally to be understood with the exception of those matters of positive compact, which would not amount to taking part in the War; for a nation then observes a friendly and impartial conduct, towards two powers at war—when it only performs to one of them what it is obliged to do by the positive stipulations of antecedent treaties; those stipulations not amounting to a participation in the war.

Neither do those expressions imply, that the UStates will not exercise their discretion, in doing kind offices to some of the parties, without extending them to the others; *so long as those offices have no relation to war:* For kind offices of that description may, consistently with neutrality, be shewn to one party and refused to another.

If the objectors mean that the UStates ought to favour France, *in thin⟨gs relating⟩ to war and where they are not bound ⟨to do it⟩ by Treaty*— they must in this case al⟨so abandon⟩ their pretension of being friends to pea⟨ce. For⟩ such a conduct would be a violation ⟨of neutrality,⟩ which could not fail to produce war.

405

⟨It⟩ follows then that the ⟨proclamation⟩ is reconcilable with all that those ⟨who⟩ censure it contend for; taking them upon their own ground—that nothing is to be done incompatible with the preservation of Peace.

But though this would be a sufficient answer to the objection under consideration; yet it may not be without use to indulge some reflections on this very favourite topic of gratitude to France; since it is at this shrine we are continually invited to sacrifice the true interests of the Country; as if *"All for love and the world well lost"* were a fundamental maxim in politics.

Faith and Justice between nations are virtues of a nature sacred and unequivocal. They cannot be too strongly inculcated nor too highly respected. Their obligations are definite and positive their utility unquestionable: they relate to objects, which with probity and sincerity generally admit of being brought within clear and intelligible rules.

But the same cannot be said of gratitude. It is not very often between nations, that it can be pronounced with certainty, that there exists a solid foundation for the sentiment—and how far it can justifiably be permitted to operate is always a question of still greater difficulty.

The basis of gratitude, is a benefit received or intended, which there was no right to claim, originating in a regard to the interest or advantage of the party, on whom the benefit is or is meant to be conferred. If a service is rendered from views *chiefly* relative to the immediate interest of the party, who renders it, and is productive of reciprocal advantages, there seems scarcely in such a case to be an adequate basis for a sentiment like that of gratitude. The effect would be disproportioned to the cause; if it ought to beget more than a disposition to render in turn a correspondent good office, founded on *mutual* interest and *reciprocal* advantage. But gratitude would require more than this; it would require, to a certain extent, even a sacrifice of the interest of the party obliged to the service or benefit of the party by whom the obligation had been conferred.

Between individuals, occasion is not unfrequently given to the exercise of gratitude. Instances of conferring benefits, from kind and benevolent dispositions or feelings towards the person benefitted, without any other interest on the part of the person, who confers the benefit, than the pleasure of doing a good action, occur every day among individuals. But among nations they perhaps never occur. It may be affirmed as a general principle, that the predominant motive of go⟨od⟩ offices from one nation to another is the interest or advantage of the Nations, which performs them.

Indeed the rule of morality is ⟨in⟩ this respect not exactly the same between Natio⟨ns⟩ as between individuals. The duty of making ⟨its⟩ own welfare the guide of its action⟨s⟩ is much stronger upon the former than upon the latter; in proportion to the greater magnitude and importance of national compared with individual happiness, to the greater permanency of the effects of national than of individual conduct. Existing Millions and for the most part future generations ar⟨e⟩ concerned in the present measures of a government: While the consequences of the private actions of ⟨an⟩ individual, for the most part, terminate with himself or are circumscribed within a narrow compass.

Whence it follows, that an individual may on numerous occasions meritoriously indulge the emotions of generosity and benevolence; not only without an eye to, but even at the expence of his own interest. But a Nation can rarely be justified in pursuing ⟨a similar⟩ course; and when it does so ought to confine itself within much stricter bounds.* Good offices, which are indifferent to the Interest of a Nation performing them, or which are compensated by the existence or expectation of some reasonable equivalent or which produce an essential good to the nation, to which they are rendered, without real detriment to the affairs of the nation rendering them, prescribe the limits of national generosity or benevolence.

It is not meant here to advocate a policy absolutely selfish or interested in nations; but to shew that a policy regulated by their own interest, as far as justice and good faith permit, is, and ought to be their prevailing policy: and that either to ascribe to them a different principle of action, or to deduce from the supposition of it arguments for a self-denying and self-sacrificing gratitude on the part of a Nation, which may have received from another good offices, is to misconceive or mistake what usually are and ought to be the springs of National Conduct.

These general reflections will be auxiliary to a just estimate of our real situation with regard to France; of which a close view will be taken in a succeeding Paper.

*This conclusion derives confirmation from the reflection, that under every form of government, RULERS are only TRUSTEES for the happiness and interest of their nation, and cannot, consistently with their trust, follow the suggestions of kindness or humanity towards others, to the prejudice of their constituent.

THE TULLY LETTERS, AN INTRODUCTION

The Whiskey Rebellion broke out in 1794 when the farmers of the western counties of Pennsylvania refused to pay the whiskey excise levied by the national government as a revenue-raising device. In the following letters, Hamilton discusses the importance of respect for the law in retaining freedom as he defends the policies of the Washington administration in suppressing the rebellion.

TULLY NO. III
AUGUST 28, 1794

Philadelphia, August 28, 1794

For the American Daily Advertiser.
To the PEOPLE *of the* UNITED STATES.
LETTER III.

If it were to be asked, What is the most sacred duty and the greatest source of security in a Republic? the answer would be, An inviolable respect for the Constitution and Laws—the first growing out of the last. It is by this, in a great degree, that the rich and powerful are to be restrained from enterprises against the common liberty—operated upon by the influence of a general sentiment, by their interest in the principle, and by the obstacles which the habit it produces erects against innovation and encroachment. It is by this, in a still greater degree, that caballers, intriguers, and demagogues are prevented from climbing on the shoulders of faction to the tempting seats of usurpation and tyranny.

Were it not that it might require too lengthy a discussion, it would not be difficult to demonstrate, that a large and well organized Republic can scarcely lose its liberty from any other cause than that of anarchy, to which a contempt of the laws is the high road.

But, without entering into so wide a field, it is sufficient to present to your view a more simple and a more obvious truth, which is this—that a sacred respect for the constitutional law is the vital principle, the sustaining energy of a free government.

Government is frequently and aptly classed under two descriptions, a government of FORCE and a government of LAWS; the first is the definition of despotism—the last, of liberty. But how can a government of laws exist where the laws are disrespected and disobeyed? Government supposes controul. It is the POWER by which individuals in society are kept from doing injury to each other and are bro't to co-operate to a common end. The instruments by which it must act are either the AUTHORITY of the Laws or FORCE. If the first be destroyed, the last must be substituted; and where this becomes the ordinary instrument of government there is an end to liberty.

Those, therefore, who preach doctrines, or set examples, which undermine or subvert the authority of the laws, lead us from freedom to slavery; they incapacitate us for a GOVERNMENT of LAWS, and consequently prepare the way for one of FORCE, for mankind MUST HAVE GOVERNMENT OF ONE SORT OR ANOTHER.

There are indeed great and urgent cases where the bounds of the constitution are manifestly transgressed, or its constitutional authorities so exercised as to produce unequivocal oppression on the community, and to render resistance justifiable. But such cases can give no colour to the resistance by a comparatively inconsiderable part of a community, of constitutional laws distinguished by no extraordinary features of rigour or oppression, and acquiesced in by the BODY OF THE COMMUNITY.

Such a resistance is treason against society, against liberty, against every thing that ought to be dear to a free, enlightened, and prudent people. To tolerate were to abandon your most precious interests. Not to subdue it, were to tolerate it. Those who openly or covertly dissuade you from exertions adequate to the occasion are your worst enemies. They treat you either as fools or cowards, too weak to perceive your interest and duty, or too dastardly to pursue them. They therefore merit, and will no doubt meet your contempt.

To the plausible but hollow harangues of such conspirators, ye cannot fail to reply, How long, ye Catilines, will you abuse our patience.

TULLY.

TULLY NO. IV
SEPTEMBER 2, 1794

Philadelphia, September 2, 1794

For the American Daily Advertiser.
To the PEOPLE *of the* UNITED STATES
LETTER IV.

The prediction mentioned in my first letter begins to be fulfilled. Fresh symptoms every moment appear of a dark conspiracy, hostile to your government, to your peace abroad, to your tranquility at home. One of its orators dares to prostitute the name of FRANKLIN, by annexing it to a publication as insidious as it is incendiary. Aware of the folly and the danger of a direct advocation of the cause of the Insurgents, he makes the impudent attempt to inlist your passions in their favour—by false and virulent railings against those who have heretofore represented you in Congress. The fore ground of the piece presented you with a bitter invective against that wise, moderate, and pacific policy, which in all probability will rescue you from the calamities of a foreign war, with an increase of true dignity and with additional lustre to the American name and character. Your Representatives are delineated as corrupt pusylanimous and unworthy of your confidence; because they did not plunge headlong into measures which might have rendered war inevitable; because they contented themselves with preparing for it, instead of making it, leaving the path open to the Executive for one last and solemn effort of negociation—because they did not display either the promptness of gladiators, or the blustering of bullies—but assumed that firm, yet temperate attitude which alone is suited to the Representatives of a brave, but rational People—who deprecated war, tho' they did not fear it—and who have a great and solid interest in peace which ought only to be abandoned when it is unequivocally ascertained that the sacrifice is absolutely due to the vindication of their honor and the preservation of their essential rights—because in fine, your Representatives wished to give an example to the world that the boasted moderation of republican governments was not (like the patriotism of our political barkers) an empty declamation, but a precious reality.

The sallies of a momentary sensibility, roused and stung by injury were excusable. It was not wonderful that the events of war, were under the first impressions heard from good, and even prudent men. But to revive them at this late hour, when fact and reflection unite to condemn them; to arraign a conduct which has elevated the national character to the highest point of true glory—to hope to embark you in the condemnation of that conduct, and to make your indignation against it useful to the cause of Insurrection and Treason, are indications of a wrong-headedness, perverseness, or profligacy, for which it is not easy to find terms of adequate reprobation.

Happily the plotters of mischief know ye not. They derive what they mistake for your image, from an original in their own heated and crooked imaginations and they hope to mould a wise, reflecting and dispassionate people, to purposes which presuppose an ignorant unthinking and turbulent herd.

But the declamations against your Representatives for their love of peace is but the preface to the main design. That design is to alienate you from the support of the laws by the spectre of an "odious excise system, baneful to Liberty, engendered by corruption and nurtured by the INSTRUMENTALITY (favoured word, fruitful source of mountebank wit) of the enemies of Freedom." To urge the execution of that system would manifest it is said an intemperate spirit; and to excite your disapprobation of that course, you are threatened with the danger of a civil war, which is called the consummation of human evil.

To crown the outrage upon your understandings; the Insurgents are represented as men who understand the principles of freedom & know the horrows and distresses of anarchy, and who therefore must have been tempted to hostility against the laws by a RADICAL DEFECT EITHER in the government, or in those entrusted with its administration. How thin the partition which divides the insinuation from the assertion, that the government is in fault, and the insurgents in the right.

Fellow-Citizens; a name, a sound has too often had influence on the affairs of nations; an EXCISE has too long been the successful watch-word of party. It has even sometimes led astray well meaning men. The experiment is now to be tried, whether there be any spell in it of sufficient force to unnerve the arm which it may be found necessary to raise in defence of law and order.

The jinglers who endeavor to cheat us with the sound, have never dared to venture into the fair field of argument. They are conscious that it is easier to declaim than to reason on the subject. They know it to be better to play a game with the passions and prejudices than to engage seriously with the understanding of the auditory.

You have already seen, that the merits of excise Laws are immaterial to the question to be decided—that you have prejudged the

411

point by a solemn constitutional act, and that until you shall have revoked or modified that act, resistance to its operation is a criminal infraction of the social compact, an inversion of the fundamental principles of Republican Government, and a daring attack upon YOUR sovereignty, which you are bound by every motive of duty, and selfpreservation to withstand and defeat. The matter might safely be suffered to rest here; but I shall take a future opportunity to examine the reasonableness of the prejudice which is inculcated against excise laws—and which has become the pretext for excesses tending to dissolve the bands of Society.

Fellow Citizens—You are told, that it will be intemperate to urge the execution of the laws which are resisted—what? will it be indeed intemperate in your Chief Magistrate, sworn to maintain the Constitution, charged faithfully to execute the Laws, and authorized to employ for that purpose force when the ordinary means fail—will it be intemperate in him to exert that force, when the constitution and the laws are opposed by force? Can he answer it to his conscience, to you not to exert it?

Yes, it is said; because the execution of it will produce civil war, the consummation of human evil.

Fellow-Citizens-Civil War is undoubtedly a great evil. It is one that every good man would wish to avoid, and will deplore if inevitable. But it is incomparably a less evil than the destruction of Government. The first brings with it serious but temporary and partial ills— the last undermines the foundations of our security and happiness— where should we be if it were once to grow into a maxim, that force is not to be used against the seditious combinations of parts of the community to resist the laws? This would be to give a CARTE BLANCH to ambition—to licentiousness; to foreign intrigue; to make you the prey of the gold of other nations—the sport of the passions and vices of individuals among yourselves. The Hydra Anarchy would rear its head in every quarter. The goodly fabric you have established would be rent assunder, and precipitated into the dust. You knew how to encounter civil war, rather than surrender your liberty to foreign domination—you will not hesitate now to brave it rather than surrender your sovereignty to the tyranny of a faction—you will be as deaf to the apostles of anarchy now, as you were to the emissaries of despotism then. Your love of liberty will guide you now as it did then—you know that the POWER of the majority and LIBERTY are inseparable—destroy that, and this perishes. But in truth that which can properly be called a civil war is not to be apprehended—Unless, from the act of those who endeavour to fan the flame, by rendering the Government odious. A civil war is a contest between two GREAT parts of the same empire. The exertion of the strength of the nation to suppress resistance to its laws by a sixtieth part of itself, is not of that description.

After endeavouring to alarm you with the horrors of civil war—an attempt is made to excite your sympathy in favour of the armed faction by telling you that those who compose it are men, who understand the principles of freedom, and know the horrors and distresses of anarchy, and must therefore have been prompted to hostility against the laws by a radical defect EITHER in the government or in its administration.

Fellow Citizens! For an answer to this you have only to consult your senses. The natural consequence of radical defect in a government, or in its administration is national distress and suffering—look around you—where is it? do you feel it? do you see it?

Go in quest of it beyond the Alleghaney, and instead of it, you will find that there also a scene of unparralleled prosperity upbraids the ingratitude and madness of those, who are endeavouring to cloud the bright face of our political horizon, and to mar the happiest lot that beneficent Heaven ever indulged to undeserving mortals.

When you have turned your eyes towards that scene—examine the men whose knowledge of the principles of freedom is so emphatically vaunted—where did they get their better knowledge of those principles than that which you possess? How is it that you have been so blind or tame as to remain quiet, while they have been goaded into hostility against the laws by a RADICAL DEFECT in the government, or its administration?

Are you willing to yield them the palm of discernment, or patriotism or of courage? TULLY.

VIEWS ON THE FRENCH REVOLUTION
1794

Hamilton strongly attacks revolutionary statesmanship in the following unfinished writing on the French Revolution. The doctrine of revolution is the doctrine of extreme medicine, and its practical defect is the application of extreme medicine when circumstances require a less drastic cure. If improvement is the intention of the statesman, the improvement must accept those limits imposed by the character of the particular political order, as well as those imposed by human nature.

[1794]

Facts, numerous and unequivocal, demonstrate that the present AERA is among the most extraordinary, which have occurred in the history of human affairs. Opinions, for a long time, have been gradually gaining ground, which threaten the foundations of Religion, Morality and Society. An attack was first made upon the Christian Revelation; for which natural Religion was offered as the substitute. The Gospel was to be discarded as a gross imposture; but the being and attributes of a GOD, the obligations of piety, even the doctrine of a future state of rewards and punishments were to be retained and cherished.

In proportion as success has appeared to attend the plan, a bolder project has been unfolded. The very existence of a Deity has been questionned, and in some instances denied. The duty of piety has been ridiculed, the perishable nature of man asserted and his hopes bounded to the short span of his earthly state. DEATH has been proclaimed an ETERNAL SLEEP—"the dogma of the *immortality* of the soul a *cheat* invented to torment the living for the benefit of the dead." Irreligion, no longer confined to the closets of conceiled sophists, nor to the haunts of wealthy riot, has more or less displayed its hideous front among all classes.

Wise and good men took a lead in delineating the odious character of Despotism; in exhibiting the advantages of a moderate and well-balanced government, in inviting nations to contend for the enjoyment of rational liberty. Fanatics in political science have since exaggerated and perverted their doctrines. Theories of Government unsuited to the nature of man, miscalculating the force of his passions, disregarding the lessons of experimental wisdom, have been projected and recommended. These have every where attracted sectaries and every where the fabric of Government has been in different degrees undermined.

A league has at length been cemented between the apostles and disciples of irreligion and of anarchy. Religion and Government have both been stigmatised as abuses; as unwarrantable restraints upon the freedom of man; as causes of the corruption of his nature, intrinsically good; as sources of an artificial and false morality, which tyrannically robs him of the enjoyments for which his passions fit him; and as cloggs upon his progress to the perfection for which he was destined.

As a corollary from these premisses, it is a favourite tenet of the sect that religious opinion of any sort is unnecessary to Society; that the maxims of a genuine morality and the authority of the Magistracy and the laws are a sufficient and ought to be the only security for civil rights and private happiness.

As another corollary, it is occasionally maintained by the same sect, that but a small portion of power is requisite to Government; that even this portion is only temporarily necessary, in consequence of the bad habits which have been produced by the errors of ancient systems; and that as human nature shall refine and ameliorate by the operation of a more enlightened plan, government itself will become useless, and Society will subsist and flourish free from its shackles.

If all the votaries of this new philosophy do not go the whole length of its frantic creed they all go far enough to endanger the full extent of the mischiefs which are inherent in so wild and fatal a scheme; every modification of which aims a mortal blow at the vitals of human happiness.

The practical developement of this pernicious system has been seen in France. It has served as an engine to subvert all her antient institutions civil and religious, with all the checks that served to mitigate the rigour of authority; it has hurried her headlong through a rapid succession of dreadful revolutions, which have laid waste property, made havoc among the arts, overthrow cities, desolated provinces, unpeopled regions, crimsonned her soil with blood and deluged it in crime poverty and wretchedness; and all this as yet for no better purpose than to erect on the ruins of former things a despotism unlimited and uncontrouled; leaving to a deluded, an abused, a plundered, a scourged and an oppressed people not even the shadow of liberty, to console them for a long train of substantial misfortunes, of bitter sufferings.

This horrid system seemed awhile to threaten the subversion of civilized Society and the introduction of general disorder among mankind. And though the frightful evils, which have been its first and only fruits, have given a check to its progress, it is to be feared that the poison has spread too widely and penetrated too deeply, to be as yet eradicated. Its activity has indeed been suspended, but the elements remain concocting for new eruptions as occasion shall permit. It is greatly to be apprehended, that mankind is not near the end of the misfortunes, which it is calculated to produce, and that it still portends a long train of convulsion. Revolution, carnage, devastation, and misery.

Symptoms of the too great prevalence of this system in the United States are alarmingly visible. It was by its influence, that efforts were made to embark this country in a common cause with France in the early period of the present war; to induce our government to sanction and promote her odious principles and views with the blood and treasure of our citizens. It is by its influence, that every succeeding revolution has been approved or excused—all the horrors that have been committed justified or extenuated—that even the last usurpation, which contradicts all the ostensible principles of the Revolution, has been regarded with complacency; and the despotic constitution engendered by it slyly held up as a model not unworthy of our Imitation.

THE DEFENCE OF THE FUNDING SYSTEM
JULY 1795

The portion of the essay that follows, written after Hamilton resigned as secretary of the Treasury, contains his most revealing reflections on true statesmanship and, by indirection, what constituted its opposite. The term "empyric," as it was defined in the late eighteenth century, meant "without rational foundation."

A Government which does not rest on the basis of justice rests on that of force. There is no middle ground. Establish that a Government may decline a provision for its debts, though able to make it, and you overthrow all public morality, you unhinge all the principles that must preserve the limits of free constitutions—you have anarchy, despotism or, what you please, but you have no *just* or *regular* Government.

In all questions about the advantages or disadvantages of national Credit, or in similar questions, which it has been seen may be raised (and it may be added have been raised), with respect to all the sources of social happiness and national prosperity—the difference between the true politician and the political-empyric is this: The latter will either attempt to travel out of human nature and introduce institutuions and projects for which man is not fitted and which perish in the imbecility of their own conception & structure, or without proposing or attempting any substitute they content themselves with exposing and declaming against the ill sides of things and with puzzling & embrassing every practicable scheme of administration which is adopted. The last indeed is the most usual because the easiest course and it embraces in its practice all those hunters after popularity who knowing better make a traffic of the weak sides of the human understanding and passions.

The true politican on the contrary takes human nature (and hu-

416

man society its aggregate) as he finds it, a compound of good and ill qualities of good and ill tendencies—endued with powers and actuated by passions and propensities which blend enjoyment with suffering and make the causes of welfare the causes of misfortune.

With this view of human nature he will not attempt to warp or distort it from its natural direction—he will not attempt to promote its happiness by means to which it is not suited, he will not reject the employment of the means which constitute its bliss because they necessarily involve alloy and danger; but he will seek to promote his action according to the byass of his nature, to lead him to the developpement of his energies according to the scope of his passions, and erecting the social organisation on this basis, he will favour all those institutions and plans which tend to make men happy according to their natural bent, which multiply the sources of individual enjoyment and increase those of national resource and strength—taking care to infuse in each case all the ingredients which can be devised as preventives or correctives of the evil which is the eternal concomitant of temporal blessing.

LETTER TO GEORGE WASHINGTON
MARCH 29, 1796

The Jay Treaty covering commercial and boundary disputes between Great Britain and the United States was approved by the Senate on June 25, 1795, and was officially ratified on August 14, 1795. Washington proclaimed the treaty on February 29, 1796, but all of its provisions could not be put into effect until Congress voted appropriations for the commissions provided for in the treaty. With a view to that, a House resolution requested that the papers relating to the negotiations over the treaty be made available to that body. The following letter contains Hamilton's draft of a proposed presidential reply to that resolution. Washington never used the Hamilton draft, but one prepared by Timothy Pickering.

New York March 29, 1796

Sir

I wish the inclosed could have been sent in a more perfect State. But it was impossible. I hope however it can be made out & may be useful.

417

It required more time to say all that was proper in a more condensed form.

In considering the course to be pursued by the President it may be well he should be reminded that the same description of men who call for the papers have heretofore maintained that they were not bound by any communication in confidence but were free afterwards to do as they pleased with papers sent them.

Respect & Aff

A Hamilton

Enclosure

Gentlemen

I have received your resolution   and have considered it with the attention always due to a request of the House of Representatives. I feel a consciousness (not conradicted I trust by any part of my conduct) of a sincere disposition to respect the rights privileges and authorities of Congress collectively and in its separate branches—to pay just deference to their opinions and wishes—to avoid intrusion on their province—to communicate freely information pertinent to the subjects of their deliberation. But this disposition, keeping steadily in view the public good, must likewise be limited and directed by the duty, incumbent upon us all, of preserving inviolate the constitutional boundary between the several departments of the Government: a duty enjoined by the very nature of a constitution which defines and distributes the powers delegated among different depositories, enforced by the solemn sanction of an oath, and only to be fulfilled by a regard no less scrupulous for the rights of the Executive than for those of every other Department.

When I communicated to the House of Representatives the Treaty lately made with Great Britain, I did not transmit the papers respecting its negotiation, for reasons which appeared to me decisive.

It is contrary to the general practice of Governments to promulge the intermediate transactions of a foreign negotiation without weighty and special reasons. The motives for great delicacy and reserve on this point are powerful. There may be situations of a Country, in which particular occurrences of a negotiation, though conducted with the best views to its interest and even to a satisfactory issue, if immediately disclosed, might tend to embarrassment and mischief in the interior affairs of that Country. Confidential discussions and overtures are inseparable from the nature of certain negotiations and frequently occur in others—essays are occasionally made by one party to discover the views of another in reference to collateral objects—motives are sometimes assigned for what is yielded by one party to another: which, if made public, might kindle the resentment or jealousy of other powers, or might raise in them pretensions not expedient to be gratified. Hence it is a rule of mutual convenience and security among nations that neither shall without adequate cause and proper reserves promulge the details of a Negotiation between them: otherwise one party might be injured by the disclosures of the other, and sometimes without being aware of the injury likely to be done.

Consequently, The general neglect of this rule in the practice of a Government would naturally tend to destroy that confidence in its prudence and delicacy—that freedom of communication with it; which are so important in the intercourses between Nation and Nation, towards the accommodation of mutual differences, and the adjustment of mutual interests.

Neither would it be likely to promote the advantage of a Nation, that the Agents of a foreign Government, with which it was at any time in Treaty, should act under the apprehension that every expression, every step of theirs would presently be exposed, by the promulgation of the other party, to the criticism of their political adversaries at home. The disposition to a liberal and perhaps for that very reason a wise policy in them might be checked by the reflection that it might afterwards appear from the disclosures on the other side, that they had not made as good bargains as they might have made. And while they might be stimulated by this to extraordinary effort and perseverance; maxims of greater secrecy and reserve in their Cabinet would leave their competitors in the negotiation without the same motive to exertion. These having nothing to fear from the indiscretion of the opposite Government would only have to manage with caution their communications to their own. The consequences of such a state of things would naturally be an increase of obstacles to the favourable close of a negotiation, and the probability of worse bargains for the Nation, in the habit of giving indiscreet publicity to its proceedings.

The Agents of such a Nation, themselves, would have strong inducements to extreme reserve in their communications with their own government; lest parts of their conduct might subject them in other quarters to unfriendly and uncandid constructions—which might so narrow the information they gave as scarcely to afford sufficient light either with regard to the fitness of their own course of proceeding or the true state and prospects of the negotiation with which they were charged.

And thus in different ways the channels of information to a Government might be materially obstructed by the impolitic practice of too free disclosure in regard to its foreign negotiations.

Moreover—It is not uncommon for the instructions to negotiat-

419

ing Agents, especially where differences are to be settled, to contain observations on the views and motives of the other party, which after an amicable termination of the business, it would be contrary to decorum, unfriendly and offensive, to make public. Such instructions also frequently manifest views, which, if disclosed, might renew sources of jealousy and ill will which a Treaty had extinguished—might exhibit eventual plans of proceeding which had better remain unknown for future emergencies, & might even furnish occasion for suspicion, and pretext for discontent, to other powers. And, in general, where more had been obtained by a Treaty than the *ultimata* prescribed to the negotiation, it would be inexpedient to publish those *ultimata:* Since, among other ill effects, the publication of them might prejudice the interest of the Country in future negotiations with the same or with different powers.

These reasons explain the grounds of a prevailing rule of Conduct among prudent Governments, (viz) not to promulge without weighty cause nor without due reserves the particulars of a foreign negotiation. It so happens indeed that many of them have no immediate application to the case of the present Treaty. And it would be unadviseable to discriminate here between such as may and such as may not so apply. But it would be very extraordinary, situated as the UStates were in relation to Great Britain, at the commencement of the negotiation if some of them did not operate against a full disclosure of the papers, in which it is recorded.

Connected with these general reasons against the transmission of the papers with the Treaty, it was proper to consider if there were any special reasons which recommended in the particular case a departure from the rule, and especially whether there was any purpose to which the house of Representatives is constitutionally competent, which might be elucidated by those papers.

This involved a consideration of the nature of the constitutional agency of that house, in regard to Treaties.

The Constitution of the U States empowers the President with the advice and consent of the Senate two thirds concurring to "MAKE Treaties." It no where professes to authorise the House of Representatives, or any other branch of the Government, to partake with the President and Senate in the making of Treaties. The whole Power of making Treaties is therefore by the terms of the Constitution vested in the President and Senate.

To *make* a Treaty, as applied to Nations, is to *conclude* a contract between them *obligatory on their faith*. But that cannot be an (obligatory) contract, to the validity and obligation of which the assent of another power in the state is constitutionally necessary.

420

Again: The Constitution declares that a Treaty made under the authority of the U States shall be a supreme law of the land—let it be said "a law." A law is an obligatory rule of action prescribed by the competent authority. But that cannot be an obligatory rule of action, or a *law*, to the validity and obligation of which the assent of another power in the state is constitutionally necessary.

Hence, a discretionary right in the House of Representatives, to assent or not to a Treaty, or what is equivalent to execute it or not, would negative these two important propositions of our constitution I That the President and Senate shall have power to make Treaties II That a Treaty made by them shall be a law—and in the room of them would establish this proposition "That the power of making Treaties resides in the President, Senate and House of Representatives." For whatever coloring may be given a right of discretionary assent to a contract is in substance a right to participate in the making of it.

Is there any thing in the constitution which by *necessary* implication changes the force of the express terms that regulate the deposit of the Power to make Treaties?

If there is, it must be found in those clauses which regulate the deposit of the Legislative Power. Here two questions arise—

I Can the Power of Treaty reach and embrace objects upon which the legislative power is authorised to act, as the regulation of Commerce, the defining of piracy &c or are these objects virtually excepted out of the operation of that power?

II If it can reach and embrace those objects, is there any principle which as to them gives to Congress or more properly the House of Representatives, a discretionary right of assent or dissent?

The affirmative of the first question is supported by these considerations.

I The words which establish the Power of Treaty are manifestly broad enough to comprehend all Treaties.

II It is a reasonable presumption, that they were meant to extend to all treaties usual among nations, and so to be commensurate with the variety of exigencies and objects of intercourse which occur between nation and nation; in other words that they were meant to enable the Organ of the Power to manage with efficacy the external affairs of the Country in all cases in which they must depend upon compact with another nation.

III The Treaties usual among nations are principally those of Peace, Alliance and Commerce. It is the office of Treaties of peace to establish the cessation of hostilities and the conditions of it, including frequently indemnifications, sometimes pecuniary ones. It is the

421

office of Treaties of alliance to establish cases in which nations shall succour each other in war stipulating a union of forces, the furnishing of troops, ships of war, pecuniary and other aids. It is the office of Treaties of Commerce to establish rules and conditions according to which nations shall trade with each other, regulating as far as they go the external commerce of the nations in Treaty—whence it is evident that Treaties naturally bear in different ways upon many of the most important objects, upon which the legislative power is authorised to act, as the appropriation of money, the raising of armies, the equipment of fleets, the declaring of war, the regulation of Trade. But

IV This is no objection to the Power of Treaty having a capacity to embrace those objects 1 Because that latitude is essential to the great ends for which the Power is instituted 2 Because unless the Power of Treaty can embrace objects upon which the legislative power may also act, it is essentially nugatory—often inadequate to mere treaties of Peace—always inadequate to Treaties of Alliance or Commerce 3 Because it is the office of the legislative power to establish separate rules of action for the nation of which it is—its arms being too short to reach a single case in which a common obligatory rule of action for two nations is to be established IV Because inasmuch as a common rule of action, for independent nations can only be established by compact, it necessarily is of the office of the Power of Treaty to effect its establishment V Because the power of legislation being unable to effect what the power of Treaty must effect, it is unreasonable to suppose that the former was intended to exclude the action of the latter VI Because on the other hand there is no incongruity in the supposition that the Power of Treaty, in establishing a joint rule of action with another nation, may act upon the same subject which the Legislative Power may act upon, in establishing a separate rule of action for one nation VII Because it is a common case for the different powers of Government to act upon the same subject within different spheres and in different modes. Thus the legislative power lays and provides for the collection of a particular tax—the Executive Power collects the tax and brings it into the Treasury. So the power of Treaty may stipulate pecuniary indemnification for an injury and the Legislative power may execute the stipulation by providing & designating the fund out of which the indemnification shall be made. As in the first case the Executive Power is auxiliary to the Legislative, so in the last legislative Power is auxiliary to the Power of Treaty. VIII Because this doctrine leads to no collision of powers, inasmuch as the stipulations of a Treaty may reasonably be considered as restraints upon the legislative discretion. Those stipulations operate by pledging the faith of a nation and restricting its will by the force of moral obligation, and it is a fundamental principle of social right that the will of a nation as well as that of an individual may be bound by the moral obligation of a contract. IX Because the organ of the Power of Treaty is as truly the Organ of the Will of a Nation as that of its legislative Power; and there is no incongruity in the supposition, that the will of a Nation, acting through one organ, may be bound by the pledge of its faith through another Organ. From these different views of the subject it results, that the position that the Power of Legislation, acting in one sphere, and the power of Treaty, acting in another sphere, may embrace in their action the same objects, involves no interference of constitutional Powers; and of course that the latter may reach and comprehend objects which the former is authorised to act upon; which it is necessary to suppose it does do since the contrary supposition would essentially destroy the Power of Treaty: whereas the stipulations of Treaties being only particular exceptions to the discretion of the Legislative Power, this power will always still have a wide field of action beyond and out of the exceptions.

The latitude of the Power of Treaty granted by analogous terms in the articles of our late confederation as practiced upon for years in treaties with several foreign Powers and acquiesced in by the Governments and citizens of these states, is an unequivocal comment upon the meaning of the provision in our present constitution and a conclusive evidence of the sense in which it is understood by those who planned and those who adopted the Constitution—supporting fully the foregoing construction of the Power. That latitude cannot be indebted to the circumstance of all the power granted by the confederation being in one body—for that body had legislative power in but very few cases & none in some very important cases embraced by its treaties. The examples of past practice under our present Government without the least question of its propriety afford a further corroboration of the intended & accepted sense of the Constitutional instrument.

The negative of the second question above stated is supported by these considerations.

I A discretionary right of assent in the House of Representatives (as before shewn) would contradict the two important propositions of the Constitution—That the President with the Senate shall have power to make Treaties—That the Treaties so made shall be laws.

II It supposes the House of Representatives at liberty to contravene the faith of the Nation engaged in a Treaty made by the declared constitutional Agents of the Nation for that purpose—and thus implies the contradiction that a Nation may rightfully pledge its faith through one organ, and without any change of circumstances to dissolve the obligation may revoke the pledge through another organ.

III The obvious import of the terms which grant the Power of Treaty can only be controuled, if at all, by some manifest necessary implication in favour of the discretionary right which has been mentioned. But it has been seen that no such implication can be derived from the mere grant of certain powers to the House of Representatives *in common* with the other branch of the legislative body. As there is a rational construction which renders the due exercise of these powers in the cases to which they are competent compatible with the operation of the power of Treaty in all the necessary latitude, excluding the discretionary cooperation of the house of Representatives, that construction is to be preferred. It is far more natural to consider the exercise of those powers as liable to the exceptions which the power of Treaty granted to the President and Senate may make; than to infer from them a right in the House to share in this power in opposition to the terms of the grant and without a single expression in the constitution to designate the right. It is improbable that the constitution intended to vest in the house of Representatives so extensive a controul over treaties, without a single phrase that would look directly to the object. It is the more improbable, because the Senate being in the first instance a party to treaties, the right of discretionary cooperation in the House of Representatives, in virtue of its legislative character, would in fact terminate in itself, though but a part of the legislative body—which suggests this question,— Can the House of Representatives have any right in virtue of its *general* legislative character which is not effectually participated [in] by the Senate?

IV The claim of such a right on the ground that the Legislative power is essentially deliberative, that wherever its agency is in question it has a right to act or not—and that consequently where provision by law is requisite to execute a Treaty there is liberty to refuse it—cannot be acceded to without admitting in the legislative body and in each part of it an absolute discretion incontroulable by any constitutional injunctions limits or restrictions; thereby overturning the fabric of a fixed & definite constitution and erecting upon its ruins a legislative Omnipotence.

It would, for example, give to Congress a discretion to allow or not a fixed compensation to the Judges, though the constitution expressly enjoins "that they shall at stated times receive for their services a compensation, which shall not be diminished during their continuance in office"; and would sacrifice this solemn & peremptory command of the Constitution to the opinion of Congress respecting a more essential application of the public money. Can this be true? Can any thing but absolute inability excuse a compliance with this injunction, and does not the constitution presuppose a moral impossib[il]ity of such inability? If there be a legal discretion if any case to contravene this injunction, what limit is there to the legal discretion of the legislative body? What injunction, what restriction of the constitution may they not supersede? If the Constitution cannot direct the exercise of their authority in particular cases how can it limit it in any? What becomes of the appeal to our Courts on the constitutionality of a legislative act? What becomes of the power they solemnly assert to test such an act by the constitutional Commission and to pronounce it operative or null according to its conformity with a repugnance to that Commission? What in fine becomes of the Constitution itself?

This inquiry suggests a truth fundamental to the principles of our Government and all important to the security of the People of the U States—namely that the legislative body is not deliberative in all cases, that it is only deliberative and discretionary where the constitution and the laws lay it under no command nor prohibition—that where they command, it can only execute—where they prohibit it cannot act. If the thing be commanded and the means of execution are undefined it may then deliberate on the choice of the means—but it is obliged to devise some means. It is true that the Constitution provides no method of compelling the legislative body to act, but it is not the less under a Constitutional legal and moral obligation to act, where action is prescribed, & in conformity with the rule of action prescribed.

In asserting the authority of laws as well as of the constitution to direct and restrain the position is to be understood with this difference. The constitution obliges always—the laws 'till they are annulled or repealed by the proper authority. But till then they oblige the legislative body as well as individuals; and all their antecedent effects are valid and binding. And the abrogation or repeal of a law must be by an act of the regular organ of the national will for that purpose in the forms of the constitution; not by a mere refusal to give effect to its injunctions and requisitions; especially by a part of the legislative body. A legal discretion to refuse the execution of a preexisting law is virtually a power to repeal it—and to attribute this discretion to a part of the legislative body is to attribute to it the whole instead of a part of the legislative power in the given case. When towards the execution of an antecedent law further legislative provision is necessary, the past effects of the law are obligatory; and a positive repeal or suspension by the whole legislature is requisite to arrest its future operation.

425

The idea is essential in a government like ours that there is no body of men or individual above the law; not even the legislative body till by an act of legislation they have annulled the law.

The argument from the principle of an essentially deliberative faculty in the legislative body is the less admissible, because it would result from it that the Nation could never be conclusively bound by a Treaty. Why should the inherent discretion of a future legislature be more bound by the assent of a preceding one than this was by a pledge of the public faith through the President & Senate.

Hence it follows that the house of representatives have no moral power to refuse the execution of a treaty, which is not contrary to the constitution, because it pledges the public faith, and have no legal power to refuse its execution because it is a law—until at least it ceases to be a law by a regular act of revocation of the competent authority.

The ingredient peculiar to our Constitution, in that provision, which declares that Treaties are laws, is of no inconsiderable weight in the question. It is one thing whether a Treaty pledging the faith of the Nation shall by force of moral duty oblige the legislative will to carry it into effect; another whether it shall be of itself a law. The last is the case in our constitution which by a fundamental decree gives the character of a law to every Treaty, made under the authority which it designates. Treaties therefore in our government of themselves and without any additional sanction have full legal perfection as laws.

Questions may be made as to the cases in which and the authority by which under our constitution a Treaty consonant with it may be pronounced to have lost or may be divested of its obligatory force; a point not necessary now to be discussed. But admitting that authority to reside in the legislative body—still its exercise must be by an act of Congress declaring the fact and the consequence, or declaring war against the power with whom the Treaty is. There is perceived to be nothing in our constitution, no rule of Constitutional law, to authorise one branch alone, or the House of Representatives in particular, to pronounce the existence of such cases, or from the beginning to refuse compliance with such a Treaty without any new events to change the original obligations. A right in the whole Legislative body consisting of the two houses of Congress by a collective act to pronounce the cases of non operation & nullity of a Treaty asserts every thing that can reasonably be claimed in favour of the legislative Power, presents a consistent rule & obviates all pretence of collision.

How discordant might be the results of a doctrine that the House of Representatives may at discretion execute or not a constitutional

Treaty! What confusion, if our Courts of Justice should recognise & enforce as laws treaties, the obligation of which was denied by the House of Representatives!—and that on a principle of inherent discretion which no decision of the Courts could guide. We might see our commercial & fiscal systems disorganised by the breaches made in antecedent laws by posterior treaties, through the want of some collateral provisions requisite to give due effect to the principle of the new rule.

Can that doctrine be true which may present a Treaty operating as a law upon all the citizens of a country and yet legally disregarded by a portion of the legislative body?

The sound conclusion appears to be—that when a Treaty contains nothing but what the constitution permits, it is conclusive upon ALL and ALL are bound to give it effect. When it contains more than the constitution permits it is void either in the whole or as to so much as it improperly contains.

While I can discover no sufficient foundation in the constitution for the claim of a discretionary right in the House of Representatives to participate in giving validity to Treaties; I am confirmed in the contrary inference by the knowledge I have that the expediency of this participation was considered by the Convention which planned the Constitution and was by them overruled.

The greatness of the power of Treaty under this construction is no objection to its truth. It is doubtless a great power, and necessarily so, else it could not answer those purposes of national security and interest in the external relations of a Country for which it is designed. Nor does the manner in which it is granted in our constitution furnish any argument against the magnitude which is ascribed to it—but the contrary. A treaty cannot be made without the actual cooperation and mutual consent of the Executive and two thirds of the Senate. This necessity of positive cooperation of the Executive charges him with a high responsibility, which cannot but be one great security for the proper exercise of the Power. The proportion of the Senate requisite to their valid consent to a treaty approaches so near to unanimity, that it would always be very extraordinary, if it should be given to one really pernicious or hurtful to the State. These great guards are manifest indications of a great power being meant to be deposited. So that the manner of its deposit is an argument for its magnitude rather than an argument against it, and an argument against the intention to admit with a view to security the discretionary cooperation of the House of Representatives rather than in favour of such a right in them.

Two thirds of the two houses of Congress may exercise their

whole legislative power, not only without but against the consent of the Executive. It is not evident on general principles, that in this arrangement, there is a materially greater security against a bad law than in the other against a bad Treaty. The frequent absolute necessity of secrecy not only in the conduct of a foreign negotiation, but at certain conjunctures as to the very articles of a Treaty is a natural reason why a part and that the least numerous part of the legislative body was united with the Executive in the making of Treaties in exclusion of the other and the most numerous. But if the deposit of the Power of Treaty was less safe & less well guarded, than it is conceived to be, this would not be a good argument against its being in fact exclusively deposited, as the terms of the Constitution which establish it import it to be. It would only be an argument for an amendment to the Constitution modifying the deposit of the power differently & superadding new guards.

If the House of Representatives called upon to act in aid of a Treaty made by the President & Senate believe it to be unwarranted by the cons[ti]tution which they are sworn to support—it will not be denied that they may pause in the execution; until a decision, on the point of constitutionality, in the Supreme Court of the United States shall have settled the question.

But this is the only discretion in that House, as to the obligation to carry a Treaty made by the President & Senate into effect, in the existence of which I can acquiesce, as being within the intent of the constitution.

Hence there was no question in my opinion of the competency of the House of Representatives, which I could presuppose likely to arise, to which any of the papers now requested could be deemed applicable; nor does it yet appear that any such question has arisen, upon which the request has been predicated.

Were even the course of reasoning which I have pursued less well founded than it appears to me to be—the request of papers, as a preliminary proceeding of the House, would still seem to be premature.

A question on the Constitutionality of a Treaty can manifestly only be decided by comparing the instrument itself with the Constitution.

A question whether a Treaty be consistent with or adverse to the interests of the U States must likewise be decided by comparing the stipulations which it actually contains with the situation of the U States in their internal and external relations.

Nothing extrinsic to the Treaty, or in the manner of the negotiating, can make it constitutional or unconstitutional, good or bad, salutary or pernicious. The internal evidence it affords is the only proper standard of its merits.

Whatever therefore be the nature of the duty or discretion of the house, as to the execution of the Treaty, it will find its rule of action in the Treaty. Even with reference to an animadversion on the conduct of the Agents who made the Treaty—the presumption of a criminal mismanagement of the interests of the U States ought first it is conceived to be deduced from the intrinsic nature of the Treaty & ought to be pronounced to exist previous to a further inquiry to ascertain the guilt or the guilty.

Whenever the House of Representatives, proceeding upon any Treaty, shall have taken the ground that such a presumption exists in order to such an inquiry, their request to the Executive to cause to be laid before them papers which may contain information on the subject will rest on a foundation that cannot fail to secure to it due efficacy.

But under all the circumstances of the present Request (circumstances which I forbear to particularise) and in its present indefinte form, I adopt with reluctance and regret but with intire conviction the opinion that a just regard to the Constitution and to the duty of my office forbid on my part a compliance with that request.

(G W)

If the President should conclude to send the papers reserving parts not proper to be sent instead of the last paragraph the conclusion may be this

"But though under all the circumstances of the present request (circumstances which have produced great hesitation) I should deem myself warranted in withholding the papers—I am nevertheless induced by a desire to cultivate harmony and to obviate unfavourable inferences in a case which has excited so much sensibility, to transmit to the House all such parts of the papers requested as can be material in any event for their information and as can be communicated without impropriety. These comprehend the commissions given to our Envoy, so much of the instructions to him as shew the extent & limits of his discretion & all the material parts of his correspondence."

(G W)

LETTER TO GEORGE WASHINGTON CONTAINING HAMILTON'S DRAFT OF WASHINGTON'S FAREWELL ADDRESS

JULY 30, 1796

Hamilton, on Washington's request, furnished the president with two drafts of a farewell address to be delivered at the end of his second term. The first draft was a revision of what Madison had written for the president when he considered retiring at the end of his first term, and the second draft was composed by Hamilton himself. Washington decided to use the Hamilton draft rather than Hamilton's revision of the Madison draft. Washington's Farewell Address may be regarded as a landmark speech, for it includes a statement of the principles that were to dominate American foreign policy in the 1790s.

New York July 30, 1796

Sir

I have the pleasure to send you herewith a certain draft which I have endeavoured to make as perfect as my time and engagements would permit. It has been my object to render this act *importantly* and *lastingly* useful, and avoiding all just cause of present exception, to embrace such reflections and sentiments as will wear well, progress in approbation with time, & redound to future reputation. How far I have succeeded you will judge.

I have begun the second part of the task—the digesting the supplementary remarks to the first address which in a fortnight I hope also to send you—yet I confess the more I have considered the matter the less eligible this plan has appeared to me. There seems to me to be a certain awkwardness in the thing—and it seems to imply that there is a doubt whether the assurance without the evidence would be believed. Besides that I think that there are some ideas which will not wear well in the former address, & I do not see how any part can be omitted, if it is to be given as the thing formerly prepared. Nevertheless when you have both before you you can better judge.

If you should incline to take the draft now sent—and after perusing and noting any thing that you wish changed & will send it to me I will with pleasure shape it as you desire. This may also put it in my power to improve the expression & perhaps in some instances condense.

I rejoice that certain clouds have not lately thickened & that there is a prospect of a brighter horison.

With affectionate & respectful attachment I have the honor to be Sir Yr. Very Obed Serv   A Hamilton

The President of the UStates

ENCLOSURE

Draft of Washington's Farewell Address

∧ of a Citizen to administer the Executive Gov of the U States
The period for a new election ∧ being not very distant and the
arrived   your
time actually ∧ when ~~the~~ thoughts ~~of my fellow Citizens~~ must be employed in designating ~~the Citizen who is to administer the Execu-~~
∧the person who is to be cloathed with that important trust
~~tive Government of the United States~~ ∧ for another term, ~~it may~~
∧it   especially as it
~~conduce to~~ ∧ appears to me proper, and ∧ may conduce to a more distinct expression of the public voice, that I should now apprize you
among
of the resolution I have formed to ~~desire~~ decline being considered ∧ ~~of~~
out
the number of those ∧ of whom a choice is to be made.
at the same time
I beg you nevertheless to be assured that the resolution, which I
connected with
announce, has not been taken without a strict regard to all the con-
connected with   bears
siderations attached to the relation which|as|a dutiful Citizen|I bear
his
to|my|Country; and that in withdrawing the tender of my service, which silence in my situation might imply, I am influenced by no diminution of zeal for its future interest nor by any deficiency of grateful respect for its past kindness, but by a full conviction that
such a step
~~my retreat~~ is compatible with both.
acceptance of and
The ∧ continuance hitherto in the office to which your ~~unani-~~ ~~mous~~ suffrages have twice called me has been a uniform sacrifice of
∧the opinion of public duty coinciding with
combined with a deference for

431

private inclination to ∧ ~~your~~ what appeared to be your wishes ~~and to~~

constantly

~~the opinion of public duty.~~ I |had| ~~constantly~~ hoped that it would have been much earlier in my power ~~consistently~~ consistently with motives which I was not at liberty to disregard to return to that

they

retirement from which those motives had reluctantly drawn me.

~~The conflict betwe between those motives and inclination previous to the last election~~

The strength of my desire to withdraw previous to the last election had even led to the preparation of an address to declare it to

mature

you—but deliberate reflection on the very critical and perplexed posture of our affairs with foreign nations and the unanimous advice

persons   impelled

of|men of every way|intitled to my confidence obliged me to abandon the idea.

I rejoice that ~~that~~ the state of your national Concerns external as well as internal no longer ~~appa~~ renders the pursuit of my inclination

whatever

incompatible with the sentiment of duty or propriety, and that ~~the~~

You   retain

partiality ~~which~~ any portion of ∧ ~~my fellow citizens~~ may still ~~cherish~~ for my services, ~~will not~~ they, ~~will~~ under the existing circumstances of

our   will   my   to retire

~~the~~ Country, ∧ not disapprove the resolution I have formed.

The impressions under which I first accepted the arduous trust|of chief Magistrate of the U States|were explained on the proper occa-

∧with pure intentions

sion. In the discharge of this trust I can only say that I have ∧ contributed ~~towa~~ towards the organisation and administration of the Government the best exertions of which a very fallible judgment was

in

capable. ~~I am not uncon~~ Not unconscious|at|the outset of the inferiority of my qualifications|for the station|, experience in my own eyes and perhaps still more in those of others has not diminished ~~the~~ in me the diffidence of myself—and every day the increasing weight of years admonishes me more and more that the shade of retirement is

to me

as necessary ∧ as it will be welcome|to me.|~~If any circumst~~ Satisfied that if any circumstances have given|a|peculiar value to my services

consolation

they were temporary, I have the ~~satisfaction~~ to believe that ~~patriotism~~

while inclination and prudence urge me to recede from the political
                                                it   knowing
scene patriotism does not forbid ∧ —|May I also have that of perceiv-
                    retirement
ing in my retreat that ~~my invol~~ the involuntary errors which I have
probably committed have been the causes of no serious or lasting
                                                                        ∧the anguish of
mischief to my Country and thus be spared ∧ regrets which would
disturb the repose of my retreat and embitter the remmant of my life!
                                      ∧without alloy
I may then expect to realize ∧ the purest enjoyment of partaking, in
                    ∧of
the midst of my fellow citizens ∧ the benign influence of good laws
under a free Government; the ultimate object of all my wishes and|to
                                                            I hope
which I look as|the happy reward ∧ of our mutual cares labours and
dangers.

In looking forward to the moment which is to terminate the
carreer of my public life, my sensations do not permit me to ~~suppress~~
suspend the deep acknowlegements required by that debt of gratitude which I owe to my beloved country for the many honors it has
                    ∧still more   ∧steadfast
conferred upon me ∧ for the distinguished and ∧ ~~persevering~~
                                                                            I have thence
confidence it has reposed in me and for the opportunities it has thus
enjoyed
afforded me of manifesting my inviolable attachment by services ~~at~~
~~least~~ faithful and persevering—however the inadequateness of my
            have rendered these efforts unequal to
                                            my
faculties may have ill seconded my zeal. If benefits have resulted to
∧my fellow Citizens
you ∧ from these services, let it always be remembered to your praise
and as an instructive example in our annals that the constancy of your
                                            frequently sometimes
support amidst appearances ~~sometimes~~ dubious ~~discouraging~~ vicis-
                        often discouraging
situdes of fortune ∧ and ~~not infrequently want of success~~ in situations
in which not infrequently want of success has seconded the ~~suggesti~~
criticisms of malevolence was the essential prop ~~and guarantee~~ of ~~of~~
                    ∧the guarantee of the
the efforts and ∧ measures by which they were atchieved. ~~I will not be~~
~~restrained by personal considerations of personal delicacy from pay-~~

~~ing you the tribute of declaring~~ Profoundly penetrated with this idea, I shall carry it with me to my retirement and to my grave as a lively incitement to unceasing vows (the only returns I can henceforth make) that Heaven may continue to You the choicest tokens of the beneficence merited by national piety and morality—that your union and brotherly affection may be perpetual—that the free constitution, which is the work of your own hands may be sacredly maintained— that its administration in every department may be stamped with wisdom and virtue—that in fine the happiness of the People of these States under the auspices of liberty may be made complete by so careful a preservation & so prudent a use of this blessing as will acquire them the glorious satisfaction of recommending it to the affection the praise—and the adoption of every nation which is yet a stranger to it.

Here perhaps I ought to stop. But a solicitude for your welfare,
which cannot ~~expire~~ ^{end} but with my life, ~~urges me to offer~~ and the fear
that ∧_{there may exist} projects unfriendly to it ~~are in train~~ against which it ~~is very~~
~~important~~ ^{may be necessary} you should be ~~carefully~~ guarded, urge me ~~to~~ in taking
leave of you to offer to your ∧_{solemn} consideration and frequent review
some sentiments the result of mature reflection confirmed by ∧_{observation &} experience which appear to me ~~all import~~ essential to the permanency of your felicity as a people. These will be offered with the more freedom as you can only see in them the ~~advice~~ disinterested advice of a parting friend who can have no personal motive to tincture or byass his counsel.

Interwoven as is the love of Liberty ~~in~~ ^{with} every fibre of your hearts
no recommendation ~~can be~~ ^{is} necessary to fortify your attachment to it.
~~After~~ ^{Next to} this ~~and as very materially connected with it~~ that unity ∧_{of Government} ~~of that~~
~~Republic~~ which constitutes you one people claims your ~~most cordial~~
~~affection and anxious~~ ^{vigilant & a} care ~~and vigilant~~ guardianship—as ~~one of the~~
main pillars of ~~so~~ your real independence of your peace safety ~~liberty~~ ^{freedom}
and happiness ~~and as the one against which the efforts of your inter-~~
~~most~~ ~~though covertly and~~

~~nal and external enemies will be most constantly & actively but insidiously levelled~~.

This being the point in your political fortress against which the batteries of internal and external enemies will be most constantly and actively however covertly and insidiously levelled, it is of the utmost importance that you should appreciate in its full force the immense value of your political Union to your national and individual happiness—that you should cherish towards it an affectionate and immoveable attachment and that you should watch for its preservation

ʌ~~and eagle eyed~~

with jealous ʌ solicitude.

For this you have every motive of sympathy and interest. Children for the most part of a common country, that country ~~ought~~ claims and ought to concentrate your affections. The name of Ameri-

and exalt

can must always ~~exalt your character &~~ gratify ʌ the just pride of patriotism more than any denomination which can be derived from

You have

local discrimination. ~~Religion morality~~ with slight shades of differ-

~~laws~~   institutions &

ence the same religion manners habits & political ʌ principles. You have in a common cause fought and triumphed to gether. The inde-

joint councils

pendence and liberty you enjoy are the work of ~~your united~~ ʌ efforts—dangers sufferings & successes. By your Union you atchieved

The

them, by your union you will most effectually maintain them. ~~This name of American is more flattering more exalting and ought to be more dear to you than any which you derive from the discriminations of State boundaries~~.

~~But considerations addressed to your sensibility, however persuasive to virtuous minds~~

The considerations which address themselves to your sensibility

even outweighed

are greatly strengthened by those which apply to your interest. Here every portion of our Country will find the most urgent and commanding motives for ~~cherishing~~ guarding and preserving the Union of the Whole.

free & unfettered

The North in ~~an~~ intercourse with the South under the equal laws

in the production of the latter many of them peculiar

of one Government will ʌ find vast additional resources of maritime

and precious materials of their manufacturing industry.

435

and commercial enterprise ∧ The South in the same intercourse will
share in the benefits of the Agency of the North will find its agricul-

turning into its own channels <s>those</s>

ture promoted and its commerce extended by <s>the employment of
those</s> means of Navigation which the North more abundantly affords

the national

and while it contributes to extend ∧ navigation <s>which</s> will participate
in the protection of a maritime strength to which itself is unequally
adapted. The East in a like intercourse with the West finds and in the
progressive improvement of internal navigation will more & more
find, a valuable vent for the commodities which it brings from abroad
or manufactures at home. The West derives through this Channel an

far

essential supply of its wants—and what is ∧ more important to it, it
must owe the secure and permanent enjoyment of the <s>essent</s> indispensable outlets for its own productions to the weight influence &

   maritime resources <s>& indissol</s>

<s>and future marine</s> of the Atlantic States directed by an indissoluble
community of interest. The tenure by which it could hold this advantage either from its own separate <s>power</s> strength or by an apostate
and unnatural connection with any foreign Nation must be intrinsically & necessarily precarious at every moment liable to be disturbed

   fluctuating   European

by the ∧ combinations of those primary ∧ interests which <s>every portion of Europe must</s> constantly <s>be governed by</s> regulate the conduct

And where every part finds a particular interest in the Union

of every portion of Europe—∧ All the parts of our Country will find in
their Union greater independence from the superior abundance &
variety of production incident to <s>different soils</s> the diversity of soil
& climate, all the parts of it must find in the aggregate assemblage &

greater

reaction of their mutual population production strength, proportional

frequent

security from external danger, <s>less frequency of foreign wars</s> less ∧
interruption of their peace with foreign nations and what is far more
valuable an exemption <s>those</s> from those broils & wars between the

own

parts if disunited which their ∧ rivalships <s>of inflamed</s> fomented by
foreign intrigue, or the opposite alliances <s>with which mu</s> with foreign
nations engendered by their mutual jealousies would inevitably pro-

   consequent

duce—a <s>corespondent</s> exemption from the necessity of those military establishments upon a large scale which bear in every country so menacing an aspect toward Liberty.

These considerations speak a conclusive language to every ~~considerate an~~ virtuous and considerate mind. ~~The diversities~~ They place the continuance of our Union among the first objects of patriotic desire. Is there a doubt whether a common government can long embrace so extensive a sphere? Let Time & Experience decide the question. Speculation in such a case ought not to be listened to—And

tis rational to hope that the auxiliary ∧ *agency of the* governments of the subdivisions, ~~if~~ with a proper organisation of the whole will secure a favourable issue to the Experiment. Tis allowable to believe that the spirit of party the intrigues of foreign nations, the corruption & the ambition of Individuals are likely to prove more formidable adversaries to the unity of our Empire than any inherent difficulties in the scheme. Tis

mounds
against these that the guards of national opinion national sympathy national prudence & virtue are to be erected. With such obvious motives to Union there will be always cause from the fact itself to

in any quarter
distrust the patriotism of those who ∧ may endeavour to weaken its

conjure
bands. And by all the love I bear you My fellow Citizens I ~~exhort~~ you

often
as ~~far~~ as it appears to frown upon the attempt.

at
Besides the more serious causes which have been hinted, as endangering our Union there is ~~one~~ another less dangerous but against which it is necessary to be on our guard. I mean the petulance of

collisions & disgusts
party differences of Opinion. It is not uncommon to hear the irritations which these excite vent themselves in declarations that the different parts of the Union are ill assorted and cannot remain together—in menaces from the inhabitants of one part to those of another that it will be dissolved by this or that measure. Intimations of the kind ar[e] as indiscreet as they are intemperate. Though frequently made with levity and without being in earnest they have a tendency to produce the consequence which they indicate. They teach the minds of men to consider the Union as precarious as an object to which they are not to attach their hopes and ~~desires~~ fortunes and thus weaken the sentiment in its favour. By rousing the resentment and ~~piquing the~~ alarming the pride of those to whom they are

437

addressed they set ingenuity to work to depreciate the value of the
object and ∧ to discover motives of Indifference to it. This is not wise.
Prudence demands that ~~all our words~~ we should habituate ourselves
in all our words and actions to reverence the Union as a sacred and
inviolable palladium of our happiness ~~as a thing which in even~~ and
should discountenance ~~the supposed~~ whatever can lead to a suspicion that it can in any event be abandonned.

Tis matter of serious concern
~~There is cau much cause to regret that the organisation of parties
has for some~~ that parties in this Country for some time past have been
too much characterised by ~~local and~~ geographical discriminations—
Northern and Southern States Atlantic and Western Country. These
discriminations which are the mere artifice of the spirit of party of party ~~(over~~
always
dexterous to avail itself of every source of sympathy of every handle
by which the passions can be taken hold of and which has been
sympathy of neighborhood
careful to turn to account the circumstance of territorial vicinity) have
furnished ~~in the difference of p an evidence in the difference of party
opinions~~ an argument against the Union as evidence of a real difference of local interests and views and serve to hazard it by organising
the leaders of
large districts of country under the direction of ∧ different factions
whose passions & prejudices rather than the true interests of the
Country, will be too apt to regulate the use of their influence. If it be
of our Country
possible to correct this poison in the affairs ∧ it is worthy the best
endeavours of moderate & virtuous men to effect it.

One of the expedients which the partisans of Faction employ
within local spheres
towards ~~fostering~~ strengthening their influence by local discriminations is to misrepresent the opinions and views of rival districts—The
People at large cannot be too much on their guard against the
jealousies which grow out of these misrepresentations. ~~The~~ They
tend to render aliens to each other those who ought to be tied together by fraternal affection. The Western Country have lately had a
in the negotiation by the Executive &
useful lesson on this subject. They have seen ∧ in the unanimous
ratification of the Treaty with Spain by the Senate ~~the conclusive~~
in all parts of the Country
~~proof~~ & in the universal satisfaction at that event ∧ a decisive proof
propagated

how ~~in~~ unfounded have been the suspicions [that] have been instilled
among
in them of a policy ~~hostile~~ in the Atlantic States & in the different
departments of the General Government
~~states~~ hostile to their interests in relation to the Mississipian. They
      two
have seen ∧ ~~too~~ treaties formed which secure to them every thing
that they could desire to confirm their prosperity. Will they not
henceforth rely for the preservation of these advantages on that union by which they were procured? Will they not reject those counsellors who would render them alien to their brethren & connect them
with Aliens?

To the duration and efficacy of your Union a Government extending over the whole is indispensable. ~~Without this~~ No alliances
however strict between the parts could ~~have the necessary solidity or
afford the necessarily~~ be an adequate substitute. These could not fail
to be liable to the infractions and interruptions which all alliances in
all times have suffered. Sensible of this important truth ~~and with a
view to a more intimate Union~~ you have lately established a Constitution of General Government, better calculated than the former ~~one~~ for
an intimate union and more adequate to the direction of your common concerns. This Government the offspring of your own choice
uninfluenced and unawed, completely free in its principles, in the
distribution of its powers uniting energy with safety and containing
in itself a provision for its own amendment is well entitled to your
confidence and support—~~Complian~~ Respect for its authority, compliance with its laws, acquiescence in its measures, are duties dictated
by the fundamental maxims of true Liberty. The basis of our political
systems is the right of the people to make and to alter their constitutions of Government. But the ~~existing~~ constitution for the time, and
until changed by an explicit and authentic act of the whole people, is
sacredly binding upon all. The very idea of the right and power of the
people to establish Government presupposes the duty of every individual to obey ~~it~~ the established Government.

All ~~irregular~~ obstructions ~~therefore~~ to the execution of the laws—
all <u>combinations</u> and <u>associations</u> under whatever plausible character
          direct   influence   deliberation or
with the real design to ∧ counteract countroul ∧ or awe the regular ∧
action of the constituted authorities are contrary to ~~the true principles
of a representative Government~~ this fundamental principle & of the
      fatal   to give it an artificial force;
most ~~dangerous~~ tendency. They serve to organise Faction ∧ and to
put in the stead of the delegated will of the whole nation the will of a

439

but artful & enterprising

party. A often a small ∧ minority of the community—and according to

triumphs   parties

the alternate ~~victories~~ of ~~party~~ different ~~factions~~ to make the public

ill concerted

administration ~~reflecting~~ the ∧ schemes and projects of faction rather than the wholesome plans of common councils and deliberations. However combinations or assoc[i]ations of this description may occasionally promote popular ends and purposes they are likely to produce in the course of time and things the most effectual engines by which artful ambitious and unprincipled ~~in~~ men will be enabled to subvert the power of the people and usurp the reins of Government.

Towards the preservation of your government and the permanency of your present happy state, it is not only requisite that you steadily discountenance irregular oppositions to its authority but that you should be upon your guard against the spirit of innovation upon

specious

its principles however ~~plausible~~ the pretexts. One method of assault may be to effect alterations in the forms of the constitution tending to impair the energy of the system and so to undermine what cannot be directly overthrown. In all the changes to which you may be invited remember that time and habit are as necessary to fix the true character

other

of governments as of any ∧ human institutions, that experience is the surest standard by which the real tendency of existing constitutions

facility in

of government can be tried—that changes upon the credit of mere hypothesis and opinions exposes you to perpetual change from the

success   ni

~~exse~~ssive and endless variety of hypothesis and opion—and remem-

~~always~~∧also

ber ∧ that for the efficacious management of your common interests in a country so extensive as ours a Government of as much force and strength as is consistent with the perfect security of liberty is indispensable. Liberty itself will find in such a Government, ~~its surest~~ with powers properly distributed and arranged, its surest guardian—and protector. In my opinion the real danger in our system is that the General Government organised as at present will prove too weak rather than too powerful.

already   founding

I have ∧ observed the danger to be apprehended from ~~charac-~~ ~~terising~~ our parties ~~by~~ on Geographical discriminations. Let me now

440

most
enlarge the view of this point and caution you in the ∧ solemn manner against the baneful effects of party spirit in general. This spirit
unfortunately is inseperable from human nature and has its root in
heart.
the strongest passions of the human—It exists under different shapes
in different degrees stifled controuled or repressed
in all governments ~~more or l~~ but ∧ in those of the popular form it is
utmost
always seen in its ~~most~~ vigour & rankness and it is their worst
extent   ~~usual~~
enemy. In republics of narrow ~~dimensions, the combination of a it is~~
rule
~~easy for those who at any time possess the power of the State~~ it is not
difficult~~y~~ for those who at any time possess the reins of administration, or even for partial combinations of men, who from birth riches
and other sources of distinction have an ~~habitual influence~~ extraordi-
possessing   force
nary influence by ~~having~~ or acquiring the direction of the military ∧ or
by sudden efforts of partisans & followers to overturn the established
order of things and effect a usurpation. But in republics of large
extent the one or the other is scarcely possible. The powers and
opportunities of resistance of a numerous and wide extended nation
~~compared with the ordinary~~ defy the successful efforts of the ordi-
assemblages
nary military force or of any collections which wealth and patronage
may call to their aid—especially if there be no city of overbearing
for[c]e resources and influence. In such Republics it is perhaps safe to
assert
~~say~~ that the conflict of popular faction offer the only avenues to ~~usur-~~
~~pation & tyrann~~ tyranny & usurpation. ~~Perhaps it may be safely as-~~
~~serted that in those which occupy a large extent of territory it is the~~
& usurpation
~~only channel through which tyranny~~ ∧ ~~can approach. The dep despos-~~
~~ition of one faction despotic~~ domination of one faction over another
apt to be
stimulated by that spirit of Revenge which is ∧ gradually ~~and invari-~~
~~ably~~ engendered and which in different ages and countries have produced the greatest enormities is itself a frightful despotism. But this
leads at length to a more formal and permanent despotism. The disorders and miseries which ~~resolution~~ result predispose the minds of
∧absolute   some
men to seek repose & security in the ∧ power of a single man. And ~~the~~

441

leader of a prevailing faction more able or more fortunate than his competitors turns this disposition to the purpose of an ambitious and criminal self aggrandisement.

Without looking forward to such an extremity (which however ought not to be out of sight) the ordinary and continual ~~fact~~ mischief of the spirit of party ~~demand the endeavours of moderate~~ make it the interest and the duty of a wise people to discountenance and repress it.

always

It serves ∧ to distract the Councils & enfeeble the administration of the Government. It agitates the community with ~~false alarms~~ ill founded jealousies and false alarms ~~and~~ embittering one part of the community against another, & producing occasionaly riot & insurrection. It opens inlets for foreign corruption and influence—which find an easy access through the channels of party passions—and

∧true policy & interest

cause the ∧ ~~interests~~ of our own country to be ~~sacrificed to~~ made subservient to the policy and interest of one and another foreign

Nation

~~Power~~; sometimes enslaving ~~the~~ our own Government to the will of a foreign Government.

There ~~It~~ is an opinion ~~which has some vogue and is intirely without true~~ that parties in free countries are salutary checks upon

invigorate

the administration of the Government & serve to ~~keep alive~~ ∧ the spirit of Liberty. This within certain limits is true and in governments

cast

∧a monarchical character or byass

of ∧ ~~particular kind~~ patriotism may look with some favour on the

kind

spirit of party. But in those of the popular ∧ in those purely elective, it

or

is a spirit not to be fostered ~~&~~ encouraged. From the natural tendency of such governments, it is certain there will always be enough of it for every salutary purpose and there being constant danger of excess the effort ought to be by force of public opinion to mitigate & correct it.

not to   demanding

Tis a fire which cannot be quenched but demands a uniform vigilance to prevent its bursting into a flame—lest it should not only warm but consume.

It is important likewise that the habits of thinking of the people should ~~tend~~ tend to produce caution in their ~~public~~ agents in the several departments of Government, to retain each within its proper permit one to

~~shere~~ sphere and not to ∧ encr[o]ach ~~one~~ upon ~~the~~ another—~~The~~
~~spirit of approach encroachment in this particular and~~ that every

∧from whatever quarter   reprobation   the

attempt of the kind ∧ ~~are~~ should meet with the discountenance of ∧
community, ~~so~~ and that in every case in which a precedent of ~~encour-~~

shall   corrective be sought in

~~age~~ encroachment ~~should~~ have been given, a ~~careful election of~~ (revo-

election

cation be effected by) a careful attention to the ~~choice~~ next choice of

& consolidate

public Agents. The spirit of encroachment ~~ab~~ tends to absorb ∧ the

into one

powers of the several branches and departments, and thus to establish under whatever forms a despotism. A just knowledge of the
human heart, of that love of power which predominates in it, is alone
sufficient to establish this truth. Experiments ancient and modern—
some in our own country and under our own eyes serve to confirm it.
If in the public opinion the distribution of the constitutional powers
be in any instance ~~and~~ wrong or inexpedient—let it be corrected by

course

the authority of the people in a legitimate constitutional ~~way~~—Let
there be no change by usurpation, for though this may be the instru-

∧and natural

ment of good in one instance, it is the ordinary ∧ ~~ord~~ instrument of

death

the destruction of free Government—and the influence of the ~~presede~~
precedent is always infinitely ~~worse~~ more pernicious than any thing
which it may atchieve can be beneficial.

prosperity

To all those dispositions which promote ~~the~~ political happiness,

that man

Religion and Morality are essential props. In vain does ~~he~~ ∧ claim the
praise of patriotism who labours to subvert or undermine these great
pillars of human happiness these ~~sure foundations~~ firmest foundations of ~~all~~ the duties of men and citizens. The mere politician equally
with the pious man ought to respect and cherish them. A volume
could not trace all their connections with private and public happiness. Let it simply be asked where is the security for ~~reputation~~
property for reputation for life if the sense of moral and religious

the instruments of Investigation

obligation deserts the oaths which are administered in ~~the~~ Courts of
Justice? Nor ought we to flatter ourselves that morality can be sepa-

443

rated from religion. Concede as much as may be asked to the effect of

a

refined education in minds of peculiar structure—can we believe—can we in prudence suppose that national morality can be maintained in exclusion of religious principles? Does it not require the aid of a generally received and divinely authoritative Religion?

∧a main & necessary

Tis essentially true that virtue or morality is ∧ ~~an indispensable~~

spring

~~prop~~ of popular or republican Governments. The rule indeed extends with more or less force to all free Governments. Who that is a prudent & sincere friend to them can look with indifference on the ravages which are making in the foundation of the Fabric? Religion? The uncommon means which of late have been directed to this fatal end seem to make it in a particular of manner the duty of the Retiring

a

Chief of ~~his~~ nation to warn his country against tasting of the poisonous draught.

Cultivate also industry and frugality. They are auxiliaries of good morals and ~~sour~~ great sources of private and national prosperity. Is there not room for regret that our propensity to expence exceeds the maturity of our Country for expense? Is there not more luxury among us, in various classes, than ~~the~~ suits the actual period of our national

∧the apology for

progress? Whatever may be ∧ ~~said of~~ luxury in a Country mature ~~in wealth and~~ in all the arts which are its ministers and the means of national opulence—can it promote the advantage of a young agricultural Country little advanced in manufactures and not much advanced in wealth?

Cherish public Credit as a mean of strength and security. ~~But œconomise the resource by the using it as little as possible~~ As one method of preserving it, use it as little as possible. Avoid occasions of expense by cultivating peace—remembering always that the prepara-

∧against danger

tion ∧ ~~for danger defence~~ by timely and provident disbursements is often a mean of avoiding greater disbursements to repel it. Avoid the

of

accumulation of ~~expence~~ debt by avoiding occasions ~~and~~ expence and

peace

by vigorous exertions in time of ∧ to discharge the debts which unavoidable wars may have occasionned—not transferring to posterity

which

the burthen ∧ we ought to bear ourselves. Recollect that towards the

444

~~dischar~~ payment of debts there must be Revenue, that to have revenue there must be taxes, ~~and that a chearful acquiesence which in those whie~~ that it is impossible to devise taxes which are not more or less inconvenient and unpleasant—that they are always a choice of difficulties—that ~~from~~ the intrinsic embarrassment which ~~always~~ never fails to attend a selection of objects ought to be a motive for a candid construction of the conduct of the Government in making it—and that a spirit of acquiescence in those measures for obtaining revenue which the public exigencies dictate is in an especial manner the duty and interest of the citizens of every State.

Cherish good faith and Justice towards, and peace and harmony
enjoins
with all nations. Religion and morality ~~demand~~ this conduct And It
demands ~~dictates~~
cannot be, but that true policy equally ∧ ~~demands~~ it. It will be worthy of a free enlightened and at ~~not~~ no distant period a great nation to
∧to mankind
give ∧ the magnanimous and too novel example ~~to mankind~~ of a
an exalted justice & benevolence.
people ~~and go~~ invariably governed by those exalted views. Who can
a
~~say~~ doubt that in ~~the~~ long course of time and events the fruits of such a conduct would richly repay any temporary advantages which might be lost by a steady adherence to the plan? Can it be that Providence
permanent felicity
has not connected the ∧ ~~happiness~~ of a nation with its virtue? The
recommended by   which
experiment is ~~worthy of~~ every sentiment ~~that~~ ennobles human nature. Alas! is it rendered impossible by its vices?

Toward the execution of such a plan <u>nothing is</u> more essential than that antipathies against particular nations and passionate attach-
for
ments ~~towards~~ others should be ~~discarded~~ avoided—and that instead
cultivate
of them we should ∧ just and amicable feelings towards all. That nation, which indulges towards another a habitual hatred or a habitual fondness is in some degree a slave. It is a slave to its animosity or to its ~~attach~~ affection—either of which is sufficient to lead it astray from its duty and interest. Antipathy against one nation which never fails to beget a similar sentiment in the other disposes each more readily to ~~violate the rights~~ offer injury and insult to the other—to lay hold of slight causes of umbrage and to be haughty and intractable when accidental or trifling differences arise. Hence frequent

445

broils
quarrels and bitter and obstinate contests. The nation urged by resentment and rage sometimes impels the Government to War contrary to its own calculations of policy ~~& interest~~. The Gover[n]ment ~~frequ~~ sometimes participates in this propensity & does through passion what reason would forbid—at other times it makes the animosity of the nations ~~subservient~~ subservient to hostiles projects which originate in ambition & other sinister motives. The peace often and sometimes the liberty of Nations has been the victim of this cause.

So likewise   one nation

In like manner a passionate attachment of ~~one~~ ∧ to another pro-
                                        facilitating
duces multiplied ills. Sympathy for the favourite nations, ~~promote~~
                              ∧in cases where it does not exist
promoting the illusion of a supposed common interest ∧ and a ~~participation in the enmities of the favourite leads to embark commun~~ and communicating to one the enmities of the one betrays into a participation in its quarrels & wars without adequate inducements or justifications. It leads to the concession of privileges to one nation and to the denial of them to others—which is apt doubly to injure the nation making the concession by an unnecessary ~~sacrifice~~ yielding of what ought to have been retained and by exciting jealousy ill will and retaliation in the party from whom an equal privilege is witheld. And it gives to ambitious ~~or~~ corrupted or deluded citizens, who devote
                                      power,
themselves to the views of the favourite foreign ~~nation the~~ facility in
                                      without odium &
betraying or sacrificing the interests of their own country even with
            gilding with the appearance   a virtuous impulse
~~the advantage of~~ popularity ~~to themselves~~ of ∧ ~~virtue & justness of~~
               yieldings
~~sentiment~~ the base ~~sacrifices~~ of ambition ~~of~~ or corruption.

As avenues to foreign influence in ~~innume~~ innumerable Ways such attachments are peculiarly alarming to the enlightened indepen-
                   Patriot   do they
dent ~~friend of his Country~~. How many opportunities ~~does it~~ afford to intrigue with domestic factions ~~to seduce even~~ to practice with suc-
                seduction—to   mislead
cess the arts of ~~success—to misdirect the~~ public opinion—to influence or awe the public Councils! Such an attachment of a small or weak towards a great & powerful Nation destines the former to revolve round the latter as its satellite.

Against the Mischiefs of Foreign Influence all ~~are~~ the Jealousy of

446

a free people ought to be constantly ~~directed~~ *continually* exerted. All History & Experience ~~in different ages and nations has~~ proved that foreign influence is one of the most ~~formidable~~ *baneful* foes of republican Governt—but the jealousy ~~at~~ ∧ *of it* to be useful must be impartial else it becomes an instrument ~~instead of a defence~~—of ~~that~~ ∧ *the very* influence ∧ *to be avoided* instead of a defence *guard* against. *it*

~~An~~ Excessive partiality for one foreign nation & excessive dislike of another, leads to see danger only on one side and serves to viel ∧ *& second* the arts of influence on the other. ~~This is a mo~~ Real Patriots who resist the intrigues of the favorite become suspected & odious. Its tools & dupes usurp the applause & confidence of the people to betray their interests.

The great rule of conduct for us in regard to foreign Nations ought to be to have as little <u>political</u> connection with them as possible—so far as we have already formed engagements let them be fulfilled—with circumspection indeed but with perfect good faith. ~~But~~ Here let us stop.

Europe has a set of primary interests ~~foreign to us~~ which have none or a very remote relation to us. Hence she must be involved in frequent contests the causes of which will be essentially foreign to us. Hence therefore it must necessarily be unwise ~~in us~~ on our part to implicate ourselves by an artificial connectione in the ordinary vicissitudes of European politics—in the combination, & collisions of her friendships or enmities.

Our detached and distant situation invites us to a different course & enables us to pursue it. If we remain a united people under an efficient Government the period is not distant when we may defy material injury from external annoyance—when we may take such an attitude as will cause the neutrality we shall at any time resolve to observe to be ~~duly~~ violated with caution—~~when menacing more than ear~~ when it will be the interest of belligerent nations under the impossibility of making acquisitions upon us to be very careful how either forced us to throw our weight into the opposite scale—when we may choose peace or war as our interest guided by justice shall dictate.

Why should we forego the advantages of so ~~ha~~ felicitous a situation? Why ~~should we~~ quit our own ground to stand upon ~~European~~ *Foreign* ground? Why by interweaving our destiny with any part of Europe should we intangle our ~~prospect~~ prosperity and peace in the nets of European Ambition rivalship interest or Caprice?

Permanent alliance, intimate connection with any part of the foreign ~~ea~~ world is to be avoided. (I mean) ~~I mean~~ so far ∧ as we are now at liberty to do it: for let me never be understood ~~as infedily to~~ as patronising infidelity to preexisting engagements. These must be observed in their true and genuine sense. But tis not necessary nor will it be prudent to extend them. Tis our true policy as a general principle to avoid permanent or ~~a~~ close alliance—Taking care always to keep ourselves by suitable establishments in a respectably defensive posture we may safely trust to occasional alliances ~~in~~ for extraordinary emergencies. ~~But I mean to submit to you my fellow citizens a general principle of policy which I think ought to govern you as far as you are at present free. In extraordinary exigencies temporary alliances will suffice for the occasion.~~

Harmony ∧ ~~friendly~~ liberal intercourse and commerce with all nations are recommended by justice humanity & interest. But even our commercial policy should hold an equal hand—neither seeking nor granting ∧ ~~particular~~ exclusive favours or preferences—consulting the natural course of things—_diffusing_ and _diversifying_ by gentle means the streams of Commerce but forcing nothing—establishing ~~by treaty~~ with powers so disposed in order to give to ∧ Trade a stable course, to ~~trade~~ define the rights of our Merchants and enable the Government to support them— ~~temporary~~ ∧ conventional rules of intercourse the best that present circumstances and mutual opinion of interest will permit but temporary—and liable to be abandonned or varied as time experience & future circumstances may dictate—remembering that tis folly ~~to expect a disinterested~~ alway in one nation to expect disinterested favour in another—that to accept ∧ any thing under that character ~~it~~ is to part with a portion of ~~our~~ its independence—and that ~~we~~ it may ~~frequently~~ find ~~ourselves~~ itself in the condition of having given ~~an~~ equivalents for nominal favours and of being reproached with ingratitude in the bargain. There can be no greater error in national policy than to desire expect or calculate upon real favours. Tis an illusion that experience must cure, that a just pride ought to discard.

My Countrymen!

In offering to you ∧ ~~fellow Citizens~~ these counsels of an old and affectionate friend—counsels suggested by labourious reflection and matured by a various experience—I dare not hope that they will make the strong and lasting impressions I wish—that they will controul the current of the passions or prevent our nation from running the course

I may flatter myself that

~~of~~ which has hitherto marked the destiny of all nations. But if they

some   some   that they

~~may~~ even produce ∧ partial benefits, occasional good—~~if the shall~~ sometimes recur to moderate the violence of party spirit—to warn against the evils of foreign intrigue—to guard against the impositions of pretended patriotism—the having offered them must always afford me a precious consolation.

How far in the execution of my present Office I have been guided

inculcated

by the principles which have been ~~recommended~~ the public records & the external evidences of my conduct must witness. ~~to an~~ My conscious assures me that I have at least believed myself to be guided by them.

In reference to the present War of Europe my Proclamation of the

plan

22d of April 1793 is the key to my ~~sentiments~~. Sanctioned by your approving voice and that of your representatives in Congress ~~has continually governed me~~ the spirit of that measure has continually governed me uninfluenced and unawed by the attempts of any of the warring powers their agents or partizans to deter or divert from it.

After deliberate consideration and the best lights I could obtain (and from men who did not agree in their views of the ~~original~~ progress & nature of that war) I was satisfied that our Country, ~~had~~ under all the circumstances of the case, had a right and was bound in propriety and interest to take a neutral position—And having taken it, I

far as

determined as ∧ should depend on me to maintain it steadily and firmly.

incidents

Though in reviewing the ~~events~~ of my administration I am unconscious of intentional error—I am yet too sensible of my own deficiencies not to think it probable that I have committed many errors. I deprecate the evils to which they may tend—and fervently implore the Almighty to avert or mitigate them. I shall carry with me

449

nevertheless the hope that my motives will continue to be viewed by my Country with indulgence & that after forty five years of my life devoted with an upright zeal to the public service the faults of inadequate abilities will be consigned to oblivion as myself must soon be to the mansions of rest.

Neither Ambition nor interest has been the impelling cause of my actions. I never designedly misused any power confided to me. The fortune with which I came into office is not bettered otherwise than by that ~~value~~ improvement in the value of property which the natural progress and peculiar prosperity of our country have produced. I

without cause for a blush—

retire with ~~an~~ a pure heart ~~with no sentiment alien to your true interests~~ with no alien sentiment to the ardor of those vows for the happiness of his Country which is so natural to a Citizen who sees in it ~~with undefiled hand and with ardent~~ vows for ~~the happiness of a~~

which is   himself   his

~~Country,~~ ∧ the native soil of ~~myself~~ and ∧ progenitors for four generations.

LETTER TO WILLIAM HAMILTON
MAY 2, 1797

Hamilton's brief sketch of his political career in a letter to his uncle in Scotland constitutes an autobiographical statement.

Albany State of New York
May the 2d. 1797

My Dear Sir

Some days since I received with great pleasure your letter of the 10th. of March. The mark, it affords, of your kind attention, and the particular account it gives me of so many relations in Scotland are extremely gratifying to me. You no doubt have understood that my fathers affairs at a very early day went to wreck; so as to have rendered his situation during the greatest part of his life far from eligible. This state of things occasionned a separation between him and me, when I was very young, and threw me upon the bounty of my mothers relations, some of whom were then wealthy, though by vicissitudes to which human affairs are so liable, they have been since much reduced and broken up. Myself at about sixteen came to this Country. Having always had a strong propensity to literary pursuits, by a course of steady and laborious exertion, I was able, by the age of Ninteen to qualify myself for the degree of Batchelor of Arts in the College of New York, and to lay a foundation, by preparatory study, for the future profession of the law.

The American Revolution supervened. My principles led me to take part in it. At nineteen I entered into the American army as Captain of Artillery. Shortly after, I became by his invitation Aide De Camp to General Washington, in which station, I served till the commencement of that Campaign which ended with the seige of York, in Virginia, and the Capture of Cornwallis's Army. This Campaign I made at the head of a corps of light infantry, with which I was present at the seige of York and engaged in some interesting operations.

At the period of the peace with Great Britain, I found myself a member of Congress by appointment of the legislature of this state.

After the peace, I settled in the City of New York in the practice of the law; and was in a very lucrative course of practice, when the derangement of our public affairs, by the feebleness of the general confederation, drew me again reluctantly into public life. I became a member of the Convention which framed the present Constitution of the U States; and having taken part in this measure, I conceived myself to be under an obligation to lend my aid towards putting the machine in some regular motion. Hence I did not hesitate to accept the offer of President Washington to undertake the office of Secretary of the Treasury.

In that office, I met with many intrinsic difficulties, and many artificial ones proceeding from passions, not very worthy, common to human nature, and which act with peculiar force in republics. The object, however, was effected, of establishing public credit and introducing order into the finances.

Public Office in this Country has few attractions. The pecuniary emolument is so inconsiderable as too amount to a sacrifice to any man who can employ his time with advantage in any liberal profession. The opportunity of doing good, from the jealousy of power and the spirit of faction, is too small in any station to warrant a long continuance of private sacrifices. The enterprises of party had so far succeeded as materially to weaken the necessary influence and energy of the Executive Authority, and so far diminish the power of doing good in that department as greatly to take the motives which a virtuous man might have for making sacrifices. The prospect was even bad for gratifying in future the love of Fame, if that passion was to be the spring of action.

The Union of these motives, with the reflections of prudence in relation to a growing family, determined me as soon as my plan had attained a certain maturity to withdraw from Office. This I did by a resignation about two years since; when I resumed the profession of the law in the City of New York under every advantage I could desire.

It is a pleasing reflection to me that since the commencement of my connection with General Washington to the present time, I have possessed a flattering share of his confidence and friendship.

Having given you a brief sketch of my political career, I proceed to some further family details.

In the year 1780 I married the second daughter of General Schuyler, a Gentleman of one of the best families of this Country; of large fortune and no less personal and public consequence. It is impossible to be happier than I am in a wife and I have five Children, four sons and a daughter, the eldest a son somewhat passed fifteen, who all promise well, as far as their years permit and yield me much satisfaction. Though I have been too much in public life to be wealthy, my situation is extremely comfortable and leaves me nothing to wish but a continuance of health. With this blessing, the profits of my profession and other prospects authorise an expectation of such addition to my resources as will render the eve of life, easy and agreeable; so far as may depend on this consideration.

It is now several months since I have heared from my father who continued at the Island of St Vincents. My anxiety at this silence would be greater than it is, were it not for the considerable interruption and precariousness of intercourse, which is produced by the War.

I have strongly pressed the old Gentleman to come to reside with me, which would afford him every enjoyment of which his advanced age is capable. But he has declined it on the ground that the advice of his Physicians leads him to fear that the change of Climate would be fatal to him. The next thing for me is, in proportion to my means to endeavour to increase his comforts where he is.

It will give me the greatest pleasure to receive your son Robert at my house in New York and still more to be of use to him; to which end my recommendation and interest will not be wanting, and, I hope, not unavailing. It is my intention to embrace the Opening which your letter affords me to extend intercourse with my relations in your Country, which will be a new source of satisfaction to me.

LETTER TO OLIVER WOLCOTT, JUNIOR
JUNE 29, 1798

The Alien and Sedition Acts were passed by Congress in 1798 with the avowed intention of protecting the nation from dangerous foreign influence in the midst of an undeclared war with France. In the following letter, Hamilton criticizes Senator James Lloyd's first draft of the sedition law, which was introduced in the Senate on June 26 but was recommitted by the Senate before this letter was written. The final sedition law passed by Congress in July was less restrictive of free speech.

New York, June 29, 1798

Dear Sir

I have this moment seen a Bill brought into the Senate intitled a Bill to define more particularly the crime of Treason &c. There are provisions in this Bill which according to a cursory view appear to me highly exceptionable & such as more than any thing else may endanger civil War. I have not time to point out my objections by this post but I will do it tomorrow. I hope sincerely the thing may not be hurried through. Let us not establish a tyranny. Energy is a very different thing from violence. If we make no false step we shall be essentially united; but if we push things to an extreme we shall then give to faction *body* & solidarity.

  Yrs. truly

A Hamilton
June 29. 1798

O Wolcott Esq

HAMILTON'S DRAFT OF A LETTER FROM GEORGE WASHINGTON TO JAMES MCHENRY
DECEMBER 13, 1798

The following portion of a letter that Hamilton wrote for Washington contains his thoughts on foreign policy during the period of America's undeclared war with France and should be read in conjunction with his draft of Washington's Farewell Address.

Though it may be true that some late occurrences have rendered the prospect of invasion by France, less probable or more remote: Yet duly considering the rapid vicissitudes, at all times, of political and military events; the extraordinary fluctuations which have been peculiarly characteristic of the still subsisting contest in Europe; and the more extraordinary position of most of the principal nations of that quarter of the globe; it can never be wise to vary our measures of security with the continually varying aspect of European affairs. A very obvious policy dictates to us a strenuous endeavour as far as may be practicable, to place our safety out of the reach of the casualties which may befal the contending parties and the powers more immediately within their vortex. The way to effect this is to pursue a steady system—to organise all our resources and put them in a state of preparation for prompt action. Regarding the overthrow of Europe at large as a matter not intirely chimerical—it will be our prudence to cultivate a spirit of self-dependence—and to endeavour by unremitting vigilance and exertion under the blessing of providence to hold the scales of our destiny in our own hands. Standing, as it were, in the midst of falling empires, it should be our aim to assume a station and attitude which will preserve us from being overwhelmed in their ruins.

It has been very properly the policy of our Government to cultivate peace. But in contemplating the possibility of our being driven to unqualified War, it will be wise to anticipate that frequently the most effectual way to defend is to attack. There may be imagined enterprises of very great moment to the permanent interests of this Country which would certainly require a disciplined force. To raise and prepare such a force will always be a work of considerable time; and it ought to be ready for the conjuncture whenever it shall arrive. Not to be ready then may be to lose an opportunity which it may be difficult afterwards to retrieve.

LETTER TO MARQUIS DE LAFAYETTE
JANUARY 6, 1799

Lafayette had written a letter to Hamilton stating his political principles and asserting that he believed the establishment of liberty on the continent of Europe ought to be conducted on American rather than British principles. Hamilton's response in the following letter suggests that he is doubtful about the simple application of political principles in the construction of regimes without consideration of circumstances.

New York January 6. 1799

I have been made happy my dear friend by the receipt of your letter of the 12th of August last. No explanation of your political principles was necessary to satisfy me of the perfect consistency and purity of your conduct. The interpretation may always be left to my attachment for you. Whatever difference of opinion may on any occasion exist between us can never lessen my conviction of the goodness both of your head and heart. I expect from you a return of this sentiment so far as concerns the heart. Tis needless to detail to you my political tenets. I shall only say that I hold with *Montesquieu* that a government must be fitted to a nation as much as a Coat to the Individual, and consequently that what may be good at Philadelphia may be bad at Paris and ridiculous at Petersburgh.

I join with you in regretting the misunderstanding between our two countries. You will have seen by the Presidents speech that a door is again opened for terminating them amicably. And you may be assured that we are sincere, and that it is in the power of France by reparation to our merchants for past injury and the stipulation of justice in future to put an end to the controversy.

But I do not like much the idea of your being any way implicated in the affair, lest you should be compromitted in the opinion of one or the other of the parties. It is my opinion that it is best for you to stand aloof. Neither have I abandonned the idea that 'tis most adviseable for you to remain in Europe 'till the difference is adjusted. It would be very difficult for you here to steer a course which would not place you in a party and remove you from the broad ground which you now occupy in the hearts of all. It is a favorite point with me that you shall find in the universal regard of this country all the consolations which the loss of your own (for so I consider it) may render requisite.

Mrs Church and Mrs Hamilton unite in assurance of their affectionate remembrance. Believe me always

Your very cordial & faithful friend   A H

Marquis de la Fayette

LETTER TO TOBIAS LEAR
JANUARY 2, 1800

The following letter was written on the occasion of Washington's death in December 1799. Tobias Lear was Washington's military secretary at that time.

N. York Jany. 2d. 1800

Dr. Sir

Yr. letter of the 15 of Decr. last was delayed in getting to hand by the circumstance of its having gone to N. York while I was at Phila. and of its having arrived at Phila. after I had set out on my return to N. York.

The very painful event which it announces had, previously to the receipt of it, filled my heart with bitterness. Perhaps no man in this community has equal cause with myself to deplore the loss. I have been much indebted to the kindness of the General, and he was an Aegis very essential to me. But regrets are unavailing. For great misfortunes it is the business of reason to seek consolation. The friends of General Washington have very noble ones. If virtue can secure happiness in another world he is happy. In this the Seal is now put upon his Glory. It is no longer in jeopardy from the fickleness of fortune.

Adieu &c

P.S. In whose hands are his papers gone? Our very confidential situation will not permit this to be a point of indifference to me.

LETTER CONCERNING THE PUBLIC CONDUCT AND CHARACTER OF JOHN ADAMS ESQ. PRESIDENT OF THE UNITED STATES
OCTOBER 24, 1800

Hamilton thought that the United States under the Adams presidency was like a country without a ruler. The following portion of his famous letter criticizing the Adams presidency contains Hamilton's reflections on the manner in which the chief executive should make use of his cabinet officers.

A President is not bound to conform to the advice of his Ministers. He is even under no positive injunction to ask or require it. But the Constitution presumes that he will consult them; and the genius of our government and the public good recommend the practice.

As the President nominates his Ministers, and may displace them when he pleases, it must be his own fault if he be not surrounded by men, who for ability and integrity deserve his confidence. And if his ministers are of this character, the consulting of them will always be likely to be useful to himself and to the State. Let it even be supposed that he is a man of talents superior to the collected talents of all his ministers, (which can seldom happen, as the world has seen but few FREDERICKS) he may, nevertheless, often assist his judgment by a comparison and collision of ideas. The greatest genius, hurried away by the rapidity of its own conceptions, will occasionally overlook obstacles which ordinary and more phlegmatic men will discover, and which, when presented to his consideration, will be thought by himself decisive objections to his plans.

When, unhappily, an ordinary man dreams himself to be a FREDERICK, and through vanity refrains from counselling with his constitutional advisers, he is very apt to fall into the hands of miserable intriguers, with whom his self-love is more at ease, and who without difficulty slide into his confidence, and by flattery, govern him.

The ablest men may profit by advice. Inferior men cannot dispense with it; and if they do not get it through legitimate channels, it will find its way to them, through such as are clandestine and impure.

Very different from the practice of Mr. ADAMS was that of the modest and sage WASHINGTON. He consulted much, pondered much, resolved slowly, resolved surely.

And as surely, Mr. ADAMS might have benefited by the advice of his ministers.

The stately system of not consulting Ministers is likely to have a further disadvantage. It will tend to exclude from places of primary trust, the men most fit to occupy them.

Few and feeble are the interested inducements to accept a place in our Administration. Far from being lucrative, there is not one which will not involve pecuniary sacrifice to every *honest* man of preeminent talents. And has not experience shewn, that he must be fortunate indeed, if even the successful execution of his task can secure to him consideration and fame? Of a large harvest of obloquy he is sure.

457

If excluded from the counsels of the Executive Chief, his office must become truly insignificant. What able and virtuous man will long consent to be so miserable a pageant?

Every thing that tends to banish from the Administration able men, tends to diminish the chances of able counsels. The probable operation of a system of this kind, must be to consign places of the highest trust to incapable honest men, whose inducement will be a livelihood, or to capable dishonest men, who will seek indirect indemnifications for the deficiency of direct and fair inducements.

LETTER TO GOUVERNEUR MORRIS
DECEMBER 26, 1800

In the presidential contest of 1800, both Aaron Burr and Thomas Jefferson received seventy-three electoral votes; thus the choice devolved upon the House of Representatives. In addition to the following letter, Hamilton wrote to several other Federalists urging them to support Jefferson rather than Burr for the presidency.

New York 26 Decr. 1800

Dr Sir

The post of yesterday gave me the pleasure of a letter from you. I thank you for the communication. I trust that a letter which I wrote you the day before the receipt of yours will have duly reached you as it contains some very free & confidential observations ending in two results—1 That The Convention with France ought to be ratified as the least of two evils 2 That *on the same ground Jefferson* ought to be preferred to *Burr*.

I trust the Fœderalists will not finally be so mad as to vote for the *latter*. I speak with an intimate & accurate knowledge of character. His elevation can only promote the purposes of the desperate and profligate. ⟨If t⟩here be ⟨a man⟩ in the world I ought to hate it is Jefferson. With *Burr* I have always been personally well. But the public good must be paramount to every private consideration. My opinion may be freely used with such reserves as you shall think discreet.

Yrs. very truly A H

G Morris Esq

458

LETTER TO JAMES A. BAYARD
DECEMBER 27, 1800

The most arresting event of Hamilton's political career was his support of Thomas Jefferson for president over Aaron Burr in the deadlocked election of 1800. He confessed that if there was a man in the world whom he ought to hate it was Jefferson, but he added that the public good must take precedence over every private consideration. He regarded Burr as unprincipled and a greater danger to political life than Jefferson. See also his later letter to James A. Bayard of January 16, 1801.

New-York December, 27th. 1800.

Dear Sir

Several letters to myself & others from the City of Washington, excite in my mind extreme alarm on the subject of the future President. It seems nearly ascertained that *Jefferson* & *Burr* will come into the house of Rs. with equal votes, and those letters express the probability that the Fœderal Party may prefer the latter. In my opinion a circumstance more ruinous to them, or more disastrous to the Country could not happen. This opinion is dictated by a long & close attention to the character, with the best opportunities of knowing it; an advant[ag]e for judging which few of our friends possess, & which ought to give some weight to my opinion. Be assured my dear Sir, that this man has no principle public or private. As a politician his sole spring of action is an inordinate ambition; as an individual he is believed by friends as well as foes to be without *probity*, and a voluptuary by system, with habits of expence that can be satisfied by no fair expedients. As to his talents, great management & cunning are the predominant features—he is yet to give proofs of those solid abilities which characterize the statesman. Daring & energy must be allowed him but these qualities under the direction of the worst passions, are certainly strong objections not recommendations. He is of a temper to undertake the most hazadrous enterprizes because he is sanguine enough to think nothing impracticable, and of an ambition which will be content with nothing less than *permanent* power in his own hands. The maintenance of the existing institutions will not suit him, because under them his power will be too narrow & too precarious; yet the innovations he may attempt will not offer the substitute of a system *durable* & *safe*, calculated to give lasting prosperity, & to unite liberty

459

with strength. It will be the system of the day, sufficient to serve his own turn, & not looking beyond himself. To execute this plan as the good men of the country cannot be relied upon, the worst will be used. Let it not be imagined that the difficulties of execution will deter, or a calculation of interest restrain. The truth is that under forms of Government like ours, too much is practicable to men who will without scruple avail themselves of the bad passions of human nature. To a man of this description possessing the requisite talents, the acquisition of permanent power is not a Chimæra. I *know* that Mr Burr does not view it as such, & I am sure there are no means too atrocious to be employed by him. In debt vastly beyond his means of payment, with all the habits of excessive expence, he cannot be satisfied with the regular emoluments of any office of our Government. Corrupt expedients will be to him a *necessary* resource. Will any prudent man offer such a president to the temptations of foreign gold? No engagement that can be made with him can be depended upon. While making it he will laugh in his sleeve at the credulity of those with whom he makes it—and the first moment it suits his views to break it he will do so.* Let me add that I could scarcely name a discreet man of either party in our State, who does not think Mr Burr the most unfit man in the U.S. for the office of President. Disgrace abroad ruin at home are the probable fruits of his elevation. To contribute to the disappointment and mortification of Mr J. would be on my part, only to retaliate for unequivocal proofs of enmity; but in a case like this it would be base to listen to personal considerations. In alluding to the situation I mean only to illustrate how strong must be the motives which induce me to promote *his* elevation in exclusion of another. For Heaven's sake my dear Sir, exert yourself to the utmost to save our country from so great a calamity. Let us not be responsible for the evils which in all probability will follow the preference. All calculations that may lead to it must prove fallacious.

Accept the assurances of my esteem,   A Hamilton.

*A recent incident will give you an idea of his views as to foreign politics. I dined with him lately. His toasts were "The French Republic." "The commissioners who negotiated the convention." "Buonaparte" "The Marquis La Fayette." His doctrines that it would be the interest of this country to permit the indiscriminate sale of Prizes by the Belligerent *powers* & the building & equipment of vessels; a project amounting to nothing more nor less (with the semblance of equality,) than to turn all our naval resources into the channel of France, and compel G. Britain to war. Indeed Mr Burr must have war as the instrument of his Ambition & Cupidity. The peculiarity of the occasion will excuse my mentioning *in confidence* the occurrences of a private Table.

LETTER TO JAMES A. BAYARD
JANUARY 16, 1801

In giving his support to Jefferson over Burr in the presidential election of 1800, Hamilton knew very well that the man he was supporting represented the antithesis of the entire Federalist program. Yet, he was willing to risk the undermining of that program in preference to having Burr in the presidential office. The difference in perspectives between Hamilton and Jefferson was not sufficient to make up for Burr's dangerous disregard of principle, which in Hamilton's view constituted a far more serious threat to the established political regime and to the continued preeminence of the Constitution.

New-York Jany. 16th. 1801

I was glad to find my dear sir, by your letter, that you had not yet determined to go with the current of the Fœderal Party in the support of Mr *Burr* & that you were resolved to hold yourself disengaged till the moment of final decision. Your resolution to separate yourself, in this instance, from the Fœderal Party if your conviction shall be strong of the unfitness of Mr Burr, is certainly laudable. So much does it coincide with my ideas, that if the Party Shall by supporting Mr Burr as President adopt him for their official Chief—I shall be obliged to consider myself as an *isolated* man. It will be impossible for me to reconcile with my notions of *honor* or policy, the continuing to be of a Party which according to my apprehension will have degraded itself & the country. I am sure nevertheless that the motives of many will be good, and I shall never cease to esteem the individuals, tho' I shall deplore a step which I fear experience will show to be a very fatal one. Among the letters which I receive assigning the reasons *pro* & *con* for prefering Burr to J. I observe no small exaggeration to the prejudice of the latter & some things taken for granted as to the former which are at least questionable. Perhaps myself the first, at some expence of popularity, to unfold the true character of Jefferson, it is too late for me to become his apologist. Nor can I have any disposition to do it. I admit that his politics are tinctured with fanaticism, that he is too much in earnest in his democracy, that he has been a mischevous enemy to the principle measures of our past administration, that he is crafty & persevering in his objects, that he is not scrupulous about the means of success, nor very mindful of truth, and that he is a contemptible hypocrite. But it is not true as is alleged that he is an enemy to the power of the Executive, or that he is for confounding all the powers in the House of Rs. It is a fact which I have frequently mentioned that while we were in the administration together he was generally for a large construction of the Executive authority, & not backward to act upon it in cases which coincided with his views. Let it be added, that in his theoretic Ideas he has considered as improper the participations of the Senate in the Executive Authority. I have more than once made the reflection that viewing himself as the reversioner, he was solicitous to come into possession of a Good Estate. Nor is it true that Jefferson is zealot enough to do anything in pursuance of his principles which will contravene his popularity, or his interest. He is as likely as any man I know to temporize—to calculate what will be likely to promote his own reputation and advantage; and the probable result of such a temper is the preservation of systems, though originally opposed, which being once established, could not be overturned without danger to the person who did it. To my mind a true estimate of Mr J.'s character warrants the expectation of a temporizing rather than a violent system. That Jefferson has manifested a culpable predilection for France is certainly true; but I think it a question whether it did not proceed quite as much from her *popularity* among us, as from sentiment, and in proportion as that popularity is diminished his zeal will cool. Add to this that there is no fair reason to suppose him capable of being corrupted, which is a security that he will not go beyond certain limits. It is not at all improbable that under the change of circumstances Jefferson's Gallicism has considerably abated.

As to Burr these things are admitted and indeed cannot be denied, that he is a man of *extreme* & *irregular* ambition—that he is *selfish* to a degree which excludes all social affections & that he is decidedly *profligate*. But it is said, 1st. that he is *artful* & *dexterous* to accomplish his ends—2nd. that he holds no pernicious theories, but is a mere *matter of fact* man—3rd. that his very selfishness* is a guard against mischevous foreign predilections. 4th That his *local situation* has enabled him to appreciate the utility of our Commercial & fiscal systems, and the same quality of selfishness will lead him to support & invigorate them. 5th. that he is now disliked by the Jacobins, that his elevation will be a mortal stab to them, breed an invincible hatred to him, & compel him to lean on the Federalists. 6th. That Burr's ambition will be checked by his good sense, by the manifest impossibility of succeeding in any scheme of usurpation, & that if attempted, there

*It is always very dangerous to look to the *vices* of men for *Good*.

is nothing to fear from the attempt. These topics are in my judgment more plausible than solid. As to the 1st point the fact must be admitted, but those qualities are objections rather than recommendations when they are under the direction of bad principles. As to the 2nd point too much is taken for granted. If Burr's conversation is to be credited he is not very far from being a visionary.* It is ascertained in some instances that he has talked perfect *Godwinism*. I have myself heard him speak with applause of the French system as unshackling the mind & leaving it to its natural energies, and I have been present when he has contended against Banking Systems** with earnestness & with the same arguments that Jefferson would use. The truth is that *Burr* is a man of a very subtile imagination, and a mind of this make is rarely free from ingenious whimsies. Yet I admit that he has no fixed theory & that his peculiar notions will easily give way to his interest. But is it a recommendation to have *no theory?* Can that man be a systematic or able statesman who has none? I believe not. *No general principles* will hardly work much better than erroneous ones. As to the 3rd. point—it is certain that Burr generally speaking has been as warm a partisan of France as Jefferson—that he has in some instances shewn himself to be so with passion. But if it was from calculation who will say that his calculations will not continue him so? His selfishness* so far from being an obstacle may be a prompter. If corrupt as well as selfish he may be a partisan for gain—if ambitious as well as selfish, he may be a partisan for the sake of aid to his views. No man has trafficked more than he in the floating passions of the multitude. Hatred to G. Britain & attachment to France in the public mind will naturally lead a man of his selfishness, attached to place and power, to favour France & oppose G. Britain. The Gallicism of many of our patriots is to be thus resolved, & in my opinion it is morally certain that Burr will continue to be influenced by this calculation. As to the 4th point the instance I have cited with respect to Banks proves that the argument is not to be relied on. If there was much in it, why does Chancellor Livingston maintain that we ought not to cultivate navigation but ought to let foreigners be our Carriers? France is of this opinion too & Burr for some reason or other, will be very apt to be of the opinion of *France*. As to the 5th point—nothing

*He has quoted to me *Connecticut* as an example of the success of the Democratic theory, and as authority, serious doubts whether it was not a good one.
**Yet he has lately by a trick established a *Bank*, a perfect monster in its principles; but a very convenient instrument of *profit* & *influence*.

*Unprincipled selfishness is more apt to seek rapid gain in disorderly practices than slow advantages from orderly systems.

can be more fallacious. It is demonstrated by recent facts** that Burr is *solicitous* to keep upon *Antifœderal ground*, to avoid compromitting himself by any engagements † with the Fœderalists. With or without such engagements he will easily persuade his former friends that he does stand on that ground, & after their first resentment they will be glad to rally under him. In the mean time he will take care not to disoblige them & he will always court those among them who are best fitted for tools. He will never choose to lean on good men because he knows that they will never support his bad projects: but instead of this he will endeavour to disorganize both parties & to form out of them a third composed of men fitted by their characters to be conspirators, & instruments of such projects. That this will be his future conduct may be inferred from his past plan, & from the admitted quality of irregular ambition. Let it be remembered that Mr Burr has never appeared solicitous for fame, & that great Ambition unchecked by principle, or the love of Glory, is an unruly Tyrant which never can keep long in a course which good men will approve. As to the last point—The propostion is against the experience of all times. Ambition without principle never was long under the guidance of good sense. Besides that, really the force of Mr Burrs understanding is much overrated. He is far more *cunning* than *wise*, far more *dexterous* than *able*. In my opinion he is inferior in real ability to Jefferson. There are also facts against the supposition. It is past all doubt that he has blamed me for not having improved the situation I once was in to change the Government. That when answered that this could not have been done without guilt—he replied—"Les grands ames se soucient peu des petits morceaux"—that when told the thing was never practicable from the genious and situation of the country, he answered, "that depends on the estimate we form of the human passions and of the means of influencing them." Does this prove that Mr Burr would consider a scheme of usurpation as visionary. The truth is with great apparent coldness he is the most sanguine man in the world. He thinks every thing possible to adventure and perseverance. And tho' I believe he will fail, I think it almost certain he will attempt usurpation. An[d] the attempt will involve great mischief.

But there is one point of view which seems to me decisive. If the Antifœderalists who prevailed in the election are left to take their own man, they remain responsible, and the Fœderalists remain *free united* and without *stain*, in a situation to resist with effect pernicious measures. If the Fœderalists substitute Burr, they adopt him and become

**My letter to Mr Morris states some of them.
†He trusts to their *prejudices* and *hopes* for support.

answerable for him. Whatever may be the theory of the case, abroad and at *home* (for so from the beginning will be taught) Mr Burr will become *in fact* the man of our party. And if he acts ill, we must share in the blame and disgrace. By adopting him we do all we can to reconcile the minds of the Fœderalists to him, and prepare them for the effectual operation of his arts. He will doubtless gain many of them, & the Fœderalists will become a disorganized and contemptible party. Can there be any serious question between the policy of leaving the Antifœderalists to be answerable for the elevation of an exceptionable man, & that of adopting ourselves & becoming answerable for a man who on all hands is acknowledged to be a complete *Cataline* in his practice & principles? 'Tis enough to state the question to indicate the answer, if reason not passion presides in the decision. You may communicate this & my former letter to discreet & confidential friends.

Your's very truly,   A H

AN ADDRESS TO THE ELECTORS OF THE STATE OF NEW YORK
MARCH 21, 1801

The occasion for the following address was the campaign for the governorship of New York, but in substance the address is a defense of Federalist principles and practice against Republican criticism. It is particularly valuable in that we get a backward glance from Hamilton at the totality of Federalist rule near the end of his career.

March 21, 1801

To the Electors of the State of New-York

FELLOW-CITIZENS!

We lately addressed you on the subject of the ensuing election for Governor and Lieutenant-Governor—recommending to your support STEPHEN VAN RENSSELAER and JAMES WATSON. Since that we have seen the address of our opponents, urging your preference of George Clinton and Jeremiah Van Rensselaer.

465

The whole tenor of our address carries with it the evidence of a disposition to be temperate and liberal; to avoid giving occasion to mutual recrimination. It would have been agreeable to us to have seen a like disposition in our adversaries; but we think it cannot be denied, that their address manifests a different one. It arraigns the principles of the federalists with extreme acrimony, and by the allusion to Great-Britain in the preposterous figure of the mantle, attributes to them a principle of action, which every signer of the address knows to have no existence, and which for its falsehood and malice merits indignation and disdain.

So violent an attack upon our principles justifies and calls for an exhibition of those of our opponents. To your good sense, to your love of country, to your regard for the welfare of yourselves and families, the comment is submitted.

The pernicious spirit which has actuated many of the leaders of the party denominated antifederal, from the moment when our national constitution was first proposed down to the present period, has not ceased to display itself, in a variety of disgusting forms. In proportion to the prospect of success it has increased in temerity. Emboldened by a momentary triumph in the choice of our national Chief Magistrate, it seems now to have laid aside all reserve; and begins to avow projects of disorganization, with the sanction of the most respectable names of the party, which before were merely the anonymous ravings of incendiary newspapers.

This precipitation in throwing aside the mask, will, we trust, be productive of happy effects. It will serve to shew that the mischievous designs ascribed to the party have not been the effusions of malevolence, the inventions of political rivalship, or the visionary forebodings of an over anxious zeal; but that they have been just and correct inferences from an accurate estimate of characters and principles. It will serve to shew, that moderate men, who have seen in our political struggles, nothing more than a competition for power and place, have been deceived; that in reality the foundations of society, the essential interests of our nation, the dearest concerns of individuals are staked upon the eventful contest. And, by promoting this important discovery, it may be expected to rally the virtuous and the prudent of every description round a common standard; to endeavour by joint efforts to oppose mounds to that destructive torrent, which in its distant murmuring, seemed harmless, but in the portentous roaring of its nearer approach, menaces our country with all the horrors of revolutionary phrenzy.

To what end, Fellow-Citizens, has your attention been carried across the Atlantic, to the revolution of France, and to that fatal war of which it has been the source? To what end are you told, that this is the most interesting conflict man ever witnessed, that it is a war of principles—a war between equal and unequal rights, between republicanism and monarchy, between liberty and tyranny?

What is there in that terrific picture which you are to admire or imitate? Is it the subversion of the throne of the *Bourbons,* to make way for the throne of the *Buonapartes?* Is it the undistinguishing massacre in prisons and dungeons, of men, women and children? Is it the sanguinary justice of a revolutionary tribunal, or the awful terrors of a guillotine? Is it the rapid succession of revolution upon revolution, erecting the transient power of one set of men upon the tombs of another? Is it the assassinations which have been perpetrated, or the new ones which are projected? Is it the open profession of impiety in the public assemblies, or the ridiculous worship of a Goddess of Reason, or the still continued substitution of Decades to the Christian Sabbath? Is it the destruction of commerce, the ruin of manufactures, the oppression of agriculture? Or, is it the pomp of war, the dazzling glare of splendid victories, the blood-stained fields of Europe, the smoking cinders of desolated cities, the afflicting spectacle of millions precipitated from plenty and comfort to beggary and misery? If it be none of these things, what is it?

Perhaps it is the existing government of France, of which your admiration is solicited?

Here, Fellow-Citizens, let us on our part invite you to a solemn pause. Mark, we beseech you, carefully mark, in this result, the fruit of those extravagant and noxious principles which it is desired to transplant into our happy soil.

Behold a Consul for ten years elected, *not by the people,* but by a Conservatory Senate, *self-created* and self-*continued for life;* a magistrate who to the plentitude of executive authority, adds the peculiar and vast prerogative of an exclusive right to originate every law of the republic.

Behold a Legislature elected, *not by the people,* but by the same Conservatory Senate, one branch for fourteen the other for ten years—one branch with a right to debate the law proposed by the Consul but not to propose—another branch with a right neither to debate nor propose; but merely to assent or dissent; leaving to the people nothing more than the phantom of representation, or the useless privilege of designating one *tenth* of their whole mass as *candidates* indiscriminately for the offices of the state, according to the *option* of the Conservatory Senate.

Behold in this magic lanthern of Republicanism the odious form of real despotism garnished and defended by the bayonets of more than Five Hundred Thousand Men in disciplined array.

Do you desire an illustration of the practical effect of this despotic system, read it in the last advices from France. Read it in the exercise of a power by the Chief Consul, recognized to belong to him by the Conservatory Senate, to banish indefinitely the Citizens of France without trial, without the formality of a legislative act. Then say, where can you find a more hideous despotism?—Or, what ought ye to think of those men, who dare to recommend to you as the bible of your political creed, the principles of a revolution, which in its commencement, in its progress, in its termination, (if termination it can have, before it has overthrown the civilized world) is only fitted to serve as a beacon to warn you to shun the gulphs, the quicksands, and the rocks of those enormous principles?

Surely ye will applaud neither the wisdom nor the patriotism of men, who can wish you to exchange the fair fabric of Republicanism which you now enjoy, moddeled and decorated by the hand of federalism, for that tremendous Form of Despotism, which has sprung up amidst the volcanic eruptions of *principles at war* with all past and present experience, at war with the nature of man.

Or, was the allusion to France and her revolution, to the war of principles of which you have heard, and intended to familiarize your ears to a war of arms, as one of the blessings of the new order of things? Facts, which cannot be mistaken, demonstrate that in the early period of the French revolution, it was the plan of our opponents to engage us in the war as associates of France. But at this late hour, when even the pretence of supporting the cause of liberty has vanished, when acquisition and aggrandizement have manifestly become the only, the exclusive objects of this war, it was surely to have been expected that we should have been left to retain the advantage of a pacific policy.

If there are men, who hope to gratify their ambition, their avarice, or their vengeance, by adding this country to the league of Northern Powers, in the fantastic purpose of an extension of neutral rights, the great body of the people will hardly, we imagine, see in this project benefits sufficiently solid and durable to counterbalance the certain sacrifices of present advantages, and the certain sufferings of positive evils inseparable from a state of war.

Let us now attend to some other parts of this extraordinary address.

You are told, that there are many in the bosom of our country, who have long aimed at unequal privileges, and who have too well succeeded; by arrogating to themselves the right to be considered as the only friends of the constitution, the guardians of order and religion, by the lavish abuse of their opponents, and by representing opposition to particular plans of administration, as hostility to the government itself.

What is meant by this aiming at unequal privileges?

If we are to judge of the end by the means stated to have been used, the charge amounts to this, that the federalists have sought to retain in their own hands, by the suffrages of the people, the exercise of the powers of the government.

Admitting the charge to be true, have not the antifederalists pursued exactly the same course? Have they not labored incessantly to monopolize the power of our national and state governments? Whenever they have had it, have they not strained every nerve to keep it? Why is it a greater crime in the federalists than in their rivals to aim at an ascendant in the councils of our country?

It is true, as alledged, that the federalists insisted upon their superior claim to be considered as the friends of our constitution, and have imputed to their adversaries improper and dangerous designs; but it is equally true, that these have asserted a similar claim, have advanced the pretension of being the only republicans and patriots, have charged their opponents with being in league with Great Britain to establish monarchy, have imputed to men of unblemished characters for probity, in high public offices, corruption and peculation, and have persisted in the foul charge after its falsity had been ascertained by solemn public inquiry; and in their wanton and distempered rage for calumny, have not scrupled to brand even a Washington as a *Tyrant*, a *Conspirator*, a *Peculator*.

It is true, that the federalists have represented the leaders of the other party as hostile to our national constitution; but it is not true that it was because they have been unfriendly to *particular plans* of its administration.

It is because, as a party, and with few exceptions, they were violent opposers of the adoption of the constitution itself; predicted from it every possible evil, and painted it in the blackest colours, as a monster of political deformity.

It is because the amendments subsequently made, meeting scarcely any of the important objections which were urged, leaving the structure of the government, and the mass and distribution of its powers where they were, are too insignificant to be with any sensible man a reason for being reconciled to the system if he thought it originally bad.

It is because they have opposed, not *particular* plans of the ad-

469

ministration, but the general course of it, and almost all the measures of material consequence; and this too, not under one man or set of men, but under all the successions of men.

It is because, as there have been no alterations of the constitution sufficient to change the opinion of its merits, and as the practice under it has met with the severest reprobation of the party, there is no circumstance from which to infer that they can really have been reconciled to it.

It is because the newspapers under their direction, have, from time to time continued to decry the constutution itself.

It is because they have openly avowed their attachment to the excessive principles of the French revolution, and to leading features in the crude forms of government which have appeared only to disappear; utterly inconsistent with the sober maxims upon which our Federal Edifice was reared, and with essential parts in its structure. As specimens of this, it is sufficient to observe that they have approved the unity of the Legislative power in one branch, and have been loud in their praises of an Executive Directory; that five-headed monster of faction and anarchy.

It is because they have repeatedly shewn, and in their present address again shew, that they contemplate innovations in our public affairs, which without doubt would disgrace and prostrate the government.

On these various and strong grounds have the federalists imputed to their opponents disaffection to the National Constitution. As yet they have no reason to retract the charge. To future proofs of repentance and reconciliation must an exculpation be referred. The antifederalists have acquired the Administration of the National Government. Let them shew by a wise and virtuous management, that they are its friends; and they shall then have all the credit of so happy a reformation; but till then their assertions cannot be received as proofs.

And if the views which the signers of the address now boldly avow should unfortunately be those which should regulate the future Administration of the Government, the tokens of their amity would be as pernicious as could possibly be the tokens of their most deadly hatred.

They enumerate, as the crimes of the federalists, the Funding System, the National Debt, the Taxes which constitute the public revenue, the British Treaty, the Federal City, the Mint, a Mausoleum, the Sedition Law, and a Standing Army; and they tell us in plain terms that these are "abuses no longer to be suffered."

Let it be observed in the first place, that these crying sins of our

470

Government are not to be placed exclusively to the account of the Federalists; that for some of them the other party are chiefly responsible, and that in others they have participated.

As to the *Federal City*—It is not to be denied, that this was a favorite of the illustrious Washington. But it is no less certain, that it was warmly patronized by Mr. Jefferson, Mr. Madison, and the great majority of the members, who at the time composed the opposition in Congress, and who are now influential in the anti-federal party. It is also certain that the measure has never been a favorite of a majority of the federal party.

As to the *Mint*, It was not at all a measure of party: With slight diversities of opinion, about some of the details, it was approved by both parties.

As to the MAUSOLEUM, it has not taken place at all. The bill for erecting it was lost in the Senate, where the federalists have a decided majority; and instead of it an appropriation of fifty thousand dollars was made for erecting an equestrian statue, *aggreeably to a resolution of Congress passed under the old confederation.* Is there an American, who would refuse this memorial of gratitude to the man, who is the boast of his country, the honour of his age?

As to the FUNDING SYSTEM, it was thus far a measure of both parties, that both agreed there should be a FUNDING SYSTEM. In the formation of it the chief points of difference were, 1. A discrimination, between original holders and transferrees of the public debt. 2. A provision for the general debt of the union, leaving to each state to make seperate provision for its particular debt.

Happily for our country, by the rejection of the first, which would have been an express violation of contracts, the faith of the government was preserved, its credit maintained and established.

Happily for our country, by not pursuing the last, unity, simplicity, and energy were secured to our fiscal system. The entanglements of fourteen conflicting systems of finance were avoided: The same mass of debt was included in one general provision, instead of being referred to fourteen separate provisions—more comprehensive justice was done, the states, which had made extraordinary exertions for the support of the common cause were relieved from the unequal pressure of burdens which must have crushed them, and the people were saved from the immense difference of expence between a collection of the necessary revenues by one set of officers or by fourteen different setts.

The truth then, Fellow-citizens, is this—Both parties agreed that there should be a *funding* system. And the particular plan which prevailed was most agreeable to the contract of the government—

471

most conducive to general and equal justice among the states and individuals—to order and efficiency in the finances—to economy in the collection.

Ought not these ideas to have governed? What is meant by holding up the funding system as an abuse no longer to be tolerated?

What is the funding system? It is nothing more nor less than the *pledging of adequate funds or revenues for paying the interest and for the gradual redemption of the principal,* of that very debt which was the sacred price of independence. The country being unable to pay off the principal, what better could have been done?

Is it recollected, that long before our revolution, most of the states had their funding systems? They emitted their paper money; which is only another phrase for certificates of debt, and they pledged funds for its redemption, which is but another phrase for *funding* it. What then is there so terrible in the idea of a funding system?

Those who may have been accustomed under some of the state governments, to gamble in the floating paper, and when they had monopolized a good quantity of it among themselves at low prices, to make partial legislative provisions for the payment of the particular kinds, would very naturally be displeased with a fixed and permanent system, which would give to the evidences of debt a stable value, and lop off the opportunities for gambling speculations; but men who are sensible of the pernicious tendency of such a state of things, will rejoice in a plan which was designed to produce and *has produced* a contrary result.

What have been the effects of this system?—An extension of commerce and manufactures, the rapid growth of our cities and towns, the consequent prosperity of agriculture and the advancement of the farming interest. All this was effected, by giving life and activity to a capital in the public obligations, which was before dead, and by converting it into a powerful instrument of mercantile and other industrious enterprize.

We make these assertions boldly, because the fact is exemplified by experience, and is obvious to all discerning men. Our opponents in their hearts know it to be so.

As to the public debt—The great mass of it was not *created* by the federalists peculiarly. It was contracted by all who were engaged in our councils during our revolutionary war. The federalists have only had a principal agency in providing for it. No man can impute that to them as a crime who is not ready to avow the fraudulent and base doctrine, that it is wiser and better to *cheat* than to *pay* the creditors of a nation.

It is a fact certain and notorious, that under the administration of the first Secretary of the Treasury, ample provision was made, not only for paying the interest of this debt but for extinguishing the principal in a moderate term of years.

But it is alledged that this debt has been increased and is increasing.

On this point we know that malcontent individuals make the assertion, and exhibit statements intended to prove it. But this we also know, that a Committee of the House of Representatives, particularly charged with the inquiry, have stated and reported the contrary; and we think that more credit is due to their representation than to that of individuals—especially as nothing is easier than in a matter of this sort to make plausible statements, which, though utterly false, cannot be detected except by those who possess all the materials of a complex calculation, who are qualified and who will take the pains to make it.

We know likewise that extraordinary events have compelled our Government to extraordinary expenditures—An Indian war, for some time disastrous, but terminated on principles likely to give durable tranquility to our frontier. Two insurrections, fomented by the opposition to the Government. The hostilities of a foreign power encouraged by the undissembled sympathies of the same opposition, which obliged the government to arm for defence and security: These things have retarded the success of the efficacious measures which have been adopted for the discharge of our debt; measures which with a peaceable and orderly course of things, accelerated by the rapid growth of our country are sufficient in a few years without any new expedient to exonerate it from the whole of its present debt.

These, Fellow-Citizens, are serious truths, well known to most of our opponents, but what they shamefully endeavor to disfigure and disguise.

As to *Taxes*, they are evidently inseparable from Government. It is impossible without them to pay the debts of the nation, to protect it from foreign danger, or to secure individuals from lawless violence and rapine.

It is always easy to assert that they are heavier than they ought to be, always difficult to refute the assertion—which cannot ever be attempted without a critical review of the whole course of public measures. This gives an immense advantage to those who make a trade of complaint and censure.

But, Fellow-Citizens, it is in our power to state to you in relation to this subject and upon good information, one material fact.

There is perhaps no item in the catalogue of our taxes, which has been more unpopular than that which is called the DIRECT TAX.

This tax may emphatically be placed to the account of the opposite party, it was always insisted upon by them as preferable to taxes of the indirect kind. And it is a truth capable of full proof, that Mr. *Madison*, second in the confidence of the antifederal party, the confidential friend of Mr. Jefferson, and now Secretary of State by his nomination, was the proposer of this tax. This was done in a Committee of the last House of Representatives of which he was a member—was approved by that committee, and referred to the late Secretary of the Treasury, Mr. Wolcott, with *instructions* to prepare a plan as to the *mode*.

Let it be added, that it was a principle of the federal party, never to resort to this species of tax but in time of war or hostility with a foreign power, that it was in such a time when they did resort to it—and that the occasion ceasing by the prospect of an accommodation, it has been resolved by them not to renew the tax.

As to the *British Treaty*, it is sufficient to remind you of the extravagant predictions of evil persons to its ratification, and to ask you in what have they been realized? You have seen our peace preserved, you have seen our Western Posts surrendered, our commerce proceed with success in its wonted channels, and our argriculture flourish to the extent of every reasonable wish. And you have been witnesses to none of the mischiefs which were foretold. You will then conclude with us, that the clamours against this treaty are the mere ebullitions of ignorance, of prejudice and of faction.

As to the *Sedition Law*, we refer you to the debates in Congress for the motives and nature of it—More, would belong too much this reply already more lengthy than we could wish. We will barely say, that the most essential object of this act is to declare the Courts of the United States competent to the cognizance of those slanders against the principal officers and departments of the federal Government, which at common law are punishable as libels; with the liberal and important mitigation of allowing the truth of an accusation to be given in evidence in exoneration of the accuser. What do you see in this to merit the execrations which have been bestowed on the measure?

As to a *Standing Army*—there is none except four small regiments of infantry insufficient for the service of guards in the numerous posts of our immense frontiers, stretching from Niagara to the borders of Florida, and two regiments of artillery which occupy in the same capacity the numerous fortifications along our widely extended seacoast. What is there in this to affright or disgust?

If these corps are to be abolished, substitutes must be found in the militia. If the experiment shall be made, it is easy to foretell that it will prove not a measure of economy, but a heavy bill of additional cost, and like all other visionary schemes, will be productive, only of repentance, and a return to a plan injudiciously renounced.

This exposition of the measures which have been represented to you as abuses, *no longer to be suffered* (mark the strength of the phrase), will, we trust, serve to satisfy you, of the violence and absurdity of those crude notions which govern our opposers, if we believe them to be sincere.

Happily for our country, however, there has just beamed a ray of hope, that these violent and absurd notions will not form the rule of conduct of the person whom the party have recently elevated to the head of our National affairs.

In the speech of the new President upon assuming the exercise of his office, we find among the articles of his creed "THE HONEST PAYMENT OF OUR DEBT, AND SACRED PRESERVATION OF THE PUBLIC FAITH." The funding system, the national debt, the British treaty are not therefore in his conception abuses, which if no longer to be tolerated would be of course to be abolished.

But we think ourselves warranted to derive from the same source a condemnation still more extensive of the opinions of our adversaries. The speech characterizes our present government "as a Republican Government, in the *full tide* of successful *experiment*." Success in the *experiment* of a government, is success in the *practice* of it, and this is but another phrase for an administration, in the main, wise and good. That administration has been hitherto in the hands of the federalists.

Here then, fellow-citizens, is an open and solemn protest against the principles and opinions of our opponents, from a quarter which as yet they dare not arraign.

In referring to this speech, we think it proper to make a public declaration of our approbation of its contents: We view it as virtually a a candid retraction of past misapprehensions, and a pledge to the community that the new President will not lend himself to dangerous innovations, but in essential points will tread in the steps of his predecessors.

In doing this, he prudently anticipates the loss of a great portion of that favor which has elevated him to his present station. Doubtless it is a just foresight. Adhering to the professions he has made, it will not be long before the body of the antifederalists will raise their croaking and ill omened voices against him: But in the talents, the patriotism, and the firmness of the federalists, he will find more than an equivalent for all that he shall lose.

All those of whatever party, who may desire to support the moderate views exhibited in the Presidential Speech, will unite against the violent projects of the men who have addressed you in favor of Mr. Clinton, and against a candidate who in all past experience has evinced that he is likely to be a fit instrument of these projects.

Fellow Citizens, we beseech you to consult your *experience*, and not listen to tales of evil, which exist only in the language, not even in the imaginations of those who deal them out. This experience will tell you, that our opposers have been uniformly mistaken in their views of our constitution, of its administration, in all the judgments which they have pronounced of our public affairs; and consequently that they are unfaithful or incapable advisers. It will teach you that you have eminently prospered under the system of public measures pursued and supported by the Federalists.

In vain are you told that you owe your prosperity to your own industry and to the blessings of Providence. To the latter doubtless you are primarily indebted. You owe to it among other benefits the constitution you enjoy and the wise administration of it, by virtuous men as its instruments. You are likewise indebted to your own industry. But has not your industry found aliment and incitement in the salutary operation of your government—in the preservation of order at home—in the cultivation of peace abroad—in the invigoration of confidence in pecuniary dealings—in the increased energies of credit and commerce—in the extension of enterprize ever incident to a good government well administered. Remember what your situation was immediately before the establishment of the present constitution. Were you then deficient in industry more than now? If not, why were you not equally prosperous? Plainly because your industry had not at that time the vivifying influences of an efficient, and well conducted government.

There is one more particular in the address which we cannot pass over in silence, though to avoid being tedious we must do little more than mention it: It is a comparison between the administration of the former and present governors of this state on the point of economy, accompanied with the observations that the former had shewn an anxious solicitude to exempt you from taxation.

The answer to this is, that under the administration of Mr. Clinton the state possessed large resources, which were the substitute for taxation. The duties of impost, the proceeds of confiscated property, and immense tracts of new land, which, if they had been providently disposed of, would have long deferred the necessity of taxation. That this was not done, Mr. Clinton, as one of the commissioners of the land-office, is, in a principal degree, responsible.

Under the administration of Mr. Jay, the natural increase of the state has unavoidably augmented the expence of the government. And the appropriations of large sums in most of which all parties have concurred, to a variety of objects of public utility and necessity, has so far diminished the funds of the state as in the opinion of all parties to have required a resort to taxes.

The principal of these objects have been, 1. The erection of fortifications, and the purchase of cannon, arms and other warlike implements for the purpose of defence. 2. The building and maintenance of the state prisons, in the laudable experiment of an amelioration of our penal code. 3. The purchase from Indians of lands which though resold have not yet been productive of revenue. 4. The payment of dower to the widows of persons whose estates had been confiscated. 5. Large appropriations for the benefit of common schools, roads and bridges. 6. The erection of an arsenal and public offices in the city of Albany.

Hence it is evident that the difference which has been remarked to you in respect to taxation has proceeded from a difference of circumstances, not from the superior providence or œconomy of the former, or from the improvidence or profusion of the existing administration. Our opponents may be challenged to bring home to Mr. Jay the proofs of prodigality, and they may be told that the purity and integrity of his conduct in relation to the public property, have never for a moment been drawn into question.

We forbear to canvass minutely the personalities in which our adversaries have indulged. 'Tis enough for us, that they acknowledge our candidate to possess the good qualities which we have ascribed to him: If he has inherited a large estate, 'tis certainly no crime.

'Tis to his honour, that his benevolence is as large as his estate. Let his numerous tenants be his witnesses;—attached as they are to him, not by the ties of dependence (for the greater part of them hold their lands in fee simple, and upon easy rents) but by the ties of affection, by those gentle and precious cords which link gratitude to kindness. Let the many indigent and distressed who have been gladdened by the benign influence of his bounty be his witnesses. And let every reflecting man well consider, whether the people are likely to suffer because the ample fortune of a virtuous and generous chief magistrate places him beyond the temptation of a job, for the accumulation of wealth.

We shall not inquire how ample may be the domains, how productive the revenues, how numerous the dependents of Mr. Clinton, or how his ample domains may have been acquired. 'Tis enough for us to say, that if Mr. Van Rensselaer is *rich*, Mr. Clinton is not *poor:* and that it is at least as innocent in the former to have been born to

477

opulence, as in the latter to have attained to it by means of the advantages of the first office of the state, long very long enjoyed, for three years at least too long, because, by an unlawful tenure—contrary to a known majority of suffrages.

We shall not examine how likely it is that a man considerably passed the meridian of life, and debilitated by infirmities of body, will be a more useful and efficient Governor, and more independent of the aid of friends and relatives, than a man of acknowledged good sense, of mature years, in the full vigor of life, and in the full energy of his faculties.

We shall not discuss how far it is probable that the radical antipathy of Mr. Clinton to the vital parts of our National Constitution has given way to the little formal amendments which have since been adopted. We are glad to be assured that it has. It gives us pleasure to see proselytes to the truth; nor shall we be over curious to enquire how men get right if we can but discover that they are right. If happily the possession of the power of our once detested government shall be a talisman to work the conversion of all its enemies, we shall be ready to rejoice that good has come out of evil.

But we dare not too far indulge this pleasing hope. We know that the adverse party has its *Dantons*, its *Robespierres*, as well as its *Brissots*, and its *Rolands*; and we look forward to the time when the sects of the former will endeavor to confound the latter and their adherents, together with the federalists, in promiscuous ruin.

In regard to these sects, which compose the pith and essence of the antifederal party, we believe it to be true, that the contest between us is indeed a war of principles—a war between tyranny and liberty, but not between monarchy and republicanism. It is a contest between the tyranny of jacobinism, which confounds and levels every thing, and the mild reign of rational liberty, which rests on the basis of an efficient and well balanced government, and through the medium of stable laws, shelters and protects, the life, the reputation, the prosperity, the civil and religious rights of every member of the community.

'Tis against these sects that all good men should form an indissoluble league. To resist and frustrate their machinations is alike essential to every prudent and faithful administration of our government, whoever may be the depositaries of the power.

THE LUCIUS CRASSUS CRITICISM OF JEFFERSON'S MESSAGE TO CONGRESS OF DECEMBER 8, 1801, AN INTRODUCTION

The Lucius Crassus papers, entitled The Examination, *were written as a criticism of President Jefferson's first annual message to Congress of December 1801 and of the actions taken by Jefferson's administration during 1801. Jefferson had observed in his message that "the Judiciary System will of course present itself to the contemplation of Congress," and soon after that the Judiciary Repeal Act of 1802 was passed. The repeal act overturned the Judiciary Act of 1801, thereby abolishing federal judgeships established by that act. Accordingly, Hamilton broadened his criticism of Jefferson's program to include a criticism of that legislation. The significance of these papers inhere in his criticism of that legislation and in the reasoning he uses to support that criticism. Hamilton regarded the passage of the Judiciary Repeal Act as a further threat to an already unstable constitutional balance of power. He had stated in* Federalist 78 *that if "the Courts of Justice are to be considered as the bulwark of a limited constitution against legislative encroachments, this consideration will afford a strong argument for the permanent tenure of judicial offices." Following this line of reasoning, the power of Congress to abolish judgeships would threaten the independence of the judiciary and therewith undermine the equilibrium of the constitutional system.*

THE EXAMINATION NO. XII
FEBRUARY 23, 1802

New York, February 23, 1802

From the manner in which the subject was treated in the fifth and sixth numbers of The Examination, it has been doubted, whether the writer did or did not entertain a decided opinion as to the power of Congress to abolish the offices and compensations of Judges, once instituted and appointed pursuant to a law of the United States. In a matter of such high constitutional moment, it is a sacred duty to be explicit. The progress of a bill lately brought into the Senate for repealing the law of the last session, entitled, "An act to provide for the more convenient organization of the courts of the U. States," with the avowed design of superceding the judges, who were appointed under it, has rendered the question far more serious than it was while it rested merely on the obscure suggestion of the Presidential Message. 'Till the experiment had proved the fact, it was hardly to have been imagined, that a majority of either house of Congress, whether from design or error, would have lent its sanction to a glaring violation of our national compact, in that article, which of all others is the most essential to the efficiency and stability of the Government; to the security of property; to the safety and liberty of person. This portentous and frightful phenomenon has, nevertheless, appeared. It frowns with malignant and deadly aspect upon our constitution. Probably before these remarks shall be read, that Constitution will be no more! It will be numbered among the numerous victims of Democratic phrenzy; and will have given another and an awful lesson to mankind—the prelude perhaps of calamities to this country, at the contemplation of which imagination shudders!

With such a prospect before us, nothing ought to be left unessayed, to open the eyes of thinking men to the destructive projects of those mountebank politicians, who have been too successful in perverting public opinion, and in cheating the people out of their confidence; who are advancing with rapid strides in the work of disorganization—the sure fore-runner of tyranny; and who, if they are not arrested in their mad career, will, ere long, precipitate our nation into all the horrors of anarchy.

It would be vanity to expect to throw much additional light upon a subject which has already exhausted the logic and eloquence of some of the ablest men of our country; yet it often happens, that the same arguments placed in a new attitudes, and accompanied with illustrations which may have escaped the ardor of a first research, serve both to fortify and to extend conviction. In the hope that this may be the case, the discussion shall be pursued with as much perspicuity and brevity, as can be attained.

The words of the constitution are, "The Judges *both* of the Supreme and Inferior Courts *shall hold their offices during good behaviour,* and shall at stated times receive for their services a compensation which *shall not be diminished during their continuance in office."*

Taking the literal import of the terms as the criterion of their true meaning, it is clear, that the *tenure* or *duration* of the office is limited by no other condition than the *good behaviour* of the incumbent. The words are imperative, simple, and unqualified: "The Judges *shall hold their offices during good behaviour."* Independent therefore of any artificial reasoning to vary the nature and obvious sense of the words, the provision must be understood to vest in the Judge a right to the office, indefeasible but by his own misconduct.

It is consequently the duty of those who deny this right, to shew either that there are certain presumptions of intention deducible from other parts of the constitutional instrument, or certain general principles of constitutional law or policy, which ought to control the literal and substitute a different meaning.

As to presumptions of intention different from the import of the terms, there is not a syllable in the instrument from which they can be inferred; on the contrary, the latter member of the clause cited, affords very strong presumption the other way.

From the injunction, that the compensation of the Judges shall not be diminished, it is manifest, that the Constitution intends to guard the Independence of those Officers against the Legislative Department: Because, to this department *alone* would have belonged the power of diminishing their compensations.

When the Constitution is thus careful to tie up the Legislature, from taking away part of the compensation, is it possible to suppose that it can mean to leave that body at full liberty to take away the whole? The affirmative imputes to the Constitution the manifest absurdity of holding to the Legislature this language, "You shall not *weaken* the Independence of the Judicial character, by exercising the power of *lessening* his emolument, but you may *destroy* it altogether, by exercising the greater power of *annihilating* the recompence with the office." No mortal can be so blind as not to see, that by such a construction, the restraint intended to be laid upon the Legislature by the injunction not to lessen the compensations, becomes absolutely nugatory.

In vain is a justification of it sought in that part of the same article which provides that "The Judicial power of the United States shall be vested in one Supreme Court and in such Inferior Courts as the Congress *may* from time to time ordain and establish." The position that a discretionary power to institute Inferior Courts includes virtually a power to abolish them, if true, is nothing to the purpose. The abolition of a Court does not necessarily imply that of its Judges. In contemplation of law, the Court and the Judge are distinct things. The Court may have a legal existence, though there may be no Judge to exercise its powers. This may be the case either at the original creation of a Court, previous to the appointment of a Judge, or subsequently by his death, resignation or removal: In the last case, it could not be pretended that the Court had become extinct by the event. In like manner, the office of the Judge may subsist, though the Court in which he is to officiate may be suspended or destroyed. The duties of a Judge, as the office is defined in our Jurisprudence, are two fold—judicial and ministerial. The latter may be performed out of Court, and often without reference to it. As conservator of the peace, which every judge is *ex officio,* many things are done not connected with a judicial controversy, or to speak technically, with a *lis pendens.* This serves to illustrate the idea, that the office is something different from the Court; which is the place or situation for its principal action, yet not altogether essential to its activity. Besides, a Judge is not the less a Judge when out of Court than when in Court. The law does not suppose him to be always in Court, yet it does suppose him to be always in office; in vacation as well as in Term. He has also a property or interest in his office, which entitles him to civil actions and to recompence in damages for injuries that affect him in relation to his office; but he cannot be said to have a property or interest in the Court of which he is a member. All these considerations confirm the hypothesis, that the Court and the Judge are distinct legal entities, and therefore may exist the one independently of the other.

If it be replied, that the office is an incident to the Court, and that the abolition of the principal includes that of the incidents—The answer to this is, that the argument may be well founded as to all subsequent appointments; but not as to those previously made. Though there be no office to be filled in future, it will not follow that one already vested in an individual by a regular appointment and commission, is thereby vacated and divested. Whether this shall or shall not happen must depend on what the Constitution or the law has declared with regard to the *tenure* of the office. Having pronounced that this shall be during good behavior, it will preserve the office, to give effect to that tenure for the benefit of the possessor. To be consistent with itself, it will require and prescribe such a modification and construction of its own acts, as will reconcile its power over the future, with the rights which have been conferred as to the past.

Let it not be said that an office is a mere trust for public benefit, and excludes the idea of a property or a vested interest in the individual. The first part of the proposition is true—the last false. Every office combines the two ingredients of an interest in the possessor, and a trust for the public. Hence it is that the law allows the officer redress by a civil action for an injury in relation to his office, which presupposes property or interest. This interest may be defeasible at the pleasure of the government, or it may have a fixed duration, according to the constitution of the office. The idea of a vested interest holden even by a permanent tenure, so far from being incompatible with the principle that the primary and essential end of every office is the public good, may be conducive to that very end by promoting a diligent, faithful, energetic, and independent execution of the office.

But admitting, as seems to have been admitted by the speakers on both sides the question, that the judge must fall with the court, then the only consequence will be, that Congress cannot abolish a court once established. There is no rule of interpretation better settled than that different provisions in the same instrument, on the same subject, ought to be so construed, as, if possible, to comport with each other, and give a reasonable effect to all.

The provision that "The Judiciary Power shall be vested in one Superior Court and in such inferior courts as the Congress *may* from time to time ordain and establish" is immediately followed by this other provision, "The judges *both* of the Supreme and Inferior Courts shall hold their offices during good behaviour."

The proposition, that a power to do, includes virtually, a power to undo, as applied to a legislative body, is generally but not universally true. All *vested rights* form an exception to the rule. In strict theory, there is no lawful or moral power to divest by a subsequent statute, a right vested in an individual by a prior: And accordingly it is familiar to persons conversant with legal studies, that the repeal of a law does not always work the revocation or divestiture of such rights.

If it be replied, that though a legislature might act immorally and wickedly in abrogating a vested right, yet the legal *validity* of its act for such a purpose could not be disputed; it may be answered that this odious position, in any application of it, is liable to question in every limited Constitution; (that is, in every Constitution which, in its theory, does not suppose the WHOLE POWER of the Nation to be lodged in the legislative body;)—and that it is certainly false in its application to a legislature, the authorities of which are defined by a positive written Constitution, as to every thing which is contrary to the actual provisions of that Constitution. To deny this is to affirm that the *delegated* is paramount to the *constituent* power. It is in fact to affirm there are *no constitutional limits to the Legislative Authority.*

The enquiry then must be, whether the power to abolish Inferior Courts, if implied in that of creating them, is not abridged by the clause which regulates the tenure of Judicial office.

The first thing which occurs in this investigation, is, that the power to abolish is at most, an implied or incidental power and as such will the more readily yield to any express provision with which it may be inconsistent.

The circumstance of giving to Congress a discretionary power to establish Inferior Courts instead of establishing them specifically in the Constitution, has, with great reason, been ascribed to the impracticability of ascertaining beforehand the number and variety of Courts, which the developement of our national affairs might indicate to be proper; especially in relation to the progress of new settlements, and the creation of new states. This rendered a discretionary power to *institute* Courts indispensable; but it did not alike render indispensable a power to abolish those which were once instituted. It was conceived, that with intelligence, caution, and care, a plan might be pursued in the institution of Courts, which would render abolitions unnecessary. Indeed it is not presumable with regard to establishments of such solemnity and importance, making part of the *organization* of a principal department of the Government, that a fluctuation of plans was anticipated. It is therefore not essential to suppose, that the power to destroy was intended to be included in the power to create: Thus the words "to ordain and establish," may be satisfied by attributing to them only the latter effect.

Consequently when the grant of the power to institute Courts, is immediately succeeded by the declaration that the Judges of those Courts shall *hold* their offices during good behaviour; if the exercise of the power to abolish the Courts cannot be reconciled with the actual holding or enjoyment of the office, according to the prescribed tenure, it will follow that the power to abolish is interdicted. The implied or hypothetical power to destroy the office must give way to the express and positive right of holding it during good behaviour. This is agreeable to the soundest rules of construction; the contrary is in subversion of them.

Equally in vain is a justification of the construction adopted by the advocates of the repeal, attempted to be derived from a distinction between the Supreme and Inferior Courts. The argument, that as the former is established by the Constitution, it cannot be annulled by a legislative act, though the latter which must owe their existence to such an act may by the same authority be extinguished, can afford no greater stability to the office of a Judge of the Supreme Court than to that of a Judge of an Inferior Court. The Constitution does indeed establish the Supreme Court; but it is altogether silent as to the number of the Judges. This is as fully left to legislative discretion as the institution of Inferior Courts; and the rule that a power to undo is implied in the power to do, is therefore no less applicable to the reduction of the number of the Judges of the Supreme Court than to the abolition of the Inferior Courts. If the former are not protected by the clause, which fixes the tenure of office, they are no less at the mercy of the legislature than the latter: And if that clause does protect them, its protection must be equally effectual for the Judges of the Inferior Courts. Its efficacy in either case must be founded on the principle that it operates as a restraint upon the legislative discretion; and if so, there is the like restraint in both cases, because the very same words in the very same sentence define conjunctly the tenure of the offices of the two classes of Judges. No sophistry can elude this conclusion.

It is therefore plain to a demonstration, that the doctrine which affirms the right of Congress to abolish the Judges of the Inferior Courts is absolutely fatal to the independence of the Judiciary department. The observation that so gross an abuse of power as would be implied in the abolition of the Judges of the Supreme Court, ought not to be supposed, can afford no consolation against the extreme danger of the doctrine. The terrible examples before us forbid our placing the least confidence in that delusive observation. Experience, sad experience warns us to dread every extremity—to be prepared for the worst catastrophe that can happen.

LUCIUS CRASSUS.

THE EXAMINATION NO. XIV
MARCH 2, 1802

New York, March 2, 1802

In the course of the debate in the Senate, much verbal criticism has been indulged; many important inferences have been attempted to be drawn from distinctions between the words *shall* and *may*. This species of discussion will not be imitated, because it is seldom very instructive or satisfactory. These terms, in particular cases, are frequently synonymous, and are imperative or permissive, directing or enabling, according to the relations in which they stand to other words. It is however certain that the arguments even from this source, greatly preponderate against the right of Congress to abolish the Judges.

But there has been one argument, rather of a verbal nature, upon which some stress has been laid, which shall be analized; principally, to furnish a specimen of the wretched expedients to which the supporters of the repeal are driven. It is this, "The tenure of an office is

485

not synonymous with its existence. Though Congress may not annul the tenure of a Judicial Office, while the office itself continues; yet it does not follow that they may not destroy its existence.

The constituent parts of an office are its authorities, duties and duration. These may be denominated the elements of which it is composed. Together they form its *essence* or *existence*. It is impossible to separate even in idea the duration from the existence: The office must cease to exist when it ceases to have duration. Let it be observed, that the word *tenure* is not used in the constitution, and that in the debate it has been the substitute for duration. The words "The Judges shall hold their offices during good behavior," are equivalent to these other words; The offices of the Judges shall endure or last so long as they behave well.

The conclusions from these principles are that existence is a *whole* which includes tenure or duration as a part; that it is impossible to annul the existence of an office without destroying its tenure; and consequently that a prohibition to destroy the tenure is virtually and substantially a prohibition to abolish the office. How contemptible then the sophism that Congress may not destroy the tenure; but may annihilate the office!

It has now been seen, that this power of annihilation is not reconcileable with the language of the constitutional instrument, and that no rule of constitutional law, which has been relied upon, will afford it support. Can it be better defended by any principle of constitutional policy?

To establish the affirmative of this question it has been argued, that if the Judges hold their offices by a title absolutely independent of the Legislative will, the Judicial Department becomes a colossal and overbearing power, capable of degenerating into a permanent tyranny, at liberty, if audacious and corrupt enough, to render the authority of the Legislature nugatory, by expounding away the laws, and to assume a despotic controul over the rights of person and property.

To this argument (which supposes the case of a palpable abuse of power) a plain and conclusive answer is, that the constitution has provided a complete safeguard in the authority of the *House of Representatives* to impeach; of the *Senate* to condemn. The Judges are in this way amenable to the public Justice for misconduct; and upon conviction, removeable from office. In the hands of the Legislature itself is placed the weapon by which they may be put down and the other branches of the government protected. The pretended danger, therefore, is evidently imaginary—the security perfect!

Reverse the Medal. Concede to the Legislature a legal discretion to abolish the Judges, where is the defence? where the security for the Judicial Department? There is absolutely none. This most valuable member of the government, when rightly constituted, the surest guardian of person and property, of which stability is a prime characteristic; losing at once its most essential attributes, and doomed to fluctuate with the variable tide of faction, degenerates into a disgusting mirror of all the various, malignant and turbulent humors of party-spirit.

Let us not be deceived. The real danger is on the side of that foul and fatal doctrine, which emboldens its votaries, with daring front and unhallowed step, to enter the holy temple of Justice and pluck from their seats the venerable personages, who, under the solemn sanction of the Constitution, are commissioned to officiate there; to guard that sacred compact with jealous vigilance; to dispense the laws with a steady and impartial hand; unmoved by the storms of faction, unawed by its powers, unseduced by its favors; shielding right and innocence from every attack; resisting and repressing violence from every quarter. 'Tis from the triumph of that execrable doctrine that we may have to date the downfall of our Government and with it, of the whole fabric of Republican Liberty. Who will have the folly to deny that the definition of despotism is the concentration of all the powers of Government in one person or in one body? Who is so blind as not to see that the right of the Legislature to abolish the Judges at pleasure destroys the independence of the Judicial Department, and swallows it up in the impetuous vortex of Legislative influence? Who is so weak as to hope that the Executive, deprived of so powerful an auxiliary will long survive? What dispassionate man can withstand the conviction that the boundaries between the departments will be thenceforth nominal; and that there will be no longer more than one active and efficient department?

It is a fundamental maxim of free government, that the three great departments of power, *Legislative, Executive* and *Judiciary*, shall be essentially distinct and independent the one of the other. This principle, very influential in most of our state constitutions, has been particularly attended to in the Constitution of the United States; which, in order to give effect to it, has adopted a precaution peculiar to itself, in the provisions that forbid the Legislature to vary in any way the compensation of the *President* to diminish that of a *Judge*.

It is a principle equally sound, that though in a government like that of Great Britain, having an hereditary chief with vast prerogatives, the danger to Liberty, by the predominance of one department over the other, is on the side of the Executive; yet in popular forms of government, this danger is chiefly to be apprehended from the Legislative branch.

The power of legislation is in its own nature the most comprehensive and potent of the three great subdivisions of sovereignty. It is the will of the government; it prescribes universally the rule of action, and the sanctions which are to enforce it. It creates and regulates the public force, and it commands the public purse. If deposited in an elective representative of the people, it has, in most cases, the body of the nation for its auxiliary, and generally acts with all the momentum of popular favor. In every such government it is consequently an organ of immense strength. But when there is an hereditary chief magistrate, cloathed with dazzling prerogatives and a great patronage, there is a powerful counterpoise; which, in most cases, is sufficient to preserve the equilibrium of the government; in some cases to incline the scale too much to its own side.

In governments wholly popular or representative, there is no adequate counterpoise. Confidence in the most numerous, or Legislative Department, and jealousy of the Executive Chief, form the genius of every such government. That jealousy, operating in the constitution of the Executive, causes this organ to be intrinsically feeble; and withholding in the course of administration accessary means of force and influence, is for the most part vigilant to continue it in a state of impotence. The result is that the Legislative body, in this species of government, possesses additional resources of power and weight; while the Executive is rendered much too weak for competition; almost too weak for self defence.

A third principle, not less well founded than the other two, is that the Judiciary department is naturally the weakest of the three. The sources of strength to the Legislative branches have been briefly delineated. The Executive by means of its several active powers; of the dispensations of honors and emoluments and of the direction of the public force is evidently the second in strength. The Judiciary, on the other hand, can ordain nothing. It commands neither the press nor the sword. It has scarcely any patronage. Its functions are not active but deliberative. Its main province is to declare the meaning of the laws; and in extraordinary cases it must even look up to the Executive aid for the execution of its decisions. Its chief strength is in the veneration which it is able to inspire by the wisdom and rectitude of its judgments.

This character of the Judiciary clearly indicates that it is not only the weakest of the three departments of power; but, also as it regards the security and preservation of civil liberty by far the safest. In a

488

conflict with the other departments it will be happy if it can defend itself—to annoy them is beyond its power. In vain would it singly attempt enterprises against the rights of the citizen. The other departments could quickly arrest its arm, and punish its temerity. It can only then become an effectual instrument of oppression, when it is combined with one of the more active and powerful organs; and against a combination of this sort, the true and best guard is a complete independence on each and both of them. Its dependence on either will imply and involve a subserviency to the views of the department on which it shall depend. Its independence of both will render it a powerful check upon the others, and a precious shield to the rights of persons and property. Safety, Liberty, are therefore inseparably connected with the real and substantial Independence of the Courts and Judges.

It is plainly to be inferred from the instrument itself, that these were governing principles in the formation of our Constitution: that they were in fact so, will hereafter be proved by the cotemporary exposition of persons who must be supposed to have understood the views with which it was framed, having been themselves members of the body that framed it. Those principles suggest the highest motives of Constitutional policy against that construction, which places the existence of the Judges at the mercy of the Legislature. They instruct us, that to prevent a concentration of powers, the *essence of despotism,* it is essential that the departments among which they shall be distributed, should be effectually independent of each other; and that it being impossible to reconcile this independence with a right in any one or two of them to annihilate at discretion the organs of the other, it is contrary to all just reasoning to imply or infer such a right. So far from its being correct, that an express interdiction is requisite to deprive the Legislature of the power to abolish the Judges, that the very reverse is the true position. It would require a most express provision, susceptible of no other interpretation, to confer on that branch of the government an authority, so dangerous to the others, in opposition to the strong presumptions, which in conformity with the fundamental maxims of free government, arise from the care taken in the Constitution, to establish and preserve the reciprocal and complete independence of the respective branches, first by a separate organization of the departments, next by a precise definition of the powers of each, lastly by precautions to secure to each a permanent support.

LUCIUS CRASSUS.

THE EXAMINATION NO. XV
MARCH 3, 1802

New York, March 3, 1802

It is generally understood that the Essays under the Title of the Federalist, which were published at New York, while the plan of our present Federal Constitution was under the consideration of the people, were principally written by two persons who had been members of the Convention which devised that plan, and whose names are subscribed to the instrument containing it. In these Essays the principles advanced in the last number of this Examination are particularly stated and strongly relied upon in defence of the proposed Constitution; from which it is a natural inference that they had influenced the views with which the plan was digested. The full force of this observation will be best perceived by a recurrence to the work itself; but it will appear clearly enough from the following detached passages.

"One of the principal objections inculcated by the more respectable *adversaries* to the Constitution, is its supposed violation of the political maxim that the *Legislative, Executive* and *Judiciary* Departments ought to be *separate* and *distinct*." "No *political truth* is certainly of *greater intrinsic value*, or is stamped with the authority of more enlightened patrons of liberty, than that on which the objection is founded. The *accumulation* of all power, Legislative, Executive, and Judiciary, in the same hands, whether of one, a few, or many; whether hereditary, self appointed or elective, may justly be pronounced the *very definition* of tryanny."* "Neither of the three Departments ought to possess *directly* or *indirectly* an *overruling influence* over the others in the administration of their respective powers." "But the most difficult task is to provide some *practical security* for each *against the invasion* of the others."

"Experience assures us that the efficacy of *parchment barriers* has been greatly overrated, and that some *more adequate defence is indispensably necessary* for the more feeble against the more powerful members of the government. The Legislative Department is every where extending the sphere of its activity, and drawing all power into its impetuous vortex." "In a representative republic, where the executive magistracy is carefully limited both in the extent and the duration of its power; and where the legislative power is exercised by an assembly, which is inspired by a supposed influence over the people with

*No. XLVII.

an intrepid confidence in its own strength; which is sufficiently numerous to feel all the passions which actuate a multitude; yet not so numerous as to be incapable of pursuing the objects of its passions, by means which reason prescribes; *it is against the enterprising ambition of this department, that the people ought to indulge all their jealousy and exhaust all their precautions."* Again, "The *tendency* of Republican Governments is to an *aggrandizement of the Legislature at the expence of the other Departments."*

These passages recognise as a fundamental maxim of free government, that the three departments of power, ought to be separate and distinct; consequently that neither of them ought to be able to exercise, either directly or indirectly, an *overruling influence* over any other. They also recognize as a truth, indicated by the nature of the system and verified by experience, that in a Representative Republic, the Legislative Department is the "AARON'S ROD" most likely to swallow up the rest, and therefore to be guarded against with particular care and caution: And they inculcate that parchment barriers, (or the formal provisions of a constitution designating the respective boundaries of authority) having been found ineffectual for protecting the more feeble against the most powerful members of the government, some more adequate defence, some practical security is necessary. What this was intended to be will appear from subsequent passages.

"To what expedient shall we finally resort for maintaining in practice the necessary partition of power among the several Departments as laid down in the Constitution?" "As all exterior provisions are found to be inadequate, the defect must be supplied by so contriving the interior structure of the government as that its several constituent Departments may, by their mutual relations, be the means of keeping each other in their proper places."*

These passages intimate the *"practical security"* which ought to be adopted for the preservation of the weaker against the stronger members of the Government. It is so to contrive its interior structure that the constituent organs may be able to *keep each other* in their *proper places;* an idea essentially incompatible with that of making the *existence* of one dependent on the *will* of another. It will be seen afterwards how this structure is to be so contrived.

"In order to lay a *foundation* for that separate and distinct exercise of the different powers of government, which to a certain extent, is admitted on all hands to be essential to the preservation of liberty; it is evident that each department should have a will of its own; and consequently should be so constituted that the members of each should have *as little agency* as possible in the appointment of the

*No. LI.

members of the others. This principle rigorously adhered to would require that all the appointments for the several departments should be drawn from the same fountain of authority, the people." But "In the constitution of the Judiciary Department it might be inexpedient to insist rigorously on the principle; first, because peculiar qualifications being essential in the members, the primary consideration ought to be [to] select that mode of choice, which best secures these qualifications; secondly, because *the permanent tenure* by which the appointments are held in that Department, must soon destroy all sense of dependence on the authority conferring them."

"It is equally evident that the members of each Department should be as little dependent as possible on those of the others for the emoluments annexed to their offices. Were the Executive Magistrate or the *Judges* not independent of the Legislature in this particular, *their Independence in every other* would be merely nominal." "The great security against a concentration of the several powers in the same Department consists in giving to those who administer each Department the *necessary constitutional means and personal motives*, to resist encroachments of the others." "But it is not possible to give to each Department an equal power of self-defence. In Republican Governments the Legislative authority necessarily predominates."

The means held out as proper to be employed, for enabling the several departments to keep each other in their proper places, are: 1. To give to each such an *organization* as will render them essentially independent of one another. 2. To secure to each a *support* which shall not be at the discretionary disposal of any other. 3. To establish between them such *mutual relations of authority* as will make one a check upon another, and enable them reciprocally to resist enroachments, and confine one another within their proper spheres.

To accomplish the first end, it is deemed material that they should have as little agency as possible in the appointment of one another, and should all emanate directly from the same fountain of authority—the people: And that it being expedient to relax the principle, in respect to the Judiciary Department, with a view to a more select choice of its organs; this defect in the creation ought to be remedied by a *permanent tenure* of office; which certainly becomes nominal and nugatory, if the existence of the office rests on the pleasure of the Legislature. The principle that the several organs should have as little agency as possible in the appointment of each other, is directly opposed to the claim in favour of one of a discretionary agency to destroy another. The second of the proposed ends, is designed to be effected by the provisions for fixing the compensations of the Executive and Judicial Departments—The third, by the qualified negative of the Executive, or the acts of the two houses of Congress;

by the right of one of these houses to accuse; of the other to try and punish the Executive and Judicial officers; and lastly, by the right of the Judges, as interpreters of the laws, to pronounce unconstitutional acts void.

These are the means contemplated by the Constitution, for maintaining the limits assigned to itself, and for enabling the respective organs of the Government to keep each other in their proper places, so that they may not have it in their power to domineer the one over the other, and thereby in effect, though not in form, to concentrate the powers in one department, overturn the Government, and establish a Tyranny. Unfortunate if these powerful precautions shall prove insufficient to accomplish the end, and to stem the torrent of the Imposter—INNOVATION disguised in the specious garb of *Patriotism!*

The views which prevailed in the formation of the Constitution are further illustrated by these additional comments from the same source.*

"As liberty can have nothing to fear from the Judiciary alone, but would have every thing to fear from its union with either of the other departments; that as all the effects of such an union must ensue from a dependence of the former on the latter, notwithstanding a nominal and apparent separation; that as from the natural feebleness of the Judiciary, it is in continual jeopardy of being overpowered, awed or influenced by its co-ordinate branches; and that as nothing can contribute so much to its firmness and independence, as *permanency in office*, this quality may therefore be justly regarded as an indispensable ingredient in its constitution; and in a great measure as the citadel of the public justice and the public security."

"The complete Independence of the Courts of Justice is peculiarly essential in a limited constitution. Limitations can be preserved in practice no other way, than through the medium of the Courts of Justice to declare all acts contrary to the manifest tenor of the Constitution void."

Then follows a particular discussion of the position, that it is the right and the duty of the Courts to exercise such an authority: to repeat which, would swell this number to an improper size.

The essence of the argument is, that every act of a delegated authority, contrary to the tenor of the commission under which it is exercised is void; consequently that no legislative act, inconsistent with the Constitution, can be valid. That it is not a natural presumption that the Constitution intended to make the legislative body the final and exclusive judges of their own powers; but more rational to suppose that the courts were designed to be an intermediate body

*No. LXXVIII.

between the people and the legislature, in order, among other things, to keep the latter within the bounds assigned to its authority. That the interpretation of the laws being the peculiar province of the Courts, and a Constitution being in fact a fundamental law, superior in obligation to a statute, if the Constitution and the statute are at variance, the former ought to prevail against the latter; the will of the people against the will of the agents; and the Judges ought in their quality of interpreters of the laws, to pronounce and adjudge the truth, namely, that the unauthorised statute is a nullity.

"Nor (continues the commentator) does this conclusion by any means suppose a superiority of the judicial to the legislative power. It only supposes that the power of the people is superior to both; and that where the will of the legislature declared in its statute, stands in opposition to that of the people declared in the constitution, the Judges ought to be governed by the latter, rather than the former. They ought to regulate their decisions by the fundamental laws, rather than by those which are not fundamental."

"If then the Courts of Justice are to be considered as the bulwarks of a limited constitution, against legislative encroachments, this consideration will afford a strong argument for the permanent tenure of Judicial offices."

But no proposition can be more manifest, than that this permancy of tenure must be nominal, if made defeasible at the pleasure of the Legislature, and that it is ridiculous to consider it as an obstacle to encroachments of the Legislative Department; if this department has a discretion to vacate or abolish it directly or indirectly.

In recurring to the comments which have been cited, it is not meant to consider them as evidence of any thing but of the views with which the Constitution was framed. After all, the Instrument must speak for itself. Yet to candid minds, the co-temporary explanation of it, by men, who had had a perfect opportunity of knowing the views of its framers, must operate as a weighty collateral reason for believing the construction agreeing with this explanation to be right, rather than the opposite one. It is too cardinal a point, to admit readily the supposition, that there was misapprehension; and whatever motives may have subsequently occurred to bias the impressions of the one or the other of the purposes alluded to, the situation in which they wrote, exempts both from the suspicion of an intention to misrepresent in this particular. Indeed a course of argument more accommodating to the objections of the adversaries of the Constitution would probably have been preferred as most politic, if the truth, as conceived at the time, would have permitted a modification. Much trouble would have been avoided by saying, "The Legislature will have a complete controul over the Judges, by the discretionary power of reducing the number of those of the Supreme Court, and of abolishing the existing Judges of the Inferior Courts, by the abolition of the Courts themselves." But this pretension is a novelty reserved for the crooked ingenuity of after discoveries.

LUCIUS CRASSUS.

THE EXAMINATION NO. XVI
MARCH 19, 1802

New York, March 19, 1802

The President, as a politician, is in one sense particularly unfortunate. He furnishes frequent opportunities of arraying him against himself—of combating his opinions at one period by his opinions at another. Without doubt, a wise and good man may, on proper grounds relinquish an opinion which he has once entertained, and the change may even serve as a proof of candour and integrity. But with such a man, especially in matters of high public importance, changes of this sort must be rare. The contrary is always a mark either of a weak and versatile mind, or of an artificial and designing character, which, accommodating its creed, to circumstances, takes up or lays down an article of faith, just as may suit a present convenience.

The question, in agitation, respecting the Judiciary Department, calls up another instance of opposition, between the former ideas of Mr. Jefferson, and his recent conduct. The leading positions which have been advanced as explanatory of the policy of the Constitution, in the structure of the different departments, and as proper to direct the interpretation of the provisions which were contrived to secure the independence and firmness of the Judges, are to be seen in a very emphatical and distinct form in the Notes on Virginia. The passage in which they appear, deserves to be cited at length, as well for its intrinsic merit, as by way of comment upon the true character of its author; presenting an interesting contrast between the maxims, which experience had taught him while Governor of Virginia, and those which now guide him as the official head of a great party in the United States.

It is in these words—

"All the powers of government, legislative, executive and judiciary, result to the legislative body. The concentrating these in the

495

same hands is precisely the definition of despotic government. It will be no alleviation that these powers will be exercised by a plurality of hands, and not by a single one. One hundred and seventy-three despots would surely be as oppressive as one. Let those who doubt it turn their eyes on the Republic of Venice. As little will it avail us that they are chosen by ourselves. An *elective despotism* was not the government we fought for; but one which should not only be founded on free principles, but in which the powers of government should be so divided and balanced among several bodies of magistracy, as that no one could transcend their legal limits, without being effectually *checked* and *restrained* by the others. For this reason that Convention which passed the ordinance of government, laid its foundation on this basis, that the legislative, executive and judiciary departments, should be separate and distinct, so that no person should exercise the powers of more than one of them at the same time. *But no barrier was provided between these several powers.* The judiciary and executive members were left dependent on the legislative for their subsistence in office, and some of them for their continuance in it. If therefore the legislature assumes executive and judiciary powers, no opposition is likely to be made; nor if made can be effectual; because in that case, they may put their proceedings into the form of an act of assembly, which will render them obligatory on the other branches. They have accordingly *in many instances decided rights* which should have been left to *judiciary controversy;* and *the direction of the executive, during the whole time of their session, is becoming habitual and familiar."*

This passage fully recognises these several important truths: that the tendency of our governments is towards a CONCENTRATION of the POWERS of the different departments in the LEGISLATIVE BODY; that such a CONCENTRATION, is precisely the DEFINITION of DESPOTISM, and that an effectual *barrier* between the respective departments ought to exist. It also, by a strong implication, admits that offices during *good behaviour* are independent of the Legislature for their continuance in office. This implication seems to be contained in the following sentence: "The Judiciary and Executive members were left dependent on the Legislature for their subsistence in office, and *some* of them *for their continuance in it."* The word 'some,' implies that *others* were not left thus dependent; and to what description of officers can the exception be better applied, than to the Judges, the tenure of whose offices was *during good behaviour?*

The sentiments of the President delivered at a *period* when he can be supposed to have been under no improper bias, must be regarded by all those, who respect his judgement, as no light evidence of the truth of the doctrine for which we contend. Let us, however, resume and pursue the subject on its merits, without relying upon the aid of so variable and fallible an authority.

At an early part of the discussion in this Examination, a construction of the Constitution was suggested, to which it may not be amiss to return: It amounts to this, that Congress have power to new-model, or even to abrogate an Inferior Court, but not to abolish the office or emoluments of a Judge of such court previously appointed. In the Congressional debates, some of the speakers against the repealing law, appear to have taken it for granted, that the *abrogation of the court* must draw with it the *abolition of the Judges,* and therefore, have denied in totality, the power of abrogation. In the course of these papers too, it has been admitted, that if the preservation of the Judges cannot be reconciled with the power to annul the Court, then the existence of this power is rightly denied. But in an affair of such vast magnitude, it is all-important to survey with the utmost caution the ground to be taken, and then to take and maintain it with inflexible fortitude and perseverence. Truth will be most likely to prevail, when the arguments which support it stop at a temperate mean, consistent with practical convenience. Excess is always error. There is hardly any theoretic hypothesis, which, carried to a certain extreme, does not become practically false. In construing a Constitution, it is wise, as far as possible to pursue a course, which will reconcile essential principles with convenient modifications. If guided by this spirit, in the great question which seems destined to decide the fate of our Government, it is believed that the result will accord with the construction, that *Congress have a right to change or abolish Inferior Courts, but not to abolish the actual Judges.*

Towards the support of this construction, it has been shewn in another place, that the Courts and the Judges are distinct legal *entities,* which, in contemplation of law, may exist, independently the one of the other—mutually related, but not inseparable. The act proposed to be repealed exemplifies this idea in practice. It abolishes the District Courts of Tennessee and Kentucky, and transfers their Judges to one of the Circuit Courts. Though the authorities and jurisdiction of those Courts are vested in the Circuit Court, to which the Judges are transferred; yet the *identity of the Courts* ceases. It cannot be maintained that Courts so different in their organization and jurisdiction, are the same; nor could a legislative transfer of the Judges have been constitutional, but upon the hypothesis, that the office of a Judge may survive the Court of which he is a member: a *new appointment* by the Executive, of two additional Judges for the Circuit Court, would otherwise have been necessary.

This precedent in all its points is correct, and exhibits a rational

497

operation of the construction which regards the office of the Judge, as distinct from the Court, as one of the elements or constituent parts of which it is composed: not as a mere incident that must perish with its principal.

It will not be disputed, that the Constitution might have provided *in terms*, and with effect, that an Inferior Court which had been *established by law*, might by law be abolished; nevertheless, that the Judges of such Courts should retain the offices of Judges of the United States, with the emoluments before attached to their offices. The operation of such a provision would be, that when the Court was abolished, all the functions to be executed in that Court, would be suspended, and the Judge could only continue to exert the authorities and perform the duties which might before have been performed, without reference to causes pending in Court; but he would have the capacity to be annexed to another Court; without the intervention of a new appointment, and by that annexation, simply to *renew* the exercise of the authorities and duties which had been suspended.

If this might have been the effect of positive and explicit provision, why may it not likewise be the result of provisions, which, presenting opposite considerations, point to the same conclusion, as a compromise calculated to reconcile those considerations with each other and to unite different objects of public utility? Surely the affirmative infringes no principle of legal construction, transgresses no rule of good sense.

Let us then enquire, whether there are not in this case opposite and conflicting considerations, demanding a compromise of this nature? On the one hand, it is evident that if an inferior court once instituted, though found inconvenient, cannot be abolished, this is to entail upon the community the mischief, be it more or less, of a first error in the administration of the government. On the other hand, it is no less evident, that if the judges hold their offices at the discretion of the legislature, they cease to be a co-ordinate, and become a dependent branch of the government; from which dependence mischiefs infinitely greater are to be expected.

All these mischiefs, the lesser as well as the greater, are avoided by saying, *"Congress may abolish the Courts, but the Judges shall retain their offices with the appurtenant emoluments."* The only remaining inconvenience then, will be one too insignificant to weigh in a national scale, that is, the expence of the compensations of the Incumbents, during their lives. The future and permanent expence will be done away.

But will this construction secure the benefits proposed by the

Constitution from the independent tenure of Judicial Office? Substantially it will. The main object is to preserve the judges from being influenced by an apprehension of the loss of the advantages of office. As this loss could not be incurred, that influence would not exist. Their firmness could not be assailed by the danger of being superseded, and perhaps *consigned to want*. Let it be added, that when it was understood not to be in the power of the Legislature to deprive the Judges of their offices and emoluments, it would be a great restraint upon the factious motives, which might induce the abolition of a court. This would be much less likely to happen unless for genuine reasons of public utility; and of course there would be a much better prospect of the stability of Judiciary establishments.

LUCIUS CRASSUS.

REMARKS ON THE REPEAL
OF THE JUDICIARY ACT
FEBRUARY 11, 1802

The Judiciary Repeal Act of 1802 overturned the Judiciary Act of 1801 and therewith abolished federal judgeships established under that previous act. Hamilton regarded the repeal act as a serious threat to the independence of the judiciary and hence to the balance of the Constitution.

New York, February 11, 1802

First Version

After some pause, Gen. HAMILTON rose. He began with stating his own decided opinion, that the contemplated repeal of the late act, *taken in connexion with the known and avowed object of that repeal,* was an unequivocal violation of the constitution in a most vital part. However, he did expect that on that point, the gentlemen present would be unanimous. Neither had he any hope that any representations whatever, would arrest the contemplated blow. In this opinion, and because he thought the Bar ought to hold themselves too high to idly

499

commit their own dignity by an opposition which they must know would be fruitless, he was opposed to the idea of memorializing Congress at all. He observed also, that the reception which the petition of the Pennsylvania Bar had met with, and the manner in which the bill had been immediately afterwards hastened in its progress, gave no encouragement to the hope that ours would be better received. He then said that from respect to our brethren of Philadelphia, and since we were called upon to express an opinion, he inclined to the idea of a letter to those gentlemen, rather than a memorial. In this view he submitted the draft of a letter to the meeting, in which it had been endeavoured so to express, as that gentlemen of every political opinion might join in. . . .

Mr. HARISON and Gen. HAMILTON followed, and in a very able, dispassionate and conclusive manner, demonstrated the inefficacy of the former Judiciary system—the importance of an independent Federal Judiciary—and the trivial amount of its expence, compared with the benefits resulting from it, to every individual in the community. . . .

Gen. HAMILTON again rose. He felt little zeal upon this subject, because he believed that no possible exertions could arrest the blow aimed at the constitution. Respecting what was observed of secret popular societies, he said, the baneful effects of them were not confined to modern times, but had been felt in some of the ancient republics, as was noticed by Montesquieu. He repeated, that they were the most dangerous engines ever employed against free governments. He mentioned the example of a great kingdom subverted by their influence, and which had found no relief but in the horrid calm of despotism. An occasional and public meeting of individuals to petition the legislature, have no resemblance to a secret, organized and extensive combination of political societies. He declared in the most emphatic manner, that if the bill for the repeal passed, and the independence of the Judiciary was destroyed, the constitution was but a shadow, and we should, e'er long, be divided into separate confederacies, turning our arms against each. He solemnly called heaven to witness his devout desire that the system of government adopted among us might prosper; but his hope in their prosperity was much weakened, when he perceived them becoming the spoil of popular intrigue, and one after another "crumbling beneath him." Between a government of laws, administered by an independent Judiciary, or a despotism supported by an army, there was no medium. If we relinquish one, we must submit to the other. He pathetically deplored the event to which we hasten, but intimated no hope that any human exertions could avert it. . . .

Second Version

He [Hamilton] confessed with seeming sincerity, he felt little zeal on the present occasion. He *could prove* that to repeal the judiciary law and to with-hold the salaries of the judges, would be an infringement of the constitution. He did not intend, however, to dwell on the constitutionality of the question. He allowed that gentlemen might have different opinions concerning it. His primary object was to obtain the unanimous vote of the Bar against the *expediency* of the repeal. He admitted that the present, as well as the old judiciary system, were defective. He was well disposed, nevertheless, towards the present one, since he thought it an improvement on the old judiciary law. He was averse to presenting a memorial to Congress on the subject. Still he thought that the opinions of the gentlemen of the Bar of this city on it ought to be made known. He conceived that the gentlemen of the Bar of Philadelphia had been indecorously treated by the Senate. And he thought the profession in this city ought more duly to appreciate their worth, than to subject themselves, by memorializing Congress, to that ill treatment which the Bar of Philadelphia had received from the Senate. . . . He was solicitous to unite the profession in one sentiment. To this end, he had, with much caution, formed an answer to the letter received from Philadelphia, and submitted it to the consideration of the gentlemen as a basis of a resolution. (This letter was approbatory of the proceedings of the profession in Philadelphia.) . . .

General Hamilton delivered what is termed a most eloquent speech. He found that the gentlemen of the Bar were nearly equally divided. He therefore threw off that imposing but *veiled modesty* with which he commenced the business of the evening: attacked the passions, but kept aloof from the understanding, although addressing the profession. He declared that he would "give one drop of blood from his heart to unite them in sentiment on that occasion." The want of zeal which he felt in the early part of the evening, vanished when he found the pretended absence answered not the intended end. He said that if the judiciary law should be repealed he should consider the constitution as a dead letter. He had long foreseen what had come to pass. He hinted that he often doubted the *practicability* of a *government like ours*. He dreaded the consequences of a repeal. He desired them to remember what he was about to say, to wit, that we should soon see State "arrayed against State to embrue their hands in each other's blood." In which case, some daring usurper (he did not mention himself) would arise, seize the reins of government, and, like Bonaparte, establish a despotism. In this threatening manner he harangued about twenty minutes, intending to produce by terror, what he could not effect by reason.

Third Version

To these remarks General Hamilton rose again to reply—he remarked in substance that he had fostered the hope, that on this occasion, by cautiously avoiding to say any thing on the point of the constitutionality of the proposed repeal, and stating only the opinion of the New-York bar on that of its *inexpediency*, there would have been but one sentiment—He regretted, deeply regretted, that on this point there was a diversity of sentiment; he foresaw the unhappy effects that would hence result; he deplored them, not from any private or contracted view, but turning his eye inward on his heart, and looking to heaven as the witness of his motives, he declared he knew of none that influenced him but the sincerest attachment to the public good. So far as respected the unconstitutionality of the proposed repeal, he had no hesitation in avowing his own opinion. He considered it a most direct, and fatal violation of the most essential, the most *vital* principle of the constitution. The independence of the judges once destroyed, the constitution is gone, it is a dead letter; it is a vapor which the breath of faction in a moment may dissipate, and this boasted union the labor of true patriots, the hope of our country, which in the last 12 years has raised us to the most enviable height of prosperity, dissolves and dies.

He had cherished the idea, he said, that this part of the Constitution was the last that party violence would attack. That although certain extensions of executive authority, certain changes in the finances, or in diplomatic arrangements abroad might take place, yet that the essential rights of the judiciary in which foreigners and citizens, but more especially the mercantile interests of the U. States are so deeply concerned, would have been preserved inviolate. He had looked forward to many evils that he thought likely to flow from the known principles of the leading characters now in authority, but indeed, he had not calculated on such a rapid progression of evil. He had little hope that any thing that could now be *said* or done, would assist in averting the impending blow. He [k]new full well that the plan now going into effect had long been meditated and resolved on, and hence, his zeal was much abated, yet could any thing he could do have any effect in saving the constitution from the final blow that now menaced it, he would labor day and night; he would not give 'sleep to his eyes, nor slumber to his eye-lids,' while he had hope to support his exertions; nay, 'I would give a drop of my heart's blood,' said he, to save this *vital* principle of the constitution. There is no motive which induced me to put my life at hazard through our revolutionary war, that would not now as powerfully operate on me, to put it again in jeopardy, in defence of the independence of the judiciary; for remember what is said this night; if this fatal measure is not by *some means* arrested, if the *laws* are not suffered to controul the passions of individuals, thro the organs of an extended, firm and independant judiciary, the bayonet must. There is no alternative; we must be ruled by municipal law, or by—a military force: and I beg gentlemen to recollect what I now say, without aspiring to the character of a prophet, that if this rash unadvised repeal takes place, mutual confidence will be destroyed—the union will gradually crumble to pieces and in a few, very few years, the present confederation will either be parcelled out into separate territories, with clashing interests, and you will see the hand of brother, raised to shed a brother's blood, or you will see this country become the prey of a usurper, and sink into the calm of a military despotism. On those gentlemen, then, who truly value our republican government, I call, to banish for an instant, the influence of party-spirit, and to lend their aid in extinguishing a rising conflagration, which threatens to involve this devoted country in miseries incalculable. On the point of *expediency*, he observed, that he could, in no one point of view, consider the proposed repeal as defensible. Every gentleman present, who had been concerned in business depending in the circuit court of the United States, knew, without his going into details, the vices of the *old system*. Many of its defects were indeed removed by the present, which, however, was not to be considered as perfect. On this, certain improvements could be advantageously engrafted—which would render it a very eligible and convenient system. But he was surprised, greatly surprised indeed, to hear any gentleman who had any respect to his own character, risk an opinion, that the district courts, with the supreme court of the United States, were fully competent to all the business of the United States. The business of the former he said, from revenue and admiralty causes, and from what arose under the late bankrupt law, furnished full employ for the most industrious judge. Beside, if all suits were originally to be commenced in the district courts, no suitor would rest satisfied with the decision of a single man, but would remove the cause for a final hearing to the supreme court of the United States, in which case parties would be constantly obliged to travel with papers and vouchers from the extremities of the Union to the seat of government, there to retain new counsel, be at heavy expences, and far from their families, which would produce inconveniences that would not long be submitted to.

LETTER TO THE NEW YORK EVENING POST
FEBRUARY 24, 1802

Hamilton throughout his lifetime was harassed by the charge that the Plan of Government he proposed to the Constitutional Convention was intended as an introduction to monarchy. He consistently maintained, however, that his plan was wholly republican in character. Hamilton argues in the following reply to an editorial in the New York Evening Post *that the two essential criteria of republicanism are that the executive and legislative officers are chosen directly or indirectly by the people and that they hold their offices during a responsible and defeasible tenure, and that his plan meets this republican test.*

New York, February 24, 1802

We might well be excused from taking any notice of such a writer as the author of the leading article in the Citizen of this morning; but as in one instance he has pretended to state facts, in reply to what was said in the Evening Post, respecting the opinions held in the Convention by Mr. Hamilton and by Mr. Maddison, some answer may be expected. Mr. Hamilton had been charged with holding an opinion in favor of monarchy, and it had been said he proposed a monarchy to the Convention. This was denied. It is now replied, that he proposed a "system composed of three branches, an Assembly, a Senate, and a Governor; that the Assembly should be *elected by the people* for three years, and that the Senate and Governor should likewise be *elected by the people* during good behaviour." Thus the charge is at length reduced to specific terms. Before it can be decided, however, whether this would be a *monarchy* or a *republic,* it seems necessary to settle the meaning of those terms.

No exact definitions have settled what is or is not, a *Republican Government,* as contradistinguished from a *Monarchical.* Every man who speaks or writes on the subject, has an arbitrary standard in his own mind. The mad Democrat will have nothing republican which does not accord with his own mad theory—He rejects even representation. Such is the opinion held by a man now one of Mr. Jefferson's ministers. Some authors denominate every government a Monarchy, in which the Executive Authority is placed in a single hand; whether for life or for years, and whether conferred by election or by de[s]cent. According to this definition the actual Government of the United States, and of most states, is a *Monarchy.*

In practice, the terms Republic and Republican, have been applied with as little precision. Even the government of England, with a powerful hereditary King, as been repeatedly spoken of by authors, as a Commonwealth or Republic. The late government of Holland, with a hereditary Stadtholder, was constantly so denominated. That of Poland, previous to the dissolution of the state, with an Executive, for life, was never called by any other name.

The truth seems to be, that all Governments have been deemed Republics, in which a large portion of the sovereignty has been vested in the whole, or in a considerable body of the people; and that none have been deemed Monarchies as contrasted with the Republican standard, in which there has not been an *hereditary* Chief Magistrate.

Were we to attempt a correct definition of a Republican Government, we should say, "That is a Republican Government, in which both the Executive and Legislative organs are appointed by a popular Election, and hold their offices upon a responsible and defeasible tenure." If this be not so, then the tenure of good behavior, for the Judicial Department is Anti-republican; and the Government of this state is not a Republic: If the contrary, then a Government would not cease to be Republican, because a branch of the Legislature, or even the Executive, held their offices during good behavior. In this case the two essential criteria would still concur—The creation of the Officer, by a popular Election, and the possibility of his removal in the course of law, by accusation before, and conviction by a competent Tribunal.

How far it may be expedient to go, even within the bounds of the theory, in framing a Constitution, is a different question, upon which we pretend not to give our opinion. It is enough for the purpose of our assertion if it be *in principle* correct. For even then, upon the statement of the Citizen himself, General Hamilton did never propose *a monarchy.*

Thus much too we will add, that whether General Hamilton at any stage of the deliberations of the Convention did or did not make the proposition ascribed to him, it is certain that his more deliberate and final opinion, adopted a moderate term of years for the duration of the office of President; as also appears by a plan of a Constitution *in writing now in this city,* drawn up by that Gentleman in detail.

Whether the first system presented by Mr. Hamilton, was the one to which he gave a decided preference, it would be difficult to say, since we find him adopting and proposing a different one in the course of the sitting of the convention. It may have been his opinion

505

was nearly balanced between the two; nay it is possible he may have really preferred the one last proposed, and that the former, like many others, was brought forward to make it the subject of discussion, and see what would be the opinions of different gentlemen on so momentous a subject. And it is now repeated with confidence, that the *Virginia* delegation did vote for the most energetic form of government, and that Mr. Maddison was of the number. But we desire to be distinctly understood, that it was never intended by mentioning this circumstance, to impeach the purity of Mr. Maddison's motives. To arraign the morals of any man because he entertains a speculative opinion on government different from ourselves, is worse than arrogance. He who does so, must entertain notions in ethics extremely crude, and certainly unfavourable to virtue.

LETTER TO GOUVERNEUR MORRIS
FEBRUARY 29, 1802

Gouverneur Morris was a close political associate of Hamilton's throughout his career and certainly someone in whom Hamilton could confide, as the following letter reveals.

New York, February 29, 1802

My Dr. Sir

Your letter of the 22d is the third favour for which I am indebted to you since you left N York.

Your frankness in giving me your opinion as to the expediency of an application of our bar to Congress obliges me. But you know we are not readily persuaded to think we have been wrong. Were the matter to be done over I should pursue the same course. I did not believe the measure would be useful as a preventative, and for the people an expression of an opinion by letter would be as good as in a memorial. It appeared to me best because it saved our delicacy and because in the abstract I am not over fond of the precedent of the bar addressing Congress. But I did what I thought likely to do more good—*I induced* the Chamber of Commerce to send a memorial.

As to the rest, I should be a very unhappy man, if I left my tranquillity at the mercy of the misinterpretations which friends as well as foes are fond of giving to my conduct.

Mine is an odd destiny. Perhaps no man in the UStates has sacrified or done more for the present Constitution than myself—and contrary to all my anticipations of its fate, as you know from the very begginning I am still labouring to prop the frail and worthless fabric. Yet I have the murmurs of its friends no less than the curses of its foes for my rewards. What can I do better than withdraw from the Scene? Every day proves to me more and more that this American world was not made for me.

The suggestions with which you close your letter suppose a much sounder state of the public mind than at present exists. Attempts to make a show of a general *popular* dislike of the pending measures of the Government would only serve to manifest the direct reverse. Impressions are indeed making but as yet within a very narrow sphere. The time may ere long arrive when the minds of men will be prepared to make an offer to *recover* the Constitution, but the many cannot now be brought to make a stand for its preservation. We must wait awhile.

I have read your speech⟨es⟩ with great pleasure. They are truly worthy of you. Your real friends had many sources of satisfaction on account of them. The conspiracy of Dulness was at work. It chose to misinterpret your moderation in certain transactions of a personal reference. A public energetic display of your talents and principles was requisite to silence the Cavillers. It is now done. You, friend Morris, are by *birth* a native of this Country but by *genius* an exotic. You mistake if you fancy that you are more a favourite than myself or that you are in any sort upon a theatre s⟨uited⟩ to you.

Adieu   Yrs. ever   A H

LETTER TO JAMES A. BAYARD
APRIL 6, 1802

The following letter contains Hamilton's commentary on Federalist party politics in 1802 and expresses his fears about Burr's intrusion into that party.

New-York April 6th. 1802

Amidst the humiliating circumstances which attend our country, all the sound part of the community must find cause of triumph in the brilliant display of talents which have been employed though without success, in resisting the follies of an infatuated administration. And your personal friends will not have much reason for mortification on account of the part you have performed in the interesting scene. But my dear Sir we must not content ourselves with a temporary effort to oppose the approach of the evil. We must derive instruction from the experience before us; and learning to form a just estimate of the things to which we have been attached, there must be a systematic & persevering endeavour to establish the fortune of a great empire on foundations much firmer than have yet been devised. What will signify a vibration of power, if it cannot be used with confidence or energy, & must be again quickly restored to hands which will prostrate much faster than we shall be able to rear under so frail a system? Nothing will be done till the structure of our National Edifice shall be such as naturally to controul excentric passions & views, and to keep in check demagogues & knaves in the disguise of Patriots. Yet I fear a different reasoning will prevail, and an eagerness to recover lost power will betray us into expedients which will be injurious to the country, & disgraceful & ruinous to ourselves. What meant the *apparition* & the *toast* which made part of the *afterpiece* of the *birth day festival?* Is it possible that some new intrigue is about to link the Fœderalists with a man, who can never by anything else than the bane of a good cause? I dread more from this, than from all the contrivances of the bloated & senseless junta of Virginia. The Fœds. & Antifœds. of this state united in certain amendments to the constitution now before your house, having for objects, 1st to discriminate the candidates for the Presidency & Vice-Presidency, 2nd to have the electors of these officers chosen by the people in districts under the direction of Congress. Both these appear to me points of importance in true Fœderal calculation. Surely the scene of last session ought to teach us the intrinsic demerits of the existing plan. It proved to us, how possible it is for a man in whom no party has confidence, & who deserves the confidence of none, by mere intrigue & accident, to acquire the first place in the Government of our Nation; and it also proved to us how serious a danger of convulsion & disorder is incident to the plan. On this point things have come to my knowledge, improper for a letter, which would astonish you. Surely we ought by this time to have learnt, that whatever multiplied the opportunities &

means of Cabal is more favorable to our adversaries than to us. They have certainly the advantage in the game, by greater zeal activity and subtlety, & especially by an abandonment of principle. On all these accounts it is our true policy to abridge the facilities to Cabal as Much as possible in all our public institutions & measures. As to the Second of the amendments, it has ever appeared to me as sound principle, to let the Fœderal Government rest as much as possible on the shoulders of the people, and as little as possible on those of the State Legislatures. The proposition accords with this principle & in my view it is further recommended by its tendency to exclude *combination* which I am persuaded in the general & permanent course of things will operate more against, than for us. Col: Burr without doubt will resist these amendments. And he may induce some of our friends to play into his hands. But this will be a very bad calculation even admitting the inadmissible idea, that he ought to be adopted as a Chief of the Fœderal Party. We never can have him fairly in our power, till we render his situation absolutely hopeless with his old friends. While the indiscriminate voting prevails he will find it his interest to play fast & lose and to keep himself in a state to be at the head of the Antifœderal Party. If these hopes are cut off, he will immediately set about forming a third party of which he will be the head, and then if we think it worth the while we can purchase him with his flying squadron. These observations are of course hypothetical. For to My Mind the elevation of Mr Burr by Fœderal Means to the Chief Magistracy of the U. States will be the worst kind of political suicide.

Adieu my dear Sir   Yours very sincerely   A. Hamilton

LETTER TO JAMES A. BAYARD
APRIL 16–21, 1802

In the following letter, Hamilton responds to an argument that an improved Federalist rhetoric might have enabled that party to maintain itself in its partisan political struggles with the Jeffersonian Republicans, that is, that the Federalists required a rhetoric which would appeal to the popular passions if they were to remain in power for a longer time. The Jeffersonian rhetoric promised Americans an emanci-

pation from the burdens and restraints of government. Reflecting on the Republican victory of 1800, Hamilton observes that for the Federalists to win the vicious passions to their side would require renouncing their principles and further corrupting popular opinion. He counsels that, whatever plan the Federalists adopt, it must, to be successful, be founded on the truth of their propositions. The rhetoric that Hamilton recommends is not the art of gratifying multitudes. While he regrets that, as leader of the Federalist party, he had not given more effort to educating the broad electorate concerning the purposes of that party, he refuses to be guided by depraved popular passions in refashioning party doctrine. It may very well be that Jeffersonian rhetoric was more consistent with American prejudices than Hamiltonian rhetoric was, but it does not follow that Hamiltonian rhetoric should have departed from its principles or purposes to become more successful politically. Hamiltonian rhetoric reflected Hamiltonian purposes.

New-York April 16–21, 1802

Dear Sir.

Your letter of the 12th inst. has relieved me from some apprehension. Yet it is well that it should be perfectly understood by the truly sound part of the Fœderalists, that there do in fact exist intrigues in good earnest, between several individuals not unimportant, of the Fœderal Party, and the person in question; which are bottomed upon motives & views, by no means auspicious to the real welfare of the country. I am glad to find that it is in contemplation to adopt a plan of conduct. It is very necessary; & to be useful it must be efficient & comprehensive in the means which it embraces, at the same time that it must meditate none which are not really constitutional & patriotic. I will comply with your invitation by submitting some ideas which from time to time have passed through my mind. Nothing is more fallacious than to expect to produce any valuable or permanent results, in political projects, by relying merely on the reason of men. Men are rather reasoning tha[n] reasonable animals for the most part governed by the impulse of passion. This is a truth well understood by our adversaries who have practised upon it with no small benefit to their cause. For at the very moment they are eulogizing the reason of men & professing to appeal only to that faculty, they are courting the strongest & most active passion of the human heart—*VANITY!*

It is no less true that the Fœderalists seem not to have attended to the fact sufficiently; and that they erred in relying so much on the rectitude & utility of their measures, as to have neglected the cultivation of popular favour by fair & justifiable expedients. The observation has been repeatedly made by me to individuals with whom I particularly conversed & expedients suggested for gaining good will which were never adopted. Unluckily however for us in the competition for the passions of the people our opponents have great advantages over us; for the plain reason, that the vicious are far more active than the good passions, and that to win the latter to our side we must renounce our principles & our objects, & unite in corrupting public opinion till it becomes fit for nothing but mischief. Yet unless we can contrive to take hold of & carry along with us some strong feelings of the mind we shall in vain calculate upon any substantial or durable results. Whatever plan we may adopt, to be successful must be founded on the truth of this proposition. And perhaps it is not very easy for us to give it full effect; especially not without some deviations from what on other occasions we have maintained to be right. But in determining upon the propriety of the deviations, we must consider whether it be possible for us to succeed without in some degree employing the weapons which have been employed against us, & whether the actual state & future prospect of things, be not such as to justify the reciprocal use of them. I need not tell you that I do not mean to countenance the imitation of things intrinsically unworthy, but only of such as may be denominated irregular, such as in a sound & stable order of things ought not to exist. Neither are you to infer that any revolutionary result is contemplated. In my opinion the present Constitution is the standard to which we are to cling. Under its banners, *bona fide* must we combat our political foes—rejecting all changes but through the channel itself provides for amendments. By these general views of the subject have my reflections been guided. I now offer you the outline of the plan which they have suggested. Let an Association be formed to be denominated, "The Christian Constitutional Society." It's objects to be

1st The support of the Christian Religion.

2nd The support of the Constitution of the United States.

Its Organization.

1st A directing council consisting of a President & 12 Members, of whom 4 & the President to be a quorum.

2nd A sub-directing council in each State consisting of a Vice-President & 12 Members, of whom 4 with the Vice-President to be a quorum & 3rd As many societies in each State, as local circumstances may permit to be formed by the Sub-directing council.

511

The Meeting at Washington to Nominate the *President & Vice-President* together with *4 Members of each* of the councils, who *are to complete* their own numbers respectively.

Its Means.

1st The diffusion of information. For this purpose not only the Newspapers but pamphlets must be la[r]gely employed & to do this a fund must be created. 5 dollars annually for 8 years, to be contributed by each member who can really afford it, (taking care not to burden the less able brethren) may afford a competent fund for a competent time. It is essential to be able to disseminate *gratis* useful publications. Whenever it can be done, & there is a press, clubs should be formed to meet once a week, read the newspapers & prepare essays paragraphs &ct.

2nd The use of all lawful means in concert to promote the election of *fit men*. A lively correspondence must be kept up between the different Societies.

3rd The promoting of institutions of a charitable & useful nature in the management of Fœderalists. The populous cities ought particularly to be attended to. Perhaps it will be well to institute in such places 1st Societies for the relief of Emigrants—2nd. Academies each with one professor for instructing the different Classes of Mechanics in the principles of Mechanics & Elements of Chemistry. The cities have been employed by the Jacobins to give an impulse to the country. And it is believed to be an alarming fact, that while the question of Presidential Election was pending in the House of Rs. parties were organized in several of the Cities, in the event of there being no election, to cut off the leading Fœderalists & sieze the Government. An Act of association to be drawn up in concise general terms. It need only designate the "name" "objects" & contain an engagement to promote the objects by all lawful means, and particularly by the diffusion of Information. This act to be signed by every member.

The foregoing to be the principal Engine. In addition let measures be adopted to bring as soon as possible the repeal of the Judiciary law before the Supreme Court. Afterwards, if not before, let as many Legislatures as can be prevailed upon, instruct their Senators to endeavour to procure a repeal of the repealing law. The body of New-England speaking the same language will give a powerful impulse. In Congress our friends to *propose* little, to agree candidly to all good measures, & to resist & expose all bad. This is a general sketch of what has occurred to me. It is at the service of my friends for so much as it may be worth. With true esteem & regard

  Dr Sir Yours   AH

LETTER TO TIMOTHY PICKERING
SEPTEMBER 16, 1803

Hamilton wrote the following letter in response to a query concerning the charge that he had intended to introduce monarchy in this country in the Constitutional Convention. This charge was used against Hamilton throughout his political career.

New York September 16
1803

My Dear Sir

I will make no apology for my delay in answering your inquiry some time since made, because I could offer none which would satisfy myself. I pray you only to believe that it proceeded from any thing rather than want of respect or regard. I shall now comply with your request.

The highest toned propositions, which I made in the Convention, were for a President, Senate and Judges during good behaviour—a house of representatives for three years. Though I would have enlarged the Legislative power of the General Government, yet I never contemplated the abolition of the State Governments; but on the contrary, they were, in some particulars, constituent parts of my plan.

This plan was in my conception conformable with the strict theory of a Government purely republican; the essential criteria of which are that the principal organs of the Executive and Legislative departments be elected by the people and hold their offices by a *responsible* and temporary or *defeasible* tenure.

A vote was taken on the proposition respecting the Executive. Five states were in favour of it; among those Virginia; and though from the manner of voting, by delegations, individuals were not distinguished, it was morally certain, from the known situation of the Virginia members (six in number, two of them *Mason* and *Randolph* possessing popular doctrines) that *Madison* must have concurred in the vote of Virginia. Thus, if I sinned against Republicanism, Mr. Madison was not less guilty.

I may truly then say, that I never proposed either a President, or Senate for life, and that I neither recommended nor meditated the annihilation of the State Governments.

And I may add, that in the course of the discussions in the

513

Convention, neither the propositions thrown out for debate, nor even those voted in the earlier stages of deliberation were considered as evidences of a definitive opinion, in the proposer or voter. It appeared to me to be in some sort understood, that with a view to free investigation, experimental propositions might be made, which were to be received merely as suggestions for consideration.

Accordingly, it is a fact, that my final opinion was against an Executive during good behaviour, on account of the increased danger to the public tranquil[i]ty incident to the election of a Magistrate of this degree of permanency. In the plan of a Constitution, which I drew up, while the convention was sitting & which I communicated to Mr. Madison about the close of it, perhaps a day or two after, the Office of President has no greater duration than for three years.

This plan was predicated upon these bases—1 That the political principles of the people of this country would endure nothing but republican Government. 2 That in the actual situation of the Country, it was in itself right and proper that the republican theory should have a fair and full trial—3 That to such a trial it was essential that the Government should be so constructed as to give it all the energy and stability reconciliable with the principles of that theory. These were the genuine sentiments of my heart, and upon them I acted.

I sincerely hope, that it may not hereafter be discovered, that through want of sufficient attention to the last idea, the experiment of Republican Government, even in this Country, has not been as complete, as satisfactory and as decisive as could be wished.

Very truly   Dear Sir   Yr friend & servt   A Hamilton

Timothy Pickering Esqr.

especially confidential

Appendix

GEORGE WASHINGTON TO ALEXANDER HAMILTON
AUGUST 28, 1788

The following letter contains Washington's assessment of the The *Federalist Papers, a copy of which had been sent to him by Hamilton. This letter deserves to be included in this volume because of Washington's thoughtful recognition of the value of* The *Federalist Papers beyond the ratification controversy.*

Mount Vernon Augt. 28th. 1788

Dear Sir,

I have had the pleasure to receive your letter dated the 13th.—accompanied by one addressed to General Morgan. I will forward the letter to Gener[a]l Morgan by the first conveyance, and add my particular wishes that he would comply with the request contained in it. Although I can scarcely imagine how the Watch of a British Officer, killed within their lines, should have fallen into his hands (who was many miles from the scene of action) yet, if it so happened, I flatter myself there will be no reluctance or delay in restoring it to the family.

As the perusal of the political papers under the signature of Publius has afforded me great satisfaction, I shall certainly consider them as claiming a most distinguished place in my library. I have read every performance which has been printed on one side and the other of the great question lately agitated (so far as I have been able to obtain them) and, without an unmeaning compliment I will say that I have seen no other so well calculated (in my judgment) to produce conviction on an unbiassed mind, as the *Production* of your *Triumvirate*—when the transient circumstances & fugitive performances which attended this *crisis* shall have disappeared, that work will merit

515

the notice of Posterity; because in it are candidly discussed the principles of freedom & the topics of government, which will be always interesting to mankind so long as they shall be connected in Civil Society.

The Circular Letter from your Convention, I presume, was the equivalent by wch. you obtained an acquiescence in the proposed Constitution: Nothwithstanding I am not very well satisfied with the tendency of it; yet the Fœderal affairs have proceeded, with few exceptions, in so good a train, that I hope the political Machine may be put in motion, without much effort or hazard of miscarrying.

On the delicate subject with which you conclude your letter, I can say nothing; because the event alluded to may never happen; and because, in case it should occur, it would be a point of prudence to defer forming one's ultimate and irrevocable decision, so long as new data might be afforded for one to act with the greater wisdom & propriety. I would not wish to conceal my prevailing sentiment from you. For you know me well enough, my good Sir, to be persuaded that I am not guilty of affectation, when I tell you, it is my great and sole desire to live and die, in peace and retirement, on my own farm. Were it ever indispensable, a different line of conduct should be adopted; while you and some others who are acquainted with my heart would *acquit*, the world and Posterity might probably *accuse* me of *inconsistency* and *ambition*. Still I hope I shall always possess firmness and virtue enough to maintain (what I consider the most enviable of all titles) the character of *an honest man*, as well as prove (what I desire to be considered in reality) that I am, with great sincerity & esteem,

Dear Sir   Your friend and   Most obedient Hble Ser

Go: Washington

The Honble. Alexr. Hamilton Esqr.

Index

How Democratic Is the Constitution?

Robert A. Goldwin and William A. Schambra, editors

When the question, How democratic is the Constitution? was answered with a resounding, Not at all, by Charles A. Beard in 1913, an intense debate resulted that has not subsided to this day. The essays in this collection, written by leading spokesmen for a wide range of opposing views, will give the reader a sense of the intensity and complexity of the continuing debate.

Some of the authors accept a version of Beard's thesis, arguing that the Constitution was designed to protect the wealthy by frustrating popular rule, that it is an aristocratic document garbed in democratic rhetoric, or that it is a middle-of-the-road compromise between radical democrats and "accommodating conservatives." Other authors reject the Beardian thesis, maintaining that the Constitution is unqualifiedly democratic, that it was designed to establish a "deliberative democracy," or that its seemingly undemocratic institutions are intended to secure rights for all.

These subjects, and others, are argued vigorously and authoritatively in essays by:

WALTER BERNS
American Enterprise Institute

WILSON CAREY MCWILLIAMS
Rutgers University

JOSEPH M. BESSETTE
Catholic University

MICHAEL PARENTI
Institute for Policy Studies

ANN STUART DIAMOND
American Enterprise Institute

GORDON S. WOOD
Brown University

ALFRED F. YOUNG
Northern Illinois University

150 pp./1980/paper $5.25/cloth $12.25

How Capitalistic Is the Constitution?

Robert A. Goldwin and William A. Schambra, editors

What is the relationship between democratic government and a capitalist economic system? That is the central issue discussed in these essays by leading spokesmen for diverse points of view when they answer the question asked in the title of this volume.

Some of the authors argue that there is a deep contradiction between the promises of democratic equality in the Constitution and the material inequalities generated by American capitalism. Other authors reject that view and maintain that capitalism is not only compatible with but essential for democratic liberty.

The controversy on how to understand and to reconcile our political and economic systems is presented in its full political, historical, economic, legal, and philosophic complexity in essays by:

WALTER DEAN BURNHAM
Massachusetts Institute of Technology

EDWARD S. GREENBERG
University of Colorado

ROBERT LEKACHMAN
City University of New York

FORREST MCDONALD
University of Alabama

STEPHEN MILLER
American Enterprise Institute

MARC F. PLATTNER
United States Mission to the United Nations

BERNARD H. SIEGAN
University of San Diego Law School

This book is the second in a series in AEI's project "A Decade of Study of the Constitution." The first book was *How Democratic Is the Constitution?* edited by Robert A. Goldwin and William A. Schambra.

172 pp./1981/paper $6.25/cloth $14.25